EYEBLINK CLASSICAL CONDITIONING VOLUME 2:
Animal Models

EYEBLINK CLASSICAL CONDITIONING
VOLUME 2:
Animal Models

edited by

Diana S. Woodruff-Pak
Temple University

Joseph E. Steinmetz
Indiana University

SPRINGER SCIENCE+BUSINESS MEDIA, LLC

Library of Congress Cataloging-in-Publication Data

Eyeblink classical conditioning / edited by Diana Woodruff-Pak, Joseph E. Steinmetz.
p. cm.
Contents: v. 1. Applications in humans.
Includes bibliographical references and index.
ISBN 978-1-4757-8354-4 ISBN 978-0-306-46897-1 (eBook)
DOI 10.1007/978-0-306-46897-1
1. Neuropsychological tests. 2. Clinical neuropsychology. 3. Eyelid conditioning. I. Woodruff-Pak, Diana S., 1946- II. Steinmetz, Joseph E., 1955-

RC386.6.N48 E94 1999
153.1'526--dc21

99-049487

Originally published by Kluwer Academic Publishers in 2000
Softcover reprint of the hardcover 1st edition 2000

Printed on acid-free paper.

TABLE OF CONTENTS

LIST OF CONTRIBUTORS

M. Todd Allen
Center for Molecular and
Behavioral Neuroscience
Rutgers University
197 University Avenue
Newark, NJ 07102

Yukiko Asaka
Department of Psychology
Miami University
Oxford, OH 45056

Stephen D. Berry
Department of Psychology
Miami University
Oxford, OH 45056

Ramie L. Borgnis
Department of Psychology
Miami University
Oxford, OH 45056

M. Claire Cartford
Department of Psychology
Hedco Neuroscience Building 501
University of Southern California
Los Angeles, CA 90089-2520

Mark Chachich
Shirley L. Buchanan Neuroscience
Research Laboratory (151A)
Wm. Jennings Bryan Dorn
VA Medical Center
6439 Garners Ferry Road
Columbia, SC 29209-1639

John F. Disterhoft
Department of Cell and
Molecular Biology
Northwestern Univ. Medical School
303 East Chicago Avenue
Chicago, IL 60611-3008

Michael Ewers
Department of Psychology
Temple University
1701 N. 13th Street
Philadelphia, PA 19122

John H. Freeman, Jr.
Department of Psychology
University of Iowa
Seashore Hall
Iowa City, IA 52242

Mark A. Gluck
Center for Molecular and
Behavioral Neuroscience
Rutgers University
197 University Avenue
Newark, NJ 07102

Charles R. Goodlett
Department of Psychology
Science Building 120G
Indiana University–Purdue
University Indianapolis
Indianapolis, IN 46202-3272

John T. Green
Department of Psychology
Indiana University
1101 E. 10th Street
Bloomington, IN 47405-7007

David G. Lavond
Department of Psychology
Hedco Neuroscience Building 501
University of Southern California
Los Angeles, CA 90089-2520

Michael D. Mauk
Department of Neurobiology
and Anatomy
University of Texas Houston
Medical School
P.O. Box 20708
Houston, TX 77225

Matthew D. McEchron
Department of Cell and
Molecular Biology
Northwestern Univ. Medical School
303 East Chicago Avenue
Chicago, IL 60611-3008

Joselyn McLaughlin
Shirley L. Buchanan Neuroscience
Research Laboratory (151A)
Wm. Jennings Bryan Dorn
VA Medical Center
6439 Garners Ferry Road
Columbia, SC 29209-1639

Javier F. Medina
Department of Neurobiology
and Anatomy
University of Texas Houston
Medical School
P.O. Box 20708
Houston, TX 77225

Catherine E. Myers
Center for Molecular and
Behavioral Neuroscience
Rutgers University
197 University Avenue
Newark, NJ 07102

William L. Nores
Department of Neurobiology
and Anatomy
University of Texas Houston
Medical School
P.O. Box 20708
Houston, TX 77225

Donald A. Powell
Shirley L. Buchanan Neuroscience
Research Laboratory (151A)
Wm. Jennings Bryan Dorn
VA Medical Center
6439 Garners Ferry Road
Columbia, SC 29209-1639

Bernard G. Schreurs
Behavioral Neuroscience Unit
National Institutes of Health
Building 36, Room B205
Bethesda, MD 20892

Matthew A. Seager
Department of Psychology
Miami University
Oxford, OH 45056

Mark E. Stanton
U.S. Environmental Protection Agency
Neurotoxicology Division MD -74B
Research Triangle Park, NC 27711

Phillip M. Steele
Department of Neurobiology and Anatomy
University of Texas Houston Medical School
P.O. Box 20708
Houston, TX 77225

Joseph E. Steinmetz
Department of Psychology
Indiana University
1101 E. 10th Street
Bloomington, IN 47405-7007

Richard F. Thompson
Neuroscience Program
Hedco Neuroscience Building 522
University of Southern California
Los Angeles, CA 90089-2520

Diana S. Woodruff-Pak
Department of Psychology
Temple University
1701 N. 13th Street
Philadelphia, PA 19122

1 ANIMAL MODELS IN EYEBLINK CLASSICAL CONDITIONING

Joseph E. Steinmetz
Indiana University

Diana S. Woodruff-Pak
Temple University

INTRODUCTION

One of the oldest and most challenging of problems that has interested behavioral and brain scientists is how the nervous system encodes learning and memory. Over the years, a variety of approaches have been adopted to study this problem and these approaches have attacked the problem at different levels of organization and analysis. The level that is the focus of this volume is the animal model. This level provides the opportunity for a fine-grained analyses of the anatomy, physiology and neurochemistry of neuronal systems known to be involved in learning and memory.

The use of the model systems approach to explore the neural correlates of learning and memory has proven very productive. In this approach, a simplified preparation that shows clear behavioral plasticity is used to make an analysis of the neuronal substrates of the behavioral change tractable. Over the past 25 years or so, a variety of model systems have been developed including invertebrate systems such as *Aplysia* (e.g., Carew, Walters & Kandel, 1981) and *Hermissenda* (e.g., Farley & Alkon, 1982), reduced systems such as the hippocampal slice and cell culture preparations (e.g., Linden, 1994; Teyler, Cavas & Coussens, 1995), and observations of simple forms of learning in a variety of non-human species.

In 1972, Thompson, Patterson and Teyler detailed the advantages and power of using simplified "model" biological systems to study the neural mechanisms of learning and in doing so pointed out three major obstacles that have to be overcome to most successfully use this approach: 1) the behavioral properties of plasticity in the model system that is adopted has to correspond to those of intact higher vertebrates; 2) neural mechanisms that form the substrates of plasticity in the model system must be amenable to analysis; and 3) the mechanisms that underlie plasticity in the model system must also be shown to be present in intact higher organisms (Thompson, Patterson & Teyler, 1972).

Arguably, rabbit eyeblink classical conditioning has proven to be the most valuable model system for studying the neural correlates of learning and memory. The success of this model system may be largely due to the fact that the three problems identified by Thompson and his colleagues (1972) have been adequately addressed by use of the paradigm. First, behavioral eyeblink conditioning data collected from human and several species of non-human animals have shown similar patterns of acquisition, retention and extinction of this form of simple learning. Second, using recording, stimulation, lesion and pharmacological methods, analysis of the neural systems and structures involved in eyeblink classical conditioning has been possible. Clearly, the neural mechanisms of conditioning are certainly amenable to virtually all levels of analysis using this model system. Third, data collected to date have consistently demonstrated that the brain networks used in eyeblink conditioning are virtually identical across all vertebrate species studied, which include humans, monkeys, rabbits, rats, cats and mice. Indeed, the power of this model system for analyzing the neural correlates of learning and memory are apparent upon reading the various chapters in this volume that covers non-human research as well as the various chapters in its companion volume which covers human eyeblink classical conditioning (Woodruff-Pak & Steinmetz, 2000).

THE PARADIGM

Eyeblink classical conditioning is a simple associative learning and memory procedure that involves pairing two stimuli, one called a conditioned stimulus (the CS) and a second called an unconditioned stimulus (the US). At a behavioral level, the CS is typically considered to be a neutral stimulus in that its presentation does not generally elicit overt responses. Conversely, the US is chosen for its ability to consistently produce a reflexive response called the unconditioned response (the UR)—in the case of eyeblink classical conditioning, a vigorous movement of the eyelids. Typically tones, lights or tactile stimuli are used as CSs while air puffs or mild periorbital shocks are used as USs. Several CS-US pairings eventually produce learning, i.e., the CS becomes capable of eliciting an eyeblink response even in the absence of the US. The learned response is called a conditioned response (the CR). Eyeblink classical conditioning also has another interesting feature: The CR is timed such that the peak amplitude of the response occurs at the time of US onset—the performance of the CR is incredibly well-timed.

Most studies of eyeblink classical conditioning have employed delay conditioning procedures. In delay conditioning, the CS and US overlap for a period of time. This can be considered the simplest form of eyeblink classical conditioning because on delay trials presentation of the two stimuli overlap. Some studies have employed trace conditioning procedures. In trace conditioning, the CS is presented, a time period then elapses during which no stimuli are presented (i.e., the trace period), and then the US is presented. This procedure places an additional demand on the subject—the CS and US do not co-occur in time and thus the occurrence of the CS must be "remembered" by the nervous system over the trace period. The discrimination/reversal conditioning procedure has also been used successfully to explore the neural correlates of eyeblink classical conditioning. In discrimination training, two different CSs are used. One CS (the CS+) is paired with the US while the second CS (the CS-) is presented by itself. Often two tones of different frequencies are used as the CS+ and CS- but sometimes the CS+ and CS- may be in different modalities (such as using tones and lights for the CS+ and CS-, respectively). In discrimination training, the subjects learn to respond to the CS+ while not responding to the CS-. Reversal training follows discrimination training and simply entails a switch in the CS assignments. In the reversal task, the subjects must learn to respond to the former CS- while suppressing responses to the former CS+.

After paired CS-US acquisition training, extinction of the eyeblink CR is often studied. Normally, CS-alone presentations delivered over a few sessions will produce CR extinction. Extinction can also be obtained with unpaired presentations of the CS and US. In fact, unpaired CS and US training is an important control procedure used to rule out pseudoconditioning and simple sensitization effects. Finally, presentation of the US before the CS (called backwards conditioning) does not produce overt conditioned responses and this procedure has been occasionally used to study the effects of CS-US temporal overlap in a situation where acquisition of CRs does not occur.

A LITTLE HISTORY: FROM HUMANS TO RABBITS

As detailed in the companion volume to this book, *Eyeblink Classical Conditioning: Volume I – Applications in Humans* (Woodruff-Pak & Steinmetz, 2000), eyeblink classical conditioning was first performed on humans subjects. The first known published eyeblink conditioning study was reported by Zwaademaker and Lans in 1899. Dodge (1913) published a paper in English concerning the blink reflex and Cason published a series of papers on the conditioned eyeblink response between 1922 and 1925 in the *American Journal of Psychology* and in the *Journal of Experimental Psychology*. In this country, Ernest Hilgard was among the first researchers to use classical eyeblink conditioning in humans to study associative learning (e.g., Hilgard, 1933). Over the last 100 years, a number of papers detailing the results of human eyeblink conditioning experiments have been published each year.

While some progress was made in advancing the field's understanding of learning and memory processes using the human eyeblink conditioning preparation, the development of the rabbit model of eyeblink conditioning resulted in an explosion of data concerning both behavioral and biological aspects of classical conditioning. In their 1983 paper,"Twenty Years of Classical Conditioning with the Rabbit," Gormezano, Kehoe and Marshall elegantly detailed the origin of the rabbit eyeblink classical conditioning preparations. In the early 1960s, Gormezano and associates developed the rabbit preparations "to remedy long-term deficiencies and difficulties in the study of classical conditioning (Gormezano et al., 1983, p. 202)." Of particular note for the present discussion, Gormezano and co-workers recognized the potential use of classical conditioning for studying neuronal function associated with associative learning and also recognized the limitations of the Pavlovian procedures that had been developed, including human eyeblink conditioning procedures. Some of the problems inherent in human eyeblink conditioning included some measurement difficulties, variability in responding, difficulties in applying physiological manipulations, and the presence of voluntary responding in the human subject. In short, Gormezano and his colleagues developed the rabbit classical eyeblink conditioning "to focus attention on the objective determinants of conditioning and to provide the robust data necessary to address both physiological and theoretical questions (Gormezano et al., 1983, p. 202)."

Behavioral Experiments

For a variety of reasons, rabbits proved to be ideal subjects for eyeblink classical conditioning experiments. First, they adapt well to restraint with little or no training and therefore can be held calmly and quietly within restraint boxes for experiments that last 60-90 minutes. This allows for the use of many behavioral (and neural) manipulations in awake, behaving animals. Second, recording the CR/UR is relatively easy. Investigators have used mechanical potentiometers, electromyographic methods, and photodiode and infrared technologies to monitor nictitating membrane or external eyelid movements (both of which are typically conditioned with paired CS-US trials). Third, rabbits show relatively low spontaneous blinking rates thus very few trials are lost to random blinking that might interfere with conditioned or reflexive responding. Forth, depending on the exact training parameters used, the rabbits learn the response in 100-200 trials. This rate of learning produces enough training trials to track a gradual acquisition (and extinction) of the learned response without requiring extended training over many tedious sessions. Fifth, naive rabbits show few "alpha" responses to the CS—that is, overt behavioral responses that occur to presentation of the CS before training is begun. The lack of alpha responses makes it easier to evaluate conditioned responding during paired training sessions.

Over the years, due largely to the efforts of Gormezano and colleagues as well as other researcher such as Moore, Wagner, Patterson, Kehoe and their associates, a great deal is known about behavioral aspects of classical eyeblink conditioning. Moreover, these procedures have been used to study a number of learning and memory phenomena such as the interstimulus interval function (e.g., Smith 1968), CS- and US-intensity effects on acquisition and extinction (e.g., Ashton, Bitgood & Moore, 1969; Scavio & Gormezano, 1974), differences between delay and trace conditioning (e.g., Smith, Coleman & Gormezano, 1969), effects of massed versus distributed training (e.g., Levinthal, Tartell, Margolin & Fishman, 1985), transfer of training effects (e.g., Scavio & Gormezano, 1980), response timing effects (e.g., Kehoe, Horn & Horn, 1993), bidirectional and backward conditioning (e.g., Smith et al., 1969), mechanisms of reinforcement (e.g., Coleman & Gormezano, 1979), stimulus generalization and discrimination (e.g., Macrae & Kehoe, 1995) and a number of "higher-order" conditioning effects such as sensory preconditioning (e.g., Port & Patterson, 1984), conditioned inhibition (e.g., Blazis & Moore, 1991), latent inhibition (e.g., Solomon & Moore, 1975) and blocking (Giftakis & Tait, 1998). In short, use of the rabbit eyeblink classical conditioning paradigm has significantly advanced our understanding of learning and memory processes.

Neural Experiments

Background

As should be evident upon reading the various chapters in this volume, more is known about the neural structures and systems that are involved in eyeblink classical conditioning than any other learning and memory task. A large part of this success is directly due to the nature of the conditioning task as well as the choice of the rabbit as a subject for the neural experiments that were undertaken over the years.

Classical conditioning procedures afford the experimenter maximum control over the training situation and this has proven extremely beneficial for collecting and interpreting neural data. The experimenter determines when trials are delivered along with the timing and arrangement of stimuli within individual trials. Also, the individual trials are relatively brief. These advantages were especially important for the early neural recording experiments that were conducted in the late 1970s and early 1980s, before high-speed computer digitization and high-capacity storage were available to researchers. Individual trials of 500 - 1500 msec could be delivered with the researchers knowing precisely when the trial would be given (i.e., when to examine neural activity). These relatively small, discrete chunks of behavioral and neural data could be analyzed and examined, even with the relatively early computers. The discrete nature of the classical conditioning procedure can be contrasted with operant situations where the subject, for the most part, is in control of stimulus presentations and/or response generation. The relatively low capacity and low speed of computers of the 1970s and 1980s made it very difficult to record the long streams of behavioral and neural data that were necessary to capture when the subject decided to issue an operant response. Hence, until technological developments in the computer industry occurred, progress with instrumental and operant procedures was slower than progress with eyeblink classical conditioning.

Variations of the eyeblink conditioning procedure are easy to perform and under the control of the experimenter (e.g., interstimulus interval shifts, altering the CS or US, adopting trace versus delay procedures, evaluating stimulus pre-exposure effects, etc.). These manipulations have allowed for very thorough examinations of the role of brain structures and systems in the various aspects of the eyeblink classical conditioning task. Also, the response requirement of the eyeblink classical conditioning task (i.e., a simple, discrete movement of the eyelids) enabled rather tight correlations to be established between neural activation and manipulations and behavioral responding.

The nature of responding in the eyeblink conditioning task also allowed researchers to separate learning from performance variables. Because the UR elicited on US-alone trials could be recorded and compared with CRs elicited on CS trials, the effects of biological manipulations on learning versus performance could be examined. For example, lesions could potentially disrupt associative learning processes or cause deficits in the motor system that affect performance of the reflexive response as well as the learned response. These effects are separable by delivering US-alone as well as paired CS-US trials and assessing changes in the UR as well as the CR. In addition, CS-alone trials can be given along with US-alone and CS-US paired trials during recording experiments when attempting to distinguish between CS- and US-related activity.

The choice of the rabbit as a subject for behavioral/neural studies was fortuitous. First, the size of the rabbit brain is somewhere between the brain of a rat and the brain of a cat. Thus, recording procedures required less miniaturization than required for rat and mouse recording experiments. Second, the docile nature of the rabbit also made recording experiments and drug infusion studies extremely easy to perform. The rabbits sit quietly in restraint boxes or cloth slings with very little head movements. It has actually been possible to record single-unit activity from rabbits without restraining the head. Third, the left and right eyeblink responses can be conditioned independently in the rabbit. Therefore, each rabbit can act as its own control in lesion and recording experiments. This has proven very useful for ruling out motivation and arousal effects as explanations for some of the results of lesion, stimulation, pharmacological and recording studies that have been performed over the years.

In summary, the choice of eyeblink classical conditioning as a paradigm and the choice of the rabbit as an experimental subject were largely responsible for the great deal of success that researchers have had in exploring the neural substrates of this form of classical conditioning. A brief history of the use of this procedure to study neural correlates of learning and memory is presented here. This history is not meant to be an exhaustive review of studies that explored the neural substrates of eyeblink classical conditioning, but rather a sampling of research that has been conducted over the years. Much of the history of research in this area is covered in the chapters that follow in this volume.

Early Neural Studies

Some of the earliest studies of the involvement of the brain in eyeblink classical conditioning concentrated on the involvement of cerebral cortex in acquisition and performance of the eyeblink CR and on studying the sensory and motor pathways involved in conditioning. Interest in the involvement of cerebral cortex as a location for the memory trace for eyeblink conditioning is explicable given the emphasis that Pavlov (1927), Lashley (1929) and others gave to the cortical mediation of learning. Interest in the sensory and motor pathways involved in eyeblink conditioning also seems natural as defining input and output pathways in a system would seem important for determining where in the brain convergence of the CS and US occurs.

In a series of studies that were first published in 1968, Oakley and Steele Russell provided convincing data that pointed to a subcortical storage location for classically conditioned eyeblink responses (e.g., Oakley & Steele Russell, 1968; 1972; 1977). They showed that various lesions of neocortex, delivered either before training or after asymptotic responding was established, failed to affect conditioned responding. Indeed, the lack of effect of neocortical lesion was striking and indicated that lower brain areas were involved in acquisition and performance of the eyeblink CR. In more recent work, Mauk and Thompson (1987) similarly demonstrated that decerebration did not affect conditioned responses. These studies ruled out cerebral cortex as the critical structure for acquisition and memory of eyeblink conditioning.

An early example of studies designed to explore the CS and US systems engaged in eyeblink conditioning is Bruner's (1966) study of the effect of electrical brain stimulation on the rate of conditioning. He delivered hypothalamic stimulation that was demonstrated to be either positively or negatively reinforcing in an operant situation simultaneously with the presentation of a periorbital shock US during eyeblink conditioning and observed a facilitation in conditioning. These data were interpreted by Bruner to demonstrate the importance of the reinforcement mechanisms in classical conditioning. Studies by Patterson (1970; 1971) illustrate early attempts to study and define critical pathways involved in projecting CS information into the brain. Patterson substituted electrical stimulation of the inferior colliculus for the normal peripheral CSs used in conditioned and observed robust conditioning. He argued the activation of the inferior colliculus served as a sufficient CS input for conditioning and suggested that auditory CSs may utilize this pathway.

Early studies also examined the final common pathway for generating the conditioned eyeblink response and also examined potential plasticity in brain stem motor nuclei that made up these pathways. For example, in a series of experiments conducted in Richard Thompson's laboratory at the University of California, Irvine, the involvements of the abducens and accessory abducens nuclei in generating the nictitating membrane UR and CR were studied (e.g., Cegavske, Patterson & Thompson, 1979; Cegavske, Thompson, Patterson & Gormezano, 1976). Other studies showed that electrical stimulation of the abducens and accessory abducens nuclei could be substituted for a peripheral US and produce conditioned responding (Mis, Gormezano & Harvey, 1979; Powell & Moore, 1980). Additional experiments showed that these nuclei were capable of pairing-specific plasticity. For example, Ison and Leonard (1971) first reported that the excitability of the eyeblink UR to facial shock was increased during and following tone presentations. A potential neural basis for this effect was explored by Young, Cegavske & Thompson (1976) who demonstrated tone-induced alterations in excitability of abducens nucleus motoneurons that accompanied the behavioral excitability changes.

In addition to collecting early data concerning the neural structures involved in eyeblink conditioning, these early studies laid the foundation for later studies involving the brainstem and cerebellum. Indeed, many of the experimental techniques and strategies pioneered in these early studies were successfully used in subsequent studies that have established the cerebellum as critical for eyeblink conditioning. A number of these subsequent studies are described in this volume.

Hippocampal and Limbic System Studies

Schmaltz and Thieos (1972) demonstrated that acquisition and extinction of a classically conditioned response in rabbits was, for the most part, not affected by large aspiration lesions of the hippocampus. However, given the growing body of literature in the 1970s that implicated the hippocampus in learning and memory processes, interest remained high in exploring the involvement of the limbic system in associative learning. Eyeblink classical conditioning proved ideal for further studies, especially neuronal recording experiments.

In a series of studies, Berger, Thompson, and their colleagues demonstrated that hippocampal neurons fired in a pattern that was related to the performance of the behavioral CR (Berger, Alger & Thompson, 1976; Berger, Rinaldi, Weisz & Thompson, 1983; Berger & Thompson, 1977, 1978a, 1978b). Specifically, pyramidal cells in the hippocampus exhibited learning-related neuronal plasticity that developed over the course of conditioning. Within individual training trials, the pattern of discharge of these cells correlated strongly with the amplitude-time course of the behavioral response. This initial study was followed by a series of other recording and lesion experiments that explored the involvement of the hippocampus and limbic system in the acquisition and performance of the classically conditioned eyeblink response. For example, the effects of medial septal lesions were evaluated (Berry & Thompson, 1979) as were recordings taken from the medial septum during conditioning (Berger & Thompson, 1978).

The data collected in the late 1970s indicated that the hippocampus, while not necessary for basic delay conditioning, was somehow involved in encoding some aspects of the learning. Subsequent lesion and recording studies used in conjunction with variations of the classical conditioning procedure have further demonstrated an hippocampal involvement in conditioning. For example, lesions of the hippocampus are known to impair trace conditioning (Moyer, Deyo & Disterhoft, 1990) and neural recordings taken during trace conditioning reveal training-related activity in pyramidal cells (Disterhoft, Thompson & Moyer, 1994). Also, critical hippocampal involvement in latent inhibition, sensory preconditioning and discrimination/reversal learning has been demonstrated (e.g., Solomon & Moore, 1975). Work continues on defining a more specific role for the hippocampus in eyeblink classical conditioning.

Cerebellar and Brainstem Studies

When it was clear that the hippocampus and neocortex was not critical for basic delay conditioning, attention turned to the involvement of lower brain systems in eyeblink conditioning. In the early 1980s, in a series of papers, Thompson and colleagues reported an intriguing finding. Lesions of the cerebellum, ipsilateral to the side being trained, prevented naive rabbits from learning the conditioned eyeblink response and abolished CRs in rabbits trained before the lesion was delivered (McCormick et al., 1981). Further, there appeared to be no recovery of responding in the lesioned rabbits. This basic discovery led to an extensive series of experiments in the Thompson laboratory, and other laboratories around the world, that explored the involvement of the brain stem and cerebellum in eyeblink classical conditioning. These studies employed a variety of experimental techniques such as brain lesions, brain microstimulation, multiple- and single-unit recording, pharmacological manipulations, and anatomical tract-tracing. In total, these studies identified key areas of cerebellar cortex and the deep cerebellar nuclei that appear to encode conditioning. In addition, the CS and US pathways have largely been defined as well as the output pathway from the cerebellum to brain stem motor nuclei responsible for generating the CRs (see Steinmetz, 1998, for review).

These data have indicated that CSs used in eyeblink conditioning are projected to discrete regions of the cerebellar cortex and the interpositus nucleus via mossy fibers that originate in the basilar pontine nuclei. The USs used in eyeblink conditioning appear to be projected to regions of cerebellar cortex and the interpositus nucleus via climbing fibers that originate in the dorsolateral region of the inferior olive complex. Conditioning is thought to be the product of plasticity induced in cerebellar cortical and nuclear regions due to the conjunctive activation of these regions by the CS and the US. It is hypothesized that the pairing-induced alteration of cerebellar activity is then capable of exciting brainstem motor neurons (via red nucleus activation) that are responsible for the generations of the behavioral CR. In essence, this defined neural circuit provides the sufficient and essential substrates for basic eyeblink classical conditioning.

Much of the current work in this system is in defining the roles of various areas in the conditioning process along with uncovering the cellular mechanisms that may be responsible for the induction and maintenance of plasticity in the cerebellar system. In addition, the interactions of the cerebellar system with other brain systems known to be engaged in conditioning (such as the limbic system) are actively being studied. In sum, it is clear that we know more about the neural substrates of eyeblink classical conditioning than any other type of mammalian learning and memory. This is likely due to the choice of paradigm, experimental subject, and the ingenuity of many of the researchers who have studied this basic problem. Much of this research is presented and summarized in this volume.

Eyeblink Classical Conditioning in Species Other than Rabbits

For many of the reasons detailed above, the rabbit for the most part has been the species of choice for behavioral and neural research concerning eyeblink classical conditioning. However, over the years, other species have been used to explore behavioral and neural correlates of eyeblink conditioning such as cats (Patterson, Olah & Clement, 1977) and ferrets (Hesslow, Svensson & Ivarsson, 1999). In fact, the eyeblink classical conditioning procedure was first developed using humans as subjects and human eyelid conditioning has been "rediscovered" as of late. For coverage of human eyeblink conditioning, interested readers should see the companion volume to this book, *Eyeblink Classical Conditioning: Volume I – Applications in Humans* (Woodruff-Pak & Steinmetz, 2000).

There has been a great deal of interest lately in using rats and mice in eyeblink classical conditioning experiments (e.g., Chen et al., 1986; Stanton, Freeman & Skelton, 1992 and Chapters 2, 4, 5, 6 and 11, this volume). Standard rat and mouse conditioning procedures have been established and there are a growing number of investigators who are publishing papers detailing experiments with these species. There are some advantages to using rats and mice in this area of research. Compared to rabbits, rats are generally less expensive to purchase and maintain, rats are capable of displaying a wider repertoire of well-defined behaviors that can be studied simultaneously or in addition to eyeblink conditioning, and rats have been used in a wider variety of neurobiological experiments (i.e., we know relatively more about the anatomy, pharmacology and physiology of the rat brain than many other species). Mice show tremendous promise for use in genetic studies of brain function. Indeed, mutants and transgenic mice are now being studied in a variety of laboratories and eyeblink classical conditioning has proven to be an ideal behavioral manipulation to study in combination with genetic manipulations.

In total, use of the variety of species as animal models during eyeblink classical conditioning studies, in addition to the rabbit, is adding to the ever-growing base of data concerning the neural correlates of simple associative learning.

AN OVERVIEW OF THIS VOLUME

We had three major goals in assembling the contributions to this volume. First, we wanted to present the current state of knowledge concerning the neural substrates of eyeblink classical conditioning. To this end, we have included chapters that detail the involvement of a variety of brain areas in eyeblink conditioning, brain areas that include the cerebellum and brainstem, the hippocampus and limbic system, the cerebral cortex, the thalamus, and the neostriatum. Second, we wanted to highlight the myriad of experimental approaches that have been used to delineate the neuronal networks and processes involved in eyeblink conditioning. These experimental approaches include electrophysiology, microstimulation, lesion, cellular/molecular, pharmacological, and computational methodologies. Third, we wanted to show the usefulness of eyeblink conditioning for studying a number of phenomena related to behavioral and brain function such as development, aging, pathology, drug effects, and motivation.

In addition to the brief history and overview of the neurobiology of eyeblink classical conditioning that is presented in this introductory chapter, Richard Thompson's contribution to this volume (Chapter 2) provides his frank and personal insight into his laboratory's efforts to establish the cerebellum as the "engram" for eyeblink classical conditioning using the rabbit as a model system. As detailed in this chapter, not everyone in the neuroscience community readily embraced the idea that the cerebellum was capable of showing plasticity because the cerebellum was considered to be a motor and postural control structure and not a structure capable of associating two stimuli in time. As Thompson vividly describes in Chapter 2, the early lesion and recording studies sparked lively debate on both sides of the issue, a debate that underscores how passionate beliefs can be held as data are collected.

Chapters 3 and 4 provide an overview of neurobiological approaches that have been used in conjunction with eyeblink classical conditioning. In Chapter 3, David Lavond and M. Claire Cartford review the results of several lesions experiments that have been used to study neural structures involved in eyeblink conditioning. The original discovery of the involvement of the cerebellum in eyeblink conditioning was based on the observation that cerebellar lesions produced a non-recoverable deficit in conditioning—i.e., the lesion technique has been key in establishing the involvement of the cerebellum in conditioning. In their chapter, Lavond and Cartford discuss data and issues concerning the use of non-reversible lesions and present recent data collected with a related technique, reversible brain inactivation. This latter technique has provided perhaps the most convincing data to date of the essential involvement of the cerebellum in eyeblink conditioning.

In Chapter 4, Joseph Steinmetz reviews the results of electrophysiological and microstimulation experiments that have been undertaken to study the neural substrates of eyeblink conditioning in animals. Neural recordings have been taken from a wide variety of brain regions concomitantly with eyeblink conditioning including the limbic system, cerebral cortex, the neostriatum, brainstem areas, and the cerebellum. The high degree of stimulus control and response control afforded by this preparation has enabled the establishment of strong relationships between activity in well-defined brain areas and the acquisition and performance of the conditioned response. The use of microstimulation is also reviewed. In general, this technique was used extensively to establish CS and US pathways involved in conditioning in several experiments that substituted electrical stimulation of brain regions for presentation of the peripheral stimuli typically used as CSs or USs.

The use of eyeblink classical conditioning to studies issues related to life span development are presented in Chapters 5, 6, and 7. In Chapter 5, Mark Stanton and John Freeman review the research that has been undertaken to study the time course of the development of eyeblink conditioning with reference to the development of brain function. Stanton and his associates have developed rat conditioning procedures so these developmental data are based on a rat model. Thus, information about the use of the rat as a subject in eyeblink conditioning studies is also presented in this chapter. In Chapter 6, Charles Goodlett, Mark Stanton and Joseph Steinmetz discuss how the rat eyeblink conditioning model can be used to study abnormalities in development. They review their work, to date, in studying the effects of neonatal alcohol exposure on conditioning and brain function assessed in young and adult rats. In this model, neonatal ethanol exposure produces abnormalities in cerebellar and brainstem function—eyeblink classical conditioning is being used in conjunction with anatomical and brain recording techniques to assess the impact of the ethanol exposure on behavioral and brain functioning. In Chapter 7, John Green and Diana Woodruff-Pak review the large body of data concerning the use of eyeblink classical conditioning in the animal model to study normal aging processes. They detail the power of analysis that is realized by using this behavioral procedure to study aging effects on brain and behavioral function.

Chapters 8, 9, and 10 present a variety of data and ideas that are related to viewing the neurobiological substrates of eyeblink conditioning from two different levels of analysis; a cellular/molecular level versus a systems level. Bernard Schreurs details in Chapter 8 a variety of research conducted on the cellular correlates of eyeblink conditioning. To develop a full understanding of the plasticity processes that take place in neurons that are involved in encoding conditioning, it is very important that studies into cellular and molecular nature of these changes are undertaken. Schreurs summarizes the studies that have been conducted to date, especially those involving cellular processes related to long-term depression (LTD) at the synapses of cerebellar neurons. In Chapter 9, William Nores, Javier Medina, Phillip Steele and Michael Mauk describe how they have studied and modeled the relative contributions of cerebellar cortex and the deep cerebellar nuclei to the conditioning process using cortical lesions, behavioral variations, and computational modeling techniques. This chapter details the controversy that has existed in defining the critical roles of cortex and the deep nuclei in conditioning. In addition, the chapter emphasizes a systems-level approach to understanding how a neural network can be defined and studied to develop a comprehensive understanding of the neural substrates of a learned behavior. In Chapter 10, M. Todd Allen, Catherine Myers and Mark Gluck summarize their computational modeling and experimental approaches to studying the neural network involved in eyeblink classical conditioning. In this chapter, computational models are described that have been constrained by known behavioral and neural data. These models include descriptions of the involvement of the cerebellum and limbic system in basic delay eyeblink conditioning and a general conceptual framework for viewing interactions between brain areas during conditioning. In addition, they provide details of models that account for variations in the basic conditioning procedure such as those required for trace conditioning, sensory preconditioning and latent inhibition.

The last section of this book includes four chapters that represent extensions and uses of the eyeblink classical conditioning procedure to study an array of issues that are related to general learning and memory processing in the brain. In Chapter 11, Donald Powell, Jocelyn McLaughlin, and Mark Chachich detail the efforts of Powell and his colleagues, over the years, to study the similarities and differences between behavioral and neural correlates of autonomic and somatic classical conditioning. Differences in brain systems that encode the autonomic and somatic learning are presented and discussed and a behavioral stages model of classical conditioning is then described. This interesting model is described within the context of neural systems that support the early stages of the model, in which autonomic responses are learned and later stages in which somatomotor responses are learned. In Chapter 12, Stephen Berry, Matthew Seager, Yukiko Asaka, and Ramie Borgnis focus on classical conditioning of appetitively and aversively motivated responding (i.e., jaw-movement and eyeblink conditioning). Berry and his colleagues describe their recording, lesion and drug studies that have been undertaken to study neurobiological correlates of motivation. For the most part, discussion centers around the function of the hippocampus and related structures in processing conditioning-related information.

In Chapter 13, John Disterhoft and Matthew McEchron discuss the key role played by the hippocampus and forebrain structures in the acquisition and consolidation of trace eyeblink classical conditioning, a variation of eyeblink conditioning that is highly dependent on hippocampal activation. Their chapter details extracellular neuronal recording experiments that have provided insight into the function of higher brain areas during conditioning. In addition, they summarize a series of intracellular recording studies involving hippocampal neurons that were undertaken to describe biophysical properties of neurons that may be related to conditioning-induced plasticity. Finally, in Chapter 14, Diana Woodruff-Pak and Michael Ewers describe how eyeblink classical conditioning has been used to study the behavioral and pharmacological effects of cognitive-enhancing drugs on basic associative learning. Above all, this chapter serves to underscore the usefulness of this paradigm for investigating drug effects. Indeed, the parallel in the human and non-human neural circuitry required to learn and remember this simple behavioral task makes it ideal for future studies in humans involving drugs such as the cognitive-enhancing compounds described in this chapter.

CONCLUSIONS

Upon reading the individual chapters in the volume, it should become apparent that a wealth of information concerning the neural substrates of eyeblink classical conditioning is now available. While there still remain some differences of opinions concerning the relative roles of specific brain structures during eyeblink conditioning, there is a growing consensus that the basic neural circuits in the brain that are engaged during learning and performance of this task have been defined. Progress in two research areas should be especially important in the coming years. First, now that specific brain areas involved in conditioning have been identified, it should now be possible to uncover the essential molecular and cellular processes that occur within neurons and between neurons to promote the acquisition and memory of this simple, associative learning procedure. Second, it is important to conduct further studies aimed at delineating interactions between parts of the neural circuit known to be engaged in the conditioning. Indeed, use of the eyeblink conditioning procedure seems ideal for advancing our understanding of how activity in interacting brain systems and structures can produce more complex behaviors and cognitions.

REFERENCES

Ashton, A.B., Bitgood, S.C., & Moore, J.W. (1969). Differential conditioning of the rabbit nictitating membrane response as a function of US shock intensity and duration. *Psychonomic Science, 15*, 127-218.

Berger, T.W., Alger, B., & Thompson, R.F. (1976). Neuronal substrate of classical conditioning in the hippocampus. *Science, 192*, 483-485.

Berger, T.W., Rinaldi, P.C., Weisz, D.J., & Thompson, R.F. (1983). Single-unit analysis of different hippocampal cell types during classical conditioning of rabbit nictitating membrane response. *Journal of Neurophysiology, 50*, 1197-1219.

Berger, T.W., & Thompson, R.F. (1977). Identification of pyramidal cells as the critical elements in hippocampal neuronal plasticity during learning. *Proceedings of the National Academy of Sciences (U.S.A.), 75*, 1572-1576.

Berger, T.W., & Thompson, R.F. (1978a). Neuronal plasticity in the limbic system during classical conditioning of the rabbit nictitating membrane response: I. the hippocampus. *Brain Research, 145*, 323-346.

Berger, T.W., & Thompson, R.F. (1978b). Neuronal plasticity in the limbic system during classical conditioning of the rabbit nictitating membrane response: II. septum and mammillary bodies. *Brain Research, 156*, 293-314.

Berry, S.D., & Thompson, R.F. (1979). Medial septal lesions retard classical conditioning of the nictitating membrane responses in rabbits. *Science, 205*, 208-209.

Blazis, D.E.J., & Moore, J.W. (1991). Conditioned inhibition of he nictitating membrane response in rabbits following hypothalamic and mesencephalic lesions. *Behavioural Brain Research, 46*, 71-81.

Bruner, A. (1966). Facilitation of classical conditioning in rabbits by reinforcing brain stimulation. *Psychonomic Science, 6*, 211-212.

Carew, T.J., Walters, E.T., & Kandel, E.R. (1981). Associative learning in *aplysia*: cellular correlates supporting a conditioned fear hypothesis. *Science, 211*, 501-504.

Cason, H. (1922). The conditioned eyelid reaction. *Journal of Experimental Psychology, 5*, 153-195.

Cason, H. (1923). A note on the conditioned eyelid reaction. *Journal of Experimental Psychology, 6*, 82-83.

Cason, H. (1924). The concept of backward association. *American Journal of Psychology, 35*, 217-221.

Cason, H. (1925). General aspects of the conditioned response. *Psychological Review, 32*, 285-331.

Cegavske, C.F., Patterson, M.M., & Thompson, R.F. (1979). Neuronal unit activity in the abducens nucleus during classical conditioning of the nictitating membrane response in the rabbit (*oryctolagus cuniculus*). *Journal of Comparative Physiological Psychology, 93*, 595-609.

Cegavske, C.F., Thompson, R.F., Patterson, M.M., & Gormezano, I. (1976). Mechanisms of efferent neuronal control of the reflex nictitating membrane response in rabbit (*oryctolagus cuniculus*). *Journal of Comparative and Physiological Psychology, 90*, 411-423.

Chen, L., Bao, S., Lockard, J.M., Kim, J.J., & Thompson, R.F. (1996). Impaired classical eyeblink conditioning in cerebellar-lesioned and Purkinje cell degeneration (pcd) mutant mice. *Journal of Neuroscience, 16*, 2829-2838.

Coleman, S.R., & Gormezano, I. (1979). Classical conditioning and the "law of effect": Historical and empirical assessment. *Behaviorism, 7,* 1-33.

Disterhoft, J.F., Thompson, L.T., & Moyer, J., Jr. (1994). Cellular mechanisms of associative learning in the hippocampus. In J. Delacour (Ed.), *The Memory System of the Brain,* (pp. 431-492). New Jersey: World Scientific.

Dodge, R. (1913). The refractory phase of the normal wink reflex. *American Journal of Psychology, 24,* 1-7.

Farley, J., & Alkon, D. (1982). Associative neural and behavioral changes in *hermissenda*: consequences of neural system orientation for light and pairing specificity. *Journal of Neurophysiology, 48,* 785-807.

Giftakis, J.E., & Tait, R.W. (1998). Blocking of the rabbit's classically conditioned nictitating membrane response: Effects of modifications of contextual associative strength. *Learning and Motivation, 29,* 23-48.

Gormezano, I., Kehoe, E.J., & Marshall, B.S. (1983). Twenty years of classical conditioning with the rabbit. *Progress in Psychobiology and Physiological Psychology, 10,* 197-275.

Hesslow, G., Svensson, P., & Ivarsson, M. (1999). Learned movements elicited by direct stimulation of cerebellar mossy fiber afferents. *Neuron, 24,* 179-185.

Hilgard, E.R. (1933). Modification of reflexes and conditioned reaction. *Journal of General Psychology, 9,* 210-215.

Ison, J.R., & Leonard, D.W. (1971). Effects of auditory stimului on the amplitude of the nictitating membrane reflex of the rabbit (*oryctolagus cuniculus*). *Journal of Comparitive Physiological Psychology, 75,* 157-164.

Kehoe, E.J., Horne, P.S., & Horne, A.J. (1993). Discrimination learning using different CS-US intervals in classical conditioning of the rabbit's nictitating membrane response. *Psychobiology, 21,* 277-285.

Lashley, K.S. (1929). Learning: I. Nervous-mechanisms of learning. In: L. Morechison (Ed.), *The Foundations of Experimental Psychology,* Clark University Press: Worcester, MA.

Levinthal, C.F., Tartell, R.H., Margolin, C.M., & Fishman, H. (1985). The CS-US interval (ISI) function in rabbit nictitating membrane response conditioning with very long intertrial intervals. *Animal Learning & Behavior, 13,* 228-232.

Linden, D.J. (1994). Long-term synaptic depression in the mammalian brain. *Neuron, 12,* 457-472.

Mauk, M.D., & Thompson, R.F. (1987). Retention of classically conditioned eyelid responses following acute decerebration. *Brain Research, 403,* 89-95.

Macrae, M., & Kehoe, E.J. (1995). Transfer between conditional and discrete discriminations in conditioning of the rabbit nictitating membrane response. *Learning and Motivation, 26,* 380-420.

McCormick, D.A., Lavond, D.G., Clark, G.A., Kettner, R.R., Rising, C.E., & Thompson, R.F. (1981). The engram found? Role of the cerebellum in classical conditioning of nictitating membrane and eyelid responses. *Bulletin of the Psychonomic Society, 18,* 103-105.

Mis, F.W., Gormezano, I., & Harvey, J.A. (1979). Stimulation of abducens nucleus supports classical conditioning of the nictitating membrane response. *Science, 206,* 473-475.

Moyer, J.R., Deyo, R.A., & Disterhoft, J.F. (1990). Hippocampectomy disrupts trace eye-blink conditioning in rabbits. *Behavioral Neuroscience, 104,* 243-252.

Oakley, D.A., & Russell, I.S. (1968). Mass action and Pavlovian conditioning. *Psychonomic Science, 12,* 91-92.

Oakley, D.A., & Russell, I.S. (1972). Neocortical lesions and Pavlovian conditioning. *Physiology & Behavior, 8,* 915-926.

Oakley, D.A., & Russell, I.S. (1977). Subcortical storeage of Pavlovian conditioning in the rabbit. *Physiology & Behavior, 18,* 931-937.

Patterson, M.M. (1970). Classical conditioning of the rabbit's (*oryctolagus cuniculus*) nictitating membrane response with fluctuating ISI and intracranial CS1. *Journal of Comparative Physiological Psychology, 72,* 193-202.

Patterson, M. M. (1971). Inferior colliculus CS intensity effect on rabbit nictitating membrane conditioning. *Physiology & Behavior, 6,* 273-278.

Patterson, M.M., Olah, J., & Clement, J. (1977). Classical nictitating membrane conditioning in the awake, normal, restrained cat. *Science, 196,* 1124-1126.

Pavlov, I.P. (1927). *Conditioned Reflex* (translated by G.V. Anrep). Oxford University Press: London.

Port, R.L, & Patterson, M.M. (1984). Fimbrial lesions and sensory preconditioning. *Behavioral Neuroscience, 98,* 584-589.

Powell, G.M., & Moore, J.W. (1980). Conditioning of the nictitating membrane response in rabbit (*orytolagus cuniculus*) with electrical brain-stimulation as the unconditioned stimulus. *Physiology & Behavior, 25*, 205-216.

Scavio, M.J., & Gormezano, I. (1974). CS intensity effects upon rabbit nictitating membrane conditioning, extinction, and generalization. *Pavlovian Journal of Biological Sciences, 9*, 25-34.

Scavio, J.J., & Gormezano, I. (1980). Classical-classical transfer: Effects of prior appetitive conditioning upon aversive conditioning in rabbits. *Animal Learning and Behavior, 8*, 218-224.

Schmaltz, L. W., & Theios, J. (1972). Acquisition and extinction of a classically conditioned response in hippocampectomized rabbit (*oryctolagus cuniculus*). *Journal of Comparative Physiological Psychology, 79*, 328-333.

Smith, M.C. (1968). CS-US interval and US intensity in classical conditioning of the rabbit's nictitating membrane response. *Journal of Comparative and Physiological Psychology, 66*, 679-687.

Smith, M.C., Coleman, S.R., & Gormezano, I. (1969). Classical conditioning of the rabbit's nictitating membrane response at backward, simultaneous, and forward CS-US intervals. *Journal of Comparative and Physiological Psychology, 69*, 226-331.

Solomon, P.R., & Moore, J.W. (1975). Latent inhibition and stimulus generalization of the classically conditioned nictitating membrane response in rabbits (*Oryctolagus cuniculus*) following dorsal hippocampal ablation. *Journal of Comparative and Physiological Psychology, 89*, 1192-1203.

Stanton, M.E., Freeman, J.H., & Skelton, R.W. (1992). Eyeblink conditioning in the developing rat. *Behavioral Neuroscience, 106*, 657-665.

Steinmetz, J.E. (1998). The localization of a simple type of learning and memory: The cerebellum and classical eyeblink conditioning. *Current Directions in Psychological Research, 7*, 72-77.

Teyler, T.J., Cavus, I., & Coussens, C. (1995). Synaptic plasticity in the hippocampal slice: Functional consequences. *Journal of Neuroscience Methods, 59*, 11-17.

Thompson, R.F., Patterson, M.M., & Teyler, T.J. (1972). The neurophysiology of learning. *Annual Review of Psychology, 23*, 73-104.

Woodruff-Pak, D.S., & Steinmetz, J.E. (2000). *Eyeblink Classical Conditioning, Vol 1: Human Applications*, Boston: Kluwer.

Young, R. A., Cegavske, C. F., & Thompson, R. F. (1976). Tone-induced changes in excitability of abducens motoneurons and of the reflex path of nictitating membrane response in rabbit (*oryctolagus cuniculus*). *Journal of Comparative and Physiological Psychology, 90*, 424-434.

Zwaardemaker, H. & Lans, L.J. (1899). Uber ein Stadium relativer Unerregparkeit als Ursache des intermitterenden Charakters des Lidschlagreflexes. *Centbl. F. Physiol. 13*, 325-329.

2 DISCOVERING THE BRAIN SUBSTRATES OF EYEBLINK CLASSICAL CONDITIONING

Richard F. Thompson
University of Southern California

INTRODUCTION

This chapter is of necessity a rather personal document. From the beginning of my scientific career I had a deep interest in the brain mechanisms of learning and memory, stemming in part from the writings of Pavlov, Lashley and Hebb. I had the good fortune to obtain a Ph.D. at the University of Wisconsin with W.J. Brogden, a pioneering figure in this field who discovered sensory preconditioning and did classic work with Gantt on the possible role of cerebellum in classical conditioning (Brogden & Gantt, 1942). My good fortune continued in a postdoctoral fellowship with Clinton Woolsey at the University of Wisconsin School of Medicine. Woolsey was an eminent neurophysiologist whose pioneering work first demonstrated the exquisitely detailed representations of sensory projections to the cerebral cortex and the organization of motor cortex, as well as the organization of sensory and motor cortical projections to the cerebellar cortex.

SPINAL PLASTICITY

From the time of my graduate studies I searched for behavioral paradigms that would permit analysis of the neuronal mechanisms that seemed to code and store memories. In initial work in my own laboratory I collaborated with a colleague, W. Alden Spencer (we had become good friends as college students at Reed) when we both took assistant professor positions at the University of Oregon Medical School in Portland, I in Psychiatry and Alden in Physiology. We focused on habituation of the spinal flexion reflex as a model system of behavioral plasticity, e.g., nonassociative learning. In these studies we characterized the basic properties of habituation and sensitization, ruled out a number of then current hypotheses of mechanisms and concluded that the basic mechanism of habituation appeared to be a form of synaptic depression (Thompson & Spencer, 1966). On the other hand, dishabituation was clearly a superimposed facilitation process of sensitization. At the University of California,

Irvine, a graduate student, Philip Groves, and I developed these notions into the "dual-process" theory, which accounted for a wide range of neural and behavioral phenomena of habituation, a theory that remains influential in the field today (Groves & Thompson, 1970).

Beginning at Oregon and continuing at the University of California, Irvine, I and my students were able to show that classical conditioning of the hindlimb flexion reflex in the acute spinal cat was indeed a candidate model for analysis of mechanisms of associative learning (Patterson, Cegavske & Thompson, 1973). For both habitation and conditioning of spinal reflexes we were able to rule out changes in the cutaneous afferent terminals and changes in motor neuron excitability as mechanisms. (Reflex sensitization did involve increases in motor neuron excitability). However, in both cases the technology of the time was such that we were unable to identify the interneurons critically involved and hence could not definitively characterize the neural mechanisms underlying these forms of behavioral plasticity.

THE EYEBLINK RESPONSE

In part because of my work with Woolsey, I had hoped to identify a learning paradigm where the cerebral cortex was necessary. At the University of California, Irvine, we tried several approaches, including classical conditioning of the relayed pyramidal response (Roemer, Teyler & Thompson, 1974) and neuronal activity of the cerebral cortex in instrumental avoidance learning (Gabriel, Wheeler & Thompson, 1973) but none seemed entirely satisfactory to me. (The avoidance study was really Michael Gabriel's work and he continued this approach to this day in a most successful research program, see, e.g., Gabriel, 1993). During this period at Irvine, Michael Patterson was a post-doctoral fellow in my laboratory, having obtained his Ph.D. with I. Gormezano at the University of Iowa. (Gormezano and I had been fellow graduate students at the University of Wisconsin; he worked with David Grant, a pioneering figure in the field of human eyeblink conditioning). Patterson strongly proselytized Gormezano's preparation, classical conditioning of the nictitating membrane response in the rabbit, as a suitable preparation for analysis of brain substrates of associative learning and memory (e.g., Gormezano et al., 1962). I was of course familiar with Gormezano's work and a great admirer of it. Len Ross and Allan Wagner had independently developed classical conditioning of the rabbit eyelid closure response as a model system; actually I believe their work preceded Gormezano's (see Wagner, 1999). In any event we set up a rabbit nictitating membrane (NM) response preparation at Irvine. I was indeed impressed with the high degree of behavioral control, thanks to Gormezano's many studies (Gormezano et al., 1983), the fact that the learning exhibited the basic phenomena of Pavlovian conditioning and the possibilities for analysis of neuronal mechanisms (see, e.g., Thompson et al., 1976). At this time (1973) we moved to Harvard, established a rabbit NM conditioning laboratory and obtained an NSF grant to support this work. We had no idea where the memory traces for this basic form of associative learning and memory were formed and stored.

THE MOTOR NERVES AND NUCLEI

We began our analysis with a focus on the motor nerves and nuclei that generated the reflex and learned NM responses (Cegaske et al., 1976; Young et al., 1976; Cegarske et al., 1979). To oversimplify from our work and the work of others, the 6th nerve was critically important for the NM response but the 3rd and 4th nerves were also involved and the 7th nerve was critical for closure of the external eyelid (obicularis oculi muscles). In terms of motor nuclei, the 7th nucleus of course controlled external eyelid closure and the accessory portion of the 6th nucleus innervated the retractor bulbus muscle, which retracted the eyeball and forced the nictitating membrane out across the front surface of the eye. The 4th and 6th nuclei acted synergistically with the accessory 6th.

It is important to stress the fact that the pathways mediating the reflex eyeblink are in the brainstem and do not involve "higher" brain systems such as the cerebellum and hippocampus. Specifically, there are direct projections from the trigeminal nucleus (activated by stimulation of the cornea and surrounding tissues) to the relevant motor nuclei and indirect projections relaying via the brainstem reticular system to the motor nuclei (Hiraoka & Shimamura, 1977) (see Figure 8).

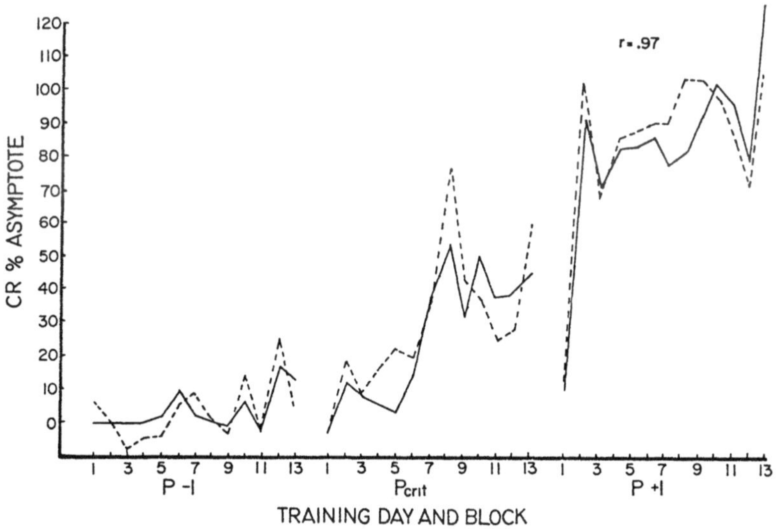

Figure 1. The rates of learning of nictitating membrane (NM) and eyelid responses recorded simultaneously from the left eye (rabbit). NM extension (solid line) is measured with a potentiometer and the external eyelid response (dashed line) is measured as a quantified EMG recording from the obicularis oculi muscle (controlling the external eyelid). Both measures are expressed as percent asymptotic response level. Pcrit is the day on which criterion CR performance was reached, P-1 is the day before and P+1 is the day after. The correlation between the two measures is virtually perfect. [From McCormick et al., 1982.]

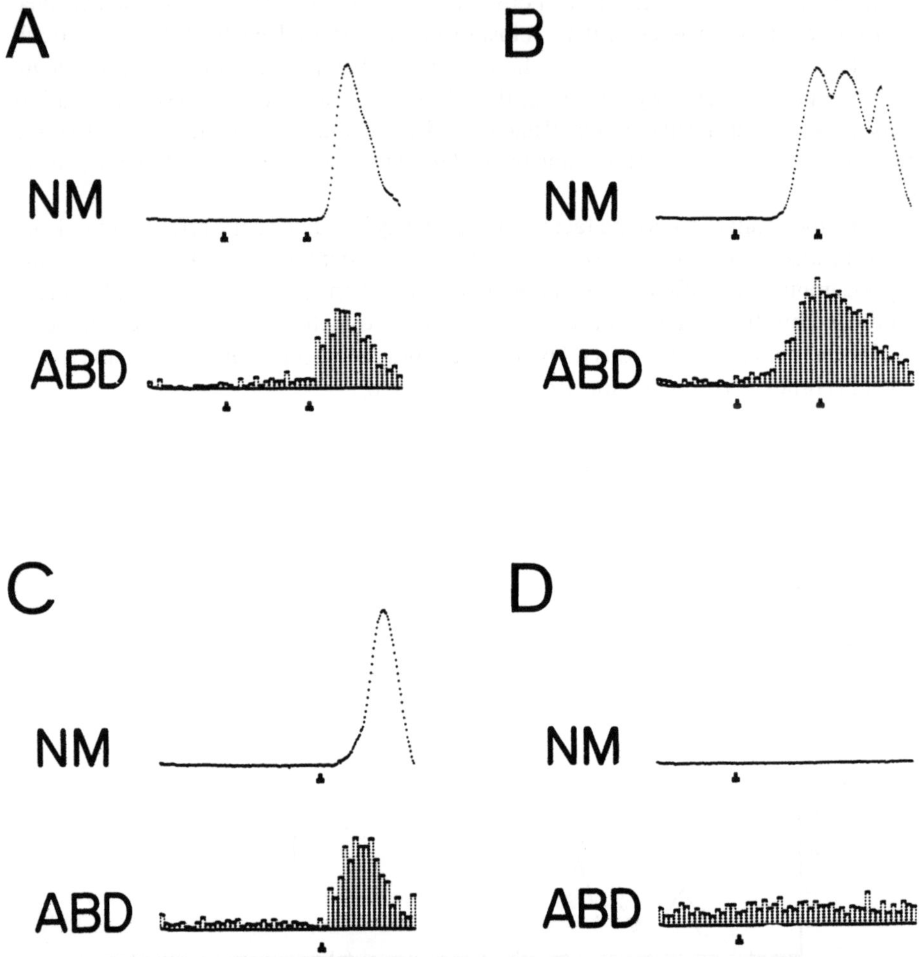

Figure 2. Examples of eight-trial data comparing averaged NM responses and abducens nucleus unit histograms (15-msec time bins) for a conditioning (A,B) and a control (C,D) animal. For the NM response, upward movement of the trace represents extension of the NM across the cornea. For the conditioning animal, A is an eight-trial block at beginning of training, and B is an eight-trial block after the animal had learned to criterion. For the control animal, C is an eight-trial block of air puff-US-alone trials, and D is an eight-trial block of tone-CS-alone trials. Note the close correspondence in the amplitude-time course between the behavioral and the neural measures. NM = nictitating membrane; ABD = abducens nucleus; Left cursor, tone CS onset; right cursor, corneal air puff US onset. [From Cegavske et al., 1979.]

For a time much was made of the critical importance of the accessory 6th nucleus (e.g., Welsh & Harvey, 1989). However, years earlier Gormezano had shown that eyeball retraction, NM extension and external eyelid closure responses all exhibited the same learning curves (Deaux et al., 1963; Gormezano et al., 1962; Schneiderman, et al., 1962) and we later showed with simultaneous recordings that NM extension and external eyelid closure (actually EMG activity of the obicularis oculi muscles) were essentially perfectly correlated over the course of learning (McCormick et al., 1982c) (Figure 1). Indeed, obicularis oculi EMG appears to be the most robust and sensitive measure of learning (Lavond et al., 1990). Recordings from the relevant motor nuclei, particularly the 6th, accessory 6th and 7th, showed essentially identical patterns of learning-induced increases in neuronal activity.

The basic logic of our approach seemed reasonable–identify the critical motor neurons involved in control of the learned response and trace the essential circuitry backward to the source, the "engram." The fact that several motor nuclei showed the same pattern of learning-induced activation argued against any plasticity unique to one motor nucleus (e.g., the accessory 6th) or in fact to processes of plasticity at the level of the motor nuclei. Instead, it seemed most likely that the learning-induced response in the motor nuclei was driven from a common central source. The pattern of learning induced increase in the activity of neurons in the motor nuclei in the CS period in paired trials and on CS alone trials (i.e., the neuronal CR) was strikingly similar in form to the amplitude-time course of NM extension, external eyelid closure and of course the EMG recorded from the obicularis oculi muscles. Indeed, an envelope of increased frequency of discharge of neurons in the motor nuclei preceded in time and closely predicted the form of the behavioral eyeblink/NM response (Figure 2). This close predictive parallel was most evident with unit cluster recordings but was also true for single unit recordings in the motor nuclei.

Our initial logic–to work backwards from the motor nuclei–was not as simple as it might have seemed because of the very large number of central brain systems that project to the motor and premotor nuclei. So at this point we adopted a different strategy. It was apparent that the amplitude–time course form of the conditioned eyeblink/NM response closely paralleled and followed the pattern of increased unit activity in the motor nuclei. So we focused on this behavioral model of the learning-induced increase in neural activity in the motor nuclei and used it as a template or model (Figure 2). The higher brain systems that acted to generate and drive the learning-induced neuronal CR, the "model" in the motor nuclei, must show the same pattern of learning-induced activity as do the motor nuclei, and hence the amplitude-time course of the learned eyeblink-NM response. Thus, we searched through higher brain systems looking for learning-induced neuronal activity that correlated closely with and preceded in time the form of the learned eyeblink-NM response. In essence, we mapped the brain of the rabbit, searching for neuronal models of the learned behavioral response (see, e.g., McCormick et al., 1983; Thompson et al., 1976). We did not of course search blindly but rather system by system.

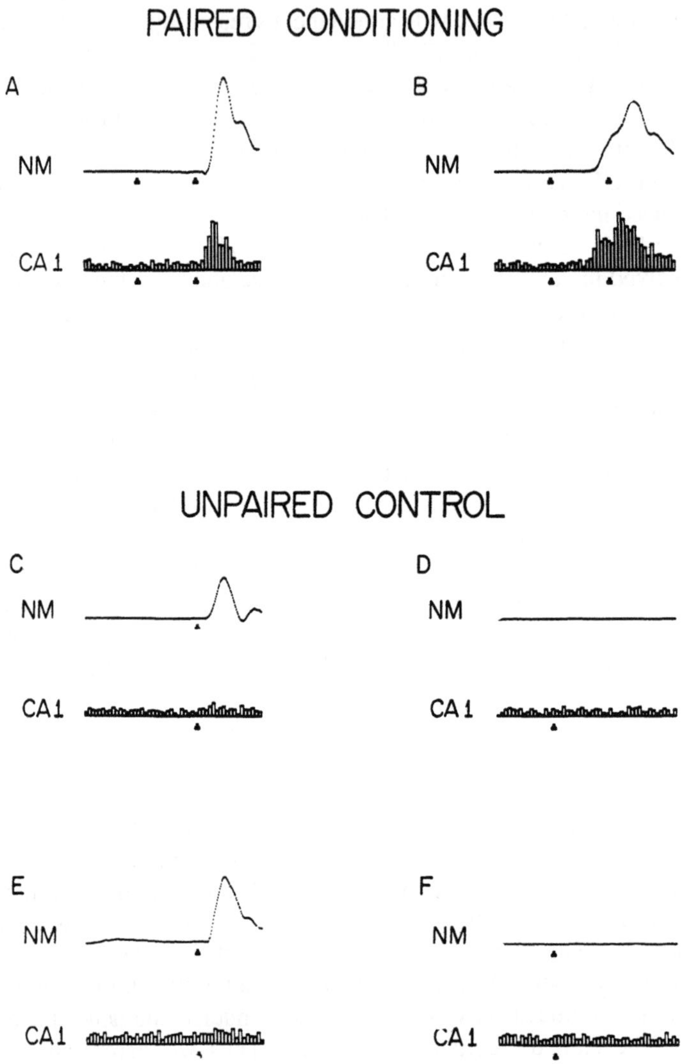

Figure 3. Hippocampal unit cluster responses over the course of eyeblink conditioning. In all cases upper trace is the average nictitating membrane response for one block of eight trials; lower trace is hippocampal unit post-stimulus histograms (15 msec time bins) for one block of eight trials. A and B, first and last blocks from Day 1 from an animal given paired training. C-F, eight trial blocks in an animal given unpaired stimuli: C and E, US alone trials; D & F, CS alone trials. First cursor indicates tone CS onset; second cursor corneal air puff US onset. Total trace length equals 750 msec. [From Berger & Thompson, 1978a.]

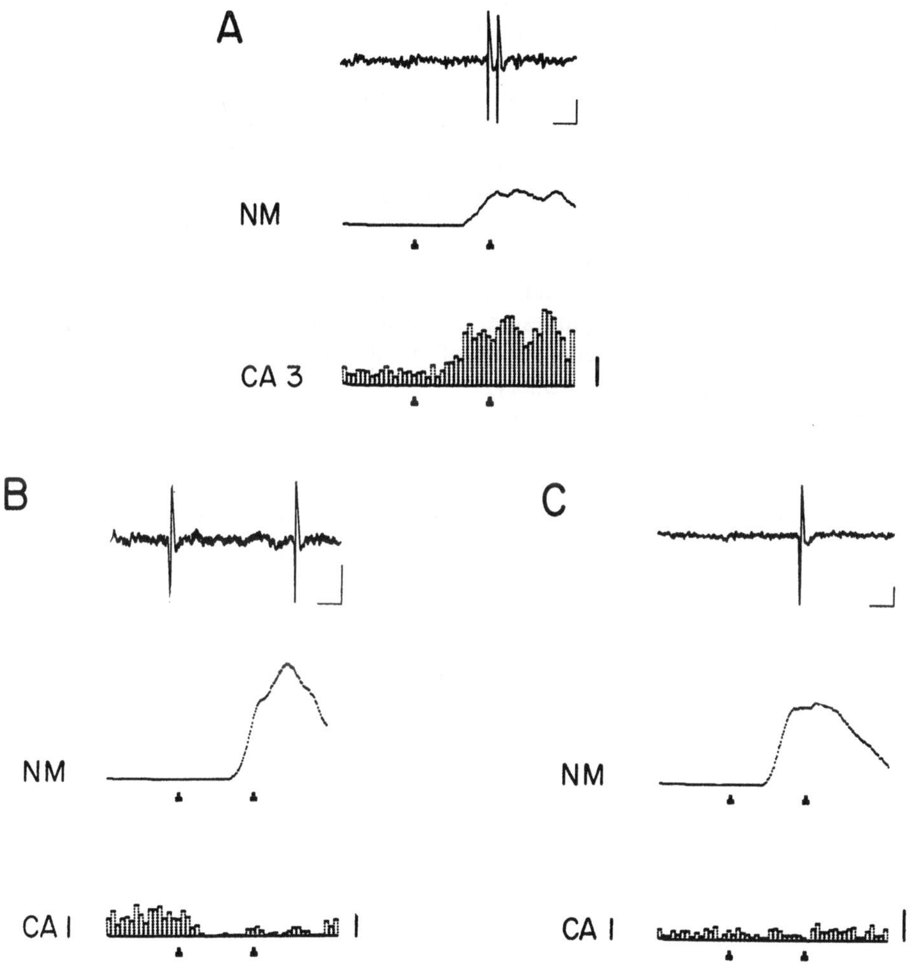

Figure 4. Responses of single hippocampal neurons recorded from animals trained in eyeblink conditioning. Middle traces show average NM responses and bottom traces post stimulus histograms generated by isolated hippocampal units recorded during paired conditioning trials. Top traces show examples of spontaneous unit activity from the single neurons that generated the respective post-stimulus histograms. Calibrations for upper raw unit tracings are 50 μv and 5 msec. Middle and lower trace duration is 750 msec. A shows a pyramidal neuron so identified by antidromic stimulation, B and C are from unidentified units. [From Berger and Thompson, 1978b.]

THE HIPPOCAMPAL STORY

Early on, at Harvard, Ted Berger and Brad Alger (graduate students in the lab) discovered the remarkable engagement of neuronal activity in the hippocampus. The pattern of learning-induced increased frequency of discharge of neurons in CA_1 and CA_3 (we showed later that the response was generated by pyramidal neurons) correlated essentially perfectly with and preceded in time over trials the form of the eyeblink-NM response (Berger et al., 1976). Furthermore, the hippocampal unit response began to develop in the US period within just a few trials of training and moved into the CS period in close association with the development of the behavioral CR (Berger & Thompson, 1978) (Figures 3 and 4). It seemed like a perfect candidate for the engram. In addition, EEG activity recorded from the hippocampus at the beginning of training predicted the rate of learning (Berry & Thompson, 1978, 1979). We characterized this learning-induced response in the hippocampus in some detail (see Berger, Berry & Thompson, 1986a; Berger et al., 1983). Unfortunately, we knew from other work that animals could learn the basic delay conditioned NM-eyeblink response following hippocampal lesions (Schmaltz & Theios, 1972). This apparent enigma may reflect a fundamental aspect of the functions of higher brain systems in basic associative learning and memory.

Paul Solomon (visiting professor) and Donald Weisz (postdoctoral fellow), working in our laboratory after we returned to Irvine, showed that if very large bilateral lesions of the hippocampus were made before training, then learning of the *trace* CR (500 msec interval between CS offset and US onset) was markedly impaired (Solomon et al., 1986a). More recently, Disterhoft and associates replicated these findings in detail (Moyer et al., 1990). More recently, Jeansok Kim and Robert Clark, working now in the lab at USC, showed that if animals were first trained in the trace procedure and then given large bilateral hippocampal lesions immediately after training, the CR was abolished (Kim et al., 1995). However, if the lesions were made a month after training the CR was unaffected (Figure 5). Interestingly if animals were trained on the standard delay procedure, the lesion (immediately after training) had no effect on the CR but when the animals were then shifted to the trace procedure, the CR extinguished. More recently we made use of scopolamine, a drug with actions on the hippocampal system (Soloman et al., 1983, 1993), to explore its effects on the trace conditioned response (Kaneko & Thompson, 1997). In brief, doses of scopolamine that have little effect on delay conditioning (0.1mg/kg) completely prevent learning of the trace conditioned response.

A Model of Declarative Memory

In sum, hippocampal lesions induced antereograde amnesia (impairment of post-lesion learning) and marked but time-limited retrograde amnesia. These are precisely the effects that such lesions have on declarative memory in humans (McGlinchey-Berroth et al., 1997). Consequently, trace eyeblink conditioning would seem an excellent simplified model of the role of the hippocampus in declarative memory. In humans, declarative memory refers to memory for one's own experiences, often modeled as

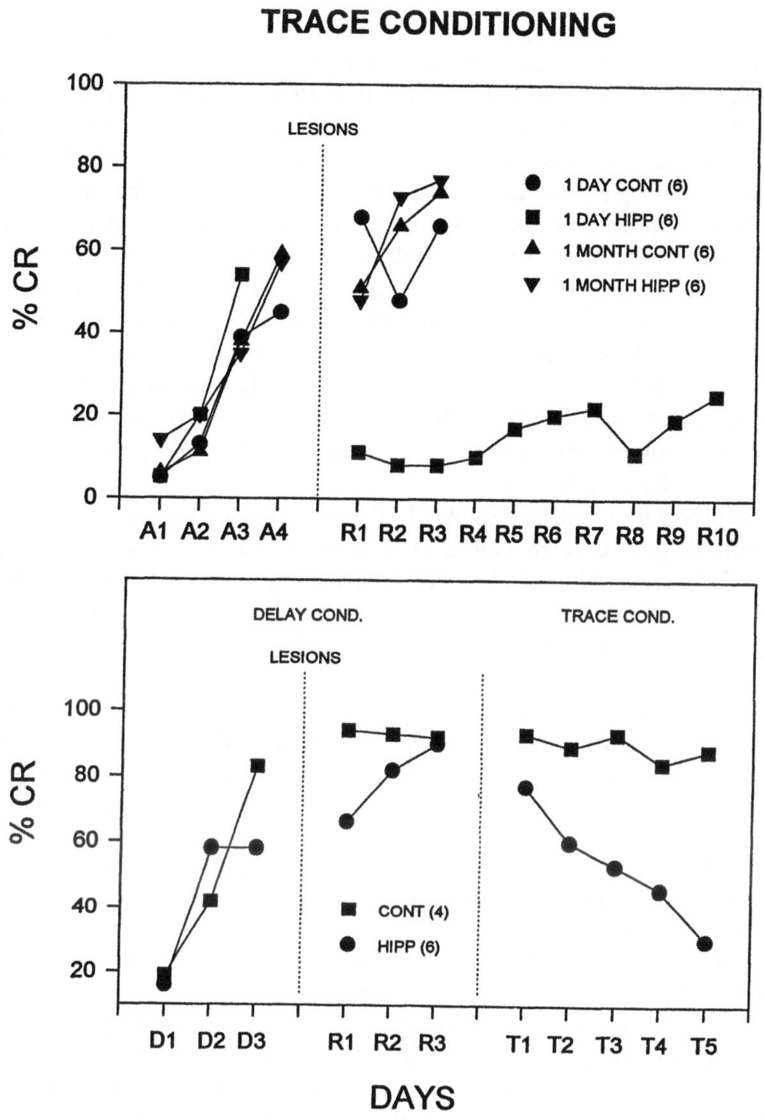

Figure 5. Top. Four groups of rabbits trained using a 500 msec trace conditioning procedure. Large bilateral lesions of the hippocampus are made one day or one month after training (1 day Hipp; 1 month Hipp) or sham lesions (1 day cont; 1 month cont). Note that the memory is fully preserved if the lesion is made one month after training but completely abolished by a lesion one day after training. Bottom. Two groups of animals trained on the standard delay procedure, followed by hippocampal lesions one day after training (Hipp) or by sham lesions (cont). The delay learning is not much impaired by the hippocampal lesion. Following this the animals were shifted to the trace procedure (see above). The sham animals transferred with no difficulty but the hippocampal lesion animals extinguished with continued training. [From Kim, Clark & Thompson, 1995.]

recognition memory in monkeys. A key aspect of human declarative memory is "awareness"–people are aware of the memories they can describe.

A recent study from Larry Squire's laboratory strongly supports the view that trace eyeblink conditioning is indeed a model of declarative memory (Clark & Squire, 1998). Normal and amnesic humans were trained on both the standard short delay procedure and a long (1,000 msec) trace interval procedure. Subjects in both groups learned the delay procedure normally, although the amnesics could not recall (verbally describe) the experience, consistent with the early study by Weiskranz and Warrington (1979). In marked contrast, amnesics were unable to learn the long-trace procedure, a result also reported by McGlinchey-Berroth et al. (1997). Interestingly, performance of the normal subjects on the long-trace procedure showed considerable intersubject variability. Normal subjects who learned the trace CR could describe the stimulus contingencies, but normal subjects who did not learn the trace CR well could not describe the contingencies. It appears that at least in humans awareness is necessary for learning of the trace procedure.

The results of the Clark and Squire (1998) study strongly support the view that the trace eyeblink procedure in rabbits is a viable elementary model of declarative memory. This preparation would seem to have many advantages for analysis of the brain circuits and processes critical for declarative memory formation and storage because so much is known about the brain circuitry essential for eyeblink conditioning, as will be detailed below. In animals (and to the degree tested in humans, see below) the cerebellum is necessary for all aspects of eyeblink learning and memory, including the trace CR (Woodruff-Pak et al., 1985). Consequently, it will be possible to identify the entire circuitry involved in the "read in" and "read out" of the hippocampal-dependent trace memory system. In marked contrast, essentially nothing is known about the read-out of declarative memory from the hippocampus and related medial temporal lobe cortex to behavior in monkeys and humans. Identification of the necessary circuitry for trace conditioning in the rabbit would seem to be an extremely important priority for future research.

Gregory Clark completed an initial study in our laboratory of relations between the cerebellar and hippocampal systems in eyeblink conditioning (Clark et al, 1984). In brief, unilateral cerebellar interpositus lesions that completely abolished the conditioned eyeblink response ipsilateral to this lesion (see below) also abolished the learning-induced increase in unit activity in the hippocampus in the CS period. When training was shifted to the other eye, this eye rapidly developed the CR and the hippocampal response in the CS period reappeared. Ted Berger and his students explored possible anatomical pathways interrelating the cerebellum and hippocampus in some detail (e.g. Berger et al, 1986b).

THE CEREBELLAR STORY

Our initial hunch that the cerebellum was involved in eyeblink conditioning came from several sources, e.g., the brain mapping studies by David McCormick in the laboratory (e.g., McCormick et al., 1983), a lesion study in the laboratory by David Lavond (Lavond et al., 1981) and an ongoing series of studies in our laboratory begun at Irvine by Ronald Kettner (Kettner et al., 1980; Kettner & Thompson, 1982). Kettner's project involved recording neuronal unit activity from auditory nuclei in rabbits detecting threshold level acoustic stimuli (eyeblink conditioning). Some of Kettner's recordings missed the dorsal cochlear nucleus and ended up in the cerebellar interpositus nucleus, which lies just dorsal to the dorsal cochlear nucleus. These recordings showed a neuronal model of the behavioral CR, which we never saw in the auditory nuclei. Kettner's elegant work, incidentally, using a signal detection theory approach, provided definitive evidence that the auditory relay nuclei play no role in learning and memory of the conditioned eyeblink response (Kettner & Thompson, 1985).

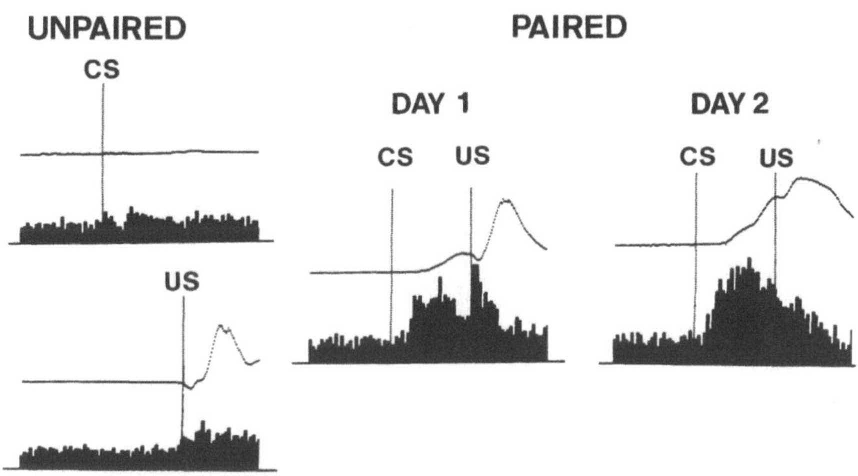

Figure 6. Averaged NM response (upper traces) and histograms of multiple unit activity recorded from the cerebellar anterior interpositus nucleus to unpaired tone and corneal air puff stimuli and then over the course of paired training for one animal. Each histogram is for one entire session. The Day 1 paired data are also shown in Figure 7 (next to right, bottom). [From McCormick & Thompson, 1984a and unpublished data.]

The Basic Discovery

The fact that a neuronal model of the behavioral CR developed in the cerebellum (see Figure 6) (McCormick & Thompson, 1984a,b; McCormick et al., 1981; 1982a; Berthier & Moore, 1990) was suggestive of a memory trace but we knew from our earlier work on the hippocampus that neuronal recordings, per se, could not identify the essential memory trace. We completed a series of lesion studies, initially involving large cerebellar lesions (e.g., McCormick et al., 1981; 1982a) and later lesions limited to the interpositus nucleus (e.g., McCormick & Thompson, 1984a,b; Clark et al., 1984) (Figure 7). The key players in these initial studies were David McCormick, David Lavond and Gregory Clark. I will never forget the first polygraph record McCormick showed me of a rabbit with a cerebellar lesion–the CR was completely abolished.

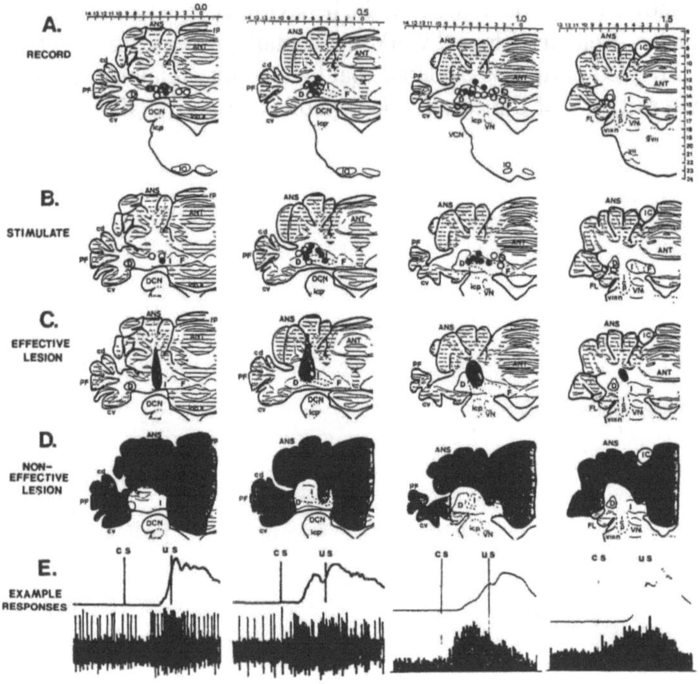

Figure 7. Spatial distribution of recording, stimulating, effective, and noneffective lesion sites within the ipsilateral cerebellum. (A) Recording sites that did (filled circles) and did not (open circles) develop neuronal "models" (E) of the learned eyeblink response. Only the recording sites that developed robust responses or no response at all are plotted. The larger numbers above each section represent millimeters anterior to lambda and the numbers to the side represent millimeters below bone at lambda. (B) Sites that, when stimulated, did (filled circles) and did not (open) elicit eyeblink responses. (C) An example of a lesion of the dentate and interpositus (D-1) nuclei which permanently abolished the learned response (3). (D) Composite from three animals of cortical lesions that were not effective in abolishing the learned eyeblink response. (E) Neuronal responses of four different recording sites within the cerebellum. The first recording is an example of multiple-unit activity from the ansiform cortex. The second recording and the two histograms on the right were obtained from the D-1 nuclei. The histograms are averages of an entire session of training. The first vertical line represents the onset of the tone, and the second represents the onset of the air puff. Each histogram bar is 9 msec wide, and the length of the entire trace is 750 msec. The top trace in each set is the movement of the NM with "up" being extension across the eyeball. [From McCormick & Thompson, 1984a.]

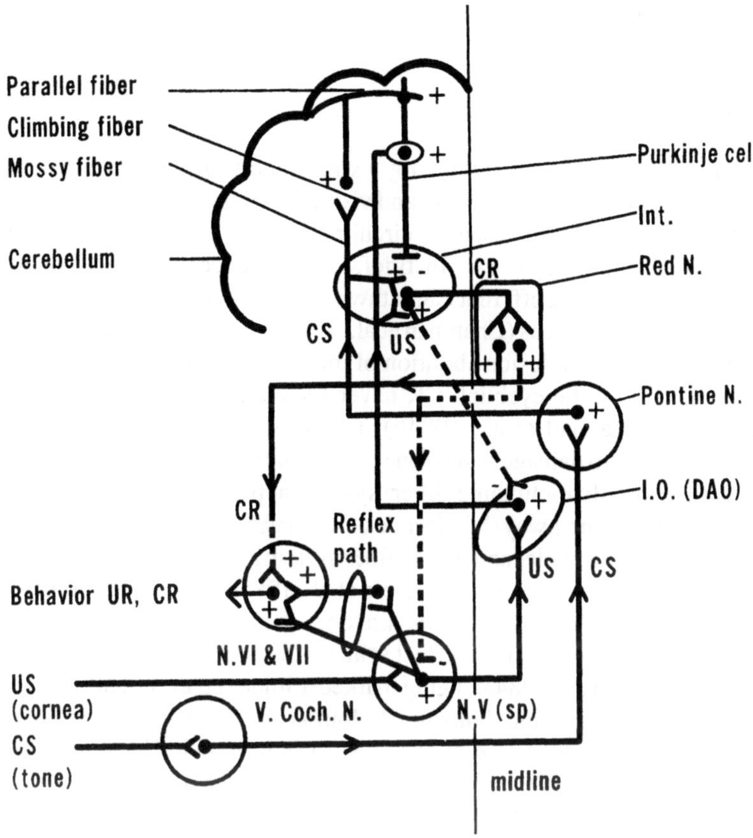

Figure 8. Simplified schematic of hypothetical memory trace circuit for discrete behavioral responses learned as adaptations to aversive events. The US (corneal air puff) pathway seems to consist of somatosensory projections to the dorsal accessory portion of the inferior olive (DAO) and its climbing fiber projections to the cerebellum. The tone CS pathway seems to consist of auditory projections to pontine nuclei (Pontine N) and mossy fiber projections to the cerebellum. The efferent (eyelid closure) CR pathway projects from the interpositus nucleus (Int) of the cerebellum to the red nucleus (Red N) and via the descending rubral pathway to act ultimately on motor neurons. The interpositus nucleus sends a direct GABAergic inhibitory projection to the inferior olive and the red nucleus may also exert inhibitory control over the transmission of somatic sensory information about the US to the inferior olive (IO), so that when a CR occurs (eyelid closes), the red nucleus dampens US activation of climbing fibers and the interpositus directly inhibits the inferior olive. Evidence is most consistent with storage of the memory traces in localized regions of cerebellar cortex and interpositus nucleus. Pluses indicate excitatory and minuses inhibitory synaptic action. Additional abbreviations: N V (sp), spinal fifth cranial nucleus; N VI, sixth cranial nucleus; N VII, seventh cranial nucleus; V Coch N, ventral cochlear nucleus. [Modified from Thompson, 1986.]

There was no response at all, even later than the CS period on CS alone trials, and no effect at all on the reflex response.

The Essential Circuitry

In a subsequent series of key studies my extraordinary group of undergraduates, graduate students, post-doctoral fellows and visiting professors at Stanford University succeeded in identifying the essential circuitry for this basic form of associative learning and memory (Figure 8). In brief, our evidence strongly supported the following conclusions: The efferent CR pathway was the superior cerebellar peduncle and magnocellular red nucleus (Chapman et al., 1988; McCormick et al., 1982b, Haley et al., 1983); the cerebellar lesion abolition of the eyeblink CR was strictly ipsilateral (Lincoln et al., 1982); the eyeblink CR never recovered at all following effective cerebellar lesions (Lavond et al., 1984b); the interpositus lesion abolition of the eyeblink CR was due to damage to neuron somas, not fibers of passage (Lavond et al., 1985); the inferior olive-climbing fiber system appeared to be the critical US reinforcing or teaching pathway (McCormick et al., 1985; Mauk et al., 1986; Steinmetz et al, 1984); the pontine nuclei and mossy fiber system appear to convey the necessary CS information to the cerebellum (Steinmetz et al., 1985; 1986; 1987; Solomon et al., 1986b; Knowlton & Thompson, 1988; Lavond et al., 1987a); interpositus lesion abolition of the eyeblink CR had no effect at all on the conditioned heart rate response in the rabbit (Lavond et al., 1984a); aging markedly impaired the conditioned eyeblink response in both rabbits and humans (Solomon et al., 1989; Woodruff-Pak & Thompson, 1985; Woodruff-Pak et al., 1987; 1988; Woodruff-Pak & Thompson, 1988), as did Alzheimer's Disease in humans (Solomon et al., 1991; Woodruff-Pak et al., 1990); electrical stimulation of sensory areas of the neocortex served as an effective CS in classical conditioning of discrete responses (e.g. Doty et al., 1956) because it activated the cerebellar memory system (Knowlton & Thompson, 1992; Knowlton et al., 1993); the cerebellar flocculus and paraflocculus were not involved at all in eyeblink conditioning (Logan et al., 1994); and many other findings as well (see Thompson & Krupa, 1994; Thompson & Kim, 1996, for overviews). Allan Wagner and associates had developed elegant conceptual/computational models of classical conditioning that mapped very closely onto the circuitry we had been characterizing (Wagner, 1981; Wagner & Brandon, 1989; Wagner & Donegan, 1989).

A particularly satisfying aspect of our discovery of the essential role of the cerebellum in classical conditioning of discrete responses is the relevance of our work to the human condition. Irene Daum and associates, working in Germany, replicated in humans the fact that appropriate cerebellar damage completely prevents learning of the eyeblink CR (Daum et al., 1993). Christine Logan (a former graduate student of mine) and Scott Grafton, a neurologist then at USC, completed an extensive PET study of eyeblink conditioning in humans. Their results indicated significant activation in the cerebellar interpositus nucleus and several loci in cerebellar cortex, in close agreement with our recording studies in the rabbit cerebellum (Logan & Grafton, 1995).

A point that is obvious from our studies but seems not to be widely understood is that our results on the role of the cerebellum in classical conditioning apply to the learning of any discrete movement: eyeblink, headturn, forelimb flexion, hindlimb flexion, etc. (See Mauk et al., 1986; Steinmetz et al., 1989; Donegan et al., 1983; as shown initially in the classic study by Brogden & Gantt, 1942). Eyeblink conditioning is simply a convenient response to measure. Our findings to date seem to have identified perhaps *the* critical function of the cerebellum, namely the learning of discrete skilled movements, a basic notion proposed in classic theories of the cerebellum as a learning machine (see Albus, 1971; Eccles, 1977; Ito, 1984; Marr, 1969). Indeed, our work constitutes a compelling verification of these theories.

In the context of theoretical aspects of cerebellar function in learning and memory Nelson Donegan and Mark Gluck in my laboratory contributed careful analytic thinking about the cerebellar circuit (see e.g., Donegan et al., 1989). Gluck developed most important connectionist level models of the cerebellar circuitry (Gluck et al., 1990; Gluck et al., 1994) and was able through his modeling to identify two key aspects of the circuitry: recurrent feedback to the cerebellum from the output of the interpositus appeared necessary to yield appropriate timing of the CR (in his models), and the inhibitory projection from the interpositus to the inferior olive could subserve the behavioral phenomenon of blocking. More recently, Gluck has focused his modeling on the hippocampus and its interactions with the cerebellum in associative learning. As a result of our cerebellar work, several other groups have also developed models of how the cerebellum can code and store memories (e.g., Buonomano & Mauk, 1994; Desmond & Moore; 1988; Fiala et al., 1996; Grossberg & Schmajak, 1989).

As I noted earlier, our search strategy using the amplitude-time course of the eyeblink-NM response as a label or template led us to the cerebellum, as it had done earlier to the hippocampus. At the time we first reported our discovery of the cerebellar involvement (McCormick et al., 1981) we were unaware of an earlier Russian literature exploring the role of the cerebellum in conditioned reflexes. However, we soon discovered this literature and cited it extensively in our first detailed analysis of effects of lesions of the cerebellar interpositus nucleus on the conditioned eyeblink-NM response (Clark et al., 1984). Actually, this early Russian literature was quite inconclusive (see e.g., Karamian et al., 1960). The Brogden and Gantt (1942) study was far and away the most convincing early demonstration of cerebellar involvement in classical conditioning of discrete responses. In brief, they found that stimulation of the cerebellar white matter, particularly in lobule HVI, evoked discrete organized movements–eyelid closure, forelimb flexion, hindlimb flexion, head turn, pinna movement, etc.–and all these discrete movements so elicited could easily be conditioned to neutral auditory and visual stimuli. This study was so far ahead of its time that it was subsequently ignored. We think now that the effective stimulus was to climbing fibers (Mauk et al., 1986; Steinmetz et al., 1989). We repeated and extended the Brogden and Gantt findings (see below).

Incredibly enough, this work and the many subsequent studies demonstrating beyond all reasonable doubt the essential role of the cerebellum in classical conditioning of discrete responses is still being ignored and even disputed by a few cerebellar workers (e.g., Llinas et al., 1997). This is particularly unfortunate since learning and storing the memories for discrete, skilled movements may be the most important thing the cerebellum does.

We were clearly the first to demonstrate essential involvement of the cerebellum in classical conditioning of discrete responses, using the eyeblink-NM response in the rabbit as a model system. Soon after our initial reports were published, Glickstein, Yeo and associates, then working in Steele-Russell's MRC unit in London, replicated our basic findings (Yeo et al., 1985a), as did other groups (e.g., Rosenfield & Moore, 1983; Rosenfield et al., 1985).

Cerebellar Cortex

Over the years Yeo, Glickstein and associates basically repeated many of our lesion and other studies and for the most part replicated our findings. (Indeed, at times we felt as though we were the directors of their laboratory). One area of disagreement concerned the effects of cerebellar cortical lesions, Yeo and associates claiming that such lesions abolished the CR (Yeo et al., 1985b). We found that such lesions at most caused a transient but sometimes substantial impairment in the CR and residual impairment but never permanent abolition, unless the interpositus nucleus was damaged (McCormick & Thompson, 1984a; Lavond et al., 1987b). This issue proved to be unresolvable with the lesion method–it is not possible to remove all cerebellar cortex without damaging the cerebellar nuclei.

This problem led us to the use of the Purkinje cell degeneration (pcd) mutant mouse (see below). In this mutant, the cerebellum develops normally until about two weeks after birth, at which point all Purkinje neurons in the cerebellar cortex die over a period of about two weeks. For a period of about two months, all other neuronal systems appear to be normal but the cerebellar cortex is of course completely non-functional (Figure 9).

These animals are markedly impaired in eyeblink conditioning–they learn much more slowly and to a much lower degree than wild type controls and extinguish more rapidly, but they do show significant learning (Figure 9) (Chen et al., 1996). If the interpositus nucleus is lesioned before training in pcd mice they are completely unable to learn, demonstrating that the residual learning pcd mice exhibit requires the interpositus, i.e., does not involve extracerebellar loci (Chen et al., 1999a). This would seem to resolve the controversy, consistent with my long-held hypothesis that both the cerebellar cortex and the interpositus nucleus are critically involved in normal learning of discrete behavioral responses. It also would seem to argue against the hypothesis by Mauk and associates (e.g., Perrett & Mauk, 1995) that the cerebellar cortex is necessary for extinction of the behavioral CR.

The "Performance" Argument

Perhaps the most ironic chapter in the cerebellar memory saga concerns the attack upon us by Welsh and Harvey (1989) over the issue of "performance." One of the primary reasons we chose classical conditioning of eyeblink and other discrete responses is that performance of the reflex response can be evaluated independently

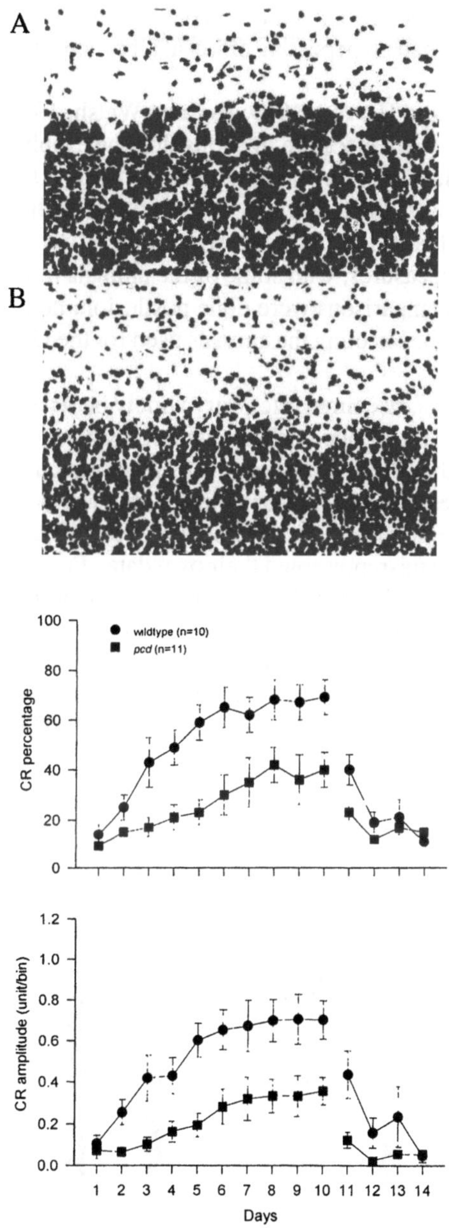

Figure 9. Top. Transverse sections of the cerebellum stained with cresyl violet from a wild-type (A) and from a pcd mutant mouse (B). Both animals are young adults. Bottom. The pcd animals are much impaired in learning. Shown are percentage of CRs (top) and CR amplitudes (bottom) exhibited by pcd (solid squares) and wild-type (solid circles) mice during ten days of acquisition and four days of extinction. [From Chen et al., 1996.]

of performance of the learned response. From the very beginning, we found that cerebellar lesions effective in completely and permanently abolishing the conditioned eyeblink/NM response had no persisting effect at all on any aspect of the performance of the reflex response.

In contrast, Welsh and Harvey (1989; see also Welsh, 1987) claimed that lesions of the interpositus that were effective in abolishing the eyeblink CR did have effects on the UR on trials when only an unconditioned stimulus (US) was presented at low US intensities. However, their analysis was entirely post hoc. They selected only some of their interpositus-lesion animals in which the CR was abolished and compared them, in terms of UR measures, with some of the animals in which the lesion did not abolish the CR. All comparisons were done postlesion; no prelesion UR data were given, and the criteria for selecting the animals used for the UR comparisons were not given.

Since UR amplitudes, rise times, etc., vary widely between animals prelesion, it is possible to obtain any result one wishes post hoc by selection of animals. In fact, when we reanalyzed the Welsh & Harvey (1989) data equating URs on low intensity US alone trials post lesion to CRs prior to lesion, the lesion abolition of the CR had no effect at all on the equated URs (Steinmetz et al., 1992). In short, Welsh and Harvey (1989) actually misrepresented their own data. Furthermore, they failed even to cite our earlier initial and comprehensive study of effects of interpositus lesions on the conditioned eyeblink-NM response (Clark et al., 1984). We reported there that appropriate lesions of the interpositus nucleus completely and permanently abolished the CR with no effect on the UR. Interestingly we found that lesions not completely effective caused a marked reduction in the amplitude of the CR, *which did not recover*

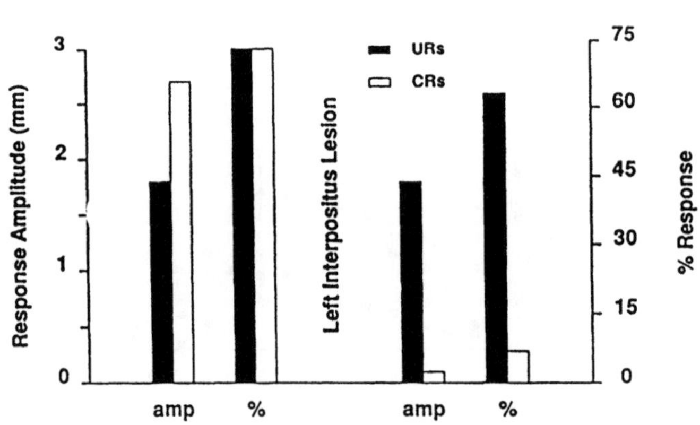

Figure 10. Response amplitudes and percentage of responses (solid bars) to 1 psi US-alone stimulus presentations and CR amplitudes and percentage of responses (open bars) for a group of animals recorded before and after cerebellar interpositus nucleus lesions. The CRs were established pairing tone and 3 psi corneal air puff US but the CRs shown are of course responses only to the CS. Note that the lesions abolish the CRs but have no significant effect on the URs (see text). [From Steinmetz et al., 1992.]

with subsequent training, a result also reported by Welsh and Harvey (1989) although they did not cite our earlier finding. In fact, when properly analyzed, the Welsh and Harvey (1989) study simply replicated the Clark et al. (1984) study. More recently we showed that if the URs on US-alone trials are compared in the same animals before and after lesion, interpositus lesions effective in completely abolishing the eyeblink CR have no persisting effect on any property of the UR over a wide range of US intensities (Steinmetz et al., 1992) (Figure 10).

Welsh and Harvey (1989) argued that "when one attempts to equate CS (conditioned stimulus) and UCS as a response-eliciting stimuli the (lesion) deficits in the CR and the UCR become more alike" (p. 309). The US intensity used for training in all these studies was well above UR threshold and elicited vigorous reflex blinks, typically considerably larger in amplitude than the asymptotic CR. It is conceivable that use of the relatively high-intensity US in training may have resulted in some as-yet-undefined effect that could influence subsequent UR performance on US-alone trials at low US intensities (i.e., could somehow mask lesion effects on the UR). The eyeblink UR itself does exhibit a degree of plasticity, increasing in amplitude with repeated US presentations independent of associative learning (Steinmetz et al., 1992), or as a result of reflex facilitation (Weisz & LoTurco, 1988), or following eyelid loading (Evinger & Manning, 1988). Consequently we trained animals with very low intensity USs such that the CRs and URs were identical in amplitude before lesion (Ivkovich et al., 1993). Following lesions of the interpositus nucleus the CRs were completely and permanently abolished but the URs were unaffected. The "performance" argument is simply wrong.

By the early 1980s (about 1983-84 at Stanford) it was clear to me from our ongoing lesion, recording, stimulation and anatomical studies noted earlier that the cerebellum was necessary for the learning and memory of the conditioned eyeblink and other discrete responses; that the CR pathway involved projections from the interpositus via the superior cerebellar peduncle to the magnocellular red nucleus and to motor nuclei; that the US reinforcing or teaching pathway involved the inferior olive and climbing fibers to the cerebellum; that the CS pathways involved projections via the pontine nuclei and mossy fibers to the cerebellum; and finally that the first clear sites of convergence of the CS and US pathway were in the cerebellum (see Figure 8). Given all this it seemed obvious that the memory traces were formed and stored in the cerebellum. But at this point the world outside my laboratory was not fully convinced.

Reversible Inactivation

I decided that the only fully convincing result would be to use reversible inactivation. Thus, if inactivation of the critical cerebellar region (that abolished the CR in trained animals) during training completely prevented learning, but inactivation of the output from the cerebellum, e.g., the superior cerebellar peduncle and red nucleus (lesions of these structures abolished the CR in trained animals) during training did not prevent learning, then the case for a cerebellar memory trace was solid. I asked a visiting professor in my laboratory at Stanford to develop a cooling system that could be used to reversibly inactivate the components of the eyeblink circuit. Unfortunately his efforts were not successful. When we moved to USC David Lavond, then working in my laboratory, took up the challenge and developed the very successful freon-based reversible cooling system which he describes in his chapter in this volume (see Chapter 3 and see also Clark & Lavond, 1993; Clark et al., 1992).

Eric Knudsen, a colleague at Stanford, suggested we use local infusion of muscimol to induce reversible inactivation. Muscimol is a GABA agonist and activates $GABA_A$ receptors on neuron cell bodies and dendrites, causing them to hyperpolarize (shut down) for periods of more than an hour, followed by recovery of normal function. David Krupa, then a graduate student in my laboratory at USC, took up this suggestion and completed a remarkable series of studies, initially with Judith Thompson (see Figure 11). Our results with muscimol reversible inactivation agreed completely with the reversible cooling results from Lavond's laboratory (see Chapter 3, this volume). Inactivation of the motor nuclei (a in Figure 11) during learning completely prevented expression of the CR (and UR). However, when muscimol was removed, learning had been fully established, even though there was complete absence of behavioral responding during training (Krupa et al., 1996). Inactivation of the red nucleus during training (b in Figure 11) completely prevented expression of the CR

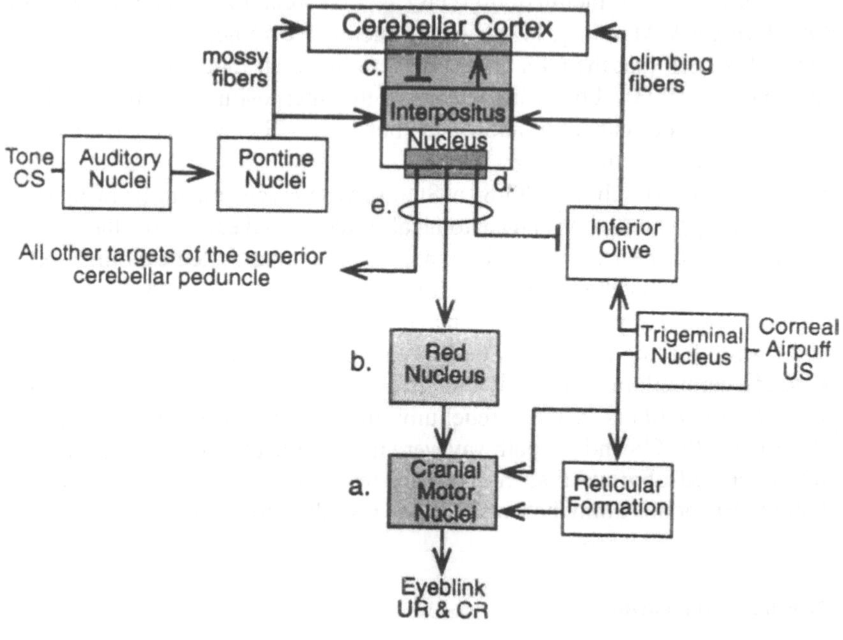

Figure 11. Simplified schematic of the essential brain circuitry involved in eyeblink conditioning. Shadowed boxes represents areas that have been reversibly inactivated during training (see text for details). (a) Inactivation of the motor nuclei including facial (seventh) and accessory sixth. (b) Inactivation of magnocellular red nucleus. (c) Inactivation of dorsal aspects of the interpositus nucleus and overlying cerebellar cortex. (d) Inactivation of ventral interpositus and of white matter ventral to the interpositus. (e) Inactivation of the superior cerebellar peduncle (scp) after it exits the cerebellar nuclei.

(but the UR was normal). When inactivation was removed, learning had been fully established, just as with inactivation of the motor nuclei (see Figure 12) (Krupa et al., 1993). Results identical to red nucleus inactivation were found with inactivation of the superior cerebellar peduncle (e in Figure 11), containing all the output axons from the interpositus-dentate nuclei (Krupa & Thompson, 1995) (we used TTX here to inactivate axons). In complete contrast, inactivation of a localized region of dorsal anterior interpositus nucleus and overlying cerebellar cortex completely prevented learning (c in Figure 11; see also Figure 12) (Krupa et al., 1993; Krupa & Thompson, 1997). Thus the memory trace must have been formed in the cerebellum.

A red herring in the reversible inactivation story was provided by Welsh and Harvey (1991). They first trained rabbits (eyeblink-NM) to a light CS and then infused lidocaine in the vicinity of the interpositus nucleus during one day of training to a tone CS. They reported that the infusion prevented CRs to test light CSs during the one day of tone training and, on the day after lidocaine infusion, the animals showed CRs to the tone. We completed a straightforward study where we infused lidocaine in the interpositus during initial training to a tone CS (Nordholm et al., 1993). We found that if lidocaine was infused in the vicinity of the dorsal interpositus during training it completely prevented learning but if it was infused ventrally, where it would inactivate the output of the nucleus (e.g., superior cerebellar peduncle) it did not prevent learning of the CR, although it did prevent performance of the CR (Welsh and Harvey result). Indeed, examination of the Welsh and Harvey histologies suggested that in some of their animals the cannula tips were ventral.

Lidocaine has many problems as an agent for reversible inactivation. Its duration of action is very short, only a few minutes, and it must be infused continuously. Also its locus of action can be extremely limited and difficult to determine with radiolabel. Furthermore, lidocaine inactivates both neuron cell bodies and axon fibers of passage. Muscimol (a $GABA_A$ agonist) has none of these disadvantages–its duration of action is at least two hours following a one minute infusion, it acts only on neuron cell bodies and not on fibers of passage and its distribution of action can be accurately determined using a radiolabel (^{3}H-muscimol).

A fundamental problem with the Welsh and Harvey study was that of transfer of training. They did not run the control group to determine the degree of transfer of CRs from light CS training to tone CS testing. Indeed, they even stated that such transfer does not occur, and cited a study by Kehoe to support their argument, when in fact Kehoe's work (Kehoe & Holt, 1984; Schreurs & Kehoe, 1987) demonstrated substantial transfer. In any event, in a pilot study we replicated conditions of the Welsh and Harvey (1991) study but infused muscimol instead of lidocaine and added the control group necessary to evaluate transfer of training (Cipriano et al., 1995). The bottom line is that our animals showed no evidence of learning CRs to the tone following the day of tone training with muscimol infusion in the interpositus.

The convergence of evidence from our muscimol and lidocaine studies, from Lavond's cooling studies and from recent inactivation studies in Yeo's laboratory (Hardiman et al., 1996) is conclusive: inactivation of the anterior interpositus nucleus during training completely prevents learning of the eyeblink-NM CR. This result, incidentally, does not eliminate a critical role for the cerebellar cortex in learning, since there are substantial direct projections from the interpositus nucleus to the cerebellar cortex. The fact that inactivation of the superior cerebellar peduncle (and red nucleus) during training does not prevent learning demonstrates that the memory trace(s) must be formed and stored in the cerebellum. The fact that appropriate lesions of the interpositus always permanently abolish the CR argues strongly that permanent memory trace is stored in the cerebellum. There is no evidence at all to the contrary.

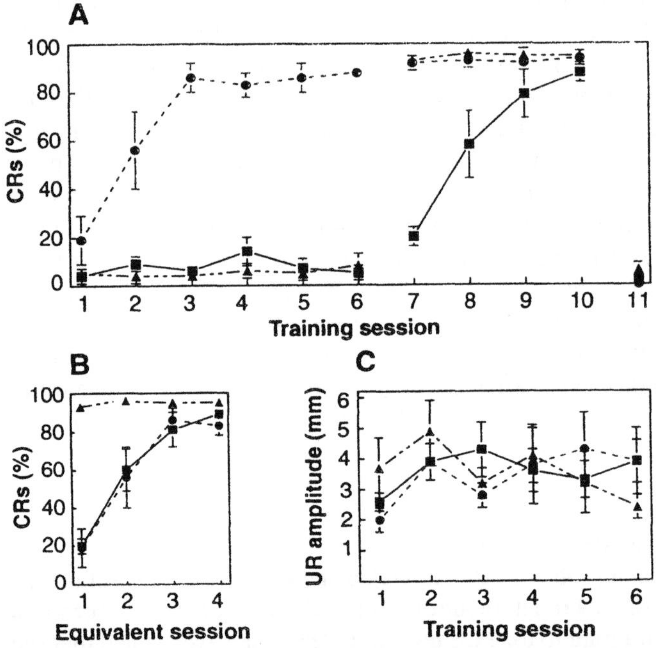

Figure 12. Effect of muscimol infusion in the cerebellum and red nucleus on CRs and URs. (A) All animals received an infusion before training on session 1 to 6. The cerebellar group (■) (n = 6) received muscimol infusions into the ipsilateral lateral cerebellum, the red nucleus group (▲) (n = 6) received muscimol in the contralateral red nucleus, and the saline group (●) (n = 6) received 1 ul of saline vehicle into the ipsilateral lateral cerebellum. No infusions were administered on Days 7 to 10. All animals received muscimol infusions before session 11. Data are expressed as percent CRs averaged over all animals in each group for each training session. (B) Percent CRs for sessions 1 to 4 of the saline group and sessions 7 to 10 of the cerebellar and red nucleus groups. (C) UR amplitudes on air puff-only test trials during the six sessions in which infusions were administered. There were no significant differences between groups on these days. All data points are means ± SEM. Symbols are the same for all charts. (From Krupa, Thompson & Thompson, 1993).

The US Pathway, Purkinje Neuron Responses and Blocking

To me, identification of the US reinforcing or teaching pathway has been perhaps the most interesting aspect of the cerebellar story. As I noted earlier, our initial studies showed that localized lesions of the dorsal accessory olive (DAO) prevented learning if made before training and after training resulted in extinction of the CR with continued paired training (McCormick et al., 1985; Steinmetz et al., 1984; see also Mintz et al., 1994). Yeo et al. (1986) made DAO lesions and reported that they immediately abolished the CR. His lesions were larger than ours and there were other procedural differences. In fact, our lesion study was done in two independent replications, one by McCormick and one by Steinmetz. In subsequent unpublished work, Jeansok Kim replicated our lesion-extinction result. Next, we found that stimulation of the DAO elicited discrete movements and these movements could be conditioned to any neutral stimulus (Mauk et al., 1986). This study was also done in two replications, one by Mauk and one by Steinmetz (in addition to being an outstanding and creative scientist, Joseph Steinmetz was a superb "mop-up" man while in my laboratory). These findings immediately provided an explanation for the results of the Brogden and Gantt (1942) study, as I noted above. Subsequently, Steinmetz and Lavond completed a tour-de-force by stimulating the pontine nuclei-mossy fibers as a CS and DAO-climbing fibers as a US and obtained normal behavioral learning (Steinmetz et al., 1989). More recently, we replicated the Brogden and Gantt result exactly, stimulating cerebellar white matter of lobule HVI as a US to evoke movements and training these movements to neutral tone CSs (Swain et al., 1992; Swain et al., 1999). We also trained these cerebellar elicited movements to stimulation of cerebellar parallel fibers in lobule HVI as a neutral CS (Shinkman et al., 1996; see also Thompson et al., 1998; 2000).

We completed extensive recordings of the activity of single Purkinje neurons before and after eyeblink training (Foy et al., 1984; Donegan et al., 1985; Foy et al., 1986; Krupa et al., 1990; Thompson, 1990; see also Krupa, 1993; Krupa et al., 1991; Kim et al., 1998). In terms of simple spike responses (presumably activated by parallel fibers) we saw several patterns of learning related activity, including one category that showed clear decreases in discharge frequency in the CS period that preceded the behavioral CR. The process of long-term depression discovered by Ito (see 1984) could underlie this result, which also makes behavioral sense in that a decrease in simple spike discharges in Purkinje neurons would disinhibit the critical neurons in the interpositus nucleus. But other patterns of learning-induced changes in Purkinje neurons, including increases in the CS period, were also seen in our work and in the studies of others (Berthier & Moore, 1986; Gould & Steinmetz, 1996; Katz & Steinmetz, 1997).

On the other hand, the complex spike responses of Purkinje neurons to climbing fiber activation showed a clear and consistent pattern of response in relation to learning. In brief, Purkinje neurons showing a clear US onset evoked complex spike (climbing fiber response) did not exhibit evoked complex spikes in paired CS-US trials where the animal gave a behavioral eyeblink CR. The occurrence of the CR somehow inhibited the US evoked complex spike. While still in my laboratory, Steinmetz began unit cluster recordings (fixed microelectrodes) from the face region of the DAO, the same region which when lesioned caused extinction of the CRs. He completed this study after moving to Indiana University, where he found a clear inverse relationship between the degree of learning and the amplitude of the US and evoked unit response in the DAO (Sears & Steinmetz, 1991). In naive animals or on US alone trials in trained animals there was a maximal US onset evoked response in the DAO. When animals gave CRs on paired trials there was no evoked unit response in the DAO. This, of course, accounted for the US evoked complex spike results in our Purkinje recordings (effect of training). We noted early that the GABAergic inhibitory pathway from the interpositus nucleus to the inferior olive could account for these results (e.g., Thompson, 1989). Although I cannot remember the exact date, I do remember that Mark Gluck and I were flying from Stanford to an ONR contractors meeting in Southern California. We were reviewing the extensive data from my laboratory on the cerebellar circuit and it became obvious to both of us that this circuit could account for the phenomenon of blocking, which Mark verified in his modeling work.

Jeansok Kim undertook to test this hypothesis (Kim et al., 1992; 1998). In brief, infusion of picrotoxin (to block the inhibitory GABAergic projection from the interpositus to the DAO) completely blocked the inhibition of Purkinje cell US evoked complex spikes on CR trials in trained animals. Further, picrotoxin infusion in the DAO during the five days of compound (tone-light) training in the blocking paradigm completely blocked subsequent behavioral blocking. This result is a most satisfying instantiation of a complex cognitive phenomenon of conditioning that is an emergent property of the cerebellar circuitry we have identified.

Eyeblink Conditioning in the Mouse

Thanks largely to the efforts of Jeansok Kim, Lu Chen and Shaowen Bao in my laboratory, we have developed eyeblink conditioning in the mouse as a useful model (as noted above). The procedure we use was actually first developed by a former postdoctoral fellow from the laboratory, Ronald Skelton, working with the rat (Skelton, 1988). It is not possible to obtain normal conditions for learning in rodents if they are restrained (because corticosterone levels skyrocket). Consequently Skelton developed a procedure for use with the freely moving animal—subcutaneous wires implanted periorbitally to deliver a shock US and record the EMG of the orbicularis oculi as the eyeblink response (see above), using a free field tone or light CS. Another former postdoc, Mark Stanton, adapted this procedure to use with infant rats and mice (Aiba et al., 1994; Freeman et al., 1995; see Chapter 5, this volume). We adopted and modified these procedures and showed that this mouse preparation exhibited normal associative learning and memory and that the interpositus was necessary, as in other mammals (Bao et al., 1998a; Chen et al., 1996, 1999a; Kim et al., 1996).

The primary motivation for developing the mouse model was of course the existence of a number of mutants with cerebellar abnormalities (e.g., the pcd mouse, see Chen et al., 1996 and above) and the proliferation of gene knockout preparations. To date, our results indicate that long-term depression (LTD) in the cerebellar cortex correlates well with eyeblink conditioning but not with motor coordination (an interesting dichotomy); that the cerebellar cortex does play a key role in learning but some degree of learning can occur in the interpositus nucleus (pcd mouse); that multiple climbing fiber innervation can lead to rapid learning but impaired motor coordination (PKCgamma KO); that BDNF plays a key role in the development of the cerebellar cortex and learning ability (stargazer and waggler); that glial cells appear to play a key role in cerebellar learning (cerebellar GFAP KO) (Bao et al., 1998b, 1999; Chen et al., 1995; Chen et al., 1996; 1999a; 1999b; Kim et al., 1996; Kim et al., 1997; Kim & Thompson, 1997; 1998; Offermanns et al., 1997; Qiao et al., 1998; Shibuki et al., 1996; Shih & Thompson, 1999). This current work is most exciting, particularly in terms of analysis of mechanisms of memory formation, and would form a chapter in itself.

CONCLUSIONS

When we began our search for the memory trace many years ago, it seemed clear to me, in spite of Lashley's pessimistic conclusion to the contrary, that memory traces could be localized and hence analyzed, at least memory traces for basic aspects of learning and memory. At present there is much hand waving in support of the counter view that memories are distributed in the brain, but very little convincing evidence. In any event, it seemed necessary to pick a simple and basic form of associative learning and memory where the CS, US, UR and CR could be well specified and controlled. Having done so there were a sequential series of problems to be solved. First, it was necessary to identify the essential (necessary and sufficient) circuitry, the CS, US, UR, and CR pathways, and the regions of CS and US convergence. Second, it was necessary to determine where in this circuitry the memory traces are formed. Having done this, the mechanisms of memory trace formations and storage can then be analyzed.

As this volume testifies, my colleagues and I have succeeded in characterizing the key essential circuitry for classical conditioning of discrete responses learned with an aversive US and have localized the sites of memory traces formation, at least within a few millimeters of tissue in the cerebellar cortex and interpositus nucleus. Several laboratories, including my own, are now focusing on mechanisms of memory storage (see e.g., Chen & Steinmetz, 2000; Gomi et al., 1999).

Discovery of the essential role of the cerebellum and its associated circuitry in classical conditioning of discrete responses, and the now very strong evidence for cerebellar localization of the memory traces, has been and is an extremely exciting intellectual adventure. Although it sounds rather self-serving, except for the pioneering study of Brogden & Gantt (1942), essentially all the major discoveries concerning the role of the cerebellum in classical conditioning of discrete responses have been made in my laboratory and/or by people who have worked in my laboratory. But there is much yet to be discovered.

REFERENCES

Aiba, A., Kano, M., Chen, C., Stanton, M.E., Gox, G.D., Herrup, K., Zwingman, T.A., & Tonegawa, S.

(1994). Deficient cerebellar long-term depression and impaired motor learning in mGluRl mutant mice. *Cell, 79*, 377-388.

Albus, J.S. 1971). A theory of cerebellar function. *Mathematical Bioscience, 10*, 25-61.

Bao, S., Chen, L., & Thompson, R.F. (1998a). Classical eyeblink conditioning in two strains of mice: Conditioned responses, sensitization and spontaneous eyeblinks. *Behavioral Neuroscience, 112*, 714-718.

Bao, S., Chen, L., Qiao, X., Knusel, B., & Thompson, R.F. (1998). Impaired eye-blink conditioning in waggler, a mutant mouse with cerebellar BDNF deficiency. *Learning & Memory, 5*, 355-364.

Bao, S., Chen, L., Qiao, X., & Thompson, R.F. (1999). Transgenic brain-derived neurotrophic factor modulates a developing cerebellar inhibitory synapse. *Learning & Memory, 6*, 276-283.

Berger, T.W., Alger, B., & Thompson, R.F. (1976). Neuronal substrate of classical conditioning in the hippocampus. *Science, 192*, 483-485.

Berger, T.W., Berry, S.D., & Thompson, R.F. (1986a). Role of the hippocampus in classical conditioning of aversive and appetitive behaviors. In R. L. Isaacson & K. H. Pribram (Eds.). *The Hippocampus. Volumes III and IV*, (pp. 203-239). New York: Plenum Press.

Berger, T.W., Rinaldi, P.C., Weisz, D.J., & Thompson, R.F. (1983). Single-unit analysis of different hippocampal cell types during classical conditioning of rabbit nictitating membrane response. *Journal of Neurophysiology, 50*, 1197-1219.

Berger, T.W., & Thompson, R.F. (1978). Identification of pyramidal cells as the critical elements in hippocampal neuronal plasticity during learning. *Proceedings of the National Academy of Sciences, (USA), 75*, 1572-1576.

Berger, T.W., Weikart, C.L., Bassett, J.L., & Orr, W.B. (1986b). Lesions of the retrosplenial cortex produce deficits in reversal learning of the rabbit nictitating membrane response: Implications for potential interactions between hippocampal and cerebellar brain systems. *Behavioral Neuroscience, 100*, 796-803.

Berry, S.D., Rinaldi, P.C., Thompson, R.F., & Verzeano, M. (1978). Analysis of temporal relations among units and slow waves in rabbit hippocampus. *Brain Research Bulletin, 3*, 509-518.

Berry, S.D., & Thompson, R.F. (1979). Medial septal lesions retard classical conditioning of the nictitating membrane response in rabbits. *Science, 205*, 209-211.

Berthier, N.E., & Moore, J.W. (1986). Cerebellar Purkinje cell activity related to the classical conditioned nictitating membrane response. *Experimental Brain Research, 63*, 341-350.

Berthier, N.E., & Moore, J.W. (1990). Activity of deep cerebellar nuclear cells during classical conditioning of nictitating membrane extension in rabbits. *Experimental Brain Research, 83*, 44-54.

Brogden, W.J. & Gantt, W.H. (1942). Interneural conditioning: Cerebellar conditioned reflexes. *Archives of Neurology and Psychiatry, 48*, 437-455.

Buonomano, D.V., & Mauk, M.D. (1994). Neural network model of the cerebellum: Temporal discrimination and the timing of motor responses. *Neural Computation, 6*, 38-55.

Cegavske, C.F., Patterson, M.M., & Thompson, R.F. (1979). Neuronal unit activity in the abducens nucleus during classical conditioning of the nictitating membrane response in the rabbit, Oryctolagus cuniculus. *Journal of Comparative and Physiological Psychology, 93*, 595-609.

Cegavske, C.F., Thompson, R.F., Patterson, M.M., & Gormezano, I. (1976). Mechanisms of efferent neuronal control of the reflex nicitating membrane response in rabbit. *Journal of Comparative & Physiological Psychology, 90*, 411-423.

Chapman, P.F., Steinmetz, J.E., & Thompson, R.F. (1988). Classical conditioning does not occur when direct stimulation of the red nucleus or cerebellar nuclei is the unconditioned stimulus. *Brain Research, 442*, 97-104.

Chen, C., Kano, M., Abeliovich, A., Chen, L., Bao, S., Kim, J.J., Hashimoto, K., Thompson, R.F., & Tonegawa, S. (1995). Impaired motor coordination correlates with persistent multiple climbing fiber innervation in PKC gamma mutant mice. *Cell, 83*, 1233-1242.

Chen, G., & Steinmetz, J.E. (2000). Microinfusion of protein kinase inhibitor H7 in the cerebellum impairs the ac1quisition but not retention of classical eyeblink conditioning in rabbits. *Brain Research, 857*, 88-104.

Chen, L., Bao, S., Lockard, J.M., Kim, J.K., & Thompson, R.F. (1996). Impaired classical eyeblink conditioning in cerebellar-lesioned and Purkinje cell degeneration (pcd) mutant mice. *Journal of Neuroscience, 16*, 2829-2838.

Chen, L., Bao, S., Qiao, X., & Thompson, R.F. (1999b). Impaired cerebellar synapse maturation in waggler, a mutant mouse with a disrupted neuronal calcium channel γ subunit. *Proceedings of the National Academy of Sciences, (USA), 96*, 12132-12137.

Chen, L., Bao, S., & Thompson, R.F. (1999a). Bilateral lesions of the interpositus nucleus completely prevent eyeblink conditioning in Purkinje cell degeneration mutant mice. *Behavioral Neuroscience, 113*, 204-210.

Cipriano, B.D., Krupa, D.J., Almanza, O.W., & Thompson, R.F. (1995). Inactivation of the interpositus nucleus prevents transfer of the rabbit's classically conditioned eyeblink response from a light to a tone CS. *Neuroscience Abstracts, 21*, 1221.

Clark, G.A., McCormick, D.A., Lavond, D.G., & Thompson, R.F. (1984). Effects of lesions of cerebellar nuclei on conditioned behavioral and hippocampal neuronal responses. *Brain Research, 291*, 125-136.

Clark, R.E., & Lavond, D.G. (1993). Reversible lesions of the red nucleus during acquisition and retention of a classically conditioned behavior in rabbit. *Behavioral Neuroscience, 107*, 264-270.

Clark, R.E., & Squire, L.R. (1998). Classical conditioning and brain systems: The role of awareness. *Science, 280*, 77-81.

Clark, R.E., Zhang, A.A., & Lavond, D.G. (1992). Reversible lesions of the cerebellar interpositus nucleus during acquisition and retention of a classically conditioned behavior. *Behavioral Neuroscience, 106*, 879-888.

Daum, I., Schugens, M.M., Ackermann, H., Lutzenberger, W., Dichgans, J., & Birbaumer, N. (1993). Classical conditioning after cerebellar lesions in human. *Behavioral Neuroscience, 107*, 748-756.

Deaux, E.B., & Gormezano, I. (1963). Eyeball retraction: Classical conditioning and extinction inthe albino rabbit. *Science, 141*, 630-631.

Desmond, J.E., & Moore, J.W. (1988). Adaptive timing in neural networks: the conditioned response. *Biological Cybernetics, 58*, 405-415.

Donegan, N.H., Foy, M.R. & Thompson, R.F. (1985). Neuronal responses of the rabbit cerebellar cortex during performance of the classically conditioned eyelid response. *Neuroscience Abstracts, 11*, 835.

Donegan, N.H., Gluck, M.A., & Thompson, R.F. (1989). Integrating behavioral and biological models of classical conditioning. In R.D. Hawkins & G.H. Bower (Eds.). *Psychology of Learning and Motivation*, (pp. 109-156). New York: Academic Press.

Donegan, N.H., Lowry, R.W. & Thompson, R.F. (1983). Effects of lesioning cerebellar nuclei on conditioned leg-flexion response. *Neuroscience Abstracts, 9*, 331.

Doty, R.W., Rutledge, L.T., & Larson, R.M. (1956). Conditioned reflexes established to electrical stimulation of cat cerebral cortex. *Journal of Neurophysiology, 19*, 401-415.

Eccles, J.C. (1977). An instruction-selection theory of learning in the cerebellar cortex. *Brain Research, 127*, 327-352.

Evinger, C., & Manning, K.A. (1988). A model system for motor learning: Adaptive gain control of the blink reflex. *Experimental Brain Research, 70*, 527-538.

Fiola, J., Grossberg, S., & Bullock, D. (1996). Metabotropic glutamate receptor activation in cerebellar Purkinje cells as a substrate for adaptive timing of the classically conditioned eye-blink response. *Journal of Neuroscience, 16*, 3760-3774.

Foy, M.R., Steinmetz, J.E. & Thompson, R.F. (1984). Single unit analysis of cerebellum during classically conditioned eyelid response. *Neuroscience Abstracts, 10*, 122.

Foy, M.R. & Thompson, R.F. (1986). Single unit analysis of Purkinje cell discharge in classically conditioned and untrained rabbits. *Neuroscience Abstracts, 12*, 518.

Freeman, J.H., Jr., Barone, S., Jr., & Stanton, M.E. (1995). Disruption of cerebellar maturation by an antimitotic agent impairs the ontogeny of eyeblink conditioning in rats. *Journal of Neuroscience, 15*, 7301-7314.

Gabriel, M. (1993). Discriminative avoidance learning: A model system. In M. Gabriel and B. Vogt (Eds.). *Neurobiology of Cingulate Cortex and Limbic Thalamus*, (pp. 478-523). Toronto: Birkhauser Publishers Inc.

Gabriel, M., Wheeler, W., & Thompson, R.F. (1973). Multiple-unit activity of the rabbit cerebral cortex in single-session avoidance conditioning. *Physiological Psychology, 1*, 45-55.

Gluck, M.A., Myers, C.E. & Thompson, R.F. (1994). A computational model of the cerebellum and motor-reflex conditioning. In S.F. Zornetzer, J.L. Davis, C. Lau, and T. McKenna (Eds.). *Introduction to Neural and Electronic Networks* (Second Edition ed., pp. 91-98). Orlando, FL: Academic Press, Inc.

Gluck, M.A., Reifsnider, J., & Thompson, R.F. (1990). Adaptive signal processing and the cerebellum: Models of classical conditioning and VOR adaptation. In M.A. Gluck & D.E. Rumelhart (Eds.). *Neuroscience and connectionist models*, (pp. 131-185). Hillsdale, NJ: Lawrence Erlbaum.

Gomi, H., Sun, W., Finch, C.E., Itohara, S., Yoshimi, K., & Thompson, R.F. (1999). Learning induces a CDC2-related protein kinase, KKIAMRE. *The Journal of Neuroscience, 19*, 9530-9537.

Gormezano, I., Kehoe, E.J., & Marshall-Goodell, B.S. (1983). Twenty years of classical conditioning research with the rabbit. In J.M. Sprague and A.N. Epstein (Eds.). *Progress in Physiological Psychology,* (pp. 197-275). New York: New York Academic.

Gormezano, I., Schneiderman, N., Deaux, E.B., & Fuentes, I. (1962). Nictitating membrane: Classical conditioning and extinction in the albino rabbit. *Science, 138,* 33-34.

Gould, T.J., & Steinmetz, J.E. (1996). Changes in rabbit cerebellar cortical and interpositus nucleus activity during acquisition, extinction and backward classical conditioning. *Neurobiology of Learning and Memory, 65,* 17-34.

Grossberg, S., & Schmajuk, N.A. (1989). Neural dynamics of adaptive timing and temporal discrimination during associative learning. *Neural Networks, 2,* 79-102.

Groves, P.M., & Thompson, R.F. (1970). Habituation: A dual-process theory. *Psychological Review, 77,* 419-450.

Haley, D.A., Lavond, D.G., & Thompson, R.F. (1983). Effects of contralateral red nuclear lesions on retention of the classically conditioned nictitating membrane/eyelid response. *Neuroscience Abstracts, 9,* 643.

Hardiman, M.J., Ramnani, N., & Yeo, C.H. (1996). Reversible inactivations of the cerebellum with muscimol prevent the acquisition and extinction of conditioned nictitating membrane responses in the rabbit. *Experimental Brain Research, 110,* 235-247.

Hiraoka, M., & Shimamura, M. (1977). Neural mechanisms of the corneal blinking reflex in cats. *Brain Research, 125,* 265-275.

Ito, M. (1984). *The Cerebellum and Neural Control.* New York: Appleton Century-Crofts.

Ivkovich, D., Lockard, J.M., & Thompson, R.F. (1993). Interpositus lesion abolition of the eyeblink conditioned response is not due to effects on performance. *Behavioral Neuroscience, 107,* 530-532.

Kaneko, T., & Thompson, R.F. (1997). Disruption of trace conditioning of the nictitating membrane response in rabbits by central cholinergic blockade. *Psychopharmacology, 131,* 161-166.

Karamian, A.I., Fanardijian, V.V., & Kosareva, A.A. (1960). The functional and morphological evolution of the cerebellum and its role in behavior. In R. Llinas (Ed.). *Neurobiology of Cerebellar Evolution and Development, First International Symposium.* Chicago, IL: American Medical Association.

Katz, D.B., & Steinmetz, J.E. (1997). Single-unit evidence for eyeblink conditioning in cerebellar cortex is altered, but not eliminated, by interpositus nucleus lesions. *Learning and Memory, 4(1),* 88-104.

Kehoe, E.J., & Holt, P.E. (1984). Transfer across CS-US intervals and sensory modalities in classical conditioning of the rabbit. *Animal Learning and Behaviora, 12,* 122-128.

Kettner, R.E., Shannon, R.V., Nguyen, T.M., & Thompson, R.F. (1980). Simultaneous behavioral and neural (Cochlear Nucleus) measurement during signal detection in the rabbit. *Perception and Psychophysics, 28,* 504-513.

Kettner, R E., & Thompson, R.F. (1982). Auditory signal detection and decision processes in the nervous system. *Journal of Comparative & Physiological Psychology, 96,* 328-331.

Kettner, R.E., & Thompson, R.F. (1985). Cochlear nucleus, inferior colliculus, and medial geniculate responses during the behavioral detection of threshold-level auditory stimuli in the rabbit. *Journal of the Acoustical Society of America, 77,* 2111-2127.

Kim, J.J., Chen, L., Bao, S., Sun., W., & Thompson, R.F. (1996). Genetic dissections of the cerebellar circuitry involved in classical eyeblink conditioning. In S. Nakanishi, A.J. Silva, and S. Aizawa, and M. Katsuki (Eds.). *Gene Targeting and New Developments in Neurobiology,* (pp. 3-15). Tokyo, Japan: Japan Scientific Societies Press.

Kim, J.J., Clark, R.E., & Thompson, R.F. (1995). Hippocampectomy impairs the memory of recently, but not remotely, acquired trace eyeblink conditioned responses. *Behavioral Neuroscience, 109,* 195-203.

Kim, J.J., Krupa, D.J. & Thompson, R.F. (1992). Intra-olivary infusions of picrotoxin prevent "blocking" of rabbit conditioned eyeblink response. *Neuroscience Abstracts, 18,* 1562.

Kim, J.J., Krupa, D.J., & Thompson, R.F. (1998). Inhibitory cerebello-olivary projections and blocking effect in classical conditioning. *Science, 279,* 570-573.

Kim, J.J., Shih, J.C., Chen, K., Chen, L., Bao, S., Shin, M. J., Maren, S.A., Anagnostaras, S.G., Fanselow, M.S., Maeyer, E.D., Seif, I., & Thompson, R.F. (1997). Selective enhancement of emotional, but not motor, learning in monoamine oxidase A-deficient transgenic mice. *Proceedings of the National Academy of Sciences (USA), 94,* 5929-5933.

Kim, J.J., & Thompson, R.F. (1997). Cerebellar circuits and synaptic mechanisms involved in classical eyeblink conditioning. *Trends in Neurosciences, 20,* 177-181.

Knowlton, B.J., Thompson, J.K., & Thompson, R.F. (1993). Projections from the auditory cortex to the pontine nuclei in the rabbit. *Behavioral Brain Research, 56,* 23-30.

Knowlton, B.J., & Thompson, R.F. (1988). Microinjections of local anesthetic into the pontine nuclei reduce the amplitude of the classically conditioned eyelid response. *Physiology & Behavior, 43*, 855-857.

Knowlton, B.J., & Thompson, R.F. (1992). Conditioning using a cerebral cortical conditioned stimulus is dependent on the cerebellum and brain stem circuitry. *Behavioral Neuroscience, 106*, 509-517.

Krupa, D.J. (1993). *Localization of the essential memory trace for a classically conditioned behavior.* Doctoral Dissertation, University of Southern California, Los Angeles.

Krupa, D.J., Tracy, J., Weiss, C., & Thompson, R.F. (1990). Single unit responses from the cerebellar cortex of naive rabbits. *Neuroscience Abstracts, 16*, 762.

Krupa, D.J., Thompson, J.K., & Thompson, R.F. (1993). Localization of a memory trace in the mammalian brain. *Science, 260*, 989-991.

Krupa, D.J., & Thompson, R.F. (1995). Inactivation of the superior cerebellar peduncle blocks expression but not acquisition of the rabbit's classically conditioned eye-blink response. *Proceedings of the National Academy of Sciences, (USA), 92*, 5097-5101.

Krupa, D.J., & Thompson, R.F. (1997). Reversible inactivation of the cerebellar interpositus nucleus completely prevents acquisition of the classically conditioned eyeblink response. *Learning & Memory, 3*, 545-556.

Krupa, D.J., Weiss, C., & Thompson, R.F. (1991). Air puff evoked Purkinje cell complex spike activity is diminished during conditioned responses in eyeblink conditioned rabbits. *Neuroscience Abstracts, 17*, 322.

Krupa, D.J., Weng, J., & Thompson, R.F. (1996). Inactivation of brainstem motor nuclei blocks expression but not acquisition of the rabbit's classically conditioned eyeblink response. *Behavioral Neuroscience, 110*, 219-227.

Lavond, D.G., Hembree, T.L., & Thompson, R.F. (1985). Effect of kainic acid lesions of the cerebellar interpositus nucleus on eyelid conditioning in the rabbit. *Brain Research, 326*, 179-182.

Lavond, D.G., Knowlton, B.J., Steinmetz, J.E., & Thompson, R F. (1987a). Classical conditioning of the rabbit eyelid response with a mossy-fiber stimulation CS: II. Lateral reticular nucleus stimulation. *Behavioral Neuroscience, 101*, 676-682.

Lavond, D.G., Lincoln, J.S., McCormick, D.A., & Thompson, R.F. (1984a). Effect of bilateral lesions of the dentate and interpositus cerebellar nuclei on conditioning of heart-rate and nictitating membrane/eyelid responses in the rabbit. *Brain Research, 305*, 323-330.

Lavond, D.G., Logan, C.G., Sohn, J.H., Garner, W.D.A., & Kanzawa, S.A. (1990). Lesions of the cerebellar interpositus nucleus abolish both nictitating membrane and eyelid EMG conditioned responses. *Brain Research, 514*, 238-248.

Lavond, D.G., McCormick, D.A., Clark, G.A., Holmes, D.T., & Thompson, R.F. (1981). Effects of ipsilateral rostral pontine reticular lesions on retention of classically conditioned nictitating membrane and eyelid responses. *Physiological Psychology, 9*, 335-339.

Lavond, D.G., McCormick, D.A., & Thompson, R.F. (1984b). A non-recoverable learning deficit. *Physiological Psychology, 12*, 103-110.

Lavond, D.G., Steinmetz, J.E., Yokaitis, M.H., & Thompson, R.F. (1987b). Reacquisition of classical conditioning after removal of cerebellar cortex. *Experimental Brain Research, 67*, 569-593.

Lincoln, J.S., McCormick, D.A., & Thompson, R.F. (1982). Ipsilateral cerebellar lesions prevent learning of the classically conditioned nictitating membrane/eyelid response. *Brain Research, 242*, 190-193.

Llinas, R., Lang, E.J., & Welsh, J.P. (1997). The cerebellum, LTD and memory: Alternative views. *Learning & Memory, 3*, 445-455.

Logan, C.G., & Grafton, S.T. (1995). Functional anatomy of human eyeblink conditioning determined with regional cerebral glucose metabolism and positron-emission tomography. *Proceedings of the National Academy of Science, (USA), 92*, 7500-7504.

Logan, C.G., Lavond, D.G., Wong, J.T., & Thompson, R.F. (1994). Acquisition of classically conditioned eyeblink response following bilateral lesions of flocculus and paraflocculus. *Behavioral & Neural Biology, 61*, 102-106.

Marr, D. (1969). A theory of cerebellar cortex. *Journal of Physiology, 202*, 437-470.

Mauk, M.D., Steinmetz, J.E., & Thompson, R.F. (1986). Classical conditioning using stimulation of the inferior olive as the unconditioned stimulus. *Proceedings of the National Academy of Sciences, (USA), 83*, 5349-5353.

McCormick, D.A., Clark, G.A., Lavond, D.G., & Thompson, R.F. (1982a). Initial localization of the memory trace for a basic form of learning. *Proceedings of the National Academy of Sciences, (USA), 79*, 2731-2735.

McCormick, D.A., Guyer, P.E., & Thompson, R.F. (1982b). Superior cerebellar peduncle lesions selectively abolish the ipsilateral classically conditioned nictitating membrane/eyelid response of the rabbit. *Brain Research, 244*, 347-350.

McCormick, D.A., Lavond, D.G., Clark, G.A., Kettner, R E., Rising, C.E., & Thompson, R.F. (1981). The engram found?: Role of the cerebellum in classical conditioning of nictitating and eyelid responses. *Bulletin of the Psychonomic Society, 18*, 103-105.

McCormick, D.A., Lavond, D.G., & Thompson, R.F. (1982c). Concomitant classical conditioning of the rabbit nictitating membrane and eyelid responses: correlations and implications. *Physiological Behavior, 28*, 769-775.

McCormick, D.A., Lavond, D.G., & Thompson, R.F. (1983). Neuronal responses of the rabbit brainstem during performance of the classically conditioned nictitating membrane (NM)/eyelid response. *Brain Research, 271*, 73-88.

McCormick, D.A., Steinmetz, J.E., & Thompson, R.F. (1985). Lesions of the inferior olivary complex cause extinction of the classically conditioned eyeblink response. *Brain Research, 359*, 120-130.

McCormick, D.A., & Thompson, R.F. (1984a). Cerebellum: Essential involvement in the classically conditioned eyelid response. *Science, 223*, 296-299.

McCormick, D.A., & Thompson, R.F. (1984b). Neuronal responses of the rabbit cerebellum during acquisition and performance of a classically conditioned nictitating membrane-eyelid response. *Journal of Neuroscience, 4*, 2811-2822.

McGlinchey-Berroth, R., Carrillo, M.C., Gabrieli, J.D., Brawn, C.M., & Disterhoft, J.F. (1997). Impaired trace eyeblink conditioning in bilateral, medial-temporal lobe amnesia. *Behavioral Neuroscience, 111*, 873-882.

Mintz, M., Lavond, D.G., Zhang, A.A., Yun, Y., & Thompson, R.F. (1994). Unilateral inferior olive NMDA lesion leads to unilateral deficit in acquisition and retention of eyelid classical conditioning. *Behavioral & Neural Biology, 61*, 218-224.

Moyer, J.R., Deyo, R.A., & Disterhoft, J.F. (1990). Hippocampectomy disrupts trace eye-blink conditioning in rabbits. *Behavioral Neuroscience, 104*, 243-252.

Nordholm, A.F., Thompson, J.K., Dersarkissian, C., & Thompson, R.F. (1993). Lidocaine infusion in a critical region of cerebellum completely prevents learning of the conditioned eyeblink response. *Behavioral Neuroscience, 107*, 882-886.

Offermanns, S., Hashimoto, K., Watanabe, M., Sun, W., Kurihara, H., Thompson, R.F., Inoue, Y., Kano, M., & Simon, M.I. (1997). Impaired motor coordination and persistent multiple climbing fiber innervation of cerebellar Purkinje cells in mice lacking Galphaq. *Proceedings of the National Academy of Sciences, (USA), 94*, 14089-14094.

Patterson, M.M., Cegavske, C.F., & Thompson, R.F. (1973). Effects of a classical conditioning paradigm on hind-limb flexor nerve response in immobilized spinal cats. *Journal of Comparative & Physiological Psychology, 84*, 88-97.

Perrett, S.P., & Mauk, M.D. (1995). Extinction of conditioned eyelid responses requires the anterior lobe of cerebellar cortex. *Journal of Neuroscience, 15*, 2074-2080.

Qiao, X., Chen, L., Gao, H., Bao, S., Hefti, F., Thompson, R.F., & Knusel, B. (1998). Cerebellar brain-derived neurotrophic factor-TrkB defect associated with impairment of eyeblink conditioning in Stargazer mutant mice. *Journal of Neuroscience, 18*, 6990-6999.

Roemer, R.A., Teyler, T.J., & Thompson, R.F. (1974). Conditioning of the pyramidal response in unanesthetized cat. *Physiological Psychology, 2*, 435-440.

Rosenfield, M.D., Dovydaitis, A., & Moore, J.W. (1985). Brachium conjunctivum and rubrobulbar tract: Brainstem projections of red nucleus essential for the conditioned nictitating membrane response. *Physiology & Behavior, 34*, 751-759.

Rosenfield, M.E., & Moore, J.W. (1983). Red nucleus lesions disrupt the classically conditioned nictitating membrane response in rabbits. *Behavioral Brain Research, 10*, 393-398.

Schmajuk, N.A., Lamoureux, J.A., & Holland, P.C. (1998). Occasion setting: a neural network approach. *Psychological Review, 105*, 3-32.

Schmaltz, L.W., & Theios, J. (1972). Acquisition and extinction of a classically conditioned response in hippocampectomized rabbits (Oryctolagus cuniculus). *Journal of Comparative and Physiological Psychology, 29*, 328-333.

Schneiderman, N., Fuentes, I., & Gormezano, I. (1962). Acquisition and extinction of the classically conditioned eyelid response in the albino rabbit. *Science, 136*, 650-652.

Schreurs, B.G., & Kehoe, E.J. (1987). Cross-modal transfer as a function of initial training level in classical conditioning with the rabbit. *Animal Learning and Behavior, 15*, 47-54.

Sears, L.L., & Steinmetz, J.E. (1991). Dorsal accessory inferior olive activity diminishes during acquisition of the rabbit classically conditioned eyelid response. *Brain Research, 545*, 114-122.

Shibuki, K., Gomi, H., Chen, L., Bao, S., Kim, J.J., Wakatsuki, H., Fujisaki, T., Fujimoto, K., Katoh, A., Ikeda, T., Chen, C., Thompson, R.F., & Itohara, S. (1996). Deficient cerebellar long-term depression, impaired eyeblink conditioning, and normal motor coordination in GFAP mutant mice. *Neuron, 16*, 587-599.

Shih, J.C., & Thompson, R.F. (1999). Monomine oxidase in neuropsychiatry and behavior. *American Journal of Human Genetics, 65*, 593-598.

Shinkman, P.G., Swain, R.A., & Thompson, R.F. (1996). Classical conditioning with electrical stimulation of cerebellum as both conditioned and unconditioned stimulus. *Behavioral Neuroscience, 110*, 914-921.

Skelton, R.W. (1988). Bilateral cerebellar lesions disrupt conditioned eyelid responses in unrestrained rats. *Behavioral Neuroscience, 102*, 586-590.

Solomon, P.R., Lewis, J.L., LoTurco, J., Steinmetz, J.E., & Thompson, R.F. (1986b). The role of the middle cerebellar peduncle in acquisition and retention of the rabbit's classically conditioned nictitating membrane response. *Bulletin of the Psychonomic Society, 241*, 75-78.

Solomon, P.R., Groccia-Ellison, M.E., Flynn, D., Mirak, J., Edwards, K.R., Dunehew, A., & Stanton, M. E. (1993). Disruption of human eyeblink conditioning after central cholinergic blockade with scopolamine. *Behavioral Neuroscience, 107*, 271-279.

Solomon, P.R., Levine, E., Bein, T., & Pendlebury, W.W. (1991). Disruption of classical conditioning in patients with Alzheimer's disease. *Neurobiology of Aging, 12*, 283-287.

Solomon, P.R., Pomerleau, D., Bennett, L., James, J., & Morse, D.L. (1989). Acquisition of the classically conditioned eyeblink response in humans over the life span. *Psychology of Aging, 4*, 34-41.

Solomon, P.R., Solomon, S.D., Schaaf, E.V., & Perry, H.E. (1983). Altered activity in the hippocampus is more detrimental to classical conditioning than removing the structure. *Science, 220*, 329-331.

Solomon, P.R., Vander Schaaf, E.R., Thompson, R.F., & Weisz, D.J. (1986a). Hippocampus and trace conditioning of the rabbit's classically conditioned nictitating membrane response. *Behavioral Neuroscience, 100*, 729-744.

Steinmetz, J.E., Lavond, D.G., Ivkovich, D., Logan, C.G., & Thompson, R.F. (1992). Disruption of classical eyelid conditioning after cerebellar lesions: damage to a memory trace system or a simple performance deficit? *Journal of Neuroscience, 12*, 4403-4426.

Steinmetz, J.E., Lavond, D.G., & Thompson, R.F. (1985). Classical conditioning of the rabbit eyelid response with mossy fiber stimulation as the conditioned stimulus. *Bulletin of the Psychonomic Society, 23*, 245-248.

Steinmetz, J.E., Lavond, D.G., & Thompson, R.F. (1989). Classical conditioning in rabbits using pontine nucleus stimulation as a conditioned stimulus and inferior olive stimulation as an unconditioned stimulus. *Synapse, 3*, 225-233.

Steinmetz, J.E., Logan, C.G., Rosen, D.J., Thompson, J.K., Lavond, D.G., & Thompson, R.F. (1987). Initial localization of the acoustic conditioned stimulus projection system to the cerebellum essential for classical eyelid conditioning. *Proceedings of the National Academy of Sciences, (USA), 84*, 3531-3535.

Steinmetz, J.E., McCormick, D.A., Baier, C.A., & Thompson, R.F. (1984). Involvement of the inferior olive in classical conditioning of the rabbit eyelid. *Neuroscience Abstracts, 10*, 122.

Steinmetz, J.E., Rosen, D.J., Chapman, P.F., Lavond, D.G., & Thompson, R.F. (1986). Classical conditioning of the rabbit eyelid response with a mossy-fiber stimulation CS: I. Pontine nuclei and middle cerebellar peduncle stimulation. *Behavioral Neuroscience, 100*, 878-887.

Swain, R.A., Shinkman, P.G. Thompson, J.K., Grethe, J.S. & Thompson, R.F. (1999). Essential neuronal pathways for reflex and conditioned response initiation in an intracerebellar stimulation paradigm. *Neurobiology of Learning & Memory, 71*, 167-193.

Swain, R.A., Shinkman, P.G., Nordholm, A.F., & Thompson, R.F. (1992). Cerebellar stimulation as an unconditioned stimulus in classical conditioning. *Behavioral Neuroscience, 106*, 739-750.

Thompson, R.F. (1989). Role of inferior olive in classical conditioning. In P. Strata (Ed.). *The Olivocerebellar System in Motor Control*, (pp. 347-362). New York: Springer-Verlag.

Thompson, R.F. (1990). Neural mechanisms of classical conditioning in mammals. *Philosophical Transactions of the Royal Society of London, B, 329*, 161-170.

Thompson, R.F., Berger, T.W., Cegavske, C.F., Patterson, M.M., Roemer, R.A., Teyler, T.J., & Young, R.A. (1976). The search for the engram. *American Psychologist, 31*, 209-227.

Thompson, R.F., & Kim, J.J. (1996). Memory systems in the brain and localization of a memory.

Proceedings of the National Academy of Sciences, (USA), 93, 13438-13444.
Thompson, R.F., & Krupa, D.J. (1994). Organization of memory traces in the mammalian brain. *Annual Review of Neuroscience, 17,* 519-549.
Thompson, R.F., Thompson, J.K., Kim, J.J., Krupa, D.J., & Shinkman, P.G. (1998). The nature of reinforcement in cerebellar learning. *Neurobiology of Learning & Memory, 70,* 150-176.
Thompson, R.F. & Spencer, W.A. (1966). Habituation: a model phenomenon for the study of neuronal substrates of behavior. *Psychological Review, 73,* 16-43.
Thompson, R.F. Swain, R., Clark, R., & Shinkman, P.S. (In press). Intracerebellar conditioning – Brogden and Gantt revisited. *Behavioral Brain Research.*
Wagner, A.R. (1981). SOP: A model of automatic memory processing in animal behavior. In N. E. Spear & R. R. Miller (Eds.). *Information Processing in Animals: Memory Mechanisms,* (pp. 5-47). Hillsdale, NJ: Erlbaum.
Wagner, A.R. (1999). Award for distinguished scientific contributions. *American Psychologist, 54,* 887-890.
Wagner, A.R., & Brandon, S.E. (1989). Evolution of a structured connectionist model of Pavlovian conditioning (ÆSOP). In S.B. Klein & R.R. Mowrer (Eds.). *Contemporary Learning Theories: Pavlovian Conditioning and the Status of Traditional Learning Theories,* (pp. 149-189). Hillsdale, NJ: Erlbaum.
Wagner, A.R., & Donegan, N. (1989). Some relationships between a computational model (SOP) and an essential neural circuit for Pavlovian (rabbit eyeblink) conditioning. In R.D. Hawkins & G.H. Bower (Eds.). *Computational Models of Learning in Simple Neural Systems: The Psychology of Learning and Motivation,* (Vol. 23, pp. 157-203). New York: Academic Press.
Weiskrantz, L., & Warrington, E.K. (1979). Conditioning in amnesic patients. *Neuropsychologia, 17,* 187-194.
Weisz, D.J. & LoTurco, J.J. (1988). Reflex facilitation of the nictitating membrane response remains after cerebellar lesions. *Behavioral Neuroscience, 102,* 203-209.
Welsh, J.P. (1987). *The effect of nucleus interpositus lesions on retention of the rabbit's classically conditioned nictitating membrane response.* MA Thesis, University of Iowa, Iowa City.
Welsh, J.P., & Harvey, J.A. (1989). Cerebellar lesions and the nictitating membrane reflex: Performance deficits of the conditioned and unconditioned response. *Journal of Neuroscience, 9,* 299-311.
Welsh, J.P., & Harvey, J.A. (1991). Pavlovian conditioning in the rabbit during inactivation of the interpositus nucleus. *Journal Physiology, (London), 444,* 459-80.
Woodruff-Pak, D.S., Finkbiner, R.G., & Sasse, D.K. (1990). Eyeblink conditioning discriminates Alzheimer's patients from non- demented aged. *Neuroreport, 1,* 45-48.
Woodruff-Pak, D.S., Lavond, D.G., Logan, C.G., & Thompson, R.F. (1987). Classical conditioning in 3-, 30-, and 45-month-old rabbits: behavioral learning and hippocampal unit activity. *Neurobiology of Aging, 8,* 101-108.
Woodruff-Pak, D.S., Lavond, D.G., & Thompson, R.F. (1985). Trace conditioning: Abolished by cerebellar nuclear lesions but not lateral cerebellar cortex aspirations. *Brain Research, 348,* 249-260.
Woodruff-Pak, D.S., Steinmetz, J.E., & Thompson, R.F. (1988). Classical conditioning of rabbits 2-1/2 to 4 years old using mossy fiber stimulation as a CS. *Neurobiology of Aging, 9,* 187-193.
Woodruff-Pak, D.S., & Thompson, R.F. (1985). Classical conditioning of the eyelid response in rabbits as a model system for the study of brain mechanisms of learning and memory in aging. *Experimental Aging Research, 11,* 109-122.
Woodruff-Pak, D.S., & Thompson, R.F. (1988). Classical conditioning of the eyeblink response in the delay paradigm in adults aged 18-83 years. *Psychology of Aging, 3,* 219-229.
Yeo, C.H., Hardiman, M.J., & Glickstein, M. (1985a). Classical conditioning of the nictitating membrane response of the rabbit. I. Lesions of the cerebellar nuclei. *Experimental Brain Research, 60,* 87-98.
Yeo, C.H., Hardiman, M.J., & Glickstein, M. (1985b). Classical conditioning of the nictitating membrane response of the rabbit. II. Lesions of the cerebellar cortex. *Experimental Brain Research, 60,* 99-113.
Yeo, C.H., Hardiman, M.J., & Glickstein, M. (1986). Classical conditioning of the nictitating membrane response of the rabbit. IV. Lesions of the inferior olive. *Experimental Brain Research, 63,* 81-92.
Young, R.A., Cegavske, C.F., & Thompson, R.F. (1976). Tone-induced changes in excitability of abducens motoneurons and of the reflex path of nictitating membrane response in rabbit (Oryctolagus cuniculus). *Journal of Comparative & Physiological Psychology, 90,* 424-434.

ACKNOWLEDGEMENT

The work reported here was supported in part by grants from NSF (IBN-9215069), ONR (N00014-95-1-1152), NIMH (5P01–MH52194), NIA (AF05142) and the Sankyo Co. Very special thanks to my wife Judith Thompson, who has always been totally supportive of my research odyssey and for many years the most valuable scientist in my laboratory.

3 EYEBLINK CONDITIONING CIRCUITRY: TRACING, LESION, AND REVERSIBLE LESION EXPERIMENTS

David G. Lavond and M. Claire Cartford
University of Southern California

INTRODUCTION

The search for an understanding of the biological bases of learning and memory requires the consensus of results from a number of techniques including recording, stimulation, pharmacology, anatomy and, not the least, the lesion. No one technique, in isolation of the others, can adequately resolve complexities of even the simplest form of learning. Each technique has its particular strengths, each has its fatal flaws. They balance and complement each other. This chapter concerns itself chiefly with studies using the lesion technique. Where appropriate we also highlight several anatomical tracing studies that have contributed in particular to the understanding of the rabbit eyeblink neural circuitry. The following chapter by Steinmetz considers the complementary recording and stimulation experiments. Together, they converge into a coherent story about rabbit eyeblink conditioning.

The lesion method is much maligned in terms of the relative lack of technical sophistication involved and more importantly because of the problems associated with its interpretation. There is no denying the lack of technical sophistication involved in many lesion methodologies, yet the lesion technique tells us something critically important that no other technique determines: whether a structure is necessary in some critical way, either for the association or for the performance, of learning and memory. Cerebral cortical lesions, for example, often have little or no apparent effect, ruling out a critical participation. Carefully conducted lesion studies and reversible lesions in particular have provided key evidence for localization of learning and memory in eyeblink conditioning. The lesion studies described here were necessary complements to observations made from recording and stimulation studies.

In the following, we first briefly review the problems of interpretation for lesion experiments. We then review the evidence from permanent lesion studies that led to our identification of the cerebellum as critically involved in eyeblink conditioning. Our discussion of permanent lesion studies is followed by a section dealing with studies using reversible lesion techniques as well as genetic lesions (mutations). Cumulatively, these studies lead to a better understanding of the basic organization of the brain circuitry underlying a basic form of learning and memory.

INTERPRETATIONS

A 'lesion' is often used in a colloquial sense to indicate any type or source of brain damage. That damage could be caused accidentally as in clinical conditions such as a stroke, or intentionally in the laboratory where there is some control over the timing, location and extent of the damage. For the purposes of this review, there is little reason to distinguish between ablations where tissue might be aspirated away from the rest of the surviving brain, for example, or electrolytic lesions (or chemical or radio frequency lesions) where the damaged tissue remains in place. The point is that some part of the brain is demonstrably, permanently destroyed, and the question is whether there is a concomitant loss of a specific behavior, or some isolated component of that behavior, in our case the conditioned eyeblink. Here we review some of the possible outcomes of lesion experiments and their possible interpretations.

When the Lesion Has No Effect

A common outcome of lesion experiments is that a lesion has had no effect on the measured behavior. The interpretation is fairly easy, that the structure is not essential for that behavior. (It could, of course, be important for some other behavior.) But a common mistake is to think that since there was no apparent effect that, therefore, the structure does not normally play some role in the behavior. For example, lesion of the hippocampus has no apparent effect on simple delay classical conditioning (Schmaltz & Theios, 1972) so one might conclude that the hippocampus is irrelevant. However, recording of normal hippocampus shows learning related unit activity in simple delay classical conditioning (Berger, Alger & Thompson, 1976), clearly indicating some unspecified participation.

One possible interpretation of the Schmaltz and Theios experiment is that the hippocampus might normally play a decided role in conditioning, but that its absence is not missed because, through evolution, the brain has developed several fail safe measures to protect itself from the effects of brain damage, specifically that the brain has redundant processing. Since we know of no two areas of the brain that, anatomically, have exactly the same afferent and efferent connections, the idea of redundancy in the strict sense is highly implausible, although redundancy is commonly asserted. More likely is that very similar functions, but not exactly the same, can take over some functioning (see *Substitution*, below).

When the Lesion Only Has a Temporary Effect

If a lesion disrupts a behavior, a common result in the experimental literature is that the condition is only temporary. That is, the behavior is initially lost and after some time or after some therapy there is recovery of function. It seems that some other locus has taken over that function. This observation is related to the enduring myth in neuroscience that initial learning in normal subjects involves conscious effort through the cerebral cortex and that somehow, magically, well learned behaviors migrate to unconscious residences. Learning to ride a bicycle, for example, seems to go from conscious (i.e., cortical) to unconscious (i.e., subcortical) processes. Damage to the cortex early in conditioning would have greater deleterious consequences than had the damage occurred when it was well learned and subcortically located. Learning and storage are conceived as having two different functions and locations. But there are several other possible explanations for why there is initial loss followed by recovery, and by implication for normal learning and storage. In fact, the causes of the recovery are intensely studied as mechanisms that could be used to promote recovery of functioning in clinical cases. We conceive of the possible mechanisms of recovery of function as falling into four categories – vicariation, diaschesis, reorganization, substitution – and emphasize here that these are *not* mutually exclusive possibilities.

Vicariation (Munk, 1881) is the idea that parts of the brain can take on a second hand (vicarious) function when the area that used to be responsible for the behavior has been damaged. Pavlov's (1927) studies of classical conditioning reported recovery after cerebral cortical lesions, which he explained in part as a function of the ill defined nature of cortical functions. Originally, vicariation required the existence of areas that had no previous functioning, an idea which was only plausible before we knew that the 'silent areas' of the brain really do have functions of their own. Hence, of all the theories of recovery of function, this is the least likely one to be valid. A modified version of vicariation suggests that surviving areas can take on additional functioning, usually at the expense of their primary duties.

Diaschesis (Monakow, 1914), and the comcomitant idea of *sparing* (Lashley, 1939), is the idea that normal functioning can be depressed by effects of shock caused to unrelated areas of the brain. Examples of shock could be temporary loss of circulation or loss of neural connectivity. Recovery occurs when the shock subsides and the spared tissue resumes its normal functioning – that is, recovery occurs because the area responsible for the behavior was never damaged. The phenomenon of recovery from spinal shock is a well known example. In terms of classical conditioning, perhaps the best example is the suggestion that loss of muscle and neural tone following cerebellar lesions can account for an apparent loss of learning (Welsh & Harvey, 1989). Schemes to promote recovery from diaschesis include (among others) serial lesions, interoperative retraining, extensive retraining and drugs, whose primary purpose is to inhibit or counter the effects of shock.

Reorganization has received the greatest attention as a mechanism for recovery of function. The idea is that a lesion has in fact destroyed the tissue responsible for the behavior, and that the brain has mechanisms to correct the damage. Among others, these mechanisms include regeneration (Cajal, 1928), reactive synaptogenesis/sprouting (Liu & Chambers, 1958), supersensitivity (Cannon, 1949), unmasking (Wall, 1980; Merzenich, Kaas, Wall, Nelson, Sur & Felleman, 1983), and recently, neural mitosis in adults (Kempermann, Brandon & Gage, 1998; Kuhn, Dickinson-Anson & Gage, 1996). The recovered behavior is the same as the originally lost behavior. With respect to classical conditioning, one example of reorganization would be the idea that learning normally occurs in cerebellar cortex but when it is damaged this allows learning to occur in the cerebellar interpositus nucleus. This concept is closely related to the bicycle analogy above, where normal learning is said to occur in one location, to be moved to another for storage.

Substitution – of sensory cues, of motor behaviors, of strategies – can result in functional recovery of the lost behavior. By that we mean that the original behavior has been permanently damaged and can never return, however adequate substitutes can stand in for the lost functioning. The paradox of substitution is that just because one observes recovered behavior it does not necessarily mean that the original behavior has returned. For example, rats without visual cortical areas can discriminate between horizontal and vertical stripes, but they do so on the basis of brightness and contour cues, not on the basis of the orientation of the lines (Lavond, Hata, Gray, Geckler, Meyer & Meyer, 1978; Lavond & Dewberry, 1980). To give one example in classical conditioning, it was possible that the learned nictitating membrane responses that are abolished by cerebellar lesions could be substituted for with eyeblinks from the external eyelids (this turned out not to be the case; Lavond, Logan, Sohn, Garner & Kanzawa, 1990).

It is generally appreciated that these mechanisms of recovery of function from nervous system injury are the *same* ones that operate throughout development and in plasticity. An injury exaggerates normal processes. As such, study of recovery of function reveals aspects of the nature of normal brain organization. The interpretation of the results of lesions is therefore a fundamental skill to understanding the brain.

The acute nature of the results of many lesion studies confounds the interpretation of lesion experiments. In some instances the original behavior returns, in others a different behavior may be affected, and discriminating between the two may be nearly impossible. These observations fuel the idea that functions can not be localized to any part of the brain, or that functions move from location to location. On the other hand, diaschesis, reorganization and substitution are mechanisms that are localized functions. That behaviors may return through diaschesis, reorganization or substitution after once appearing to be lost gives rise to the question of whether behaviors that appear to be permanently lost (next section) *could be* recovered if only there were the right conditions to promote recovery.

When the Lesion Has a Permanent Effect

If a lesion permanently abolishes a behavior then the *ideal interpretation* is that the area was actually responsible for that behavior. Establishing this interpretation for learning and memory has been a Holy Grail that is predicated upon two conditionals: that recovery cannot be induced, and that recording and stimulation studies are consistent. However, alternative, more parsimonious interpretations must be addressed, such as that the loss of functioning could be due to sensory, motor or motivational impairment rather than direct loss of functioning. In behaviorist learning terms, one must distinguish between effects on learning and effects on performance. Even then, one can never be sure if the ideal interpretation is correct. For instance, it is always possible that recovery is just around the corner if one had been persistent enough, or that the effect is due to a motor performance deficit if only one had done the right measure. The best that we can offer is a qualified statement: given our current state of knowledge, this is the best interpretation that is consistent with all the data.

Finally, in terms of the precise localization of function, the issue of fibers of passage must be addressed. The tendency is to attribute the lost function to the obvious area of damaged cell bodies. It is also possible, however, that damage to axons that merely pass through the lesioned area are actually responsible for the lost behavior. This issue can be resolved by further systematic lesions of afferents and efferents, and by chemical lesions like kainic acid or ibotenic acid which destroy cell bodies but spare fibers of passage.

PERMANENT LESIONS AND CLASSICAL EYEBLINK CONDITIONING

In this section we review the evidence from permanent lesion experiments that indicate that the cerebellum is critically involved in classical conditioning. The lesions consisted of permanent damage to the nervous system, caused by aspiration (ablation), by electrolytic coagulation, or by neurotoxicity. These studies are discussed in terms of both the question of localization of learning and memory, and also in terms of the problems associated with interpretation of lesions. We begin with a long section dealing with the question of where the conditioned response originates, starting with cerebral cortex and then narrowing to the cerebellum, and then continue with shorter sections on the circuitry related to the conditioned and unconditioned stimuli.

The Conditioned Response Circuitry

The modern history of attempts to localize learning and memory for classical conditioning began at the very inception of classical conditioning. Ivan Pavlov (1927) postulated that some point of convergence of sensory inputs with concomitant motor output would be found. Lashley later popularized the name "engram" for this theorized site. For Pavlov the obvious site of such convergence was the cerebral cortex. He systematically removed cerebral cortex of his dogs and failed to discover a cortical localization for the association. He observed cortical lesions having a temporary effect on performance, but functioning characteristically returned. Thus, Pavlov's observation of loss followed by recovery of function led him to think that there were spheres of radiating visual, auditory and motor influences without precise localization.

In 1972 Oakley and Russell reported that cortical aspirations did not abolish classical conditioning. More recently, lesions of auditory (Knowlton, 1992) or motor (Ivkovich, 1997) cortex showed that their acute effects on eyeblink conditioning are mediated through brainstem structures associated with the cerebellum. In some sense this outcome challenges the widely held view that cortex alone is responsible for higher order cognitive functions, and suggests a cognitive role for the cerebellum.

Trace conditioning, on the other hand, is one example of a more demanding task in that it requires that the memory of one stimulus be retained in its absence for association with a second stimulus. In trace conditioning, the conditioned stimulus is presented briefly, followed by an interval where no stimulus is given, then followed by presentation of the unconditioned stimulus. To make an association in this paradigm requires that the event of the conditioned stimulus be held in memory so that it is available to associate with the unconditioned stimulus. In well-trained animals, lesions of the hippocampus cause learned eyeblink responses to become maladaptive (Solomon, Vander Schaff, Thompson, & Weisz, 1986). The argument is that hippocampal lesions abolish trace conditioning. The relationship between hippocampus and cerebellum is hierarchical: any learning of trace conditioning in the hippocampus depends upon the cerebellum, for cerebellar lesions abolish trace conditioning (Woodruff-Pak, Lavond & Thompson, 1985). Another case for hippocampal involvement in complex learning is the failure to see reversal learning in hippocampal lesioned subjects (Berger & Orr, 1983). For simple delay classical conditioning, however, hippocampal lesions have no effect (Schmaltz & Theios, 1972). Indeed, based on these observations alone, it has been proposed that the basic association for classical conditioning occurs at lower levels of the nervous system, and that higher regions become engaged as the complexity of conditioning increases (Lavond, Kim & Thompson, 1993).

That the cerebral cortex and limbic system, as represented by the hippocampus, were not responsible for the basic association for simple classical conditioning led to some radical experiments asking whether any of the other higher tissue was involved. The first of these were the decortications and decerebratations by Norman and colleagues (Norman, Buchwald & Villablanca, 1977; Norman, Villablanca, Brown, Schwafel & Buchwald, 1974) in which a midcollicular transection severed the lower brainstem from the telencephalon (cortex, limbic system, basal ganglia) and diencephalon (thalamus and hypothalamus) in their greatest extents. Despite these radical procedures, cats learned simple classical conditioning. Later, Enser (1976) decerebrated rabbits and showed the highest brain structures were not essential for conditioning. That learning, however, could be artificial in the sense that the nervous system of a brain injured individual might be compensating for that damage by using parts of the brain that normally are not involved. Mauk and Thompson (1987), however, showed that previous learning survived a midbrain decerebration, thus the remaining tissue contained the previously established memory.

Together these studies showed that all tissue above the midbrain was not necessary for simple classical eyeblink conditioning. It is worth remembering that recording studies, on the other hand, demonstrated that this higher tissue was involved, recalling that hippocampal cells reacted to simple training. What this unit activity means from the standpoint of the learning is by no means clear. However, combined with the lesion results, it suggests that higher regions become critically engaged with more complex learning. Where, then, is the basic association formed?

The earlier recording studies of the involvement of the hippocampus in simple delay classical conditioning gave an important clue as to how to find out. Unit activity in the hippocampus showed increases in activity that preceded the actual learned behavioral response. Further, the rate of this activity was highly correlated to the form of the actual eyeblink. This activity only developed over the course of training with paired trials. In essence, then, the hippocampal unit activity predicted the learned behavior, therefore it *could be* causative. This unit activity appears to reflect the engram, or more correctly put it seems to be a signature for the underlying physical plasticity associated with learning and memory. More neutrally, we can refer to this phenomenon as *learning-related unit activity*.

This learning related unit activity became the means to begin searching for brainstem areas responsible for forming the basic association for classical conditioning which are described in Thompson's Chapter 2 and Steinmetz's Chapter 4. The point here is that, having discovered suspected sites of the engram with recording techniques, the question then turned to whether or not they were essential for the basic association or, like the hippocampus, were merely involved. For this reason McCormick and colleagues lesioned the cerebellum of well-trained rabbits (McCormick, Lavond, Clark, Kettner, Rising & Thompson, 1981), finding that the learned response was abolished while the unlearned reflexive response continued. Just before this, Lavond and colleagues had found that brainstem damage also had this selective effect on learning (Lavond, McCormick, Clark, Holmes & Thompson, 1981). This effect turned out to be due to damage to fibers of passage from the cerebellum.

One of the key features of cerebellar lesion studies is the observation that a unilateral cerebellar lesion causes a unilateral loss of conditioned responses. Since the cerebellum represents the body ipsilaterally, this unilateral cerebellar lesion causes an ipsilateral loss. Training on the contralateral side results in learning a contralateral eyeblink. Returning the training to the ipsilateral side does not result in learning on the damaged side. This is a strikingly specific effect: conditioned responses are only abolished on the side of the lesion. The ipsilateral nature has been observed in humans with cerebellar damage as well (Woodruff-Pak, Papka & Irvy, 1996). This phenonmenon has important implications for lesion interpretation. It means that the rabbits can hear, otherwise they could not learn on the contralateral side. It means that the rabbits are not generally impaired for reflexes (the unconditioned responses are fine bilaterally) or for learned reflexes (the contralateral conditioned response is fine). It means that the rabbits can still make associations, so learning per se has not been disrupted generally. And finally, it means that there is no disruption of some global process like motivation, which is usually conceived as a unitary (indivisible) phenomenon. Together, the observation of a unilateral effect addresses questions about sensory, motor and motivational impairments that might have been caused by the lesion, as well as eliminating from consideration such processes as diaschesis.

The finding of cerebellar involvement in classical eyeblink conditioning was completely unexpected. It was startling. Attempts to induce recovery of function failed. For instance, retention testing over an eight month period showed no sign of recovery, nor did injection of amphetamine, two treatments associated with ameliorating effects of diaschesis (Lavond, Lincoln, McCormick & Thompson, 1984). In a truly heroic effort, Steinmetz, Logue & Steinmetz (1992) did not find any recovery after more than 200 days of postoperative retraining. Similarly, training on the side opposite the lesion (for example, McCormick, Lavond, Clark, Kettner, Rising & Thompson, 1981) did not induce recovery, nor did training on other successful learning tasks (heart rate, Lavond, Lincoln, McCormick & Thompson, 1984; operant conditioning, Holt, Mauk & Thompson, unpublished, but the same animals were used for subsequent classical conditioning; and amphetamine, in Lavond, Lincoln, McCormick & Thompson, 1984). The one suggestion that there might be transfer of training (seen in the data reported by McCormick, Lavond, Clark, Kettner, Rising & Thompson, 1981, and by Lavond & Steinmetz, 1989) turned out to be an artifact of the training protocol (Lavond, Kanzawa, Ivkovich & Clark, 1994). Thus, efforts to induce recovery have failed, and the effect of lesion of the cerebellum appears to be a permanent and selective abolition of the learned response.

The discovery of the role of the cerebellum in learning is consistent with an earlier literature implicating the cerebellum in conditioning (Brogden & Gantt, 1937; Karamian, Fanardijian & Kosareva, 1969; Lifshitz, 1947; Popov, 1929) and with modern concepts beyond its traditional role in motor coordination (Berntson & Micco, 1976; Berntson & Torello, 1982; Daum, Ackermann, Schugens, Reimold, Dichgans & Birbaumer, 1993; Ivry & Keele, 1989; Leiner, Leiner & Dow, 1986; Logan & Grafton, 1995; Watson, 1978). Despite this, and quite naturally, a number of questions and skepticism emerged.

For one, the selective effect on learning was questionable at face value. Until this time, lesions typically caused motor deficits that were inseparable from learning deficits. It was therefore unusual to make a claim for an effect on learning but not performance. And given that the cerebellum was involved, this seemed unlikely. Welsh and Harvey (1989, 1992) reported performance deficits on the unconditioned reflex. Independently, however, Yeo and colleagues found a selective effect of cerebellar lesion on the learned conditioned response but not on the unconditioned reflex (Yeo, Hardiman & Glickstein, 1984). They went on to identify the interpositus (1985a) and Larsell's lobule HVI (1985b,c) as the key parts of the cerebellum for eyeblink conditioning. Desmond and Moore (1983) had also described a brainstem lesion that selectively affected the conditioned but not unconditioned response. In at least one report, reflexive responses actually got larger after cerebellar damage (McCormick, Clark, Lavond & Thompson, 1982). Typically, there is no net change.

This issue about a performance deficit was systematically explored by Steinmetz and colleagues (Steinmetz, Lavond, Ivkovich, Logan & Thompson, 1992). First, one of the problems in the literature has been the problem of inadequate lesions of the interpositus. Steinmetz and colleagues showed that appropriate lesions result in complete and permanent abolition of the learned response. Second, they reported no systematic or persistent decrements in the reflexive unconditioned response which could account for the absence of the learned behavior. Importantly, unlike previous studies, they measured reflexive responses during several phases of conditioning both before and after cerebellar lesions. Third, direct lesions of the eyeblink motor neurons, designed to purposely cause deficits in the unconditioned response, did not have persisting effects on the learned response. Thus, damage to the interpositus or to the motor neurons differentially affect learning or performance, respectively. Subsequently, Ivkovich and colleagues (Ivkovich, Lockard & Thompson, 1993) showed that the differential effect of interpositus lesions on the learned response still persisted even when low intensity air puffs were used as the unconditioned response. That is, the unconditioned responses here were not disproportionately affected by interpositus lesions, also going against the idea of a performance deficit. Ironically, therefore, the more 'parsimonious' explanation that the loss of learned responses was due to a motor deficit is not supported.

Another question of parsimony is whether the cerebellar lesion causes a sensory deficit so that the rabbits are incapable of hearing the tone. Also there is the question of whether the lesion causes a 'motivational' problem in the sense that the subjects might be capable of hearing the tone and capable of making the motor movements, but incapable of attending to their relationships. In answer to both, it bears repeating that rabbits with unilateral cerebellar damage learn classically conditioned eyeblinks on the undamaged side, demonstrating that there are no sensory or motivational factors which also could have offered a more parsimonious explanation (McCormick, Lavond, Clark, Kettner, Rising & Thompson, 1981).

The question can be extended further to ask to what extent is an animal with cerebellar damage capable of learning. A broad interpretation that *all* memories can be explained by the cerebellum is refuted by Bloedel and colleagues (Bloedel, Bracha, Kelly & Wu, 1991). This is consistent with studies showing that the role of the cerebellum in conditioning does not include heart rate conditioning (Lavond, Lincoln, McCormick & Thompson, 1984), operant conditioning of a treadle-press response (Holt, Mauk & Thompson, unpublished), appetitive bar pressing (Steinmetz, Logue & Miller, 1993) and discriminative locomotor avoidance (Steinmetz, Sears, Gabriel, Kubota & Poremba, 1991). The effect of cerebellar lesions is qualified to classical conditioning of somatic responses to an aversive stimulus as we indicated earlier. Similarly, Helmuth, Ivry and Shimizu (1997) report normal responding by cerebellar patients on a number of cognitive tasks, while they maintain that the cerebellum is involved in timing of responses. Woodruff-Pak and colleagues (Woodruff-Pak, Papka & Irvy, 1996) also recently showed that human patients with cerebellar damage were impaired in classical conditioning but that cognitive tasks (such as the Wechsler Memory Scale subtests) were unimpaired. Interestingly, Supple and Leaton (1990) have demonstrated a double dissociation of cerebellar functions, for permanent vermal lesions disrupt heart rate conditioning but not eyeblink conditioning, whereas lateral cerebellar lesions affect eyeblink but not heart rate conditioning.

Another instance of the diaschesis interpretation is that cerebellar lesions cause a shock to the nervous system that indirectly interferes with the expression of learning. Under this conception, cerebellar damage does not actually remove the memory. To test this possibility, Kelly and colleagues (Kelly, Zuo & Bloedel, 1990) removed *both* the cerebellum *and* all tissue above the midbrain under the thesis that cerebellar lesions caused inhibition and decerebration removed the inhibition of a brainstem memory. They reported that these decerebrate-decerebellate rabbits learned the classically conditioned response. However, they did not include controls for increased reactivity to the stimuli. Nordholm and colleagues later showed that these responses could not be learned because short intertrial intervals used by Kelly and colleagues do not support conditioning (Nordholm, Lavond & Thompson, 1992).

Another question concerns the size of the lesion, the old mass action idea of Lashley (1929). Initially, the cerebellar lesions were very large, but eventually it was shown that a chemical lesion destroying as little as 1 cubic millimeter of the interpositus nucleus of the cerebellum had the selective effect of abolishing the learned response (Lavond, Hembree & Thompson, 1985). In other words, unlike previous attempts to localize learning and memory which showed effects only with large lesions, here a very precise lesion of the anterior and dorsolateral part of the interpositus nucleus was sufficient to produce complete abolition of the learned response.

Despite this localization to the interpositus, there remains to this day the question of whether the association resides in the interpositus or cerebellar cortex. The reason for this indecision is both simple and complex. Simply, if learning occurs in cerebellar cortical area HVI (Yeo, Hardiman & Glickstein, 1985b), then its necessary efferent pathway involves the interpositus. Lesioning the interpositus, therefore, could destroy the memory, or it could destroy the efferent pathway for a memory located solely in cerebellar cortex, or it could be that both cortex and interpositus develop the memory, a more complex explanation that preserves the emphasis on cortical models for conditioning.

Permanent lesion studies have provided some possible answers to the question of localization in cerebellar cortex versus cerebellar interpositus nucleus. Large aspirations of cerebellar cortex do not prevent acquisition (Lavond & Steinmetz, 1989; Logan, 1991) or retention (Lavond, Steinmetz, Yokaitis, & Thompson, 1987). Cerebellar cortical aspirations do adversely retard acquisition rates and impair the timing and size of the learned response (see also Lincoln, McCormick & Thompson, 1982; Perrett, Ruiz & Mauk, 1993). However, animals without cerebellar cortex nevertheless do form conditioned responses. The problem with the interpretation, however, is that technically it is practically impossible to remove all cerebellar cortex in the first place, and without damaging the underlying interpositus in the second place. If learning occurs after attempting cerebellar cortical damage, then it could be that learning occurred because part of the cerebellar cortex was spared. If learning does not occur, then it could be that the interpositus was damaged. How can one completely damage just the cortex without affecting the interpositus?

The answer to this problem appeared in a study that took advantage of a genetic mutation in mice. Recently, Chen and colleagues (Chen, Bao, Lockard, Kim & Thompson, 1996) classically conditioned a mutant mouse strain that has no Purkinje cells, the sole output of the cerebellar cortex. The mutant mouse strain is born with Purkinje cells but these die by about day 20 of life. This feature effectively isolates their cerebellar cortex from the rest of the nervous system. The advantage of the mutant mice preparation is that all the Purkinje cells are lost, thus the *entire* cerebellar cortex has been effectively excised. Yet despite the lack of influence of cerebellar cortex, these animals learned. Interestingly, they learned the classically conditioned eyeblink response with the same deficits of the conditioned response noted in the aspiration studies, meaning that the learned responses were not very large in amplitude and were not very well timed (they had long latencies). Further, as with aspiration, the mutant mice took significantly longer to learn the association, about seven times as long as normal animals in both cases.

Conversely, Katz and Steinmetz (1997) reported that learning related unit activity in cerebellar cortex may persist without interpositus and without overt behavioral conditioned responses. They trained for eyeblink conditioning and then lesioned the interpositus with ibotenic acid which would spare fibers that ascend to cerebellar cortex. They subsequently reported the absence of behavioral learned responses yet that learning related unit activity persisted in a subset of HVI neurons although it was disrupted. We postulate below that learning of different aspects of classical conditioning occurs throughout much of the eyeblink circuitry. The efferent pathway from the site of learning in the cerebellum to the motor units responsible for the behavior passes through the red nucleus on the way to the cranial motor nuclei (accessory abducens, abducens, facial, oculomotor). This reciprocal pathway, identified anatomically in 1966 by Courville and Brodal, has been confirmed by lesions of the superior cerebellar peduncle (McCormick, Guyer & Thompson, 1982), the decussation of the superior cerebellar peduncle (Lavond, McCormick, Clark, Holmes & Thompson, 1981) and the red nucleus (Haley, Lavond & Thompson, 1983; Rosenfield & Moore, 1983). In contrast to lesions of the interpositus which do not affect the reflexive eyeblink, damage to the red nucleus causes a significant but temporary disruptive effect on the reflexive eyeblink (Haley, Lavond & Thompson, 1983). Unlike lesions of the interpositus, then, lesion of the red nucleus has an effect on performance. In and of itself, however, this does not rule out the possibility that the red nucleus could be the site of the basic association. Indeed, recordings of learning related unit activity in the red nucleus are consistent with this view (McCormick, Lavond & Thompson, 1983). Furthermore, studies by Tsukahara and colleagues implicate the red nucleus over the interpositus as a site of plasticity (for example, Tsukahara, Oda & Notsu, 1981). While it is clear that the red nucleus is an important part of the system for expression of classical eyeblink conditioning, traditional lesions could not solve the dilema of whether the red nucleus is the essential site of plasticity. Reversible lesion studies, combined with neural recordings, discussed further on in this chapter, were necessary to solve this dilemma. As the following will show, red nucleus is important for the expression of the learned response, but red nucleus is not essential for associative learning.

The Unconditioned Response Circuitry

The literature about the role of the cerebellum in learning cited above (Karamian, Fanaralijian & Kosareva, 1969; Brogden and Gantt, 1942; Lifshitz, 1947; Popov, 1929), predated many of the experimental results mentioned in this article. Educating ourselves about this literature actually guided the logic of subsequent studies. Principle among these early studies were the efforts to understand the pathways involved in conveying the unconditioned stimulus to the cerebellum. According to the suggestions of Marr (1969) and Albus (1971) the inferior olive conveys information about the unconditioned stimulus to the cerebellar Purkinje cells by way of its climbing fiber innervation and serves the role as the reinforcing stimulus (the 'teaching' pathway). The first study supporting this role for the classically conditioned eyeblink response showed that well trained rabbits showed extinction-like behavior (diminished numbers of conditioned responses; spontaneous recovery at the start of each day) following lesion of the inferior olive (McCormick, Steinmetz & Thompson, 1985). In contrast, Yeo and colleagues showed that inferior olive lesions abolished conditioned responses (Yeo, Hardiman & Glickstein, 1986). Mintz and colleagues (Mintz, Lavond, Zhang, Yun & Thompson, 1994) showed both effects, immediate abolition or extinction, using unilateral chemical lesions created by NMDA injections, and suggested that the exact location and the character of the damage explained the difference. Thus, an inferior olive lesion which causes massive Purkinje cell discharge will result in disassociation before behavioral extinction training.

Supporting the idea that the inferior olive is involved in the unconditioned response pathway are the recent results of the blocking experiment by Kim and colleagues (1998). Blocking is the phenomenon where previous learning prevents learning to a new conditioned stimulus in the presence of the original conditioned stimulus (Kamin 1968). That is, if an animal has learned to associate a tone with an unconditioned stimulus, then subsequent training with tone-light stimuli paired with the unconditioned stimulus does not result in subsequent learning of an association between the light and air puff. Kim and colleagues reasoned that the inhibitory projection from interpositus to inferior olive was responsible for suppressing new learning. They disrupted the inhibitory projection by injection of muscimol, a long lasting GABA agonist, into the inferior olive during tone-light training. Subsequent testing showed that the light conditioned stimulus had acquired an association with the unconditioned stimulus. This result supports the idea that the inferior olive normally plays a role as reinforcement for classical eyeblink conditioning.

The Conditioned Stimulus Circuitry

Identifying the route of the auditory projection that conveyed the conditioned stimulus to the cerebellum proved more difficult. Although the theories of Marr and Albus posited the 'learning' role along the mossy fiber inputs to the cerebellum, there are numerous sources of mossy fibers. Further, the nature of the auditory system is such that, even if the auditory stimulus could be confined to one ear, the neural projections are bilateral and highly divergent. The known direct auditory projections from the dorsal cochlear nucleus were primarily to the vermis (Huang, Liu & Huang, 1982) rather than to the interpositus, and it was known that the vermis did not play a critical role in classical eyeblink conditioning.

An obvious source of mossy fibers to the cerebellum is the pons (Brodal and Jansen, 1946; Mihailoff, 1994). Aitken and Boyd (1978) and later Kandler and Herbert (1991) have shown that the dorsal cochlear nucleus projects to the lateral pons. Steinmetz and colleagues (Steinmetz, Logan, Rosen, Thompson, Lavond & Thompson, 1987) showed that bilateral lesions of the lateral pons abolished conditioned responses to a tone conditioned stimulus, but that conditioned responses continued to a light as the conditioned stimulus. The latter observation is significant because it showed that the lesions did not damage the actual memory. Previously, an auditory projection through the pons to the cerebellum was not known, so Steinmetz and colleagues also confirmed by anatomical tracing experiments that the lateral pons received projections from the cochlear nuclei. The projection of the pons to the interpositus had previously been questioned (Brodal, Dietrichs & Walberg, 1986), but Steinmetz and Sengelaub (1992) as well as Tracy, Thompson, Krupa & Thompson (1998) have confirmed this connection.

Summary of the Basic Circuitry for Classical Eyeblink Conditioning

Figure 1 shows a summary of the circuitry just outlined. The cerebellum has the two prerequisites for creating a memory for classical conditioning: first, a convergence of conditioned and unconditioned stimuli, and second, a modifiable motor output for the conditioned response. The conditioned stimulus comes through cochlear projections to the lateral pons, and from the lateral pons by way of mossy fiber projections to the cerebellum. The unconditioned stimulus comes through the trigeminal projections to the inferior olive, and from the inferior olive by way of climbing fiber projections to the cerebellum. The basic association for classical eyeblink conditioning occurs in the cerebellum. Learning and memory can be formed solely within the interpositus nucleus. Additionally, an association might be formed in cerebellar cortex. The conditioned response projects from the interpositus to the red nucleus by way of the superior cerebellar peduncle. The red nucleus, in turn, projects the conditioned response to the cranial motor nuclei involved in the unconditioned reflex, the accessory abducens, the abducens, the facial and the oculomotor nuclei.

Three comments should be made with respect to this summary. First, except for the anatomical connections discussed for the conditioned stimulus, the afferent and efferent connections of the cerebellum were already pretty well known. Second, the theories of Marr and Albus guided much of the thinking about the later lesion experiments, and in important respects these theories have been borne out. The details of the critical area within the cerebellum, however, are slightly different, in that the interpositus nucleus emerged as a point of focus rather than the cerebellar cortex. Third, it bears repeating that this schema is consistent not only with the lesion experiments described here, but also with the results of recording and stimulation experiments. The recording experiments often preceded the lesion experiments, and the stimulation experiments often confirmed them.

TEMPORARY LESIONS AND CLASSICAL EYEBLINK CONDITIONING

The preceding results strongly suggest that the cerebellum, and specifically the interpositus nucleus, is the locus of plasticity for forming the association for simple eyeblink conditioning. However, using permanent lesions creates an additional problem: all the testing is done on brain damaged animals, with all the associated problems of interpretation, and with the concomitant problem that the nervous system may compensate with mechanisms of recovery of function. For example, it could be that the cerebellum is merely a relay for an association formed elsewhere, but that the cerebellum is essential for the expression of the learning. Ideally, we would like to disable the function of the interpositus only during a critical phase of training, but to be able to test a fully functioning individual to see if learning had occurred elsewhere. Over the past decade, techniques have been applied for creating temporary, reversible lesions in select areas of the eyeblink neural system. Reversible lesions can be created by using local anesthetics like lidocaine or tetrodotoxin, or by activating the GABAa inhibitory system with the GABAa receptor agonist muscimol, or by temporary cooling.

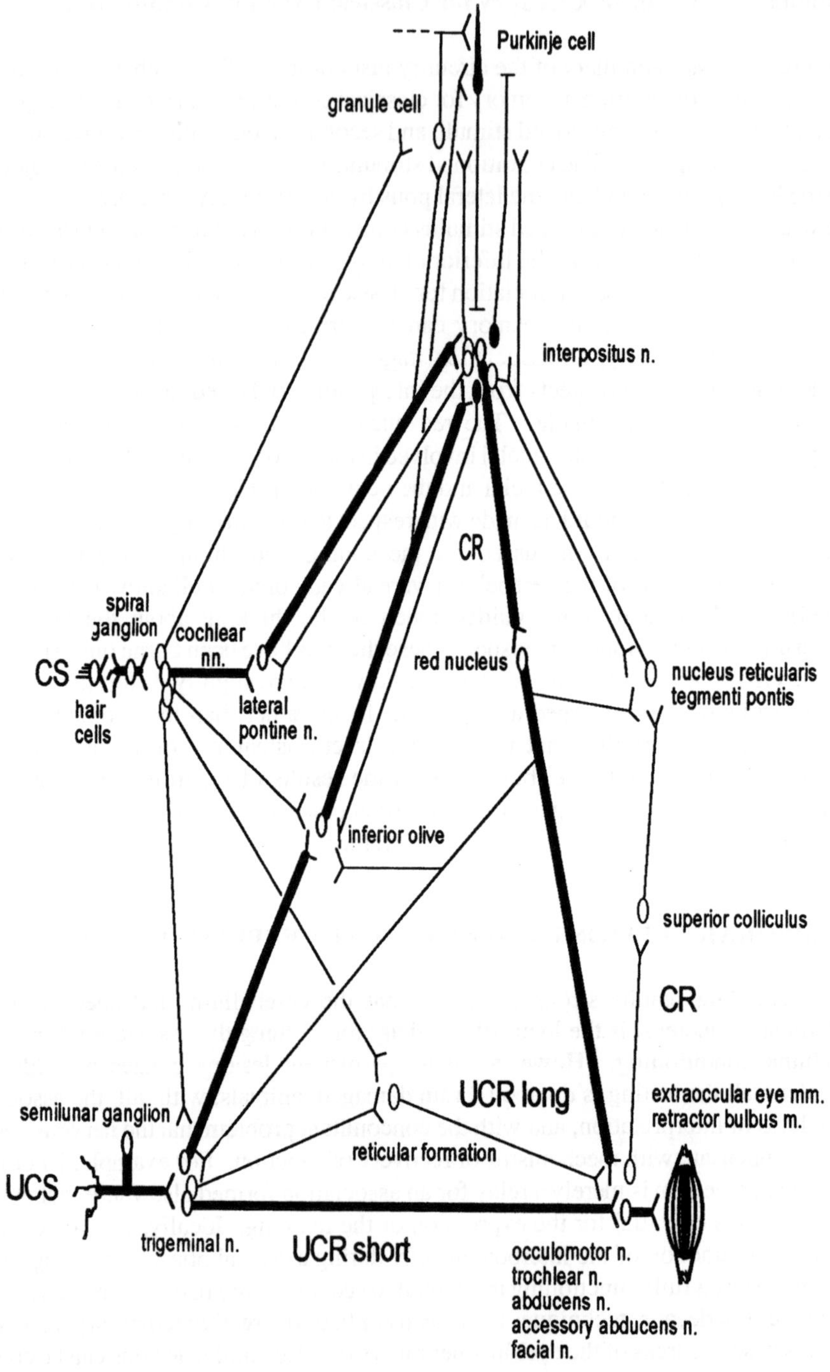
Purkinje cell
granule cell
interpositus n.
CR
spiral ganglion
cochlear nn.
CS
hair cells
lateral pontine n.
red nucleus
nucleus reticularis tegmenti pontis
inferior olive
superior colliculus
CR
UCR long
extraoccular eye mm.
retractor bulbus m.
semilunar ganglion
reticular formation
UCS
trigeminal n.
UCR short
occulomotor n.
trochlear n.
abducens n.
accessory abducens n.
facial n.

Figure 1. Putative eyeblink circuit. The major CS, US, UR and CR pathways for the conditioned eyeblink (including functional as well as anatomical pathways) are marked with heavier lines. The CS and US converge in the interpositus where an association is formed and expressed as the CR. When the interpositus is inactivated, all learning related activity that is found in other locations is abolished. Additional structures, however, participate in promoting or enhancing conditioning as show by the anatomical connections marked in thin lines. Also indicated are important feedback connections that mediate important psychological phenomenon such as blocking.

Methods of Reversible Lesions

Reversible Lesions Created by Cooling

Brooks (1983) has a good discussion of the history of cooling as a method for creating temporary lesions in physiological research. Early experimenters such as Stefani (1895), Deganello (1900) and Trendelenburg (1910) were successful in demonstrating that localized cooling resulted in reversible, localized changes in behavioral and physiological activities. A cryoprobe suitable for implantation deep in the brain was developed in the 1960s in both France and the US chiefly as a tool for the treatment of Parkinson's disease but also as a research tool (see Bracco, 1980, for a history of the medical use of cryolesions and cryosurgery, and Skinner and Lindsley, 1969, for early experiments). The version of this "depth" probe that has been used in rabbit eyeblink conditioning, using Freon as the coolant, was designed and tested by Zhang, Ni & Harper in 1986.

In simplest terms the cryoprobe used in eyeblink conditioning is designed such that a freon-like compressed coolant flows through a small inner cannula (30 gauge at about 0.3 mm outer diameter), expands into a limited reservoir chamber at the distal tip of a slightly larger outer cannula (19 gauge at about 1.1 mm outer diameter), and is drawn out of the outer cannula by a vacuum (see Figures 2 and 3). During the expansion of the compressed coolant, heat is drawn from surrounding tissue. As soon as the flow of coolant through the inner cannula is stopped, cooling stops. This allows for rapid and repeated onset and cessation of cannula with heater wire. This allows the shaft of the cannula to be maintained at body temperature while coolant flows to the distal tip. This system has been designed to limit the extent of cooling so that placement of the probe within 1 mm of a target structure will result in cessation of transynaptic propagation of signals but will not affect fibers of passage (except for those damaged by the probe itself). The probe has been used to inactivate target nuclei for periods as long as one whole training session (approximately 50 minutes), as well as to inactivate a nucleus during one block of training trials (approximately 4 minutes), without causing any permanent damage or cell loss within the target structure.

The direct, physiological effects of cooling on nervous tissue are complex. Janssen (1991) has summarized a large body of literature dealing with this issue. In the rabbit eyeblink preparation cooling the tip of the cold probe to 0^0 C results in cooling.

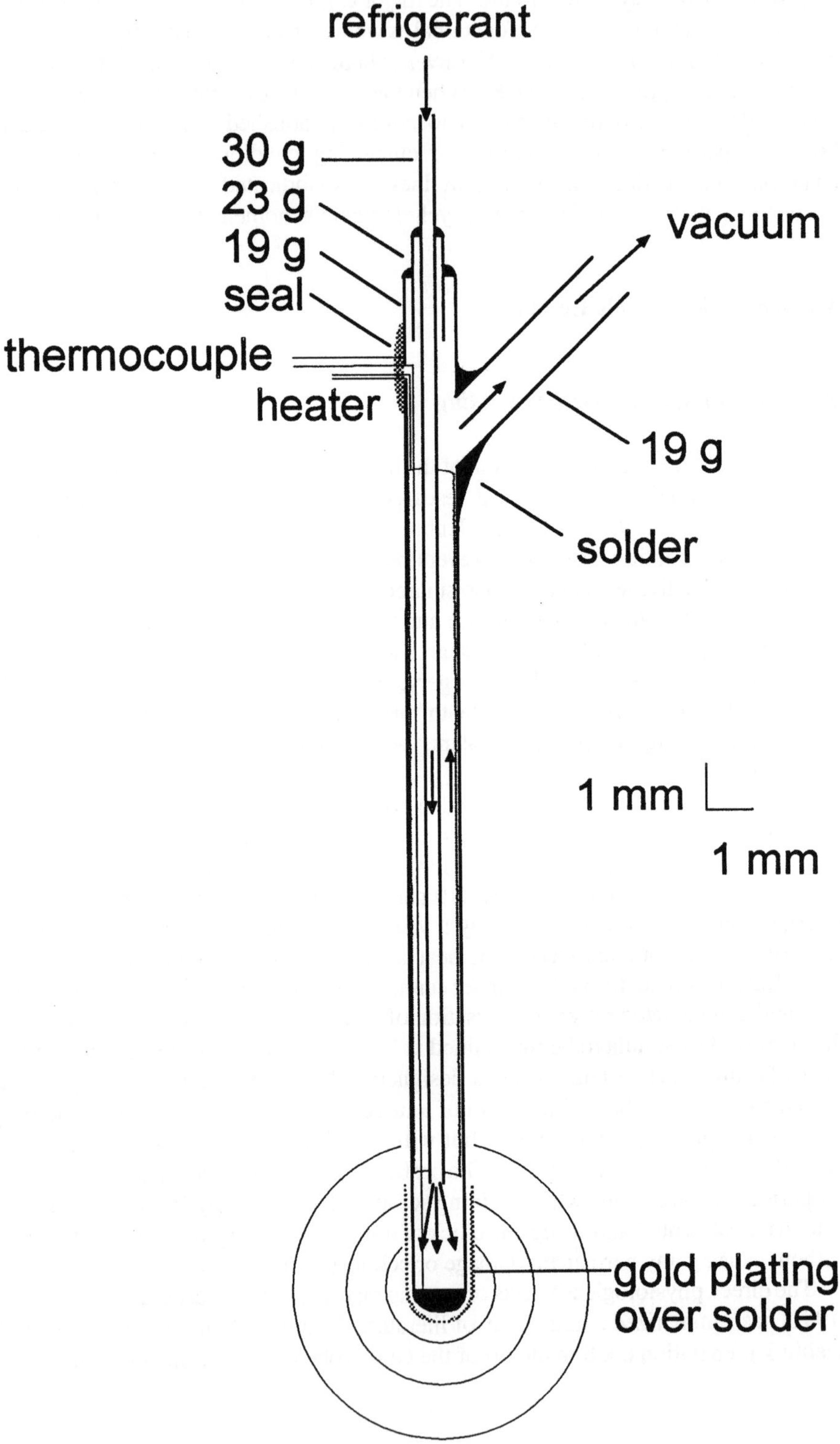
refrigerant
30 g
23 g
19 g
seal
thermocouple
heater
vacuum
19 g
solder
1 mm
1 mm
gold plating
over solder

Cooling can be limited to the distal tip of the probe by wrapping the outer in a temperature range between 8.5^0 C and 20^0 C in surrounding tissue over a distance of 2.5mm from the tip of the cold probe (Zhang, Ni & Harper, 1986). Cooling within this range blocks synaptic transmission but does not abolish spontaneous firing rates nor does it block propagation of fibers of passage (Benita & Conde, 1972; Brooks, 1983; Clark, Zhang & Lavond, 1992).

The effective range of cooling can be measured by probing the surrounding tissue with a thermocouple and measuring the isotherms. A large number of measurements, however, effectively damage the tissue so one is limited to sampling a few places and/or using acute animals rather than experimental subjects. Alternatively, cooling inhibits activity and therefore limits the uptake of glucose, so radioactively labeled 2-deoxyglucose injections could be used to estimate the range of cooling. Problems with this method of estimation include the problem of low glucose uptake by fiber tracts and the difficulty in relating amount of uptake to actual temperatures. Combinations using thermoprobes and 2-deoxyglucose are a compromise solution. Ultimately, effective cooling is best determined by comparing the accuracy and results of different probe placements.

Reversible Lesion Created by Chemical Application

Temporary acting chemicals such as anesthetics can be applied locally within the brain via a small injection cannula. Factors that influence the effectiveness of this method include the duration of action of the chemical, the accurate placement of the cannula and the molecular composition of the brain area to be inactivated. The area of effective action of the chemical can be difficult to determine even when radiolabeled forms of the chemical are available, for the boundary is a function of the film exposure to some extent, and the boundary of effective chemical is often left to one's judgement.

Figure 2. Construction of a cooling probe. The essential features are that stainless steel tubing is soldered together so that a refrigerant (for example HFC 134a, a freon-like substance) can be injected through a small 30 gauge tubing that extends inside a larger 19 gauge tubing. As the refrigerant escapes the 30 gauge tubing, it expands and is confined by the 19 gauge tubing. This expansion of the refrigerant absorbs heats, thus cooling the surround area. The amount of cooling is regulated by the rate of flow. The solder at the end of the 19 gauge tubing is plated with gold to prevent tissue reactivion to the lead in the solder. The refrigerant is withdrawn by vacuum through a Y-shaped 19 gauge extension. This basic version of a cooling probe is sufficient for most studies. Where it is critical to confine cooling to the tip of the cooling probe, an internal heating wire is coiled inside the 19 gauge tubing. The heating wire compensates for cooling and maintains the surrounding tissue at body temperature. Finally, an internal circuit using constantan wire to create a thermocouple can be added to monitor the temperature of the probe. Cooling probe design and the associated electronic circuitry are described by Zhang, Ni & Harper (1986).

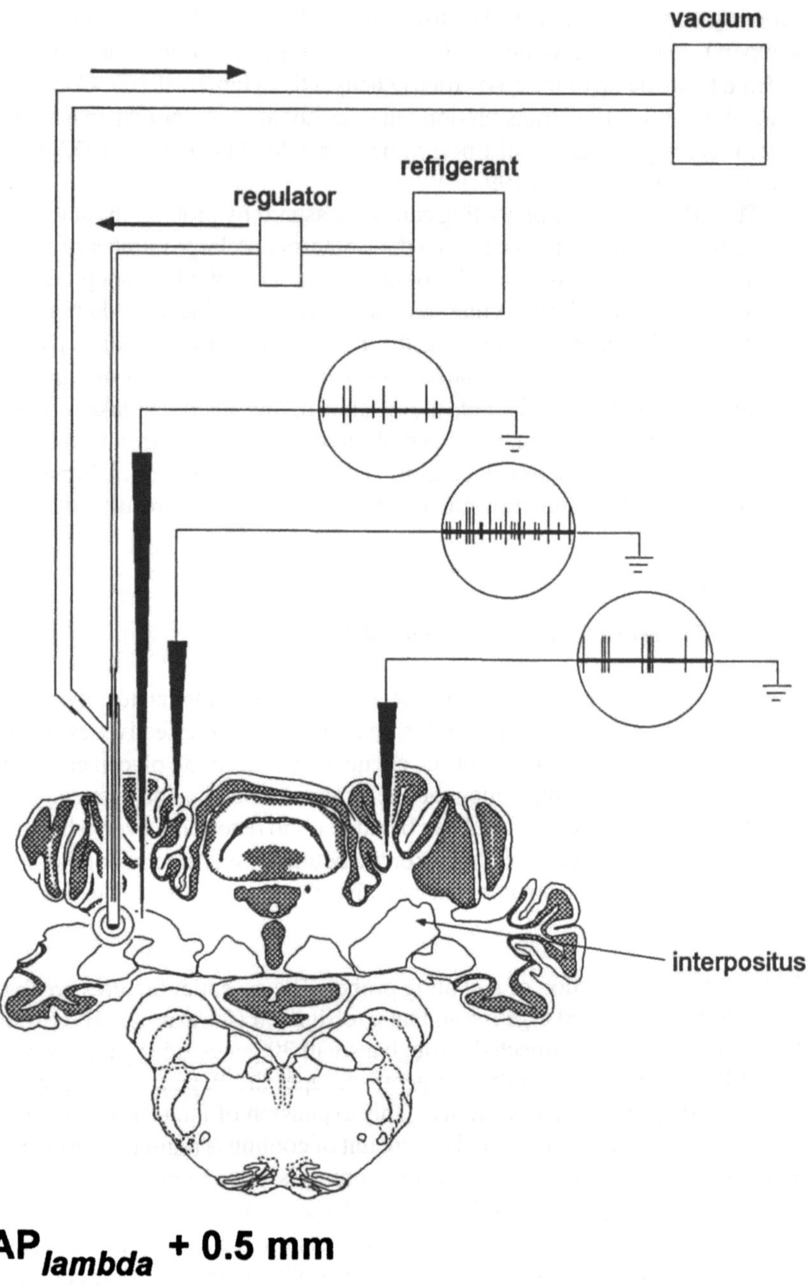
vacuum
refrigerant
regulator
interpositus
AP*lambda* + 0.5 mm

Figure 3. Design of experiments using cooling. A cooling probe is implanted close to the location one desires to cool (1-2 mm away). The extent of cooling has been ascertained by acute studies using an external (to the probe), moveable thermocouple. In the example here, the cooling probe is implanted in the dentate nucleus in order to cool the interpositus nucleus. In operation, Teflon tubing delivers the refrigerant from a tank of HFC 134a refrigerant via a solenoid regulator to the cooling probe. Teflon is used because it is more resistant to degradation from the refrigerant. The regulator is turned on and off at a rate to control the amount of refrigerant to the probe, and thus the amount of cooling, using electronic circuitry based upon that described by Zhang, Ni & Harper (1986). A vacuum is used to assist the flow and removal of the refrigerant. At the time of cooling, single or multiple simultaneous neural recordings can be made using fixed or moveable extracellular recording electrodes in the awake animal. Here, recordings are simulated from ipsilateral interpositus and cerebellar HVI cortex, and contralateral cerebellar HVI cortex.

As with cooling, the effective placement is best determined by comparing the accuracy and results of different placements.

Lidocaine, tetrodotoxin and muscimol have been used in eyeblink studies with selective localized effects. Lidocaine is a fast acting sodium channel blocker. Its effects are short-lived and variable. Our experience is that a single injection of lidocaine, depending on the dosage, has effects lasting anywhere from a few minutes to 10 minutes, sometimes longer. This short duration of effective anesthesia is awkward for eyeblink work where training sessions can last 50 minutes or longer. Results obtained using this method have been mixed (Chapman, Steinmetz, Sears & Thompson, 1990; Bracha, Wu, Cartwright & Bloedel, 1991; Bracha, Stewart & Bloedel, 1993; Knowlton & Thompson, 1988; Welsh, Bormann, Iannuzzelli & Harvey, 1987; Welsh & Harvery, 1991), with some studies showing that learning can be prevented and others not. By far the greatest problem, whether with a single injection or with continuous infusion, is the question of whether the lidocaine is consistently effective.

In contrast to lidocaine, the longer lasting sodium channel blocker tetrodotoxin has proven effective for inactivation of efferent cerebellar fibers (Krupa & Thompson, 1995). Krupa and Thompson injected tetrodotoxin into the superior cerebellar peduncle during acquisition training. Tetrodotoxin blocks axonal conduction from the interpositus to the red nucleus or anywhere else, and vice versa. During the injection, no behavioral conditioned responses were observed. When allowed to recover from tetrodotoxin, the animals immediately showed learned responses. This suggests that learning had to occur prior to the red nucleus.

The most used chemical so far has been muscimol, the GABAa receptor agonist. Muscimol binds to bicucullin methochloride sensitive GABAa receptors (Krosgaard-Larsen & Arnt, 1979), opening chloride channels and causing hyperpolarization of the cell (Bormann, 1988; Curtis, Game, Johnston & McCulloch, 1974; Curtis, Phillis & Watkins, 1959; Matsumoto, 1989). Inactivation by muscimol has a duration of hours but is completely dissipated within 24 hours of administration (Krupa, 1993). Muscimol does not affect fibers of passage (Matsumoto, 1989; Velazquez, Thompson,

Barnes & Angelides, 1989). The advantages of muscimol as a lesion method are its specificity for GABAa receptors, its lack of effect on fibers of passage, and the ability to determine the extent of muscimol lesions by using tritiated muscimol to estimate the extent of a lesion based on the amount and rate of injection (McCabe & Wamsley, 1986). Again, this estimate of the spread of effect is subject to the two problems of varying film exposure and to the observer's judgement of when the label is no longer considered effective. The best method for determining the effective placement is by correlating results of different histological placements with their effects. The disadvantage of using muscimol is that the effects of the lesion last for several hours and so, unlike cooling, immediate before and after measurements cannot be made. The effectiveness of muscimol can also be compromised by the relative density of GABAa receptors in any given area of the brain that is targeted for inactivation. Muscimol has been used extensively, in many behavioral paradigms, for reversible inactivation of localized areas of the brain (see for example Mink & Thach, 1991; Martin & Ghez, 1988; Van Neerven, Pompeiano & Collewijn, 1989).

Studies Using Reversible Lesions

The first attempts to use a temporary lesion had a more limited goal and involved using the local anesthetic lidocaine to temporarily inactivate either the interpositus, the suspected site of memory, or the red nucleus, the suspected site for the expression of the memory, in well-trained animals. Chapman and colleagues (Chapman, Steinmetz, Sears & Thompson, 1990) first trained rabbits on eyeblink classical conditioning, then injected lidocaine into either the interpositus or the red nucleus in two different groups of rabbits while they were given retention training, while at the same time recording from the opposite nucleus. In both instances the learned behavioral responses were abolished with lidocaine and reappeared when the drug wore off. Importantly, inactivation of the interpositus nucleus also abolished the learning related unit activity in the red nucleus, whereas inactivation of the red nucleus did not abolish the learning related unit activity in the interpositus. This indicates that the flow of information goes from interpositus to red nucleus, and not vice versa.

It is worth noting that, like lesions of the red nucleus (Haley, Lavond & Thompson, 1983), reversible inactivation of red nucleus by lidocaine (Bracha, Stewart & Bloedel, 1993) or cooling (Clark & Lavond, 1993; Cartford, Gohl, Singson & Lavond, 1997) results in abolition of conditioned responses and acute deficits of unconditioned responses. However, an advantage of muscimol inactivation reported by Krupa and colleagues (1993) is that inactivation of red nucleus abolished conditioned responses but had no effect on unconditioned responses.

The problem with lidocaine as an agent for creating a temporary lesion is that it wears off quickly. To maintain its effectiveness over longer periods of time requires continuous infusion, so that its use is a delicate balance between causing damage due to the volume of the injection and not using enough (Knowlton & Thompson, 1988). Carelessness alone could cause some of the discrepancies between lidocaine studies.

The promise of using reversible lesions to dissociate learning from performance deficits was better realized by using localized cooling. Clark and colleagues cooled either the interpositus (Clark, Zhang & Lavond , 1992) or red nucleus (Clark & Lavond, 1993) in two different groups of rabbits who were given five days of acquisition training. During this time no learned behaviors were noted. The rabbits were then tested for retention under normal conditions (i.e., without cooling). The results were that the rabbits who had been cooled in the red nucleus showed very good retention, whereas those that had been cooled in the interpositus had to learn as if they were naive to eyeblink conditioning. Further, as with the experiments by Chapman and colleagues, recordings during cooling showed that learning related unit activity developed in the interpositus when the red nucleus was cooled, but did not develop in the red nucleus when the interpositus was cooled. It is possible to conclude that the interpositus nucleus is essential for making the association. This finding was replicated by Krupa, Thompson & Thompson (1993) using reversible inactivation with the GABA agonist muscimol. Yeo and associates (Hardiman, Ramnani & Yeo, 1996; and Ramnani & Yeo, 1996) have also used muscimol to show that the cerebellum, and particularly the anterior interpositus nucleus, are necessary for acquisition and extinction of the conditioned eyeblink response. Most recently, Bracha, Irwin, Webster, Wunderlich, Stachowiak & Bloedel (1998) have employed the protein synthesis inhibitor anisomysin as a lesion technique in eyeblink learning. This study shows that inhibition of protein synthesis in the interpositus nucleus has a significant effect on retention of learning (the conditioned response) but not on performance (the unconditioned response) of the nictitating membrane response.

Although it would be a parsimonious explanation to invoke the interpositus as the essential site of plasticity, the cerebellar cortex cannot be entirely ruled out in these experiments. The shaft of the cooling probe could affect the temperature of cerebellar cortex HVI directly, or the tip of the probe where the cooling is most intense could disrupt critical afferent fibers to that cortex. Similarly, spread of muscimol into HVI could also directly affect the cortex. However, Krupa and Thompson (1997) subsequently found the same results with very small injections of muscimol into interpositus. The study by Bracha and his colleagues (1994, 1998) using protein synthesis inhibition also supports this explanation. The role of the cerebellum per se in forming the association is clear – the essential association is not formed elsewhere in the absence of the cerebellum.

Reversible inactivation and tracing studies have also been used to explore the role of important sensory and motor nuclei involved in eyeblink conditioning. The facial and abducens nuclei are involved in the motor expression of the eyeblink. Zhang and colleagues (Zhang & Lavond, 1991; Clark, Zhang & Lavond, 1997) cooled facial nucleus and surround during acquisition training, at which time they abolished both conditioned and unconditioned motor output of the eye. Nevertheless, subsequent testing without cooling demonstrated that learning had taken place. Thus, the expression of a behavior is not necessary for learning. Krupa and colleagues (Krupa, Weng & Thompson, 1996) subsequently replicated this finding using muscimol to inactivate the brainstem motor nuclei (facial and accessory abducens) that control the eyeblink response.

The trigeminal nuclear region is involved in the sensory aspects of eyeblink conditioning. Bracha, Wu, Cartwright & Bloedel (1991) used lidocaine to implicate the trigeminal nucleus and surrounding reticular formation in eyeblink conditioning.

However, Clark, Zhang & Lavond (1997) found that cooling the parvocellular reticular formation did not have an effect on acquisition of the conditioned response. The pontine reticular tegmental nucleus has a strong reciprocal relationship with the interpositus nucleus. Cartford (1998) used muscimol to inactivate the pontine reticular tegmental nucleus. Inactivation of the reticular tegmental nucleus resulted in a deficit in expression of the learned behavior but did not disrupt learning.

Finally, it may be recalled that this series of studies into the role of the cerebellum in classical eyeblink conditioning began with the observation that learning related unit activity could be found in much of the brainstem (McCormick, Lavond & Thompson, 1983). The experiments with reversible inactivation indicate that the sensory and motor brainstem structures involved in eyeblink learning do not form the association. This begs the question of what the learning related unit activity that is recorded in each of these structures is, where it comes from and how it develops. Since the cerebellum is strongly implicated in learning, the obvious question is whether the cerebellum is also the source of the learning related unit activity found throughout the eyeblink circuitry.

In the next series of cooling experiments we initially trained all subjects, then cooled the interpositus or red nucleus while monitoring both the behavioral responses and the unit activity in these other locations: cerebellar cortex (Clark, Zhang & Lavond, 1997), lateral pons (Clark, Gohl & Lavond, 1997; Cartford, Gohl, Singson & Lavond, 1997), trigeminal nucleus (Clark & Lavond, 1996), reticular formation and facial nucleus (Clark, Zhang & Lavond, 1997), and reticular tegmental nucleus (Cartford, 1998). In all instances of interpositus cooling, behavioral learned responses were abolished as well as learning related unit activity. Importantly, in the examples where conditioned stimulus evoked unit activity also was observed, that activity remained with cooling. Thus, cooling the interpositus had the effect of selectively abolishing learned unit activity but not affecting sensory evoked unit activity. This observation would seem to rule out a generalized or nonspecific effect of inactivation. In contrast, cooling red nucleus sometimes affected both learning related and sensory evoked unit activity in the lateral pons and reticular tegmental nucleus.

Consistent with this conclusion was the failure of cooling red nucleus, reticular formation, cerebellar cortex or facial nucleus to prevent acquisition. In the cases of red nucleus and facial nucleus inactivations, cooling prevented expression of learned responses. Nevertheless, subsequent testing without cooling showed that the association had been formed. In the case of the facial nucleus this was an unexpected finding because cooling during acquisition training had also completely blocked the reflexive unconditioned response. This confirms earlier behavioral work that showed that learning can occur without performance.

A MODEL OF THE NEURAL SUBSTRATES OF EYEBLINK CONDITIONING

The results of lesion experiments on learning have commonly yielded equivocal interpretations that have pitted localization versus non-localization conceptions of brain organization against each other. The advantage of the classical conditioning paradigm is that the stimuli and responses are well defined and the unconditioned stimulus can be used to assess effects on performance as the reversible inactivation studies show so clearly. Today the conflict in the interpretation of the cerebellar findings might be restated, not as to whether memory can be localized but rather whether there is a single memory or multiple copies of the same memory. For this discussion the question is whether the memory for this simple classical conditioning is to be found entirely within the interpositus or whether it is distributed among the many cerebellar and brainstem structures that show learning related unit activity?

One answer can be called the *distributed memory hypothesis* as suggested by the presence of learning related unit activity in neural structures throughout the eyeblink system. For example, Desmond and Moore (1983) proposed that equal but *not* independent memories for classical conditioning could be found in the supratrigeminal nucleus and the interpositus – a lesion of either nucleus would abolish learned behavioral responses but the memory still existed in the other nucleus, it simply could not be expressed. A similar conception has been proposed for the relationship of the cerebellar cortex with its deep nucleus, the interpositus (Lavond, Kim & Thompson, 1993). On the surface it seems like a reasonable, redundant feature of the nervous system. However, more recent experimental evidence suggests that the interpositus, or the interpositus with the cerebellar cortex, forms the association for classical eyeblink conditioning and transmits that information to other structures. Thus, inactivation of the interpositus abolishes all learning related unit activity elsewhere, yet inactivation of these efferent structures do not abolish learning related unit activity in the interpositus.

The reason this alternative hypothesis is more fruitful than the distributed memory hypothesis is that we can then ask what are the functions of these other regions? For example, we already know that cerebellar cortex shows plasticity – learning – and that cerebellar cortex is important for the normal rate of acquisition and for the quality of the response (timing and amplitude). It seems reasonable to us that the interpositus forms the basic association, and that the cerebellar cortex takes advantage of this plasticity to enhance the functions of the interpositus with more efficient learning and with additional learned features. Thus, while the distributed memory hypothesis says that the memory is the same in each location and in some sense cannot be localized by lesions, the *cooperative memories hypothesis* says that there is a hierarchy of memories – not just a single memory – that depend upon the central association, that the memories are different in each location, and that these memories collectively contribute to the ultimate behavioral manifestation of conditioning.

This is not a new idea – for classical conditioning it has long been suggested that the hippocampus builds upon the associational apparatus of the cerebellum to effect more complex conditioning contingencies (Lavond, Kim & Thompson, 1993; Thompson, Berger, Berry, Clark, Kettner, Lavond, Mauk, McCormick, Solomon & Weisz, 1982). Other forebrain structures may have a similar relationship; for example, Steinmetz and colleagues (e.g., White, Miller, White, Dike, Rebec & Steinmetz, 1994) report unit activity related to conditioning in the neostriatum. We propose here that learning in the interpositus feeds back to and influences secondary learning.

It is our contention that the distributed memory hypothesis has distracted both experimental and computational efforts from the simplest explanation of eyeblink learning. Using the bicycle analogy introduced earlier, normal learning to ride always occurs and remains at the level of the interpositus, but early in training other structures like cerebral cortex, hippocampus, and cerebellar cortex act to guide and correct that learning. The locus of the associative engram does not move. For classical conditioning, the focus should be on the nature of the various types of learning that occur in the interpositus, cerebellar cortex, brainstem structures, and hippocampus, that act together for the final behavior. Each locus may preferentially learn a particular aspect of conditioning. Presumably, long term potentiation and long term depression will be the mechanisms by which the associations are instantiated. In any event, it bears repeating that the cooperative memories hypothesis assumes that each locus has a unique contribution to the overall learned behavior. This idea is not unique. Disterhoft and his colleagues recently published a nearly identical expression of the cooperative memories hypothesis (Blaxton, Zeffiro, Gabrieli, Bookheimer, Carrillo, Theodore & Disterhoft, 1996).

Consider just one testable implication of the cooperative memories hypothesis. We have specifically hypothesized that the learning in the interpositus nucleus allows auditory cells in the lateral pons to sharpen their tuning curves. This sharpening could allow for learning of the conditioned stimulus properties in the lateral pons. We think of this as a mechanism for selective attention. Note, however, that this learning is different and at the same time dependent upon the learning that has occurred in the interpositus. Without the basic association formed in the interpositus, the lateral pons could not contribute learning of its different function. Such a concept could apply equally well to the contribution of cerebellar cortex for timing and amplitude of the learned response, or to the reactivity of cells to the unconditioned response in the trigeminal nucleus. Together these different forms of plasticity combine to give the ensemble effort that we recognize as learning. This insight, we believe, is the real contribution of the lesion technique to recording and stimulation studies of the biological bases of learning and memory.

REFERENCES

Aitkin, L.M., & Boyd, J. (1978). Acoustic input to the lateral pontine nuclei. *Hearing Research, 1*, 67-77.

Albus, J.S. (1971). A theory of cerebellar function. *Mathematical Biosciences, 10*, 25-61.

Benita, M., & Conde, H. (1972). Effects of local cooling upon conduction and synaptic transmission. *Brain Research, 36*, 133-151.

Berger, T.W., Alger, B., & Thompson, R.F. (1976). Neuronal substrates of classical conditioning in the hippocampus. *Science, 192*, 483-485.

Berger, T.W., & Orr, W.B. (1983). Hippocampectomy selectively disrupts discrimination reversal conditioning of the rabbit nictitating membrane response. *Behavioural Brain Research, 8*, 49-68.

Berntson, G.G., & Micco, D.J. (1976). Organization of brain stem behavioral systems. *Brain Research Bulletin, 1*, 471-483.

Berntson, G.G., & Torello, M.W. (1982). The paleocerebellum and the integration of behavioral function. *Physiological Psychology, 10*, 2-12.

Blaxton, T.A., Zeffiro, T.A., Gabrieli, J.D.E., Bookheimer, S.Y., Carrillo, M.C., Theodore, W.H., & Disterhoft, J.F. (1996). Functional mapping of human learning: a positron emission tomography activation study of eyeblink conditioning. *Journal of Neuroscience, 16*, 4032-4040.

Bloedel, J.R., Bracha, V., Kelly, T.M., & Wu, J.Z. (1991). Substrates for motor learning: does the cerebellum do it all? *Annals of the New York Academy of Sciences, 627*, 305-318.

Bormann, J. (1988). Electrophysiology of $GABA_A$ and $GABA_B$ receptor subtypes. *Trends in Neuroscience, 11(3)*, 112-116.

Bracco, D. (1980). Historical Developments. In R.J. Ablin,. (Ed.), *Handbook of Cryosurgery*. New York, Marcel Dekker, Inc.

Bracha, V., Wu, J.Z., Cartwright, S., & Bloedel, J.R. (1991). Selective involvement of the spinal trigeminal nucleus in the conditioned nictitating membrane response of the rabbit. *Brain Research, 556(2)*, 317-320.

Bracha, V., Stewart, S. L., & Bloedel, J.R. (1993). The temporary inactivation of the red nucleus affects performance of both conditioned and unconditioned nictitating membrane responses in the rabbit. *Experimental Brain Research, 94(2)*, 225-236.

Bracha, V., Webster, M.L., Winters, N.K., Irwin, K.B., & Bloedel, J.R. (1994). Effects of muscimol inactivation of the cerebellar interposed-dentate nuclear complex on the performance of the nictitating membrane response in the rabbit. *Experimental Brain Research, 100*, 453-468.

Bracha, V., Irwin, K.B., Webster, M.L., Wunderlich, D.A., Stachowiak, M.K., & Bloedel, J.R. (1998). Microinjections of anisomysin into the intermediate cerebellum during learning affect the acquisition of classically conditioned responses in the rabbit. *Brain Research, 788(1-2)*, 169-178.

Brodal, A., & Jansen, J. (1946). The pontocerebellar pojection in the rabbit and cat: Experimental investigations. *Journal of Comparative Neurology, 84*, 31-118.

Brodal, P., Dietrichs, E., & Walberg, F. (1986). Do pontocerebellar mossy fibres give off collaterals to the cerebellar nuclei? An experimental study in the cat with implantation of crystalline HRP-WGA. *Neuroscience Research, 4(1)*, 12-24.

Brogden, W.J., & Gantt, W.H. (1942). Interneural conditioning: Cerebellar conditioned reflexes. *Archives of Neurology and Psychiatry, 48*, 437- 455.

Brooks, V.B. (1983). Study of Brain Function By Local, Reversible Cooling.. In R.H. Adrian, H. sur Hausen, E. Helmreich, H. Holzer, R. Jung, O. Krayer, R.J. Linden, P.A. Miescher, J. Piiper, H. Rasmussen, U. Trendelenburg, K. Ullrich, W. Vogt, & A. Weber (Eds.), *Reviews of Physiology, Biochemistry and Pharmacology*. (pp.2-109). New York, Springer-Verlag.

Cajal, S.R. (1928). *Degeneration and regeneration of the nervous system*. London, Oxford University Press.

Cannon, W.F., & Rosenblueth, A. (1949). *The supersensitivity of denervated structures*. New York: Macmillan.

Cartford, M.C., Gohl, E., Singson, M., & Lavond, D.G. (1997). The effects of reversible inactivation of the red nucleus on learning-related and auditory-evoked unit activity in the pontine nuclei of classically conditioned rabbits. *Learning & Memory, 3*, 519-531.

Cartford, M.C. (1998). Studies on the organization of learning and memory in a classical conditioning model system: Participation of nuclearis reticularis tegmenti pontis (NRTP) and lateral pons in rabbit eyeblink conditioning. *Ph.D. Dissertation*, University of Southern California.

Chapman, P.F., Steinmetz, J.E., Sears, L.L., & Thompson, R.F. (1990). Effects of lidocaine injection in the interpositus nucleus and red nucleus on conditioned behavioral and neuronal responses. *Brain Research, 537*, 140-156.

Chen, L., Bao, S., Lockard, J.M., Kim, J.J., & Thompson, R.F. (1996). Impaired classical eyeblink conditioning in cerebellar-lesioned & Purkinje cell degeneration (pcd) mutant mice. *Journal of Neuroscience, 16*, 2829-2838.

Clark, R.E., & Lavond, D.G. (1993). Reversible lesions of the red nucleus during acquisition and retention of a classically conditioned behavior in rabbits. *Behavioral Neuroscience, 107*, 264-270.

Clark, R.E., Zhang, A.A., & Lavond, D.G. (1992). Reversible lesions of the cerebellar interpositus nucleus during acquisition and retention of a classically conditioned behavior. *Behavioral Neuroscience, 106*, 879-888.

Clark, R.E., Zhang, A.A., & Lavond, D.G. (1997). The importance of cerebellar cortex and facial nucleus in acquisition and retention of eyeblink/NM conditioning: evidence for critical unilateral regulation of the conditioned response. *Neurobiology of Learning and Memory, 67*, 96-111.

Clark, R.E., Gohl, E.B., & Lavond, D.G. (1997). The learning related activity which develops in the pontine nuclei during classical eyeblink conditioning is dependent upon the interpositus nucleus. *Learning & Memory, 3*, 532-544.

Clark, R.E., & Lavond, D.G. (1996). Neural unit activity in the trigeminal complex with interpositus or red nucleus inactivation during classical eyeblink conditioning. *Behavioral Neuroscience, 110*, 1-9.

Courville, J., & Brodal, A. (1966). Rubrocerebellar connections in the cat: An experimental study with silver impregnation methods. *Journal of Comparative Neurology, 126*, 471-485.

Curtis, D.R., Game, C.J.A., Johnston, G.A.R., & McCulloch, R.M. (1974). Central effects of ß-(*p*-chlorophenyl)-gamma-amino-n-butyric acid and ß-alanine. *Brain Research, 70*, 493-499.

Curtis, D.R., Phillis, J.W., & Watkins, J.C. (1959). The depression of spinal neurons by gamma-amino-n-butyric acid and ß-alanine. *Journal of Physiology, 146*, 185-203.

Daum, I., Ackermann, H., Schugens, M.M., Reimold, C., Dichgans, J., & Birbaumer, N. (1993). The cerebellum and cognitive functions in humans. *Behavioral Neuroscience, 107*, 411-419.

Deganello, U. (1900). Action de la temperature sur le centre bulbaire inhibiteur du coeur et sur le centre bulbaire vaso-constricteur. *Archives Italian Biology, 33*, 186-188.

Desmond, J.E., & Moore, J.W. (1983). A supratrigeminal region implicated in the classically conditioned nictitating membrane response. *Brain Research Bulletin, 10*, 765-773.

Enser, D. (1976). A study of classical nictitating membrane conditioning in neodecorticate, hemidecorticate and thalamic rabbits. University of Iowa, Dissertation.

Hardiman, M.J., Ramnani, N., & Yeo, C.H. (1996). Reversible inactivations of the cerebellum with muscimol prevent the acquisition and extinction of conditioned nictitating membrane response in the rabbit. *Experimental Brain Research, 110(2)*, 235-247.

Helmuth, L., Ivry, R.B., & Shimizu, N. (1997). Preserved performance by cerebellar patients on tests of word generation, discrimination learning, and attention. *Learning & Memory, 3*, 456-474.

Haley, D.A., Lavond, D.G., & Thompson, R.F. (1983). Effects of contralateral red nuclear lesions on retention of the classically conditioned nictitating membrane/eyelid response. *Neuroscience Abstracts, 9*, 643.

Holt, L., Mauk, M.D., & Thompson, R.F. (1984). Effects of lateral cerebellar lesions on classical and operant conditioning. Unpublished manuscript.

Huang, C., Liu, G., & Huang, R. (1982). Projections from the cochlear nucleus to the cerebellum. *Brain Research, 244*, 1-8.

Ivkovich, D., & Thompson, R.F. (1997). Motor cortex lesions do not affect learning or performance of the eyelid response in rabbits. *Behavioral Neuroscience, 111*, 727-738.

Ivkovich, D., Lockard, J.M., & Thompson, R.F. (1993). Interpositus lesion abolition of the eyelid conditioned response is not due to effects on performance. *Behavioral Neuroscience, 107*, 530-532.

Ivry, R.I., & Keele, S.W. (1989). Timing functions of the cerebellum. *Cognitive Neuroscience, 1*, 134-150.

Janssen, R. (1992). Thermal Influences on Nervous System Function. *Neuroscience and Biobehavioral Reviews, 16*, 399-413.

Kamin, L.J. (1968). Attention-like processes in classical conditioning. In M.R. Jones (Ed.), Miami Symposium on the prediction of behavior, 1967: Aversive Stimulation. Coral Gables: University of Miami Press.

Kandler, K., & Herbert, H. (1991). Auditory projections from the cochlear nucleus to pontine and mesencephalic nuclei in the rat. *Brain Research, 562*, 230-242.

Karamian, A.I., Fanaralijian, V.V., & Kosareva, A.A. (1969). The functional and morphological evolution of the cerebellum and its role in behavior. In R. Llinas (Ed.), *Neurobiology of cerebellar evolution and development*, First International Symposium. Chicago: American Medical Association.

Katz, D.B., & Steinmetz, J.E. (1997). Single unit evidence for eye-blink conditioning in cerebellar cortex is altered but not eliminated by interpositus nucleus lesions. *Learning & Memory, 3*, 88-104.

Kelly, T.M., Zuo, C.C., & Bloedel, J.R. (1990). Classical conditioning of the eyeblink reflex in the decerebrate-decerebellate rabbit. *Behavioural Brain Research, 38*, 7-18.

Kempermann, G., Brandon, E.P., & Gage, F.H. (1998). Environmental stimulation of 129/SvJ mice causes increased cell proliferation and neurogenesis in the adult dentate gyrus. *Current Biology, 8*, 939-942.

Kim, J., Krupa, D.J., & Thompson, R.F. (1998). Inhibitory cerebello-olivary projections and blocking effect in classical conditioning. *Science, 279*, 570-573.

Knowlton, B.J., & Thompson, R.F. (1992). Conditioning using a cerebral cortical conditioned stimulus is dependent on the cerebellum and brainstem circuitry. *Behavioral Neuroscience, 106(3)*, 509-517.

Knowlton, B.J., & Thompson, R.F. (1988). Microinjections of local anesthetic into the pontine muclei reduce the amplitude of the classically conditioned eyelid response. *Physiology & Behavior, 43*, 855-857.

Krogsgaard-Larsen, P., & Arnt, J. (1979). GABA receptor agonists: Relationship between structure and biological activity IN VIVO and IN VITRO. In P. Mandel, & F.V. DeFeudis,. (Eds.), GABA-Biochemistry and CNS Functions. New York, Plenum Press.

Krupa, D.J. (1993). Localization of the essential memory trace for a classically conditioned behavior. *Ph.D. Dissertation*, University of Southern California.

Krupa, D.J., & Thompson, R.F. (1995). Inactivation of the superior cerebellar peduncle blocks expression but not acquisition of the rabbit's classically conditioned eye-blink response. *Proceedings of the National Academy of Sciences (USA), 92*, 5097-5101.

Krupa, D.J., & Thompson, R.F. (1997). Reversible inactivation of the cerebellar interpositus nucleus completely prevents acquisition of the classically conditioned eye-blink response. *Learning & Memory, 3(6),* 545-556.

Krupa, D.J., Thompson, J.K., & Thompson, R.F. (1993). Localization of a memory trace in the mammalian brain. *Science, 260,* 989-991.

Krupa, D.J., Weng, J., & Thompson, R.F. (1996). Inactivation of brainstem motor nuclei blocks expression but not acquisition of the rabbit's classically conditioned eyeblink response. *Behavioral Neuroscience, 110(2),* 219-227.

Kuhn, H.G., Dickinson-Anson, H., & Gage, F.H. (1996). Neurogenesis in the dentate gyrus of the adult rat: age-related decrease of neuronal progenitor proliferation. *Journal of Neuroscience, 16,* 2027-2033.

Lashley, K.S. (1929). *Brain mechanisms and intelligence.* Chicago: University of Chicago.

Lashley, K.S. (1939). The mechanism of vision. XVI. The functioning of small remnants of the visual cortex. *Journal of Comparative Neurology, 70,* 45-67.

Lavond, D.G., & Dewberry, R.G. (1980). Visual form perception is a function of the visual cortex: II. The rotated horizontal-vertical and oblique-stripes pattern problems. *Physiological Psychology, 8,* 1-8.

Lavond, D.G., Hata, M.G., Gray, T.S., Geckler, C.L., Meyer, P.M., & Meyer, D.R. (1978). Visual form perception is a function of the visual cortex. *Physiological Psychology, 6,* 471-477.

Lavond, D.G., Hembree, T.L., & Thompson, R.F. (1985). Effect of kainic acid lesions of the cerebellar interpositus nucleus on eyelid conditioning in the rabbit. *Brain Research, 326,* 179-182.

Lavond, D.G., Kanzawa, S.A., Ivkovich, D., & Clark, R.E. (1994). Transfer of learning but not memory after unilateral cerebellar lesion in rabbits. *Behavioral Neuroscience, 108,* 284-293.

Lavond, D.G., Kim, J.J., & Thompson, R.F. (1993). Mammalian brain substrates of aversive classical conditioning. *Annual Review of Psychology, 44,* 317-342.

Lavond, D.G., Lincoln, J.S., McCormick, D.A., & Thompson, R.F. (1984). Effect of bilateral lesions of the dentate and interpositus cerebellar nuclei on conditioning of heart-rate and nictitating membrane/eyelid responses in the rabbit. *Brain Research, 305,* 323-330.

Lavond, D.G., Logan, C.G., Sohn, J.H., Garner, W.D.A., & Kanzawa, S.A. (1990). Lesions of the cerebellar interpositus nucleus abolish both nictitating membrane and eyelid EMG conditioned responses. *Brain Research, 514,* 238-248.

Lavond, D.G., McCormick, D.A., Clark, G.A., Holmes, D.T., & Thompson, R.F. (1981). Effects of ipsilateral rostral pontine reticular lesions on retention of classically conditioned nictitating membrane and eyelid responses. *Physiological Psychology, 9,* 335-339.

Lavond, D.G., & Steinmetz, J.E. (1989). Acquisition of classical conditioning without cerebellar cortex. *Behavioural Brain Research, 33,* 113-164.

Lavond, D.G., Steinmetz, J.E., Yokaitis, M.H., & Thompson, R.F. (1987). Reacquisition of classical conditioning after removal of cerebellar cortex. *Experimental Brain Research, 67,* 569-593.

Leiner, H.C., Leiner, A.L., & Dow, R.S. (1986). Does the cerebellum contribute to mental skills? *Behavioral Neuroscience, 100,* 443-454.

Lifshitz, N.N. (1947). Influence of the cerebellar ablation on conditioned reflexes in dogs. *Trudy fiziol Inst Pavlova Acad Sci, 2,* 11-50.

Lincoln, J.S., McCormick, D.A., & Thompson, R.F. (1982). Ipsilateral cerebellar lesions prevent learning of the classically conditioned nictitating membrane eyelid response. *Brain Research, 242,* 190-193.

Liu, C.N., & Chambers, W.W. (1958). Intraspinal sprouting of dorsal root axons. *Archives of Neurology & Psychiatry, 79,* 46-61.

Logan, C.G. (1991). Cerebellar cortical involvement in excitatory and inhibitory classical conditioning. *Ph.D. Dissertation,* Stanford University.

Logan, C.G., & Grafton, S.T. (1995). Functional anatomy of human eyeblink conditioning determined with regional cerebral glucose metabolism and positron-emission tomography. Proceedings of the *National Academy of Sciences* (USA), *92,* 7500-7504.

Marr, D. (1969). A theory of cerebellar cortex. *Journal of Physiology (London), 202,* 437-470.

Martin, J.H., & Ghez, C. (1988). Red nucleus and motor cortex: parallel motor systems for the initiation and control of skilled movement. *Behavioural Brain Research,* 28, 217-223.

Matsumoto, R.R. (1989). GABA receptors: are cellular differences reflected in function? *Brain Research Reviews, 14,* 203-225.

Mauk, M.D., & Thompson, R.F. (1987). Retention of classically conditioned eyelid responses following acute decerebration. *Brain Research, 403,* 89-95.

McCabe, R.T., & Wamsley, J.D. (1986). Autoradiographic localization of subcomponents of the

macromolecular GABA receptor complex. *Life Sciences, 39*, 1937-1945.
McCormick, D.A., Guyer, P.E., & Thompson, R.F. (1982). Superior cerebellar peduncle lesions selectively abolish the ipsilateral classically conditioned nictitating membrane/eyelid response of the rabbit. *Brain Research, 244*, 347-350.
McCormick, D.A., Lavond, D.G., Clark, G.A., Kettner, R.E., Rising, C.E., & Thompson, R.F. (1981). The engram found? Role of the cerebellum in classical conditioning of nictitating membrane and eyelid responses. *Bulletin of the Psychonomic Society, 18*, 103-105.
McCormick, D.A., Clark, G.A., Lavond, D.G. & Thompson, R.F. (1982). Initial Localization of the memory trace for a basic form of learning. *Proceedings of the National Academy of Sciences* (USA), *79(8)*, 2731-2742.
McCormick, D.A., Lavond, D.G., & Thompson, R.F. (1983). Neuronal responses of the rabbit brainstem during performance of the classically conditioned nictitating membrane (NM)/eyelid response. *Brain Research, 271*, 73-88.
McCormick, D.A., Steinmetz, J.E., & Thompson, R.F. (1985). Lesions of the inferior olivary complex cause extinction of the classically conditioned eyeblink response. *Brain Research, 359*, 120-130.
Merzenich, M.M., Kaas, J.H., Wall, J., Nelson, R.J., Sur, M., & Felleman, D. (1983). Topographic reorganization of somatosensory cortical areas 3b and 1 in adult monkeys following restricted deafferentation. *Neuroscience, 8*, 33-55.
Mihailoff, G.A. (1994). Identification of pontocerebellar axon collateral synaptic boutons in the rat cerebellar nuclei. *Brain Research, 648*, 313-318.
Mink, J.W., & Thach, W.T. (1991). Basal Ganglia Motor Control. III. Pallidal Ablation: Normal Reaction Time, Muscle Cocontraction, and Slow Movement. *Journal of Neurophysiology, 65(2)*, 330-351.
Mintz, M., Lavond, D.G., Zhang, A.A., Yun, Y., & Thompson, R.F. (1994). Unilateral inferior olive NMDA lesion leads to unilateral deficit in acquisition and retention of eyelid classical conditioning. *Behavioral and Neural Biology, 61*, 218-224.
Monakow, C. von (1914). *Die lokalisation im grosshirn und der abbau der funktion durch kortikale herde*. Wiesbaden, Bergmann.
Munk, H. (1881). *Uber die funktionen der groshirnrinde*. Berlin, A. Hirschwald.
Neerven, J. van, Pompeiano, O., & Collewijn, H. (1991). Effects of GABAergic and noradrenergic injections into the cerebellar flocculus on vestibulo-ocular reflexes in the rabbit. *Progress in Brain Research, 88*, 485-497.
Nordholm, A.F., Lavond, D.G., & Thompson, R.F. (1991). Are eyeblink responses to tone in the decerebrate, decerebellate rabbit conditioned responses. *Behavioural Brain Research, 44*, 27-34.
Norman, R.J., Buchwald, J.S., & Villablanca, J.R. (1977). Classical conditioning with auditory discrimination of the eyeblink in decerebrate cats. *Science, 196*, 551-553.
Norman, R.J., Villablanca, J.R., Brown, K.A., Schwafel, J.A., & Buchwald, J.S. (1974). Classical conditioning in the bilateral hemispherectomized cat. *Experimental Neurology, 44*, 363-380.
Oakley, D.A., & Russell, I.S. (1972). Neocortical Lesions and classical conditioning. *Physiology & Behavior, 8*, 915-926.
Pavlov, I.P. (1927). *Conditioned reflexes*. Oxford: Oxford University Press.
Perrett, S.P., Ruiz, B.P., & Mauk, M.D. (1993). Cerebellar cortex lesions disrupt learning-dependent timing of conditioned eyelid responses. *Journal of Neuroscience, 13*, 1708-18.
Popov, N.F. (1929). The role of the cerebellum in elaborating the motor conditioned reflexes. In *Higher Nervous Activity*. Moscow, Com. Acad. Press.
Ramnani, N., & Yeo, C.H. (1996). Reversible inactivations of the cerebellum prevent the extinction of conditioned nictitating membrane responses in rabbit. *Journal of Physiology (London), 495(1)*, 159-168.
Rosenfield, M.E., & Moore, J.W. (1983). Red nucleus lesions disrupt the classically conditioned nictitating membrane response in rabbits. *Behavioural Brain Research, 10(2-3)*, 393-398.
Schmaltz, L.W., & Theios, J. (1972). Acquisition and extinction of a classically conditioned response in hippocampectomized rabbits *Oryctolagus cuniculus*. *Journal of Comparative & Physiological Psychology, 79*, 328-333.
Skinner, J.E., & Lindsey, D.B. (1968). Reversible cryogenic blockade of neural function in the brain of unrestrined animals. *Science, 161*, 595-597.
Solomon, P.R., Vander Schaff, E.F., Thompson, R.F., & Weisz, D.G. (1986). Hippocampus and trace conditioning of the rabbit's classically conditioned nictitating membrane response. *Behavioral Neuroscience, 100*, 729-744.
Stefani, A. (1895). De l;action de la temperature sur les centres bulbaires du coer et des vaiss eaux.

Archives of Italian Biology, 24, 424-437.
Steinmetz, J.E., Lavond, D.G., Ivkovich, D., Logan, C.G., & Thompson, R.F. (1992). Disruption of classical eyelid conditioning after cerebellar lesions: damage to a memory trace system or a simple performance deficit. *Journal of Neuroscience, 12*, 4403-4426.
Steinmetz, J.E., Logan, C.G., Rosen, D.J., Thompson, J.K., Lavond, D.G., & Thompson, R.F. (1987). Initial localization of the acoustic conditioned stimulus projection system to the cerebellum essential for classical eyelid conditioning. *Proceedings of the National Academy of Sciences* (USA), *84*, 3531-3535.
Steinmetz, J.E., Logue, S.F., & Miller, D.P. (1993). Using signaled barpressing tasks to study the neural substrates of appetitive and aversive learning in rats: Behavioral manipulations and cerebellar lesions. *Behavioural Neuroscience, 107*, 941-954.
Steinmetz, J.E., Logue, S.F., & Steinmetz, S.S. (1992). Rabbit classically conditioned eyelid responses do not reappear after interpositus nucleus lesion and extensive post-lesion training. *Behavioural Brain Research, 51*, 103-114.
Steinmetz, J.E., Sears, L.L., Gabriel, M., Kubota, Y., & Poremba, A. (1991). Cerebellar interpositus nucleus lesions disrupt classical nictitating membrane conditioning but not discriminative avoidance learning in rabbits. *Behavioural Brain Research, 45*, 71-80.
Steinmetz, J.E., & Sengelaub, D.R. (1992). Possible conditioned stimulus pathway for classical eyelid conditioning in rabbits. I. Anatomical evidence for direct projections from the pontine nuclei to the cerebellar interpositus nucleus. *Behavioral and Neural Biology, 57*, 103-115.
Supple, W.F., & Leaton, R.N. (1990). Lesions of the cerebellar vermis and cerebellar hemispheres: effects on heart rate conditioning in rats. *Behavioral Neuroscience, 104*, 934-947.
Thompson, R.F., Berger, T.W., Berry, S.D., Clark, G.A., Kettner, R.E., Lavond, D.G., Mauk, M.D., McCormick, D.A., Solomon, P.R., & Weisz, D.J. (1982). Neuronal substrates of learning and memory: hippocampus and other structures. In C.D. Woody (Ed.), *Conditioning: Representation of Involved Neural Functions*. (pp.115-130). New York, Plenum Press.
Tracy, J., Thompson, J.K., Krupa, D.J., & Thompson, R.F. (1998). Evidence of plasticity in the pontocerebellar conditioned stimulus pathway during classical conditioning of the eyeblink response in the rabbit. *Behavioral Neuroscience, 112(2)*, 267-285.
Trendelenburg, W. (1910). Ausschaltungam Zentralnervensystem. II. Zur Lehre van den bulbairen und spinalen Atmungs-und GefaBzentren. Pfluegers Arch., *135*, 469-505.
Tsukahara, N., Oda. Y., & Notsu, T. (1981). Classical conditioning mediated by the red nucleus in the cat. *Journal of Neuroscience, 1*, 72-79.
Velazquez, J.L., Thompson, C.L., Barnes, E.M., & Angelides, K.J. (1989). Distribution and lateral mobility of GABA/Benzodiazepine receptors in nerve cells. *Journal of Neuroscience*, 9(6), 2163-2169.
Wall, P.D. (1980). Mechanisms of plasticity of connection following damage in adult mammalian nervous systems. In P. Bach-y-Rita (Ed.), *Recovery of function: Theoretical considerations for brain injury rehabilitation*. Baltimore, MD: University Park Press.
Watson, P.J. (1978). Nonmotor functions of the cerebellum. *Psychological Bulletin, 85*, 944-967.
Welsh, J.P., Bormann, N., Iannuzzelli, P., & Harvey, J.A. (1987). Intracerebellar lidocaine produces a reversible decrement in conditioned and unconditioned nictitating membrane responses in the rabbit. *Neuroscience Abstracts, 13*, 804.
Welsh, J.P., & Harvey, J.A. (1989). Cerebellar lesions and the nictitating membrane reflex: performance deficits of the conditioned and unconditioned response. *Journal of Neuroscience, 9*, 299-311.
Welsh, J.P., & Harvey, J.A. (1991). Pavlovian conditioning in the rabbit during inactivation of the interpositus nucleus. *Journal of Physiology, 444*, 459-480.
Welsh, J.P., & Harvey, J.A. (1992). The role of the cerebellum in voluntary and reflexive movements: History and current status. In R. Llinas & C. Sotelo (Eds.), *The cerebellum revisited*. (pp. 301-334). New York, Springer-Verlag.
White, I.M, Miller, D.D., White, W., Dike, G.L., Rebec, G.V., & Steinmetz, J.E. (1994). Neuronal activity in rabbit neostriatum during classical eyelid conditioning. *Experimental Brain Research, 99*, 179-190.
Woodruff-Pak, D.S., Lavond, D.G., & Thompson, R.F. (1985). Trace conditioning: abolished by cerebellar nuclear lesions but not lateral cerebellar cortex aspirations. *Brain Research, 348*, 249-260.
Woodruff-Pak, D. S., Papka, M., & Ivry, R. B. (1996). Cerebellar involvement in eyeblink classical conditioning in humans. *Neuropsychology, 10*, 443-458.
Yeo, C.H., Hardiman, M.J., & Glickstein, M. (1984). Discrete lesions of the cerebellar cortex abolish the classically conditioned nictitating membrane response of the rabbit. *Behavioural Brain Research, 13*,

261- 266.

Yeo, C.H., Hardiman, M.J., & Glickstein, M. (1985a). Classical conditioning of the nictitating membrane response of the rabbit. I. Lesions of the cerebellar nuclei. *Experimental Brain Research, 60*, 87-98.

Yeo, C.H., Hardiman, M.J., & Glickstein, M. (1985b). Classical conditioning of the nictitating membrane response of the rabbit. II. Lesions of the cerebellar cortex. *Experimental Brain Research, 60*, 99-113.

Yeo, C.H., Hardiman, M.J.. & Glickstein, M. (1985c). Classical conditioning of the nictitating membrane response of the rabbit III. Connections of cerebellar lobule HVI. *Experimental Brain Research, 60(1)*, 114-126.

Yeo, C.H., Hardiman, M.J., & Glickstein, M. (1986). Classical conditioning of the nictitating membrane response of the rabbit. IV. Lesions of the inferior olive. *Experimental Brain Research, 63*, 81-92.

Zhang, A.A., & Lavond, D.G. (1991). Effects of reversible lesion of reticular or facial neurons during eyeblink conditioning. *Neuroscience Abstracts, 17*, 869.

Zhang, J., Ni, H., & Harper, R.M. (1986). A miniaturized cryoprobe for functional neuronal blockade in freely moving animals. *Journal of Neuroscience Methods, 16*, 79-87.

4 ELECTROPHYSIOLOGICAL RECORDING AND BRAIN STIMULATION STUDIES OF EYEBLINK CONDITIONING

Joseph E. Steinmetz
Indiana University

INTRODUCTION

Extracellular recording of the electrical activity of the brain and direct electrical stimulation of brain tissue have been important tools used to study relationships between brain function and behavior. Both research tools have been used extensively over the years to study how the brain encodes classical eyeblink conditioning. The eyeblink conditioning preparation has proven ideal for using neural recording methods. Because the experimenter defines when the conditioned stimulus (CS) and unconditioned stimulus (US) are presented, it has been possible to examine neural activity recorded during single conditioning trials and define those brain sites that respond to the conditioning stimuli, those sites that show activity related to the unconditioned response (UR) or conditioned response (CR), and those sites that respond to more than one feature of the conditioning process. Likewise, brain microstimulation methods have proven useful during eyeblink conditioning. Because discrete stimuli are typically used for CSs and USs, electrical stimulation has been substituted for these stimuli in several different experiments. In this chapter, I will review a portion of the rather large volume of eyeblink conditioning data that has been collected using neural recording and brain stimulation techniques.

THE BASICS OF NEURAL RECORDING

Neural recording typically involves lowering high-impedance, insulated, metal microelectrodes into areas of the brain and monitoring the electrical activity of neurons near the exposed tip of the microelectrode. For chronic recording experiments, the microelectrodes are lowered in a brain area of interest and then held into place with acrylic cement that affixes the electrode to the skull. This preparation allows for the long term monitoring of neural activity from a single brain area. Recording can take place over periods of days, weeks, or even months. Some researchers use moveable microelectrodes for neural recording. For these studies, an electrode manipulator is

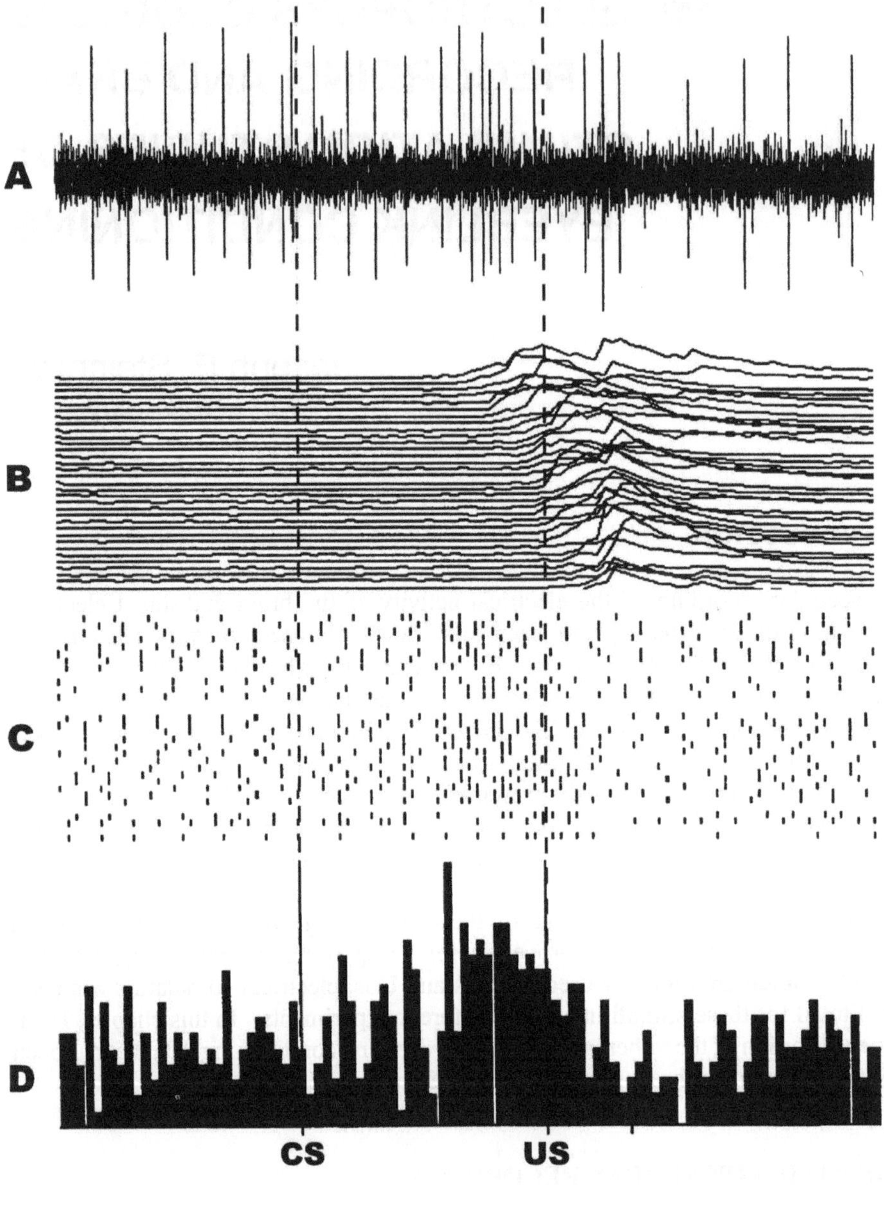
A
B
C
D
CS
US

cemented to the skull before training. A manipulator is a device that is designed to lower microelectrodes into the brain during conditioning sessions. This preparation allows for repositioning of the electrode during or between conditioning sessions thus enabling a variety of sites to be monitored during training. The advantage of chronic recording is that it is possible to monitor the activity of the same population of neurons during several phases of conditioning (e.g., acquisition and extinction). The advantage of recording with moveable electrodes is that it is possible to monitor the activity of several populations of neurons over the course of training.

Over the years, both multi-unit and single-unit recording experiments have been conducted. In multi-unit recording experiments, the action potentials of several neurons are recorded simultaneously by the electrode. The output of the electrode is typically amplified then routed to an electronic window discriminator that isolates action potentials with amplitudes that exceed a pre-set threshold that has been defined by the experimenter. During multi-unit recording, the threshold is typically set to discriminate 2-5 action potentials with the greatest amplitudes. In single-unit recording, the action potentials of one neuron are recorded by the electrode (i.e., the discriminator threshold is set by the experimenter to isolate the activity of one neuron). Multi-unit recording has proven valuable for initial assessments of the activity of populations of neurons. However, multi-unit recordings do not allow the investigator to analyze patterns of activity of single neurons in the population. For example, it is difficult to determine if individual neurons in a population are displaying excitatory patterns of action potentials versus inhibitory patterns of action potentials.

Figure 1. (Opposite page). Typical behavioral responses and neural activity during classical eyeblink conditioning. (A) Example of raw unit activity recorded during one trial of training. The trial depicted here is 1000 msec in length with 300 msec between onset of the trial and onset of the CS (first dashed vertical line), 300 msec between onset of CS and onset of US (second dashed vertical line) and 400 msec between US onset and the end of the trial. Action potentials from 2-3 neurons can be seen in this raw record. (B) Traces of eyeblink responses monitored via an infrared detection device on 36 trials are shown. Note that early in training (lower traces), response onsets are after US onset while later in training learned responses (CRs) are seen (upper traces). (C) Raster plot showing when discriminated action potentials occurred during the 36 trials relative to CS and US onset. This is a standard method that is often used to depict temporal patterns of neural activity. (D) Peristimulus-time histogram of the activity. This histogram represents neural activity summed across the 36 trials shown in the raster plot. Standard statistics are used to compare the amount of activity before CS onset with activity that occurs after. This histogram shows CR-related activity recorded from the rabbit cerebellum during classical eyeblink conditioning.

Recent advances in neural recording, however, now allow experimenters to combine the advantages of multi-unit and single-unit recording. Instead of relying on window discriminators to separate action potentials on the sole basis of amplitude, several commercial systems are now available to discriminate action potentials on the basis of waveform. These systems use waveform template matching algorithms to identify the activity of individual neurons from a cluster of several neurons being recorded simultaneously. Coupled with new multi-wire electrodes that are used to simultaneously monitor activity from more than one brain site, these new multi-unit recording techniques should prove valuable for describing brain activity associated with learning -- procedures such as classical eyeblink conditioning.

During classical eyeblink conditioning, researchers look for patterns of action potentials that are in some way related to the learning situation. Typically, neural activity is summed over several trials and peristimulus time histograms representing trial-related activity across trials are produced. These histograms are examined for patterns of activation related to stimulus presentation or conditioning. For example, if the amplitude of the peristimulus histograms is greatest just after presentation of a tone CS and the activity is invariant (i.e., does not move in time from trial-to-trial), we are likely to classify the pattern as tone-CS-related. Activity that occurs invariantly after air puff-US presentation might be classified as US or UR-related. Activity that is found in the interval between CS and US presentation and moves in a fashion that is correlated with CR performance might be classified as CR- or learning-related. Standard score calculations and cross-correlational techniques are often used to establish relationships between neural activity and behavioral responding (see Katz & Steinmetz, 1997 or Sears & Steinmetz, 1990, for examples of the use of these computational techniques).

THE BASICS OF BRAIN STIMULATION

For brain stimulation studies, stimulating microelectrodes are typically implanted chronically into brain areas of interest prior to behavioral training. The stimulation microelectrodes are usually stainless steel and lower impedance than recording microelectrodes (i.e., the tip size of the stimulating electrodes are larger than recording electrodes). Most studies use either monopolar or bipolar stimulation techniques. For monopolar stimulation, one electrode is lowered into the target brain region and the reference electrode for the stimulation is affixed to the skull. For bipolar stimulation, two electrodes with tips quite close to each other are lowered into the target brain region; one electrode delivers current while the second electrode serves as the reference for the stimulation. These techniques result in somewhat different stimulation results with regard to the extent, intensity and spread of the stimulating current that is applied to the brain tissue.

Once implanted, the electrodes are used to deliver current to specific brain regions in hopes of electrically exciting the neurons near the tip of the stimulating electrode. As detailed below, this technique has been used successfully as a substitute for external stimuli presented during conditioning, as a means to disrupt normal activity in the brain, and as a means to activate neurons in establishing connectivity in the brain. The choice of parameters used during brain stimulation is very important. If the goal of the brain stimulation is to mimic electrical activity in the brain, current levels delivered as well as stimulus frequency and pulse duration must be chosen as to not exceed normal, physiological levels. If disruption of brain activity is the goal, super-physiological levels of brain stimulation are usually desired. Also, consideration is normally given as to where in the nervous system the stimulation is being delivered. For example, different techniques are used if axons are to be excited as opposed to neuron cell bodies. When done properly, microstimulation of the brain has proven to be a valuable tool for studying the involvement of brain structures and systems in classical eyeblink conditioning (See Yeomans, 1990, for a review of brain stimulation techniques).

NEURAL RECORDING EXPERIMENTS

Hippocampal Recordings During Eyeblink Conditioning

The first systematic neural recording studies that explored correlations between brain activity and eyeblink conditioning were undertaken by Berger, Thompson and their colleagues and involved recordings from the hippocampus and limbic system. Using multi-unit recording techniques and recording from populations of neurons in the CA1 and CA3 regions of the hippocampus, Berger and Thompson (1978a) reported that populations of neurons in the hippocampus increased their firing rates above spontaneous levels during initial phases of paired CS-US training. The activity increases began during the US period and moved forward in time, eventually forming an amplitude-time course "model" that preceded the onset of the behavioral response (i.e., the hippocampal neurons began discharging prior to the onset of the CR with a firing pattern that closely resembled the topography of the behavioral response in timing and amplitude). Berger and colleagues followed up this study with a single-unit analysis of hippocampal activity (Berger, Rinaldi, Weisz & Thompson, 1983) and showed that different subpopulations of hippocampal cells correlated with different within-trial distributions of activity. For example most pyramidal cells showed significant, positive correlations with the topography of the behavioral CR while a few showed inhibition. Other pyramidal cells did not alter their firing patterns from spontaneous levels. Hippocampal theta cells were found that responded during paired conditioning trials with a rhythmic bursting. Theta cells are neurons that show slow, rhythmic bursting patterns at or near theta rates (8 Hz).

Other limbic system structures were also showed patterns of activation related to eyeblink conditioning (Berger, Clark & Thompson, 1980). Recordings were made from two structures that send projections to the hippocampus; the medial septum and the entorhinal cortex. Medial septum recordings did not resemble those taken from the hippocampus (Berger & Thompson, 1978b). Units in the medial septum seemed to encode the presentation of the CS and US (i.e., they showed rather sharp, short-duration increases in unit activity just after CS and US presentation) and this activity decreased with training. The peristimulus time histograms created from recordings taken from the entorhinal cortex, however, did resemble the learning-related activity seen in the hippocampus demonstrating within-trial similarities (Berger et al., 1980). Across trials, however, there was less similarity; entorhinal cortex showed no significant increases in activity with training. Conditioning-related recordings were also taken from several hippocampal efferents including the lateral septum, the anterior thalamic nucleus and the mammillary nuclei (Berger et al., 1980; Berger & Thompson, 1978b). A high degree of correspondence between the neuronal activity in the hippocampus and lateral septum was observed. The anterior thalamic and medial and lateral mammillary nuclei, however, did not show activity patterns similar to the hippocampus.

These early recording experiments most certainly demonstrated that the hippocampus was somehow involved in encoding eyeblink conditioning. However, lesions studies revealed that for at least delay conditioning (the conditioning process used in the limbic system recording studies) the hippocampus was not essential for conditioning to occur (e.g., Schmaltz & Theios, 1972). Indeed, the recording studies of Berger, Thompson, and colleagues, while demonstrating the engagement of the hippocampus during conditioning, did not speak to the role of the observed hippocampal learning-related activity. Recording studies conducted since these initial experiments have attempted to address the role of the hippocampus in conditioning.

Disterhoft and colleagues have examined hippocampal activity during classical trace conditioning, a variation of eyeblink conditioning that is known to be dependent on an intact hippocampus. Using a short-interval (300 msec) trace eyeblink conditioning procedure, Disterhoft and associates showed some differences between delay and trace conditioning in patterns of hippocampal neuronal responses (Disterhoft, Thompson & Moyer, 1994). A rather pronounced tone-evoked response was observed early in the CS period, unit responsiveness decreased substantially during the trace period, then showed a pronounced CR-related response late in the trace period just before US onset. The early excitation and later reduction in hippocampal neuronal responsiveness is not seen in delay conditioning (even with relatively long ISIs) thus suggesting that this pattern may have something to do with encoding the trace or temporal characteristics of the trace procedure.

Using newer template-matching techniques, Disterhoft and colleagues have recorded from populations of hippocampal neurons during trace conditioning (McEchron & Disterhoft, 1997). They reported large increases in activity following both the CS and US early in conditioning when CRs began to appear. Theta cells showed an activity pattern opposite to that of the pyramidal cells. While most pyramidal cells showed increases in activity specific to the day when initial CRs were observed, other pyramidal responses profiles appeared to be involved in assessing the temporal properties of the CS-US trace conditioning trials.

Using another variation of eyeblink conditioning, classical discrimination/reversal conditioning, Miller and Steinmetz (1997) have examined conditioning-related, multiple-unit activity in the hippocampus. In discrimination training, rabbits are presented with two CSs, a CS+ that is followed by the US and a CS- that is presented in isolation. The rabbits learn to respond to the CS+ and suppress responding to the CS-. During the reversal phase of training, the CS+ and CS- are reversed so that the rabbit is required to respond to the initial CS- and suppress responding to the initial CS+. Miller and Steinmetz (1997) showed learning-related patterns of hippocampal activity to the CS+ (a tone) when CRs were present and no learning-related hippocampal activity on CS- trials (a second tone of different frequency) when CRs were absent. Interestingly, during early phases of reversal training, learning-related activity in the hippocampus disappeared even though rabbits were performing CRs on both CS+ and CS- trials. Learning-related activity reappeared, however, when the reversal conditioning began to emerge. These data suggest that the hippocampus is encoding more then performance of the CR. It seems to be signaling when acquisition of a new CR is occurring.

A few recent studies have suggested that regardless what the hippocampus is encoding during classical eyeblink conditioning, it may be doing so on a rather short-term, temporary basis. For example, Sears and Steinmetz (1990) recorded multi-unit activity from the hippocampus over eight days of training which is somewhat longer than the number of days recorded in previous studies. Similar to Berger and Thompson (1978a), a rather rapid development of learning-related activity in the hippocampus that peaked about 3-4 days into training was observed. Hippocampal activity declined, however, with additional days of training until it returned to levels comparable to the first day of training. This same pattern was reported by McEchron and Disterhoft (1997) during their study of hippocampal cellular activity associated with classical trace conditioning. These recording studies are in agreement with hippocampal lesions studies that have shown a temporary involvement of the hippocampus in encoding eyeblink conditioning. For example, Kim, Clark and Thompson (1995) reported that hippocampal lesions delivered immediately after trace eyeblink conditioning abolished CRs, but that lesions delivered one month after training had no affect on the learned response.

There is some evidence that learning-related activity in the hippocampus, at least for delay conditioning procedures, may depend on input from the cerebellum and associated brain structure (which are now known to play critical roles in the acquisition and performance of the eyeblink CR). Clark, McCormick, Lavond and Thompson (1984) overtrained rabbits using a tone CS and air puff US while recording hippocampal activity. They then delivered electrolytic lesions to the region of the interpositus nucleus. The lesions abolished CRs in the rabbits and also abolished conditioned increases in hippocampal CA1 activity. The learning-related activity could be reestablished when training was switched to the opposite eye. Sears and Steinmetz (1990) examined the effects of cerebellar lesions on the acquisition of CR-related activity in the hippocampus. Lesions of the left interpositus nucleus before training prevented acquisition of the eyeblink CR. The lesions also prevented the development of CR-related activity in the hippocampus. When training was switched to the unlesioned right side, CR-related activity was seen in the hippocampus along with the appearance of behavioral CRs. Neither learning-related hippocampal activity nor CRs were seen when training was once again delivered to the left, lesioned side. These studies suggest that the learning-related activity in the hippocampus is critically dependent on the presence of behavioral CRs and that the cerebellum may provide the hippocampus with important information needed to establish the learning-related pattern of neural discharges.

Some attempts have been made to trace how cerebellar interpositus nucleus activity might influence hippocampal activity. For example, Miller and Steinmetz (1992) monitored medial and lateral septal activity before and after lesions of the interpositus nucleus. The lesions abolished behavioral CRs and CR-related activity in the lateral septum but did not affect CS- and US-related activity characteristic of the medial septum. We interpreted these data to show that the interpositus lesions affected hippocampal output (i.e., the lateral septum) but did not affect activity in at least one hippocampal input (i.e., the medial septum). In a similar study, we examined the effects of interpositus and red nucleus lesions on activity in a cerebellar-thalamic projection area with the idea that this area may provide a critical relay site for information flow from the cerebellum to the hippocampus (Sears, Logue & Steinmetz, 1996). Neural activity in the ventrolateral thalamic nucleus was monitored before and after lesions of either the interpositus nucleus or the red nucleus. Interpositus lesions, but not red nucleus lesions disrupted conditioning-related activity in the thalamus thus demonstrating that an efferent copy of learning-related activity is projected from the interpositus nucleus to the ventrolateral thalamus. We then lesioned this area of the thalamus and recorded hippocampal activity during conditioning. In animals with thalamic lesions, learning-related activity could be seen in the hippocampus, thus eliminating the ventrolateral thalamus as a potential relay site for information flowing from the interpositus nucleus to the hippocampus. To date, it is unknown precisely how interpositus activity influences the establishment of learning-related activity in the hippocampus, although projections through frontal cortex remain a viable and unchecked possibility.

Since the earliest recording studies of Berger and Thompson (1978a) it has been clear that the hippocampus and limbic system play some role in classical eyeblink conditioning. However, the precise role for the hippocampus in this simple associative learning procedure has yet to be delineated. What is clear is that more complicated forms of the procedure, such as trace conditioning and discrimination/reversal conditioning, seem to require the involvement of the hippocampus. Indeed, the hippocampal activity might be signaling a variety of processes such as short-term memory, context encoding or temporal aspects of conditioning.

Cerebellar Recordings During Eyeblink Conditioning

When it was clear that the hippocampus and other higher brain areas were not essential for classical eyeblink conditioning, attention was focused on the brain stem and other lower brain areas. As detailed in other chapters of this volume, a great deal of data has been collected in support of the idea that the cerebellum and associated brain stem areas are essential for the acquisition and performance of the conditioned eyeblink response. Neural recording experiments were critical in establishing a role for the cerebellum and associated brain stem areas in eyeblink conditioning. These studies are presented here.

McCormick, Thompson and colleagues used multi-unit recording methods to provide important evidence for an involvement of the cerebellum in eyeblink conditioning (e.g., McCormick & Thompson, 1984). Using basic mapping techniques in which electrodes were systematically moved through the cerebellar cortex and the deep cerebellar nuclei and also chronically implanted electrodes, these investigators showed that areas in the neocerebellar cortex and the region of the interpositus and dentate nuclei contained neurons that discharged in a pattern that appeared to be related to eyeblink conditioning. Activity of the populations of neurons in the deep cerebellar nuclei and cerebellar cortex formed peristimulus activity histograms that closely resembled the topography of the behavioral CR. Moreover, the onset of the unit activity occurred before the onset of the behavior thus suggesting that the activity could be producing the behavioral CR. The formation of the neural "model" occurred simultaneously with the appearance of CRs. Other populations of cerebellar neurons showed invariant activation patterns that seemed to be linked to presentation of either the CS or the US (i.e., they were not related to CR performance). These data supported the idea that the cerebellum encoded the acquisition and performance of the classically conditioned eyeblink response.

In two experiments, Berthier and Moore (1986; 1990) examined the activity of single units in the cerebellar cortex and the deep cerebellar nuclei to better define the participation of these areas in the learning process. Using a differential conditioning procedure with tonal CSs and a periorbital shock US, Berthier and Moore (1986) first recorded from a number of Purkinje cells located in Larsell's lobule HVI (an area of cerebellar cortex previously identified as important for classical eyeblink conditioning). They showed that a number of Purkinje cells discharged with simple spikes to presentation of the US although complex spiking was rarely seen. Simple spike discharges in the cerebellum indicate that the mossy fiber system is being activated while complex spike discharges indicate an activation of the climbing fiber system (that originates in the inferior olive). The HVI Purkinje cells showed a variety of responses to the CSs including an increase in simple spiking that was correlated with CRs and preceded the CRs by 20-200 msec. Some cells showed a decrease in firing rate to the presentation of the CS thus demonstrating that both excitatory and inhibitory patterns of learning-related activity could be seen in cerebellar cortex. More recently, Schreurs and colleagues have conducted elegant intracellular analyses of Purkinje cells obtained from rabbits that have undergone classical eyeblink conditioning (e.g., Schreurs, Sanchez-Andres & Alkon, 1991; Schreurs, Oh and Alkon, 1996). They have described cellular processes that appear to be related to conditioning (see Chapter 8 by Schreur in this volume).

Using the differential conditioning procedure, Berthier and Moore (1990) recorded single unit activity in the interpositus and dentate nuclei. They reported that 47% of the cells responded to the orbital shock US while 21% of the cells responded with short latencies to the CSs used. Some cells responded when either CS+ or CS- were presented while other cells responded only when a CR was present. Further, about one-half of the CR-related cells followed trial-by-trial variations of CR latency while the other half seemed to be time-locked to CS onset. These single unit recording studies have provided good evidence that individual neurons in the cerebellar cortex and the deep cerebellar nuclei seem to encode the CS, US, UR and CR associated with eyeblink conditioning. It is likely that the activity of these individual neurons produced the variety of patterns of activity seen in the populations of neurons monitored in the multi-unit recording studies of McCormick, Thompson and colleagues (e.g., McCormick & Thompson, 1984).

While it is clear that the cerebellar cortex and the cerebellar deep nuclei both encode eyeblink conditioning, it is not clear what specific role each plays in acquisition and performance of the learned response. We have recently conducted some recording studies aimed at delineating differences between these areas. In one study (Gould &

Steinmetz, 1996), we recorded multi- and single-unit activity from cerebellar cortex and the interpositus nucleus during a number of variations of conditioning including acquisition and extinction training and forward, backward, and unpaired presentations of the CS and US. Overall, we observed the development of learning-related activity in the interpositus nucleus only when the CS was presented before the US in normal forward-paired fashion. Conversely, changes in cerebellar cortical unit activity were seen regardless of the order in which the stimuli were presented. Increases in responsiveness of Purkinje cells were even seen after explicitly unpaired presentations of the CS and US. Finally, extinction produced a rather rapid loss of learning-related activity in the interpositus nucleus as CRs disappeared whereas learning-related activity in the cerebellar cortex far outlasted the performance of behavioral CRs by several sessions.

In another study (Gould & Steinmetz, 1994) we recorded multi-unit activity from the cerebellar cortex and deep nuclei during discrimination/reversal conditioning. During both discrimination and reversal phases of conditioning, we saw a similar pattern of activation in the cerebellar cortex – CR-related activity was present on CS+ trials when CRs were present but not on CS- trials when CRs were absent. Activity in the interpositus nucleus was different. During discrimination training, CR-related activity was present on CS+ but not CS- trials but after reversal training only a very weak activation of the interpositus on CS+ trials could be detected. We have interpreted these data to indicate that the interpositus nucleus is relatively pairing-specific as to encoding the learning while the cortex is not. Furthermore, these data suggest that these two areas are encoding different features of the conditioning and that discrimination/reversal encoding likely involves other brain structures. We have speculated that while plasticity in the interpositus nucleus is responsible for issuing a motor "command" to lower brain stem areas for the conditioned eyeblink response, cerebellar cortex may be responsible for timing functions or perhaps enhancing the nuclear response (i.e. a response gain-setting mechanism).

We examined the dependency of the learning-related activity in cerebellar cortex on learning-related activity in the interpositus nucleus in another study (Katz & Steinmetz, 1997). In this study, we delivered kainic acid lesions to the interpositus nucleus to eliminate CR-related plasticity (as well as behavioral CRs). Purkinje cell recordings were then made. We showed the development of normal learning-related activity in the cerebellar cortex even though the interpositus nucleus was lesioned (although the balance between inhibitory and excitatory type units may have been slightly altered). These data suggest that plasticity is independently established in these two areas of the cerebellum.

Recordings in the CS and US Pathways During Conditioning

Recordings studies have also been used to provide evidence for the pathways from the periphery that carry the CS and the US. We have hypothesized that a tone CS is projected from the ear to the cochlear nuclei to the basilar pontine nuclei which, in turn, sends mossy fiber axons to both cerebellar cortex and the deep cerebellar nuclei (see Steinmetz, 1996, for review). We have also hypothesized that an air puff US is

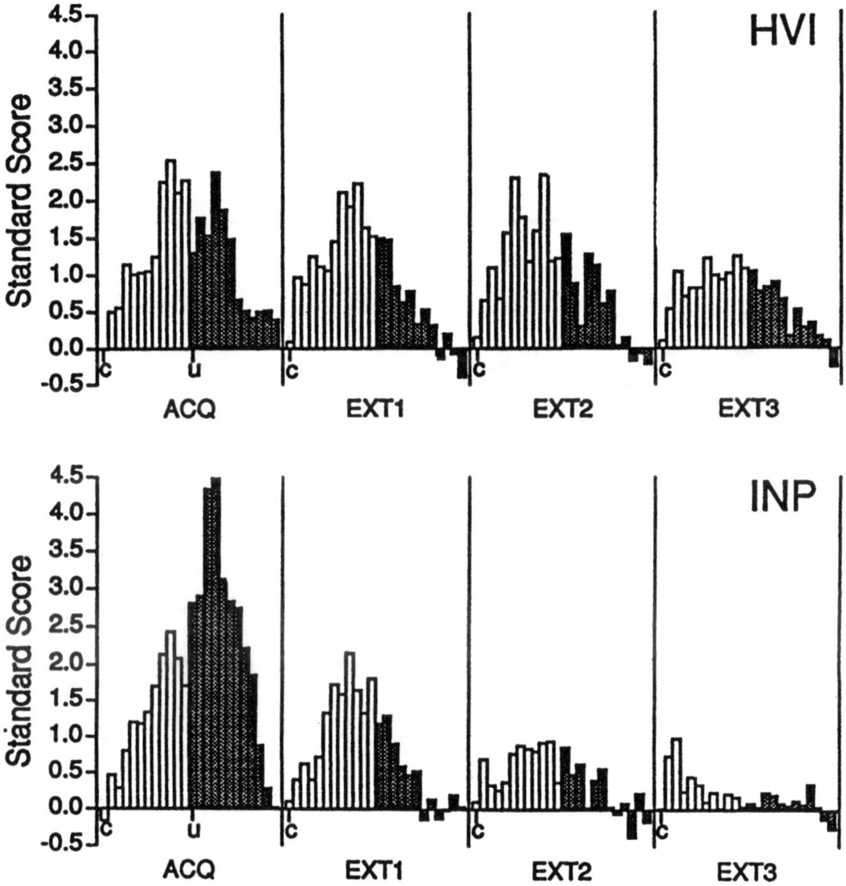

Figure 2. Histograms depicting standardized scores of neural activity recorded from neurons in Larsell's lobule VI of cerebellar cortex (HVI) and from neurons in the interpositus nucleus of the cerebellum (INP). The white bars show activity recorded between CS onset and US onset and the dark bars show activity recorded after US onset. Four sessions of training are shown, the last day of paired CS-US acquisition training (ACQ) and three consecutive days of CS-alone extinction data (EXT1 - EXT3). These recordings showed that learning-related unit activity in the cerebellar cortex persisted for several days into extinction training even though CRs were no longer present while learning-related unit activity in the interpositus nucleus diminished as the CR was extinguished (Reprinted with permission from Gould & Steinmetz, 1996).

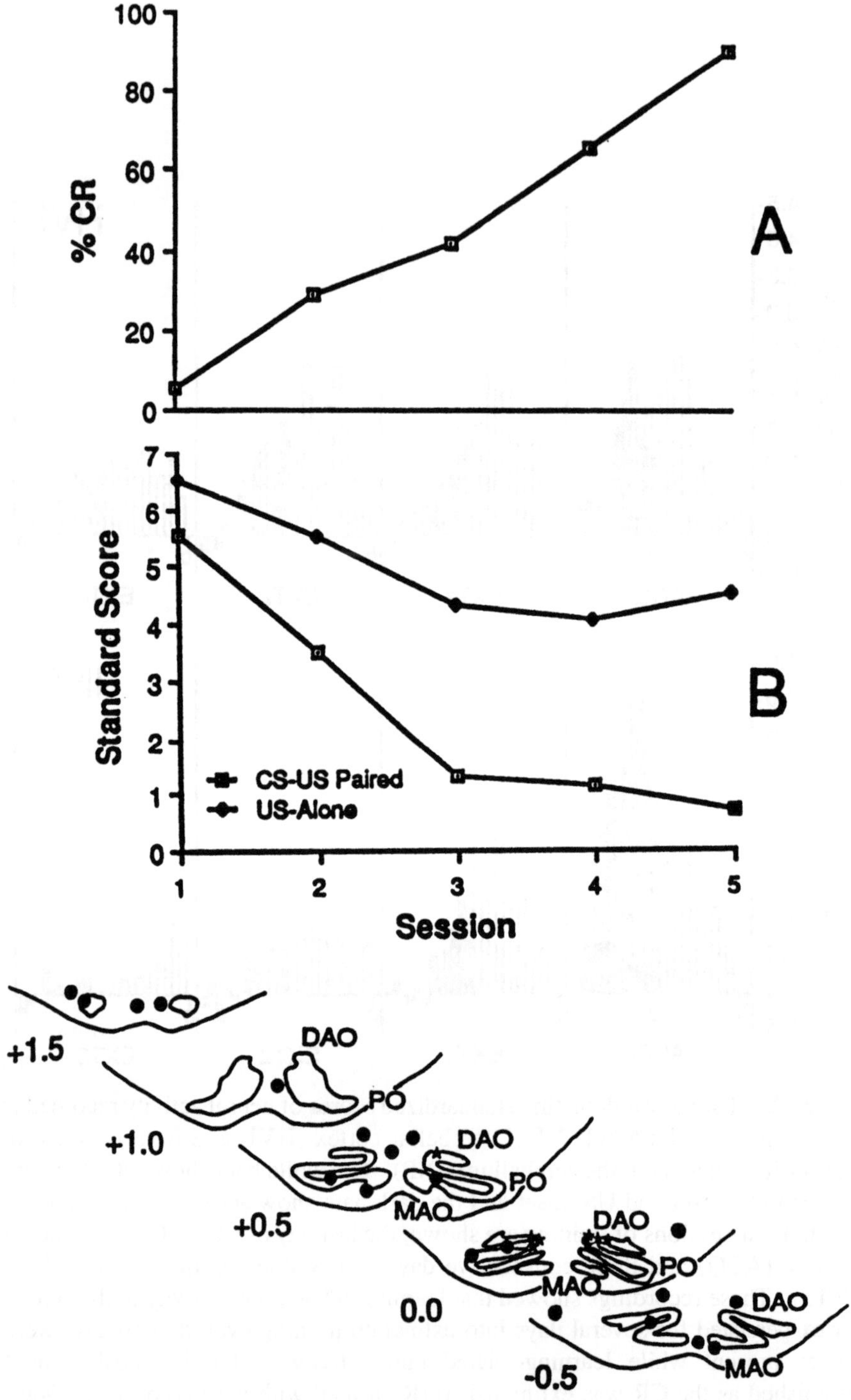

100
80
60
40
20
0
% CR
A
7
6
5
4
3
2
1
0
Standard Score
B
CS-US Paired
US-Alone
1
2
3
4
5
Session
+1.5
DAO
PO
+1.0
DAO
PO
MAO
+0.5
DAO
PO
MAO
0.0
DAO
MAO
-0.5

projected from receptors on the cornea to the trigeminal nucleus to the dorsal accessory inferior olive which in turn, sends axons to both cerebellar cortex and the deep cerebellar nuclei. On the CS side, recordings from anesthetized rabbits have demonstrated that a tone evokes activity in lateral and medial regions of the pontine nuclei (Steinmetz et al., 1987). Similarly, tone-evoked activity can be seen in the pontine nuclei during training in the awake rabbit. In fact, some cells show CR-related activity that is abolished when the interpositus nucleus is deactivated (Cartford, Gohl, Singson & Lavond, 1997).

On the US side, discrete regions of the trigeminal nucleus showed US-evoked activity when a corneal air puff was presented as well as CR-related activity that was similar in form to activity recorded in the interpositus nucleus (Richards, Ricciardi & Moore, 1991). However, when the interpositus nucleus was deactivated by cooling with a cold probe, the CR-related activity in the trigeminal nucleus disappeared thus suggesting that the CR-related activity seen in the trigeminal nucleus originated in the interpositus nucleus (Clark & Lavond, 1996). US-evoked activity can be seen in the dorsal accessory olive before learning occurs (Sears & Steinmetz, 1991), but this activity diminishes as CRs are formed. A similar result has been reported by Hesslow and Ivarsson who classically conditioned eyeblink responses in decerebrate ferrets (Hesslow & Ivarsson, 1996). It appears that there are inhibitory connection between the interpositus nucleus and the inferior olive. As the interpositus begins to build learning-related activity, it appears to phasically inhibit the inferior olive. This mechanism may be important for control of timing of the CR.

Figure 3. Neuronal activity in the dorsal accessory inferior olive decreases as classical eyeblink conditioning occurs. (A) Percent CRs increases across five days of paired CS-US training in a group of rabbits. (B) Standard scores of neuronal activity in the dorsal accessory inferior olive actually decrease over the five days of paired training. The squares show standard scores of olivary activity recorded on CS-alone trials interspersed during paired training while the circles show activity recorded on US-alone trials interspersed during training. Note that the decrement in responsiveness is only seen on trials when the CS was presented (i.e., when a CR was present) thus demonstrating that the decrement in neuronal responding is pairing specific and possibly dependent on execution of the CR. (C) Schematic of the ventral brain stem showing recording sites from this experiment. Stars depict locations where decrements in activity were seen (Reprinted with permission from Sears & Steinmetz, 1991).

Recordings in Other Brain Regions During Eyeblink Conditioning

Other areas of the brain stem are involved in encoding various aspects of the conditioning process. The red nucleus receives output from the interpositus nucleus and relays information concerning the CR to motor nuclei responsible for generating the eyeblink. Early multi-unit recording experiments demonstrated the development of CR-related activity in the red nucleus (e.g., Chapman, Steinmetz, Sears & Thompson, 1990). These results were replicated in single-unit studies by Desmond and Moore (1991). Using a differential conditioning procedure with a orbital shock US, they showed many units with altered firing rates that were either time-locked to the CS or the CR. In essence, these response patterns were similar to those seen in the interpositus nucleus thus suggesting the possibility that basic cellular plasticity responsible for CR formation occurs in the red nucleus (i.e., perhaps "learning" occurs in the red nucleus and is projected elsewhere, including to the cerebellum). This possibility has been ruled out by other studies. For example, Chapman, Sears, Steinmetz and Thompson (1991) trained two groups of rabbits; a group that had recording electrodes in the red nucleus and a cannula aimed at the interpositus nucleus, and a second group that had recording electrodes in the interpositus nucleus and a cannula aimed at the red nucleus. While delivering training trials and recording from the electrodes, lidocaine was delivered via the cannulae to inactivate either the red nucleus or the interpositus nucleus. When the interpositus nucleus was inactivated, CRs were abolished and no CR-related activity was seen in the red nucleus. Conversely, when the red nucleus was inactivated, CRs were abolished but CR-related activity was still observed in the interpositus nucleus. This study has established that the direction of CR flow in this system is from the interpositus nucleus to the red nucleus and not in the opposite direction.

Activity in cranial motor nuclei responsible for various components of the eyeblink response (e.g., abducens, accessory abducens and facial nuclei) have been observed. For example, Cegavske, Patterson and Thompson (1979) recorded multi-unit neuronal activity from the abducens nucleus during classical eyeblink conditioning with a tone CS and an air puff US. Between-blocks comparisons of neural and behavioral responses showed an almost perfect correlation during acquisition training while within-block comparisons showed a close correspondence between the peristimulus histograms of activity and the topography of the CR or UR. In short, these recordings revealed CR and UR activity characteristic of the motor neurons responsible for activating musculature that produces eyeblinks. It appears that these areas received input from the red nucleus thus forming a part of the basic CR pathway. These areas also receive input indirectly from the trigeminal nucleus thus forming part of the UR pathway as well.

Neural activity related to eyeblink conditioning has also been recorded in a number of other brain regions. Using extracellular and intracellular recording techniques coupled with a conditioning procedure that produced increases of a very short latency eyeblink response (e.g., > 20 msec), Woody and his associates demonstrated an important involvement of motor cortex in encoding plasticity for this short-latency response (e.g., Aou, Woody & Birt, 1992; Brons & Woody, 1980; Woody & Black-Cleworth, 1973). Recordings from an anterior "nonspecific", polysensory, sensorimotor area in the rabbit, however, failed to reveal CR-related activity. Small unlearned responses to a tone CS and air puff US were present but neuronal activity associated with classical eyeblink conditioning was not observed (Hoehler & Thompson, 1980). Unit activity during classical eyeblink conditioning has been recorded from the neostriatum (White, Miller, White, Dike, Rebec & Steinmetz, 1994). Neostriatal neurons were shown to process information regarding the CS and CR as well as the US/UR. A close temporal correlation between neuronal activity and CR onset was observed. These data demonstrated that the neostriatum encoded all aspects of conditioning including occurrence of the stimuli and integration of sensorimotor information. This finding is consistent with other experiments that have demonstrated that neostriatal neurons respond to movement and movement-related sensory stimuli (e.g., Rolls & Williams, 1987). These studies demonstrate that several regions of the brain encode the classically conditioned eyeblink response. The roles of the various structures in conditioning, however, have not been delineated.

MICROSTIMULATION EXPERIMENTS

There is a relatively long history of using electrical brain stimulation as a substitute for peripheral stimuli during classical conditioning. These studies were generally designed to demonstrate that activation of a given brain region was sufficient to support conditioning. Loucks (1933), for example, showed that direct stimulation of visual cortex as a CS could elicit CRs when paired with a forelimb shock US. Doty, Rutledge, and Larsen (1956) conditioned the cat foreleg flexion response by activating several cerebral cortical sites as a US. Subcortical structures have also served as effective CS-stimulation sites. Neilson, Knight and Porter (1962) effectively conditioned a forepaw shock-avoidance response by delivering a stimulation CS to 21 different subcortical structures. In addition, Patterson (1970, 1971) showed that the rabbit nictitating membrane response could be classically conditioned when inferior colliculus stimulation was forward paired with a periorbital shock US.

Brain stimulation studies have been conducted to establish the involvement of cranial nerve motor nuclei in activating musculature that produce eyelid closure and nictitating membrane movement (the responses typically recorded during classical eyeblink conditioning). Mis, Gormezano and Harvey (1979) and Martin, Land and Thompson (1980) substituted electrical stimulation of the abducens nucleus for a periorbital shock US or an air puff US and produced robust conditioning when the stimulation US was paired with a tone CS. These basic studies were replicated and extended by Powell and Moore (1980) who performed a careful analysis of the location of successful brain stem stimulation-US sites. They reported that the electrode locations that produced the most successful maintenance of conditioning were located caudal and ventrolateral to the abducens nucleus in a region containing cells that comprise the accessory abducens nucleus.

Microstimulation in the Hippocampus During Eyeblink Conditioning

Because of interest in the role of the hippocampus and limbic system in classical eyeblink conditioning, a few experiments involving hippocampal microstimulation have been performed. Salafia, Romano, Tynan and Host (1977) delivered stimulation to the hippocampus just after each CS-US paired trial. They reported a massive disruption of acquisition if the stimulation was delivered before learning occurred. However, the stimulation had no effect if delivered after CRs were established. They interpreted their data to indicate that hippocampal stimulation somehow disrupted the consolidation of the learning. It should be noted, however, that Prokasy, Kesner and

Calder (1983) conducted a similar experiment using posttrial dorsal hippocampal stimulation and reported a facilitation of eyeblink conditioning.

Robinson, Port and Berger (1989) investigated the effects of kindling the hippocampal perforant path - dentate projection on discrimination/reversal conditioning. Kindling is a progressive intensification of electrophysiological and behavioral responsiveness to repetitively presented subconvulsive stimulation. They showed that kindling facilitated learning of the initial discrimination but severely impaired reversal learning in that responding to the CS- remained at high levels. In a subsequent study, Robinson (1992) showed that hippocampal kindling significantly potentiated the population spike, EPSP and magnitude of twin pulse inhibition recorded in granule cells activated by perforant path activation. Subsequent discrimination/reversal conditioning revealed a retardation in the rate of reversal while kindling-induced potentiation, within excitatory and inhibitory circuits in the hippocampus, persisted for the duration of training.

A few studies have attempted to substitute limbic system stimulation for peripheral CSs during eyeblink conditioning. Prokasy, Kesner and Calder (1983) showed that low levels (i.e., sub-seizure levels) of stimulation of the CA1 layer of the hippocampus did not serve as an effective CS during eyeblink conditioning. Knowlton and Thompson (1989) examined the effectiveness of stimulating the medial or lateral septum as a substitute for a CS during eyeblink conditioning. The medial septum sends input into the hippocampus while the lateral septum receives output from the hippocampus. They showed that stimulation of the medial septum was a far less effective CS than stimulation of the lateral septum, perhaps due to the different roles these nuclei play during conditioning (i.e., the lateral septum projects to a variety of brain stem structures that may be involved in conditioning).

Microstimulation in the Cerebellum and Brainstem During Eyeblink Conditioning

When attention became focused on the cerebellum and associated brain stem structures as critical for classical eyeblink conditioning, microstimulation studies were undertaken to delineate CS and US pathways from the periphery to the cerebellum and further establish a role for the cerebellum in conditioning.

The first series of experiments undertaken used microstimulation of the lateral pontine nuclei to provide evidence that this region of the brain stem relayed tone CS information into the cerebellum during conditioning (Steinmetz, Rosen, Chapman, Lavond & Thompson, 1986). In brief, stimulating electrodes were placed in lateral regions of the pontine nuclei and electrical stimulation delivered through the electrodes was paired with an air puff US (i.e., the stimulation served as a CS). Normal acquisition and extinction were seen with the pontine-stimulation-CS. Also, unpaired presentation of the stimulation CS and air puff US produced no CRs while lesions of the interpositus nucleus abolished CRs established with the pontine-stimulation-CS. Other studies provided evidence that the pontine stimulation activates neurons normally engaged by a peripheral, tone CS. For example, a normal "inverted-U" ISI function was observed when rabbits were trained with various ISIs and with the

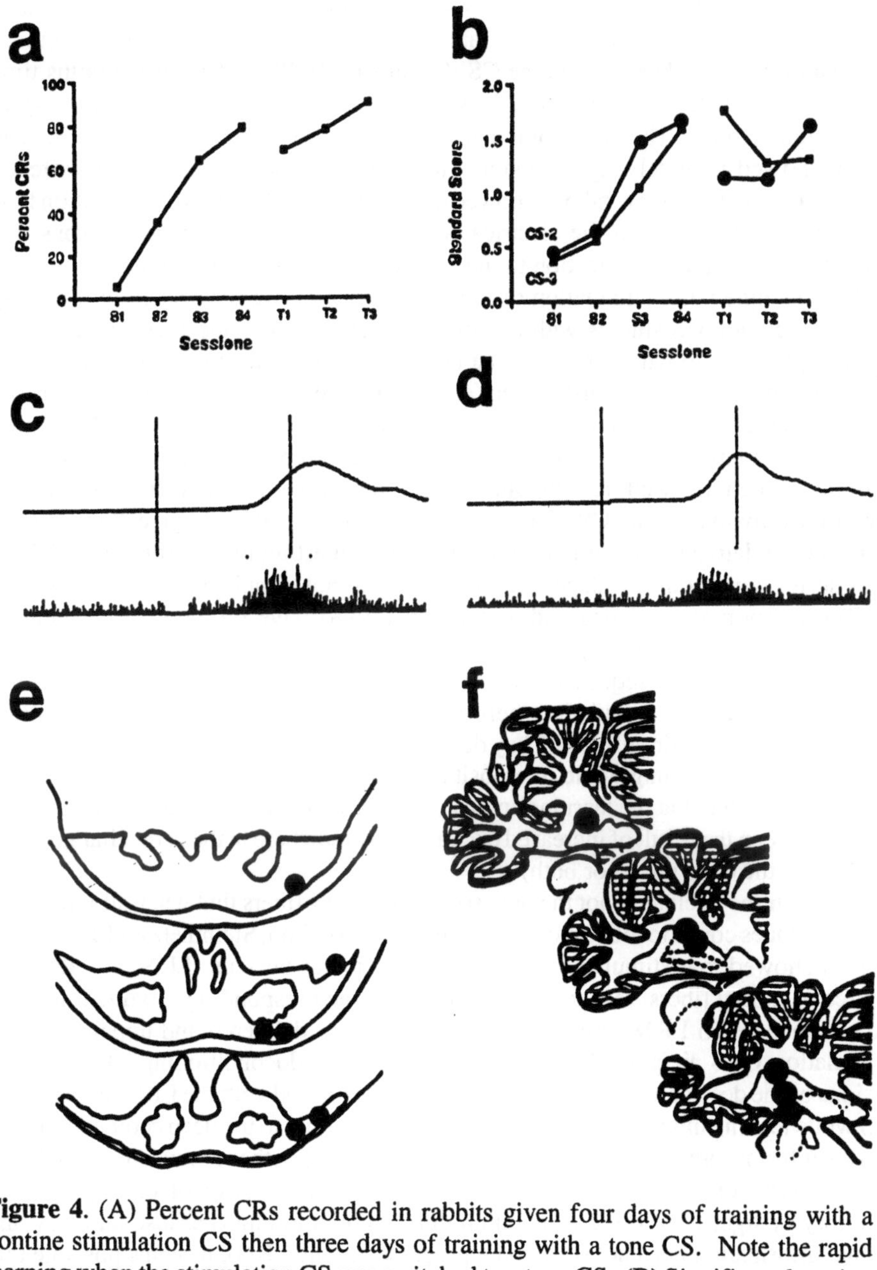

Figure 4. (A) Percent CRs recorded in rabbits given four days of training with a pontine stimulation CS then three days of training with a tone CS. Note the rapid learning when the stimulation CS was switched to a tone CS. (B) Significant learning related activity was recorded in the interpositus nucleus with both stimulation and tone CSs. (C and D) Examples of behavioral responding and unit activity evoked with a stimulation CS (C) and tone CS (D). (E) Stimulation sites in the pontine nuclei. (F) Recording sites in the interpositus nucleus. (Preprinted with permission from Steinmetz, 1990).

pontine-stimulation-CS (Steinmetz, 1990a). In another study, interpositus nucleus recordings were made in a group of rabbits that were trained first with a pontine-stimulation-CS and then with a tone CS (Steinmetz, 1990b). The peristimulus time histograms produced with the two CSs were virtually identical, both showing strong CR-related activity. The behavioral data from this study were also interesting. The rabbits showed extremely rapid transfer of training when the pontine CS was switched to a tone CS. In fact, a few rabbits showed CRs on the very first tone presentation thus arguing very strongly that the electrical stimulation activated pontine neurons that normally project tone information to the cerebellum during conditioning.

Using single pulse stimulation of the pontine nuclei, we have since followed up these stimulation-CS studies with mapping studies in acute, anesthetized rabbits to identify precisely to where in cerebellar cortex and the deep cerebellar nuclei inputs from the pontine nuclei are distributed (e.g., Gould, Sears & Steinmetz, 1993). More recently, Tracy and Steinmetz (1998) recorded from single Purkinje cells using a pontine stimulation CS and an air puff US. The cerebellar cortical cells showed learning-related as well as stimulus-related discharge patterns (i.e., similar to recordings involving tone CSs). Few inhibitory patterns of Purkinje cell discharges were seen, relative to tone-trained rabbits, thus suggesting that recruitment of these cells during conditioning is dependent on brain areas not stimulated in this experiment.

Tracy, Thompson, Krupa and Thompson (1998) have provided some indirect evidence of plasticity in the pontocerebellar CS pathway. They measured electrical stimulation thresholds required to elicit eyeblinks with either pontine or cerebellar interpositus nucleus stimulation before and after conditioning with a pontine-stimulation-CS and air puff US. They demonstrated a decrease in pontine stimulation thresholds after learning while interpositus nucleus threshold remained stable. The authors suggested that the learning-induced decrease in pontine stimulation threshold may have been the result of increased excitability somewhere in the cerebellar network (in cortex, the deep nuclei or both).

The pontine nucleus is not the only source of mossy fibers that when stimulated as a CS produces conditioned responding. Lavond, Knowlton, Steinmetz and Thompson (1987) showed that stimulation of the lateral reticular nucleus (LRN), an alternate source of mossy fibers, resulted in robust conditioned responding. Extinction could be obtained when LRN-stimulation-alone trials were delivered and unpaired LRN-stimulation CS - air puff US trials produced no pseudoconditioning. In addition, lesions of the deep cerebellar nuclei abolished CRs formed with the LRN-stimulation-CS while leaving intact the UR. The LRN projects mainly to the deep cerebellar nuclei via the inferior cerebellar peduncle and receives input from the red nucleus, spinal cord and cerebral cortex. While it is unlikely that this nucleus is involved in projecting auditory or light CSs to the cerebellum during conditioning (because auditory and visual information does not seem to be processed in the LRN), it seems possible that proprioceptive and tactile CSs may be processed via this route as these fibers are known to convey proprioceptive information involved in developing motor skills.

Similar microstimulation experiments have been conducted concerning the US pathway from the periphery to the cerebellum. Mauk, Steinmetz and Thompson (1986) showed that inferior olive stimulation could evoke discrete responses that included head and trunk movements, limb movements and eye blinks. Furthermore, when a tone CS preceded the electrical stimulation of the inferior olive, normal rates of classical conditioning could be produced. The response that was conditioned was the response elicited by the olive-stimulation-US (including eyeblinks). Furthermore, lesions of the interpositus nucleus abolished not only the CR produced by the CS-US pairings, but also the UR elicited by stimulation. These data provide strong evidence that neurons in the inferior olive are responsible for relay information about the US to the cerebellum during conditioning.

We have also shown that rather normal rates and levels of conditioning can be obtained when a pontine-stimulation-CS was paired with an olive-stimulation-US (Steinmetz, Lavond, & Thompson, 1989). The CRs established with this procedure could be extinguished with either CS-alone or unpaired CS and US presentations. The results of this experiment provide strong evidence that critical sites of plasticity associated with acquisition and performance of the conditioned eyeblink response reside in areas of the cerebellum, the only structure efferent to the points of stimulation.

Other investigations have employed brain stimulation methods to delineate the US pathway. Schreurs (1987) showed that stimulation of the spinal trigeminal nucleus elicited eyeblink URs. Furthermore, trigeminal stimulation as a US has been shown to support conditioning (Nowak & Gormezano, 1990; Schreurs, 1988). These results are compatible with the idea that the inferior olive is involved in projecting US information to the cerebellum; a major target of trigeminal axons is the area of the inferior olive stimulated by Mauk et al (1986). Nowak, Marshall-Goodell, Kehoe and Gormezano (1997) further reported that when electrical stimulation was delivered to the interpositus nucleus or red nucleus as a US and paired with an auditory CS, eye blink CRs could be produced. This finding was not in agreement with an earlier report by Chapman, Steinmetz & Thompson (1988) who observed no eyeblink CRs with paired tone CS and stimulation USs delivered to either the red nucleus or interpositus nucleus (although CR acquisition was very rapid in animals that had received interpositus nucleus stimulation once tone CS - air puff US trials were begun). One possible explanation for these discrepant findings may be differences in stimulation parameters used for training (i.e., the Nowak et al. study used more intense, higher frequency stimulation than did Chapman et al.).

Finally, studies involving stimulation of the cerebellum have also been conducted to provide further evidence on the involvement of the structure in encoding classical eyeblink conditioning. Brogden and Gantt (1937, 1942) were the first to use cerebellar stimulation during classical conditioning. They showed that discrete motor responses (URs) could be elicited by activating induction coils that were implanted into the cerebellum. When the cerebellar-stimulation-US was paired with an auditory CS, CRs were observed. Swain, Shinkman, Nordholm and Thompson (1992) similarly reported successful eyeblink conditioning in rabbits when an auditory CS was paired with electrical stimulation of the cerebellar white matter as a US. Taking this preparation one step further, Shinkman, Swain and Thompson (1996) implanted two sets of electrodes into the cerebellum. One set was placed in cortical parallel fibers and was used to deliver a CS while the second set was placed in underlying cerebellar white matter and was used to deliver a US (which generated a variety of discrete responses). Paired stimulation-CS and -US trials resulted in the development of conditioned responses that could be extinguished with CS-alone presentations. A substantial reduction in the CS threshold for response elicitation was observed in all subjects thus suggesting that local excitability changes accompanied the paired stimulations. These results provided additional support for the idea that critical plasticity underlying acquisition and performance of the classically conditioned eyeblink response occurred in the cerebellum.

SOME CONCLUDING REMARKS

It should be clear from the data presented above that neural recording and microstimulation methods have played key roles in the delineation of neural structures and systems involved in classical eyeblink conditioning. The single-unit and multi-unit recording studies have been particularly useful for identifying those areas of the brain that are activated during conditioning. These studies have shown areas such as the pontine nuclei, trigeminal nucleus, and inferior olive are involved in projecting information about the conditioning stimuli to more central brain areas where critical associations between the stimuli are made. Other studies have demonstrated that structures like the hippocampus, neostriatum, and perhaps most importantly, the cerebellum are important loci where critical cellular plasticity processes associated with conditioning occur. Future studies using template matching algorithms coupled with multi-electrode recording should further our understanding of how neurons change with experience and how the firings of individual members of populations of neurons are related to one another. Microstimulation experiments have also proven valuable for delineating neural circuits involved in eyeblink conditioning. The CS and US pathways responsible for projecting information to central brain areas, such as the cerebellum, were for the most part discovered using these techniques. Of particular note were the stimulus substitution experiments where electrical stimulation was substituted for peripheral CSs and USs during conditioning. Important future experiments will likely couple microstimulation methods with neural recording, especially those experiments designed to test threshold changes in excitability along important links in the neural circuitry that underlies this simple form of associative learning.

REFERENCES

Aou, S., Woody, C.D., & Birt, D. (1992). Increases in excitability of neurons of the motor cortex of cats after rapid acquisition of eye blink conditioning. *Journal of Neuroscience, 12*, 560-569.

Berger, T.W., Clark, G.A., & Thompson, R.F. (1980). Learning-dependent neuronal responses recorded from limbic system brain structures during classical conditioning. *Physiological Psychology, 8*, 155-167.

Berger, T.W., Rinaldi, P.S., Weisz, D.J., & Thompson, R.F. (1983). Single-unit analysis of different hippocampal cell types during classical conditioning of rabbit nictitating membrane response. *Journal of Neurophysiology, 50*, 1197-1219.

Berger, T.W., & Thompson, R.F. (1978a). Neuronal plasticity n the limbic system during classical conditioning of the rabbit nictitating membrane response: I. The hippocampus. *Brain Research, 145*, 323-346.

Berger, T.W., & Thompson, R.F. (1978b). Neuronal plasticity n the limbic system during classical conditioning of the rabbit nictitating membrane response: II. Septum and mammillary bodies. *Brain Research, 156*, 293-314.

Berthier, N.E., & Moore, J.W. (1986). Cerebellar Purkinje cell activity related to the classically conditioned nictitating membrane response. *Experimental Brain Research, 63*, 341-350.

Berthier, N.E. & Moore, J.W. (1990). Activity of deep cerebellar nucleus cells during classical conditioning of nictitating membrane extension in rabbits. *Experimental Brain Research, 83*, 44-54.

Brogden, W.J., & Gantt, W.H. (1937). Cerebellar conditioned reflexes. *American Journal of Physiology, 119*, 277-278.

Brogden, W.J., & Gantt, W.H. (1942). Intraneural conditioning. *Archives of Neurology and Psychiatry, 48*, 437-455.

Brons, J.F., & Woody, C.D. (1980). Long-term changes in excitability of cortical neurons after Pavlovian conditioning and extinction. *Journal of Neurophysiology, 44*, 605-615.

Cartford, M.C., Gohl, E., Singson, M., & Lavond, D.G. (1997). The effects of reversible inactivation of the red nucleus on learning-related and auditory-evoked unit activity in the pontine nuclei of classically conditioned rabbits. *Learning & Memory, 3*, 519-531.

Cegavske, C.F., Patterson, M.M., & Thompson, R.F. (1979). Neuronal unit activity in the abducens nucleus during classical conditioning of the nictitating membrane response in the rabbit (*Orytalagus cuniculus*). *Journal of Comparative and Physiological Psychology, 93*, 595-609.

Chapman, P.F., Steinmetz, J.E., Sears, L.L., & Thompson, R.F. (1990). Effects of lidocaine injection in the interpositus nucleus and red nucleus on conditioned behavioral and neuronal responses. *Brain Research, 537*, 149-156.

Chapman, P.F., Steinmetz, J.E., & Thompson, R.F. (1988). Classical conditioning does not occur when direct stimulation of the red nucleus or cerebellar nuclei is the unconditioned stimulus. *Brain Research, 442*, 97-104.

Clark, G.A., McCormick, D.A., Lavond, D.G., & Thompson, R.F. (1984). Effects of lesions of cerebellar nuclei on conditioned behavioral and hippocampal neuronal responses. *Brain Research, 291*, 125-136.

Clark, R.E., & Lavond, D.G. (1996). Neural unit activity in the trigeminal complex with interpositus or red nucleus inactivation during classical eyeblink conditioning. *Behavioral Neuroscience, 110*, 13-21.

Desmond, J.E., & Moore, J.W. (1991). Single-unit activity in red nucleus during the classically conditioned rabbit nictitating membrane response. *Neuroscience Research, 10*, 260-279.

Disterhoft, J.F., Thompson, L.T., & Moyer, Jr., J.R. (1994). Cellular mechanisms of associative learning in the hippocampus. In J. Delacour (Ed.), *The Memory System of the Brain* (pp. 431-492). New Jersey: World Scientific.

Doty, R.W., Rutledge, L.T., & Larsen, R.M. (1956). Conditioned reflexes established to electric stimulation of cat cerebral cortex. *Journal of Neurophysiology, 19*, 401-415.

Gould, T.J., Sears, L.L., & Steinmetz, J.E. (1993). Possible CS and US pathways for rabbit classical eyelid conditioning: Electrophysiological evidence for projections from the pontine nuclei and inferior olive to cerebellar cortex and nuclei. *Behavioral and Neural Biology, 60*, 172-185.

Gould, T.J., & Steinmetz, J.E. (1994). Multiple unit activity from rabbit cerebellar cortex and interpositus nucleus during classical discrimination/reversal eyelid conditioning. *Brain Research, 652*, 98-106.

Gould, T.J., & Steinmetz, J.E. (1996). Changes in rabbit cerebellar cortical and interpositus nucleus activity during acquisition, extinction and backward classical conditioning. *Neurobiology of Learning and Memory, 65*, 17-34.

Hesslow, G., & Ivarsson, M. (1996). Inhibition of the inferior olive during conditioned responses in the decerebrate ferret. *Experimental Brain Research, 110*, 36-46.

Hoehler, F.K., & Thompson, R.F. (1980). Neural unit activity in an anterior "nonspecific" cortical area during classical conditioning of the rabbit's nictitating membrane response. *Bulletin of the Psychonomic Society, 15*, 61-64.

Katz, D.B., & Steinmetz, J.E. (1997). Single-unit evidence for eyeblink conditioning in cerebellar cortex is altered, but not eliminated, by interpositus nucleus lesions. *Learning & Memory, 4(1)*, 88-104.

Knowlton, B.J. & Thompson, R.F. (1989). Stimulation of the lateral septum is a more effective conditioned stimulus than stimulation of the medial septum during classical conditioning of the eye-blink response. *Behavioral Neuroscience, 103*, 206-208.

Lavond, D.G., Knowlton, B.J., Steinmetz, J.E., & Thompson, R.F. (1987). Classical conditioning of the rabbit eyelid response with a mossy-fiber stimulation CS. II. Lateral reticular nucleus stimulation. *Behavioral Neuroscience, 101*, 676-682.

Loucks, R.B. (1933). Preliminary report of a technique for stimulation or destructions of tissues beneath the integument and the establishing of conditioned responses with faradization of the cerebral cortex. *Journal of Comparative Physiology, 16*, 439-444.

Martin, G.K., Land, T., & Thompson, R.F. (1980). Classical conditioning of the rabbit (*Oryctalagus cuniculus*) nictitating membrane response using electrical brain stimulation as the unconditioned stimulus. *Journal of Comparative and Physiological Psychology, 94*, 216-226.

Mauk, M.D., Steinmetz, J.E., & Thompson, R.F. (1986). Classical conditioning using stimulation of the inferior olive as the unconditioned stimulus. *Proceedings of the National Academy of Sciences (USA), 83*, 5349-5353.

McEchron, M.D., & Disterhoft, J.F. (1997). Sequence of single neuron changes in CA1 hippocampus of rabbits during acquisition of trace eyeblink conditioned responses. *Journal of Neurophysiology, 78*, 1030-1044.

McCormick, D.A., & Thompson, R.F. (1984). Neuronal responses of the rabbit cerebellum during acquisition and performance of a classically conditioned nictitating membrane-eyelid response. *Journal of Neuroscience, 4*, 2811-2822.

Miller, D.P., & Steinmetz, J.E. (1992). Lesions of the rabbit cerebellar interpositus nucleus affect classical NM conditioned-related activity in the lateral but not the medial septum. *Physiology & Behavior, 52*, 83-89.

Miller, D.P., & Steinmetz, J.E. (1997). Hippocampal activity during discrimination/reversal eyeblink conditioning in rabbits. *Behavioral Neuroscience, 111*, 70-79.

Mis, F.W., Gormezano, I., & Harvey, J.A. (1979). Stimulation of abducens nucleus supports classical conditioning of the nictitating membrane response. *Science, 206*, 473-475.

Neilson, H.C., Knight, J.M., & Porter, P.B. (1962). Subcortical conditioning, generalization, and transfer. *Journal of Comparative and Physiological Psychology, 55*, 168-173.

Nowak, A.J., & Gormezano, I. (1990). Electrical stimulation of brainstem nuclei: Elicitation, modification, and conditioning of the rabbit nictitating membrane response. *Behavioral Neuroscience, 104*, 49-56.

Nowak, A.J., Marshall-Goodell, B., Kehoe, E.J., & Gormezano, I. (1997). Elicitation, modification, and conditioning of the rabbit nictitating membrane response by electrical stimulation in the spinal trigeminal nucleus, inferior olive, interpositus nucleus, and red nucleus. *Behavioral Neuroscience, 111*, 1041-1055.

Patterson, M.M. (1970). Classical conditioning of the rabbit's (*Oryctolagus cuniculus*) nictitating membrane response with fluctuating ISI and intracranial CS. *Journal of Comparative and Physiological Psychology, 72*, 193-202.

Patterson, M.M. (1971). Inferior colliculus CS intensity effect on rabbit nictitating membrane conditioning. *Physiology & Behavior, 6*, 273-278.

Powell, G.M., & Moore, J.W. (1980). Conditioning of the nictitating membrane response in rabbit (*Oryctolagus cuniculus*) with electrical brain stimulation as the unconditioned stimulus. *Physiology & Behavior, 25*, 205-216.

Prokasy, W.F., Kesner, R.P., & Calder, L.D. (1983). Posttrial electrical stimulation of the dorsal hippocampus facilitates acquisition of the nictitating membrane response. *Behavioral Neuroscience, 97*, 890-896.

Richards, W.G., Ricciardi, T.N., & Moore, J.W. (1991). Activity of spinal trigeminal pars oralis and adjacent reticular formation units during differential conditioning of the rabbit nictitating membrane response. *Behavioural Brain Research, 44*, 195-204.

Robinson, G.B. (1992). Reversal learning of the rabbit nictitating membrane response following kindling-induced potentiation within the hippocampal dentate gyrus. *Behavioural Brain Research, 50*, 185-192.

Robinson, G.B., Port, R.L., & Berger, T.W. (1989). Kindling facilitates acquisition of discriminative responding but disrupts reversal learning of the rabbit nictitating membrane response. *Behavioural Brain Research, 31*, 279-283.

Rolls, E.T., & Williams, G.V. (1987). Sensory and movement-related neuronal activity in different regions of the primate striatum. In J.S. Schneider & T.I. Lidsky (Eds.), *Basal ganglia and behavior: Sensory aspects of motor functioning* (pp 37-59), Toronto: Huber.

Salafia, W.R., Romano, A.G., Tynan, T., & Host, K.C. (1977). Disruption of rabbit (*Oryctolagus cuniculus*) nictitating membrane conditioning by posttrial electrical stimulation of hippocampus. *Physiology & Behavior, 18*, 207-212.

Schmaltz, L.W., & Theios, J. (1972). Acquisition and extinction of a classically conditioned response in hippocampectomized rabbits (*Oryctolagus cuniculus*). *Journal of Comparative and Physiological Psychology, 79*, 328-333.

Schreurs, B.G. (1987). Parameters and sites of brainstem stimulation capable of eliciting the rabbit nictitating membrane response. *Behavioural Brain Research, 25*, 155-160.

Schreurs, B.G. (1988). Stimulation of the spinal trigeminal supports classical conditioning of the rabbit's nictitating membrane response. *Behavioral Neuroscience, 102*, 163-172.

Schreurs, B.G., Oh, M.M., & Alkon, D.L. (1996). Pairing specific long-term depression of Purkinje cell excitatory postsynaptic potentials results from a classical conditioning procedure in the rabbit cerebellar slice. *Journal of Neurophysiology, 75*, 1051-1060.

Schreurs, B.G., Sanchez-Andres, J.V., & Alkon, D.L. (1991). Learning-specific differences in Purkinje-cell dendrites of lobule HVI (Lobus simplex): intracellular recording in a rabbit cerebellar slice. *Brain Research, 548*, 18-22.

Sears, L.L., Logue, S.F., & Steinmetz, J.E. (1996). Involvement of the ventrolateral thalamus in rabbit classical eyeblink conditioning. *Behavioural Brain Research, 74*, 105-117.

Sears, L.L., & Steinmetz, J.E. (1990). Acquisition of classically conditioned-related activity in the hippocampus is affected by lesions of the cerebellar interpositus nucleus. *Behavioral Neuroscience, 104*, 681-692.

Sears, L.L., & Steinmetz, J.E. (1991). Dorsal accessory inferior olive activity diminishes during acquisition of the rabbit classically conditioned eyelid response. *Brain Research, 545*, 114-122.

Shinkman, P.G., Swain, R.A., Thompson, R.F. (1996). Classical conditioning with electrical stimulation of cerebellum as both conditioned and unconditioned stimulus. *Behavioral Neuroscience, 110*, 914-921.

Steinmetz, J.E. (1990a). Classical nictitating membrane conditioning in rabbits with varying interstimulus intervals and direct activation of cerebellar mossy fibers as a CS. *Behavioural Brain Research, 38*, 97-108.

Steinmetz, J.E. (1990b). Neuronal activity in the cerebellar interpositus nucleus during classical NM conditioning with a pontine stimulation CS. *Psychological Science, 1*, 378-382.

Steinmetz, J.E. (1996). The brain substrates of classical eyeblink conditioning in rabbits. In J. Bloedel, T. Ebner and S. Wise (Eds.), *Acquisition of Motor behavior in Vertebrates*, (pp. 89-114), Cambridge, MA: MIT Press.

Steinmetz, J.E., Lavond, D.G., & Thompson, R.F. (1989). Classical conditioning in rabbits using pontine nucleus stimulation as a conditioned stimulus and inferior olive stimulation as an unconditioned stimulus. *Synapse, 3(3)*, 225-233.

Steinmetz, J.E., Logan, C.G., Rosen, D.J., Thompson, J.K., Lavond, D.G., & Thompson, R.F. (1987). Initial localization of the acoustic conditioned stimulus projection system to the cerebellum during classical eyelid conditioning. *Proceedings of the National Academy of Sciences (USA)*, 84, 3531-3535.

Steinmetz, J.E., Rosen, D.J., Chapman, P.F., Lavond, D.G., & Thompson, R.F. (1986). Classical conditioning of the rabbit eyelid response with a mossy fiber stimulation CS. I. Pontine nuclei and middle cerebellar peduncle stimulation. *Behavioral Neuroscience, 100*, 871-880.

Swain, R.A., Shinkman, P.G., Nordholm, A.F., & Thompson, R.F. (1992). Cerebellar stimulation as an unconditioned stimulus in classical conditioning. *Behavioral Neuroscience, 106*, 739-750.

Tracy, J., & Steinmetz, J.E. (1998). Purkinje cell responses to pontine stimulation CS during rabbit eyeblink conditioning. *Physiology & Behavior, 65(2)*, 381-386..

Tracy, J., Thompson, J.K., Krupa, D.J., & Thompson, R.F. (1998). Evidence of plasticity in the pontocerebellar conditioned stimulus pathway during classical conditioning of the eyeblink response in the rabbit. *Behavioral Neuroscience, 112*, 267-285.

White, I.M., Miller, D.P., White, W., Dike, G.L., Rebec, G.V., & Steinmetz, J.E. (1994). Neuronal activity in rabbit neostriatum during classical eyelid conditioning. *Experimental Brain Research, 99*, 179-190.

Woody, C.D., & Black-Cleworth, P. (1973). Differences in excitability of cortical neurons as a function of motor projection in conditioned cats. *Journal of Neurophysiology, 36*, 1104-1116.

Yeomans, J.S. (1990). *Principles of Brain Stimulation*. New York: Oxford University Press.

5 DEVELOPMENTAL STUDIES OF EYEBLINK CONDITIONING IN THE RAT

Mark E. Stanton
Neurotoxicology Division
United States Environmental Protection Agency
University of North Carolina at Chapel Hill

John H. Freeman Jr.
University of Iowa

INTRODUCTION

Research on classical eyeblink conditioning has come a long way since its early days (Hilgard 1931; Hilgard & Marquis 1940; Chapters 1 and 2 this volume). The range of topics encompassed by this research—theories of learning, memory, and motivation; systems and cellular neurobiology; neural network models; lifespan development and aging; human neurological disorders and cognitive neuroscience—is remarkably broad and deep (see other contributions to this volume and its companion volume on human applications). With eyeblink conditioning it is now possible to study motivational associative and cognitive processes in both laboratory animals and humans at both neurobiological and behavioral levels in an integrated manner with the same experimental procedure. This integrative power is arguably unmatched by any other single learning paradigm.

These advances in research have created an extraordinary opportunity to apply eyeblink conditioning to life-span studies of learning (Chapter 7 this volume; Stanton & Freeman 1994; Stanton, Freeman & Skelton 1992; Woodruff-Pak & Thompson 1988). Here we focus on how behavioral, neurobiological, and comparative properties of this paradigm can advance developmental psychobiology. The minimal sensory, motor, and motivational demands of eyeblink conditioning make it suitable with little or no modification for subjects from early infancy to old age. Associative learning is readily distinguished from nonassociative forms of behavioral change by comparing paired versus unpaired training conditions. Learning versus performance is also readily distinguished by comparing the conditioned and unconditioned eyeblink reflex. Parametric control of eyeblink conditioning is precise and well documented. An impressive range of nonassociative, associative, and cognitive processes can be readily probed simply by manipulating parameters of eyeblink conditioning (Wagner & Brandon 1989). This can also be done by contrasting "higher order" conditioning phenomena with simple associative learning (e.g., Schmajuk & Dicarlo 1991). These behavioral properties of the eyeblink conditioning paradigm are ideally suited for studies of mammalian development.

A great deal is known about the ontogeny of associative learning in animals, particularly the rat (Kail & Spear 1984; Krasnegor, Blass, Hofer & Smotherman, 1986; Spear & Campbell 1978; Shair, Barr & Hofer 1991; Rudy 1992; Spear & Rudy 1991). The developmental emergence of simple conditioning depends on the specific sensorimotor systems that are engaged in a given learning episode. Chemosensory conditioning appears earlier than auditory or visual conditioning; somatomotor conditioned responses (CRs) appear earlier in development than autonomic CRs and within these different sensory and effector systems simple delay conditioning often appears earlier in development than "higher order" conditioning phenomena (see Nicolle, Barry, Veronesi & Stanton, 1989; Rudy, 1992; Hunt & Campbell, 1996). However special developmental predispositions can also result in the appearance of "higher order" phenomena during transient stages of infancy (Spear, Kraemer, Molina & Smoller, 1988). This literature suggests that there are multiple "simple engrams" that develop independently but that also come to interact with sensory, motor, motivational, and cognitive processes according to overlapping, complex, and sometimes counterintuitive developmental timetables (Stanton, in press). It is therefore impossible to study the ontogeny of learning separately from the behavioral organization in which this learning is imbedded. This makes the task of unravelling these complex ontogenetic interactions very challenging. At a purely behavioral level, the analytic (and synthetic) properties of eyeblink conditioning provide a tractable approach to this difficult task.

The neurobiological properties of eyeblink conditioning are also an important advantage for developmental studies of learning. Eyeblink conditioning depends on neural structures—cerebellum and hippocampus—that show dramatic maturational changes across a protracted period of ontogeny, particularly in the altricial rat (Altman, 1982; Altman & Bayer, 1975). A great deal is known about the developmental neurobiology of these structures, not only in rodents but from a comparative standpoint as well (e.g., Altman & Bayer, 1996; Bayer et al., 1993; Kretschmann, Kammradt, Krauthausen, Sauer & Wingert, 1986; Diamond, 1990). In the rat, the volume of the cerebellar cortex increases more than 20-fold during the first three postnatal weeks. Cells of the deep nuclei, Purkinje cells, and brain stem nuclei that are afferent and efferent to the cerebellum, are formed before birth. In contrast, cerebellar granule stellate and basket cells are generated during the first 2-3 postnatal weeks. These cell types also undergo extensive morphological, physiological, and neurochemical development, which continues through the fifth postnatal week. Dendritic expansion and synaptogensis of these cell types begins during the second week and continues through postnatal day (PND) 30 (Berry & Bradley, 1976) and determines the growth and morphology of Purkinje cell dendrites. The spontaneous firing of Purkinje cells develops between PND10 and 20 and looks adult-like after PND21 (Crepel, 1972). Climbing fiber excitation of Purkinje cells can be seen at PND3 and mossy fiber excitation of Purkinje cells can be seen at PND7 but the patterns of these responses continue to develop until PND21 (Puro & Woodward, 1977; Crepel, 1971). Purkinje cells are initially innervated by multiple climbing fibers, with the adult pattern of innervation by a single climbing fiber emerging around PND15 (Crepel, 1971; Crepel,

Mariani & Bouchaud, 1976). Neurotransmitter systems and calcium mediated signal transduction mechanisms in the cerebellum also undergo dramatic postnatal development in the rat. Gamma-aminobutyric acid (GABA) immunoreactivity and glutamic acid decarboxylase (GAD; the synthesizing enzyme for GABA) mRNAs in Purkinje and Golgi cells increase through the first three postnatal weeks (Aoki, Semba & Kashiwamata, 1989; Willcutts & Morrison-Bogorad, 1991; Greif, Eflander, Tillakaratne & Tobin, 1991). Expression of glutamate receptor mRNAs in Purkinje and granule cells also increases during the first three postnatal weeks, suggesting late maturation of granule cell innervation (Pellegrini-Giampietro, Bennett & Zukin, 1991). Finally there is a wealth of information on the effects of antiproliferative agents such as methlazoxymethanol (MAM) and x-irradiation on cerebellar development (Altman & Bayer, 1996; Chen & Hillman, 1986; 1989). The duration, pattern, and timing of x-irradiation during the neonatal period targets different populations of cerebellar neurons (Altman & Bayer, 1996). This extensive knowledge of cerebellar development creates an unusual opportunity for behavioral investigation. Research on the role of the cerebellum in the conditioned eyeblink response has generated models of a brainstem-cerebellar circuit that is necessary and sufficient for learning and empirical methods for probing it (see Thompson, 1986; Chapters 4 and 10; this volume). By applying these models and methods to the developing cerebellum, there is an opportunity to specify and characterize the relation between brain maturation and learning in ways that were previously not possible. Neurobiological studies in developing rodents have focussed on the neural substrates and correlates of early olfactory conditioning (Hall, 1987; Wilson et al., 1991). These studies have provided important insights about sensory and ecological determinants of neural plasticity and behavior but they have been limited by an inability to completely specify the circuitry (particularly efferent pathways) underlying the learned behavior. This problem is overcome by eyeblink conditioning which offers for the first time the prospect of analyzing the ontogeny of learning in terms of a delineated neural circuit.

Eyeblink conditioning can also advance the effort to understand the the role of the hippocampus in the ontogeny of memory and cognition (Altman et al., 1973; Douglas, 1975; Amsel & Stanton, 1980; Nadel & Zola-Morgan, 1984; Rudy, 1992). It is clear that multiple brain memory systems show different developmental profiles and that this may reflect modulation of early developing associative systems by later developing cognitive systems (e.g., Rudy, 1992). However this developmental research has been limited by an inability to specify the neural bases of the *simpler* systems through which cognition is expressed (Stanton, in press). The eyeblink conditioning paradigm offers the potential to understand cognitive development in terms of hippocampal-cerebellar interactions that are becoming increasingly well characterized empirically and theoretically (Chapter 10, this volume; Schmajuk & DiCarlo, 1991; Schmajuk, 2000). Understanding the development of a cognitive system involving the hippocampus via its relations with an identified brainstem-cerebellar circuit for associative learning has the potential to advance developmental psychobiology in many important new ways (Stanton, in press).

One final advantage that we briefly mention is the contribution that eyeblink conditioning can make to studies of human memory development and developmental disorders (Chapter 6, this volume; Ivkovich et al., 2000; Lipsitt, 1990; Sears et al.,

1994; Sears & Steinmetz, 2000; Stanton & Freeman, 1994). There are few, if any, behavioral procedures in human infancy research that can be used as early as 10 days of age (Little, Lipsett & Rovee-Collier, 1984), can be used without modification across subsequent development, can be linked to postnatally developing neural systems and circuits, and can be linked to a developmental animal model, in the way that eyeblink conditioning can. Eyeblink conditioning therefore provides a very rare opportunity to integrate studies of the psychobiology of learning and memory in both infant humans and animals (Ivkovich et al., 2000; Rovee-Collier, 1986). This is true also for studies of developmental neurobehavioral disorders. Disorders which involve abberant maturation of the cerebellum and/or hippocampus include autism, schizophrenia, Downs Syndrome, neonatal hypoxic ischemia, undernutrition, hypoglycemia, hypothroidism, and developmental exposure to methylmercury, anticonvulsants, lead, retinoids, and alcohol (see review of Stanton & Freeman, 1994; Chapter 6, this volume; Sears & Steinmetz, 2000). Because eyeblink conditioning offers so many ways to probe cerebellar and hippocampal function, *developmental* applications of this paradigm could result in major new discoveries concerning the etiology and mechanisms of these developmental disorders (Stanton & Freeman, 1994).

Clearly developmental studies of eyeblink conditioning have vast potential. A broad program of research is already emerging which encompasses topics ranging from the developmental analysis of the neural mechanisms underlying simple associative learning (Freeman & Nicholson, 1999), to the ontogeny of multiple memory systems in animals and humans (Ivkovich et al., 2000; Stanton, in press), to the early characterization and treatment of developmental disorders (Stanton & Freeman, 1994; Chapter 6, this volume). In order to limit the scope of the present chapter, we confine our review to the initial efforts to establish a developmental rodent model of eyeblink conditioning. Our review focusses on our characterization of the ontogeny of simple delay conditioning and its disruption by early damage to the developing cerebellum. Over the long term, we expect this line of developmental research to expand in ways that both harness and enhance the power of the eyeblink conditioning paradigm.

ONTOGENY OF EYEBLINK CONDITIONING

In this section, we describe our methodology and our efforts to characterize behaviorally the ontogeny of delay conditioning in infant rats. Thus far, we have examined learning versus performance, the role of conditioning parameters, and effects of age of training versus testing. These behavioral studies provide a context for studies of the neural substrates underlying the ontogeny of delay conditioning. Studies of neural substrates, which thus far have focussed on effects of early cerebellar damage, are described in the succeeding section.

Methods and Measures

This section provides a very detailed description of our methods for those who may have a special interest in these techniques.

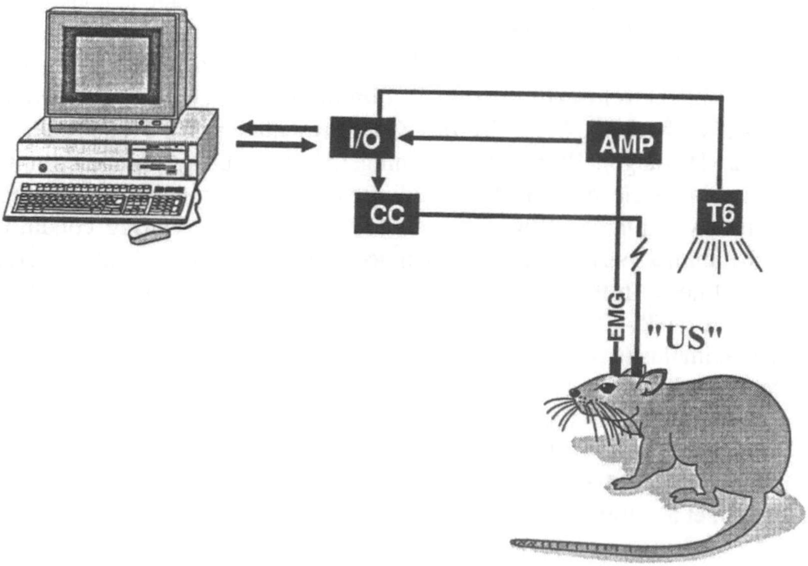

Figure 1. Schematic diagram of the conditioning preparation. The rat is free to locomote within a test chamber. Electromyographic (EMG) recording of the eyelid muscle and brief (100 msec) stimulation of the periocular region ("ZAP") from a constant current stimulator (CC) is accomplished via electrodes that terminate in plugs mounted surgically on a headstage. The EMG recording is amplified (AMP) rectified and integrated via an input/output (I/O) device that interfaces with a personal computer The computer controls via the I/O device delivery of a tone (T6) from a speaker mounted on the wall of the test chamber and of the periocular stimulus from the CC unit. The preparation is adapted from one originally developed by Skelton (1988).

Experimental Preparation

We began our developmental studies of eyeblink conditioning by adapting to infant rats a method for conditioning freely moving adult rats that was developed by Ron Skelton (Skelton, 1988; Figure 1). In our initial studies, we worked collaboratively with Skelton and with his equipment which was shipped to North Carolina for that purpose (Stanton, Freeman & Skelton, 1992; Freeman, Spencer, Skelton & Stanton, 1993). On the basis of our experiences with this equipment, a separate Eyeblink

Conditioning System was custom built "in house" (Systems Support Staff Neurotoxicology Division U.S. EPA Research Triangle Park). This apparatus was used in all of our subsequent studies.

Apparatus

The conditioning apparatus consists of a stainless steel wire mesh cage (22 x 22 x 26 cm) in which animals are allowed to move about freely. This cage is housed within a sound-attenuated chamber (BRS/LVE, Laurel MD). The chamber is lined with acoustic foam (Illbruck, Minneapolis, MN) and is equipped with an exhaust fan (background noise level 62-70 dB [SPL]), dim house light (15 W), and two audio speakers (Radio Shack #004 Fort Worth TX) for presentation of the tone conditioned stimuli (2-12 kHz range). Prior to conditioning, infant rats undergo surgery in which a bipolar stimulating electrode, EMG recording electrode, and insulted strip connector are permanently implanted (Figure 1, see *Surgery* below). During conditioning sessions, the animal's strip connector is connected to a set of wire leads which pass through small holes in the top of the cage and chamber to a commutator (Airflyte Bayonne, #CAY-675-12) suspended above the chamber. Presentations of the tone conditioned stimulus (CS; 2.8 kHz, 90 dB [SPL]) and shock unconditioned stimulus (US; 2 mA, produced by a 60 Hz constant-current square wave (World Precision Instruments, #A365D-B Sarasota FL) are controlled on-line by a personel computer. This computer and custom-built interface also processes and records electromyographic (EMG) activity from the eyelid muscle (see Figure 2; Skelton, 1988; Stanton et al., 1992; Stanton & Freeman, 1994).

Surgery

One day prior to training, rat pups undergo a procedure in which a bipolar stimulating electrode for delivery of the US, an EMG recording electrode to monitor eyelid activity, and associated plugs and connectors for attachment to peripheral equipment, are surgically installed (Figure 1). Each animal is anesthetized by inhalation of Metofane® (methoxyflurane, Pittman-Moore Mundelein, IL). We apply 3 ml of Metofane to absorbent gauze or tissue placed beneath a mesh floor in a closed chamber. Anesthesia is initially achieved by placing pups in the chamber for 3-5 minutes and maintained subsequently by delivery of supplemental Metofane via nose cone as needed. A midline incision is made to expose the surface of the skull. Two "skull hooks" fashioned from stiff wire are inserted superficially under the skull surface (Gilbert & Cain, 1980). These hooks are used to secure electrode connectors to the skull when a headstage is formed from dental acrylic at the end of surgery. (These "skull hooks" are functionally similar to "skull screws" used with adult animals. They are necessary because the infant rat's skull is too thin to support a skull screw [Gilbert & Cain, 1980]). Two (differential) fine-wire EMG electrodes (Medwire #316, SS 3T, teflon insulated) are then implanted in the upper eyelid muscle. Two 26 g needles are inserted vertically through the muscle 2-4 mm apart, an electrode wire is passed through each needle, and then the needles are removed, leaving the electrodes coursing through the eyelid muscle. A ground electrode is placed subcutaneously (s.c.) at the back of the neck. Next a bipolar stimulating electrode (Plastics One, #MS 303/2, Roanoke VA), insulated except for about 0.5 - 1.0 mm at the tip, is placed s.c. with its tips in a v-shape immediately dorsal caudal to the left eye. This electrode is used to deliver the periocular shock US. EMG and ground electrodes terminate in amphenol pins in an insulted strip connector. This strip connector and the terminal of the bipolar electrode are secured to the skull with dental acrylic. Following surgery, pups are returned to their home cages with food and water and monitored during recovery from anesthesia.

Procedure

All of the experiments reviewed in this chapter involve a simple delay conditioning procedure (Figure 2). Unless otherwise noted, a 380-ms tone CS (2.8 kHz, 90 dB [SPL]) overlaps and coterminates with a 100-ms, perioccular shock US (2 mA) producing a 280-ms interstimulus interval (ISI) between CS and US onset. Training sessions consist of 100 trials, 10 blocks of 10 trials with nine paired and one tone-alone test trial per block. The intertrial interval (ISI) averages 30 sec (range = 18-42 sec). In our unpaired control procedure, sessions consist of the same type and number of CS and US presentations. However, CS and US occur in a pseudorandom order such that no more than three presentations of either stimulus occur consecutively; and stimulus presentations occur at an average interval of 15 sec (range = 9-21 sec). Pups typically receive three sessions in one day beginning at 5-hour intervals. In some experiments, six conditioning sessions are run in this manner across two days. Multiple sessions are run over a 1-2 day period because growth and development are so rapid in rat pups that running daily sessions across several days, as is typical with adult rats, confounds maturation and learning (Amsel & Stanton, 1980).

Dependent Measures and Data Analysis

Our Eyeblink Conditioning System (Systems Engineering Staff, Neurotoxicology Division, U.S. EPA, Research Triangle Park, NC) rectifies and integrates the raw EMG signal and samples this signal in 2.5 ms bins during each trial epoch for analysis (Figure 2). Each trial epoch is divided into four time periods: (1) Pre-CS period, a baseline sampling period leading up to presentation of the tone CS; (2) Alpha- or startle-response (SR) period, the first 80 ms after tone onset; (3) CS period, beginning 80 ms after tone onset and ending at the onset of the US on paired trials, or at the end of the trial epoch on CS-alone test trials—EMG activity during this period defines the CR (Figure 2); and (4) US period, the time from offset of the US to the end of the trial—EMG activity during this period defines the UR (the recording is interupted during US presentation). The threshold for registering an EMG response is set at 0.4 arbitrary units above the average baseline amplitude. Measures of percentage, amplitude, latency, and area are calculated for each response type—SR, CR, and

UR—by trial, trial-block, or session, and subjected to appropriate between-within analysis of variance (ANOVA), depending on the design of a given experiment.

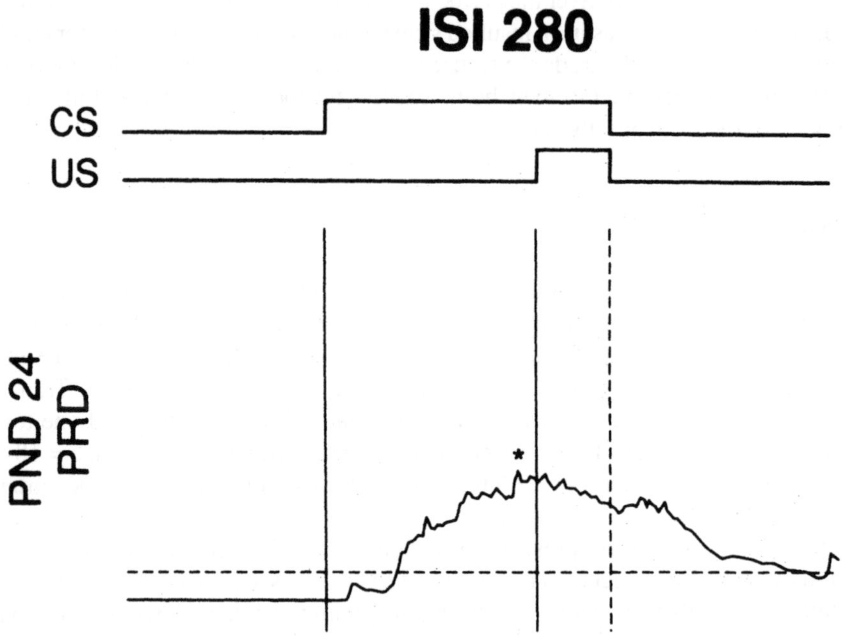

Figure 2. Drawing of a representative trial epoch taken from a 24-day-old rat illustrating a conditioned responsed (CR) on a CS-alone test trial (from Freeman et al., 1993). Upper tracing: A 380 ms conditioned stimulus (CS) overlaps and coterminates with a 100 ms unconditioned stimulus (US) yielding an interstimulus interval of 280 ms (ISI 280). Lower tracing: Vertical solid lines denote CS and US onset dashed line US offset. Horizontal dashed line denotes response threshold (four arbitrary units). Horizontal solid line depicts integrated EMG activity (in arbitrary units) which peaks (note asterisk) around the time of US onset. On paired trials (not shown) the recording is interupted during US presentation and EMG activity following US offset defines the unconditioned response (UR). Note short-latency "alpha" or startle response (SR below threshold) during first 80 ms following CS onset. SR, CR, and UR are measured and analyzed separately (see text for further explanation).

Late Postnatal Development of Auditory Eyeblink Conditioning

In our first study, separate groups of rat pups were trained with either delay conditioning or unpaired control procedures on either PND17 or 24 (Stanton, Freeman & Skelton, 1992). The PND17 age was chosen because it closely follows eye opening (typically about PND15), because auditory fear conditioning is present at this age

(PND16, Campbell & Ampuero, 1985; Rudy, 1992), and because it represents the preweanling period of development (weaning typically occurs on PND21). The PND24 age was arbitrarily chosen because it represents the weanling period of development and entails substantial neural and behavioral maturity.

The results of this experiment are shown in Figure 3. Eyeblink conditioning develops dramatically between PND17 and 24. Rats given paired training on PND17 showed fewer CRs across 10-trial blocks of training than rats tested on PND24. As a result there was a greater difference between paired and unpaired groups on PND24 than on PND17. The age difference in rate of conditioning apparently reflects a difference in the associative determinants of the eyeblink CR.

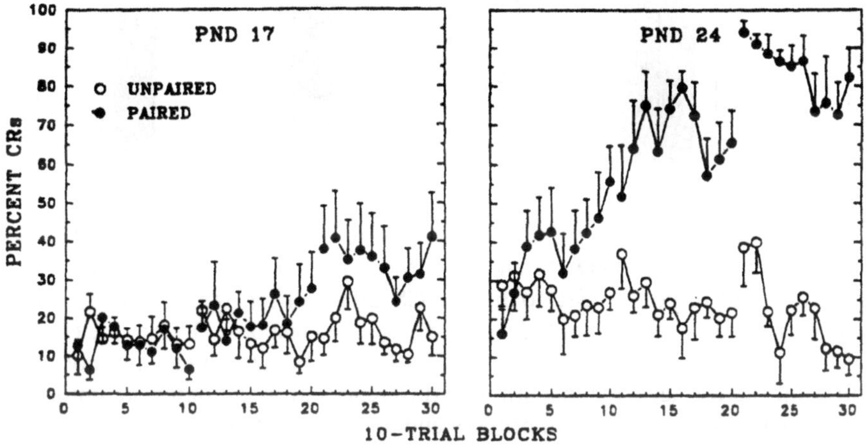

Figure 3. Postnatal development of eyeblink conditioning in rats between Postnatal Day (PND) 17 (left panel) and PND24 (right panel). Mean (± *SE*) percentage conditioned responses (CRs) are shown for separate groups of rats receiving paired training (filled symbols) or unpaired training (open symbols) across three training sessions each containing 10 blocks of 10 trials. Interuption in lines connecting data points indicate (4 -hour) break between sessions (From Stanton et al., 1992).

Dissociation of Learning and Performance

One important advantage of the eyeblink conditioning preparation is that measures of learning are readily dissociated from comparable measures of performance. Processing of the CS can be determined independently by measuring the "alpha-" or startle-response (SR) to the tone whereas processing of the US and motor performance can be determined by measuring the UR (see *Dependent Measures* above). To determine the role of learning versus performance we examined these measures in preweanling and weanling rats (Stanton et al., 1992).

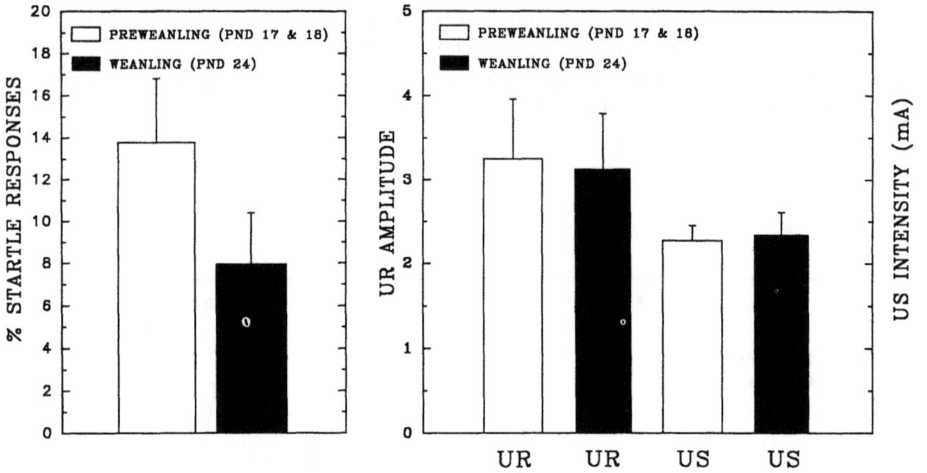

Figure 4. Sensory processing of CS (left panel) and US (right panel) does not change between Postnatal Day (PND) 17 and 24. Mean (± *SE*) percentage of unlearned "alpha" or startle responses (SR) to the tone CS did not differ significantly across age (left panel). Mean (± *SE*) amplitude of unconditioned response (UR) to the US or of the US intensity required to elicit a UR of constant amplitude did not differ significantly across age (right panel). Age differences in conditioning are unlikely to reflect developmental changes in primary auditory function in US efficacy or motor performance (from Stanton et al., 1992).

Figure 4 shows the percentage of startle responses (left panel) and the mean amplitude of the UR and mean US intensities (right panel) obtained at each age. Preweanling pups showed approximately the same percentage of startle responses to the tone CS as weanling pups (left panel). There was a trend toward elevated SRs in the *younger* rats (which showed *poorer* conditioning) but this trend was not statistically significant. In addition there were no age differences in either measure of US processing (right panel). In a separate experiment we looked for "ceiling" and "floor effects" by measuring UR amplitudes evoked by US intensities of 0, 1, 2, and 3 mA (Stanton et al., 1992; Experiment 3; not shown). There was a linear increase in UR amplitude across this range of US intensities. However no age differences were observed at any intensity (consistent with other developmental studies of shock sensitivity; e.g., Haroutunian & Campbell, 1979). Taken together these findings suggest that the difference in rate of conditioning observed over this age range is not secondary to an age difference in auditory function, US efficacy, or ability to perform the motor (eyeblink) response.

Parametric Studies

Another important advantage of eyeblink conditioning is that the parametric "laws of learning" have been well characterized with this preparation (Gormezano, Kehoe & Marshall, 1983). This is especially true for the developmental analysis of learning in which parametric variation plays such an important role (Amsel & Stanton, 1980). In this section we review studies which asked how variation in conditioning parameters would affect the ontogeny of eyeblink conditioning. We undertook these parametric studies for three reasons. First we sought to extend our analysis of learning versus performance. The contribution of, for example, age differences in CS and US processing to the ontogeny of conditioning cannot be fully appreciated without directly examining effects of variation in CS salience or US intensity on conditioning. Such studies of course also provide clues about what behavioral or neural processes are most important developmentally. A second reason is that conditioning parameters that are optimal for training adults may not be optimal for infants. If so, some combination of parameters could reveal conditioning at an earlier age than would be apparent when pups are trained with parameters that are optimal for adults. Finally, because our infant rat conditioning preparation is new, we sought to confirm that the general laws of eyeblink conditioning commonly observed in other preparations also apply to our preparation (at least at stages of development when conditioning is observed). This is important for the claim that we are in fact studying eyeblink conditioning.

Arousal

Arousal or stress can alter the rate of eyeblink conditioning (e.g., Berry & Swain, 1989; Shors, Weiss & Thompson, 1992; Taylor, 1951). For example, water deprivation increases rate of nictitating membrane response (NMR) conditioning in rabbits (Berry & Swain, 1989; Chapter 12 in this volume). We examined the role of arousal in the ontogeny of eyeblink conditioning as part of the early development of our methodology. In our first two experiments (Stanton et al., 1992), preweanling rat pups were not returned to their home litters following surgery because we were concerned that their mothers would chew or otherwise damage the pup's headstages. Instead we individually housed them and hand fed them light cream during the experiment in an attempt to mitigate the nutritive component of maternal deprivation. Nevertheless this procedure likely resulted in some stress in rat pups at this age (Stanton et al., 1988) and so we performed an experiment to directly test the effect of deprivation on eyeblink conditioning in developing rats (Stanton et al., 1992; Experiment 4). Separate groups of rat pups were either returned to their home cage following surgery where they remained except during test sessions (we discovered that maternal rats do not damage their pups headstages) or they were housed individually without food or water until the end of the experiment (24-32 hours later). We found that deprivation increased rate of conditioning in both PND17 and 24 rats, consistent with Berry & Swain (1989). Interestingly PND17 rats that were not deprived showed no conditioning whatsoever across three 100-trial sessions whereas their deprived counterparts showed a modest increase in percentage CRs in the third session (like that shown in Figure 3). However, there was a large age difference in rate of eyeblink conditioning regardless of deprivation condition. This indicates that age differences in arousal cannot explain the ontogenetic emergence of eyeblink conditioning, although arousal can modulate conditioning rate during development as it does in adulthood. In all of our subsequent experiments we have avoided deprivation and housed all subjects in their (developmentally appropriate) home environment.

Interstimulus Interval

In adult eyeblink conditioning there is an interval between CS and US onset that is optimal for conditioning. Studies of interstimulus interval (ISI) functions indicate that 250-500 ms is the optimal ISI in rabbits (Smith, Coleman & Gormezano, 1969). However studies in 10-30-day-old human neonates show better conditioning with a 1500 ms than a 500 ms ISI (Little, Lipsitt & Rovee-Collier, 1984). This suggests that optimal ISI parameters for adults may not be optimal for eyeblink conditioning in infants. To determine whether the same is true of infant rats we performed a study in which PND17 or 24 rats were trained with ISIs of 280, 560, 1120, or 1960 ms, under either paired or unpaired conditions (Freeman et al., 1993). The main result of this experiment is shown in Figure 5. At the 280 ms ISI, conditioning was seen only in 24-day-old rats trained in the paired condition. There was no evidence of conditioning —defined as significantly better performance in a paired group than its unpaired control—at any other combination of age and ISI. Thus, conditioning in PND24 rats declined at longer ISIs. This decline is similar to (though perhaps steeper than) that observed in studies of adult subjects (Kimble, 1947; Smith et al., 1969). Importantly, conditioning in PND17 rats did not improve at longer ISIs, indicating that our failure to observe conditioning at this age is not the result of an inappropriately short ISI. The finding that human infants show better conditioning at longer ISIs (Rovee-Collier et al., 1984) may not have much generality (see Ivkovich et al., 2000).

US Intensity

In eyeblink conditioning, rate and asymptote of learning increase with increasing US intensity (Smith, 1968; Spence, 1953). In order to determine the effect of this parameter on age differences in eyeblink conditioning, pups received paired or unpaired training on PND17 or 24 with either a 1 or 3 mA US. These US intensity levels "bracket" the 2 mA US used in our other experiments and match the values employed in our parametric study of UR amplitude (see above). On PND24, use of a 1.0 mA US failed to support conditioning whereas the 3.0 mA US resulted in rapid conditioning (Figure 6, right panel). Pups trained on PND17 did not show conditioning at either US intensity (Figure 6, left panel). Comparison with conditioning produced by a 2.0 mA US (Figure 5, top left panel) suggests that CR amplitude increases systematically across US intensities of 1.0 2.0 and 3.0 mA in PND24 rats but fails entirely to increase in PND17 rats. In contrast, UR amplitude increases in an identical

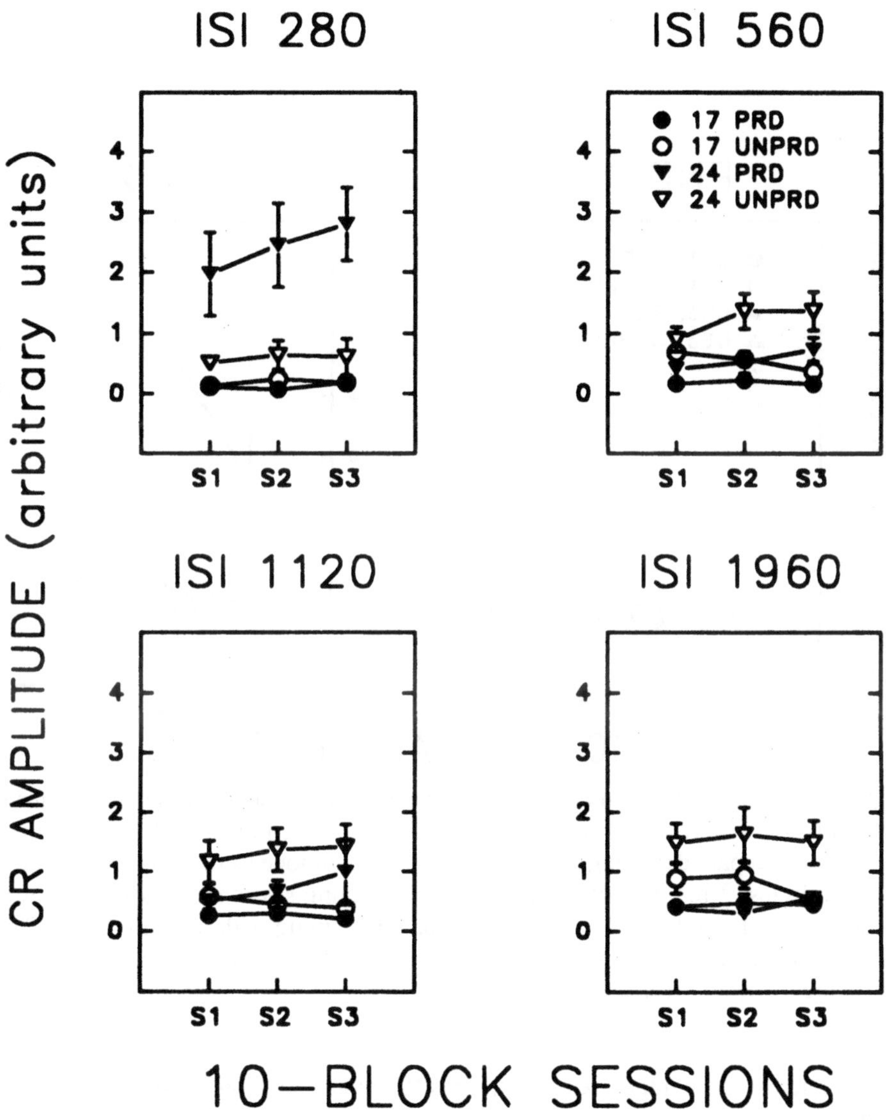

Figure 5. Mean (± *SE*) conditioned response (CR) peak amplitudes for 17-day-old (circles) and 24-day-old (triangles) rats as a function of training condition (paired filled symbols; unpaired open symbols) sessions (10 blocks of 10 trials) and interstimulus interval (ISI) in milliseconds. At 24 days of age conditioning was evident only at the shortest (280 msec) ISI. At 17 days of age conditioning failed to appear regardless of ISI (from Freeman et al., 1993).

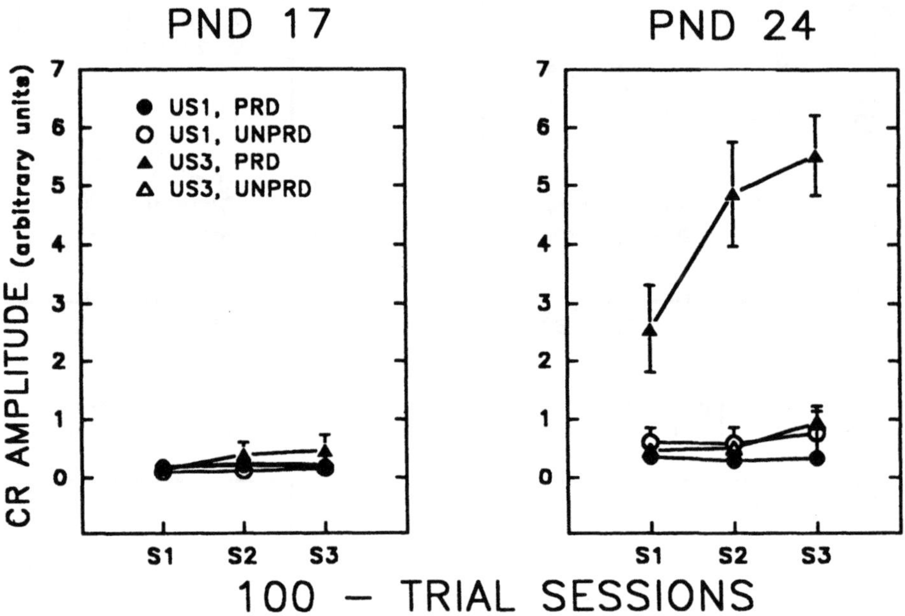

Figure 6. Mean (± *SE*) conditioned response (CR) amplitudes for rats on Postnatal Day (PND) 17 (left panel) or PND24 (right panel) as a function of paired (filled symbols) or unpaired training (open symbols), unconditioned stimulus (US) intensity (1 mA circles; 3 mA triangles), and 100-trial training sessions. Conditioning was evident only in 24-day-olds that received paired training with a 3 mA US. This conditioning is stronger than that produced by a 2 mA US (compare with top left panel of Figure 3) (from Freeman et al., 1993).

manner across these intensities at both ages (Stanton et al., 1992; Experiment 3, see above).

These results show that conditioning on PND24 increases as a function of US intensity. This agrees generally with studies of adult humans and rabbits (Spence, 1953; Smith, 1968). In contrast, conditioning in PND17 pups fails to occur regardless of US intensity. This supports our claim (Figure 4) that poor conditioning in PND17 rats is not secondary to age differences in US processing but rather seems to reflect a deficit in a associative learning.

CS Salience

Acquisition of eyeblink conditioning is a positive function of CS intensity or salience (Gormezano et al., 1983). It has been shown with an acoustic startle paradigm that tones in the 5 – 10 kHz range are more salient to preweanling rat pups than lower frequency tones (Rudy & Hyson, 1984). This led us to examine the effects of varying the frequency of the tone CS (2.8, 5.0, and 9.0 kHz) on associative conditioning in PND17 and 24 rat pups (Andrews, Freeman, Carter & Stanton, 1995). We found that the 9.0 kHz tone elicted stronger startle responses in our eyeblink conditioning preparation (see Methods above) than the 2.8 and 5.0 kHz tones and that this effect did not change with age (Andrews et al., 1995). The effect of auditory frequency of the tone CS on conditioning are shown in Figure 7.

Tone frequency did not influence conditioning in pups trained on PND24. Both paired and unpaired groups showed a modest increase in responding to the tone as a function of CS frequency but the *difference* between these groups did not change across frequencies (Figure 7). In contrast, pups trained on PND17 showed an increase in associative learning as tone frequency increased to 5.0 and 9.0 kHz (Figure 7).

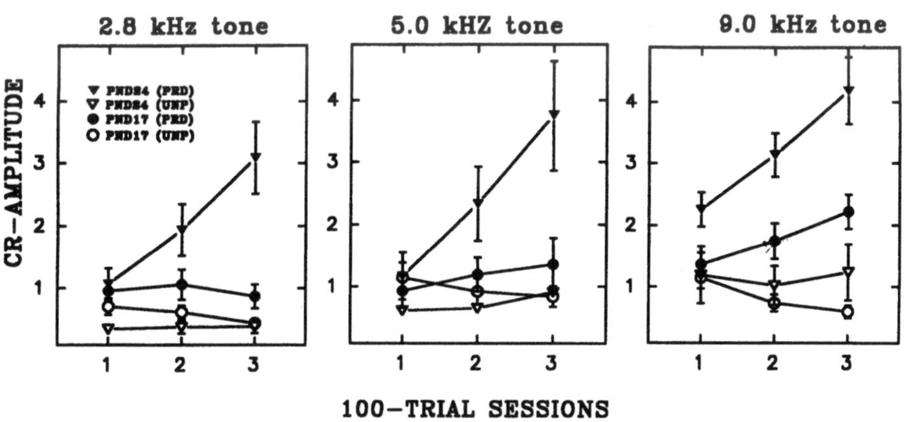

Figure 7. Mean (± *SE*) conditioned response (CR) amplitudes (in arbitrary units) for rats on Postnatal Day (PND) 17 (circles) or PND24 (triangles) as a function of paired (filled symbols) or unpaired training (open symbols), 100-trial training sessions, and auditory frequency of the tone CS (28, 50, and 90 kHz in left, middle, and right panels, respectively). On PND17 conditioning was enhanced modestly at the highest tone frequency. However large age differences in conditioning were evident at all tone frequencies (from Andrews et al., 1995).

However, the amount of conditioning seen in PND17 pups trained with a 9.0 kHz CS remained modest compared with the performance of PND24 pups. These data suggest that the ontogeny of eyeblink conditioning depends on developmental changes in processes related to the acquisition or expression of associative learning (Andrews et al., 1995). Consistent with our previous data (Figure 4), primary sensory development does not seem to account for developmental changes in the eyeblink CR. It remains possible, however, that auditory system maturation at some central level (e.g., mossy fiber projections to the cerebellum) may play a contributory role.

Amount of Training

We have also examined the effects of presenting rat pups with more training trials (Stanton, Fox & Carter, 1998). We examined eyeblink conditioning in 17-, 20-, and 24-day-old rats that received double the number of conditioning trials (600) that we typically use. The results of this experiment are shown in Figure 8. Even with this extensive amount of training, rats trained on PND17-18 (circles) showed significantly less conditioning than rats trained on PND24-25 (squares). Acquisition of CRs in the group trained on PND20-21 (triangles) was intermediate between the other two groups. Pups trained in the paired condition on PND17-18 did not differ significantly from their unpaired controls in any session (Stanton et al., 1998). In contrast, pups trained in the paired condition on PND20-21 and PND24-25 differed from their unpaired controls (and from each other) by the second training session (Stanton et al., 1998).

These data demonstrate that the poor conditioning observed in 17-day-olds cannot be reversed with extensive training. They also show that rate of eyeblink conditioning in the infant rat increases gradually and continuously between PND17 and 24. It is possible that the associative processes underlying this ontogenetic change also mature gradually during this developmental period in the rat.

Savings

In the final experiment of this section we examined the role that acquisition versus expression of associative learning plays in the developmental emergence of the eyeblink CR (Stanton et al., 1998). We thought that paired training on PND17 might result in associative learning which is not expressed at that age. Such learning might however become manifest as savings during futher training at a subsequent age when such learning can be expressed (i.e., PND20 in previous experiment; Figure 8, above). We tested that hypothesis in an experiment involving three separate groups of rat pups. These groups received three sessions of either paired, unpaired, or no training on PND17. Three days later, on PND20, these groups all received three sessions of paired training. Figure 9 shows terminal performance of the paired and unpaired groups on PND17 along with acquisition data during paired training for all three groups on PND20.

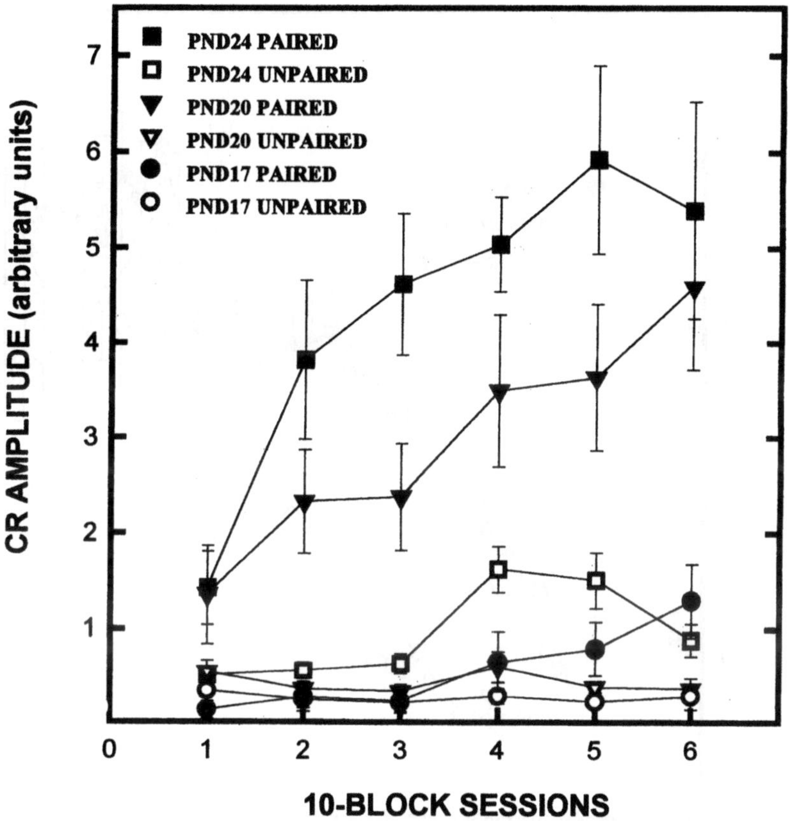

Figure 8. Mean (± *SE*) conditioned response (CR) amplitudes for separate groups of rats that received paired (filled symbols) or unpaired training (open symbols) across two successive days of training (three sessions per day each consisting of 10 blocks of 10 trials). Training began on Postnatal Day (PND) 17 (circles), PND20 (triangles), or PND24 (squares). Conditioning failed to appear on PND17-18 even after 600 trials but emerged in a graded fashion at the older ages (from Stanton et al., 1998).

A clear savings effect was observed. The group that received prior paired training on PND17 (Group PRD-PRD) learned substantially faster than the group that received no training on PND17 (Group NAÏVE-PRD). Unpaired training on PND17 (Group UNP-PRD) resulted in acquisition on PND20 that was intermediate between that of the PRD-PRD and NAÏVE-PRD groups. This finding suggests that processes related

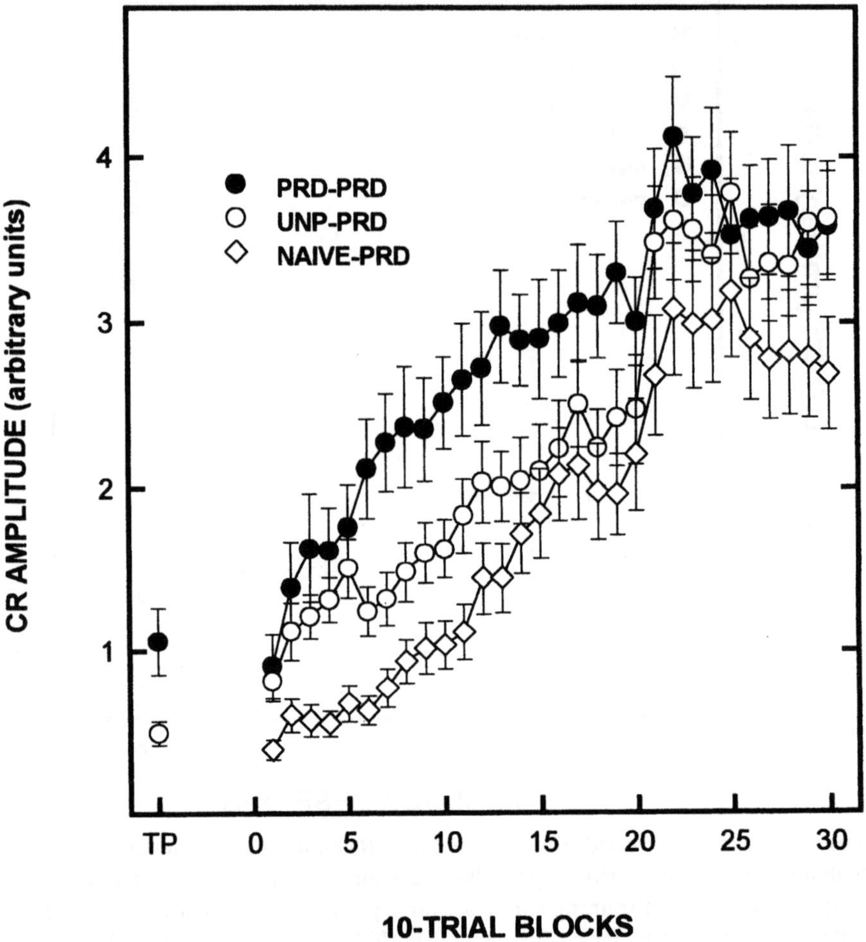

Figure 9. Mean (± *SE*) conditioned response (CR) amplitudes for three separate groups of rats that received three sessions of paired training (each consisting of 10 blocks of 10 trials) on PND20. These groups differed in their training history on PND17 (TP terminal performance at the end of training on PND17). Group PRD-PRD (filled circles) received paired training on PND17; UNP-PRD (open circles) received unpaired training on PND17; and NAÏVE-PRD (open diamonds) received no training on PND17. Prior paired training facilitated conditioning relative to the other two groups. Prior unpaired training facilitated conditioning relative to Group NAÏVE-PRD (from Stanton et al., 1998).

to acquisition and expression of eyeblink conditioning can be ontogenetically dissociated and that both contibute to the developmental emergence of the behavioral CR. Whether this dissociation results from developmental differences in acquisition versus expression within a single brain memory system or in interactions between multiple memory systems is a question for future research (for further discussion, see Stanton et al., 1998). These findings also indicate that unpaired preexposure to US and CS facilitates rather than impairs conditioning. Impairment of conditioning or "learned irrelevance" (Mackintosh, 1974) is typically observed in adults and, we've recently discovered, emerges by PND30 in the rat (Rush, Robinette & Stanton, 1999). Entorhinal cortical lesions disrupt learned irrelevance in adult rabbits (Allen, Chelius & Gluck, 1998). Perhaps immaturity of entorhinal cortex accounts for the failure to observe this phenomena in PND20 rats (Figure 9).

Summary of Parametric Studies

These studies have examined the effects of arousal, interstimulus interval, US intensity, CS salience, amount of training, and age of training versus testing, on the developmental emergence of the eyeblink CR in the rat. Taken together, the results of these studies support the view that this emergence results from developmental changes in an *associative* process rather than in sensory, motor, or motivational processes that are necessary for performance of the eyeblink CR. Factors such as arousal, CS salience, and unexpressed learning play a modulatory role in the ontogeny of eyeblink conditioning. However, all of the behavioral data point to an underlying associative system or process that is *crucial* for the ontogenetic emergence of the eyeblink CR. As an aggregate, these parametric studies also failed to uncover any evidence that the postnatal development of eyeblink conditioning is an artifact of the use of conditioning parameters that are optimal for training adults but not for infants. Other forms of parametric variation remain to be tested. However, it seems fair to argue that a shift in the burden of proof for this optimality assertion is warranted on the basis of the current data. Finally, these parametric studies generally confirm that conditioning obtained with our infant rat preparation tend to follow the same general laws of eyeblink conditioning that have been documented in other preparations.

EFFECTS OF EARLY CEREBELLAR DAMAGE

The cerebellum undergoes substantial postnatal development in the rat (Altman, 1982) and a large body of evidence indicates that eyeblink conditioning critically depends on cerebellar circuitry (Krupa, Thompson & Thompson, 1993; Lavond & Steinmetz, 1989; McCormick & Thompson, 1984; Thompson, 1986). This makes it likely that the ontogeny of eyeblink conditioning is caused primarily by the protracted postnatal development of the cerebellum. This hypothesis is supported by all of the behavioral data reviewed in the previous section. We now turn to two complementary studies which further tested this hypothesis by examining the effects of early cerebellar damage on the ontogeny of eyeblink conditioning. In one study, an antiproliferative agent, methazoxymethanol (MAM), was administered systemically in order to disrupt granule cell neurogenesis in the cerebellum (Freeman, Barone & Stanton, 1995a). The other study examined the effects of unilateral aspiration lesions of the cerebellar cortex or the cortex plus deep nuclei on the ontogeny of eyeblink conditioning (Freeman, Carter & Stanton, 1995b). The first involved a manipulation that disrupts normal developmental processes in the brain. However, because a systemically administered agent was used, there is no assurance that this disruption was confined exclusively to the cerebellum. The second study involved damage that was better localized to the cerebellum and that provided a better point of comparison with previous lesion studies performed in adult animals. Taken together these two studies provide converging evidence that cerebellar development is critical for the ontogeny of eyeblink conditioning.

Neonatal Exposure to an Antiproliferative Agent

Exposure to antiproliferative agents during the first two postnatal weeks dramatically impairs cerebellar development in the rat. The antiproliferative effects of x-irradiation on the ontogeny of cerebellar circuitry have been characterized extensively (Altman, 1982). However a similar pattern of effects has been observed following neonatal exposure to MAM (Chen & Hillman, 1986; 1989). On the basis this literature, Freeman et al. (1995a) exposed rat pups to either 20 mg/kg MAM or saline vehicle on PND4 and again on PND7. Pups from each treatment condition then received six 100-trial sessions of paired or unpaired training on PND24-25 with our standard delay eyeblink conditioning procedure (see Figures 1 and 2 above). On the following day (PND26) pups were sacrificed and perfused for histological analysis of brain tissue.

Anatomy

Effects of this MAM exposure on the cerebellum are shown in Figure 10. A clear reduction in cerebellar volume (upper panels), ectopic granule cells, and misallignment of Purkinje cells (lower panels), were evident following MAM treatment (right panels) relative to vehicle control (left panels). These effects are consistent with previous studies (Altman, 1982; Chen & Hillman, 1986; 1989). In contrast, granule cells in the dentate gyrus were unaffected and there were no signs of major abnormalities in the cerebellar deep nuclei, lateral pontine nuclei, inferior olive, or red nucleus, as assessed by examination of Nissl-stained material (Freeman et al., 1995a). Quantitative neuroanatomy revealed a 30% reduction in the area of the whole cerebellum, cerebellar white matter, molecular layer, and granule cell layer. This reduction did not differ in magnitude across these areas. Quantitative analysis failed to reveal effects on area of the deep nuclei, pontine nuclei, inferior olive, or red nucleus (Freeman et al., 1995a). In general, these effects were also observed on PND19, 22, and 33, and did not change much with age (Freeman et al., 1995a, Experiment 2).

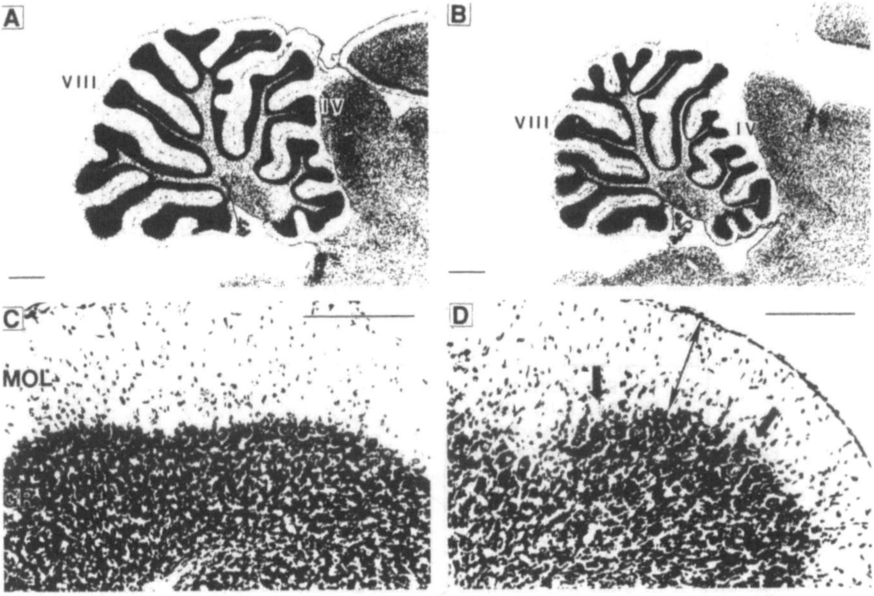

Figure 10. Nissl-stained parasagittal sections from rats sacrificed on Postnatal Day 26 (PND26) following dosing with MAM (methazoxymethanol; BD) or saline (AC) on PND4 and 7. MAM treatment produced cerebellar hypoplasia (B) and misalighment of Purkinje cells (see arrows in D). Scale bar: A and B 500 μm; C and D 100 μm. MOL, Molecular layer; GR, granule cell layer (From Freeman et al., 1995a).

Behavior

The effects of MAM exposure on eyeblink conditioning are shown in Figure 11. The increase across training session in both CR amplitude (upper panel) and CR percentage (lower panel) was reduced in MAM-exposed rats that received paired training relative

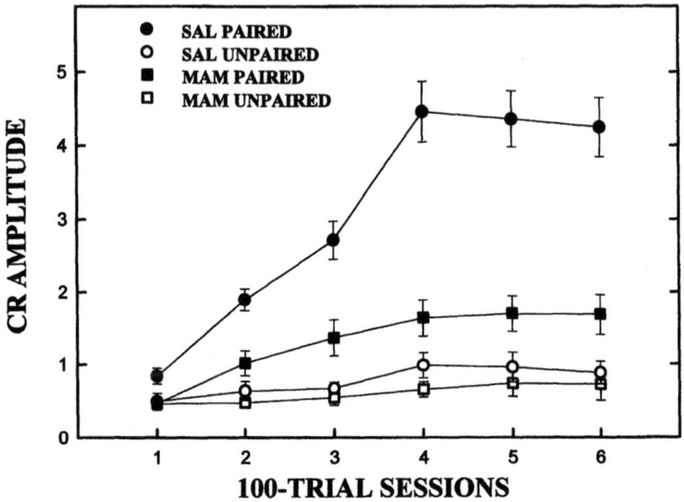

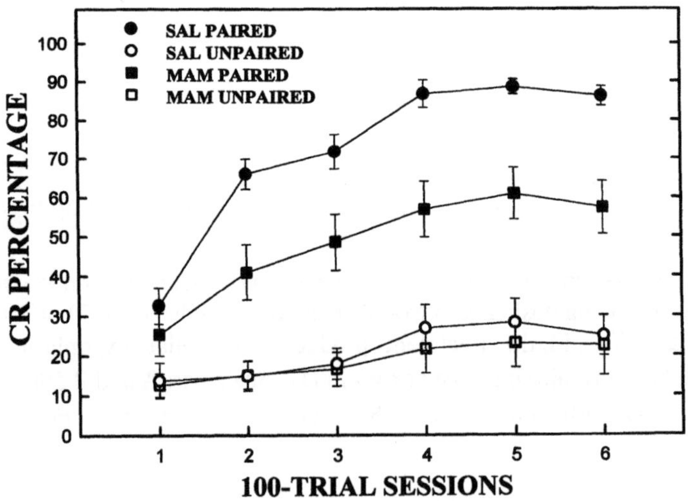

Figure 11. Mean (± *SE*) conditioned response (CR) amplitudes (upper panel) and percentage of CRs (lower panel) for 24-25-day-old rats injected on PND4 and 7 with saline (circles) or methazoxymethanol (MAM squares) as a function of training condition (paired filled symbols; unpaired open symbols) and training sessions (100-trials/session). Neonatal MAM exposure impaired but did not abolish eyeblink conditioning (from Freeman et al., 1995a).

to their saline-exposed counterparts. However, both of the paired groups performed at higher levels than their unpaired counterparts, indicating that MAM impaired but did not abolish eyeblink conditioning. Effects of MAM appeared larger with the CR amplitude measure than with CR percentage. This suggests that MAM may disrupt the function of cerebellar cortex more than that of the deep nuclei (Lavond & Steinmetz, 1989; see below). In contrast to this impairment of the eyeblink CR, MAM failed to alter the eyeblink UR or other forms of learning—spatial delayed alternation and auditory fear conditioning—that do not critically depend on the cerebellum (Freeman et al., 1995a). This indicates that this MAM exposure interfered with learning rather than performance. Both the neuroanatomical and behavioral analyses suggest that the effects of this MAM exposure were largely confined to the cerebellum (Freeman et al., 1995a).

Early Aspiration Lesions of the Cerebellum

In another study, aspiration lesions of the cerebellum were performed on PND10 and eyeblink conditioning was assessed on PND24 (Freeman, Carter & Stanton, 1995b). These lesions were performed ipsilateral or contralateral to the trained eye in a manner that either included the cerebellar cortex and deep nuclei or that was confined only to cerebellar cortex (Freeman et al., 1995b). The contralateral lesion was included in order to determine whether neural control of eyeblink conditioning is lateralized in the infant rat as it appears to be in the adult (Thompson, 1986). If so, the contralateral lesion could also serve as a control for nonspecific developmental brain damage. These lesion groups and sham controls received either paired or unpaired training with our standard procedure (see Figures 1 and 2).

Anatomy

Illustrative drawings of the lesions appear in Figure 12. Extent of the smallest and largest aspiration are shown for each lesion group. Typical lesions were intermediate in extent. Typical "deep lesions" included the deep nuclei and most of overlying cerebellar cortex. Typical "cortex lesions" were confined to hemispheric cortex. There were no differences in lesion extent in the ipsi- versus contralateral groups.

Behavior

Results for the CR percentage measure appear in Figure 13. Stong conditioning was evident in Sham-lesioned rat pups that received paired training relative to their unpaired controls (left panel). In the ipsilateral lesion groups (middle panel), aspirations that included the deep nuclei vitually abolished conditioning whereas aspirations of overlying cerebellar cortex modestly impaired conditioning relative to sham lesions (compare left and middle panels). In the contralateral lesion groups (right panel), aspirations that included the deep nuclei impaired but did not abolish conditioning whereas cortical aspirations had no effect (compare left and right panels). These effects cannot be explained by alterations in motor performance or US efficacy as reflected in the UR amplitude measure (Freeman et al., 1995b). These results are generally consistent with those from lesion studies of adult rabbits (Lavond & Steinmetz, 1989; Steinmetz et al., 1992; Thompson, 1986). The one exception is the impairment of conditioning observed in the CONTRA-DEEP condition. A follow-up experiment showed that this exception could be attributed to the age at which the aspiration lesion was performed. Contralateral lesions performed on PND10 impaired eyeblink conditioning whereas lesions performed on PND20 had no effect (Freeman et al., 1995b; Experiment 2). This effect of age of lesion may reflect reorganization of rubral projections from the cerebellum that occur following hermicerebellectomy

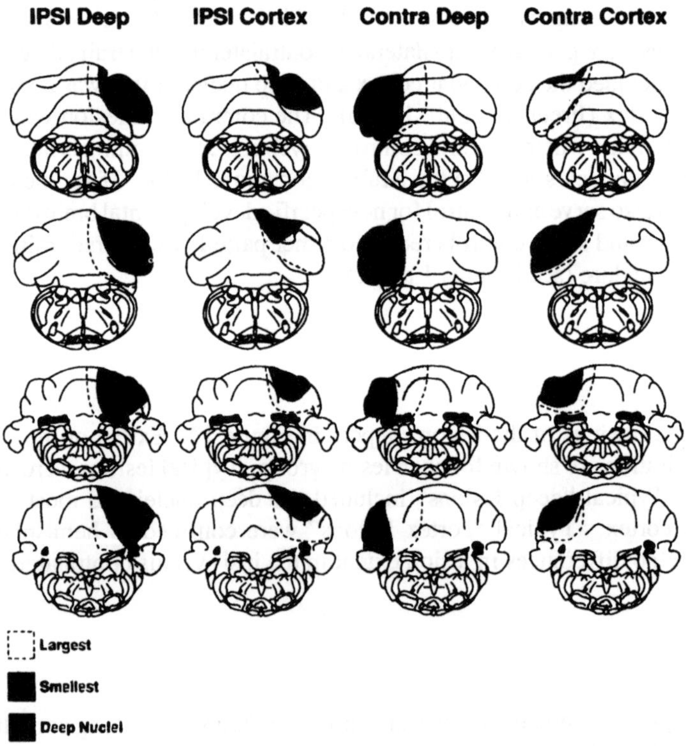

Figure 12. The rostral (bottom) to caudal (top) extent of the largest and smallest lesion for rats given aspirations on Postnatal Day (PND) 10 of either cerebellar cortex (Cortex) or cortex+deep nuclei (Deep) either ipsilateral (IPSI) or contralateral (Contra) to the trained eye. Rats were sacrificed for histology on PND25 (from Freeman et al., 1995b).

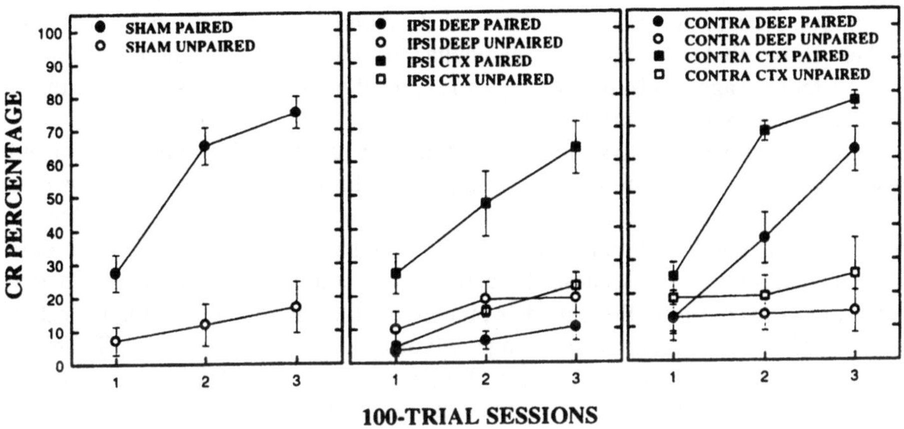

Figure 13. Mean (± *SE*) percentage of conditoned responses (CR) for Postnatal Day (PND) 24 rats that received on PND10 sham surgery (SHAM; left panel) or unilateral aspirations of ipsilateral cerebellar cortex and deep nuclei (IPSI DEEP middle panel circles) of ipsilateral cortex (IPSI CTX; middle panel squares) of contralateral cortex and deep nuclei (CONTRA DEEP; right panel circles) or of the contralateral cortex (CONTRA CTX; right panel squares) as function of paired (filled symbols) or unpaired training (open symbols) and training session (100 trials/session). Conditioning was abolished by ipsilateral "deep" lesions and impaired by contralateral "deep" lesions. Conditioning was also impaired by ipsilateral but not contralateral aspirations of cortex (from Freeman et al., 1995b).

during the neonatal period but not later developmental stages in the rat (Gramsbergen, 1982; Gramsbergen & Ijkema-Paasen, 1982). If so then eyeblink conditioning is probably lateralized at the age that it normally emerges (PND20-24; see Freeman et al., 1995b for futher discussion).

SUMMARY AND CONCLUSIONS

Our behavioral studies show that the emergence of eyeblink conditioning between 17- and 24-days of age in the rat is an extremely robust phenomenon. We have not found a parametric or motivational manipulation that will produce conditioning in preweanling rats that is as strong as the conditioning seen in weanlings. Conditioning in the preweanling is generally absent (or weak) whereas conditioning in the weanling is strong and generally conforms to the parametric laws of eyeblink conditioning. These studies show that eyeblink conditioning emerges gradually rather than abruptly over this age range and that processes of acquisition and expression of learning together contribute to the developmental emergence of the behavioral CR. Finally our behavioral studies strongly suggest that this emergence depends on maturation of an associative process rather than of sensory, motor, or motivational processes that are necessary for learning and performance. Our neurobiological studies indicate that this associative process depends on the normal development of the cerebellum. These studies show that disruption of cerebellar development by administering an antiproliferative agent or by performing early cerebellar aspirations interferes with the ontogeny of eyeblink conditioning.

Our developmental analysis is consistent in many respects with empirical data and theoretical models concerning the role of the cerebellum in eyeblink conditioning (see Thompson, 1986; Chapters 2, 3, 4 and 10, this volume). These models hold that the eyeblink CR depends on brainstem-cerebellar circuitry whereas the UR depends only on brainstem circuitry. Because the cerebellum matures later than the brainstem (Altman & Bayer, 1996), these models predict that the CR should develop later than the UR and that early cerebellar damage will disrupt the CR but not the UR. This is precisely what we have found (Figures 3, 4; Freeman et al., 1995ab; Stanton et al., 1992). Moreover, our parametric studies of the eyeblink UR (Stanton et al., 1992) clearly indicate that the cerebellum is critical for *learning* rather than merely for the generation of low amplitude eyeblink responses (Steinmetz et al., 1992). These models also hold that cerebellar control of the eyeblink CR is lateralized. Our developmental studies show that lateralized damage on PND10 has different effects on subsequent conditioning than damage on PND20 (Freeman et al., 1995b). However the eyeblink CR does not emerge until PND20 (Figure 8) and at this age it appears to be controlled by the ipsilateral cerebellum. When lesions are performed on PND20, ipsilateral but not contralateral damage impairs eyeblink conditioning (Freeman et al., 1995b). Finally, our data are consistent with models postulating that the cerebellar deep nuclei are critical for the eyeblink CR whereas cerebellar cortex modulates acquisition rate and amplitude of the CR. Changes in CR amplitude occur over a more protracted period of development than changes in CR percentage (Freeman et al., 1995a) and cerebellar cortical damage produced by both neonatal aspirations and MAM exposure has a larger effect on CR amplitude than on CR percentage (Figure 11; Freeman et al., 1995a,b). In contrast, damage that includes the deep nuclei virtually abolishes eyeblink CRs (Freeman et al., 1995b). In summary, there are many aspects of our developmental data that are consistent with models of cerebellar involvement in eyeblink conditioning. Further tests of the applicability of these models to the ontogeny of learning are clearly warranted.

The studies reviewed in this chapter have relied solely on behavioral and lesion methods. Future studies that apply a broader range of techniques—brain stimulation and recording, reversible inactivation, quantitative neural network models, etc.—to developing rats are needed in order to better characterize the relationship between cerebellar development and the ontogeny of eyeblink conditioning (e.g., Freeman & Danielson, 1999). However by comparing results from our two methods of damaging the developing cerebellum—aspiration lesions and exposure to the antimitotic agent MAM—it is possible to speculate a bit further about how this relationship may work. Although differentiating microneurons in cerebellar cortex (particularly granule cells) were the primary target of MAM in our experiments, it is likely that loss of these target neurons resulted in secondary effects on other elements of cerebellar circuitry, for example a reduction in dendritic expansion of Purkinje cells, loss of afferent and efferent fibers to and from cerebellar cortex, and abberant connectivity and physiology of remaining neurons (Altman & Bayer, 1996). It is interesting that the partial cerebellar hypoplasia produced by MAM was much more disruptive to eyeblink conditioning than aspiration of the entire hemispheric cortex but clearly less disruptive than aspirations that also included the deep nuclei (compare Figures 11 and 13). Conditioning in MAM-exposed weanling rats also bore a stronger resemblence to that of *normal* preweanling rats than did conditioning in weanling rats with either aspiration lesion. There are several explanations for this but one possibility is that the developmental emergence of the eyeblink CR reflects an "orchestra" of maturational changes that are distributed across several elements of brainstem-cerebellar circuitry rather than changes in a single element (e.g., afferent input neural plasticity or efferent expression). Future studies with other techniques and with quantitative models may help distinguish these possibilities.

The prospect of such studies highlights the power of the eyeblink conditioning paradigm for understanding the developmental psychobiology of learning at the level of neural circuitry. Studies at the systems and comparative levels also promise a bright future for developmental eyeblink conditioning research.

REFERENCES

Allen, M.T., Chelius, L., & Gluck, M.A. (1998). Selective entorhinal cortical lesions disrupt the learned irrelevance pre-exposure effect in the classically conditioned rabbit eyeblink response paradigm. *Society for Neuroscience Abstracts, 24*, 442.

Altman, J. (1982). Morphological development of the rat cerebellum and some of its mechanisms. In S.L. Palay & V. Chan-Palay (Eds.). *The Cerebellum: New Vistas.* Berlin: Springer-Velag.

Altman, J., & Bayer, S. (1975). Postnatal development of the hippocampal dentate gyrus under normal and experimental conditions. In R. L. Isaacson & K. H. Pribram (Eds.). *The Hippocampus, Part 1.* New York, NY: Plenum Press.

Altman, J., & Bayer, S. (1966). *Development of the Cerebellar System: In Relation to its Evolution Structure and Functions.* Boca Raton: CRC Press.

Altman, J., Brunner, R. L., & Bayer, S.A. (1973). The hippocampus and behavioral maturation. *Behavioral Biology, 8*, 557-596.

Amsel, A., & Stanton, M. (1980). Ontogeny and phylogeny of paradoxical reward effects. In J. S. Rosenblatt, R. A. Hinde, C. Beer & M.-C. Busnel (Eds.). *Advances in the Study of Behavior.* New York, NY: Academic Press.

Andrews, S.J., Freeman, J.H., Jr., Carter, C.S., & Stanton, M.E. (1995). Ontogeny of eyeblink conditioning in the rat: Auditory frequency and discrimination learning effects. *Developmental Psychobiology, 28*, 307-320.

Aoki, E., Semba, R., & Kashiwamata, S. (1989). When does GABA-like immunoreactivity appear in the rat cerebellar GABAergic neurons? *Brain Research, 502*, 245-251.

Bayer, S.A., Altman, J., Russo, R.J., & Zhang, X. (1993). Timetables of neurogenesis in the human brain based on experimentally determined patterns in the rat. *Neurotoxicology, 14*, 83-144.

Berry, M., & Bradley, P. (1976). The growth of dendritic trees of Purkinje cells in the cerebellum of the rat. *Brain Research, 112*, 1-35.

Berry, S.D., & Swain, R.A. (1989). Water deprivation optimizes hippocampal activity and facilitates nictitating membrane conditioning. *Behavorial Neuroscience, 103*, 71-76.

Campbell, B.A., & Ampuero, M.X. (1985). Dissociation of autonomic and behavioral components of conditioned fear during development in the rat. *Behavorial Neuroscience, 99*, 1089-1102.

Chen, S., & Hillman, D.E. (1986). Selective ablation of neurons by methylazoxymethanol during pre- and postnatal brain development. *Experimental Brain Research, 94*, 103-108.

Chen, S., & Hillman, D.E. (1989). Regulation of granule cell number by a predetermined number of Purkinje cells in development. *Developmental Brain Research, 45*, 137-143.

Crepel, F. (1971). Maturation of climbing fiber responses in the rat. *Brain Research, 35*, 272-276.

Crepel, F. (1972). Maturation of cerebellar Purkinje cells I: Postnatal evolution of the Purkinje cell spontaneous firing in the rat. *Experimental Brain Research, 14*, 463-479.

Crepel, F., Mariani, J., Delhaye-Bouchaud, N.J. (1976). Evidence for a multiple innervation of Purkinje cells by climbing fibers in the immature rat. *Neurobiology, 7*, 567-578.

Diamond, A. (1990). *The Development and Neural Basis of Higher Cognitive Functions.* New York: New York Academy of Sciences Press, 608.

Douglas, R. (1975). The development of hippocampal function: Implications for theory and therapy. In R. Isaacson & K. Pribram (Eds.). *The Hippocampus, Part 1.* New York: Plenum.

Freeman, J.H., Jr., & Nicholson, D.A. (1999). Developmental changes in eyeblink conditioning and neuronal activity in the cerebellar interpositus nucleus. *Society for Neuroscience Abstracts*, 382.

Freeman, J. H., Spencer, C.O., Skelton, R.W., & Stanton, M. E. (1993). Ontogeny of eyeblink conditioning in the rat: Effect of US intensity and interstimulus interval on delay conditioning. *Psychobiology, 21*, 233-242.

Freeman, J.H., Jr., Barone, S., Jr., & Stanton, M.E. (1995a). Disruption of cerebellar maturation by an antimitotic agent impairs the ontogeny of eyeblink conditioning in rats. *Journal of Neuroscience, 15* 7301-7314.

Freeman, J.H., Jr., Carter, C.S., & Stanton, M.E. (1995b). Early cerebellar lesions impair eyeblink conditioning in developing rats: Differential effects of unilateral lesions on postnatal day 10 or 20. *Behavioral Neuroscience, 109*, 893-902.

Freeman, J.H. Jr., Spencer, C.O., Skelton, R.W., & Stanton, M.E. (1993). Ontogeny of eyeblink conditioning in the rat: Effect of US intensity and interstimulus interval on delay conditioning. *Psychobiology, 21*, 233-242.

Gilbert, M.E., & Cain, D.P. (1980). Electrode implantation in infant rats for kindling and chronic brain recording. *Behavioural Brain Research, 1*, 553-555.

Gormezano, I., Kehoe, E. J., & Marshall, B. (1983). Twenty years of classical conditioning research with the rabbit. In J. M. Sprague & A. N. Epstein (Eds.). *Progress in Psychobiology and Physiological Psychology.* New York, NY: Academic Press.

Gramsbergen, A., & Ijkema-Paasen, J. (1982). CNS plasticity after hemicerebellectomy in the young rat: Quantitative relations between aberrant and normal cerebellorubral projections. *Neuroscience Letters, 33*, 129-134.

Gramsbergen, A. (1982). The effects of cerebellectomy in the young rat I Behavioural seuelae. *Behavioral Brain Research, 6*, 85-92.

Greif, K.F., Eflander, M.G., Tillakaratne, N.J.K., & Tobin, A.J. (1991). Postnatal expression of glutamate decarboxylases in developing rat cerebellum. *Neurochemical Research, 16*, 235-242.

Hall, W. (1987). Early motivation reward learning and their neural bases: Developmental revelations and simplifications. In N. Krasnegor, E. Blass, M. Hofer, & W. Smotherman, (Eds.). *Perinatal Development: A Psychobiological Perspective.* New York: Academic Press.

Haroutunian, V., & Campbell, B.A. (1979). Emergence of interoceptive and exteroceptive control of behavior in rats. *Science, 205*, 927-929

Hilgard, E.R., & Marquis, D.G. (1940). *Conditioning and Learning* New York: Appleton-Century-Crofts.

Hilgard, E.R. (1931). Conditioned eyelid reactions to a light stimulus based on the reflex wink to sound. *Psychological Monographs, 41*, 1.

Hunt, P.S., & Campbell, B.A. (1997). Developmental dissociation of the components of conditioned fear. In M.S. Fanselow & M.E. Bouton (Eds.). *Learning Motivation and Cognition: The Functional Behaviorism of Robert C Bolles (pp 53-74).* Washington DC: American Psychological Association.

Ivkovich, D., Eckerman, C.O., Krasnegor, N.A., Stanton, M.E. (2000). Using eyeblink conditioning to assess neurocognitive development. In D.S. Woodruff-Pak & J.E. Steinmetz (Eds.). *Eyeblink Classical Conditioning: Human Applications.* Amsterdam: Kluwer Academic Publishers.

Kail, R., & Spear, N. (1984). *Comparative Perspectives on the Development of Memory.* Hillsdale, NJ: Erlbaum.

Kimble, G.A. (1947). Conditioning as a function of the time between conditioned and unconditioned stimuli. *Journal of Experimental Psychology, 37,* 1-15.

Krasnegor, N., Blass, E., Hofer, M., & Smotherman, W. (1986). *Perinatal Development: A Psychobiological Perspective.* New York: Academic Press.

Kretschmann, H.J., Kammradt, G., Krauthausen, I., Sauer, B., & Wingert, F. (1986). Growth of the hippocampal formation in man. *Bibliography of Anatomy, 28,* 27-52.

Krupa, D.J., Thompson, J.K., & Thompson, R.F. (1993). Localization of a memory trace in the mammalian brain. *Science, 260,* 989-991.

Lavond, D.G., & Steinmetz, J.E. (1989). Acquisition of classical conditioning after removal of cerebellar cortex. *Behavioural Brain Res*earch, 33, 113-164.

Lipsitt, L. (1990). Learning processes in the human newborn: Sensitization habituation and classical conditioning. In A. Diamond, (Ed.). *The Development and Neural Basis of Higher Cognitive Functions, Volume 608.* New York: New York Academy of Sciences.

Little, A.H., Lipsitt, L.P., & Rovee-Collier, C. (1984). Classical conditioning and retention of the infant's eyelid response: Effects of age and interstimulus interval. *Journal of Experimental Child Psychology, 37,* 512-524.

Mackintosh, N.J. (1974). *The Psychology of Animal Learning.* New York: Academic Press.

McCormick, D.A., & Thompson, R.F. (1984). Cerebellum: Essential involvement in the classically conditioned eyelid response. *Science, 223,* 296-298.

Nadel, L., & Zola-Morgan, S. (1984). Infantile amnesia: A neurobiological perspective. In M. Moscovitch (Ed.). *Infant Memory.* New York: Plenum.

Nicolle, M.M., Barry, C.C., Veronesi, B., & Stanton, M.E. (1989). Fornix transections disrupt the ontogeny of latent inhibition in the rat. *Psychobiology, 17,* 349-357.

Pellegrini-Giampietr, D.E., Bennett, M.V.L., & Zukin, R.S. (1991). Differential expression of three glutamate receptor genes in developing rat brain: An *in situ* hybridization study. *Proceedings of the National Academy of Science, (USA),* 88, 4157-4161.

Puro, D.G., & Woodward, D.J. (1977). Maturation of evoked climbing fiber input to rat cerebellar Purkinje cells, I. *Experimental Brain Research, 28,* 421-427.

Rovee-Collier, C. (1986). The rise and fall of infant classical conditioning research: Its promise for the study of early development. In L. Lipsitt & C. Rovee-Collier (Eds.). *Advances in Infant Research, Volume 4.* Norwood, NJ: Ablex.

Rudy, J. (1992). Development of learning: From elemental to configural associative networks. In C. Rovee-Collier & L. Lipsitt (Eds.). *Advances in infancy research.* New Jersey: ABLEX Publishing Corporation.

Rudy, J.W., & Hyson, R.L. (1984). Ontogenesis of learning: III. Variation in the rat's differential reflexive and learned responses to sound frequencies. *Developmental Psychobiology, 17,* 285-300.

Rush, A.N., Robinette, B.R., & Stanton, M.E. (1999). Ontogeny of eyeblink conditioning in the rat: Learned irrelevance. *Society for Neuroscience,* Miami, FL (October).

Schmajuk, N.A. (2000). Neural network approaches to classical conditioning. In D.S. Woodruff-Pak & J.E. Steinmetz (Eds.). *Eyeblink Classical Conditioning: Human Applications.* Amsterdam: Kluwer Academic Publishers.

Schmajuk, N.A., & DiCarlo, J.J. (1991). A neural network approach to hippocampal function in classical conditioning. *Behavioral Neuroscience, 105,* 82-110.

Sears, L.L., Finn, P.R., & Steinmetz, J. (1994). Abnormal classical eye-blink conditioning in autism. *Journal of Autism and Developmental Disorders, 24(6),* 737-751.

Sears, L., & Steinmetz, J. (2000). Classical eyeblink conditioning in normal and autistic children. In D.S. Woodruff-Pak & J.E. Steinmetz (Eds.). *Eyeblink Classical Conditioning: Human Applications.* Amsterdam: Kluwer Academic Publishers.

Shair, H., Barr, G., & Hofer, M. (1991). *Developmental Psychobiology: New Methods and Changing Concepts.* NewYork: Oxford University Press.

Shors, T.J., Weiss, C., & Thompson, R.F. (1992). Stress-induced facilitation of classical conditioning. *Science, 24,* 537-539.

Skelton, R.W. (1988). Bilateral cerebellar lesions disrupt conditioned eyelid responses in unrestrained rats. *Behavioral Neuroscience, 102,* 586-590.

Smith, M.C. (1968). CS-US interval and US intensity in classical conditioning of the rabbit's nictitating membrane response. *Journal of Comparative and Physiological Psychology, 66,* 679-687.

Smith, M.C., Coleman, S.R., & Gormezano, I. (1969). Classical conditioning of the rabbit's nictitating membrane response at backward simultaneous and forward CS-US intervals. *Journal of Comparative and Physiological Psychology, 69*, 226-231.

Spear, N., & Campbell, B. (1978). *Ontogeny of Learning and Memory.* Hillsdale, NJ: Erlbaum.

Spear, N., & Rudy, J. (1991). Tests of the ontogeny of learning and memory: Issues methods and results. In H. Shair, G. Barr & M. Hofer (Eds.). *Developmental Psychobiology: New Methods and Changing Concepts.* New York: Oxford University Press.

Spear, N.E., Kraemer, P.J., Molina, J.C., & Smoller, D.E. (1988). Developmental change in learning and memory: Infantile disposition for unitization (pp 27-52). In J. Delacour & J.C.S. Levy (Eds.). *Systems with Learning and Memory Abilities.* Amsterdam: Elsevier.

Spence, K.W. (1953). Learning and performance in eyelid conditioning as a function of the intensity of the UCS. *Journal of Experimental Psychology, 45*, 57-63.

Stanton, M.E. (In press). Multiple memory systems, development, and conditioning. *Behavioural Brain Research.*

Stanton, M.E., & Freeman, J.H., Jr. (1994). Eyeblink conditioning in the infant rat: An animal model of learning in developmental neurotoxicology. *Environmental Health Perspectives, 102*, 131-139.

Stanton, M.E., Fox, G.D., & Carter, C.S. (1998). Ontogeny of the conditioned eyeblink response in rats: Acquisition or expression? *Neuropharmacology, 37*, 623-632.

Stanton, M.E., Freeman, J.H., Jr., & Skelton, R.W. (1992). Eyeblink conditioning in the developing rat. *Behavioral Neuroscience, 106*, 657-667.

Stanton, M.E., Gutierrez, Y.R., & Levine, S. (1988). Maternal deprivation potentiates pituitary-adrenal stress responses in infant rats. *Behavioral Neuroscience, 102*, 692-700.

Steinmetz, J.E., Lavond, D.G., Ivkovich, D., Logan, C.G., & Thompson, R.F. (1992). Disruption of classical eyelid conditioning after cerebellar lesions: Damage to a memory trace system or a simple performance deficit? *Journal of Neuroscience, 12*, 4403-26.

Taylor, J.A.. (1951). The relationship of anxiety to the conditioned eyelid response. *Journal of Experimental Psychology, 41*, 81-92.

Thompson, R.F. (1986). The neurobiology of learning and memory. *Science, 233*, 941-947.

Wagner, A.R., & Brandon, S.E. (1989). Evolution of a structured connectionist model of Pavlovian conditioning (AESOP). In S.B. Klein & R.R, Mowrer (Eds). *Contemporary Learning Theories: Pavlovian Conditioning and the Status of Traditional Learning Theory.* Hillsdale, NJ: Erlbaum.

Willcutts, M.D., & Morrison-Bogorad, M. (1991). Quantitative *in situ* hybridization analysis of glutamic acid decarboxylase messenger RNA in developing rat cerebellum. *Developmental Brain Research, 63*, 253-264.

Wilson, D., Sullivan, R., & Leon, M. (1991). A search for the neural mechanisms of olfactory learning in young rats. In H. Shair, G. Barr & M. Hofer, (Eds.). *Developmental Psychobiology: New Methods and Changing Concepts.* New York: Oxford University Press.

Woodruff-Pak, D.S., & Thompson, R.F. (1988). Cerebellar correlates of classical conditioning across the life span. In P.B. Baltes, D.M. Featherman & R.M. Lerner, (Eds.). *Life-span Development and Behavior.* Hillsdale NJ: Erlbaum.

ACKNOWLEDGMENT

This manuscript has been reviewed by the National Health and Environmental Effects Research Laboratory, U.S.E.P.A., and approved for publication. Mention of trade names or commercial products does not constitute endorsement or recommendation for use.

6 ALCOHOL-INDUCED DAMAGE TO THE DEVELOPING BRAIN: FUNCTIONAL APPROACHES USING CLASSICAL EYEBLINK CONDITIONING

Charles R. Goodlett
Indiana University-
Purdue University Indianapolis

Mark E. Stanton
United States Environmental
Protection Agency

Joseph E. Steinmetz
Indiana University

INTRODUCTION

The systematic experimental analysis of classical eyeblink conditioning over the last half-century has provided neuroscientists with a powerful tool to analyze the function of neural circuits mediating one form of associative learning. The key experimental and behavioral parameters influencing eyeblink conditioning have been empirically established, and the neural correlates of the sensory, motor, and associative processes involved have been extensively characterized (Gormezano, Kehoe & Marshall, 1983; Gormezano, Prokasy & Thompson, 1987; Thompson, 1986). Research over the last two decades has identified and confirmed that circuits in the cerebellum and brainstem are essential for acquisition, performance, and extinction of conditioned eyeblink responses. This analysis of eyeblink conditioning has also been extended to include systems-level interactions between the brainstem-cerebellar circuits and forebrain areas such as the hippocampus. These interactions account for higher-order aspects of learning, including trace conditioning, discrimination reversal, latent inhibition, and sensory preconditioning (e.g., reviewed by Schmajuk & DiCarlo, 1991). Classical eyeblink conditioning has provided a basis to compare processes and mechanisms of learning and memory in several mammalian species (e.g., Gormezano, et al., 1987; Logan & Grafton, 1995; Skelton, 1988) and across the life span (Solomon, Barth, Wood, Velazquez, Groccia-Ellison & Yang, 1995; Stanton, Freeman & Skelton, 1992; Woodruff-Pak & Thompson, 1988). Eyeblink conditioning has also been used to characterize functional consequences of clinical neuropathology of the cerebellum and brainstem (Daum, Schugens, Ackermann, Lutzenberger, Dichgans & Birbaumer, 1993; Topka, Valls-Sole, Massaquoi & Hallett, 1992; Woodruff-Pak, Papka, & Ivry, 1996), or of developmental disorders involving cerebellar abnormalities (Sears, Finn & Steinmetz, 1994; Stanton & Freeman, 1994).

A key advantage of a developmental analysis of eyeblink conditioning is that it may be useful as an early functional indicator of the type and severity of damage to the developing brain resulting from developmental exposure to drugs or toxins. Such an indicator makes it possible to characterize the nature of developmental insults by providing empirical information on the functional consequences of early brain damage and how they change with development (Spear, 1990; Stanton & Freeman, 1994). Eyeblink conditioning may also provide a useful index of function early in development, providing a means of early detection of prenatal drug-induced functional damage (Ivkovich et al., companion volume). In turn, this may also promote more effective early intervention targeted toward specific functional processes, taking fullest advantage of developmental neuroplasticity in infancy.

This chapter focuses on the neuroteratogenic effects of alcohol, a drug of abuse which, 25 years after the first English-language report identified fetal alcohol syndrome (FAS) (Jones & Smith, 1973; Jones, Smith, Ulleland & Streissguth, 1973), still carries significant liability for abuse during pregnancy (Stratton, Howe & Battaglia, 1996). As reviewed below, substantial experimental and clinical evidence indicates that the developing cerebellum and brainstem are major targets for neurotoxic damage by alcohol. The recent use of eyeblink conditioning to advance the scientific understanding of clinically relevant brain damage induced by early exposure to alcohol will be highlighted, with reference to its potential power for understanding broad aspects of alcohol-induced brain damage. The chapter will conclude with a section on prospective uses of eyeblink conditioning as a clinical tool for use in experimental assessment in cases of infants and children at risk for disorders related to prenatal alcohol exposure.

CLASSICAL EYEBLINK CONDITIONING IN NORMAL AND ABNORMAL DEVELOPMENT

One current experimental use of eyeblink conditioning addresses normal and abnormal brain development (Stanton & Freeman, 1994; Stanton & Goodlett, 1998). This functional ontogenetic approach is based on the premise that behavioral evidence of conditioning emerges over development in conjunction with the functional maturation of the brainstem-cerebellar circuits mediating the associative learning. The expression of associative conditioning develops later than sensory and motor processes required for the behavior (Stanton, et al., 1992; see also, Stanton & Freeman, this volume), suggesting that the development of neural mechanisms necessary for conditioning is relatively more protracted than for these related processes (Rudy, 1992). These mechanisms can be studied in an identified neural circuit, providing opportunities to obtain detailed knowledge of the developmental determinants of conditioning. This knowledge can reciprocally inform neuroscience both about processes of functional brain development and about the mechanisms of neural plasticity underlying learning (see Stanton & Freeman, this volume).

Analysis of abnormal brain development has been an integral component of this developmental approach, and recent studies have evaluated alterations of brain development resulting from genetic sources and from environmental insults occurring during early development. Studies of eyeblink conditioning in mice bearing specific genetic mutations that affect cerebellar development have provided important *in vivo* experimental tests of hypotheses about the cellular and molecular components of eyeblink conditioning. For example, Purkinje cell degeneration (*pcd*) mice, a neurological mutant in which cerebellar Purkinje cells undergo rapid cell death over the 3rd-4th week of postnatal life, had severe deficits in acquisition of conditioning. They reached terminal performance levels of about 40% conditioned responses (CRs), compared to about 70% for wild-type littermates (Chen, Bao, Lockard, Kim & Thompson, 1996). This subnormal conditioning in *pcd* mice supports the view provided by lesion (Lavond & Steinmetz, 1989) and electrophysiological recording studies (Berthier & Moore, 1986; see also Chapter 4 by Steinmetz, this volume), that normal conditioning involves the cerebellar cortex in addition to the interpositus nucleus (which was structurally intact in the *pcd* mice). Gene-targeting approaches have also been used to test the functional importance of specific gene products for eyeblink conditioning, as demonstrated by the impairment of the learning-related increase in CR amplitude seen in gene-targeted mutant mice lacking the mGluR1 metabotropic glutamate receptor (Aiba, Kano, Chen, Stanton, Fox, Herrup, et al., 1994).

Eyeblink conditioning also has been used to assess functional development following treatments in neonatal rats that interfere with the normal development of the cerebellum (Stanton & Freeman, 1994). Neonatal aspirations of the ipsilateral cerebellar cortex retarded acquisition and impaired CR amplitude in weanling rats, whereas neonatal aspirations that also included the interpositus nucleus eliminated subsequent conditioning. Neither lesion affected sensorimotor responsiveness to conditioning stimuli, suggesting that early cerebellar damage produces selective effects on the ontogeny of learning but not performance (Freeman, Carter & Stanton, 1995b). In this respect, early cerebellar damage has effects on eyeblink conditioning that are similar to those observed after adult damage (Thompson, 1986).

The consequences of exposure to drugs or environmental toxins during early development that have the potential to induce cerebellar dysgenesis also have been studied through a similar developmental strategy (Freeman, Barone, & Stanton, 1995a; Stanton & Freeman, 1994; Stanton & Gallagher, 1996). For example, treatment of neonatal pups with the anti-mitotic agent methylazoxymethanol interferes with cerebellar granule cell neurogenesis, and the limited granule cell acquisition produces significant cerebellar hypoplasia. Methylazoxymethanol treatment on postnatal days 4 and 7 produced selective deficits in the percentage and amplitude of conditioned eyeblink responses in weanling rats. Unconditioned responses (URs) and CRs that do not depend on the cerebellum (i.e., fear) were unaffected by this methylazoxymethanol treatment (Freeman, et al., 1995a; Chapter 5, this volume).

CLINICAL ASPECTS OF PRENATAL ALCOHOL EXPOSURE

The original descriptions of the fetal alcohol syndrome (FAS) documented a characteristic pattern of facial abnormalities, growth deficiency, and evidence of brain damage (Jones & Smith, 1973; Jones, et al., 1973; Lemoine, Harousseau, Borteyru & Menuet, 1968). Since then, studies of children and young adults diagnosed with FAS, using cognitive, behavioral, neuropsychological, and neuroimaging approaches, have indicated that heavy prenatal exposure to alcohol induces a spectrum of structural and functional CNS abnormalities (Mattson & Riley, 1998; Roebuck, Mattson & Riley, 1998a; Streissguth, Bookstein, Barr, Press & Sampson, 1998). Permanent damage to the central nervous system (CNS) and the attendant life-long disorders of learning, memory, and behavioral regulation reflect the debilitating consequences of prenatal exposure to alcohol. In recent years, studies have included groups of children known to have had heavy prenatal exposure to alcohol, but for whom the diagnosis of FAS cannot be made because the children lacked the characteristic facial dysmorphology necessary to meet the diagnostic criteria. In those studies, the extent of brain damage and cognitive/behavioral dysfunction was nearly as severe for the alcohol-exposed children without the full FAS phenotype, as that found in the children with a confirmed FAS diagnosis (Mattson, Riley, Gramling, Delis & Jones, 1997; Mattson, Riley, Gramling, Delis & Jones, 1998; Sowell, Jernigan, Mattson, Riley, Sobel & Jones, 1996). The recent report from the Institute of Medicine (Stratton, et al., 1996) recommended a classification of Alcohol-Related Neurodevelopmental Disorder (ARND) for children with CNS abnormalities related to prenatal alcohol exposure, but who do not have the FAS face. The recommendation for this diagnostic category emphasizes the fact that developmental disorders resulting from prenatal alcohol-induced brain damage are not confined just to those who are diagnosed with FAS. A recent estimate places the combined prevalence of FAS and ARND at nearly 1 in every 100 live births (Sampson, Streissguth, Bookstein, Little, Clarren, Dehaene et al., 1997).

Across individuals, brain damage and behavioral dysfunction resulting from prenatal alcohol exposure covers a wide spectrum of abnormalities in humans (Abel, 1995; Abel & Hannigan, 1995). Diminished IQ is typical, but it may range from mild-to-moderate mental retardation to normal. Recent neuropsychological studies have indicated varying degrees of cognitive deficits, including problems in executive function, working memory, planning and abstract thinking, speed of information processing, spatial abilities, arithmetic, encoding, and shifting attention (Coles, Platzman, Raskind-Hood, Brown, Falek & Smith, 1997; Jacobson, Jacobson, Sokol & Ager, 1998; Kopera-Frye, DeHaene & Streissguth, 1996; Mattson & Riley, 1998; Mattson et al., 1998; Olson, Feldman, Streissguth, Sampson & Bookstein, 1998; Streissguth, Sampson, Carmichael Olson, Bookstein, Barr, Scott et al., 1994), along with poor regulation of adaptive behavior and social skills (Streissguth et al., 1998; Thomas, Kelly, Mattson & Riley, 1998b) and motor dysfunction (Kyllerman, Aronson, Sabel, Karlberg, Sandin & Olegard, 1985). The variability in the expression of CNS structural and functional effects in populations heavily exposed to alcohol prenatally likely reflects the complex interactions of multiple risk factors. These include variation in the alcohol exposure scenario (quantity, frequency, pattern, and developmental timing of maternal drinking), together with subject and environmental variables such as maternal physiology, polydrug exposure, nutritional status, socioeconomic status and postnatal environment, and genetic contributions to vulnerability.

EXPERIMENTAL APPROACHES TO ALCOHOL-RELATED NEURODEVELOPMENTAL DISORDERS

To understand the variable severity of consequences of prenatal alcohol exposure, experimental studies are necessary in which the alcohol exposure is known and in which dependent measures of structural and functional damage are as precise as possible. One of the main barriers to effective identification, intervention, and treatment of children with ARND is the lack of systematic knowledge about the contributions of different risk factors to phenotypic variations in alcohol-affected children. It is difficult to obtain reliable, accurate, verifiable, or precise information about different patterns of drinking or changes in drinking patterns over different periods across pregnancy. Experimental studies using animal models are necessary to test the relative risk associated with different patterns of alcohol exposure, using measures of behavioral and neurobiological outcomes that are relevant to effects seen in humans.

The second barrier to understanding ARND is that there is no systematic knowledge of the specific consequences of prenatal alcohol exposure on the development and function of specifically identified neural circuits involved in learning. The analysis of learning deficits in humans has so far been limited to evaluations of performance on neuropsychological or cognitive tests, sometimes combined with structural neuroimaging data describing effects in specific regions or structures. In animal models of prenatal alcohol-induced damage, correlations between structural or functional measures for certain brain regions and behavioral impairments have been reported, e.g., for acquisition of spatial delayed alternation (Nagahara & Handa, 1997) or parallel bar traversal (Thomas, Goodlett & West, 1998a). However, these approaches are generally limited by the difficulty in specifying the locus and nature of neuronal information processing that is affected by early alcohol exposure. This difficulty results from the lack of detailed understanding of the neural substrates underlying the learned behaviors.

Classical eyeblink conditioning offers an ideal, if not unique, experimental alternative. It involves operationally defined manipulations and measures that allow precise control and measurement of an empirically valid associative learning process that generalizes from non-human mammals to humans. As a model of mammalian learning, it is currently the best-characterized in behavioral neuroscience. The empirical and logical advantages of being able to relate behavioral learning to an identified neural circuit are as crucial to the effort to localize the causes of learning disorders (Stanton & Freeman, 1994) as they are to the effort to find the "engram" (Thompson, 1986). We report here our initial efforts to use eyeblink conditioning to develop a programmatic approach to the structural, functional, and behavioral consequences of brain damage produced by prenatal alcohol exposure. After reviewing the clinical evidence that gestational alcohol exposure in humans damages the cerebellum, the remainder of this chapter describes current and future efforts to understand the principles and mechanisms of ARND through experimental studies of eyeblink conditioning in developing rodents.

CEREBELLAR DAMAGE AND MOTOR DYSFUNCTION IN CHILDREN PRENATALLY EXPOSED TO ALCOHOL

Some of the earliest indications that the cerebellum and brainstem are vulnerable to prenatal alcohol-induced damage were from the first autopsy reports of confirmed FAS cases who died in infancy, usually from cardiac or CNS complications (Clarren, 1986). The sample of autopsied cases is small and skewed toward the most extreme neuropathologic outcomes, since FAS-related malformations in live-born infants rarely compromise long-term viability. In Clarren's 1986 review, 10 of the 16 autopsy cases were rated as having cerebellar and brainstem dysgenesis, with hypocellularity being a common pathologic feature.

Identified abnormalities in development of motor function trace back to the early descriptions of FAS and children of alcoholic women (Jones et al., 1973). Developmental problems in motor coordination, fine and gross motor control, balance, and gait are commonly reported consequences in children known to have been heavily exposed to alcohol prenatally (Barr, Streissguth, Darby & Sampson, 1990; Kyllerman et al., 1985; Marcus, 1987; Olegard, Sabel, Aronson, Sandin, Johansson, Carsson et al., 1979). Recent experimental analyses comparing motor performance of prenatal alcohol-exposed children and control populations have demonstrated alcohol-related deficits in equilibrium on a dynamic tilt test of balance correction under conditions when the available somatosensory information was unreliable (Roebuck, Simmons, Mattson & Riley, 1998b; Roebuck, Simmons, Richardson, Mattson & Riley, 1998c). A recent study also reports that heavy prenatal alcohol exposure produces general deficits in measures of gross motor function on the Bruininks-Oseretsky Test of Motor Proficiency (Johnson, Goodman & Mattson, 1999).

Quantitative MRI neuroimaging studies in children with heavy prenatal alcohol exposure have confirmed the overall reduction in brain volume (microencephaly) characteristic of FAS. Although the total volume of both the forebrain and cerebellum are reduced in these children, reductions in size of the anterior vermis of the cerebellum (Sowell, et al., 1996) and of the basal ganglia (Mattson, Riley, Sowell, Jernigan, Sobel & Jones, 1996) are disproportionately greater than for the whole brain. The cerebellar reductions evident in these imaging studies, along with the neurobehavioral studies and the autopsy cases, indicate that cerebellar damage is a significant, prominent effect of heavy prenatal alcohol exposure in humans.

CEREBELLAR DAMAGE AND MOTOR IMPAIRMENT IN THE NEONATAL RAT MODEL

Animal model studies over the last 25 years have been essential for establishing that alcohol is a teratogen and for identifying and evaluating key risk factors that determine the type and severity of effects on brain and behavioral development (Becker, Diaz-Granados & Randall, 1996; Goodlett & Johnson, 1999; Hannigan, 1996; Hannigan & Abel, 1996). There is strong evidence from animal studies (Goodlett & Johnson, 1999; Maier, Chen & West, 1996) and more limited evidence from human studies (Coles, 1994; Jacobson et al., 1998; Streissguth, Bookstein, Sampson & Barr, 1993) that the wide range of observed types and severity of CNS damage and neurobehavioral effects result, in part, from variation in the pattern, duration and timing of developmental exposure to alcohol. Periods of enhanced vulnerability are evident for many effects, implying that the developmental timing of exposure in human pregnancies may be critical to the outcomes observed (Coles, 1994; Goodlett & Johnson, 1999; Maier et al., 1996). Binge patterns of drinking are associated with more adverse outcomes (Jacobson et al., 1998; Streissguth et al., 1994; West, Goodlett, Bonthius & Pierce, 1989), and drinking that extends into the third trimester appears to increase the severity of effects (Smith, Coles, Lancaster, Fernhoff & Falek, 1986a; Smith, Lancaster, Moss-Wells, Coles & Falek, 1986b).

The Neonatal Rat Model of Alcohol Exposure during the Human Third Trimester

To compare neuroteratogenic effects of drug exposure across species, it is essential to evaluate the timing of exposure based on comparable stages of brain development rather than on a time scale relative to birth. In that regard, the brain developmental processes comparable to those occurring over the human third trimester, occur in the rat after birth—over the first two postnatal weeks (Bayer, Altman, Russo & Zhang, 1993; Dobbing & Sands, 1973; West, 1987). For example, in terms of Purkinje cell development, the process of neurite outgrowth and formation of the characteristic dendritic tree during synaptogenesis occurs in humans over the third trimester, beginning around fetal week 24 (Zecevic & Rakic, 1976). In the rat, the same process occurs approximately over postnatal days 3 to 12.

Over the last two decades, a large number of studies from many labs have documented that alcohol exposure in this "third trimester equivalent" period of brain development in neonatal rats constitutes a stage of vulnerability to permanent brain damage and behavioral dysfunction (Goodlett & Johnson, 1999; Goodlett & West, 1992; Samson, 1986; West et al., 1989). In addition to being able to study effects related to third trimester exposure, the neonatal rat model also provides precise knowledge of (and control over) a primary intervening variable—blood alcohol concentration. Whether administration involves use of artificial rearing procedures to control nutritional status (West, 1993) or the recent modifications using intragastric intubation (Goodlett, Pearlman & Lundahl, 1998; Light, Kane, Pierce, Jenkins, Ge, Brown et al., 1998), the neonatal rat model allows experimental manipulation of the key variables determining the alcohol exposure scenario, including the dose, pattern and timing of each exposure episode.

Cerebellar Damage in the Neonatal Rat Model

The effects of neonatal alcohol administration on cerebellar structural development have been extensively characterized over the last decade, and the key parameters of exposure that determine the extent of damage have been identified (Goodlett & Johnson, 1999; Goodlett & West, 1992; Maier et al., 1996). The daily pattern of alcohol exposure is a key risk factor, with cerebellar cell loss being much more severe when a given amount of alcohol is administered in a relatively short period of time (2-4 hours) than when it is distributed over the whole day (Bonthius & West, 1990; Bonthius & West, 1991). The more severe damage with binge drinking is directly related to the higher episodic peak blood alcohol concentrations produced with binge drinking. The increased risk associated with binge drinking has been broadly confirmed for neurobehavioral measures in human studies (Jacobson et al., 1998; Streissguth et al., 1994), and underscores the recent emphasis on using measures of the number of drinks per episode in assessing risk for ARND.

Using the binge exposure model in neonatal rats, two other key determinants of cerebellar damage (cell loss) have been identified—the developmental timing of exposure and the amount of alcohol per binge (reviewed in Goodlett & Johnson, 1999). Most of the neonatal studies have administered alcohol over postnatal days 4-9, and neonatal exposure produces more severe Purkinje cell loss than comparable exposure spanning the prenatal period of Purkinje cell neurogenesis in rats (Marcussen, Goodlett, Mahoney & West, 1994). During the neonatal period of Purkinje cell synaptogenesis, clear temporal windows of vulnerability to alcohol-induced cell loss have been documented. Binge exposure before postnatal day 7 produces significantly more severe Purkinje cell loss than similar exposure initiated after postnatal day 7 (Goodlett & Eilers, 1997; Hamre & West, 1993; Thomas et al., 1998a). As shown in Figure 1 (from Goodlett & Eilers, 1997), just a single episode of binge alcohol exposure on postnatal day 4 (mean peak blood alcohol concentration = 387 mg/dl) resulted in significant reductions in the number of cerebellar Purkinje cells, whereas similar exposure on postnatal day 9 had no significant effect.

The amount of Purkinje cell loss is directly proportional to the dose of alcohol administered during the daily binges. For example, a recent dose-response analysis evaluated the number of surviving Purkinje cells following daily binge exposures of 4.5, 5.25, or 6.0 g/kg of ethanol administered on postnatal days 4-6 (Goodlett, Pearlman & Lundahl, 1998). As shown in Figure 2, alcohol reduced the number of Purkinje cells in a dose-dependent manner, with percent reductions relative to untreated controls reaching 50% for the 6.0 g/kg dose. As reviewed elsewhere (Goodlett & Johnson, 1999), a large number of studies from several independent investigators have confirmed that cerebellar development in the neonatal rat, a period approximately comparable to human cerebellar development occurring over human fetal weeks 24-32, appears to be a critical period of vulnerability to alcohol-induced cerebellar Purkinje cell loss.

Whether Purkinje cell death is a primary effect of alcohol exposure is not currently known. The mechanisms and pathways of pathogenesis underlying neonatal alcohol-induced cell loss have not been established, but preliminary evidence suggests that Purkinje cell death resulting from acute exposure on postnatal day 4 occurs very rapidly (Mahoney, Abbott & West, 1997). Recent anatomical studies have suggested that the neuronal populations with afferent or efferent connections with Purkinje cells are reduced in direct proportion to the alcohol-induced Purkinje cell loss. These include the cerebellar granule cells (Bonthius & West, 1991; Hamre & West, 1993; Napper & West, 1995b), the deep cerebellar nuclei (Napper, 1997), and the inferior olive (Napper & West, 1995a). The alcohol-induced cell loss in these populations may be a direct effect of alcohol on those neurons. Alternatively, the loss may be secondary to loss of Purkinje cells, since Purkinje cells are the main target of efferent projections from the inferior olive and from cerebellar granule cells, and the main source of afferent input to the deep nuclei. Regardless, it appears that the long-term consequence of heavy neonatal alcohol exposure in the rat is a dose-related reduction in neuronal numbers in the major populations of this brainstem-cerebellar network, and the reductions appear proportional across the populations evaluated so far.

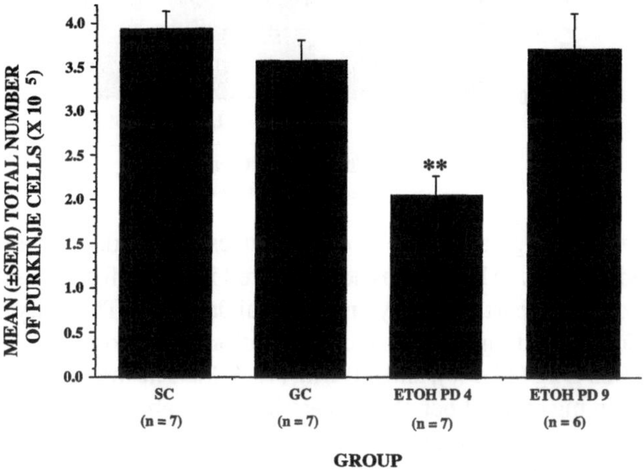

Figure 1. Temporal Windows of Vulnerability to Alcohol-induced Purkinje Cell Loss during the Early Postnatal Period. Alcohol was administered as a 15% v/v solution in milk formula, delivered via artificial rearing in two feedings, two hours apart, either on postnatal day 4 (ETOH PD 4) or on postnatal day 9 (ETOH PD 9). Compared to suckle controls (SC) or artificially reared gastrostomy controls (GC), only the postnatal day 4 exposure resulted in significant Purkinje cell loss. (Reprinted with permission from Goodlett & Eilers, Alcoholism: Clinical and Experimental Research, 1997.)

It should be noted as well that although there is substantial evidence for neonatal alcohol-induced damage to the cerebellum, there is only a single report that has evaluated physiological functioning (Backman, West, Mahoney, & Palmer, 1998). In that study, spontaneous and evoked activity of Purkinje cells, recorded from vermal lobules IX and X of adult rats under urethane anesthesia, was not different from controls. However, the proportion of Purkinje neurons generating complex spike bursts was decreased in the alcohol-exposed rats, suggesting an abnormality in the synaptic interactions between the climbing fibers (from the inferior olive) and the

Purkinje cells. Clearly, additional detailed studies of the physiology of the alcohol-damaged cerebellum are warranted. The potential to evaluate learning-related neuroplasticity in the cerebellar-brainstem circuits of behaving rats undergoing classical eyeblink conditioning should provide ground-breaking insights into the functional consequences of alcohol-induced damage to the developing brain.

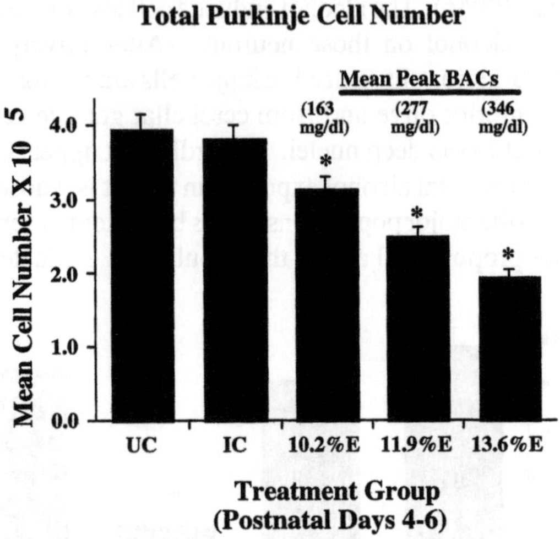

Figure 2. Neonatal binge alcohol exposure induces a dose-dependent reduction in cerebellar Purkinje cells. Alcohol was administered in a milk formula solution in two intubations, two hours apart, each day on postnatal days 4-6. The daily alcohol doses (in g/kg/day) corresponding to the v/v concentrations listed on the X-axis were 4.5 g/kg (10.2%), 5.25 g/kg (11.9%), and 6.0 g/kg (13.6%). The mean peak blood alcohol concentrations (in mg ethanol per 100 ml) are indicated above each group. The total number of Purkinje cells in the cerebellum was counted on postnatal day 10 using the stereological optical fractionator. UC: Unintubated controls; IC: Intubated controls. (Reprinted with permission from Goodlett, Pearlman & Lundahl, Neurotoxicology & Teratology, 1998.)

Motor Correlates of Cerebellar Damage in the Neonatal Rat Model

Early postnatal alcohol exposure has been shown to impair performance on a variety of tasks that challenge motor coordination and hindlimb control. Deficits have been found in gait (Meyer, Kotch & Riley, 1990a), parallel bar traversal (Goodlett & Lundahl, 1996; Klintsova, Cowell, Swain, Napper, Goodlett & Greenough, 1998; Meyer, Kotch & Riley, 1990b; Thomas, Wasserman, West & Goodlett, 1996), balance on a rotating rod (Goodlett, Thomas & West, 1991; Klintsova et al., 1998), and peg walking (McKinley & Goodlett, 1997). In general, the severity of motor performance deficits is consistent with the degree of structural damage to the cerebellum. A recent study explicitly tested the correlation between motor performance deficits and cerebellar damage using alcohol treatments at different times during the neonatal period. The number of surviving cerebellar Purkinje cells was significantly correlated (r = +0.74) with performance measures on a parallel bar traversal task tested on postnatal days 30-32 (Thomas, et al., 1998a).

CLASSICAL EYEBLINK CONDITIONING DEFICITS IN THE NEONATAL RAT MODEL

The above findings indicate clear behavioral consequences of cerebellar damage resulting from neonatal alcohol exposure in rats. However, most of the described behavioral phenomena are not understood in terms of cerebellar circuitry and, as argued previously, it is therefore difficult to integrate neuroanatomical, neurophysiological and behavioral studies of alcohol-induced cerebellar damage with these behavioral tasks. This led us to ask whether neonatal alcohol exposure would impair acquisition of eyeblink conditioning in developing rats. In our first study, we conditioned weanling (23-24 days-old) Long-Evans rats that had been given 5.25 g/kg/day of alcohol via artificial rearing procedures on postnatal days 4-9 (Stanton & Goodlett, 1998). This alcohol treatment represented a heavy binge exposure (mean peak blood alcohol concentrations were measured to be about 320 mg/dl on postnatal day 6). Our structural studies in other rats given treatments producing similar blood alcohol profiles indicated that this treatment reduces Purkinje cell numbers to about 60% of the mean number of Purkinje cells in control rats. The weanling rats were given three conditioning sessions in the delay paradigm, 100 trials per session, 5 hours apart on postnatal days 23-24 according to the general procedures of Stanton & Freeman (1994). Briefly, the conditioned stimulus (CS) was a 2.8 kHz, 380 msec, 90 dB tone and the unconditioned stimulus (US) was a 100 msec, 2 mA, periocular shock (Skelton, 1988; Stanton & Freeman, 1994). On paired trials, the CS overlapped and coterminated with the US, yielding a CS-US delay interval of 280 msec. During each training session, 9 out of 10 trials were paired trials, and the 10th trial was a CS-alone test trial (Stanton, et al., 1992).

As shown in Figure 3 (left panel), the ethanol-exposed group (filled circles) failed to show acquisition of conditioned eyeblink responses. The gastrostomy control (GC) and suckle control groups (SC) showed a large increase in CR amplitude across the 3 training sessions, but the ethanol-exposed group (ETOH) showed no such increase. This conditioning deficit was not the result of an inability to perform the eyeblink response because there were no group differences in unconditioned eyeblink responses (URs) to the unconditioned stimulus (Figure 3, right panel). There were also no group differences in "alpha" or startle-related blink responses to the tone CS (data not shown, Stanton & Goodlett, 1998). This severe and selective impairment in eyeblink conditioning is consistent with the view that cerebellar damage causes the behavioral effect. The fact that we can demonstrate this effect at an age when the rat first normally shows clear evidence of associative eyeblink conditioning indicates that this conditioning paradigm provides a promising way of integrating anatomical, physiological and behavioral studies of cerebellar development after early alcohol insults.

We have followed up the first study with a replication (Stanton & Goodlett, 1999)in which alcohol was administered via intragastric intubation (avoiding artificial rearing, see Goodlett, Lundahl & Pearlman, 1998). The amount of training that the weanling rats received was increased to 600 trials (six 100-trial sessions across two days instead of three 100-trial sessions in one day); groups of unpaired conditioning

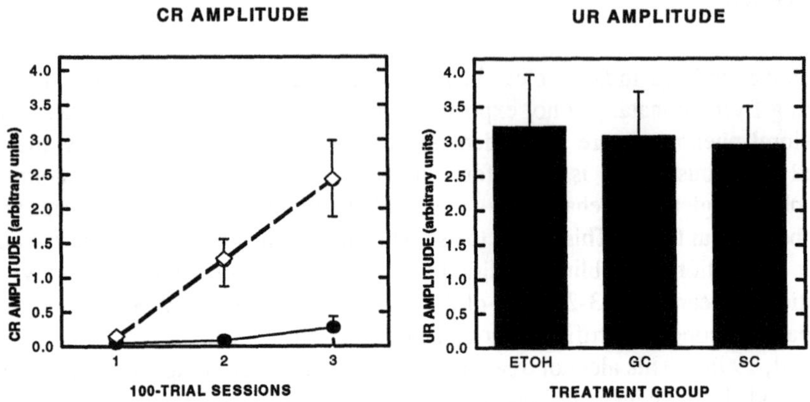

Figure 3. Neonatal Binge Alcohol Exposure Severely Impairs Classical Eyeblink CRs but not URs in Weanling Rats. Note in the left panel that the CR amplitude of the alcohol group [filled circles; ETOH] failed to increase over the three 100-trial sessions of paired training, whereas both the suckle controls [open diamonds; SC] and the gastrostromy controls [open circles, overlapped by diamonds; GC] showed CR acquisition typical for this age. Note in the right panel the absence of group differences in eyeblink amplitude measures in response to the periorbital shock used as the US. (Reprinted with permission from Stanton & Goodlett, Alcoholism: Clinical and Experimental Research, 1998).

controls were included as well (see Freeman, Carter & Stanton, 1995). In other respects, the design and procedure was essentially identical to our first study (Stanton & Goodlett, 1998). The ETOH groups were compared with Sham-intubated (SI) and Unintubated Controls (UC).

Analysis of CR amplitude in this replication study confirmed the predicted interaction of neonatal treatment and type of training, and revealed three major findings. First, the alcohol treatment produced severe acquisition impairments, confirming our previous findings from the artificial rearing study. The acquisition pattern over the three sessions on the first training day for the three groups given paired training yielded the expected significant increase in CR amplitude in the SI and UC control groups, but almost no increase in the ETOH group. The differences in exposure regimen between the two studies—artificial rearing in the first vs. intubation in the second—did not substantially alter the outcome. Second, the deficits were in the associative aspects of conditioning. CR amplitudes for the three groups that received unpaired training did not differ significantly across treatment or training sessions. Neonatal ETOH exposure altered eyeblink responding under associative training conditions, but not under unpaired training conditions. Third, with more extended training, evidence of some conditioning did emerge in the alcohol group, albeit still well below controls. The three additional 100-trial sessions on the second day of training resulted in a significant increase in CR amplitude in the ETOH group, relative to its unpaired counterpart, and relative to performance after the first three sessions. It appeared that alcohol-induced deficits in acquisition at this age reflect a severe impairment, but not an absolute failure, of associative processes underlying the generation of the eyeblink CR.

The slow acquisition of eyeblink CRs and the significantly smaller amplitudes once CRs are expressed, are remarkably parallel to behavioral deficits shown from other conditions involving damage to the cerebellar cortex, including the *pcd* mutant mice (Chen et al, 1996), experimental lesions of rabbit cerebellar cortex (Lavond & Steinmetz, 1989), as well as in human neuropathological cases involving cerebellar cortical lesions (Woodruff-Pak et al., 1996). These parallel findings could have important implications for our search for the locus and nature of ethanol-induced brain damage that is responsible for the eyeblink conditioning impairments.

We have also begun to evaluate the long-term consequences of the neonatal binge alcohol exposure, using paired and unpaired training in adult rats (Green, Rogers, Rorick, Goodlett & Steinmetz, 1999). As with the studies in weanlings, the alcohol treatments were 5.25 g/kg/day, delivered on postnatal days 4-9 via intragastric intubation. For these adult studies, the rats were given one session per day, 100 trials per session, for 10 days. Rats of the alcohol group emitted significantly fewer CRs, and the amplitudes of CRs emitted were reduced compared to controls. Given this evidence that the eyeblink conditioning deficits induced by heavy neonatal alcohol exposure endure into maturity, subsequent analyses are needed to address what aspect of neuronal function and plasticity in the cerebellar-brainstem circuits account for this learning deficit.

Taking advantage of the fact that the basic neuronal circuitry essential for classical eyeblink conditioning has been delineated, we have begun a series of experiments aimed at evaluating neuronal activity in several key areas of the brainstem and cerebellum. Of particular interest will be the single-unit recording data from the pontine nuclei, inferior olive, cerebellar cortex, and the interpositus nucleus. The pontine nuclei and inferior olive have been identified as important relay points for transmitting the CS and US, respectively, into the cerebellum. Cerebellar cortex and the interpositus nucleus are critical sites of convergence for the CS and US and are thought to contain neurons that change their firing properties to encode acquisition and performance of the classically conditioned response. We plan to systematically examine activity in these regions to test the functional integrity of this conditioning circuit, with the aim of advancing our understanding of the debilitating effects of early alcohol exposure on neural and behavioral functioning.

PROSPECTIVE USES OF EYEBLINK CONDITIONING TO STUDY ALCOHOL-RELATED NEURODEVELOPMENTAL DISORDERS

From the work completed so far using the neonatal rat model of third-trimester alcohol exposure, it is clear that heavy exposure during an identified critical period of vulnerability induces severe cerebellar damage and significant, permanent deficits in eyeblink conditioning. Some of the key questions concerning risk factors described previously, particularly those concerning different alcohol exposure scenarios (dose, timing, and duration of exposure), can now be expediently addressed, at least in terms of this cerebellar-dependent form of learning. This approach, combined with quantitative analyses of neuronal populations implicated in eyeblink conditioning (interpositus nucleus, cerebellar cortex, inferior olive, and pontine nuclei), has the potential to extend and greatly refine the correlational analysis of alcohol-induced brain damage and developmental disorders of behavior.

Perhaps the greatest advantage of eyeblink conditioning is that it provides a means to begin to identify what aspects of neuronal function are compromised by alcohol exposure. Single-unit analysis of patterns of neuronal activity—in the interpositus nucleus, the cerebellar cortex, the inferior olive, or the pontine nuclei—over the course of conditioning, can help identify whether the deficits can be attributed to specific functional abnormalities within identified sites or cell populations of the brainstem-cerebellar neural circuit. For example, the behavioral deficits may result from impaired synaptic activation in the brainstem or cerebellum related either to CS or US input. Alternatively, the deficits may involve underlying problems in cellular neuroplasticity in the interpositus or cerebellar cortex related specifically to associative changes mediating learning. The results from the electrophysiological studies, coupled with anatomical analyses, should provide data that identify causes and correlates of the deficits in learning observed in animals given early exposure to alcohol.

As a final, crucial point, the eyeblink conditioning model provides one of the most direct means of taking knowledge and information gained from scientific studies of animal models, and devising parallel applications of the paradigm to humans at risk for Alcohol-Related Neurodevelopmental Disorders. Eyeblink conditioning in adult humans has a long history of use, both for experimental studies in adults and in studies of pathological conditions (see companion volume, Woodruff-Pak & Steinmetz, 2000). Procedures have been adapted for use in studying human infant learning (Little, Lipsitt & Rovee-Collier, 1984), most recently to identify parameters useful in evaluating very young infants from normal and at-risk pregnancies (Ivkovich, Collins, Eckerman, Krasnegor & Stanton, 1999; Ivkovich, Eckerman, Krasnegor & Stanton, 2000). One of the most pressing problems in fetal alcohol research is the need for a valid, precise, and effective means to screen newborns and infants from at-risk pregnancies, to identify those with severe alcohol-induced CNS damage or with specific types of functional deficits. Eyeblink conditioning may provide an effective and practical tool to include in that process. This would be particularly true if eyeblink conditioning deficits in humans could be linked to heavier alcohol exposure or to exposure that extends into the third trimester. Toward that end, eyeblink conditioning may provide a specific behavioral correlate of cerebellar damage, and may help identify infants or children who may be targeted for intensive efforts of intervention or specific forms of rehabilitation (Klintsova et al., 1998).

REFERENCES

Abel, E.L. (1995). An update on incidence of FAS: FAS is not an equal opportunity birth defect. *Neurotoxicology and Teratology, 17*, 437-443.

Abel, E.L., & Hannigan, J.H. (1995). Maternal risk factors in fetal alcohol syndrome: Provocative and permissive influences. *Neurotoxicology and Teratology, 17*, 448-462.

Aiba, A., Kano, M., Chen, C., Stanton, M.E., Fox, G.D., Herrup, K., Zwingman, T.A., & Tonegawa, S. (1994). Deficient cerebellar long-term depression and impaired motor learning in mGluR1 mutant mice. *Cell, 79*, 377-388.

Backman, C., West, J.R., Mahoney, J.C., & Palmer, M.R. (1998). Electrophysiological characterization of cerebellar neurons from adult rats exposed to ethanol during development. *Alcoholism: Clinical and Experimental Research, 22*, 1137-1145.

Barr, H.M., Streissguth, A.P., Darby, B.L., & Sampson, P.D. (1990). Prenatal exposure to alcohol, caffeine, tobacco and aspirin: Effects on fine and gross motor performance in 4-year-old children. *Developmental Psychology, 26(3)*, 339-348.

Bayer, S.A., Altman, J., Russo, R.J., & Zhang, X. (1993). Timetables of neurogenesis in the human brain based on experimentally determined patterns in the rat. *Neurotoxicology, 14*, 83-144.

Becker, H.C., Diaz-Granados, J.L., & Randall, C.L. (1996). Teratogenic actions of ethanol in the mouse: A minireview. *Pharmacology, Biochemistry, and Behavior, 55*, 501-513.

Berthier, N.E., & Moore, J.W. (1986). Cerebellar Purkinje cell activity related to the classically conditioned nictitating membrane response. *Experimental Brain Research, 63*, 341-350.

Bonthius, D.J., & West, J.R. (1990). Alcohol-induced neuronal loss in developing rats: Increased brain damage with binge exposure. *Alcoholism: Clinical and Experimental Research, 14*, 107-118.

Bonthius, D.J., & West, J.R. (1991). Permanent neuronal deficits in rats exposed to alcohol during the brain growth spurt. *Teratology, 44*, 147-163.

Chen, L., Bao, S., Lockard, J.M., Kim, J.J., & Thompson, R.F. (1996). Impaired classical eyeblink conditioning in cerebellar-lesioned and Purkinje cell degeneration (*pcd*) mutant mice. *Journal of Neuroscience, 16*, 2829-2838.

Clarren, S.K. (1986). Neuropathology in fetal alcohol syndrome. In J.R. West (Ed.), *Alcohol and Brain Development (pp. 158-166)*. New York: Oxford University Press.

Coles, C. (1994). Critical periods for prenatal alcohol exposure: evidence from animal and human studies. *Alcohol Health & Research World, 18*, 22-29.

Coles, C.D., Platzman, K.A., Raskind-Hood, C.L., Brown, R.T., Falek, A., & Smith, I.E. (1997). A comparison of children affected by prenatal alcohol exposure and attention deficit, hyperactivity disorder. *Alcoholism: Clinical and Experimental Research, 21*, 150-161.

Daum, I., Schugens, M.M., Ackermann, H., Lutzenberger, W., Dichgans, J., & Birbaumer, N. (1993). Classical conditioning after cerebellar lesions in humans. *Behavioral Neuroscience, 107(5)*, 748-756.

Dobbing, J., & Sands, J. (1973). The quantitative growth and development of the human brain. *Archives of Disease in Childhood, 48*, 757-767.

Freeman, J.H., Jr., Barone, S., Jr., & Stanton, M.E. (1995a). Disruption of cerebellar maturation by an antimitotic agent impairs the ontogeny of eyeblink conditioning in rats. *Journal of Neuroscience, 15*, 7301-7314.

Freeman, J.H., Jr., Carter, C.S., & Stanton, M.E. (1995b). Early cerebellar lesions impair eyeblink conditioning in developing rats: Differential effect of unilateral lesions on postnatal day 10 or 20. *Behavioral Neuroscience, 109*, 893-902.

Goodlett, C.R., & Eilers, A.T. (1997). Alcohol-induced Purkinje cell loss with a single binge exposure in neonatal rats: A stereological study of temporal windows of vulnerability. *Alcoholism: Clinical and Experimental Research, 21*, 738-744.

Goodlett, C.R., & Johnson, T.B. (1999). Temporal windows of vulnerability to alcohol during the third trimester equivalent: Why "knowing when" matters. In J.H. Hannigan, L.P. Spear, N.E. Spear, & C.R. Goodlett (Eds.), *Alcohol and Alcoholism: Effects on Brain and Development (pp. 59-91)*. Hillsdale, NJ: Lawrence Erlbaum.

Goodlett, C.R., & Lundahl, K.R. (1996). Temporal determinants of neonatal alcohol-induced cerebellar damage and motor performance deficits. *Pharmacology, Biochemistry, and Behavior, 55*, 531-540.

Goodlett, C.R., Pearlman, A.D., & Lundahl, K.R. (1998). Binge neonatal alcohol intubations induce dose-dependent loss of Purkinje cells. *Neurotoxicology and Teratology, 20*, 285-292.

Goodlett, C.R., Thomas, J.D., & West, J.R. (1991). Long-term deficits in cerebellar growth and rotarod performance of rats following "binge-like" alcohol exposure during the neonatal brain growth spurt. *Neurotoxicology and Teratology, 13*, 69-74.

Goodlett, C.R., & West, J.R. (1992). Fetal alcohol effects: Rat model of alcohol exposure during the brain growth spurt. In I. Zagon & T. Slotkin (Eds.), *Maternal Substance Abuse and the Developing Nervous System (pp. 45-75).* New York: Academic Press.

Gormezano, I., Kehoe, E.J., & Marshall, B.S. (1983). Twenty years of classical conditioning research with the rabbit. In J.M. Sprague & A.N. Epstein (Eds.), *Progress in Psychobiology and Physiological Psychology (pp. 198-275).* New York: Academic Press.

Gormezano, I., Prokasy, W.F., & Thompson, R.F. (1987). *Classical Conditioning (3rd ed.).* Hillsdale, NJ: Lawrence Erlbaum Associates.

Green, J.T., Rogers, R.F., Rorick, L.M., Goodlett, C.R., & Steinmetz, J.E. (1999). Early exposure to alcohol disrupts adult cerebellar-dependent learning. *Alcoholism: Clinical and Experimental Research, 23,* 32A.

Hamre, K.M., & West, J.R. (1993). The effects of the timing of ethanol exposure during the brain growth spurt on the number of cerebellar Purkinje and granule cell nuclear profiles. *Alcoholism: Clinical and Experimental Research, 17*, 610-622.

Hannigan, J.H. (1996). What research with animals is telling us about alcohol-related neurodevelopmental disorder. *Pharmacology, Biochemistry, and Behavior, 55*, 489-499.

Hannigan, J.H., & Abel, E.L. (1996). Animal models for the study of alcohol-related birth defects. In H.-L. Sphohr, & H.-C. Steinhausen (Eds.), *Alcohol, Pregnancy and the Developing Child (pp. 77-102).* Cambridge, U.K.: Cambridge University Press.

Ivkovich, D., Collins, K.L., Eckerman, C.O., Krasnegor, N.A., & Stanton, M.E. (1999). Classical delay eyeblink conditioning in 4- and 5-month-old human infants. *Psychological Science, 10,* 4-8.

Ivkovich, D., Eckerman, C.O., Krasnegor, N.A., & Stanton, M.E. (2000). Using eyeblink conditioning to assess neurocognitive development. In D.S. Woodruff-Pak & J.E. Steinmetz (Eds.), *Eyeblink Classical Conditioning: Applications in Humans, Volume I.* Amsterdam: Kluwer Academic Publishers.

Jacobson, J.L., Jacobson, S.W., Sokol, R.J., & Ager, J.W. (1998). Relation of maternal age and pattern of pregnancy drinking to functionally significant cognitive deficits in infancy. *Alcoholism: Clinical and Experimental Research, 22*, 345-351.

Johnson, H.S., Goodman, A.M., & Mattson, S.N. (1999). Fine- and gross-motor deficits in children with heavy prenatal alcohol exposure. *Alcoholism: Clinical and Experimental Research, 23*, 32A.

Jones, K.L., & Smith, D.W. (1973). Recognition of the fetal alcohol syndrome in early infancy. *Lancet, 2*, 999-1001.

Jones, K.L., Smith, D.W., Ulleland, C N., & Streissguth, A.P. (1973). Pattern of malformation in offspring of chronic alcoholic mothers. *Lancet, 1*, 1267-1271.

Klintsova, A.Y., Cowell, R.M., Swain, R.A., Napper, R.M.A., Goodlett, C.R., & Greenough, W.T. (1998). Therapeutic effects of complex motor training on motor performance deficits induced by neonatal binge-like alcohol exposure in rats: I. Behavioral results. *Brain Research, 800,* 48-61.

Kopera-Frye, K., DeHaene, S., & Streissguth, A.P. (1996). Impairments of number processing induced by prenatal alcohol exposure. *Neuropsychologia, 34*, 1187-1196.

Kyllerman, M., Aronson, M., Sabel, K.-G., Karlberg, E., Sandin, B., & Olegard, R. (1985). Children of alcoholic mothers: Growth and motor performance compared to matched controls. *Acta Paediatrica Scandanavica, 74*, 20-26.

Lemoine, P., Harousseau, H., Borteyru, J.P., & Menuet, J.C. (1968). Children of alcoholic parents: Abnormalities observed in 127 cases. *Ouest Med, 8*, 476-482.

Light, K.E., Kane, C.J.M., Pierce, D.R., Jenkins, D., Ge, Y., Brown, G., Yang, H., & Nyamweya, N. (1998). Intragastric intubation: Important aspects of the model for administration of ethanol to rat pusps during the postnatal period. *Alcoholism: Clinical and Experimental Research, 22*, 1600-1606.

Little, A.H., Lipsitt, L.P., & Rovee-Collier, C. (1984). Classical conditioning and retention of the infant's eyelid response: Effects of age and interstimulus interval. *Journal of Experimental Child Psychology, 37*, 512-524.

Lavond, D.G., & Steinmetz, J.E. (1989). Acquisition of classical conditioning without cerebellar cortex. *Behavioural Brain Research, 33*, 113-164.

Logan, C.G., & Grafton, S.T. (1995). Functional anatomy of human eyeblink conditioning determined with regional cerebral glucose metabolism and positron-emission tomography. *Proceedings of the National Academy of Sciences, (USA), 92*, 7500-7504.

Mahoney, J.C., Abbott, L.C., & West, J.R. (1997). Time course of Purkinje cell death following a single day of ethanol exposure in the neonatal rat. *Alcoholism: Clinical and Experimental Research, 21,* 85A.

Maier, S.E., Chen, W., & West, J.R. (1996). The effects of timing and duration of alcohol exposure on development of the fetal brain. In E.L. Abel (Ed.), *Fetal Alcohol Syndrome: From Mechanism to Prevention (pp. 27-50).* Boca Raton, FL: CRC Press.

Marcus, J. C. (1987). Neurological findings in the fetal alcohol syndrome. *Neuropediatrics, 18,* 158-160.

Marcussen, B.L., Goodlett, C.R., Mahoney, J.C., & West, J.R. (1994). Developing rat Purkinje cells are more vulnerable to alcohol-induced depletion during differentiation than during neurogenesis. *Alcohol, 11,* 147-156.

Mattson, S.N., & Riley, E.P. (1998). A review of the neurobehavioral deficits in children with fetal alcohol syndrome or prenatal exposure to alcohol. *Alcoholism: Clinical and Experimental Research, 22,* 279-294.

Mattson, S.N., Riley, E.P., Gramling, L., Delis, D.C., & Jones, K.L. (1997). Heavy prenatal alcohol exposure with or without physical features of the fetal alcohol syndrome leads to IQ deficits. *Journal of Pediatrics, 131,* 718-721.

Mattson, S.N., Riley, E.P., Gramling, L., Delis, D.C., & Jones, K.L. (1998). Neuropsychological comparison of alcohol-exposed children with or without physical features of fetal alcohol syndrome. *Neuropsychology, 12,* 146-153.

Mattson, S.N., Riley, E.P., Sowell, E.R., Jernigan, T L., Sobel, D.F., & Jones, K.L. (1996). A decrease in the size of the basal ganglia children with fetal alcohol syndrome. *Alcoholism: Clinical and Clinical Research, 20,* 1088-1093.

McKinley, P.J., & Goodlett, C.R. (1997). Effects of binge ethanol exposure in neonatal rats on acquisition of novel motor learning as adults. *Alcoholism: Clinical and Experimental Research, 21,* 118A.

Meyer, L.S., Kotch, L.E., & Riley, E.P. (1990a). Alterations in gait following ethanol exposure during the brain growth spurt in rats. *Alcoholism: Clinical and Experimental Research, 14,* 23-27.

Meyer, L.S., Kotch, L.E., & Riley, E.P. (1990b). Neonatal ethanol exposure: Functional alterations associated with cerebellar growth retardation. *Neurotoxicology and Teratology, 12,* 15-22.

Nagahara, A.H., & Handa, R.H. (1997). Fetal alcohol exposure produces delay-dependent memory deficits in juvenile and adult rats. *Alcoholism: Clinical and Experimental Research, 21,* 710-715.

Napper, R.M.A. (1997). A permanent decrease in neurons in the deep cerebellar nucleus of the rat following exposure to ethanol during the postnatal growth spurt. *Alcoholism: Clinical and Experimental Research, Supplement, 21(3),* 84A.

Napper, R.M.A., & West, J.R. (1995a). Permanent neuronal cell loss in the inferior olive of adult rats exposed to alcohol during the brain growth spurt: A stereological study. *Alcoholism: Clinical and Experimental Research, 19,* 1321-1326.

Napper, R.M.N., & West, J.R. (1995b). Permanent neuronal cell loss in the cerebellum of rats exposed to continuous low blood alcohol levels during the brain growth spurt: A stereological investigation. *The Journal of Comparative Neurology, 362,* 283-292.

Olegard, R., Sabel, K.G., Aronson, M., Sandin, B., Johansson, P.R., Carsson, C., Kyllerman, M., Iversen, K., & Hrbek, A. (1979). Effects on the child of alcohol abuse during pregnancy. *Acta Paediatrica Scandinavia Paediatr, 275,* 112-121.

Olson, H.C., Feldman, J.J., Streissguth, A.P., Sampson, P.D., & Bookstein, F.L. (1998). Neuropsychological deficits in adolescents with fetal alcohol syndrome: Clinical findings. *Alcoholism: Clinical and Experimental Research, 22,* 1998-2012.

Roebuck, T.M., Mattson, S.N., & Riley, E.P. (1998a). A review of the neuroanatomical findings in children with fetal alcohol syndrome or prenatal exposure to alcohol. *Alcoholism: Clinical and Experimental Research, 22,* 339-344.

Roebuck, T.M., Simmons, R.W., Mattson, S.N., & Riley, E.P. (1998b). Prenatal exposure to alcohol affects the ability to maintain postural balance. *Alcoholism: Clinical and Experimental Research, 22,* 252-258.

Roebuck, T.M., Simmons, R.W., Richardson, C., Mattson, S.N., & Riley, E.P. (1998c). Neuromuscular responses to disturbance of balance in children with prenatal exposure to alcohol. *Alcoholism: Clinical and Experimental Research, 22,* 1992-1997.

Rudy, J.W. (1992). Development of learning: From elemental to configural associative networks. In C. Rovee-Collier & L.P. Lipsitt (Eds.), *Advances in infancy research (pp. 247-289).* New Jersey: ABLEX Publishing Corporation.

Sampson, P.D., Streissguth, A.P., Bookstein, F.L., Little, R.E., Clarren, S.K., Dehaene, P., Hanson, J.W., & Graham, J.M. (1997). The incidence of fetal alcohol syndrome and prevalence of alcohol-related neurodevelopmental disorder. *Teratology, 56*, 317-326.

Samson, H.H. (1986). Microencephaly and the fetal alcohol syndrome: Human and animal studies. In J.R. West (Ed.), *Alcohol and Brain Development (pp. 167-183).* New York: Oxford University Press.

Schmajuk, N.A., & DiCarlo, J.J. (1991). A neural network approach to hippocampal function in classical conditioning. *Behavioral Neuroscience, 105*, 82-105.

Sears, L.L., Finn, P.R., & Steinmetz, J.E. (1994). Abnormal classical eyeblink in autism. *Journal of Autism and Developmental Disabilities, 24*, 737-751.

Skelton, R.W. (1988). Bilateral cerebellar lesions disrupt conditioned eyelid responses in unrestrained rats. *Behavioral Neuroscience, 102*, 586-590.

Smith, I.E., Coles, C.D., Lancaster, J., Fernhoff, P.M., & Falek, A. (1986a). The effect of volume and duration of prenatal ethanol exposure on neonatal physical and behavioral development. *Neurobehavioral Toxicology and Teratology, 8*, 375-381.

Smith, L.E., Lancaster, J.S., Moss-Wells, S., Coles, C.D., & Falek, A. (1986b). Identifying high risk pregnant drinkers: Biological and behavioral correlates of continuous heavy drinking during pregnancy. *Journal of Studies on Alcohol, 48*, 304-309.

Solomon, P.R., Barth, C.L., Wood, M.S., Velazquez, E., Groccia-Ellison, M., & Yang, B.-Y. (1995). Age-related deficits in retention of the classically conditioned nictitating membrane response in rabbits. *Behavioral Neuroscience, 109*, 18-23.

Sowell, E.R., Jernigan, T.L., Mattson, S.N., Riley, E.P., Sobel, D.F., & Jones, K.L. (1996). Abnormal development of the cerebellar vermis in children prenatally exposed to alcohol: Size reduction in Lobules I-V. *Alcoholism: Clinical and Experimental Research, 20*, 31-34.

Spear, L.P. (1990). Neurobehavioral assessment during the early postnatal period. *Neurobehavioral Toxicology and Teratology, 12*, 489-497.

Stanton, M.E., & Freeman, J H. (1994). Eyeblink conditioning in the developing rat: An animal model of learning in developmental neurotoxicology. *Environmental Health Perspectives, 102*, 131-139.

Stanton, M.E., Freeman, J.H., & Skelton, R.W. (1992). Eyeblink conditioning in the developing rat. *Behavioral Neuroscience, 106*, 657-665.

Stanton, M.E., & Gallagher, M. (1996). Use of Pavlovian conditioning techniques to study disorders of attention and learning. *Mental Retardation & Developmental Disability Research Review, 2*, 234-242.

Stanton, M.E., & Goodlett, C.R. (1998). Neonatal ethanol exposure impairs eyeblink conditioning in weanling rats. *Alcoholism: Clinical and Experimental Research, 22*, 270-275.

Stanton, M.E., & Goodlett, C.R. (1999). Impairment of eyeblink conditioning by neonatal alcohol exposure: Effects of extended training. *Neurotoxicology & Teratology. (abstract)*

Stratton, K., Howe, C., & Battaglia, F. (Eds.). (1996). *Fetal Alcohol Syndrome: Diagnosis, Epidemiology, Prevention, and Treatment.* Washington, D. C.: National Academy Press.

Streissguth, A.P., Bookstein, F.L., Barr, H.M., Press, S., & Sampson, P.D. (1998). A fetal alcohol behavior scale. *Alcoholism: Clinical and Experimental Research, 22*, 325-333.

Streissguth, A.P., Bookstein, F.L., Sampson, P.D., & Barr, H.M. (1993). *The Enduring Effects of Prenatal Alcohol Exposure on Child Development, Birth Through 7 Years.* Ann Arbor, MI: University of Michigan Press.

Streissguth, A.P., Sampson, P.D., Carmichael Olson, H., Bookstein, F.L., Barr, H.M., Scott, M., Feldman, J., & Mirsky, A.F. (1994). Maternal drinking during pregnancy: Attention and short-term memory in 14-year-old offspring—A longitudinal prospective study. *Alcoholism: Clinical and Experimental Research, 18*, 202-218.

Thomas, J.D., Goodlett, C.R., & West, J.R. (1998a). Alcohol-induced Purkinje cell loss depends on the developmental timing of neonatal alcohol exposure and correlates with motor performance. *Developmental Brain Research, 105*, 159-166.

Thomas, J.D., Wasserman, E.A., West, J.R., & Goodlett, C.R. (1996). Behavioral deficits induced by bingelike exposure to alcohol in neonatal rats: Importance of developmental timing and number of episodes. *Developmental Psychobiology, 29*, 433-452.

Thomas, S.E., Kelly, S.J., Mattson, S.N., & Riley, E.P. (1998b). Comparison of social abilities of children with fetal alcohol syndrome to those of children with similar IQ scores and normal controls. *Alcoholism: Clinical and Experimental Research, 22*, 528-533.

Thompson, R.F. (1986). The neurobiology of learning and memory. *Science, 233*, 941-947.

Topka, H., Valls-Sole, J., Massaquoi, S.G., & Hallett, M. (1992). Deficit in classical conditioning in patients with cerebellar degeneration. *Brain, 116*, 961-969.

West, J.R. (1987). Fetal alcohol-induced brain damage and the problem of determining temporal vulnerability: A review. *Alcohol and Drug Research, 7*, 423-441.

West, J.R. (1993). Use of pup in a cup model to study brain development. *Journal of Nutrition, 123*, 382-385.

West, J.R., Goodlett, C.R., Bonthius, D.J., & Pierce, D.R. (1989). Manipulating peak blood alcohol concentrations in neonatal rats: Review of an animal model for alcohol-related developmental effects. *Neurotoxicology, 10*, 347-366.

Woodruff-Pak, D.S., Papka, M., & Ivry, R. (1996). Cerebellar involvement in eyeblink classical conditioning in humans. *Neuropsychology, 10*, 443-458.

Woodruff-Pak, D.S. & Steinmetz, J.E. (2000). Eyeblink Classical Conditioning: Applications in Humans, Volume I. Amsterdame: Kluwer Academic Publishers.

Woodruff-Pak, D.S., & Thompson, R.F. (1988). Cerebellar correlates of classical conditioning across the life span. In P.B. Baltes, D.M. Featherman, & R.M. Lerner (Eds.), *Life-span Development and Behavior.* Hillsdale, NJ: Lawrence Erlbaum Associates.

Zecevic, N., & Rakic, P. (1976). Differentiation of Purkinje cells and their relationship to other components of developing cerebellar cortex in man. *Journal of Comparative Neurology, 167*, 27-48.

7 EYEBLINK CLASSICAL CONDITIONING IN AGING ANIMALS

John T. Green
Indiana University

Diana S. Woodruff-Pak
Temple University

INTRODUCTION

The passage of time produces changes in both the behavior and the brains of organisms. For most psychologists and neuroscientists, brain-behavior relationships are studied at a single point in time. Learning and memory experiments carried out with one age group provide a snapshot of the organism. However, the passage of time adds an additional dimension that can provide insights about basic mechanisms of learning and memory. For example, Carol Barnes found age-related impairments in maze learning in rodents, and these results led her to study hippocampal place cells in older rats and make significant contributions to knowledge about spatial encoding (Barnes, Suster, Shen & McNaughton, 1997). It was the knowledge that eyeblink conditioning was impaired in normal aging that made this well-characterized model attractive for the investigation of neurobiological substrates of age-related memory impairment. Indeed, Richard F. Thompson suggested that the model system of eyeblink classical conditioning might be "the Rosetta stone for brain substrates of age-related deficits in learning and memory," (Thompson, 1988, p. 547).

Aging is most typically associated with declines in functioning, both neural and behavioral. However, individual organisms age at different rates. One organism may show a steady decline in functioning while another shows only slight changes over the years. An important goal towards an understanding of the aging process is to determine how changes in neural structures impact on behavior. As such, tasks that engage well-defined neural substrates are particularly valuable. Eyeblink classical conditioning is such a task. In this chapter, we will review research that suggests that age-associated changes in two neural substrates that have been demonstrated to be critical for eyeblink classical conditioning, the hippocampus and the cerebellum, are responsible for age-associated declines in conditioning. These findings have led to the use of eyeblink classical conditioning as a preclinical test for potential cognition-enhancing drugs intended to reverse declines in learning and memory caused by the effects of both normal and pathological aging on the brain.

EYEBLINK CLASSICAL CONDITIONING AS A MODEL SYSTEM

The model system approach is often an essential one for a detailed investigation of brain-behavior relations. A model system provides the researcher with a well-defined, simple behavior in an animal that can be objectively measured and quantified. This is important if one wants strict operational definitions of terms such as "learning" and "memory". Simple behaviors are also useful in that it is possible to correlate them with activity in discrete areas of the brain. The more complex the behavior, the more difficult it is to know with what aspect the neural activity is correlated. In particular, behaviors for which investigators can predict the timing of responses are critical for identifying neural substrates. Most importantly, the use of animals allows a full investigation of brain-behavior relations, with a view towards generalization to more complex but related behaviors and to more complex species, such as humans. Eyeblink classical conditioning in rabbits is such a model system. In this chapter, we will review the use of eyeblink conditioning as a model of age-associated changes in learning and memory.

Eyeblink classical conditioning is a simple form of learning that can be studied with little modification across a variety of species, including humans. The basic procedure involves repeated trials in which the presentation of an initially neural stimulus, such as a tone (the conditioned stimulus or CS), is followed after approximately half a second by a stimulus that evokes a reflexive eyelid closure, such as a corneal air puff (the unconditioned stimulus or US). The CS is still on when the US is delivered and the two stimuli coterminate. Initially, eyeblinks occur only after the US as a reflexive response (the unconditioned response, or UR). Eventually, eyeblinks occur after the CS but before the US. This is a learned response (the conditioned response, or CR). Thus, learning is defined as the acquisition of CRs.

The critical substrate for eyeblink conditioning in both humans (Woodruff-Pak, 1997) and non-human animals (Steinmetz, 1996) is the cerebellum ipsilateral to the eye that receives the US. The hippocampal formation appears to play a modulatory role. Abnormal functioning of the hippocampus appears to retard the rate of simple eyeblink conditioning. In addition, the hippocampal formation appears to be necessary for procedures in which there are multiple CSs (for a review, see Green & Woodruff-Pak, 2000).

There are at least four advantages to using eyeblink conditioning as an animal model of the effects of aging on learning and memory in humans (Woodruff-Pak, 1995). First, both animals and humans show age-associated deficits in conditioning, and these can be easily dissociated from age-associated changes in sensory systems (i.e., differences in CS thresholds) or motor systems (differences in UR amplitude). Second, both animals and humans show age-associated changes in the neural substrates critical for eyeblink conditioning, the cerebellum and the hippocampus. Third, age-associated deficits have been artificially-induced in both young animal and young human subjects with drugs that affect cholinergic neurotransmission. Finally, age-associated deficits can be reversed in normal older animals using cognition-enhancing drugs. Published studies demonstrating that age-associated deficits in eyeblink classical conditioning can be reversed in normal older humans with cognition-enhancing drugs have not yet appeared, to the best of our knowledge. However, the fact that the identical procedure can be tested in both animals and humans makes eyeblink conditioning a potentially valuable preclinical test.

AGE-ASSOCIATED DEFICITS IN EYEBLINK CONDITIONING

One of the strengths of using eyeblink conditioning as a model of age-associated deficits in learning and memory is that both humans and non-human animals show similar deficits as they age. Humans begin to show age-associated deficits in eyeblink conditioning at about 40-50 years of age (Durkin, Prescott, Furchgott, Cantor & Powell, 1993; Solomon, Pomerleau, Bennett, James & Morse, 1989; Woodruff-Pak & Jaeger, 1998; Woodruff-Pak & Thompson, 1988). Rabbits begin to show age-associated deficits at around two years of age (see Figure 1). Woodruff-Pak (1988) estimated that, based on declines in reproductive capacity, a 2-year-old rabbit is equivalent to a 35-40-year-old human, which suggests similar onset of age-associated declines in eyeblink conditioning in both humans and rabbits. Furthermore, the results found with rabbits and reviewed below appear to generalize to other non-human species, such as rats (Weiss & Thompson, 1991; 1992) and cats (Harrison & Buchwald, 1983).

Age-associated Deficits in the Delay Procedure

In the delay procedure, the CS remains on when the US is delivered and the stimuli coterminate. The interstimulus interval (ISI) is the amount of time between CS onset and US onset, which has been found to be important for classical conditioning. In eyeblink conditioning, ISIs of 250-750 ms are the most common, with the most rapid conditioning between 250 and 500 ms. Table 1 summarizes the studies testing the delay procedure in aging (i.e., over 2-year-old) rabbits.

Age-associated deficits are relatively small in the short-ISI (less than 500-ms) delay procedure for 2-3-year-old rabbits but may increase rapidly beyond three years of age. Powell, Buchanan and Hernandez (1981) were the first to report age-associated deficits in eyeblink conditioning in rabbits. They used a tone CS, an eyeshock US, and a 500-ms ISI in which CS offset coincided with US onset. However, interpretation of this result is complicated by the fact that these rabbits received 100 CS-alone trials before conditioning. Delivery of CS-alone trials prior to CS-US conditioning is known to slow the rate of conditioning, an effect called "latent inhibition". Thus, aging rabbits may have been slowed due to greater latent inhibition. Furthermore, Powell et al. tested rabbits that were approximately 40-month-old, which is the age when serious deficits in the short-ISI delay procedure are observed (Solomon & Groccia-Ellison, 1996).

In contrast to the study by Powell et al., other studies have found only minor deficits in aging rabbits in the short-ISI delay procedure. Using a 450-ms delay procedure with a tone CS and an eyeshock US, Graves and Solomon (1985) reported no differences between 6-month-old rabbits and 36-60-month-old rabbits in either the number of trials to emit eight CRs in 10 consecutive trials or in percentage of CRs. Solomon et al. (1995) reported somewhat slower acquisition in 36-50-month-old rabbits compared to 6-8-month-old rabbits in a 400-ms delay procedure using a tone CS and an air puff US. Using the exact same procedure but with a narrower age range of older rabbits centered at 36-months-old, Coffin and Woodruff-Pak (1993) found some impairment in conditioning, although the effect was not large.

It appears that around two years is the age of onset of significant impairments for rabbits in the short-ISI delay procedure but impairments do not become very severe until after three years of age. Solomon and Groccia-Ellison (1996) compared four different age groups in the same 400-ms delay procedure employed by Solomon et al. (1995) and Coffin and Woodruff-Pak (1993). Young rabbits (3.5-8-month-old) asymptoted at approximately 80% CRs by Day 5 of conditioning. In contrast, 24- and 36-month-old rabbits asymptoted at approximately 60% CRs by Days 5-7 of conditioning, indicating some impairment in learning. By far the greatest impairment, however, was in the 48-month-old rabbits. These rabbits asymptoted at approximately 30% CRs and it took them, on average, about nine days of conditioning to achieve even this low amount of CRs. Note, however, that the age of onset for deficits in eyeblink conditioning varies even within studies and some rabbits over two years of age learn eyeblink conditioning at the same rate as much younger rabbits. In contrast, rabbits less than 1-year-old condition at very similar rates. Increasing variability in the rate of learning with age is probably due to variability in the rate at which the critical substrates for eyeblink conditioning age. This will be discussed in more detail below.

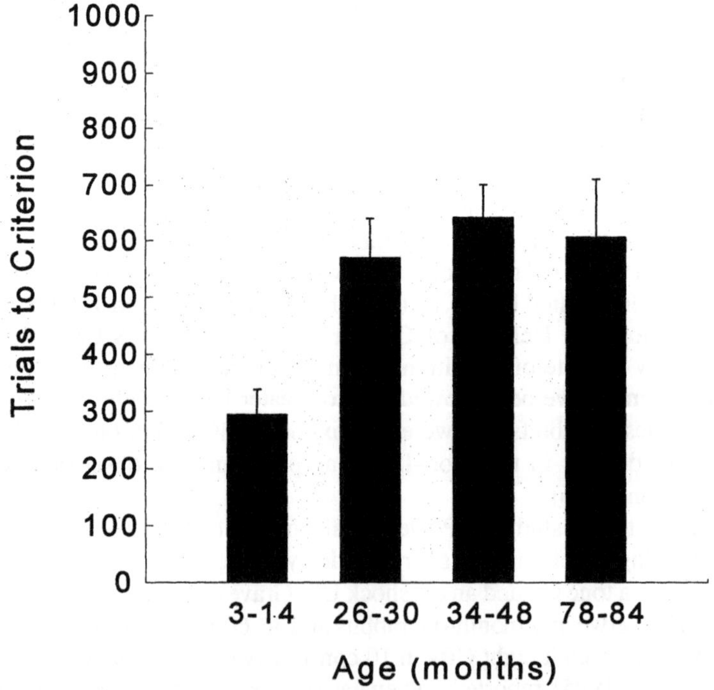

Figure 1. Trials to learning criterion (eight conditioned responses in nine consecutive trials) in the 750 msec EBCC procedure in 35 New Zealand white rabbits. Rabbits ranged in age from 3 to 84 months.

Table 1. Delay Classical Conditioning Procedure in Aging Rabbits

Study	Age (mos.)	CS	US	ISI
Coffin & Woodruff-Pak (1993)	36	tone	air puff	400-ms
Graves & Solomon (1985)	36-40	tone	shock	450-ms
Powell, Buchanan, & Hernandez (1981)	Approx. 40	tone	shock	500-ms[1]
Solomon, Barth, Wood, Velazquez et al. (1995)	36-50	tone	air puff	400-ms
Solomon & Groccia-Ellison (1996)	12-48[2]	tone	air puff	400-ms
Solomon & Groccia-Ellison (1996)	12-48[2]	tone	air puff	900-ms
Solomon, Wood, Groccia-Ellison et al. (1995)	36-42	tone	air puff	400-ms
Woodruff-Pak, Chi, Li, Pak, & Fanelli (1997)	18-44	tone	air puff	750-ms
Woodruff-Pak, Coffin, & Papka (1994)	21-55	tone	air puff	750-ms
Woodruff-Pak & Li (1994)	21-44	tone	air puff	750-ms
Woodruff-Pak, Li, Hinchliffe, & Port (1997)	24-44	tone	air puff	750-ms
Woodruff-Pak, Li, Kazmi, & Kem (1994)	27-36	tone	air puff	750-ms
Woodruff-Pak, Li, & Kem (1994)	24-55	tone	air puff	750-ms
Woodruff-Pak, Steinmetz, & Thompson (1988)	30-44	pons stim.	air puff	250-ms

[1]CS offset coincided with US onset
[2]Compared 1-year-, 2-year-, 3-year-, and 4-year-old rabbits

Eyeblink conditioning in the long-ISI (over 500-ms) delay procedure shows a somewhat earlier onset of age-associated deficits than the short-ISI delay procedure. For example, over the past several years, Woodruff-Pak and colleagues have used the 750-ms delay procedure with a tone CS and an air puff US to test the effects of various drugs on eyeblink classical conditioning (see Chapter 14 in this volume). Several of these studies included both young (3-7-month-old) and aging (over 24-months-old) rabbits that were used as vehicle-injected controls. In all cases, aging rabbits showed large deficits in conditioning relative to young, vehicle-injected controls (Woodruff-Pak, Coffin & Papka, 1994; Woodruff-Pak, Li, Kazmi & Kem, 1994; Woodruff-Pak, Li & Kem, 1994). Aging rabbits required, on average, about 800 to over 1,000 trials in order to emit eight CRs within nine consecutive trials. In comparison, young rabbits in these studies required less than 400 trials.

Solomon and Groccia-Ellison (1996) directly compared four age groups of rabbits in eyeblink conditioning in a 900-ms delay procedure using a tone CS and an air puff US. Six-month-old rabbits asymptoted at about 75% CRs by Day 5, which is very similar to the results discussed above from the same study but testing the 400-ms delay procedure in 6-month-old rabbits. In contrast, 2-year and 3-year-old rabbits took several more days of training to reach the same level of CRs as their corresponding age groups that were tested in the 400-ms delay procedure. This suggests that as the ISI is lengthened, age deficits appear somewhat earlier, although the effect is not nearly as large as when the procedure is changed from delay to trace, as discussed below.

Age-associated Deficits in the Trace Procedure

In the trace procedure, the CS begins and ends, there is a brief 'blank' period (usually about 500-ms), and then the US begins and ends. This 'blank' period makes eyeblink conditioning much more difficult for both young and aging rabbits, and they acquire CRs more slowly than in the delay procedure (Sasse & Woodruff-Pak, 1990; Sasse, Coffin & Woodruff-Pak, 1991). Older rabbits appear to be particularly impaired by the addition of the 'blank' period. The trace procedure typically uses a longer ISI than the delay procedure but this fact alone does not appear to account for the larger age-associated differences in the trace procedure compared to the delay procedure (Solomon & Groccia-Ellison, 1996).

There is some disagreement among laboratories as to how long it takes aging rabbits to learn the trace procedure. Part of this may stem from slightly different indices of learning criterion. Solomon's laboratory has used eight CRs within 10 consecutive trials as a criterion (Graves & Solomon, 1985; Solomon & Groccia-Ellison, 1996). Disterhoft's laboratory has used both eight CRs within 10 consecutive trials and 80% CRs within a session as measures of learning criterion (Deyo, Staube & Disterhoft, 1989; Kowalska & Disterhoft, 1994; Kronforst-Collins, Moriearty, Ralph et al., 1997; Kronforst-Collins, Moriearty, Schmidt & Disterhoft, 1997; Straube, Deyo, Moyer & Disterhoft, 1990; Thompson & Disterhoft, 1997; Thompson, Moyer & Disterhoft, 1997). Woodruff-Pak and colleagues have used eight CRs within nine consecutive trials as a measure of learning criterion (Woodruff-Pak, Cronholm & Sheffield, 1990; Woodruff-Pak, Lavond, Logan & Thompson, 1987), which is more stringent than eight CRs within 10 consecutive trials but probably not as stringent as 80% CRs within a session.

Despite slightly different indices of learning, there is more or less general agreement that rabbits begin to show age-associated declines in the trace procedure at about two years of age (Solomon & Groccia-Ellison, 1996; Thompson, Moyer & Disterhoft, 1996; Woodruff-Pak et al., 1987). Two-year-old rabbits are also impaired in the delay procedure with a comparable ISI, but the effect is less severe (Solomon & Groccia-Ellison, 1996). Deficits below two years of age are minimal (Thompson, Moyer & Disterhoft, 1996). Table 2 summarizes the studies testing the trace procedure in aging rabbits.

Age-associated Deficits in the Discrimination Procedure

In the basic discrimination procedure, two CSs that differ along a single dimension, such as frequency or modality, are used. One CS is always followed by the US (CS+) and the other CS is never followed by the US (CS-). The animal will emit CRs to both CSs early in training. As acquisition proceeds, CRs to the CS- will gradually disappear.

It is difficult to determine whether aging rabbits show deficits in the discrimination procedure that are unrelated to their impairment in acquisition of CRs. Powell, Buchanan, and Hernandez (1984) tested a two-tone discrimination procedure and found that aging (approximately 40-month-old) male (but not female) rabbits were

Table 2. Trace Classical Conditioning Procedure and Older Rabbits

Study	Age (mos.)	CS	US	ISI	trace
Deyo, Straube, & Disterhoft (1989)	32-48	tone	air puff	600-ms	500-ms
Graves & Solomon (1985)	36-40	tone	shock	950-ms	500-ms
Kowalska & Disterhoft (1994)	36-42	tone	air puff	600-ms	500-ms
Kronforst-Collins et al. (1997a)	33-34	tone	air puff	600-ms	500-ms
Kronforst-Collins et al. (1997b)	37-38	tone	air puff	600-ms	500-ms
Solomon & Groccia-Ellison (1996)	12-48[1]	tone	air puff	900-ms	400-ms
Straube, Deyo et al. (1990)	38-42	tone	air puff	600-ms	500-ms
Thompson & Disterhoft (1997)	37-38	tone	air puff	600-ms	500-ms
Thompson, Moyer, & Disterhoft (1996)	12-36[2]	tone	air puff	600-ms	500-ms
Woodruff-Pak, Cronholm et al. (1990)	27-50	tone	air puff	750-ms	500-ms
Woodruff-Pak, Lavond et al. (1987)	26-50[3]	tone	air puff	750-ms	500-ms

[1]Compared 1-year-, 2-year-, 3-year-, and 4-year-old rabbits
[2]Compared 1-year-, 2-year-, 2.5-year-, and 3-year-old rabbits
[3]Compared 2.5-year- and 3.75-year-old rabbits

slower to acquire CRs to the CS+ than young (approximately 6-month-old) rabbits. All rabbits were trained for 10 sessions of 64 trials (32 CS+ and 32 CS-) per session. Discrimination had only begun to develop in the young rabbits by the end of training, reaching about 20-30% difference in percentage of CRs between CS+ and CS-. Yokel (1989) found that aging rabbits (2-3.4-year-old) could learn a two-tone discrimination procedure. Unfortunately, no young rabbits were tested in this study. Thus, it is difficult to determine whether aging affects discrimination itself in addition to affecting the ability to acquire CRs.

Age-associated Deficits in Reacquisition

In reacquisition studies, animals are trained to criterion in a particular procedure and then trained again in the same procedure after a waiting period. This method can be thought of as a measure of memory (in the form of savings). In addition, an assessment of true age-associated changes in eyeblink conditioning can be made, compared to the cross-sectional comparisons between age groups that are typically made. Changes in eyeblink conditioning with age, as opposed to merely differences between age groups, can only be assessed in this type of within-subjects design where the same participants are tested multiple times over a period of months or years.

Coffin and Woodruff-Pak (1993) trained young (7-month-old) and aging (36-month-old) rabbits in the 400-ms delay procedure with a tone CS and an air puff US for seven days and then retested a subset of young and aging rabbits 12 and 18 months after initial acquisition. Young rabbits attained learning criterion in about the same number of trials in acquisition, 12-month reacquisition, and 18-month reacquisition. In contrast, aging rabbits attained learning criterion in over 100 fewer trials in each training stage. Thus, seemingly paradoxically, aging rabbits showed savings while young rabbits did not. However, the researchers suggested that it may be the case that the young rabbits aged more than the older rabbits in terms of eyeblink classical conditioning performance during the interval between initial acquisition and reacquisition. Aging may not affect reacquisition beyond three years of age but may impact heavily on reacquisition in rabbits that are initially trained when young but pass into middle-age before reacquisition training.

In contrast to Coffin and Woodruff-Pak (1993), Solomon, Barth et al. (1995) reported age-associated deficits in 3-month reacquisition after initial training in the same 400-ms delay procedure. However, aging rabbits did show substantial savings, although less than young rabbits. Aging rabbits emitted an average of approximately 35% CRs in Session 1 of reacquisition and approximately 60% CRs in Session 2 of reacquisition. In comparison, these same rabbits required five sessions during initial acquisition to attain 35% CRs and nine sessions to attain 60% CRs. Young rabbits showed faster reacquisition but this may be contaminated by the fact that 20 CS-alone retention trials were given immediately before reacquisition. It may be the case that aging rabbits showed greater extinction during these trials, causing them to take somewhat longer to reacquire CRs. Thus, it appears that aging may have some effects on reacquisition of eyeblink conditioning but the effects may not be very pronounced, at least over a period of several months.

Age-associated Deficits in Retention

Retention studies are similar to reacquisition studies except that after the waiting period, animals receive CS-alone trials instead of CS-US trials. The theory behind using CS-alone trials instead of CS-US trials is that CS-alone trials allow an assessment of memory independent of new learning. However, this may not be strictly the case. Extinction occurs during CS-alone trials and extinction also involves learning in that the CS no longer predicts the US. The difference is that learning during extinction is inhibitory rather than excitatory.

Solomon, Barth et al. (1995) compared young (6-8-month-old) and aging (36-50-month-old) rabbits in 3-month retention after 18 sessions of acquisition in the 400-ms delay procedure with a tone CS and an air puff US. Aging rabbits emitted significantly fewer CRs during the 20 CS-alone trials of retention than young rabbits. In fact, aging rabbits emitted hardly any (< 5%) CRs during retention, indicating that aging heavily impacted the ability to retain the CS-US association. This is in contrast to reacquisition, where aging had only small effects. Thus, the new excitatory learning during reacquisition may have masked any age-associated deficits in memory for the CS-US association over time.

Retention can be ameliorated by cognition-enhancing drugs. Solomon et al. (1995) administered the calcium-channel blocker, nimodipine, to older rabbits for 90 days after they had been trained in the 500 ms delay procedure for 18 sessions (1,800 trials). CS-alone retention trials were presented at the end of 30 and 90 days after training

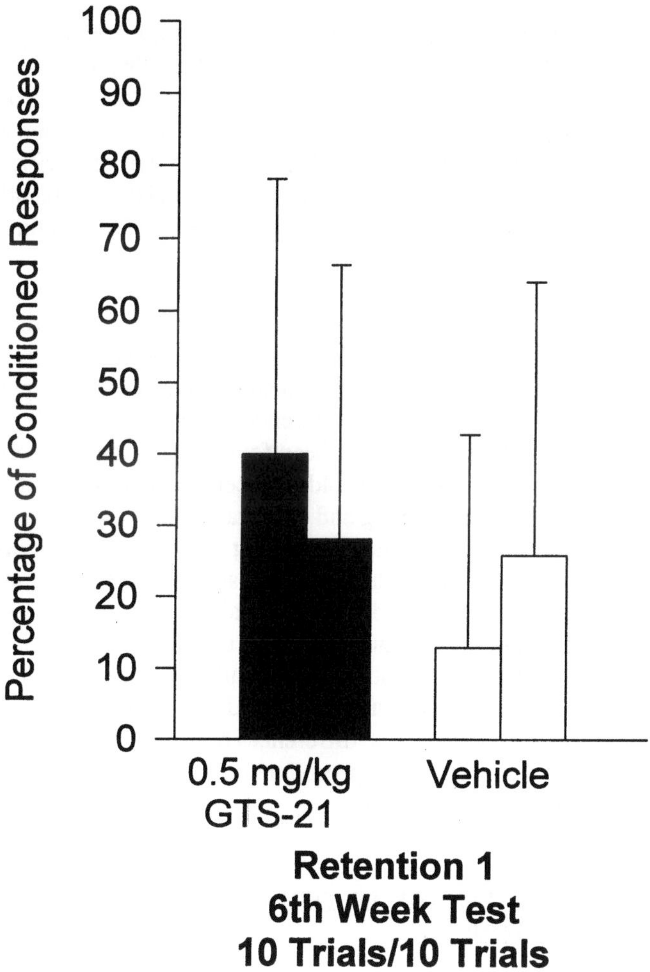

Figure 2. Percentage of CRs in older rabbits during CS-alone trials with no drug administration. Testing took place six weeks after training with drug was completed. Drug treatment during training significantly improved retention. (From Woodruff-Pak, Green, Coleman-Valencia & Pak, in press).

(during the period that nimodipine was administered). Administration of a dose of 15 mg/kg nimodipine resulted in significantly better retention. The nicotinic cholinergic agonist, GTS-21, also improved retention in older rabbits (Woodruff-Pak, Green, Coleman-Valencia & Pak, in press; Figure 2). In this experiment the drug was administered during training and then no further drug administration occurred.

Age-associated Deficits in Stimulus Processing

Age-associated deficits in eyeblink classical conditioning do not appear to be caused by changes in sensitivity to the CS or the US. Sensory thresholds have been measured using the method of constant stimuli, in which a stimulus is presented at a set of different intensities. The intensity that elicits a given response 50% of the time is said to be the threshold for that stimulus for that organism. Tone threshold for both young and older rabbits has been found to be about 60-75 decibels (Coffin & Woodruff-Pak, 1993; Graves & Solomon, 1985; Solomon Barth et al., 1995; Solomon & Groccia-Ellison, 1996; Solomon, Wood et al., 1995; Thompson & Disterhoft, 1997; Thompson, Moyer & Disterhoft, 1996), which is below the 85-90 decibel tones typically used. No differences between 2-year-, 3-year-, and 4-year-old rabbits in tone threshold have been found (Solomon & Groccia-Ellison, 1996).

Thresholds for air puff (Solomon, Barth et al., 1995; Solomon & Groccia-Ellison, 1996; Solomon, Wood et al., 1995) and periorbital shock (Graves & Solomon, 1985; Powell, Buchanan & Hernandez, 1981) have also been assessed. Air puff thresholds for both young and older rabbits have been found to be about 0.72-0.87 psi, compared to the 3 psi air puff that is standard. No differences between 2-year-, 3-year-, and 4-year-old rabbits in air puff threshold have been found (Solomon & Groccia-Ellison, 1996). Similarly, periorbital shock threshold has been found to be about 0.375-0.765 mA with no differences between young and older rabbits.

Age-associated deficits in stimulus processing can also be assessed with the explicitly unpaired procedure, in which the stimuli used for conditioning are presented separately and in a pseudorandom order. The unpaired procedure by itself may not reveal deficits in CS processing, since a lack of response to the CS is expected. Nevertheless, factors related to presenting stimuli multiple times, in a situation similar to paired conditioning, may reveal age-associated abnormalities not seen during sensory threshold testing. However, no differences between young and aging rabbits have been observed in the unpaired procedure (Coffin & Woodruff-Pak, 1993; Woodruff-Pak, Coffin & Papka, 1994).

AGE-ASSOCIATED CHANGES IN THE CRITICAL SUBSTRATES FOR EYEBLINK CONDITIONING

Both the cerebellum and the hippocampal formation are involved in eyeblink conditioning in both humans and non-human animals. The cerebellum ipsilateral to the eye that receives the US is essential in all procedures while the hippocampal formation plays a modulatory role in the delay procedure and a more essential role in more complicated procedures (for a review, see Green & Woodruff-Pak, 2000). Both the hippocampal formation and the cerebellum develop neural activity that models CRs and URs. Lesions of the ipsilateral cerebellum completely abolish CRs in all procedures and prevent acquisition when made before training. Lesions of the hippocampal formation do not affect acquisition in the basic delay or discrimination procedures but do have varying effects on other procedures, such as trace conditioning. Lesions of the medial septum, rather than the hippocampus proper, retard acquisition in the delay procedure (Berry & Thompson, 1979).

Eyeblink conditioning as a model of age-associated deficits in learning and memory is strengthened by the fact that both humans and non-human animals show age-associated changes in the both the cerebellum and the hippocampal formation. It is important to note, however, that there is increasing variability in learning rates as organisms age. Thus, a task that engages well-defined neural substrates is especially useful as a model of age-associated deficits in learning since the impact of age-associated differences in the structure and function of critical neural substrates can be assessed as potential causal factors.

Age-associated Changes in the Septo-hippocampal System

Although it is clear that some cells are lost in both the septum and the hippocampus with age, in the last few years the extent of this loss in normal aging in both humans and non-human animals has been called into question. The development of stereological cell counting techniques has been the force behind this change of view. Stereological cell counting techniques, which account for differences in neuronal density and differences in volume of the area under study, allow an unbiased estimate of total cell number in a particular brain area. Unbiased cell counting has revealed little neuronal loss in the medial temporal lobes of aging animals, in contrast to previous reports (for a review, see Gallagher & Rapp, 1997). Furthermore, the magnitude of cholinergic cell loss in the basal forebrain cholinergic system is far less than was previously thought (Muir, 1997). Normal aging also appears to only slightly reduce the number of hippocampal pyramidal cells in rabbits (Woodruff-Pak & Trojanowski, 1996). It is important to note that these results appear to apply only to normal aging. Age-associated pathologies such as Alzheimer's disease have been found to produce widespread neuronal loss even using unbiased cell counting techniques (Gallagher & Rapp, 1997). Indeed, West, Coleman, Flood, and Troncoso (1994) identified the CA1 region in hippocampus as a site with almost total loss of pyramidal cells in Alzheimer's disease, although there is relatively little loss of CA1 pyramidal cells in normal human aging (West, 1993). It is the CA1 pyramidal cells that fire in conjunction with CRs and URs during eyeblink conditioning in rabbits (Berger & Thompson, 1978).

The Septo-hippocampal Cholinergic System and Eyeblink Conditioning

Less cell loss in normal aging in the basal forebrain cholinergic system than was previously thought is particularly interesting in relation to age-associated deficits in eyeblink conditioning. The basal forebrain cholinergic system consists of neurons containing choline acetyltransferase (the enzyme that catalyzes the synthesis of acetyl coenzyme A and choline into acetylcholine) located in the medial septal nucleus, the diagonal band nuclei, the basal nucleus of Meynert (i.e., the substantia innominata), and the magnocellular preoptic field (Cooper, Bloom & Roth, 1996). Of these structures, the medial septal nucleus is the one that sends cholinergic projections to the hippocampal formation. Lesions of this structure remove cholinergic input to the hippocampus and have been found to retard the rate of eyeblink conditioning in young rabbits in the 250-ms delay procedure (Berry & Thompson, 1979).

It has been known for quite some time that disruption of the central cholinergic system retards acquisition of eyeblink classical conditioning. Systemic injections of forms of the muscarinic cholinergic antagonists atropine (Downs et al., 1972) and scopolamine (Harvey, Gormezano & Cool-Hauser, 1983; Moore, Goodell & Solomon, 1976; Salvatierra & Berry, 1989; Solomon, Solomon, Vander Schaaf & Perry, 1983) that cross the blood-brain barrier slowed acquisition in the delay procedure in young rabbits, unlike forms of these drugs that did not cross the blood-brain barrier. This effect only occurred when the hippocampus was intact (Solomon et al., 1983). Hippocampal modeling of CRs was disrupted in these subjects (Salvatierra & Berry, 1989). Systemic injections of scopolamine also disrupted acquisition in the 750-ms trace procedure with a 500-ms 'blank period' in young rabbits (Kaneko & Thompson, 1997). Furthermore, systemic injections of the nicotinic cholinergic antagonist, mecamylamine, slowed acquisition in the 750-ms delay procedure in young rabbits (Woodruff-Pak & Hinchliffe, 1997; Woodruff-Pak, Li, Kazmi & Kem, 1994). The same impairments in eyeblink conditioning produced in rabbits by injection of scopolamine can be produced in humans by oral administration of scopolamine (Bahro, Schreurs, Sunderland & Molchan, 1995; Solomon et al., 1993).

Scopolamine appears to act indirectly on the hippocampus via cholinergic inputs from the medial septum. Localized infusion of scopolamine into the medial septum retards acquisition (Powell, Hernandez & Buchanan, 1985; Solomon & Gottfied, 1981). Infusion of scopolamine directly into the dorsal hippocampus has no effect (Solomon & Gottfried, 1981). These effects are similar to those observed when the medial septum is lesioned (Berry & Thompson, 1979), which removes all cholinergic innervation of the hippocampus. Myers et al. (1996) proposed an artificial neural network model in which disruption of cholinergic innervation of the hippocampus reduces the ability to modulate new learning, which suggests that post-acquisition disruptions of the septo-hippocampal cholinergic system should have no effect.

Rather than a model of deficits in eyeblink conditioning caused by normal aging, disruption of the septo-hippocampal cholinergic system may be more appropriately thought of as a model of deficits in eyeblink conditioning caused by pathological aging, in particular Alzheimer's disease (Woodruff-Pak, 1995). Patients with probable Alzheimer's disease are impaired in eyeblink conditioning beyond the effects of normal aging (Solomon et al., 1995; Solomon, Levine, Bein & Pendlebury, 1991; Woodruff-Pak, Finkbiner & Sasse, 1990; Woodruff-Pak & Papka, 1996; Woodruff-Pak, Romano & Hinchliffe, 1996; Woodruff-Pak, Romano & Papka, 1996). As noted above, while recent evidence is mixed at best for loss of neurons with normal aging in the basal forebrain cholinergic system, there is extensive evidence for the loss of these neurons with Alzheimer's disease, even using recently developed unbiased cell counting techniques. Furthermore, there are abnormalities of the cells that remain, such as abnormally shaped axon terminal boutons associated with a central amyloid core (neuritic plaques) and protein fiber tangles in cell bodies (neurofibrillary tangles) (Muir, 1997). As mentioned previously, there is also almost complete loss in Alzheimer's disease of cells known to be engaged during eyeblink conditioning, CA1 pyramidal cells in the hippocampus. Therefore, an aging animal with a disrupted septo-hippocampal cholinergic system might be an excellent animal model of Alzheimer's disease (Woodruff-Pak & Trojanowski, 1996).

In this regard, it is interesting to note the development in recent years of immunotoxins that specifically destroy cholinergic neurons, such as 192 IgG-saporin (Gallagher & Rapp, 1997; Muir, 1997). This has allowed researchers to selectively lesion components of the basal forebrain cholinergic system without damaging non-cholinergic neurons or fibers of passage. Interestingly, selective damage to the basal forebrain cholinergic system has failed to reproduce many of the behavioral effects previously observed after non-selective damage to this region, leading some to speculate that the basal forebrain cholinergic system may be less important for learning and memory than was previously thought (Gallagher & Rapp, 1997; Muir, 1997). Recently, it has been suggested that the basal forebrain cholinergic system may be involved in attention rather than memory (Baxter, Holland & Gallagher, 1997; Waite, Wardlow & Power, 1999). Along these lines, it should be noted that systemic scopolamine has been found by some researchers to increase tone CS thresholds (i.e., a louder tone is required for scopolamine-treated rabbits to be responsive) (Harvey et al., 1983; Moore et al., 1976) which may be due to a disruption of attention.

Eyeblink conditioning may provide a better test of the effects of selective cholinergic lesions on learning, memory, and attention than the tasks typically used. Many of the tasks used have poorly defined neural substrates (outside of engagement of the septo-hippocampal system). In addition, a potentially serious problem is the lack of rigorous control over various performance factors, such as general activity levels. Testing eyeblink conditioning in aging rabbits with selective destruction of various components of the basal forebrain cholinergic system, in particular the medial septum, may provide a more useful animal model of Alzheimer's disease.

Age-associated Deficits in Hippocampal Responsivity

While pathological aging produces changes in the septo-hippocampal cholinergic system that may lead to deficits in eyeblink conditioning, normal aging may produce more general changes in hippocampal responsivity that slow eyeblink conditioning. Several studies by Disterhoft and colleagues have examined the responsiveness of aging hippocampal cells to depolarizing stimulation. Following stimulation, hippocampal cells from aging rabbits show an increased afterhyperpolarization (the hyperpolarization after an action potential) relative to cells from young rabbits (Moyer, Thompson, Black & Disterhoft, 1992). The peak amplitude and integrated area of the afterhyperpolarization of aging hippocampal neurons are approximately twice as large as those from young neurons. Furthermore, aging neurons showed fewer action potentials to an 800-ms depolarizing pulse (i.e., they showed increased accommodation). Moyer and Disterhoft (1994) provided evidence that the cause of the increase in afterhyperpolarization in aging neurons was an increase in the amount of calcium entering the neurons. The slow plateau phase of the calcium-mediated action potential in aging neurons is significantly increased in both amplitude and width (see also Chapter 13 in this volume).

The increased afterehyperpolarization of hippocampal cells may be one of the causes of age-associated deficits in eyeblink conditioning. Afterhyperpolarization of hippocampal pyramidal cells is reduced after eyeblink conditioning in either delay (Coulter et al., 1989; Disterhoft, Coulter & Alkon, 1986; Disterhoft, Golden, Read, Coulter & Alkon, 1988; LoTurco, Coulter & Alkon, 1988; Sanchez-Andres & Alkon, 1991) or trace (deJonge, Black, Deyo & Disterhoft, 1990; Moyer, Thompson & Disterhoft, 1996) conditioning, allowing these cells to fire more rapidly (for a review, see Disterhoft, Thompson, Moyer & Mogul, 1996). Until recently, afterhyperpolarization of hippocampal pyramidal cells has not been examined in cells from aging rabbits that have undergone eyeblink conditioning. These experiments are described in Chapter 13 in this volume.

In the intact animal, hippocampal pyramidal cells of aging and young rabbits do not show differences in spontaneous firing rates (Thompson, Deyo & Disterhoft, 1990). There is some evidence, however, of differences in hippocampal activity during eyeblink conditioning. Woodruff-Pak et al. (1987) recorded multiple-unit activity from young (3-month-old), middle-aged (26-33-month-old), and aging (39-50-month-old) rabbits during eyeblink conditioning in the 750-ms trace procedure with a 500-ms 'blank' period. Aging rabbits were significantly impaired in acquiring CRs. Furthermore, aging rabbits showed significantly less multiple-unit activity in the US period than young rabbits by Session 2 of training. Four of the six young rabbits reached the behavioral learning criterion of eight CRs within nine consecutive trials by Session 3 of training whereas all but two of the older rabbits required at least seven sessions to reach this criterion. Thus, less hippocampal activity in the US period in aging rabbits was correlated with a slower rate of learning.

Surprisingly, the study by Woodruff-Pak et al. (1987) is the only one in the literature to date in which neural activity was recorded from the hippocampus of aging rabbits during eyeblink conditioning. Some support for their findings comes from a study by Seager, Borgnis, and Berry (1997) that examined jaw movement conditioning, which uses parameters very similar to eyeblink conditioning but utilizes a different US (an intraoral squirt of water) and measures a different motor behavior (jaw movement). Seager et al. made multiple-unit recordings from the dorsal hippocampus during jaw movement conditioning using a trace procedure very similar to the one used by Woodruff-Pak et al. Seager et al. found less hippocampal activity at the end of the 'blank' period (i.e., just before US onset) in aging rabbits (40-49-month-old) compared to young rabbits (3-7-month-old). Unfortunately, jaw movement conditioning relies on somewhat different substrates than eyeblink conditioning. For example, the ipsilateral interpositus nucleus is not critical for jaw movement conditioning (Gibbs, 1992), which limits the generalizability of results from this type of conditioning to eyeblink conditioning. Studies using single-unit recording during eyeblink conditioning in aging rabbits would be helpful in determining the extent to which hippocampal activity during eyeblink conditioning is abnormal in aging rabbits.

Age-associated Changes in the Cerebellum

Very few studies have examined the aging cerebellum in rabbits. From the few that have been conducted, however, it appears that aging may adversely affect areas that are critically involved in acquisition of eyeblink classical conditioning, including lobule HVI and the interpositus nucleus (Woodruff-Pak & Trojanowski, 1996). In particular, Purkinje cells in lobule HVI are lost with age (Woodruff-Pak, Cronholm & Sheffield, 1990; Woodruff-Pak & Trojanowski, 1996; Figure 3). Furthermore, the number of Purkinje cells is negatively correlated with rate of learning such that acquisition of CRs takes longer with fewer Purkinje cells (Woodruff-Pak et al., 1990; Woodruff-Pak & Trojanowski, 1996). Thus, in addition to abnormalities in the septo-hippocampal system, loss of Purkinje cells in the aging rabbit cerebellum may contribute to slower learning.

Given the loss of Purkinje cells with age, an important future direction for studies of age-associated impairments in eyeblink conditioning would be to investigate both the functioning of the remaining Purkinje cells as well as the impact that loss of Purkinje cells has on neural activity in the interpositus nucleus. Electrophysiological recording may reveal abnormalities in the patterns of conditioning-related activity that normally develops in these areas. Furthermore, cognition-enhancing drugs that improve eyeblink classical conditioning (which will be discussed below) may well be impacting the cerebellum as well as the septo-hippocampal system and this may be revealed in changes in electrophysiological activity. For example, there are cholinergic projections from the tegmental nuclei to the deep cerebellar nuclei (Cooper et al., 1996). Systemic cholinergic drugs that affect eyeblink conditioning may act on this pathway, in addition to the basal forebrain cholinergic system.

Attributions of age-associated deficits in eyeblink conditioning solely to alterations in the septo-hippocampal system should be made with caution. The ipsilateral cerebellum is critical for *all* eyeblink conditioning procedures while the hippocampal formation appears to be necessary for establishing associations between multiple CSs, including the conditioning context (Green & Woodruff-Pak, 2000). Lesions of the ipsilateral interpositus nucleus, one of the deep cerebellar nuclei, abolishes or prevents conditioning in the delay (Clark, McCormick, Lavond & Thompson, 1984; Lavond, Hembree & Thompson, 1985; McCormick et al., 1981; Steinmetz, Lavond, Ivkovich, Logan & Thompson, 1992), trace (Woodruff-Pak, Lavond & Thompson, 1985), and discrimination (Gould & Steinmetz, 1994) procedures. Importantly, conditioning-related hippocampal activity during eyeblink classical conditioning is abolished after lesioning the ipsilateral interpositus nucleus (Clark et al., 1984). Furthermore, this activity never develops if the interpositus nucleus is lesioned prior to training (Sears & Steinmetz, 1990). Thus, if normal aging negatively impacts the cerebellum, age-associated declines in eyeblink conditioning may be at least partially due to changes in the critical cerebellar substrate. The extent to which this is true needs to be more fully evaluated.

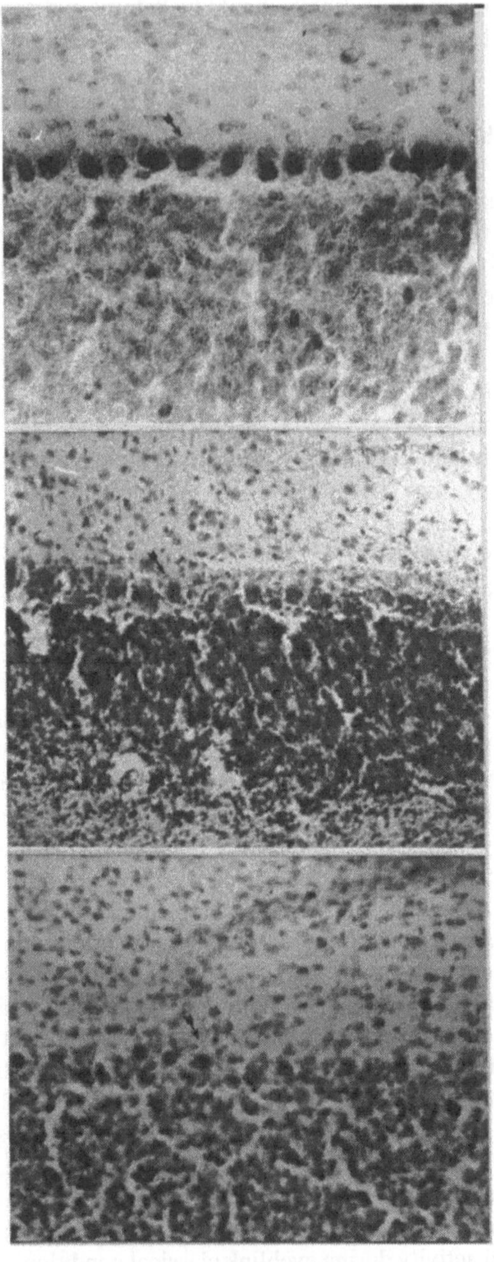

Figure 3. Photomicrograph of Nissl–stained cerebellar cortex showing molecular, Purkinje, and granule cell layers of rabbits at three ages: a 3-month-old rabbit (Top), a 40-month-old rabbit (Middle), and a 50-month-old rabbit (Bottom). These rabbits attained learning criterion in the 750 ms trace procedure (500 ms trace) in 961, 1,890, and 2,269 trials, respectively. Arrows show Purkinje cells (Data from Woodruff-Pak, Cronholm & Sheffield, 1990).

REVERSING AGE-ASSOCIATED DEFICITS IN EYEBLINK CONDITIONING

As discussed above, age-associated deficits in eyeblink conditioning may be at least partially due to less excitable neurons in the hippocampus. Furthermore, deficits in eyeblink conditioning observed in pathological aging, such as Alzheimer's disease, may be the result of a disruption in cholinergic innervation of the hippocampus. The case for eyeblink conditioning as a model of age-associated deficits in learning and memory is strengthened by the fact that age-associated deficits in eyeblink conditioning can be reversed in animals. Drugs that can reverse age-associated deficits in eyeblink conditioning may be useful in ameliorating age-associated deficits in learning and memory generally. Thus, eyeblink conditioning may be a potent preclinical test of the efficacy of cognition-enhancing drugs. In this chapter a few examples of cognition-enhancing drug effects are presented, and Chapter 14 (this volume) focuses on this topic in greater detail.

Nimodipine

The lines of evidence described above point to age-associated increases in calcium influx as a possible cause of age-associated decreases in hippocampal responsivity. Furthermore, decreased hippocampal responsivity may lead to deficits in eyeblink classical conditioning. Thus, a drug that decreases calcium influx should improve conditioning performance. One such drug is nimodipine. Nimodipine enhances spontaneous pyramidal cell activity (Thompson et al., 1990) and reduces both afterhyperpolarization and accommodation in hippocampal neurons (Moyer et al., 1992). These effects have been shown to be mediated by reductions in the amplitude and width of the slow plateau phase of calcium action potentials (Moyer & Disterhoft, 1994).

Nimodipine has been shown to improve performance in the 600-ms trace procedure with a 500-ms 'blank' period (Deyo, Straube & Disterhoft, 1989; Kowalska & Disterhoft, 1994; Straube, Deyo, Moyer & Disterhoft, 1990) and the 750-ms delay procedure (Woodruff-Pak, Chi, Li, Pak & Fanelli, 1997). The improvement is much greater for aging rabbits compared to young rabbits (Deyo, Straube & Disterhoft, 1989). The amount of nimodipine in blood plasma is significantly correlated with the number of trials required to reach 80% CRs within a session (Kowalska & Disterhoft, 1994) or eight CRs within nine consecutive trials (Woodruff-Pak, Chi et al., 1997). Nimodipine does not facilitate acquisition in the 400-ms delay procedure but does facilitate retention of this acquisition, as assessed one month and three months after initial acquisition (Solomon, Wood et al., 1995). Finally, changes in sensory thresholds (Solomon, Wood et al., 1995) or changes in sensitivity to stimuli (Woodruff-Pak, Chi et al., 1997) have been ruled out as the source of nimodipine's effects.

Nefiracetam (DM-9384)

Nefiracetam is a pyrrolidone derivative that appears to have diverse effects on the central nervous system (for a review, see Hiramatsu, Shiotani, Kameyama & Nabeshima, 1997). Repeated administration of nefiracetam enhances both cholinergic and GABAergic neurotransmission. Enhancement of the cholinergic system occurs via increases in choline acetyltransferase activity (the enzyme that catalyzes the synthesis of acetyl coenzyme A and choline into acetylcholine). Enhancement of the GABAergic system occurs via increases in GABA turnover, increases in glutamic acid decarboxylase activity (the enzyme that converts L-glutamic acid to GABA), and facilitation of the GABA uptake transporter.

Nefiracetam is able to reverse scopolamine-induced memory impairments in several animal models of amnesia, suggesting effects on central muscarinic cholinergic receptors. In addition, it has been recently shown that nefiracetam increases the excitability of rat CA1 hippocampal slices, an effect that is blocked by the nicotinic acetylcholine antagonist mecamylamine (Nishizaki et al., 1999). In support of links between behavioral impairments caused by cholinergic disruption, and amelioration of impairments by nefiracetam's action on the central cholinergic system, Woodruff-Pak and Hinchliffe (1997) demonstrated that systemically-administered nefiracetam could reverse retardation of 750-ms delay eyeblink conditioning induced by either scopolamine or mecamylamine in young rabbits.

Nefiracetam improves eyeblink conditioning in aging rabbits as well. Woodruff-Pak and Li (1994) demonstrated significantly better acquisition in the 750-ms delay procedure with a tone CS and an air puff US for 21-44-month-old rabbits. Nefiracetam appears to improve eyeblink conditioning via actions on the septo-hippocampal system. As mentioned previously, young rabbits without a hippocampus learn eyeblink conditioning in the delay procedure at the same rate as young rabbits with an intact hippocampus. This effect appears to be the same in aging rabbits (Woodruff-Pak, Li, Hinchliffe & Port, 1997). Nefiracetam facilitates acquisition of the 750-ms delay procedure in aging rabbits only when the hippocampus is intact (Woodruff-Pak et al., 1997). This strongly suggests that nefiracetam facilitates eyeblink conditioning in aging rabbits by actions on the septo-hippocampal system rather than by actions on some other brain area, such as the cerebellum. A similar test has not been performed on the other drugs mentioned in this section, making it unclear whether they are facilitating eyeblink conditioning via actions on the septo-hippocampal cholinergic system or via actions on the cerebellum.

GTS-21

GTS-21 is an arylidene anabaseine that is a partial agonist of the alpha-7 subtype of the nicotinic cholinergic receptor (for a review, see Kem, 1997). Woodruff-Pak, Li, and Kem (1994) tested aging (24-55-month-old) rabbits in the 750-ms delay procedure with a tone CS and an air puff US. Aging rabbits injected with either 0.5 or 1.0 mg/kg GTS-21 acquired CRs significantly more quickly than rabbits injected with either vehicle or 0.1 mg/kg GTS-21. In fact, the two higher concentrations of GTS-21 facilitated learning in aging rabbits to the point where it was similar to acquisition of the same procedure in young rabbits. GTS-21 did not appear to heighten sensitivity to the CS or decrease sensitivity to the US, as unpaired training was not different between aging rabbits injected with 0.5 mg/kg GTS-21 and vehicle-injected rabbits.

Metrifonate

Metrifonate is an organophosphate compound that produces long-lasting inhibition of acetylcholinesterase (the enzyme that breaks down acetylcholine in the synaptic cleft into choline and acetate). Cholinesterase inhibitors may allow more acetylcholine to remain in the synaptic cleft where it can act postsynaptically. Metrifonate has been shown to increase responsivity of CA1 pyramidal neurons from aging rabbits, both when applied directly to slice preparations and when slice preparations are made from rabbits that received chronic oral administration (Oh, Power, Thompson, Moriearty & Disterhoft, 1999). This effect was reversed by in vitro applications of the muscarinic cholinergic antagonist atropine, suggesting that metrifonate enhances hippocampal responsivity via actions on muscarinic cholinergic neurotransmission.

Oral administration of metrifonate also improves eyeblink conditioning in the 600-ms trace procedure with a 500-ms 'blank' period, a tone CS, and an air puff US (Kronforst-Collins, Moriearty, Schmidt & Disterhoft, 1997; Kronforst-Collins, Moriearty, Ralph et al., 1997). Chronic oral administration beginning one week before training and continuing daily throughout training produced better learning, as indexed by percentage of CRs and trials to eight CRs in 10 consecutive trials, as well as a dose-related inhibition of acetylcholinesterase activity in plasma and red blood cells (Kronforst-Collins, Moriearty, Ralph et al., 1997). However, it was noted that steady state values of inhibition of acetylcholinesterase activity were not reached until 2-3 weeks after the beginning of treatment, suggesting that the maximum beneficial effects of metrifonate may not have been observed in this study. A follow-up study began chronic oral administration of metrifonate three weeks before eyeblink conditioning and found even more facilitated performance compared to rabbits administered vehicle. Furthermore, retention testing (20 CS-alone trials) once per week for four weeks following the end of acquisition training and cessation of metrifonate administration showed higher percentages of CRs in groups that had been administered metrifonate compared to the group that had been administered vehicle.

SUMMARY AND CONCLUSIONS

We have presented evidence that eyeblink classical conditioning is a useful animal model of the effects of aging on learning and memory and their neurobiological substrates. Both humans and non-human animals show similar: (1) age-associated deficits in behavioral indices of eyeblink conditioning; (2) age-associated deficits in the neural substrates critical for eyeblink conditioning; and (3) artificial induction of age-associated deficits. In addition, age-associated deficits can be reversed in animals. Combined with several other advantages, such as the ease with which learning can be dissociated from performance and extensive knowledge of the underlying neural substrates, eyeblink conditioning provides an excellent model of the effects of aging on learning and memory.

There are several avenues of inquiry that deserve further investigation. Very little is known regarding the effects of aging on the functional integrity of the cerebellum. Since eyeblink conditioning is critically dependent upon the cerebellum, studies using single-unit recording and stereological cell counting may provide valuable information regarding age-associated changes in the cerebellum.

A second avenue of inquiry that deserves further attention is the extent to which the integrity of the basal forebrain cholinergic system is necessary for eyeblink conditioning. Use of immunotoxins that selectively destroy cholinergic neurons may help to elucidate more precisely the mechanisms by which cholinergic drugs affect eyeblink conditioning and, more broadly, learning and memory.

Thirdly, age-associated changes in the engagement of the hippocampal formation during eyeblink conditioning need to be examined more fully. Studies would benefit from using single-unit recording techniques, which can reveal more detailed information regarding age-associated differences in neural activity than multiple-unit techniques. Furthermore, investigation of procedures other than delay and trace may be beneficial. Procedures involving multiple CSs, such as negative patterning, may engage the septo-hippocampal system more fully (see Green & Woodruff-Pak, 2000), and thus have utility in studies of aging.

Finally, more studies examining the same subjects over time would be extremely useful. Most of the work discussed in this chapter is cross-sectional in nature. While this approach is a necessity in histological and *in vitro* work, examination of behavior and neural activity is not limited to between-age group comparisons. Testing the same subjects at several points in time, and examining corresponding neural activity would be very beneficial for specifying true age-associated *changes* as opposed to age-associated *differences* in brain-behavior relationships.

Much remains to be discovered above the complex interactions between aging, learning and memory, and the brain. Eyeblink classical conditioning provides an extremely useful tool for unraveling changes in the brain-behavior interactions of organisms as a function of the passage of time.

REFERENCES

Bahro, M., Schreurs, B.G., Sunderland, T., & Molchan, S. E. (1995). The effects of scopolamine, lorazepam, and glycopyrrolate on classical conditioning of the human eyeblink response. *Psychopharmacology, 122,* 395-400.

Barnes, C.A., Suster, M.S., Shen, J., & McNaughton, B.J. (1997). Multistability of cognitive maps in the hippocampus of old rats. *Nature, 388*, 272- 275.

Baxter, M.G., Holland, P.C., & Gallagher, M. (1997). Disruption of decrements in conditioned stimulus processing by selective removal of hippocampal cholinergic input. *Journal of Neuroscience, 17*, 5230-5236.

Berger, T.W., & Thompson, R.F. (1978a). Identification of pyramidal cells as the critical elements in hippocampal neuronal plasticity during learning. *Proceedings of the National Academy of Science (USA), 75,* 1572-157.

Clark, G.A., McCormick, D.A., Lavond, D.G., & Thompson, R.F. (1984). Effects of lesions of cerebellar nuclei on conditioned behavioral and hippocampal neuronal responses. *Brain Research, 291*, 125-

136.

Coffin, J.M., & Woodruff-Pak, D.S. (1993). Delay classical conditioning in young and older rabbits: Initial acquisition and retention at 12 and 18 months. *Behavioral Neuroscience, 107*, 63-71.

Cooper, J.R., Bloom, F.E., & Roth, R. H. (1996). *The Biochemical Basis of Neuropharmacology* (7th ed.). New York: Oxford University Press.

Coulter, D.A., LoTurco, J.J., Kubota, M., Disterhoft, J.F., Moore, J.W., & Alkon, D. L. (1989). Classical conditioning reduces amplitude and duration of calcium-dependent afterhyperpolarization in rabbit hippocampal pyramidal cells. *Journal of Neurophysiology, 61*, 971-981.

de Jonge, M.C., Black, J., Deyo, R.A., & Disterhoft, J.F. (1990). Learning-induced afterhyperpolarization reductions in hippocampus are specific for cell type and potassium conductance. *Experimental Brain Research, 80*, 456-462.

Deyo, R.A., Straube, K.T., & Disterhoft, J.F. (1989). Nimodipine facilitates associative learning in aging rabbits. *Science, 243*, 809-811.

Disterhoft, J.F., Coulter, D.A., Alkon, D.L. (1986). Conditioning-specific membrane changes of rabbit hippocampal neurons measured *in vitro*. *Proceedings of the National Academy of Sciences (USA), 83*, 2733-2737.

Disterhoft, J.F., Golden, D.T., Read, H.L., Coulter, D.A., & Alkon, D.L. (1988). AHP reductions in rabbit hippocampal neurons during conditioning correlate with acquisition of the learned response. *Brain Research, 462*, 118-125.

Disterhoft, J.F., Thompson, L.T., Moyer, J.R., & Mogul, D.J. (1996). Calcium-dependent afterhyperpolarization and learning in young and aging hippocampus. *Life Sciences, 59*, 413-420.

Downs, D., Cardozo, C., Schneiderman, N., Yehle, A. L., VanDercar, D.H., & Zwilling. G. (1972). Central effects of atropine upon aversive classical conditioning in rabbits. *Psychopharmacologia, 23*, 319-333.

Durkin, M., Prescott, L., Furchtgott, E., Cantor, J., & Powell, D.A. (1993). Concomitant eyeblink and heart rate classical conditioning in young, middle-aged, and elderly human subjects. *Psychology and Aging, 8*, 571-581.

Gallagher, M., & Rapp, P.R. (1997). The use of animal models to study the effects of aging on cognition. *Annual Review of Psychology, 48*, 339-370.

Gibbs, C.M. (1992). Divergent effects of deep cerebellar lesions on two different conditioned somatomotor responses in rabbits. *Brain Research, 585*, 395-399.

Graves, C.A., & Solomon, P.R. (1985). Age-related disruption of trace but not delay classical conditioning of the rabbit's nictitating membrane response. *Behavioral Neuroscience, 99*, 88-96.

Green, J.T., & Woodruff-Pak, D.S. (2000). Eyeblink classical conditioning: Hippocampal formation is for neutral stimulus associations as cerebellum is for association-response. *Psychological Bulletin, 126*, 138-158.

Harvey, J.A., Gormezano, I., & Cool-Hauser, V.A. (1983). Effects of scopolamine and methylscopolamine on classical conditioning of the rabbit nictitating membrane response. *Journal of Pharmacology and Experimental Therapeutics, 225*, 42-49.

Hiramatsu, M., Shiotani, T., Kameyama, T., & Nabeshima, T. (1997). Effects of nefiracetam on amnesia animals models with neuronal dysfunctions. *Behavioural Brain Research, 83*, 107-115.

Kaneko, T., & Thompson, R.F. (1997). Disruption of trace conditioning of the nictitating membrane response in rabbits by central cholinergic blockade. *Psychopharmacology, 131*, 161-166.

Kem, W.R. (1997). Alzheimer's drug design based upon an invertebrate toxin (anabaseine) which is a potent nicotinic receptor agonist. *Invertebrate Neuroscience, 3*, 251-259.

Kowalska, M., & Disterhoft, J.F. (1994). Relation of nimodipine dose and serum concentration to learning enhancement in aging rabbits. *Experimental Neurology, 127*, 159-166.

Kronforst-Collins, M.A., Moriearty, P.L., Ralph, M., Becker, R.E., Schmidt, B., Thompson, L.T., & Disterhoft, J.F. (1997). Metrifonate treatment enhances acquisition of eyeblink conditioning in aging rabbits. *Pharmacology, Biochemistry and Behavior, 56*, 103-110.

Kronforst-Collins, M.A., Moriearty, P.L., Schmidt, B., & Disterhoft, J.F. (1997). Metrifonate improves associative learning and retention in aging rabbits. *Behavioral Neuroscience, 111*, 1031-1040.

LoTurco, J.J., Coulter, D.A., & Alkon, D.L. (1988). Enhancement of synaptic potentials in rabbit CA1 pyramidal neurons following classical conditioning. *Proceedings of the National Academy of Sciences, (USA), 85*, 1672-1676.

Moore, J.W., Goodell, N.A., & Solomon, P.R. (1976). Central cholinergic blockade by scopolamine and habituation, classical conditioning, and latent inhibition of the rabbit's nictitating membrane response. *Physiological Psychology, 4*, 395-399.

Moyer, J.R., & Disterhoft, J.F. (1994). Nimodipine decreases calcium action potentials in rabbit hippocampal CA1 neurons in an age-dependent and concentration-dependent manner. *Hippocampus, 4,* 11-18.

Moyer, J.R., Thompson, L.T., Black, J.P., & Disterhoft, J.F. (1992). Nimodipine increases excitability of rabbit CA1 pyramidal neurons in an age- and concentration-dependent manner. *Journal of Neurophysiology, 68,* 2100-2109.

Muir, J.L. (1997). Acetylcholine, aging, and Alzheimer's disease. *Pharmacology Biochemistry and Behavior, 56,* 687-696.

Myers, C.E., Ermita, B.R., Harris, K., Hasselmo, M., Solomon, P., & Gluck, M.A. (1996). A computational model of cholinergic disruption of septo-hippocampal activity in classical eyeblink conditioning. *Neurobiology of Learning and Memory, 66,* 51-66.

Nishizaki, T., Matsouka, T., Nomura, T., Matsuyama, S., Watabe, S., Shiotani, T., & Yoshii, M. (1999). A 'long-term-potentiation-like' facilitation of hippocampal synaptic transmission induced by the nootropic nefiracetam. *Brain Research, 826,* 281-288.

Oh, M.M., Power, J.M., Thompson, L.T., Moriearty, P.L., & Disterhoft, J.F. (1999). Metrifonate increases neuronal excitability in CA1 pyramidal neurons from both young and aging rabbit hippocampus. *Journal of Neuroscience, 19,* 1814-1823.

Powell, D.A., Buchanan, S.L., & Hernandez, L.L. (1981). Age-related changes in classical (Pavlovian) conditioning in the New Zealand albino rabbits. *Experimental Aging Research, 7,* 453-465.

Powell, D.A., Buchanan, S.L., & Hernandez, L.L. (1984). Age-related changes in Pavlovian conditioning: Central nervous system correlates. *Physiology & Behavior, 32,* 609-616.

Sanchez-Andres, J.V., & Alkon, D.L. (1991). Voltage-clamp analysis of the effects of classical conditioning on the hippocampus. *Journal of Neurophysiology, 65,* 796-807.

Salvatierra, A.T., & Berry, S.D. (1989). Scopolamine disruption of septo-hippocampal activity and classical conditioning. *Behavioral Neuroscience, 103,* 715-721.

Sasse, D.K., Coffin, J.M., & Woodruff-Pak, D.S. (1991). Age differences in rabbits in the delay classical conditioning paradigm using 400 and 750 msec CS-US intervals. *Society for Neuroscience Abstracts, 17,* 1140.

Sasse, D.K., & Woodruff-Pak, D.S. (1990). Classical conditioning in young and older rabbits in delay and trace paradigms with a 750 msec CS-US interval. *Society for Neuroscience Abstracts, 16,* 841.

Schneiderman, N. (1966). Interstimulus interval function of the nictitating membrane response of the rabbit under delay versus trace conditioning. *Journal of Comparative and Physiological Psychology, 62,* 397-402.

Seager, M.A., Borgnis, R.L., & Berry, S.D. (1997). Delayed acquisition of behavioral and hippocampal responses during jaw movement conditioning in aging rabbits. *Neurobiology of Aging, 18,* 631-639.

Sears, L.L., & Steinmetz, J.E. (1990). Acquisition of classically conditioned-related activity in the hippocampus is affected by lesions of the cerebellar interpositus nucleus. *Behavioral Neuroscience, 104,* 681-692.

Solomon, P.R., Barth, C.L., Wood, M.S., Velazquez, E., Groccia-Ellison, M., & Yang, B.-Y. (1995). Age-related deficits in retention of the classically conditioned nictitating membrane response in rabbits. *Behavioral Neuroscience, 109,* 18-23.

Solomon, P.R., Brett, M., Groccia-Ellison, M., Oyler, C., Tomasi, M., & Pendlebury, W.W. (1995). Classical conditioning in patients with Alzheimer's disease: A multiday study. *Psychology and Aging, 10,* 248-254.

Solomon, P.R., & Gottfried, K.E. (1981). The septo-hippocampal cholinergic system and classical conditioning of the rabbit's nictitating membrane response. *Journal of Comparative and Physiological Psychology, 95,* 322-330.

Solomon, P.R., & Groccia-Ellison, M. (1996). Classic conditioning in aged rabbits: Delay, trace, and long-delay conditioning. *Behavioral Neuroscience, 110,* 427-435.

Solomon, P.R., Groccia-Ellison, M., Flynn, D., Mirak, J., Edwards, K.R., Dunehew, A., & Stanton, M.E. (1993). Disruption of human eyeblink conditioning after central cholinergic blockade with scopolamine. *Behavioral Neuroscience, 107,* 271-279.

Solomon, P.R., Levine, E., Bein, T., & Pendlebury, W.W. (1991). Disruption of classical conditioning in patients with Alzheimer's disease. *Neurobiology of Aging, 12,* 283-287.

Solomon, P.R., Pomerleau, D. Bennett, L., James, J., & Morse, D.L. (1989). Acquisition of the classically conditioned eyeblink response in humans over the lifespan. *Psychology and Aging, 4,* 34-41.

Solomon, P.R., Wood, M.S., Groccia-Ellison, M.E., Yang, B.-Y., Fanelli, R.J., & Mervis, R.F. (1995). Nimodipine facilitates retention of the classically conditioned nictitating membrane response in aged

rabbits over long retention intervals. *Neurobiology of Aging, 16*, 791-796.
Steinmetz, J.E. (1996). The brain substrates of classical eyeblink conditioning in rabbits. In J.R. Bloedel, T.J. Ebner, & S.P. Wise (Eds.). *The Acquisition of Motor Behavior in Vertebrates*, (pp. 89-114). MIT Press.
Straube, K.T., Deyo, R.A., Moyer, J.R., & Disterhoft, J.F. (1990). Dietary nimodipine improves associative learning in aging rabbits. *Neurobiology of Aging, 11*, 659-661.
Thompson, L.T., Deyo, R.A., & Disterhoft, J.F. (1990). Nimodipine enhances spontaneous activity of hippocampal pyramidal neurons in aging rabbits at a dose that facilitates associative learning. *Brain Research, 535*, 119-130.
Thompson, L.T., & Disterhoft, J.F. (1997). Age- and dose-dependent facilitation of associative eyeblink conditioning by D-cycloserine in rabbits. *Behavioral Neuroscience, 111*, 1303-1312.
Thompson, L.T., Moyer, J., James R., & Disterhoft, J.F. (1996). Trace eyeblink conditioning in rabbits demonstrates heterogeneity of learning ability both between and within age groups. *Neurobiology of Aging, 17*, 619-629.
Thompson, R.F. (1988). Classical conditioning: The Rosetta stone for brain substrates of age-related deficits in learning and memory? *Neurobiology of Aging, 9*, 547-548.
Waite, J.J., Wardlow, M.L., & Power, A.E. (1999). Deficit in selective and divided attention associated with cholinergic basal forebrain immunotoxic lesion produced by 192-saporin; Motoric/sensory deficit associated with Purkinje cell immunotoxic lesion produced by OX7-saporin. *Neurobiology of Learning and Memory, 71*, 325-352.
West, M.J. (1993). Regionally specific loss of neurons in the aging human hippocampus. *Neurobiology of Aging, 14*, 287-293.
West, M.J., Coleman, P.D., Flood, D.G., & Troncoso, J.C. (1994). Differences in the pattern of hippocampal neuronal loss in normal aging and Alzheimer's disease. *Lancet, 344*, 769-772.
Woodruff-Pak, D.S. (1988). Aging and classical conditioning: Parallel studies in rabbits and humans. *Neurobiology of Aging, 9*, 511-522.
Woodruff-Pak, D.S. (1995). Evaluation of cognition-enhancing drugs: Utility of the model system of eyeblink classical conditioning. *CNS Drug Reviews, 1*, 107-128.
Woodruff-Pak, D.S. (1997). Evidence for the role of the cerebellum in classical conditioning in humans. *International Review of Neurobiology, 41*, 385-410.
Woodruff-Pak, D.S., Coffin, J.M., & Papka, M. (1994). A substituted pyrrolidinone, BMY 21502, and classical conditioning of the nictitating membrane response in young and old rabbits. *Psychobiology, 22*, 312-319.
Woodruff-Pak, D.S., Cronholm, J.F., & Sheffield, J.B. (1990). Purkinje cell number related to rate of classical conditioning. *Neuroreport, 1*, 165-168.
Woodruff-Pak, D.S., Finkbiner, R.G., & Sasse, D.K. (1990). Eyeblink conditioning discriminates Alzheimer's patients from non-demented aged. *Neuroreport, 1*, 45-49.
Woodruff-Pak, D.S., & Hinchliffe, R.M. (1997). Mecamylamine- or scopolamine-induced learning impairment: Ameliorated by nefiracetam. *Psychopharmacology, 131*, 130-139.
Woodruff-Pak, D.S., & Jaeger, M. (1998). Predictors of eyeblink classical conditioning over the adult age span. *Psychology and Aging, 13*, 193-205.
Woodruff-Pak, D.S., Lavond, D.G., Logan, C.G., & Thompson, R.F. (1987). Classical conditioning in 3-, 30- and 45-month-old rabbits: behavioral learning and hippocampal unit activity. *Neurobiology of Aging, 8*, 101-108.
Woodruff-Pak, D.S., & Li, Y.-T. (1994). Nefiracetam (DM-9384): effect on eyeblink classical conditioning in older rabbits. *Psychopharmacology, 114*, 200-208.
Woodruff-Pak, D.S., Li, Y.-T., Hinchliffe, R.M., & Port, R.L. (1997). Hippocampus in delay eyeblink classical conditioning: essential for nefiracetam amelioration of learning in older rabbits. *Brain Research, 747*, 207-218.
Woodruff-Pak, D.S., Li, Y.-T., Kazmi, A., & Kem, W.R. (1994). Nicotinic cholinergic system involvement in eyeblink classical conditioning in rabbits. *Behavioral Neuroscience, 108*, 486-493.
Woodruff-Pak, D.S., Li, Y.-T., & Kem, W.R. (1994). A nicotinic agonist (GTS-21), eyeblink conditioning, and nicotinic receptor binding in rabbit brain. *Brain Research, 645*, 309-317.
Woodruff-Pak, D.S., & Papka, M. (1996). Alzheimer's disease and eyeblink conditioning: 750 ms trace vs. 400 ms delay paradigm. *Neurobiology of Aging, 17*, 397-404.
Woodruff-Pak, D.S., Romano, S.J., & Hinchliffe, R.M. (1996). Detection of Alzheimer's disease with eyeblink classical conditioning and the pupil dilation response. *Alzheimer's Research, 2*, 173-180.
Woodruff-Pak, D.S., Romano, S., & Papka, M. (1996). Training to criterion in eyeblink classical

conditioning in Alzheimer's disease, Down's syndrome with Alzheimer's disease, and healthy elderly. *Behavioral Neuroscience, 110*, 22-29.

Woodruff-Pak, & Trojanowski, J.Q. (1996). The older rabbit as an animal model: Implications for Alzheimer's disease. *Neurobiology of Aging, 17*, 283-290.

Yokel. R.A. (1989). Aluminum produces age related behavioral toxicity in the rabbit. *Neurotoxicology and Teratology, 11*, 237-242.

8 CELLULAR CORRELATES OF EYEBLINK CLASSICAL CONDITIONING

Bernard G. Schreurs
National Institutes of Health

INTRODUCTION

The purpose of the present chapter is to explore the cellular mechanisms proposed to be involved in the associative learning demonstrated by classical conditioning of the rabbit nictitating membrane response (NMR) preparation. In addition to a theoretical treatment of these cellular mechanisms, there is a methods section at the end of this chapter for readers interested in technical details.

As noted in previous chapters, classical conditioning of the rabbit NMR was first reported by Gormezano and his colleagues when they paired a tone CS with a corneal air puff US (Gormezano, Schneiderman, Deaux & Fuentes, 1962; Gormezano, 1966). As also noted in the preceding chapters, the sensory inputs of the rabbit NMR include the brain stem auditory pathways and corneal inputs that travel via the spinal trigeminal nucleus to the inferior olive and cerebellum and to the motor output of the accessory abducens nucleus that controls eyeball retraction and the resultant sweep of the nictitating membrane (Cegavske, Thompson, Patterson & Gormezano, 1976; Harvey, Land & McMaster, 1984; Van Ham & Yeo, 1996). In addition to these primary pathways, CS and US information also travels to many other parts of the brain including the hippocampus, cerebellum, and cortex. A great deal of lesion and recording research, initiated, in large part, by Thompson and his colleagues has revealed the important role played by the hippocampus and cerebellum in classical conditioning of the rabbit NMR (Thompson, 1986).

HIPPOCAMPUS

Single and multiple unit neural activity that mimics and precedes conditioned nictitating membrane responding has been recorded in the hippocampus (e.g., Berger, Alger & Thompson, 1978; Berger, Rinaldi, Weisz & Thompson, 1983; McEchron & Disterhoft, 1997). Electrodes placed in the region of the CA1 pyramidal cells of the hippocampus show that the CA1 cells respond to a tone CS at a higher frequency and shorter latency as a consequence of classical conditioning of the NMR than as a consequence of unpaired stimulus presentations. Intracellular recording of CA1 cells in a slice of hippocampus obtained from classically conditioned rabbits revealed an increase in membrane excitability indexed by reduced CA1 after hyperpolarization

(Coulter, LoTurco, Kubato, Disterhoft & Alkon, 1989) and enhanced postsynaptic potential summation (Coulter, LoTurco, Kubato, Disterhoft & Alkon, 1989). The conditioning-specific increase in excitability was found to result from a reduction in the flow of potassium ions through the cell membrane. In fact, voltage-clamp recordings in CA1 cells showed that potassium-ion currents active in the presence of calcium were modified as a function of classical conditioning (Sanchez-Andres & Alkon, 1991). Measurements made after classical conditioning of a critical enzyme which controls membrane excitability, protein kinase C (PKC), indicate that there is an increase in membrane-associated PKC near the CA1 cell bodies even one day after all training has been completed (Olds, Anderson, McPhie, Staten & Alkon, 1989). Three days after training (i.e., well into the period of memory retention) maximal PKC labeling moved from the cell bodies to the region of the CA1 dendrites (Olds et al., 1989). Interestingly, the movement of PKC in CA1 cells can be artificially induced by the drug phorbol ester which also causes the same potassium-ion flow reduction that takes place during conditioning (Bank, De Weer, Kuzirian, Rasmussen & Alkon, 1988). Translocation of PKC to the CA1 membrane by phorbol ester also causes enhanced summation of excitatoıy post synaptic potentials (EPSPs) elicited by activation of pre-synaptic fibers known as Schaeffer collaterals. This same enhanced EPSP summation was demonstrated to occur only in rabbits previously trained with a classical conditioning procedure. Memory-specific translocation of PKC in the hippocampus has also been reported for other learning paradigms such as cue and platform rat spatial maze learning (e.g., Golski, Olds, Mishkin, Olton & Alkon, 1995). Furthermore, different laboratories using different paradigms and different methodologies (e.g., monoclonal antibodies to PKC) independently confirmed the role of PKC in associative memory (for review see Van der Zee, Luiten & Disterhoft, 1997).

CEREBELLUM

In Vivo

Extensive lesion and recording data have implicated the deep nuclei and cortex of the cerebellum in classical conditioning of the rabbit NMR (e.g., Berthier & Moore, 1986; Gould & Steinmetz, 1996; Gruart & Yeo, 1995; McCormick & Thompson, 1984; Thompson & Krupa, 1994; Yeo, Hardiman & Glickstein, 1985a,b). Lesions of lobule HVI and ansiform of the cerebellar cortex ipsilateral to the stimulated eye disrupt conditioned responses and although conditioned responses eventually return, they are of lower frequency and amplitude than before the lesion (e.g., Lavond & Steinmetz, 1989; Lavond, Steinmetz, Yokaitis & Thompson, 1987; Yeo et al., 1985a). Bilateral lesions of lobule HVI abolish or severely impair conditioned responses in trained animals without affecting the unconditioned response and, even more importantly, bilateral lesions prevent relearning of the conditioned response (Gruart & Yeo, 1995). These lesions did not affect the underlying deep nuclei. *In vivo* extracellular recordings in and around lobule HVI made during learning have suggested that some

Purkinje cells show conditioned response-related increases and others show conditioned response-related decreases in spike activity (e.g., Berthier & Moore, 1986; Gould & Steinmetz, 1996; Thompson, 1990).

In Vitro

The application of electrophysiological techniques to the study of the cellular correlates of learning and memory in the cerebellum (see Methods section for technical details) has met with some success because it has taken advantage of the unique architecture of the cerebellar cortex. The cerebellar cortex contains five cell types including basket, Golgi, granule, Purkinje and stellate cells (Eccles, Ito & Szentagothai, 1967). Inputs from mossy fibers and climbing fibers that convey auditory and air puff information to the cerebellum, synapse onto the Purkinje cells which, in turn, provide the only output from the cerebellar cortex to the deep cerebellar nuclei. Slices of cerebellar cortex from specific areas identified to be involved in classical conditioning of the rabbit NMR such as lobule HVI (lobulus simplex) allow access to these individual neurons and their synaptic inputs. Purkinje cell dendritic recordings in slices of cerebellar cortex following learning allow an examination of cellular properties that change as a function of learning and memory. These recordings have documented changes in dendritic excitability in specific areas within lobule HVI ipsilateral to the side of training. Intracellular recording from Purkinje cell dendrites has also permitted the exploration of changes in intrinsic synaptic properties as a result of electrical stimulation of the mossy/parallel fiber and climbing fiber inputs. The change most often studied is known as long-term depression. Due to the importance of the cerebellum in classical conditioning of the rabbit NMR, researchers have sought to find evidence of cerebellar plasticity in the hope of finding a mechanism that can account for classical conditioning. Long-term depression has been suggested as one form of synaptic plasticity that may play a significant role in classical conditioning (e.g., Ito, 1984, 1989; Thompson, 1986).

Long-Term Depression

Cerebellar long-term depression (LTD) is a decrease in the sensitivity (desensitization) of Purkinje cell dendritic glutamate receptors that results from the conjunction of (1) intracellular calcium elevation and (2) elicitation of parallel fiber excitatory post synaptic potentials (for review see Linden & Connor, 1995). Long-term depression has most often been obtained as a result of conjoint stimulation of climbing fiber and mossy /parallel fiber inputs to the cerebellar cortex. The order of events comprising "conjoint stimulation" is important because LTD has only been obtained when climbing fiber stimulation has occurred before or at the same time as mossy/parallel fiber stimulation. In cerebellar slice preparations, LTD has been reported in guinea pigs (e.g., Sakurai, 1987) and immature rats (e.g., Crepel & Jaillard, 1991) and has been shown to result from the desensitization of glutamate receptors as a result of the conjunction of climbing fiber-induced elevations of the intracellular calcium concentration and parallel fiber EPSPs (e.g., Kano & Kato, 1987). More recently, LTD has been obtained in an immature rat slice preparation as a result of the conjunction of depolarization-induced elevation of intracellular calcium and parallel fiber EPSPs (Konnerth, Dreessen & Augustine, 1992). However, in each of the foregoing cases, LTD only occurred in the presence of the GABA antagonist bicuculline or picrotoxin, a substance which blocks the inhibition of Purkinje cells by the stellate and/or basket cell interneurons.

To examine LTD in the rabbit cerebellar slice and evaluate its potential as a form of plasticity underlying classical conditioning of the rabbit NMR, we conducted experiments (Schreurs & Alkon, 1993) using stimulation parameters and sequences used to induce LTD in other slice preparations. We found that stimulation of *climbing fibers and then parallel fibers* could produce long-term depression in the rabbit cerebellar slice but only in the presence of the GABA antagonist, bicuculline (Figure 1A). However, stimulation of *parallel fibers and then climbing fibers* using LTD-inducing parameters did not result in any long term change (Figure 1B) and stimulation of parallel fibers alone using these same parameters produced mild potentiation (Figure 1C). Interestingly, depression could be obtained in the absence of bicuculline if parallel fibers were stimulated in the presence of depolarizing current sufficient to induce local, calcium-dependent dendritic spikes (Figure 1C). Taken together, these initial experiments showed that LTD in the rabbit cerebellar slice could be obtained if climbing fiber stimulation occurred before parallel fiber stimulation in the presence of the GABA antagonist, bicuculline. However, no LTD occurred when the order of stimulation was reversed or when bicuculline was removed.

If LTD were to function as the synaptic mechanism proposed to underlie classical conditioning, the temporal and pharmacological conditions required to produce LTD or their functional equivalent would have to exist in the rabbit cerebellum during the CS-US pairings required to produce the classically conditioned response. However, classical conditioning of the rabbit nictitating membrane response only occurs reliably when the CS (e.g., tone) precedes the US (e.g., air puff). Similarly, when *in vivo* brain stimulation of the mossy/parallel fibers replaces the tone CS and stimulation of climbing fibers replaces the air puff US, classical conditioning only occurs when mossy fiber stimulation precedes climbing fiber stimulation and not when they occur simultaneously or when climbing fiber stimulation precedes mossy fiber stimulation (Gould, Sears & Steinmetz, 1993). Consequently, the temporal sequence used to produce classical conditioning using either peripheral stimulation or direct stimulation of parallel and climbing fiber pathways is the opposite of that used to produce LTD.

Pairing-Specific Depression

The fact that information about tone and air puff reach Purkinje cells via parallel and climbing fibers (e.g., Gould et al., 1993; Yeo et al., 1985c) and that synaptic plasticity in the form of LTD occurs as a result of stimulation of climbing and parallel fibers (e.g., Ito, 1989) continues to generate interest in the hypothesis that LTD is a synaptic mechanism underlying classical conditioning of the NMR (e.g., Ito, 1989; Thompson, 1986). However, as we have noted, there is a significant discrepancy between the

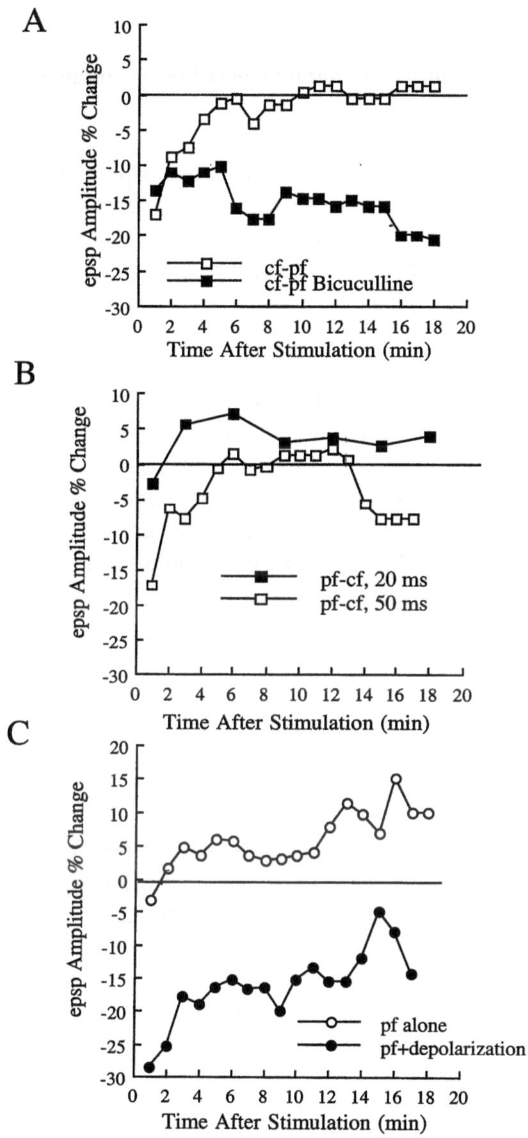

Figure 1. Mean changes in parallel fiber excitatory postsynaptic potentials (EPSPs) from prestimulation values expressed as a percent change as a result of A: stimulation of climbing fibers followed 50 ms later by stimulation of the parallel fibers for 30 seconds at a frequency of 4 Hz either in the presence (filled square, n = 8) or absence (open square, n = 13) of 20-50 mM bicuculline. B: stimulation of parallel fibers followed 20 ms (filled square, n = 10) or 50 ms (open square, n = 14) later by climbing fiber stimulation for 30 seconds at a frequency of 4 Hz. C: parallel fiber stimulation alone (open circle, n = 19) or during depolarization of the Purkinje cell dendrite by current injection sufficient to elicit local, calcium-dependent spikes (filled circle, n = 8).

timing of events that produce LTD and those that produce classical conditioning (Schreurs & Alkon, 1993; Thompson, 1986). As discussed in the previous section, LTD results from stimulation of climbing fibers before stimulation of parallel fibers whereas classical conditioning results from stimulation of parallel fibers (tone) before stimulation of climbing fibers (air puff).

Although attempts have been made to explain the disparity in timing between LTD and classical conditioning, none have been extremely successful. For example, it has been argued that in the case of delay conditioning where the tone and air puff overlap and coterminate, parallel and climbing fiber inputs do occur together. Nevertheless, conditioning of the rabbit NMR is readily achieved using a trace conditioning paradigm where the tone is terminated several hundreds of milliseconds before the onset of air puff (e.g., Gormezano, Kehoe & Marshall, 1983). In the case of trace conditioning, delay lines in the mossy/parallel fiber circuit have been proposed which modify the timing of the tone input so that it is coincident with the air puff input to the cerebellar cortex (Thompson, 1986). This is reminiscent of the original concept of the CS trace as a perseverating neural signal that ensures contiguity of the CS and US (e.g., Gormezano & Kehoe, 1981). However, Huang and Liu (1985) have shown that peak latencies of evoked auditory potentials recorded in lobule VI and VII of the cerebellum are an order of magnitude shorter (range 8 to 18 milliseconds) than those required by the delay-line hypothesis. Moreover, Gould et al. (1993) have shown that stimulation of pontine nuclei and the inferior olive - areas where stimulation has been substituted for tone and air puff to classically condition the rabbit NMR - produce cerebellar population and single unit potentials with latencies of 1 to 5 milliseconds.

We endeavored to find whether there was a form of long-term reduction in Purkinje cell EPSPs that would result from stimulation of parallel fibers that preceded stimulation of climbing fibers (Schreurs, Oh & Alkon, 1996). Our earlier LTD experiments (Schreurs & Alkon, 1993) suggested that trains of parallel fiber stimulation sufficient to depolarize the Purkinje cell dendritic membrane potential could lead to depression of parallel fiber EPSPs. Stimulation of climbing fibers also depolarized the Purkinje cell dendrites. Because stimuli such as tones and air puff lasted for tens to hundreds of milliseconds, we presented our parallel and climbing fiber stimulation as trains of pulses at durations similar to those employed in classical conditioning experiments. More importantly, our experiments used nonoverlapping trains of stimulation (Figure 2) that were presented at interstimulus and intertrial intervals that were similar to those used in *in vivo* conditioning experiments.

We tested EPSP peak amplitude to single parallel fiber test pulses before and after the parallel fibers were stimulated by a brief, high frequency train of eight constant-current pulses and climbing fibers were stimulated by a brief, lower frequency train of three constant-current pulses (Figure 3).

Consistent depression of EPSP peak amplitude only resulted when parallel fiber stimulation was paired with climbing fiber stimulation and not when presented in an unpaired manner or when parallel fiber trains were presented alone (Figure 4). Consequently, pairing-specific long-term depression (PSD) resulted from stimulation of Purkinje cells with parallel fiber frequencies observed in the cerebellum (e.g., Thach, 1970) but with a sequence and timing more normally used to classical condition an intact animal (e.g., Patterson 1970; Smith, Coleman & Gormezano, 1968).

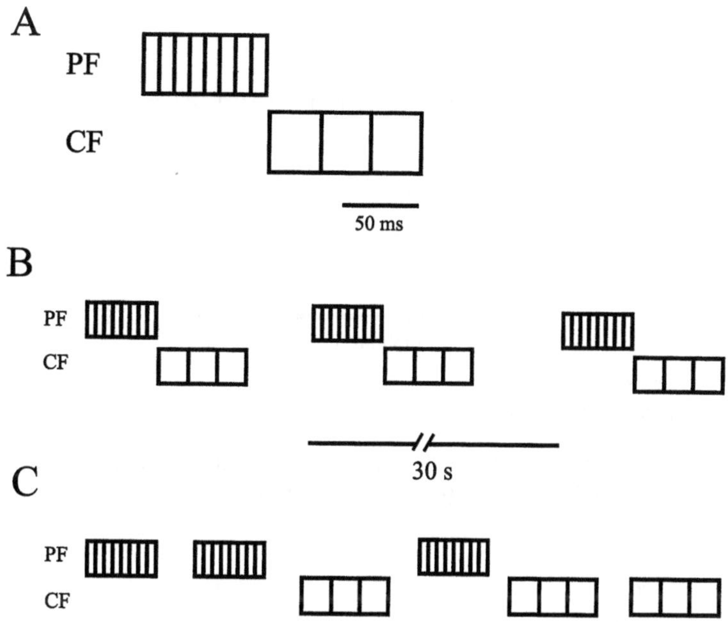

Figure 2. Schematic Diagram of Pairing-Specific Depression Protocol. A: Stimulation of parallel fibers (PF) and climbing fibers (CF) occurred at a pulse frequency of 100 Hz for 80 ms (8 pulses) and 20 Hz for 100 ms (3 pulses), respectively. B: Paired presentation of PF and CF trains occurred 20 times at an intertrial interval of 30-40 s with PF stimulation terminating before the start of CF stimulation (individual trains are illustrative and not to scale). C: Unpaired stimulation of PF and CF occurred twenty times each at an intertrial interval of 15-20 s and each train was presented separately in a pseudo-random manner. PF-alone stimulation (not shown) occurred twenty times at an intertrial interval of 30-40 s.

Apart from the obvious fact that LTD and PSD result from stimulation of parallel and climbing fiber inputs to Purkinje cells, PSD has a number of other features in common with LTD. First, in both PSD and LTD there is not only a measurable change in EPSP but we showed there is also a reduction in the response to glutamate (Schreurs et al., 1996), the transmitter at the parallel fiber-Purkinje cell synapse (e.g., Kano & Kato, 1987; Linden & Connor, 1991). The reduction in response to glutamate induced by both depression-inducing protocols suggests that both forms of depression have a substantial postsynaptic component. We found that paired-pulse facilitation occurred both before and after the stimulation protocols and that there did not appear to be any decrease in the paired-pulse facilitation as a function of those protocols (Schreurs et al., 1996). These EPSP facilitation data add to support the suggestion that PSD is postsynaptic in nature. In fact, in many other cases, activation of a synapse in rapid succession results in the second response being facilitated relative to the first. This facilitation has been shown to result from increased transmitter release and as such is presynaptic in nature (e.g., Katz & Miledi, 1968; Magleby, 1987; Zucker, 1989). The fact that depression of EPSP peak amplitude occurred after the pairing protocol

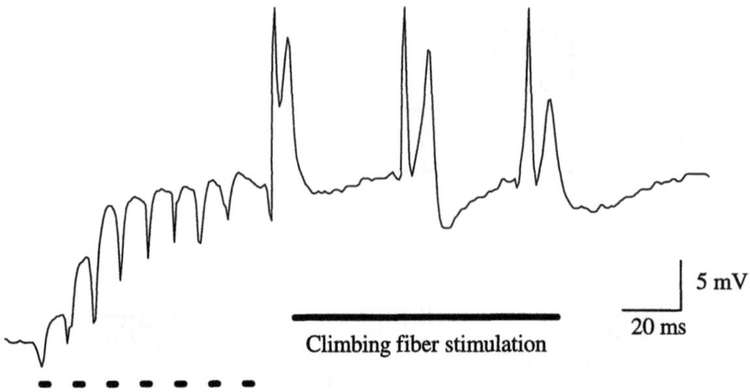

Figure 3. Sample recording of one pairing of parallel fiber stimulation (80 ms, 100 ms, 8 pulses) and climbing fiber stimulation (100 ms, 20 Hz, 3 pulses) in the PSD protocol.

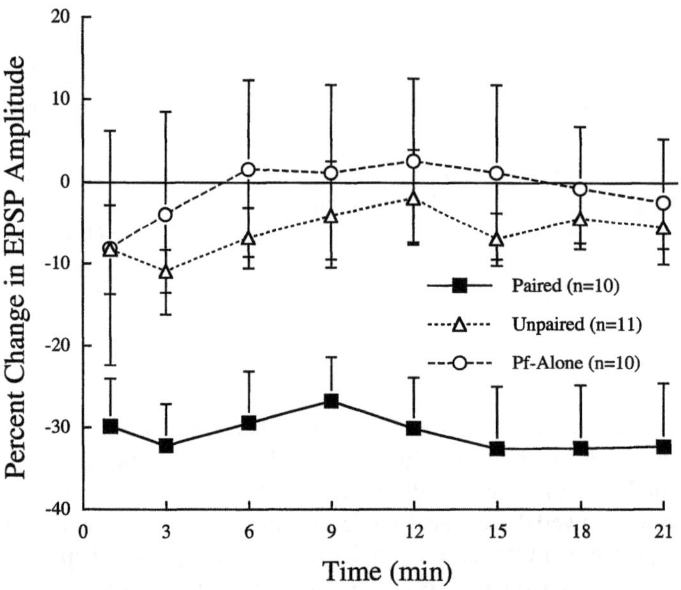

Figure 4. Mean (±sem) percent change in EPSP peak amplitude to parallel fiber test pulses measured at 1 and 3 minute and then at 3-minute intervals over the course of 21 minutes after paired parallel fiber and climbing fiber stimulation, Unpaired parallel fiber and climbing fiber stimulation, and parallel fiber stimulation (PF-Alone) protocols.

without a reduction in presynaptic facilitation suggests that the depression was postsynaptic rather than presynaptic in origin.

A second similarity between the two forms of depression is that both appear to involve protein kinases. Specifically, pairing-specific long-term depression was partially blocked by H-7 (Schreurs et al., 1996) and LTD has been blocked by calphostin C and R-31-8220 (Linden & Connor, 1991). All of these compounds are protein kinase inhibitors. Interestingly, LTD can be mimicked by the addition of protein kinase activators such as phorbol ester (Crepel & Krupa, 1988; Linden & Connor, 1991) and appears to involve protein kinase C and protein kinase G (Hartell, 1994). More recently, we have shown that a form of PSD involving postsynaptic membrane depolarization rather than climbing fiber stimulation can also be blocked by the protein kinase C inhibitor, calphostin C (Freeman, Shi & Schreurs, 1998).

Pairing-specific long-term depression and LTD are also different in a number of respects. First, PSD was obtained with trains of stimulation rather than with individual pulses typically used to produce LTD. As in a previous experiment (Schreurs & Alkon, 1993), the train of parallel fiber stimulation used in the present experiments produced substantial membrane depolarization as the EPSPs summated (Figure 3). The pairing of a parallel fiber train with a train of climbing fiber pulses was observed to depolarize the membrane to levels beyond that produced by unpaired or parallel fiber alone stimulation. Previous experiments have shown that depression only occurs if EPSPs are elicited in the presence of elevated calcium and that, in fact, elevated calcium can be substituted for climbing fiber stimulation (Crepel & Jaillard, 1991; Freeman et al., 1998; Sakurai, 1990; Schreurs & Alkon, 1993). However, because there was no overlap between the parallel fiber and climbing fiber train of stimulation in the PSD experiments, the EPSPs would have already occurred before climbing fiber stimulation could have further elevated the intracellular calcium concentration. Presumably, the train of parallel fiber pulses produced an increased susceptibility in the Purkinje cell-parallel fiber synapse to the climbing-fiber induced calcium elevation. For example, prolonged activation of a specific subtype of glutamate receptor, mGLUR1, by a train of parallel fiber stimulation would give rise to the production of the signaling molecules inositol 1,4,5-trisphosphate (IP_3) and diacylglycerol (DAG) and subsequent production of protein kinase C as well as the release from stores of significant amounts of calcium (e.g., Linden & Connor, 1995). In the present experiments, these increases in IP_3, DAG, and calcium would still be occurring at the time of climbing fiber stimulation and could interact with the additional calcium elevation induced by that stimulation. In a previous experiment, Schreurs and Alkon (1993) found that a 250-ms, high-frequency train of parallel fiber stimulation whether paired or unpaired with a climbing fiber train of stimulation was sufficient to induce a long-term reduction in EPSP amplitude. Although a presynaptic component cannot be ruled out (Schreurs & Alkon, 1993; see below), such an extended train of stimulation produced significant membrane depolarization. Indeed, Schreurs and Alkon (1993) also confirmed a previous report showing that deliberately depolarizing the membrane using a positive current step during parallel fiber stimulation was sufficient to produce a long term reduction in EPSP peak amplitude (e.g., Crepel & Jaillard, 1991). Moreover, Freeman et al. (1998) used a depolarizing current step that elicited dendritic calcium spikes as a substitute for climbing fiber stimulation and found significant levels of pairing-specific depression. This form of depression could be completely blocked by binding the intracellular calcium with the calcium binding compound EGTA (Freeman et al., 1998).

A second difference between PSD and LTD is that the former can occur without bicuculline, a potent blocker of $GABA_A$ responses in Purkinje cells including those of the rabbit (Schreurs et al., 1992). When LTD is induced in immature rat or guinea pig, a GABA antagonist such as bicuculline or picrotoxin is always present (e.g., Crepel & Jaillard, 1991; Ekerot & Kano, 1985; Hemart, Daniel, Jaillard & Crepel, 1994; Sakurai, 1987; Schreurs & Alkon, 1993). Similarly, Schreurs and Alkon (1993) showed that LTD can only be induced in the adult rabbit cerebellar slice in the presence of bicuculline. In contrast, PSD can occur in either the presence or absence of a concentration of bicuculline sufficient to block $GABA_A$ responses in the rabbit Purkinje cell (Schreurs et al., 1992) suggesting that this form of depression may not be affected by $GABA_A$-mediated inhibitory post synaptic potentials (Schreurs et al., 1996).

Long-lasting depression has been obtained when a single pulse of parallel fiber stimulation preceded a single pulse of climbing fiber stimulation by 250 ms (Chen & Thompson, 1995). This pairing of parallel and climbing fiber stimulation occurred once every second for ten minutes (600 pairings). Although such an experiment used classical conditioning-like interstimulus intervals, the interval between stimulus pairings (intertrial interval) was totally inadequate to support classical conditioning in an intact animal. In fact, an intertrial interval even nine times longer than the one second interval used by Chen and Thompson (1995) has been shown incapable of supporting conditioning of the rabbit NMR (Nordholm, Lavond & Thompson, 1991).

Cellular Correlates

Extracellular recordings in and around lobule HVI suggest that some Purkinje cells show conditioned response-related increases and others show conditioned response-related decreases in spike activity as a function of learning (e.g., Berthier & Moore, 1986; Gould & Steinmetz, 1996; Thompson, 1990). We adopted the cerebellar slice preparation in order to identify the cellular correlates of these conditioning-specific changes in Purkinje cell activity (Schreurs et al., 1991, 1997, 1998). In a typical experiment, rabbits are given sessions of paired or explicitly unpaired presentations of a tone and electrical stimulation around the right eye. Twenty four hours later, slices are prepared of lobule HVI from the right side of the cerebellum (Figure 5 B) and Purkinje cell electrophysiological properties are measured including membrane excitability (measured as threshold for dendritic spikes, Schreurs et al., 1991, 1997, 1998), synaptic excitability (measured as current required to elicit an EPSP, Schreurs et al., 1997), and potassium channel function (measured as the effects of potassium channels antagonists, Schreurs et al., 1998). The technical details of these experiments can be found in the Methods section at the end of the chapter.

Our experiments show that membrane excitability was higher in Purkinje cell dendrites in lobule HVI of rabbits given paired stimulus presentations than of rabbits given unpaired stimulus presentations (Schreurs et al., 1991, 1997, 1998). This excitability was indexed, in part, by the lower minimum current required to elicit dendritic calcium spikes in cells from paired animals than in cells from unpaired animals (Figure 5C). A second index of a change in excitability was a decrease in the size of a potassium channel-mediated transient membrane hyperpolarization in cells from paired rabbits (Schreurs et al., 1998). A third index of excitability was a decrease in the threshold current required tc elicit EPSPs and Purkinje cell spikes which was found to be lower in cells from paired animals than in cells from unpaired control animals (Schreurs et al., 1997). A fourth index of excitability was an increase in membrane-bound protein kinase C which as specific to lobule HVI of paired animals (Freeman, Scharenberg, Olds & Schreurs, 1998).

There are a number of issues raised by conditioning-specific changes in Purkinje cell excitability. First, changes in excitability may be an epiphenomenon and have little to do with conditioning. In fact, it has been argued that cerebellar structure and function are sufficiently well-understood to conclude that there is no learning-specific cerebellar plasticity and that the cerebellum is only involved in timing and coordination (e.g., Welsh & Harvey, 1989; Llinas & Welsh, 1993; Perrett, Ruiz & Mauk, 1993; Bloedel & Bracha, 1995; Anderson & Keifer, 1997). However, there is a substantial body of evidence from electrophysiological and functional imaging studies that indicates a clear role for the cerebellum in a large variety of learning tasks beyond simple timing and coordination (for review see Fiez, 1996). Second, it has been suggested that learning-specific cerebellar plasticity exists but that it takes the form of long-term depression rather than increased excitability (Linden & Connor, 1991; Schreurs & Alkon, 1993). Long-term depression is posited to reduce Purkinje cell excitability which, in turn, reduces inhibition of deep nuclei allowing CRs to occur via the red nucleus and accessory abducens nucleus (Ito, 1989; Thompson, 1986). We have already argued that LTD may not be the synaptic mechanism underlying classical conditioning of the rabbit NMR. We will show evidence below that PSD may not be involved in classical conditioning of the rabbit NMR (Schreurs et al., 1997).

A third issue raised by a conditioning-specific increase in membrane excitability is whether these findings agree with other data. *In vivo* recordings in and around lobule HVI during classical conditioning of the rabbit NMR/eyelid have identified cells with activity correlated with the tone, air puff, unconditioned response to air puff and conditioned responses to the tone (e.g., Berthier & Moore, 1986; Gould & Steinmetz, 1996; Thompson, 1990). In a discrimination experiment, Berthier and Moore (1986) identified 13 of 22 Purkinje cells that had increased simple spike activity correlated with a conditioned response that occurred to either CS+ or CS-. Only 5 of 22 Purkinje cells showed decreased simple spikes correlated with a conditioned response to CS+ or CS-. In other words, 59% of Purkinje cells recorded *in vivo* showed increased excitability during conditioned responses whereas only 23% showed decreased excitability. These numbers correspond well with a recent study by Gould and Steinmetz (1996) who found that 32 of 142 Purkinje cells (22.5%) in and around HVI identified by their complex spikes had activity that was correlated with conditioning and that 22 of these cells (68.8%) showed increased activity during conditioning and 6 cells (18.8%) showed decreased activity (Gould & Steinmetz, 1996,p. 22). In contrast, Thompson (1990) cited reports in which 31% of the Purkinje cells recorded - mostly from lobule HVI (p. 166) - showed an increase in simple spike activity as a result of classical conditioning whereas 69% showed a decrease in activity.

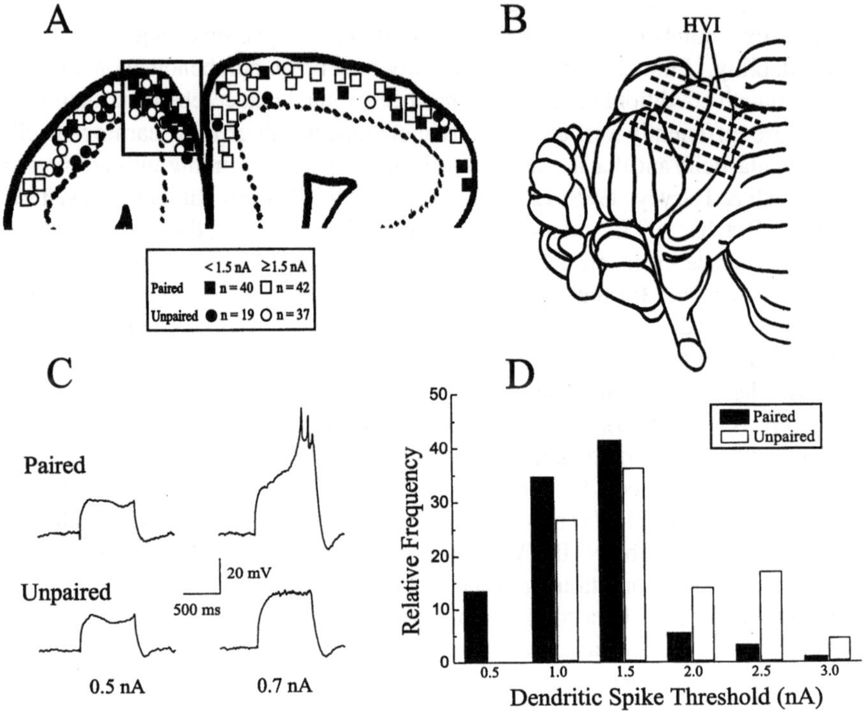

Figure 5. Learning-specific membrane excitability following three days of classical conditioning. A: Composite of recording sites for individual Purkinje cells located on a representative parasagittal slice from Larsell's lobule HVI. The slice is depicted so that the rabbit's left folium of lobule HVI is on the left and the rabbit's right folium is on the right. The cell locations for Paired (squares) and Unpaired (circles) animals are based on visual inspection (12 X magnification) of the electrode position in the slice at the time of recording. Locations are divided between those below (filled) or at and above (open) the mean dendritic spike threshold for cells from Paired animals (1.5 nA). The black square identifies the medial edge of the left folium where the largest concentration of low-threshold Purkinje cells were located. B: An anterior view of the right cerebellum indicating the area from which the slices were cut (dashed lines). C: Individual intradendritic recordings show depolarized responses to 700-ms current injections of 0.5 and 0.7 nA for a cell from a Paired animal with dendritic spikes occurring at 0.7 nA and for a cell from an Unpaired animal which remains below threshold at 0.7 nA. D: The relative frequency distribution shows a clear shift in thresholds to the left for Paired animals with only cells from Paired animals in the lowest threshold bin (0.5 - 0.9 nA).

There appears to be considerable between-study variability in the proportion of cells that show conditioning-specific changes in excitability. One reason for this apparent variability is the criteria used to select these cells. For example, Thompson (1990) found that in trained rabbits, 87% of cells showed changes in simple spike activity to the tone conditioned stimulus. The observed conditioning-specific excitability changes (69% decrease vs 31% increase) reported by Thompson (1990) are based on these 87% of cells. In contrast, Gould and Steinmetz (1996) found that only 22.5% of cells showed conditioning-specific changes in excitability. These cells were selected on the basis of the presence of complex spike activity between or during training trials. Berthier and Moore (1986) selected their cells on the basis of changes in simple spike activity that antedated conditioned responses (28.6%) and although 63.6% of these cells had complex spikes, only 13.6% showed conditioning-specific changes in those complex spikes. In other words, the criteria for selecting cells differed between Thompson (1990) and Gould and Steinmetz (1996) and Berthier and Moore (1986). The Purkinje cells in our *in vitro* studies were recorded 24 hours after training and the criteria for selection included location (anterior portion of HVI) and intrinsic membrane properties (at least -50 mV membrane potential and 28 MΩ input resistance). Although there was a significant overall increase in excitability for cells from paired rabbits, we found that less than 15% of these cells had threshold current values that did not overlap with cells from unpaired animals (Schreurs et al., 1997, 1998).

Another reason for differences in excitability between *in vivo* studies and *in vitro* experiments concerns the nature of the data obtained from the two types of studies. Specifically, the *in vivo* data are based on changes in simple and/or complex spikes resulting from stimulus- or response-elicited activity within an entire integrated network of cells in which there may be presynaptic, postsynaptic, and interneuron changes. In contrast, our *in vitro* experiments remove individual Purkinje cells from the network by hyperpolarization and examine the membrane and synaptic properties of specific dendrites.

A fourth issue raised by increases in excitability is the relevance of these increases for classical conditioning of the rabbit NMR. The prevailing view of cerebellar output circuitry is that Purkinje cells inhibit the deep nuclei of the cerebellum which, in turn, send excitatory outputs to the red nucleus (e.g., Eccles et al., 1967). In the case of a conditioned NMR/eyelid response, CS and US inputs reach both the cerebellar cortex and deep nuclei and excitation of the red nucleus by the deep nuclei drives motoneurons in accessory abducens and facial motor nuclei responsible for nictitating membrane sweeps and eyelid closure (e.g., Thompson, 1986). Accordingly, an increase in Purkinje cell excitability should result in an increase in inhibition of the deep nuclei with a consequent decrease in excitation of cells in the red nucleus and a decrease in elicitation of the CR. The same outcome should have resulted in experiments that found a two-to-one increase in conditioning-related *in vivo* activity of Purkinje cells.

There are findings which question these prevailing assumptions about cerebellar structure and function. De Zeeuw and Berribe (1995) have shown that deep cerebellar neurons receive excitatory as well as inhibitory inputs from Purkinje cells. They also found that individual Purkinje cells innervate both inhibitory and excitatory deep cerebellar neurons (Chan-Palay, 1977). Consequently, a conditioning-specific increase in Purkinje cell dendrite excitability could produce CRs through selective excitation and/or disinhibition of deep cerebellar nuclei. Even if the relevant corticonuclear connections associated with the NMR/eyelid were all inhibitory (De Zeeuw & Berribe, 1995; Teune, Van Der Burg, De Zeeuw, Voogd & Ruigrok, 1998), recent information about cerebellar function suggests testable hypotheses about the role Purkinje cell excitability might play in conditioning. First, increased Purkinje cell output could induce long-term depression of inhibitory corticonuclear synapses leading to an increased excitatory cascade to the red nucleus and motoneurons. Evidence for depression of an inhibitory synapse comes from a cerebellar slice experiment in which pairings of depolarizing current and application of the $GABA_B$ agonist, baclofen, resulted in a pairing-specific reduction in the size of the baclofen response (Schreurs et al., 1992). Experiments in hippocampus show that following pairings, GABA synapses can be converted from inhibitory to excitatory (Collin, Devan, Dahl, Lee, Axelrod & Alkon, 1995). Second, increased Purkinje cell excitability induces an increased firing of local dendritic calcium spikes which has been shown to result in a pronounced membrane after hyperpolarization (Midtgaard, 1995). Consequently, following an initial, excitability-induced burst of calcium spikes, the ensuing after hyperpolarization would silence the Purkinje cell which, in turn, would allow deep nuclei to excite the red nucleus and the CR could ensue. The relatively long latency of CRs from CS onset are consistent with a delayed hyperpolarization.

An examination of electrode recording locations following our standard three day training experiments identified clusterings of Purkinje cells with increased excitability at the medial edge of the left folium of lobule HVI (Figure 5A; Schreurs et al., 1997). These areas may represent learning "microzones" and correspond to an area of c3 shown to be involved in eyelid responses in the cat and ferret (Hesslow, 1994a, 1994b, Hesslow & Ivarsson, 1994). Our most recent experiments have focused on this "learning microzone" to maximize the likelihood of finding cells with increased excitability in two situations with potentially lower excitability yields. First, we took advantage of the fact that rabbits can begin to acquire conditioned responses (Crs) during a single 80-trial session (Scharenberg, Olds, Schreurs, Craig & Alkon, 1991) and looked early in training at the correlation between membrane excitability and learning.

After a single, 80-trial training session recordings from Purkinje cell dendrites showed that there was a strong linear relationship between the level of classical conditioning and membrane excitability (Figure 6A, 6B). In other words, the higher the level of conditioning the higher the membrane excitability (measured as threshold current for dendritic spikes, $r = -.8$) although there was no overall difference in membrane excitability between cells from paired and unpaired rabbits, we again found a unique group of cells from paired animals that had lower thresholds than any of the cells from unpaired animals (Figure 6B).

Second, we capitalized on long term memory experiments that show animals can elicit CRs to a tone CS at a level of 80% one month after training (Schreurs, 1993, range: 49 to 99%) and studied the longevity of increased Purkinje cell excitability. One month after three days of conditioning, increases in Purkinje cell excitability in the medial edge of the left lobule of HVI were still present (Figure 7). In both the one

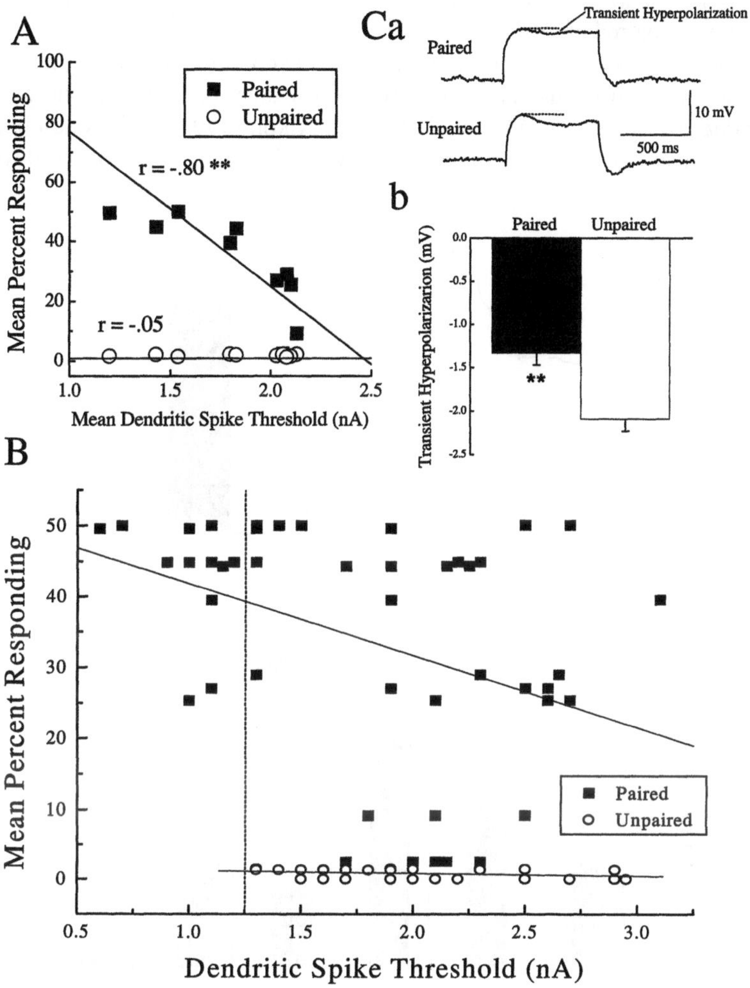

Figure 6. Learning-specific membrane excitability following one day of classical conditioning. A: A strong linear relationship between level of conditioning and mean dendritic spike threshold (at least two measures per rabbit) for Paired rabbits (filled squares, $r = -.80$, $p < .01$) relative to Unpaired rabbits (open circles, $r = -.05$, $p > .8$). B: Scatterplot of Purkinje cell dendritic spike thresholds from cells obtained in slices from paired and unpaired rabbits in A. Although mean threshold values for Paired and Unpaired rabbits overlap, the scatterplot shows that to the left of the dotted line there is a unique group of cells from Paired rabbits that have low thresholds. Lines of best fit show a significant correlation for Paired rabbits ($r = -.39$, $p < .01$) but not for Unpaired rabbits ($r = -.27$, $p > .1$). Ca: An example of the transient hyperpolarization reduced in a cell from a Paired animal (Paired, top) but not in a cell from an Unpaired animal (Unpaired, bottom). Cb: Mean transient hyperpolarization for all cells from Paired animals and all cells from Unpaired animals. (** $p < .01$).

day (Figure 6C) and the one month case (Figure 8), the second measure of excitability, transient hyperpolarization, was significantly smaller in cells from paired animals than in cells from unpaired animals.

Previous studies of neural correlates of classical conditioning have found changes in cellular excitability that last for only several days after conditioning. In the invertebrate, *Hermissenda*, Matzel, Collin and Alkon (1992) found that changes in input resistance following conditioning were detectable up to six days after

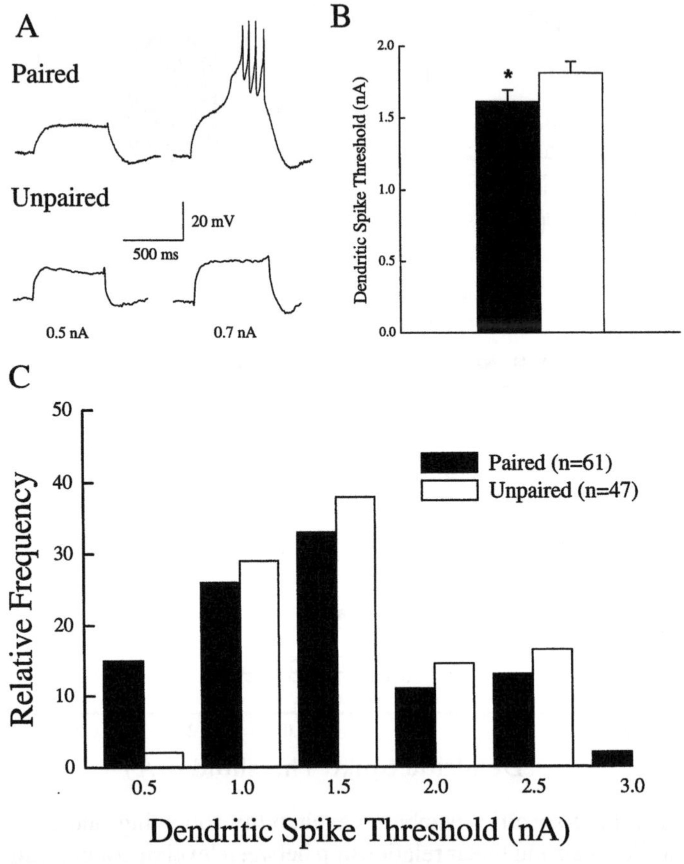

Figure 7. Learning-specific membrane excitability one month following three days of classical conditioning. A: Sample depolarizing current steps in a Purkinje cell dendrite with a low dendritic spike threshold from a trained rabbit (Paired) one month after classical conditioning showing spike threshold with a 700-ms current pulse of 0.7 nA compared to sample depolarizing current steps in a cell from an Unpaired control rabbit (Unpaired) which did not reach spike threshold at a current step of 0.7 nA. B: Mean dendritic spike thresholds showing a significantly lower threshold for cells (n = 61) from Paired rabbits than in cells (n = 47) from Unpaired rabbits. * $p < .05$. C: Relative frequency distribution shift to the left of Purkinje cell dendritic spike thresholds from cells obtained in slices from Paired compared to cells in slices from Unpaired rabbits. χ^2 (Chi square) < .05.

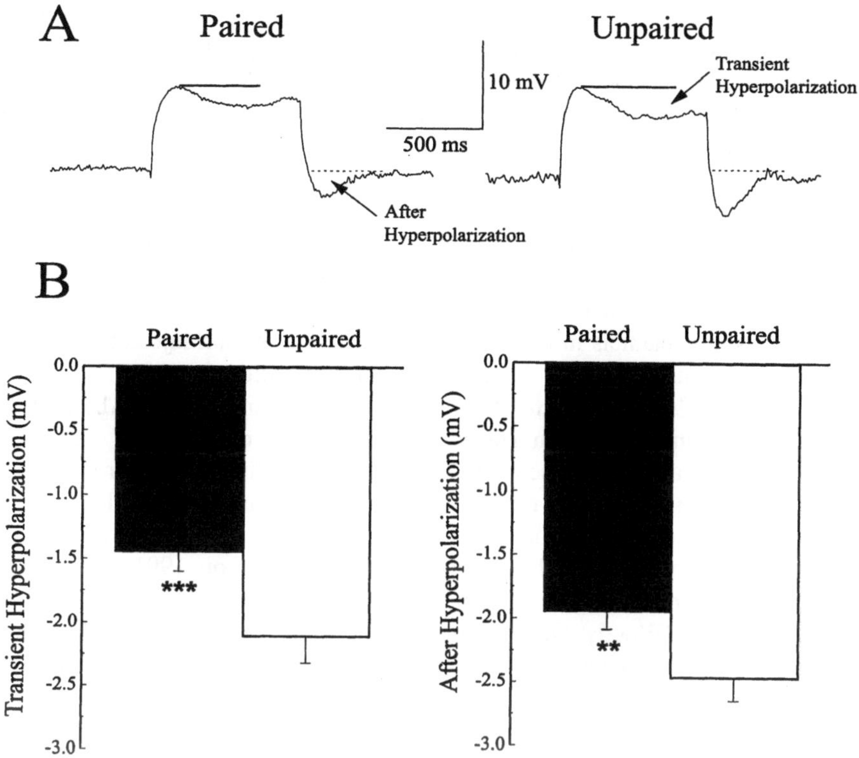

Figure 8. Changes in transient and after hyperpolarization one month after conditioning. A: Example depolarizing current steps showing smaller transient and after hyperpolarization in a cell from a Paired rabbit than in a cell from an Unpaired rabbit B: Mean transient and after hyperpolarization for all recorded cells from Paired and Unpaired animals. (*** $p < .001$, ** $p < .01$).

conditioning. Interestingly, Matzel et al. (1992) noted that conditioning-specific changes in input resistance of the *Hermissenda* B photoreceptor could be reinstated 14 days after original conditioning by renewed training. In rabbit NMR/eyelid conditioning, Moyer, Thompson and Disterhoft (1996) and Thompson, Moyer and Disterhoft (1996) found changes in the AHP of hippocampal CA1 cells returned to baseline levels seven days after conditioning. Moyer et al. (1996) and Thompson et al. (1996) failed to reinstate conditioning-specific changes in hippocampal CA1 cells 14 days after training even if renewed pairings produced asymptotic levels of conditioning. In contrast, our data provide evidence for neural correlates of learning that persist for one month after conditioning in the absence of further training. The only other data on learning-specific changes in the cerebellar cortex which lasted for

4 weeks after the end of training document an increase in synapses on Purkinje cells (Kleim, Ballard, Vij & Greenough, 1997). These synapses appear to come exclusively from parallel fibers (Kleim, Swain, Armstrong, Napper, Jones & Greenough, 1998).

The consistent, conditioning-specific increases in membrane excitability indexed by decreases in dendritic spike threshold (Figure 5D, 7C) and transient hyperpolarization (Figure 6C, 8) suggest that there is a role for Purkinje cell dendritic potassium channels in classical conditioning of the rabbit NMR. Potassium channels are responsible for regulating excitability of the membrane and the less active the potassium channels, the more excitable the membrane becomes. In fact, we were able to mimic a decrease in dendritic spike threshold in cells from naive animals by blocking potassium channels with tetramethylammonium chloride (TEA), iberiotoxin or 4 aminopyridine (4-AP) (Schreurs et al., 1997, 1998). Interestingly, the learning-specific decrease in transient hyperpolarization could only be mimicked in naive cells by application of 4-AP, an antagonist of the I_A-like potassium current. This potential role of potassium channels in learning-specific changes in Purkinje cell membrane excitability is consistent with observations of a conditioning-specific role for potassium channels in *Hermissenda* and rabbit hippocampus (e.g., Alkon, 1989; Schreurs & Alkon, 1992). In *Hermissenda*, classical conditioning induces an inactivation of I_A and Ca^{2+}-dependent K^+ channels resulting in an increase in cell excitability (Alkon, 1983). In rabbit hippocampal CA1 pyramidal cells, classical conditioning induces a reduction in a Ca^{2+}-dependent K^+ current through the cell membrane (e.g., Coulter et al., 1989; Sanchez-Andres & Alkon, 1991). Woody has reported changes in cat motor cortex pyramidal cell I_A following pairings of a click with a glabella tap (Woody, Guen & Birt, 1991). In the cerebellum, local dendritic calcium spikes are correlated with changes in local internal calcium concentration and controlled by transient outward potassium current (I_A) inactivation (Llinas & Sugimori, 1980; Midtgaard, Lasser-Ross & Ross, 1993; Midtgaard, 1995). Our experiments suggest that conditioning-specific increases in dendritic excitability are mediated by changes in I_A-like potassium currents.

PSD and Classical Conditioning

In order to evaluate the hypothesis that LTD is involved in learning, we measured parallel fiber mediated EPSPs and examined whether PSD could be obtained in Purkinje cell dendrites following classical conditioning of the rabbit NMR. Measurements of parallel fiber threshold current required to elicit EPSPs and Purkinje cell spikes were found to be significantly lower for cells from trained animals than for cells from unpaired control animals (Schreurs et al., 1997). Although Purkinje cell EPSPs were found to undergo a significant, long-term reduction in peak amplitude to parallel fiber test pulses following paired stimulation of parallel and climbing fiber inputs in cells from unpaired rabbits, there was no such reduction in cells from paired rabbits (Figure 9). One possible interpretation of these PSD data is that classical conditioning brought about synaptic depression and once Purkinje cell EPSPs were depressed, no further depression could be induced (e.g., Ito, 1989, Thompson, 1986;

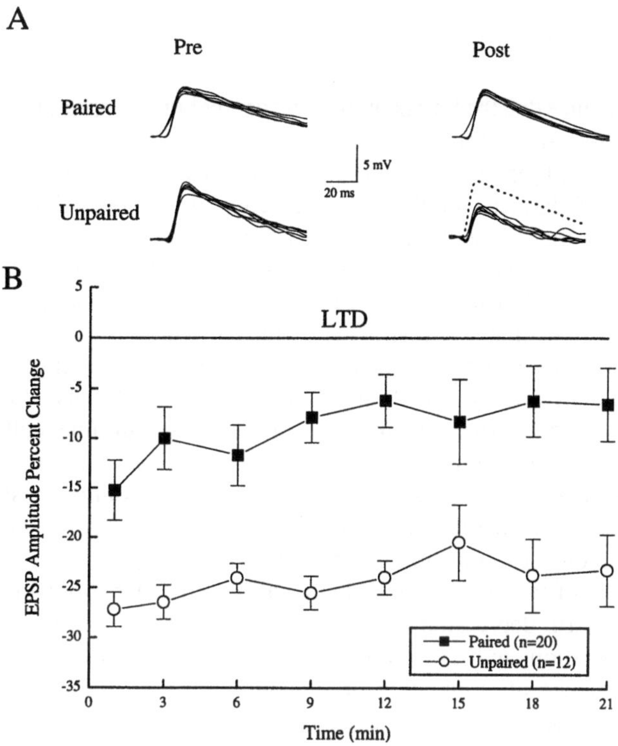

Figure 9. Effects of classical conditioning on PSD. A: Individual EPSPs in response to parallel fiber test pulses for a cell from a Paired and an Unpaired rabbit before (pre) and 21 minutes after (post) the LTD protocol. B: Mean percent change in EPSP amplitude for cells from trained (Paired) and control (Unpaired) rabbits across the 21-minute observation interval following the PSD protocol.

Shibuki, Gomi, Chen, Bao, Kim, Wakatsuki, Fujisaki, Fujimoto, Katoh, Ikeda, Chen, Thompson & Itohara, 1996). However, there are several pieces of evidence that suggest an alternative interpretation. First, there was no evidence of LTD in our EPSP recordings. In fact, in cells where threshold measurements were made, significantly less parallel fiber stimulation (current) was required to elicit EPSPs in cells from paired animal than in cells from unpaired animals (Schreurs et al., 1997). In addition, the level of parallel fiber stimulation required to cause the Purkinje cell to spike was lower in slices from conditioned animals. Consequently, the EPSPs in slices from paired animals appeared to be more excitable rather than less excitable (i.e., potentiated rather than depressed). Second, the lower threshold for dendritic spikes in cells from paired rabbits also suggests that Purkinje cells in these animals were more excitable rather than more depressed. Third, if cells were not depressed by the PDS protocol, we found that they could be depressed with further stimulation. This finding suggests that learning-induced EPSP potentiation can be depressed with a sufficiently potent protocol (e.g., Hartell, 1966).

SUMMARY AND CONCLUSIONS

There is strong evidence that the hippocampus and cerebellum comprise two areas that are involved in classical conditioning of the rabbit NMR. Both *in vivo* and *in vitro* recordings made in the hippocampus and cerebellum show changes in neural activity that are a function of classical conditioning. Moreover, in both locations, there is *in vitro* evidence that changes in neural activity are a function of an increase in membrane excitability that is mediated by a reduction in potassium channel function. A detailed analysis of Purkinje cell dendritic recordings in slices of lobule HVI shows a consistent increase in excitability that is (a) correlated with acquisition of classical conditioning, (b) at its strongest immediately following conditioning and (c) still detectable one month after the end of conditioning. Electrophysiological and pharmacological evidence suggests that this increase in Purkinje cell dendritic excitability is the result of changes in a specific type of potassium channel known as I_A. In sum, the cellular correlates of eyeblink classical conditioning consist, at least in part, of an increase in membrane excitability in identifiable cells mediated by specific changes in one or more types of potassium channel.

Our examination of synaptic plasticity in the rabbit cerebellar cortex indicates that Purkinje cell long-term depression can be obtained but it requires both a specific sequence of stimulation and the presence of the GABA inhibitor, bicuculline. However, the sequence of stimulation of synaptic inputs that produces long-term depression is very different from that used to produce classical conditioning in the intact animal. If parameters of stimulation that mimic classical conditioning are used to stimulate the parallel and climbing fiber inputs to a Purkinje cell, a long-lasting form of pairing-specific depression can be obtained that does not require bicuculline. Although this pairing-specific long term depression is an interesting form of synaptic plasticity with many similarities to traditional long-term depression, is not inducible in slices of the cerebellar cortex following classical conditioning of the intact animal. This failure to induce pairing-specific long term depression does not appear to be the result of a classical conditioning-induced depression of the Purkinje cell. Rather, there is considerable evidence from a number of different measures that the Purkinje cell becomes more excitable as a result of conditioning. Specifically, we have indexed increased excitability by measuring a decrease in dendritic threshold for dendritic calcium spikes, a decrease in transient hyperpolarization, a decrease in the current required to elicit EPSPs and an increase in PKC binding.

The conditioning-specific increase in Purkinje cell excitability that has been observed both *in vitro* and *in vivo* may interact with the deep nuclei of the cerebellum by inducing either corticonuclear long-term depression, nuclear rebound excitation, or nuclear excitation due to an excitability-induced Purkinje cell afterhyperpolarization. Each of these potential mechanisms could translate the conditioning-specific increase in Purkinje excitability into an increased cerebellar nuclear output to the red nucleus and the ensuing generation of a conditioned response.

METHODOLOGY

Slice Preparation

Rabbits are anesthetized with sodium pentobarbital (30 mg/kg) and decapitated. A rapid craniotomy which removes the occipital bone and mastoid processes allows the cerebellum and brain stem to be detached, removed, and chilled in 95% O_2 - 5% CO_2 saturated artificial cerebrospinal fluid (ACSF) within approximately 70-90 seconds. Next, the vermal area or the area surrounding the right HVI is isolated and attached with cyanoacrylate to an agar block in the cutting chamber. The isolated tissue is then immersed in room-temperature (20° -24° C) ACSF and 400-μm parasagittal slices are cut with a vibrating slicer (Vibratome 1000). Following this procedure, slices are incubated in saturated ACSF at room temperature for at least one hour before being placed in the recording chamber. The ACSF contains (mM): NaCl (124), KCl (3), MgSO4 (1.2), CaCl2 (2.1), Na2PO_4 (1.4), $NaHCO_2$ (26), Dextrose (10) and is saturated with a mixture of 95% O_2 and 5% CO_2 which maintains the pH at 7.4.

Recording Chamber

The recording chamber is a modified constant-flow (2 ml/min) surface chamber (Haas top, Medical Systems). The modifications consist of (1) a silicon wall which allows ACSF to fill the chamber to a depth of approximately 1 mm, (2) a nylon mesh used to submerge the slice and hold it in place against a second piece of nylon mesh attached to the base of the chamber, (3) a darkening of the underside of the chamber surface and, (4) a fiber-optic light positioned to direct light onto the bottom of the chamber refracting light through the plane of the slice. This pseudo dark-field illumination aids in visualization of the different layers of the cerebellar cortex.

Electrophysiology

Intracellular recordings from Purkinje-cell dendrites are obtained blindly by advancing a glass microelectrode (Leitz micromanipulator) through the Purkinje cell layer of the cerebellar slice. Microelectrodes of thick-walled glass (2 mm OD, 1 mm ID, FHC Inc.) are fabricated on a Narishige (NE-2) puller, filled with 4 M potassium acetate, and have a d.c.-resistance of 80-120 MW. An Axoprobe 1A (Axon Instruments) bridge amplifier or an Axoclamp 2B in bridge mode (axon Instruments) is used for recording intracellular electrophysiological properties.

Parallel fibers are stimulated using a bipolar electrode (150 μm separation, Rhodes) placed in the molecular layer at the cortical edge of the lobule from which the recording are made. Climbing fibers are stimulated using a bipolar electrode (100 μm separation, Rhodes) placed in the white matter of the lobule. Timing of all stimulation parameters including pulse duration, frequency, and train duration are controlled by an Anapulse stimulator (302-T, WPI) or a Master-8 stimulator (AMPI). Constant current pulses are controlled by stimulus isolation units (305-1, WPI or Isoflex,

AMPI).

Stimulation Protocols

The pulse width for both parallel and climbing fiber constant-current stimulation are set at 80 μs for all protocols. Climbing fiber-parallel fiber stimulation used to induce LTD was presented at a pulse frequency of 4 Hz for 30 s with an interval of 50 ms between the climbing fiber pulse and the parallel fiber pulse. Activation of parallel fibers and then climbing fibers in a classical conditioning-like order occurred at a pulse frequency of 4 Hz for a total of 30 s with an interval of either 50 ms or 20 ms between the parallel fiber pulse and the climbing fiber pulse. Stimulation of parallel fibers alone with or without depolarization-induced local dendritic calcium spikes also occurred at a pulse frequency of 4 Hz for 30 s.

Stimulation of parallel fibers and climbing fibers with classical conditioning parameters (PSD) occur at a pulse frequency of 100 Hz for 80 ms (8 pulses) and 20 Hz for 100 ms (3 pulses), respectively (see Figure 2). Paired presentation of parallel fiber and climbing fiber trains occurs 20 times at an intertrial interval of 30-40 s with 80 ms of parallel fiber stimulation terminating before the start of 100 ms of climbing fiber stimulation. Unpaired stimulation of parallel fibers and climbing fibers occurs twenty times each at an intertrial interval of 15-20 s and each stimulation is presented separately in a pseudo-random manner with no more than three of the same type of stimulation occurring sequentially. Parallel fiber alone stimulation occurs twenty times at an intertrial interval of 30-40 s. All PSD stimulation protocols are delivered at resting membrane potential.

Solution Application

Compounds are delivered to the slice via whole-bath perfusion or focally via pressure injection using a Picospritzer II (General Valve Corp.). Solutions for pressure injection are placed in a patch pipette and focally applied using a single pulse of the picospritzer. The pipette tip is placed at the top of the molecular layer as close as possible to the parallel fiber stimulating electrode. Picospritzer duration (5-20 ms) and pressure (1-5 psi) are adjusted to produce a reliable solution delivery.

Data Analyses

All data are recorded on video cassette tape using a PCM-VCR (DX-900, Toshiba) and digitized using pClamp software. The majority of Purkinje-cell dendrites revealed autorhythmic spontaneous activity (e.g., Llinas & Sugimori, 1980; Schreurs et al., 1991, 1992). Membrane potential is determined as the potential for somatic activity phase (Schreurs et al., 1991,1996). Input resistance measures are based on a 0.5 nA, 700-ms hyperpolarizing current step. The current necessary to hyperpolarize the dendrite 20 mV below the somatic spike activity level is determined and applied to the membrane in order to measure the dendritic spike threshold. The dendritic spike threshold is established by applying current steps starting at -.5 nA and increasing in 0.2-nA steps to 3.1 nA. Threshold measurements are based on the specific 700-ms current step required to elicit local, dendritic, calcium spikes. Due to the inability of the electrodes to pass current reliably above 3 nA, only cells that reach a threshold at or below the 3.1-nA step are included in the analysis.

Changes in Purkinje cell dendrite EPSPs are expressed as percentage change in EPSP peak amplitude calculated from an average of at least 5 EPSPs elicited by single parallel fiber pulses at between 0.1 and 0.5 Hz before the stimulation protocol and compared to sets of at least 5 single parallel fiber pulses first presented at 1 minute after the protocol and then every 3 minutes until at least 21 minutes after the protocol. The peak amplitude of single EPSPs is measured during a current step which hyperpolarized the membrane potential to 20 mV below the level of somatic spiking (Schreurs et al., 1991).

The size of the transient hyperpolarization is determined by measuring the difference between the maximum and minimum voltage during the depolarization current step prior to the occurrence of somatic spikes. In addition, the size of the after hyperpolarization is assessed by measuring the difference between the baseline voltage before and the minimum voltage after the depolarizing current step used to measure the transient hyperpolarization.

REFERENCES

Alkon, D.L. (1983) Learning in marine snails. *Scientific American, 249*, 70-84.

Alkon, D.L. (1989) Memory storage and neural systems. *Scientific American, 261*, 42-50.

Anderson, C. W. & Keifer, J. (1997). The cerebellum red nucleus are not required for *in vitro* classical conditioning of the turtle abducens nerve response. *Journal of Neuroscience, 17*, 9736-9745.

Bank, B., De Weer, A., Kuzirian, A. M., Rasmussen, H., & Alkon, D. L. (1988). Classical conditioning induces long-term translocation of protein kinase C in rabbit hippocampal CA1 cells. *Proceedings of the National Academy of Sciences (USA), 85*, 1988-1992.

Berger, T. W., Alger, B. E., & Thompson, R. F. (1978). Neuronal substrates of classical conditioning in the hippocampus. *Science, 192*, 483-485

Berger, T. W., Rinaldi, P. C., Weisz, D. J., & Thompson, R.F. (1983). Single-unit analysis of different hippocampal cell types during classical conditioning of rabbit nictitating membrane response. *Journal of Neurophysiology, 50*, 1197-1219.

Berthier, N. E., & Moore, J. W. (1986). Cerebellar Purkinje cell activity related to the classically conditioned nictitating membrane response. *Experimental Brain Research, 63*, 341-350.

Bloedel, J. R., & Bracha, V. (1995). On the cerebellum, cutaneomuscular reflexes, movement control and the elusive engrams of memory. *Behavioural Brain Research, 68*, 1-44.

Cegavske, C. F., Thompson, R. F., Patterson, M. M., & Gormezano, I. (1976). Mechanisms of efferent neuronal control of the reflex nictitating membrane response in the rabbit. *Journal of Comparative and Physiological Psychology, 90*, 411-423.

Chan-Palay, V. (1977). *Cerebellar dentate nucleus.* Berlin: Springer-Verlag.

Chen, C., & Thompson, R. F. (1995). Temporal specificity of long-term depression in parallel fiber-Purkinje synapses in rat cerebellar slices. *Learning & Memory, 2*, 185-198.

Collin, C., Devan, W. A., Dahl, D, Lee, C. J., Axelrod, J., & Alkon, D. L. (1995). Long-term synaptic transformation of hippocampal CA1 gamma-aminobutyric acid synapses and the effect of anandamide. *Proceedings of the National Acadamey of Science (USA), 92*, 10167-10171.

Coulter, D. A., Lo Turco, J., Kubato, M., Disterhoft, J. F., & Alkon, D. L. (1989). Classical conditioning alters the amplitude and time course of the calcium-dependent after hyperpolarization in rabbit hippocampal pyramidal cells. *Journal of Neurophysiology, 61*, 971-981.

Crepel, F., & Jaillard, D. (1991). Pairing of pre- and postsynaptic activities in cerebellar Purkinje cells induces long-term changes in synaptic efficacy *in vitro*. *Journal of Physiology (London), 432*, 123-141.

Ekerot, C.-F., & Kano, M. (1989). Stimulation parameters influencing climbing fibre induced long-term depression of parallel fibre synapses. *Neuroscience Research, 6*, 264-268.

Ito, M. (1984). *The cerebellum and neural control.* New York: Raven.

Crepel, F., & Krupa, M. (1988). Activation of protein kinase C induces long-term depression of glutamate sensitivity of cerebellar Purkinje cells. An in vitro study. *Brain Research, 458*, 397-401.

De Zeeuw, C. I., & Berrebi, A. S. (1995). Postsynaptic targets of Purkinje cell terminals in the cerebellar and vestibular nuclei of the rat. *European Journal of Neuroscience, 7*, 2322-2333.

Eccles, J. C., Ito, M., & Szentagothai, J. (1967). *The cerebellum as a neuronal machine*. Berlin: Springer-Verlag.

Fiez, J. A. (1996). Cerebellar contribution to cognition. *Neuron, 16*, 3-15.

Freeman, J. H., Jr., Scharenberg, A. M., Olds, J. L., & Schreurs, B. G. (1998). Classical conditioning increases membrane-bound protein kinase C in rabbit cerebellum. *NeuroReport, 9*, 2669-2673.

Freeman, J. H., Jr., Shi, T., & Schreurs, B. G. (1998). Pairing-specific long-term depression prevented by blockade of PKC or intracellular Ca^{2+}. *NeuroReport, 9*, 2237-2241.

Golski, S., Olds, J. L., Mishkin, M., Olton, D., & Alkon, D. L. (1995). Protein kinase C in the hippocampus is altered by spatial but not cued discriminations: A component task analysis. *Brain Research, 676*, 53-62.

Gormezano, I. (1966). Classical conditioning. In J. B. Sidowski (Ed.), *Experimental Methods and Instrumentation in Psychology*. (pp.385-420). New York: McGraw-Hill.

Gormezano, I., & Kehoe, E .J. (1981). Classical conditioning and the law of contiguity. In P. Harzem and M. D. Zeiler (Eds.), *Advances in Analysis of Behavior. Vol 2. Predictability, Correlation, and Contiguity*. (pp.1-45). Sussex, England: Wiley and Sons.

Gormezano, I., Kehoe, E. J., & Marshall, B. S. (1983). Twenty years of classical conditioning research with the rabbit. *Progress in Psychobiology and Physiology Psychology, 10*, 197-275.

Gormezano, I., Schneiderman, N., Deaux, E. G., & Fuentes, I. (1962). Nictitating membrane: Classical conditioning and extinction in the albino rabbit. *Science, 138*, 33-34.

Gould, T. J., Sears, L. L., & Steinmetz, J. E. (1993). Possible CS and US pathways for rabbit classical eyelid conditioning: electrophysiological evidence for projections from the pontine nuclei and inferior olive to cerebellar cortex and nuclei. *Behavioral and Neural Biology, 60*, 172-185.

Gould, T. J., & Steinmetz, J. E. (1996). Changes in rabbit cerebellar cortical and interpositus nucleus activity during acquisition, extinction, and backward classical eyelid conditioning. *Neurobiology of Learning Memory, 65*,17-34.

Gruart, A., & Yeo, C. H. (1995). Cerebellar cortex and eyeblink conditioning - bilateral regulation of conditioned responses. *Experimental Brain Research, 104*, 431-438.

Harvey, J. A., Land, T., & McMaster, S. E. (1984). Anatomical study of the rabbit's corneal-VIth nerve reflex: Connections between cornea, trigeminal sensory complex, and the abducens and accessory abducens nuclei. *Brain Research, 301*, 307-321.

Hartell, N. A. (1994). cGMP acts within cerebellar Purkinje cells to produce long term depression via mechanisms involving PKC and PKG. *NeuroReport, 5*, 833-836.

Hartell, N. A. (1996). Strong activation of parallel fibers produces localized calcium transients and a form of LTD that spreads to distant synapses. *Neuron, 16*, 601-610.

Hemart, N., Daniel, H., Jaillard, D., & Crepel, F. (1994). Properties of glutamate receptors are modified during long-term depression in rat cerebellar Purkinje cells. *Neuroscience Report, 19*, 213-221.

Hesslow, G. (1994a). Correspondence between climbing fibre input and motor output in eyeblink-related areas in cat cerebellar cortex. *Journal of Physiology (London), 476*, 229-244.

Hesslow, G. (1994b). Inhibition of classically conditioned eyeblink responses by stimulation of the cerbellar cortex in the decerebrate cat. *Journal of Physiology (London), 476*, 245-256.

Hesslow, G., & Ivarsson, M. (1994). Suppression of cerebellar Purkinje cells during conditioned responses in ferrets. *Neuroreport, 4*, 1127-1130.

Huang, C., & Liu, G. (1990). Organization of the auditory area in the posterior cerebellar vermis of the cat. *Experimental Brain Research, 81*, 377-383.

Ito, M. (1989). Long-term depression. *Annual Review of Neuroscience, 12*, 85-102.

Kano, M., & Kato, M. (1987). Quisqualate receptors are specifically involved in cerebellar synaptic plasticity. *Nature, 325*, 276-279.

Katz, B., & Miledi, R. (1968). The role of calcium in neuromuscular facilitation. *Journal of Physiology*

(London), 195, 481-492.

Kleim, J. A., Ballard, D., Vij, K., & Greenough, W. T. 1997. Learning-dependent synaptic plasticity modifications in the cerebellar cortex persists for at least four weeks. *Journal of Neuroscience*, 17, 717-721.

Kleim, J. A., Swain, R. A., Armstrong, K. A., Napper, R. M. A., Jones, T. A., & Greenough, W. T. (1998). Selective synaptic plasticity within the cerebellar cortex following complex motor skill learning. *Neurobiology of Learning and Memory*, 69, 274-289.

Konnerth, A., Dreessen, J., & Augustine, G. J. (1992). Brief dendritic calcium signals initiate long-lasting synaptic depression in cerebellar Purkinje cells. *Proceedings of the National Academy of Sciences (USA), 89*, 7051-7055.

Lavond, D. G., Steinmetz, J. E., Yokaitis, M. H., & Thompson, R. F. (1987). Reacquisition of classical conditioning after removal of cerebellar cortex. *Experimental Brain Research, 67*, 569-593.

Linden, D. J., & Connor, J. A. (1991). Participation of postsynaptic PKC in cerebellar long-term depression in culture. *Science, 254*, 1656-1659.

Linden, D. J., & Connor, J. A. (1995). Long-term depression. *Annual Review of Neuroscience, 18*, 319-357.

Llinas, R. R., & Sugimori, M. (1980). Electrophysiological properties of in vitro Purkinje cell dendrites in mammalian cerebellar slices. *Journal of Physiology (London), 305*, 197-213,.

Llinas, R. R., & Welsh, J. P. (1993). On the cerebellum and motor learning. *Current Opinion in Neurobiology, 3*, 958-965.

Magleby, K. L. (1987). Short-term changes in synaptic efficacy, In G. M. Edelman, W. E. Gall and W. M. Cowan (Eds.), *Synaptic function*. (pp. 21-56). New York: Wiley.

McCormick, D. A., & Thompson, R. F. (1984). Cerebellum: essential involvement in the classically conditioned eyelid response. *Science, 223*, 296-299.

McEchron, M. D., & Disterhoft, J. F. (1997). Sequence of single neuron changes in CA1 hippocampus of rabbits during acquisition of trace eyeblink conditioned responses. *Journal of Neurophysiology, 78*, 1030-1044.

Midtgaard, J. (1994). Processing of information from different sources: spatial synaptic integration in the dendrites of vertebrate CNS neurons. *Trends In Neuroscience, 17*, 166-173.

Midtgaard, J. (1995). Spatial synaptic integration in Purkinje cell dendrites. *Journal of Physiology (Paris), 89*, 23-32.

Midtgaard, J., Lasser-Ross, N., & Ross, W. N. (1993). Spatial distribution of Ca^{2+} influx in turtle Purkinje cell dendrites in vitro: role of a transient outward current. *Journal of Neurophysiology, 70*, 2455-2469.

Moyer, J. R., Jr., Thompson, L. T., & Disterhoft, J. F. (1996). Trace eyeblink conditioning increases CA1 excitability in a transient and learning-specific manner. *Journal of Neuroscience, 16*, 5536-5546.

Nordholm, A. F., Lavond, D. G., & Thompson, R. F. (1991). Are eyeblink responses to tone in the decerebrate, decerebellate rabbit conditioned responses? *Behavioural Brain Research, 44*, 27-34.

Olds, J. L., Anderson, M., McPhie, D., Staten, L., & Alkon, D. L. (1989). Imaging memory-specific changes in the distribution of protein kinase C within the hippocampus. *Science, 245*, 866-869.

Patterson, M. M. (1970). Classical conditioning of the rabbit's (*Oryctolagus cuniculus*) nictitating membrane response with fluctuating ISI and intracranial CS. *Journal of Comparative and Physiological Psychology, 72*, 193-202.

Perrett, S. P., Ruiz, B. P., & Mauk, M. D. (1993). Cerebellar cortex lesions disrupt learning-dependent timing of conditioned eyelid responses. *Journal of Neuroscience, 13*, 1708-1718.

Sakurai, M. (1987). Synaptic modification of parallel fibre-Purkinje cell transmission in in vitro guinea-pig cerebellar slices. *Journal of Physiology (London), 394*, 463-480.

Sakurai, M. (1990). Calcium is an intracellular mediator of the climbing fiber in induction of cerebellar long-term depression. *Proceedings of the National Academy of Science (USA), 87*, 3383-3385.

Sanchez-Andres, J. V., & Alkon, D. L. (1991). Voltage-clamp analysis of the effect of classical conditioning on the hippocampus. *Journal of Neurophysiology, 65*,796-807.

Scharenberg, A. M., Olds, J. L., Schreurs, B. G., Craig, A. M., & Alkon, D. L. (1991). Protein kinase C redistribution within CA3 stratum oriens during acquisition of NM conditioning in the rabbit. *Proceedings of the National Academy of Sciences (USA), 88*, 6637-6641.

Schreurs, B. G. (1993). Long-term memory and extinction of the classically conditioned rabbit nictitating membrane response. *Learning & Motivation, 24*, 93-302.

Schreurs, B. G., & Alkon, D. L. (1992). Memory storage mechanisms, conservation across species. In G. Adelman and B. H. Smith (Eds.), *Neuroscience year: Supplement 2 to the encyclopedia of neuroscience*. (pp 99-101). Boston: Birkhauser.

Schreurs, B. G., & Alkon, D. L. (1993). Rabbit cerebellar slice analysis of long-term depression and its role in classical conditioning. *Brain Research, 631*, 235-240.

Schreurs, B.G., Oh, M. M., & Alkon, D.L. (1993). Pairing-specific long-term depression of Purkinje cell excitatory postsynaptic potentials results from a classical conditioning procedure in the rabbit cerebellar slice. *Journal of Neurophysiology, 75*, 1051-1060.

Schreurs, B. G., Sanchez-Andres, J. V., & Alkon, D. L. (1991). Learning-specific differences in Purkinje-cell dendrites of lobule HVI (lobulus simplex): intracellular recording in a rabbit cerebellar slice. *Brain Research, 548*, 18-22.

Schreurs, B. G., Sanchez-Andres, J. V., & Alkon, D. L. (1992). GABA-induced responses in Purkinje-cell dendrites of the rabbit cerebellar slice. *Brain Research, 597*, 79-87.

Schreurs, B. G., Tomsic, D., Gusev, P. A., & Alkon, D. L. (1997). Dendritic excitability microzones and occluded long-term depression after classical conditioning of the rabbit's nictitating membrane response. *Journal of Neurophysiology, 77*, 86-92.

Schreurs, B. G., Gusev, P. A., Tomsic, D., Alkon, D. L, & Shi, T. (1998). Intracellular correlates of acquisition and long-term memory of classical conditioning in Purkinje cell dendrites in slices of rabbit cerebellar lobule HVI. *Journal of Neuroscience, 18*, 5498-5507.

Shibuki, K., Gomi, H., Chen, L., Bao, S., Kim, J. J., Wakatsuki, H., Fujisaki, T., Fujimoto, K., Katoh, A., Ikeda, T., Chen, C., Thompson, R. F., & Itohara, S. (1996). Deficient cerebellar long-term depresssion, impaired eyeblink conditioning, and normal motor coordination in GFAP mutant mice. *Neuron, 16*, 587-599.

Smith, M. C., Coleman, S. R., & Gormezano, I. (1968). Classical conditioning of the rabbit's nictitating membrane response and backward, simultaneous, and forward CS-US intervals. *Journal of Comparative and Physiological Psychology, 69*, 226-231.

Teune, T. M., Van Der Burg, J., De Zeeuw, C. I., Voogd, J., & Ruigrok, T. J. H. (1998). Single Purkinje cell can innervate multiple classes of projection neurons in cerebellar nuclei of the rat: a light microscopic and ultrastructural triple-tracer study in the rat. *Journal of Comparative Neurology, 392*, 164-178.

Thach, W. T. (1970). Discharge of cerebellar neurons related to two maintained postures and two prompt movements. II. Purkinje cell output and input. *Journal of Neurophysiology, 33*, 537-547.

Thompson, L. T., Moyer, J. R., Jr., & Disterhoft, J. E. (1996). Transient changes in excitability of rabbit CA3 neurons with a time couirse appropriate to support memory consolidation. *Journal of Neurophysiology, 76*, 1836-1849.

Thompson, R. F. (1986). The neurobiology of learning and memory. *Science, 233*, 941-947.

Thompson, R. F. (1990). Neural mechanisms of classical conditioning in mammals. *Philosophical Transactions of the Royal Society of London, 329*, 161-170.

Thompson, R. F., & Krupa, D. J. (1994). Organization of memory traces in the mammalian brain. *Annual Review of Neuroscience, 17*, 519-549.

Van der Zee, E. A., Luiten, P. G. M., & Disterhoft, J. F. (1997). Learning-induced alterations in hippocampal PKC-immunoreactivity: a review and hypothesis of its functional significance. *Progress in Neuro-Psychopharmacology and Biological Psychiatry, 21*, 531-572.

Van Ham, J. J., & Yeo, C. H. (1996). The central distribution of primary afferents from the external eyelids, conjuctiva, and cornea in the rabbit, studied using WGA-HRP and B-HRP as transganglionic tracers. *Experimental Neurology, 142*, 217-225.

Welsh, J. P., & Harvey, J. A. (1989). Cerebellar lesions and the nictitating membrane reflex: performance deficits of the conditioned and unconditioned response. *Journal of Neuroscience, 9*, 299-311.

Woody, C. D., Gruen, E., & Birt, D. (1991). Changes in membrane currents during Pavlovian conditioning of single cortical neurons. *Brain Research, 539*, 76-84.

Yeo, C. H., Hardiman, M. J., & Glickstein, M. (1985a). Classical conditioning of the nictitating membrane response of the rabbit. I. Lesions of the cerebellar nuclei. *Experimental Brain Research, 60*, 87-98.

Yeo, C. H., Hardiman, M. J., & Glickstein, M. (1985b). Classical conditioning of the nictitating membrane response of the rabbit. II. Lesions of the cerebellar cortex. *Experimental Brain Research, 60*, 99-113.

Yeo, C. H., Hardiman, M. J., & Glickstein, M. (1985c). Classical conditioning of the nictitating membrane response of the rabbit. III. Connections of cerebellar lobule HVI. *Experimental Brain Research, 60*, 114-126.

Zucker, R. S. (1989). Short-term synaptic plasticity. *Annual Review of Neuroscience, 12*, 13-31.

9 RELATIVE CONTRIBUTIONS OF THE CEREBELLAR CORTEX AND CEREBELLAR NUCLEUS TO EYELID CONDITIONING

William L. Nores, Javier F. Medina, Philip M. Steele and Michael D. Mauk

Department of Neurobiology and Anatomy and Keck Center for the Neurobiology of Learning and Memory

University of Texas Medical School at Houston

INTRODUCTION

The role of the cerebellum in Pavlovian eyelid conditioning has been debated for a number of years. Although several chapters in this volume present evidence for a role of the cerebellum in eyelid conditioning, there are alternative views that strongly criticize this position (see Bloedel, 1992; Bloedel & Bracha, 1995; De Schutter, 1995; De Schutter & Maex, 1996; Llinas et al., 1997; Llinas & Welsh, 1993; Welsh & Harvey, 1991). We have been guided by the belief that the best way to resolve this issue is by addressing how different components of the cerebellar circuitry may interact to mediate eyelid conditioning. Should a clear picture emerge, then the question as to whether the cerebellum is involved would be obviated.

In pursuing this approach, the relative contributions of the cerebellar cortex and the cerebellar nuclei has emerged as an informative yet controversial issue. It has been informative in the sense that separating the contributions of each region has provided a clearer indication of the mechanisms that appear to be operating during eyelid conditioning. The controversy has stemmed mostly from disagreements regarding the necessity of the cerebellar cortex for the acquisition and expression of conditioned eyelid responses. We acknowledge that our findings have contributed to this controversy in that they differ substantially from the results of other laboratories. Here we will outline these findings and present arguments as to why we believe our approach permits exclusion of confounds that other experimental designs cannot. From these findings, we will build a model of cerebellar mechanisms responsible for the acquisition, expression, extinction, and timing of conditioned eyelid responses.

SYNAPTIC ORGANIZATION OF THE CEREBELLUM

Considerable evidence, much coming from the work of R.F. Thompson and his colleagues, suggests that the acquisition and expression of conditioned eyelid responses are mediated by the cerebellum. Electrical stimulation and lesion studies indicate that information about the CS and US is conveyed to the cerebellum via mossy fibers and climbing fibers, respectively, (Lewis et al., 1987; Mauk et al., 1986; McCormick et al., 1985; Steinmetz et al., 1986, 1987, 1989; Steinmetz, 1990). Similar evidence indicates that CS-elicited activity of cerebellar output from the anterior interpositus nucleus drives the expression of conditioned responses (Hesslow, 1994; McCormick et al., 1982; McCormick & Thompson, 1984a; Tracy et al., 1998). This correspondence between stimuli and cerebellar afferents on the one hand, and cerebellar output and the expression of conditioned responses on the other, indicates how analysis of eyelid conditioning can be distilled to one key question: how does training endow CS-activated mossy fibers the ability to activate the appropriate neurons in the anterior interpositus nucleus? Our first efforts were directed at identifying the relative contributions of the cerebellar cortex and the interpositus nucleus to the acquisition and expression of conditioned responses.

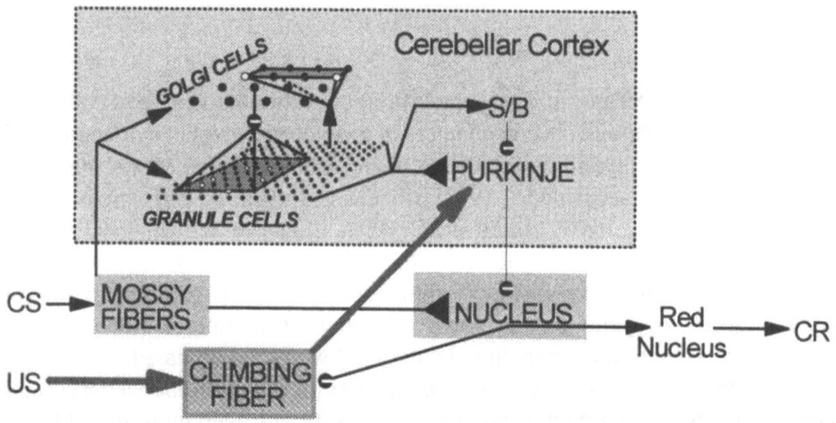

Figure 1. The synaptic organization of the cerebellum and its relation to the stimulus and response pathways involved in eyelid conditioning. Information about the CS and US are conveyed to the cerebellum via mossy fibers and climbing fibers, respectively. Mossy fibers project to the output cells of the cerebellar nuclei and the granule and Golgi cells of the cerebellar cortex. In response to mossy fiber input, subpopulations of granule and Golgi cells reciprocally interact and influence the excitatory projections of granule cells onto Purkinje cells, which inhibit nucleus output. Inhibitory interneurons, the stellate and basket cells (S/B) are excited by granule cells and inhibit Purkinje cells. Climbing fibers make excitatory synapses onto a small number of Purkinje cells. An efferent pathway from the nucleus to the red nucleus is necessary for the expression of the conditioned eyelid responses.

The synaptic organization of the cerebellum presents several challenges in this regard. Output neurons in the anterior interpositus nucleus are influenced by direct excitatory connections from mossy fiber inputs, and by inhibitory inputs from Purkinje cells in the cerebellar cortex (Figure 1). Thus, although there are in a sense two processing streams in the cerebellum, a lesion of the anterior interpositus nucleus also, in effect, disconnects the cerebellar cortex. Further complications, at least for eyelid conditioning, are introduced by 1) the close proximity of the cortex in relation to the anterior interpositus nucleus as well as to input (middle cerebellar peduncle) and output (superior cerebellar peduncle) pathways that are necessary for response expression, and 2) the relative inaccessibility of the relevant region of cerebellar cortex that appears to be involved. Together, these factors make it quite difficult to make selective lesions of the cerebellar cortex. Moreover, histological analysis is very poor at providing assurance that the cerebellar nuclei are functionally intact after a lesion of the cerebellar cortex. As all slice physiologists know, brain tissue that looks healthy under the light microscope can display a complete absence of synaptic transmission. Thus, we have generally rejected the use of histological analysis as a sole criterion for the presence of healthy brain tissue following a lesion. Instead, we have employed experimental designs that permit evaluation of the health of the anterior interpositus nucleus and input/output pathways following a cerebellar cortex lesion. This approach forms the basis for our explanations for the differences between our findings and those reported by others.

CEREBELLAR CORTEX AND EYELID CONDITIONING

Much of the debate over the relative contributions of the cerebellar cortex and anterior interpositus nucleus has centered around the effects that lesions of the cerebellar cortex have on eyelid conditioning. The original studies showed that large lesions of the cerebellar cortex spared the expression of previously acquired conditioned responses (McCormick & Thompson, 1984a,b). Soon after, others reported that more discrete lesions, which targeted deep portions of lobule HVI of the cerebellar cortex, abolished the expression of conditioned responses (Yeo et al., 1984; Yeo et al., 1985). Although subsequent studies attempted to clear up this odd discrepancy, the water only seemed to get muddier, and the controversy extended to effects on acquisition. Studies showed that large lesions of lobule HVI either retarded acquisition (Lavond & Steinmetz, 1989) or transiently abolished conditioned responses (Lavond et al., 1987), with further post-lesion training resulting in reacquisition of conditioned responses. Another study suggested that conditioned responses cannot be reacquired with more extensive lesions of lobule HVI (Yeo & Hardiman, 1992). Still later, others found that post-lesion conditioned responses are only temporarily abolished with extensive lesions of lobule HVI (Harvey et al., 1993; Woodruff-Pak et al., 1993). Clearly then, these studies have not moved anywhere near a consensus regarding the role of the cerebellar cortex in the acquisition and expression of conditioned responses. In addressing the role of cerebellar cortex, one consensus has emerged. Virtually all studies have focused on the HVI lobe, even though the original HVI observations have been called into question. This is an important point that we will return to later.

We believe the crux of this issue, and the route to its resolution, rests with verifying the specificity of the lesions (Mauk, 1997; Steele et al., 1998). As with all lesion studies, results are equivocal to the extent that the *functional* spread of the lesion is in question. This is true for both positive and negative effects. To demonstrate convincingly that lesions of the cerebellar cortex abolish conditioned responses or prevent acquisition, it is necessary to exclude the possibility that the lesions included damage to critical afferent or efferent pathways to and from the anterior interpositus nucleus. Likewise, to make a convincing demonstration that cerebellar cortex lesions do not affect acquisition or expression of conditioned responses, it is necessary to confirm that all potentially relevant regions of the cerebellar cortex were damaged. These considerations highlight how little can be learned from experiments in which lesions of the cerebellar cortex are made, and then the animal is tested for its ability to acquire conditioned responses. If the animals learn, it calls into question whether relevant regions of cerebellar cortex were sufficiently damaged. If the animals fail to learn, it calls into question whether the lesions involved damage to input or output pathways known to be necessary for response expression.

Fortunately, it seems that the organization of the cerebellum provides a solution to this problem. The first hint about this solution came when McCormick and Thompson (1984b) presented results from a single, seemingly anomalous animal in which a lesion of the cerebellar cortex spared conditioned responses, but abolished conditioned response timing. We have since shown that this effect on conditioned response timing was not anomalous, but was an accurate indication of the effects of a lesion in the critical region of cerebellar cortex in the absence of damage to the anterior interpositus nucleus. We will describe below the evidence for this assertion and outline how this finding was used to exclude the confounds described above so that the effects of cerebellar cortex lesions on the acquisition and extinction of conditioned responses could be determined.

CEREBELLAR CORTEX IS NECESSARY FOR CONDITIONED RESPONSE TIMING

We have used both lesions of the cerebellar cortex and pharmacological blockade of its output to show that the cerebellar cortex is necessary for the timing of already-learned conditioned eyelid responses. A variety of studies have shown that the inter-stimulus interval (ISI) affects the timing of conditioned eyelid responses (Figure 2*A*). The latency to onset is delayed and the rise-time gauged such that the peak eyelid closure occurs near the time that the US is normally presented. Evidence indicates that this represents true timing and is not, for example, a simple function of the strength of learning (Mauk & Ruiz, 1992; Millenson et al., 1977). Perrett et al. (1993) showed that lesions of the cerebellar cortex abolished this learned timing and yielded responses with a relatively fixed and very short-latency to onset (Figure 2*B*). This study employed a training protocol that permitted within-animal comparison of the effects of cerebellar cortex lesions on differently timed responses (Mauk & Ruiz, 1992). In this procedure, one CS was trained using a relatively short ISI (150 – 250 ms), whereas a second CS was trained with a longer ISI (500 – 1000 ms). As shown in Figure 2*B*

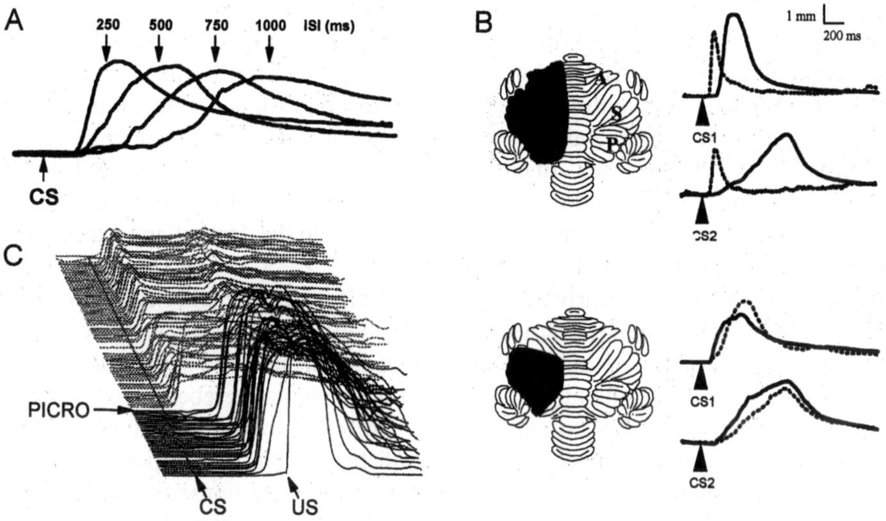

Figure 2. The cerebellar cortex is responsible for the learned timing of conditioned eyelid responses. (*A*) These are individual sweeps for CS-alone trials from four animals trained at different ISIs (250, 500, 750, and 1000 ms). CS-onset is indicated by the upward arrow. Downward arrows show the time of US-onset during training for each animal. Note how the onset latencies are delayed and rise times gauged such that peak eyelid closure occurs near the time that the US is normally presented. (*B*) Examples of the effects of cerebellar cortex lesions on the learned timing of conditioned eyelid responses using a differential conditioning procedure. The solid lines are pre-lesion responses, and the dashed-lines are post-lesion responses. In each panel, the upper sweeps represent responses to a short ISI, whereas the lower sweeps correspond to a longer ISI. Although the pre-lesion responses are appropriately timed, post-lesion responses of the animal in the upper panel exhibit short-latency to onset and reduced amplitude. Responses in the control animal in the lower panel were unchanged. From the schematic reproduction of the rabbit cerebellum taken from Brodal (1940), it is evident that the animal in the upper panel had more extensive lesions which included the (A) anterior lobe, (S) ansiform lobe, and (P) paramedian lobe. The lesions of the animal in the lower panel only included S and P. *(C)* The effects on response timing produced by temporary blockade of cerebellar cortex output by infusion of picrotoxin into the anterior interpositus nucleus. Figure 2*A* is adapted from Mauk & Ruiz (1992), Figure 2*B* is adapted from Perrett et al. (1993), and Figure 2*C* is adapted from Garcia & Mauk (1998b).

the pre-lesion timing of the conditioned responses for both conditioned stimuli was appropriate for the respective ISI. Independent of the pre-lesion timing in each animal, responses seen after lesions of the cerebellar cortex were smaller in amplitude and displayed a characteristic short-latency to onset. Garcia and Mauk (1998b) observed the same effect with reversible blockade of cerebellar cortex output via infusion of the GABA antagonist picrotoxin into the anterior interpositus nucleus (Figures 2*C* and 3). In this experiment, trained animals were infused on consecutive sessions with picrotoxin, saline, or the GABA agonist, muscimol. Saline infusions had no measurable effect on response timing or amplitude. Infusion of muscimol abolished responses, which replicates previous findings (Krupa et al., 1993; Krupa & Thompson, 1997) and indicates that the infusion had access to the interpositus neurons involved in the expression of conditioned responses. In contrast, infusion of picrotoxin abolished response timing and decreased response amplitude in a manner similar to lesions of the cerebellar cortex. In preliminary studies, we have also observed similar effects on timing and amplitude with inactivation of the cerebellar cortex via infusion of the glutamate antagonist kynurenic acid directly into the cerebellar cortex of rats (Mauk & Taylor, unpublished observations).

Combined, these data clearly indicate that the effect of cerebellar cortex removal on the expression of already-learned conditioned eyelid responses is a decrease in amplitude and disruption of timing. The infusion data in particular support this notion independent of any bias one might have about the region of cerebellar cortex that is involved. This indicates that any experiment where lesions of the cerebellar cortex did not affect response timing, or where lesions abolished conditioned responses entirely, must be viewed with caution. Lesions that did not affect response timing appear to have spared regions of cerebellar cortex relevant for eyelid conditioning, whereas lesions that abolished responses appear to have involved inadvertent damage to underlying pathways necessary for response expression.

Although it is not directly relevant to the arguments that follow, identifying the action of cerebellar cortex removal on response timing also facilitated analyses of the regions of cerebellar cortex that are relevant to eyelid conditioning. We began with no particular anatomical bias, but the picture that has slowly emerged indicates that the original emphasis on the HVI lobe was a misdirection. The original studies implicated the HVI lobule, and most subsequent work has continued to focus on this lobule. However, our results have clearly demonstrated that lesions of HVI have no measurable effects on the expression of responses, whereas lesions of the anterior lobe are required to abolish response timing and diminish response amplitude. In early studies using aspiration lesions (Perrett et al., 1993) we were unable to make lesions of the anterior lobe without also damaging HVI. These studies showed that combined lesions of anterior lobe and HVI abolished the timing of responses, whereas large lesions that included HVI but not anterior lobe had no effect on response timing. Based on these findings we concluded that either the anterior lobe alone was involved, or anterior lobe and HVI together, but that HVI lesions alone were not sufficient to produce effects on response timing or amplitude. Subsequent studies where we employed electrolytic lesions have shown that lesions of the anterior lobe are necessary and sufficient to abolish response timing and diminish response amplitude (Figure 4) (Garcia et al., in press). Based on these findings, we have suggested that the anterior lobe, not lobule HVI, is involved in Pavlovian eyelid conditioning and that removal of the anterior lobe alone abolishes response timing and diminishes response amplitude.

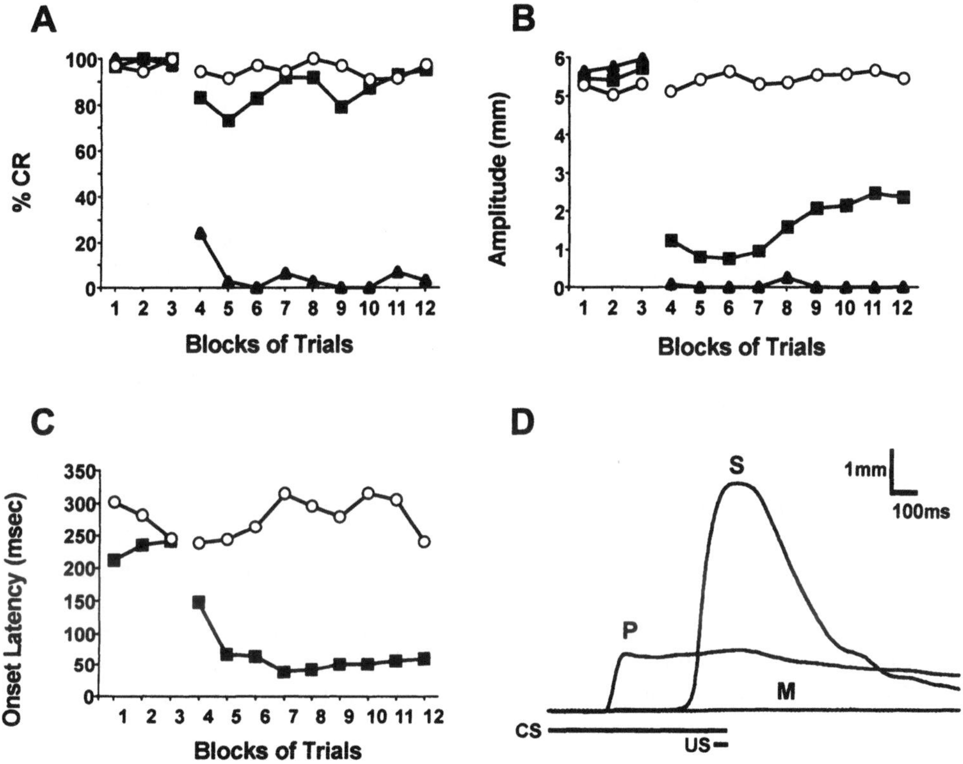

Figure 3. Group data showing the effects of picrotoxin (■), muscimol (▲), and saline (○) infused into the anterior interpositus nucleus (n = 4) on the expression of conditioned eyelid responses. (*A*) The mean percentage of conditioned responses (%CR) was almost completely abolished by muscimol, but unaffected by picrotoxin and saline. (*B*) Picrotoxin and muscimol significantly decreased the mean amplitude of the responses, and muscimol produced a decrease in amplitude that was significantly different from picrotoxin. (*C*) Picrotoxin significantly decreased the latency to onset of the conditioned responses. Because muscimol abolished most CRs, the data for the effects of muscimol on the latency to onset are not shown, but the latencies of the few responses seen were comparable to controls. (*D*) Average responses of the nine CS-alone trials following infusion of picrotoxin, muscimol, and saline. Bold lines correspond to times at which the CS and US were present. This figure is adapted from Garcia & Mauk (1998b).

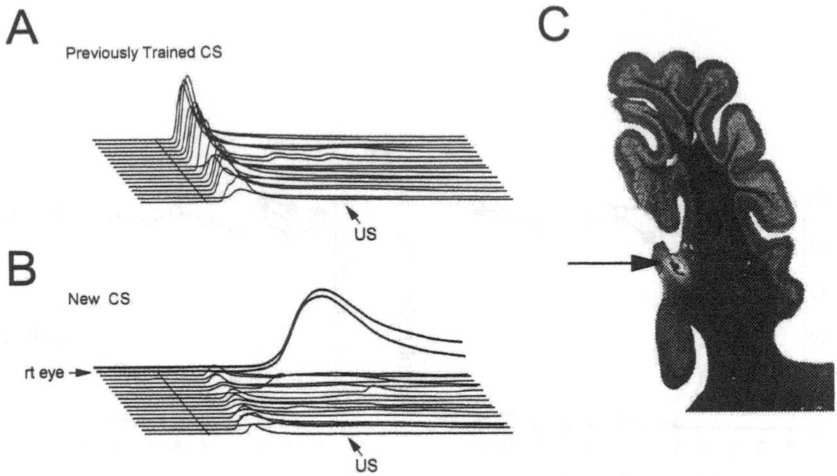

Figure 4. Small electrolytic lesions that disrupt timing to a previously trained CS prevent acquisition to a new CS. (*A*) Presentations of the previously trained CS were used to assess retention and persistence of short-latency responses throughout 15 days of post-lesion acquisition training to a new CS. Each sweep is the average response per day on CS-alone trials. The line and arrow denotes CS- and US-onset, respectively. (*B*) Acquisition to the new CS was blocked by the lesion of the anterior lobe. As in (*A*), each sweep is the average of CS-alone trials per day. This animal was able to rapidly acquire timed conditioned responses to the novel CS when the eye contralateral to the lesion was trained (rt eye). (*C*) Sagittal section through the cerebellum at the level of the anterior lobe shows the site of the electrolytic lesion (arrow) that effectively unmasked the short-latency response in (*A*) and prevented learning to a new CS (*B*). Adapted from Gracia et al. (in press).

CEREBELLAR CORTEX IS NECESSARY FOR CONDITIONED RESPONSE ACQUISITION AND EXTINCTION

That cerebellar cortex lesions abolish response timing but do not abolish responses completely provides an assay for the *functional* extent of cerebellar cortex lesions. This approach can circumvent the inherent limitations of histological analysis. If already-learned responses are abolished by a lesion, the animal should be excluded from further study, as it is likely that the lesion damaged the anterior interpositus nucleus, the mossy fiber inputs, or the outputs of the cerebellum coursing in the superior cerebellar peduncle. Similarly, if the lesion spares responses but otherwise has no effect on response timing, then the animal should also be excluded, or used as a control, as this constitutes evidence that the relevant region of cerebellar cortex was not damaged. Conversely, spared post-lesion responses with abolished timing can be taken as assurance that 1) the relevant region of cerebellar cortex was damaged, and 2) the critical input and output pathways necessary for response expression are intact. In these animals, CS-alone training can then be used to test extinction, and paired CS-US trials using a new CS can be used to test acquisition.

With this approach, we have shown that lesions of the cerebellar cortex prevent both the acquisition (Garcia et al., in press) and extinction (Perrett & Mauk, 1995) of conditioned eyelid responses. The effects of cerebellar cortex lesions on the acquisition of conditioned responses are shown in Figure 5. Animals that displayed

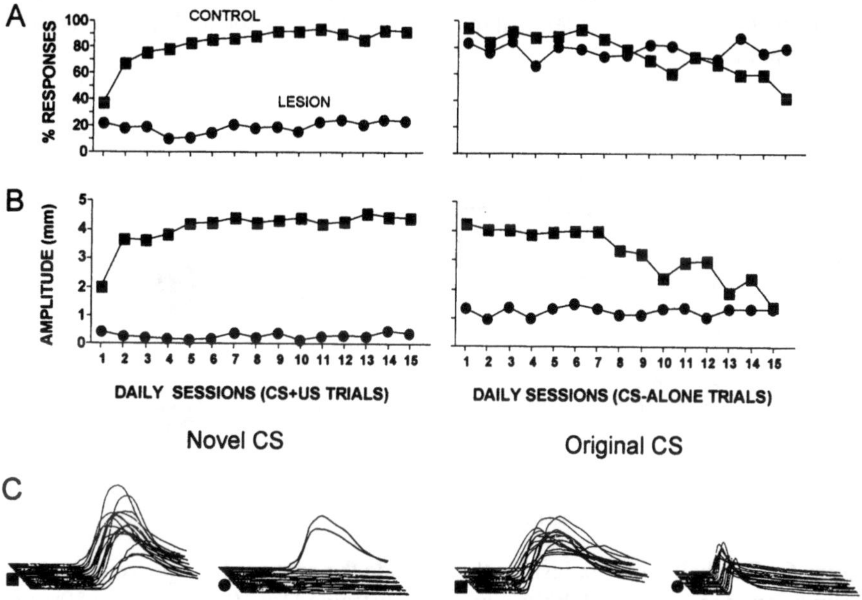

Figure 5. Lesions of the anterior lobe prevents the acquisition of conditioned eyelid responses. The group data shown reflect post-lesion mean % responses (*A*) and mean amplitudes (*B*) to a novel CS (left panel) and to the original CS (right panel). Training consisted of eight CS-US pairings of the novel CS with interspersed CS-alone trials to the original CS. Animals with lesions of the anterior lobe are denoted with closed circles (●), and those that had lesions of other regions of the cerebellar cortex are denoted with closed squares (■). (*C*) Sweeps from a control animal (■) and an animal with a lesion of the anterior lobe (●) are shown for the novel CS and original CS. Together, these data show that animals with lesions of regions of the cerebellum other than the anterior lobe acquired conditioned responses to the novel CS at a normal rate and responding to the pre-lesion CS was unaffected by the lesion. In addition, amplitudes to each CS was not affected by the lesion. Animals with lesions of the anterior lobe were unable to acquire conditioned responses to the novel CS, but continued to show a high percentage of responding to the original CS, although these responses were characterized by short-latencies and diminished amplitudes. Adapted from Garcia et al. (in press).

short-latency responses following the lesion were included in the lesion group whereas animals that showed normal response timing were included as controls. When these animals were retrained to a novel conditioned stimulus, the control animals showed normal acquisition whereas the lesion animals were unable to acquire conditioned eyelid responses, even after 15 days of training. Histological analyses confirmed that only lesions of the anterior lobe prevented acquisition to the novel CS, whereas lesions of lobule HVI had no effect on acquisition. A similar protocol was used to examine the effects of anterior lobe lesions on extinction of previously learned responses (Figure 6). Lesion animals showing short-latency responses after surgery showed almost no decrement in conditioned response probability over ten days of CS-alone training. Animals in which the lesions did not damage the anterior lobe continued to show well-timed responses identical to those before the lesion and showed relatively rapid extinction.

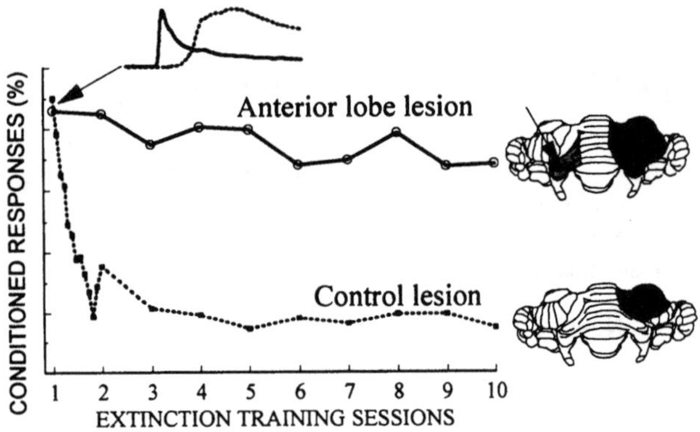

Figure 6. Cerebellar cortex lesions that include the anterior lobe prevent extinction of conditioned responses. Rabbits were initially trained for 10 days using a 500 ms ISI (not shown). Lesions that included the anterior lobe (top, right panel) abolished response timing (inset, solid trace) whereas lesions sparing the anterior lobe (bottom, right panel had no effect on timing (inset, dotted trace). In 10 days of subsequent CS-alone training, control animals showed robust extinction, whereas there was no significant decline in responding in animals with anterior lobe lesions. Adapted from Perrett and Mauk (1995).

IMPLICATIONS FOR SITES OF PLASTICITY IN THE CEREBELLUM

The above findings are consistent with the hypothesis that eyelid conditioning is mediated by two sites of plasticity in the cerebellum, one in the anterior lobe of cerebellar cortex and the other in the anterior interpositus nucleus. Plasticity in the anterior lobe is supported by the lesion-induced abolition of the learned timing of conditioned responses and by the inability to acquire or extinguish conditioned responses after the lesions. Conversely, the conditioned responses that are spared by lesions of the anterior lobe are consistent with learning-induced plasticity in the anterior interpositus nucleus as well.

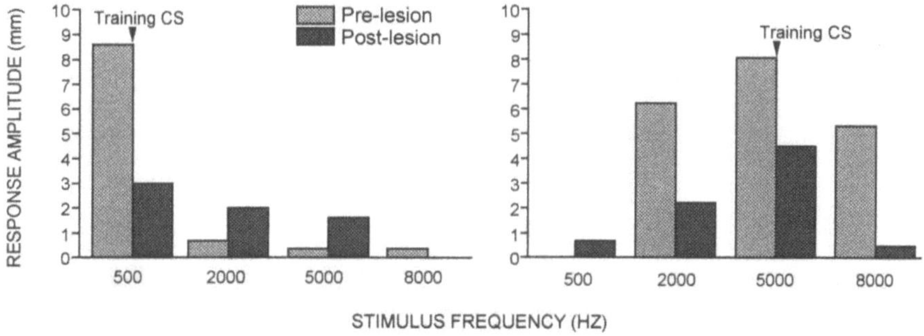

Figure 7. Post-lesion conditioned eyelid responses display stimulus specificity. Four different probe stimuli were presented to animals on the last day prior to the lesions and again on the second session after the lesion. For half of the animals the training CS was a 0.5 kHz tone (Left panel) and for the remaining animals the CS was a 5 kHz tone (Right panel). In each case the post lesion responses were larger for the training CS than for the other three probe stimuli. This specificity to the training CS indicates that the post-lesion responses are learned. Adapted from Perrett and Mauk (1995).

The presence of short-latency responses following anterior lobe lesions or following blockade of cerebellar cortex output indicates a second site of plasticity only if the short-latency responses are learned. Two lines of evidence indicate that this is true. In early studies we demonstrated that the short-latency responses display stimulus specificity. When the frequency of the auditory conditioned stimulus is varied, the amplitude of the short-latency responses decreases to the extent that the probe CS differs from the original training CS. (Garcia & Mauk, 1995; Perrett & Mauk, 1995). Animals in this study were initially trained to either a 0.5 kHz or 5 kHz tone followed by ablation lesions of the cerebellar cortex. In animals where the lesion included the anterior lobe, the post-lesion responses to each original tone had a short-latency to onset. When tones of different frequencies were substituted as CSs, the amplitude of the short-latency response decreased gradually with less similar frequencies (Figure 7). This demonstration of stimulus control is consistent with the notion that the short-latency responses are learned.

We have since made use of the ability to produce reversible disconnection of the cerebellar cortex to provide more direct evidence that the short-latency responses are learned. In these experiments, the cerebellar cortex was functionally disconnected at various stages of acquisition via pharmacological blockade of cerebellar cortex output

(Garcia & Mauk, 1998a). The time course of short-latency responses was determined by infusing picrotoxin into the anterior interpositus nucleus i) on the day before training (Pre), and ii) after each of five days of acquisition training (A1-A5). The test sessions following infusion of picrotoxin consisted of 12 CS alone presentations, which were chosen to minimize extinction. As illustrated in Figure 8, the amplitude and probability of short-latency responses increased over the five days of training, indicating that these movements are learned. We have also recently shown that the acquisition of short-latency responses is associative. Unpaired CS/US training over five days does not increase the amplitude or probability of short-latency responses

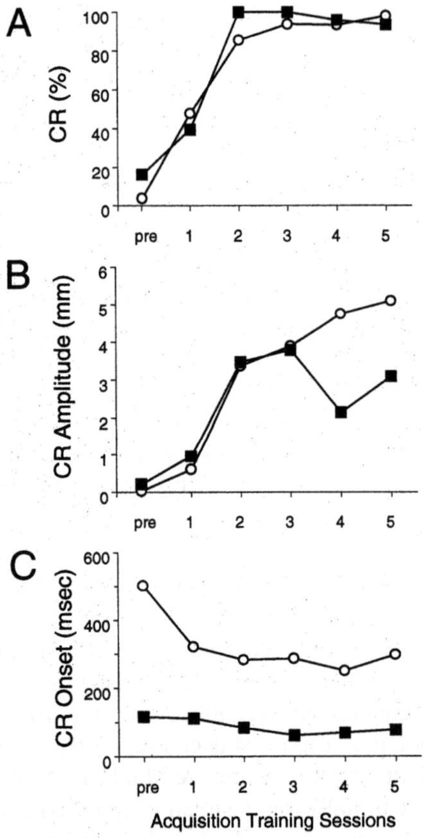

Figure 8. The amplitude and probability of short-latency responses increase with training. Group means for percentage (*A*), amplitude (*B*), and onset latency of conditioned responses (*C*) are depicted for the 12 CS-alone presentations before (○) and after (■) infusion of picrotoxin into the anterior interpositus nucleus. In this manner, the effects of intra-interpositus nucleus infusions of picrotoxin on the probability, amplitude, and latency to onset of responses were measured on the day before training commenced (pre) and after each day of normal acquisition training (1-5). Picrotoxin produced short-latency responding, which increased in amplitude and probability with training. Adapted from Garcia and Mauk (1998a).

(Steele et al., unpublished observations). Together, these data indicate that the short-latency responses produced by disconnection of the cerebellar cortex reveal a second site of plasticity that is not in the cerebellar cortex.

What is the evidence that this second site of plasticity is in the anterior interpositus nucleus? Firstly, analysis of cerebellar contributions to VOR adaptation provides a precedent for learning-related plasticity in the cerebellar nuclei (e.g. Lisberger, 1988; Miles & Lisberger, 1981; Raymond et al., 1996). Recordings from monkeys suggest that changes in VOR gain can be accounted for at least in part by changes in strength of the mossy fiber synapses in the vestibular nucleus, which functionally is a cerebellar nucleus. Secondly, several studies using reversible lesions provide evidence that plasticity in the anterior interpositus nucleus is required for the acquisition of conditioned eyelid responses. Although pharmacological blockade of synapses downstream from the anterior interpositus nucleus in the contralateral red nucleus prevents the expression of conditioned responses, it does not prevent their acquisition (Krupa et al., 1993). In contrast, pharmacological blockade of the anterior interpositus nucleus prevents learning (Krupa et al., 1993; Krupa & Thompson, 1997). Together, these data suggest that a site of plasticity essential for acquisition of eyelid responses is upstream from the red nucleus and either downstream from, or in the anterior interpositus nucleus. With strictly linear thinking, the only alternative is the anterior interpositus nucleus. However, it will be important to address the possibility that blockade of the anterior interpositus nucleus prevents learning due to the requirement of this nucleus for induction of plasticity in the cerebellar cortex. Although there is no evidence to support such a mechanism, there is also presently no evidence to exclude it.

Thus, plasticity in both the anterior lobe of cerebellar cortex and the anterior interpositus nucleus appears to play a role in the acquisition and extinction of conditioned eyelid responses. Plasticity in the cortex is supported by the abolition of the learned timing of conditioned eyelid responses, whereas plasticity in the anterior interpositus nucleus is supported by analysis of the short-latency responses unmasked by disconnection of the cerebellar cortex and by the inability to acquire responses produced by blockade of the anterior interpositus nucleus. Obviously, identifying sites of plasticity is only a first step. It is equally important to understand the rules that govern the induction of plasticity at each site as well as how these rules relate to the stimuli that produce learning and to observed changes in behavior (see Mauk et al., 1998).

RULES FOR PLASTICITY AT *gr*→*Pkj* SYNAPSES IN THE CEREBELLAR CORTEX

The original propositions by Marr (1969) and Albus (1971) regarding plasticity at granule cell to Purkinje cell (*gr*→*Pkj*) synapses in the cerebellar cortex were compelling in part because they suggested specific and important ways in which the plasticity relates to learning. Marr proposed that plasticity at these synapses was controlled by the presence or absence of climbing fiber inputs, that climbing fiber inputs could be activated in ways that lead to the induction of plasticity *in vivo*, and that the induction of plasticity would be capable of adaptively altering movements. As first observed by Ito and colleagues (1982a,b) and later by many others (Linden & Connor, 1993; Linden et al., 1991), co-activation of *gr→Pkj* synapses and the climbing fiber input to a Purkinje cell leads to the induction of LTD at the *gr→Pkj* synapses. Sakuri (1987) and later others (e.g. Salin et al., 1996) found that strong activation of *gr→Pkj* synapses without a climbing fiber input leads to the induction of LTP. If this climbing fiber-controlled LTD and LTP of *gr→Pkj* synapses is involved in motor learning in general and in eyelid conditioning in particular, its properties should satisfy three criteria: necessity for convergence, sufficiency for induction, and capacity for expression (see Mauk et al., 1998; Mauk et al., 1997).

Eyelid conditioning studies suggest with reasonable certainty that two of these criteria, necessity of convergence and capacity for expression, are satisfied. The evidence that the CS is conveyed to the cerebellum via mossy fibers (and thus to the Purkinje cell via granule cells) and that the US is conveyed to the Purkinje cells via climbing fibers is a clear indication that the *gr→Pkj* synapses are a site of convergence between the CS and the US. There is both anatomical and physiological evidence that the induction of LTD at *gr→Pkj* synapses could contribute to the expression of a learned eyelid response. Purkinje cells are known to generate action potentials at fairly high ongoing rates of around 50 to 100 Hz. Since Purkinje cells inhibit anterior interpositus cells, the type of change that LTD would produce – a learned decrease in this activity during the CS – would be appropriate to contribute to the expression of conditioned responses. Indeed, Hesslow and colleagues have presented clear evidence that such decreases in Purkinje activity not only occur, but also that they are required for response expression. In trained ferrets, single unit recordings from Purkinje cells that show a climbing fiber response to the US show a biphasic response during the expression of the response. Early in the CS Purkinje cell activity increases, whereas activity decreases just before the onset of the response (Hesslow & Ivarsson, 1994). The necessity of decreases in Purkinje cell activity is supported by the suppression of conditioned responses in trained animals by stimulation of Purkinje cells during the CS (Hesslow, 1994). Thus, the potential role of climbing fiber-induced LTD at *gr→Pkj* synapses in the acquisition of eyelid responses is supported by evidence that the necessity of convergence and capacity for expression criteria are satisfied.

These data are consistent with the notion that LTP at *gr→Pkj* synapses also satisfies the capacity for expression criteria for the extinction of conditioned responses. In a trained animal presentation of the CS without the US leads to extinction of conditioned responses. If an LTD-mediated decrease in Purkinje cell activity is required for the expression of conditioned responses, it follows that an LTP-mediated restoration of activity during the CS would be capable of contributing to extinction of the responses. Although the involvement of LTP at *gr→Pkj* in extinction has not been examined directly, Ivarsson and Hesslow have shown that the pauses in Purkinje cell activity are reversed during extinction. Work from Hesslow's group also suggests that such changes would be *capable* of contributing to response extinction.

In contrast, the apparent inability to satisfy the sufficiency of induction criterion has prompted several arguments that cerebellar LTD cannot be involved in motor learning (De Schutter, 1995; Matzel & Shors, 1997; Schreurs & Alkon, 1993). This argument focuses on the mismatch between the timing of inputs required for the induction of LTD and the timing of CS and US required for acquisition of conditioned responses. Whereas *in vitro* studies suggest that LTD is best induced with approximately simultaneous activation of granule cells and climbing fibers, simultaneous presentations of CS and US do not support conditioning. As we have argued previously (Mauk et al., 1997), viewing this as a mismatch is based in the implicit assumption that it is only the onset of the CS that is reinforced. As schematized in Fig. 9A, the temporal properties of LTD would necessarily have to match the temporal properties of eyelid conditioning if the CS were to activated activity in the cerebellum only at its onset. In this circumstance it is also difficult to imagine how the adaptive timing of the conditioned responses would occur as well. In contrast, if a CS produced tonic granule cell activity throughout its duration, the temporal properties of LTD would permit conditioning. As illustrated in Fig. 9B, the timing of conditioned eyelid responses would again be difficult to explain. Indeed, it is the timing of conditioned responses that suggests the CS is encoded in the cerebellum via activity of different subsets of granule cells at different times. As shown schematically in Figure 9*C*, a time-varying representation of the CS would not only explain response timing, but it also shows how the temporal properties of cerebellar LTD are desirable rather than problematic. Thus, by considering how granule cells may be active throughout the duration of the stimuli, the temporal requirements of LTD do not pose a problem for Marr/Albus-like theories of motor learning. Instead, these requirements seem perfectly suited to allow for the appropriate timing of conditioned responses when time-varying patterns of granule cell activity are taken into account.

Recent work by Raymond and Lisberger offer another angle on this issue (Raymond & Lisberger, 1998). Recordings from monkeys in the context of VOR adaptation suggest that LTD could only be involved in adaptation of VOR, as first suggested by Ito (1982), if climbing fiber inputs modify *gr→Pkj* synapses that were active about 100 msec prior to the climbing fiber response. This very interesting finding is consistent with the arguments presented above, but also suggests a simple mechanism for the failure of short ISIs to support eyelid conditioning. Behavioral studies have shown that with ISIs less than about 100 msec, eyelid conditioning does not occur. The data of Raymond and Lisberger suggest that the failure of conditioning at these short intervals occurs because the US-activated climbing fiber input would only be able to modify *gr→Pkj* synapses that were active before the CS was presented. Obviously more work needs to be done in this area, in part to explain the differences in LTD timing suggested by the *in vivo* studies and by *in vitro* studies.

In sum, while there are no data that directly link LTD at *gr→Pkj* synapses with acquisition of conditioned eyelid responses, there are a variety of indirect indications that support this possibility. As we have argued previously (Mauk et al., 1998) factors exists that make establishing direct links between forms of plasticity and changes in behavior extremely difficult. As such, one useful approach is to establish criteria that it should be possible to satisfy if cerebellar LTD is involved in the acquisition of

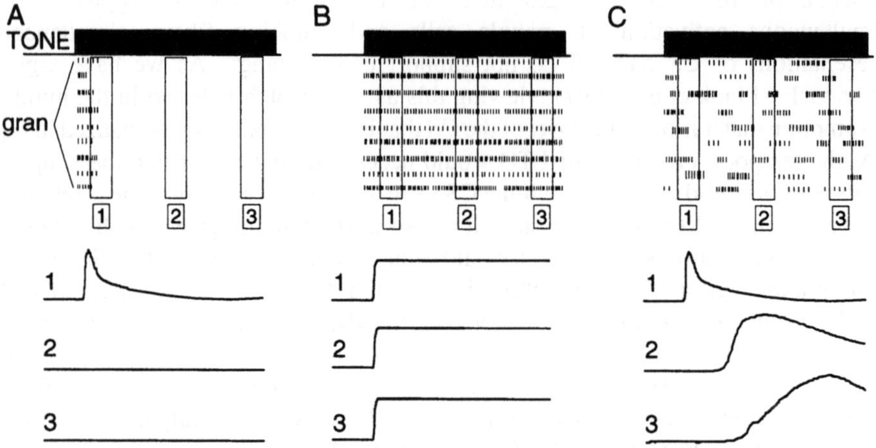

Figure 9. Temporal properties of LTD and sufficiency for induction. LTD appears to be an approximately simultaneous plasticity rule; co-active parallel fiber and climbing fiber inputs induce LTD. Since simultaneous presentation of CS and US do not support conditioning, these temporal properties have been taken as evidence that LTD cannot be involved in motor learning. This interpretation carries implicit assumptions about how granule cells are activated by the CS. The hypothetical raster plots of granule activity (black) illustrate these assumptions. The numbered panels depict presentation of the US at three different times and the window of time that a granule cell would need to be active to undergo LTD. The corresponding, numbered, traces shown below illustrate the predicted learned responses that would be acquired. (*A*) With granule cell activity occurring only at CS onset, LTD would only support learning at short CS-US intervals. (*B*) With tonic granule cell activity during the CS, responses would show the same short latency. Since the same granule cell synapses would be modified regardless of the ISI, and since these synapses would always be active at CS onset, the responses would show a fix short latency to onset independent of the ISI used in training. (*C*) In contrast, with granule cell activity that varies during the CS, an approximately simultaneous rule for LTD could contribute to the acquisition of responses that are delayed until just before the US.

responses. Data from divergent sources suggest that LTD satisfies these criteria reasonably well, as does cerebellar LTP in relation to the extinction of conditioned responses With this in mind, the model of eyelid conditioning that we will describe below will assume the following rule for plasticity at *gr→Pkj* synapses: when these synapses are activated, LTD is induced if there follows approximately 100 msec later a climbing fiber input, whereas LTP is induced if not.

RULES FOR PLACTICITY AT *mf→nuc* SYNAPSES IN THE INTERPOSITUS NUCLEUS

Evidence both from VOR adaptation studies and eyelid conditioning studies indicates that cerebellar-mediated motor learning is accompanied by plasticity at *mf→nuc* synapses. Miles and Lisberger (1981) first proposed ideas about plasticity at these synapses in the context of motor learning. Like Marr's theory, 12 years earlier, the Miles and Lisberger hypothesis is compelling due to the specifically stated rules presumed to be responsible for induction of *mf→nuc c* plasticity. They proposed that changes in VOR gain are mediated in part by plasticity at *mf→nuc* synapses and that the error signal that leads to the induction of these changes derives from the Purkinje cells in the cerebellar cortex. This hypothesis is consistent with two key findings, *i)* under normal circumstances Purkinje cell responses do not modulate much during VOR, but *ii)* lesions of the cerebellar cortex prevent VOR adaptation. Subsequently, evidence for changes in *mf→nuc* synapses has been derived from extensive analysis of cerebellar neuron activity before and after adaptation of the VOR (Lisberger, 1988; Lisberger et al., 1994).

Although evidence for plasticity at *mf→nuc* synapses during eyelid conditioning has existed for some time (Krupa & Thompson, 1995; McCormick & Thompson, 1984a,b; Perrett & Mauk, 1995; Perrett et al., 1993), more recent studies suggest that the induction of this plasticity requires input from Purkinje cells, consistent with the Miles and Lisberger hypothesis. Lesions of the anterior lobe of cerebellar cortex abolish the timing of responses. The short-latency responses that are spared are evidence for plasticity in the anterior interpositus nucleus (Perrett & Mauk, 1995; Perrett et al., 1993). Pharmacological blockade of cerebellar cortex output reversibly produces the same effect (Garcia & Mauk, 1998b). As shown in Figures 4-6 animals with anterior lobe lesions are unable either to extinguish previously learned responses or to acquire new responses (Perrett & Mauk, 1995; Garcia et al., in press). Combined with the data shown in Figure 8 that the short-latency responses are learned, these data indicate that the plasticity in the anterior interpositus nucleus that mediates the short-latency responses cannot happen without input from Purkinje cells (Garcia et al., in press; Steele et al., unpublished observations; Steele et al., 1999).

Although nothing specific is known about the specific Purkinje cell signals that induce plasticity at *mf→nuc* synapses, we have proposed an hypothesis based on known electrophysiological properties of cerebellar nucleus cells (Mauk & Donegan, 1997). Recording studies have revealed a t-like calcium conductance in cerebellar nucleus cells that is best activated by release from hyperpolarization (Llinas & Muhlethaler, 1988). Because Purkinje cells normally fire action potentials at high rates inhibiting cerebellar nucleus cells, it seems that a transient pause in this activity would be an adequate stimulus to activate the calcium conductance. We have hypothesized that the resulting increase in intracellular calcium could be a signal to induce LTP at coactive *mf→nuc* synapses. Precedent for this hypothesis comes from the work of Aizenman and Linden (1998) who have shown that plasticity at Purkinje to nucleus synapses is controlled by rebound excitation mediated by these calcium

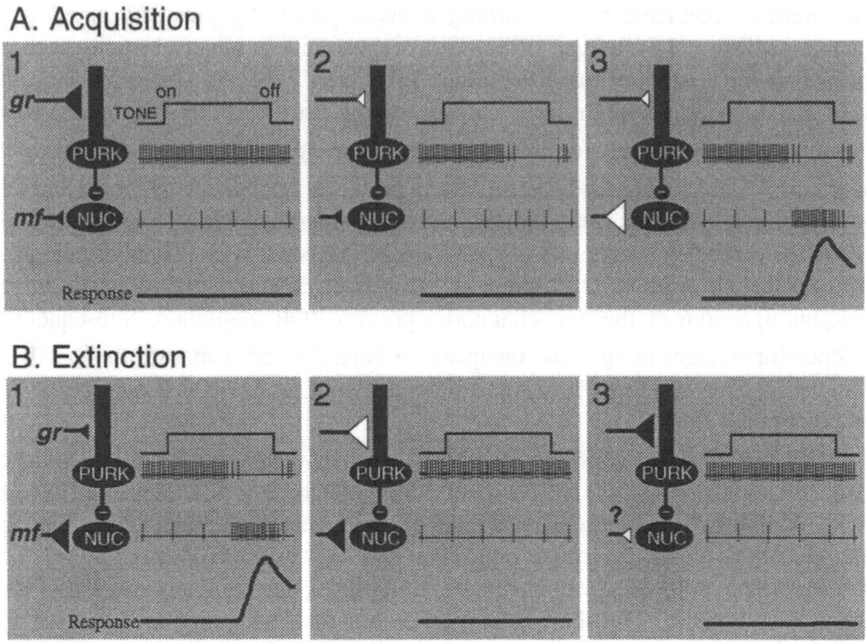

Figure 10. *A*) A schematic representation of the events that we hypothesize are responsible for acquisition of conditioned eyelid responses. Panel 1) Prior to training the granule (gr) cells activated by the CS make relatively strong synapses onto Purkinje cells (PURK) whereas the CS-activated mossy fibers (mf) make relatively weak synapses. Because of this, presentation of the CS does not change the ongoing activity of the Purkinje cell, does not increase the activity of the nucleus cell, and thus does not elicit a response. Panel 2) Training leads to the induction of LTD at CS-activate granule cell synapses (white triangle), which makes the Purkinje cell activity decrease during CS presentation. This does not produce a conditioned response due to the absence of plasticity at the CS-activated mossy fiber synapses in the nucleus. Panel 3) With further training the decrease in Purkinje cell activity during the CS leads to the induction of LTP at CS-activated mossy fiber synapses (white triangle). This permits the expression of a conditioned response. *B*) Extinction. Panel 1 shows the same circumstances as acquisition panel 3. Panel 2) Extinction training leads to the induction of LTP at CS-activated granule cell synapses (white triangle), which restores Purkinje activity during the CS and prevents the expression of conditioned responses, despite the persistence of plasticity in the cerebellar nucleus. This residual plasticity may contribute to savings. Panel 3) Continued extinction training may eventually decrease the strength of the mossy fiber synapses in the nucleus (white triangle), which might reduce or preclude savings.

conductances (see also Mauk, 1998). This hypothesis is consistent with the need for Purkinje cell input for the induction of plasticity at *mf→nuc* synapses. As yet there is no evidence for LTD at these synapses, although first principles dictate that any synapses that can get stronger can also probably get weaker. With these factors in mind the model developed in the next section assumes nothing about LTD at *mf→nuc*, but is based on the following rule for the induction of LTP: *mf→nuc* synapses undergo LTP when they are active during a transient pause in Purkinje cell activity and the corresponding increase in intracellular calcium.

A MODEL OF ACQUISITION, EXPRESSION, AND EXTINCTION OF CONDITIONED RESPONSES

Based on these sites and rules for plasticity we have previously proposed a model for cerebellar involvement in the acquisition, extinction, and expression of conditioned responses (Mauk & Donegan, 1997). Here we will summarize the key features of this model. Evidence suggests (Miall et al. 1998: Keynon et al. 1998a; 1998b) that prior to training the cerebellum is in an equilibrium in which background mossy fiber inputs produce fairly high rates of Purkinje cell activity and lower rates of ongoing nucleus and climbing fiber activities. The model assumes that presentation of a tone CS would be similar to the background in that it would not significantly alter the number of mossy fibers that are active. Thus, during the CS in an untrained animal the Purkinje cells would fire at a high rate whereas the CS would provide only weak excitatory input to the interpositus nucleus cells (Figure 10*A* Panel 1). Moreover, during paired trials the US-evoked climbing fiber input would provide the signals required for the induction of LTD at *gr→Pkj* synapses activated by the CS. Repeated CS+US pairings would decrease the average strength of *gr→Pkj* synapses causing a pause in Purkinje cell inhibition of the interpositus nucleus. Because blockade of the anterior interpositus nucleus prevents learning, we assume that this learning in the cerebellar cortex may not be sufficient to elicit a conditioned response. However, this learned pause in Purkinje cell firing would provide the required signals for the induction of LTP at the *mf→nuc* synapses activated by the CS. Presumably, as this plasticity is induced in the anterior interpositus nucleus, the CS acquires the ability to elicit conditioned responses (Fig 10*A* Panel 3).

During extinction, a complementary series of events would result in a conditioned eyelid response decrement (Figure 10*B*). Beginning with relatively weak *gr→Pkj* synapses and relatively strong *mf→nuc* synapses in the well-trained animal (Figure 10*B* Panel 1), CS-alone presentations would promote the induction of LTP at *gr→Pkj* synapses, eliminate the acquired pause in Purkinje cell activity, and reinstate the inhibition of the anterior interpositus nucleus. Having restored the high rates of Purkinje cell activity during the CS, the conditioned eyelid response diminishes (Figure 10*B* Panel 2). Further extinction training may, or may not, also induce LTD at *mf→nuc* synapses (Figure 10*B* Panel 3).

While these events provide a possible explanation for acquisition and extinction, they address neither the learned timing of the response nor the ISI function. As schematized in Figure 9, our ideas on response timing have focused on the ways in which interactions in the cerebellar cortex between granule and Golgi cells may produce time-varying activation of granule cells. In this general way, learning could be somewhat specific to the time at which the US is presented, in much the same way the learning is somewhat specific to the frequency of tone used as the CS.

To pursue such ideas further, and as a test of the plasticity rules we proposed above, we have investigated the ability of computer simulations of the cerebellum to produce the basic behavioral properties of eyelid conditioning. Although the construction of the simulations is beyond the scope of this chapter, the data in Figure 11 illustrate that the simulations are able to learn with appropriate response timing. Although not shown, the simulations display an ISI function and appropriate variation of response timing for intervals within the effective range. While the meaning of such results is debatable, we can think of the simulations as an elaborate set of hypotheses. As such, we can also use the way in which the simulations perform as predictions of our current model of eyelid conditioning.

PREDICTIONS OF THE MODEL

The predictions that we list below are based on analysis of how the simulations learn while displaying appropriate response timing and an ISI function. We emphasize again that the modeling results represent the current status of our working hypothesis of cerebellar involvement in eyelid conditioning. Each prediction will obviously require empirical test before it can be seriously considered as a candidate mechanism.

1) Whereas acquisition of conditioned responses may require plasticity at CS-activated synapses in both the cerebellar cortex and nucleus, extinction may occur with only plasticity in the cerebellar cortex.

2) The plasticity in the cerebellar nucleus remaining after extinction may in part explain savings – the observation that reacquisition after extinction is faster than original acquisition.

3) The timing of conditioned responses is produced by a combination of time-varying granule cell activity and a within-trials differential conditioning process formally similar to Pavlov's inhibition of delay. The simulations suggest that the cortex both learns to respond at times during the CS that are reinforced and learns not to respond at non-reinforced times during the CS.

4) Similarly, the ISI function may result from a combination of a gradual decline in the across-trials consistency of the granule cell representation of the CS (Mauk & Donegan, 1997) and this same within-trials differential conditioning mechanism. As the CS increases in duration (i.e. the ISI increases) the extinction that occurs during unreinforced periods of the CS comes to dominate the acquisition produced at the reinforced periods of the CS.

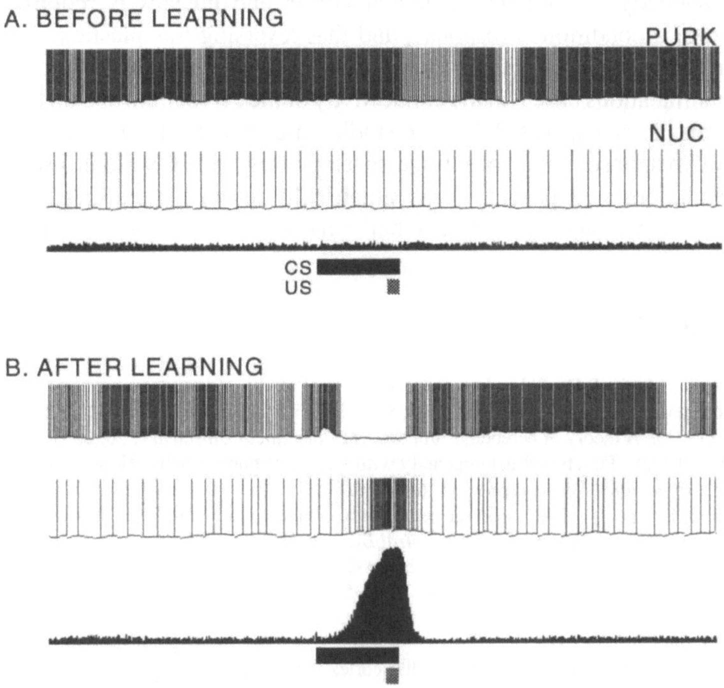

Figure 11. Results from a computer simulation of the cerebellum (Medina and Mauk, unpublished observations) showing the acquisition of an appropriately timed conditioned response with simulated CS+US paired training. *A*) Activity of a simulated Purkinje cell (top) and nucleus cell (middle) during the presentation of a simulated CS prior to training. The peri-stimulus histogram shows the average response of the nucleus cells at this stage in training. *B*) The same cells after 500 trials of simulated CS+US training. The simulated Purkinje cell shows a well timed pause in activity, whereas the nucleus cell shows a well time increase in activity as illustrated by the peri-stimulus histogram. CS presentation is indicated by the black bars, time that the US was presented in training trials is indicated by the smaller gray bars.

CONCLUSIONS

We have presented data addressing the relative contributions of the cerebellar cortex and nuclei in the acquisition and expression of conditioned eyelid responses. Data from a series of studies support the notion that while plasticity occurs in both the cerebellar cortex and nucleus, the cerebellar cortex is essential for acquisition, extinction, and for the proper expression of conditioned eyelid responses. We have presented arguments that the experiments that support this position were designed in ways to preclude confounds that were present in other attempts to identify the role of the cerebellar cortex in eyelid conditioning. We have also presented evidence that suggests plasticity in both the cerebellar cortex and nucleus is required for the expression of a conditioned response, and that reversing this plasticity only in the cerebellar cortex may be sufficient to produce extinction of conditioned responses. Computer simulations based on the connectivity of the cerebellum and on the sites and rules for plasticity suggested by our studies are able to acquire properly timed conditioned responses, and to extinguish responses with CS-alone presentations. These simulations will provide many empirically testable predictions that should facilitate our understanding of the cerebellar mechanisms of eyelid conditioning.

REFERENCES

Aizenman, C.D., Manis, P.B., & Linden, D.J. (1998). Polarity of long-term synaptic gain change is related to postsynaptic spike firing at a cerebellar inhibitory synapse. *Neuron 21*, 827-835.

Albus, J.S. (1971). A theory of cerebellar function. *Mathematical Bioscience, 10*, 25-61.

Bloedel, J.R. (1992). Functional heterogeneity with structural homogeneity: How does the cerebellum operate? *Behavioral Neuroscience, 15*, 666-678.

Bloedel, J.R., & Bracha, V. (1995). On the cerebellum, cutaneomuscular reflexes, movement control and the elusive engrams of memory. *Behavioural Brain Research, 68*, 1-44.

De Schutter, E. (1995). Cerebellar long-term depression might normalize excitation of Purkinje cells: A hypothesis. *Trends in Neuroscience, 18*, 291-295.

De Schutter E., & Maex, R. (1996). The cerebellum: cortical processing and theory. *Current Opinions in Neurobiology, 6*, 759-764.

Garcia, K.S., & Mauk, M.D. (1995). Cerebellar cortex is necessary for acquisition of Pavlovian eyelid responses. *Society for Neuroscience Abstracts, 21*, 1222.

Garcia, K.S., Mauk, M.D. (1998a). Pavlovian eyelid conditioning affects the amplitude and frequency of short-latency responses observed following pharmacological block of cerebellar cortex output. *Society of Neuroscience Abstracts, 24*, 444.

Garcia, K. S., & Mauk, M. D. (1998b). Pharmacological analysis of cerebellar contributions to the timing and expression of conditioned responses. *Neuropharmacology, 37*, 471-480.

Garcia, K.S., Steele, P.M., Mauk, M.D. (in press). Cerebellar cortex lesions prevent the acquisition of Pavlovian eyelid responses. *Journal of Neuroscience.*

Harvey, J.A., Welsh, J.P., Yeo, C.H., & Romano, A.G. (1993). Recoverable and nonrecoverable deficits in conditioned responses after cerebellar cortical lesions. *Journal of Neuroscience, 13*, 1624-1635.

Hesslow, G. (1994). Inhibition of classically conditioned eyeblink responses by stimulation of the cerebellar cortex in the decerebrate cat. *Journal of Physiology (London), 476*, 245-256.

Hesslow, G., & Ivarsson, M. (1994). Suppression of cerebellar Purkinje cells during conditioned responses in ferrets. *Neuroreport, 5*, 649-652.

Ito, M. (1982). Cerebellar control of the vestibulo-ocular reflex – around the flocculus hypothesis. *Annual Review of Neuroscience, 5*, 275-298.

Ito, M., & Kano, M. (1982a). Long-lasting depression of parallel fiber-Purkinje cell transmission induced by conjunctive stimulation of parallel fibers and climbing fibers in the cerebellar cortex. *Neuroscience Letters, 33*, 253-258.

Ito, M., Sakurai, M., & Tongroach, P. (1982b). Climbing fibre induced depression of both mossy fibre responsiveness and glutamate sensitivity of cerebellar Purkinje cells. *Journal of Physiology (London), 324*, 113-134.

Kenyon, G.T,, Medina, J.F., & Mauk, M.D. (1998a). A mathematical model of the cerebellar-olivary system I: Self-regulating equilibrium of climbing fiber activity. *Journal of Computational Neuroscience, 5*, 17-33.

Kenyon, G.T., Medina, J.F., & Mauk, M.D. (1998b). A mathematical model of the cerebellar-olivary system II. Motor adaptation through systematic disruption of climbing fiber equilibrium. *Journal of Computational Neuroscience, 5*, 17-33.

Krupa, D.J., Thompson, J.K., & Thompson, R.F. (1993). Localization of a memory trace in the mammalian brain. *Science, 260*, 989-991.

Krupa, D.J., & Thompson, R.F. (1995). Inactivation of the superior cerebellar peduncle blocks expression but not acquisition of the rabbit's classically conditioned eye-blink response. *Proceedings of the National Academy of Sciences, (U.S.A), 92*, 5097-5101.

Krupa, D.J., & Thompson, R.F. (1997). Reversible inactivation of the cerebellar interpositus nucleus completely prevents acquisition of the classicaly conditioned eye-blink response. *Learning and Memory, 3*, 545-556.

Lavond, D.G., & Steinmetz, J.E. (1989). Acquisition of classical conditioning without cerebellar cortex. *Behavioural Brain Research, 33*, 113-164.

Lavond, D.G., Steinmetz, J.E., Yokaitis, M.H., & Thompson, R.F. (1987). Reacquisition of classical conditioning after removal of cerebellar cortex. *Experimental Brain Research, 67*, 569-593.

Lewis, J.L., LoTurco, J.J., & Solomon, P.R. (1987). Lesions of the middle cerebellar peduncle disrupt acquisition and retention of the rabbit's classically conditioned nictitating membrane response. *Behavioral Neuroscience, 101*, 151-157.

Linden, D.J., & Connor, J.A. (1993). Cellular mechanisms of long-term depression in the cerebellum. *Current Opinion in Neurobiology, 3*, 401-6.

Linden, D.J., Dickinson, M.H., Smeyne, M., & Connor, J.A. (1991). A long-term depression of AMPA currents in cultured cerebellar Purkinje neurons. *Neuron, 7*, 81-9.

Lisberger, S.G. (1988). The neural basis for learning of simple motor skills. *Science, 242*, 728-35.

Lisberger, S.G., Pavelko, T.A., & Broussard, D.M. (1994). Neural basis for motor learning in the vestibuloocular reflex of primates. I. Changes in the responses of brain stem neurons. *Journal of Neurophysiology, 72*, 928-953.

Llinas, R., Lang, E.J., & Welsh, J.P. (1997). The cerebellum, LTD, and memory: alternative views. *Learning and Memory, 3*, 445-455.

Llinas, R., & Muhlethaler, M. (1988). An electrophysiological study of the in vitro, perfused brain stem-cerebellum of adult guinea-pig. *Journal of Physiology, (London), 404*, 215-240.

Llinas, R., & Welsh, ,J.P. (1993). On the cerebellum and motor learning. *Current Opinion in Neurobiology, 3*, 958-965.

Marr, D. (1969). A theory of cerebellar cortex. *Journal of Physiology, (London), 202*, 437-70.

Mauk, M.D. (1997). Roles of cerebellar cortex and nuclei in motor learning: Contradictions of clues? *Neuron, 18*, 343-346.

Mauk, M.D. (1998). More than just another modifiable synapse. *Neuron, 21*, 649-651.

Mauk, M.D., & Donegan, N.H. (1997). A model of Pavlovian eyelid conditioning based on the synaptic organization of the cerebellum. *Learning and Memory, 3*, 130-158.

Mauk, M.D., Garcia, K.S., Medina, J.F., & Steele, P.M. (1998). Does cerebellar LTD mediate motor learning? Toward a resolution without a smoking gun. *Neuron, 20*, 359-362.

Mauk, M.D., & Ruiz, B.P. (1992). Learning-dependent timing of Pavlovian eyelid responses: differential conditioning using multiple interstimulus intervals. *Behavioral Neuroscience, 106*, 666-681.

Mauk, M.D., Steele, P.M., & Medina, J.F. (1997). Cerebellar involvement in motor learning. Neuroscientist, 3, 303-313.

Mauk, M.D., Steinmetz, J.E., & Thompson, R.F. (1986). Classical conditioning using stimulation of the inferior olive as the unconditioned stimulus. *Proceedings of the National Academy of Sciences, (U.S.A.), 83*, 5349-5353.

Matzel, L.D., & Shors, T.J. (1997). Long-term potentiation: What's learning got to do with it? *Behavioural Brain Sciences, 2*, 0597-655.

McCormick, D.A., Clark, G.A., Lavond, D.G., & Thompson, R.F. (1982). Initial localization of the memory trace for a basic form of learning. *Proceedings of the National Academy of Sciences, (U.S.A.), 79*, 2731-2735.

McCormick, D.A., Steinmetz, J.E., & Thompson, R.F. (1985). Lesions of the inferior olivary complex cause extinction of the classically conditioned eyeblink response. *Brain Research, 359*, 120-130.

McCormick, D.A., & Thompson, R.F. (1984a). Cerebellum: essential involvement in the classically conditioned eyelid response. *Science, 223*, 296-299.

McCormick, D.A., & Thompson, R.F. (1984b). Neuronal responses of the rabbit cerebellum during acquisition and performance of a classically conditioned nictitating membrane-eyelid response. *Journal of Neuroscience, 4*, 2811-2822.

Miall, R.C., Keating, J.G., Malkmus, M., & Thach, W.T. (1998). Simple spike activity predicts occurrence of complex spikes in cerebellar Purkinje cells. *Nature Neuroscience, 1*, 13-15.

Miles, F.A., & Lisberger, S.G. (1981). Plasticity in the vestibulo-ocular reflex: A new hypothesis. *Annual Review of Neuroscience, 4,* 273-299.

Millenson, J.R., Kehoe, E.J., & Gormezano, I. (1977). Classical conditioning of the rabbit's nictitating membrane response under fixed and mixed CS-US intervals. *Learning and Motivation, 8,* 351-366.

Perrett, S.P., & Mauk, M.D. (1995). Extinction of conditioned eyelid responses requires the anterior lobe of cerebellar cortex. *Journal of Neuroscience, 15,* 2074-2080.

Perrett, S.P., Ruiz, B.P., & Mauk, M.D. (1993). Cerebellar cortex lesions disrupt learning-dependent timing of conditioned eyelid responses. *Journal of Neuroscience, 13,* 1708-1718.

Raymond, J.L., & Lisberger, S.G. (1998). Neural learning rules for the vestibulo-ocular reflex. *Journal of Neuroscience, 18,* 9112-9129.

Raymond, J.L., Lisberger, S.G., & Mauk, M.D. (1996). The cerebellum: a neuronal learning machine? *Science, 272,* 1126-1131.

Sakurai, M. (1987). Synaptic modification of parallel fibre-Purkinje cell transmission in in vitro guinea-pig cerebellar slices. *Journal of Physiology, (London), 394,* 463-480.

Salin, P.A., Malenka, R.C., & Nicoll, R.A. (1996). Cyclic AMP mediates a presynaptic form of LTP at cerebellar parallel fiber synapses. *Neuron, 16,* 797-803.

Schreurs, B.G., & Alkon, D.L. (1993). Rabbit cerebellar slice analysis of long-term depression and its role in classical conditioning. *Brain Research, 631,* 235-240.

Steele, P.M., Medina, J.F., Nores, W.L., & Mauk, M.D. (1998). Using genetic mutations to study the neural basis of behavior. *Cell, 95,* 879-882.

Steele, P.M., Nores, W.L., Medina, J.F., & Mauk, M.D. (1999). Induction of plasticity in the interpositus nucleus during eyelid conditioning requires input from the cerebellar cortex. *Cold Spring Harbor Abstracts.*

Steinmetz, J.E. (1990). Classical nictitating membrane conditioning in rabbits with varying interstimulus intervals and direct activation of cerebellar mossy fibers as the CS. *Behavioural Brain Research, 38,* 97-108.

Steinmetz, J.E., Lavond, D.G., & Thompson, R.F. (1989). Classical conditioning in rabbits using pontine nucleus stimulation as a conditioned stimulus and inferior olive stimulation as an unconditioned stimulus. *Synapse, 3,* 225-233.

Steinmetz ,J.E., Logan, C.G., Rosen, D.J., Thompson, J.K., Lavond, D.G., & Thompson, R.F. (1987). Initial localization of the acoustic conditioned stimulus projection system to the cerebellum essential for classical eyelid conditioning. *Proceedings of the National Academy of Sciences, (U.S.A.), 84,* 3531-3535.

Steinmetz, J.E., Rosen, D.J., Chapman, P.F., Lavond, D.G., & Thompson, R.F. (1986). Classical conditioning of the rabbit eyelid response with a mossy-fiber stimulation CS: I. Pontine nuclei and middle cerebellar peduncle stimulation. *Behavioral Neuroscience, 100,* 878-887.

Tracy, J.A., Thompson, J.K., Krupa, D.J., & Thompson, R.F. (1998). Evidence of plasticity in the pontocerebellar conditioned stimulus pathway during classical conditioning of the eyeblink response in the rabbit. *Behavioral Neuroscience, 112,* 267-285.

Welsh, J.P., & Harvey, J.A. (1991). Pavlovian conditioning in the rabbit during inactivation of the interpositus nucleus. *Journal of Physiology, (London), 444,* 459-480.

Woodruff-Pak, D.S., Lavond, D.G., Logan, C.G., Steinmetz, J.E., & Thompson, R.F. (1993). Cerebellar cortical lesions and reacquisition in classical conditioning of the nictitating membrane response in rabbits. *Brain Research, 608,* 67-77.

Yeo, C.H., & Hardiman, M.J. (1992). Cerebellar cortex and eyeblink conditioning: a reexamination. *Experimental Brain Research, 88,* 623-638.

Yeo, C.H., Hardiman, M.J., & Glickstein, M. (1984). Discrete lesions of the cerebellar cortex abolish the classically conditioned nictitating membrane response of the rabbit. *Behavioural Brain Research, 13,* 261-266.

Yeo, C.H., Hardiman, M.J., & Glickstein, M. (1985). Classical conditioning of the nictitating membrane response of the rabbit. III. Connections of cerebellar lobule HVI. *Experimental Brain Research, 60,* 114-126.

10 NEURAL NETWORK APPROACHES TO EYEBLINK CLASSICAL CONDITIONING

M. Todd Allen, Catherine E. Myers, and Mark A. Gluck
Rutgers University

INTRODUCTION

In the last 25 years, there has been an explosion in our understanding of the neural substrates of classical eyeblink conditioning. Along with this increase in empirical data, there has also been an increase in the number of attempts to understand the underlying mechanisms within this circuitry by the use of neural networks, computational models that attempt to simulate empirical results based on the theorized function of various brain structures. Neural networks rely upon large amounts of empirical data upon which to base their theoretical formulations. In turn, neural networks have the ability to propose theories and make novel predictions which serve as a guide for future empirical research. In this fashion, the use of neural networks can help advance our understanding of the neural bases of learning and memory, not only by the development of top-down theories formed from prior empirical findings but also by going beyond simple replication of prior empirical work and making novel predictions that can guide future empirical work. In this chapter, we will discuss the development of our neural network model of the cerebellar and hippocampal substrates of eyeblink classical conditioning.

A successful neural network model should simulate the basic behavior of an intact animal in a specific domain such as eyeblink classical conditioning. If a neural network model takes its architecture from the circuits and structures of the brain, then it should be able to simulate not only behavior, but also activity changes in various regions. It should also account for lesion findings; if the components of the model which represent various brain structures are disabled, the model should show behavior similar to animals with analogous lesions. A successful neural network model should also make novel predictions about the effects of yet untested lesions. It is much easier, quicker, and less expensive to test the effects of various lesions by disabling the components of a model and running the simulations on a computer than to do a comparable series of animal lesion experiments. The simulations should be able to identify the key experiments which should then be done to test the predictions of the model. Also, by analyzing the patterns of activity within model components during the learning process, we can theorize how the activity patterns in the brain might encode information during learning. In this way, neural networks can provide insight to guide both behavioral and electrophysiological work.

Our basic strategy has been to start with a well-defined and heavily-studied learning paradigm: classical eyeblink conditioning. Empirical findings in this domain have come out of a variety of experimental techniques employed by many laboratories (for review see Anderson & Steinmetz, 1994; Kim & Thompson, 1997, Thompson, 1986). Overall, the cerebellum has been implicated as the necessary site of plasticity for the acquisition and expression of the conditioned eyeblink response. In addition to the role of the cerebellum in eyeblink conditioning, there is also an older literature which indicates that the hippocampus plays a role in some forms of eyeblink classical conditioning (e.g., Berger, Alger & Thompson, 1976; Solomon & Moore, 1975; Solomon, 1977; see also Chapter 13, this volume).

Our approach has been to start with a simple model of this learning, and then try to map the model's computational sub-processes onto identified neural circuits, incrementally incorporating more biological and physiological details into the architecture. Through this approach, we have moved from simplified models of brain structures which were capable of simulating simple response acquisition at a trial level to more physiological models which can also simulate real-time characteristics of the behavioral response. These studies are described below.

CEREBELLAR SUBSTRATES OF EYEBLINK CONDITIONING

The classically conditioned eyeblink response paradigm consists of the pairing of a neutral conditioned stimulus, CS (either a tone or light), with a response-evoking unconditioned stimulus, US (either a corneal air puff or peri-orbital shock). In delay conditioning, the CS onset precedes US onset with the two stimuli partially overlapping and coterminating. Early in training, there is no behavioral response to the CS while the US elicits a reflexive eyeblink (unconditioned response or UR). Following about 100 paired presentations, the rabbit begins to give small eyeblinks (conditioned responses or CRs) in response to the tone. As training progresses, these CRs increase in amplitude and come to be timed so that maximal eyelid closure occurs at about the time of US onset. In this way, the rabbit learns not only that the CS predicts the US but also learns the precise interval between CS and US onset. For a discussion of the development and history of the classical eyeblink conditioning in the rabbit see Chapter 1 in this volume.

The brainstem and cerebellar circuitries that underlie eyeblink conditioning have been delineated through various experimental techniques. Lesions and inactivation studies of the cerebellum and brainstem have identified the cerebellum, in particular the deep interpositus nucleus as the necessary site of plasticity for eyeblink conditioning. For a complete discussion of these lesion results see Chapter 3 in this volume. Changes in neural activity in cerebellar and brainstem structures (thought to encode the CR) have been recorded in a variety of single and multiple unit electrophysiological recording studies, while the pathways which conduct CS and US information to the cerebellum have been delineated through electrical microstimulation experiments. For a complete discussion of these results see Chapter 4 in this volume.

Simply put, the cerebellar cortex and interpositus receive CS tone information from the lateral pontine nuclei and US air puff information from the dorsal accessory region of the inferior olive. Convergence of the CS and US information in the cerebellum drives learning. The conditioned response-related activity is transmitted to the brainstem motor nuclei along with positive feedback to the pontine nuclei and negative feedback to the inferior olive.

RESCORLA-WAGNER RULE

In addition to these behavioral and neurobiological foundations for our cerebellar computational models, we have based our mathematical algorithms on the Rescorla-Wagner rule. The Rescorla-Wagner rule is one of the most influential models of classical conditioning and forms the core for our modeling of cerebellar function in eyeblink conditioning. Rescorla and Wagner formalized a mathematical model that described a rule for predicting changes in CS-US associations (Rescorla & Wagner, 1972; Wagner & Rescorla, 1972). In their model, the associative changes accruing between a CS and the US on a trial are proportional to the degree to which the US is unexpected given all the CS cues that are present on that trial. To formulate the relationship, let V_A denote the strength of association between stimulus element CS_A and reinforcing unconditioned stimulus, the US. If CS_A is followed by the US, then the change in the associative strength between CS_A and the US, ΔV_A can be described by Equation (1):

$$\Delta V_A = \alpha_A \beta{\uparrow} \left(\lambda - \sum_{k \in S} V_k \right) \quad (1)$$

where α_A reflects the intensity or salience of CS_A, $\beta_{\uparrow}$ reflects the rate of learning λ is the maximum possible level of associative strength conditionable with that US intensity, and $\sum_{k \in S} V_k$ is the sum of the associative strengths of all the CSs occurring on that trial. If CS_A is presented on a trial and not followed by the US, then the association between CS_A and the US decreases analogously, viz.,

$$\Delta V_A = \alpha_A \beta{\downarrow} \left(0 - \sum_{k \in S} V_k \right) \quad (2)$$

where $\beta_{\downarrow}$ reflects the rate of change on trials when the US is absent.

The Rescorla-Wagner model and its equivalent formulations such as the Least Mean Squares (LMS) rule account for many different learning phenomena such as blocking, conditioned inhibition, overshadowing, and positive patterning (Kremer, 1978; Rescorla & Holland, 1977; Walkenbach & Haddad, 1980). However, it has been difficult to conceive how this rule is implemented in the brain, especially how the brain computes the aggregate prediction $\sum_{k \in S} V_k$ and the error $\left(\lambda - \sum_{k \in S} V_k\right)$.

DEVELOPMENT OF A CEREBELLAR MODEL OF EYEBLINK CONDITIONING

All of the efforts to model cerebellar function in eyeblink conditioning that we will discuss are based on the idea of mapping the Rescorla-Wagner rule onto the neural circuitry thought to underlie classical eyeblink conditioning. All the cerebellar models to be discussed are steps in the development of our current model of the role of the cerebellum in eyeblink conditioning.

Application of the Rescorla-Wagner Rule to the Cerebellum

The initial idea of mapping the Rescorla-Wagner rule onto cerebellar circuitry was put forth by Donegan, Gluck & Thompson (1989). The idea of error correction to improve US prediction was thought to involve the feedback of CR-related activity from the interpositus to the inferior olive. While not a computational model, per se, this early theoretical attempt to apply learning theory to the cerebellar circuitry thought to underlie eyeblink conditioning set the groundwork for subsequent computational models of the cerebellum and related brainstem structures in eyeblink conditioning. In all subsequent modeling attempts, the same basic mathematical mechanism of the Rescorla-Wagner rule is applied to a more physiologically-detailed representation of the neural circuitry.

There has been strong empirical evidence for the application of the Rescorla-Wagner error-correction rule to the US pathway involving the inferior olive. Berthier & Moore (1986) found that inferior olive-induced complex spikes decrease or cease in paired CS-US trials in well-trained animals where a CR occurred. Sears and Steinmetz (1991) recorded air puff US-related activity in the dorsal accessory inferior olive (DAO) during conditioning. Initially, the air puff US elicited strong evoked responses in the DAO, but as conditioning proceeded and the percentage of CRs increased, this DAO activity decreased on paired trials. The air puff US continued to elicit strong DAO responses in an air puff-alone trials. Taken together, these two recording studies demonstrate that as conditioning occurs, the DAO ceases to respond to the US air puff, and this results in a lack of climbing fiber-induced complex spiking in cerebellar Purkinje cells.

Further evidence for this cerebellar-olivary feedback pathway has been provided by tract tracing studies in the rabbit that have shown direct connections between the deep interpositus nucleus and the DAO (Steinmetz & Sengelaub, 1992). These projections from the cerebellum to the inferior olive have been shown to be GABA-ergic in both the rat (Angaut & Sotelo, 1989) and cat (Gibson, Robinson, Alam & Houk, 1987), and additionally, lesion to this pathway has been shown to disinhibit the inferior olive (Andersson, Garwicz & Hesslow, 1988). Taken together, these anatomical studies provide evidence for a direct inhibitory pathway through which CR-related activity in the interpositus nucleus could inhibit responding of the DAO in response to the air puff US.

Adaptive Filter Model of the Cerebellum

Gluck, Reifsnider and Thompson (1990) put forth a model of the cerebellum based on LMS spectrum analyzers. The task of CR development was viewed as a problem in adaptive signal processing. The cerebellum was thought to function as an adaptive filter that converts input signals (the CS) into the desired output (the CR) based on the training signal of the US. This model could simulate various characteristics of eyeblink conditioning such as generation of a CR that increased in amplitude across training and was timed to coincide with US presentation, and a shift in peak CR response time when the interval between CS onset and US onset was lengthened. However, the LMS spectrum analyzer model failed to correctly predict the fact that the CR onset initially occurs near the time of US onset but gradually moves earlier to the CS period. Additionally, this model did not take into account cerebellar anatomy or physiology.

Physiological LMS Spectrum Analyzer Cerebellar Model

The next step in the development of the current model of the cerebellum was to map the basic LMS spectrum analyzer model onto the basic components of the cerebellum (Bartha, Gluck & Thompson, 1991). The LMS spectrum analyzer model was extended by incorporating anatomical details of the cerebellar circuit, a learning rule based on Purkinje cell physiology, the existence of two sites of plasticity within the cerebellum, and more plausible assumptions for the CS representations.

The basic circuit for the Bartha et al., (1991) model incorporated the connectivity between the cerebellar cortex, the interpositus nucleus, and the inferior olive. A single neural element was used to represent populations of neurons in each of the structures. Information about the US passed through the inferior olive and had collaterals connecting to both the interpositus element and the cerebellar cortex element. CS information also had collaterals to both the interpositus and the cerebellar cortex.

The output of the cortex element, which represents the activity of Purkinje cells, had an inhibitory connection to the interpositus element, which in turn had an inhibitory connection to the inferior olive element. Based on recordings from the interpositus, Bartha et al., interpreted the activity in the interpositus element as a measure of the CR. Plasticity (learning) in the model occurred at the CS connections to both the cerebellar cortex and interpositus elements. The learning rule at the CS-cortex connections was based on a rule by Houk (1989) which was derived from plasticity observed in Purkinje cells.

The Bartha et al., (1991) model was able to simulate CR acquisition for standard delay conditioning. There was a high level of background activity in the CS-cortex inputs during non-CS periods, which was responsible for the baseline activity of the cortex element. The CS-cortex weights were initialized so that the CS elicited no response. No baseline activity was assumed for the interpositus element. The cortex element's activity was completely depressed at about the time of the US onset. Activity in the interpositus, which was taken to represent the CR, initially began after US onset. As training progressed, the CR gradually moved forward in time and grew in amplitude. Meanwhile, the inhibitory projections of the interpositus element reduced the activity of the inferior olive, decreasing plasticity in the cerebellar cortex element.

This model was capable of simulating real-time CR response topography along with simulating acquisition, extinction, and reacquisition at the trial level.

This model was also capable of simulating the blocking effect. As proposed by Donegan et al., (1989), the inhibitory feedback of the CR to the inferior olive could be a mechanism for the Kamin (1969) blocking effect, a learning phenomenon whereby previous training to a one cue blocks subsequent learning to second cue. An example of this effect would be to train a rabbit with tone and air puff presentations. A second phase of training would consist of a tone-light compound paired with the air puff. Subsequent test trials of the light alone show little responding, as if prior learning about the tone "blocked" learning about the light.

In the model, training with tone will lead to a reduction of the activity in the inferior olive due to the negative feedback loop from the interpositus to the inferior olive. As the tone-air puff association is learned, olivary activity decreases, and learning slows. Continued training with a tone-light compound results in little or no additional learning, since olivary activity is still low. Subsequent tests with the light alone result in no CR.

Fully Recurrent Error Correcting Real-Time Cerebellar Model

The most recent cerebellar modeling effort (Gluck, Allen, Myers & Thompson, in press) is an expansion on the model presented by Gluck, Myers, and Goebel (1994) which now includes a more physiologically-accurate representation of the cerebellum and its recurrent connections. It also focuses on the negative feedback pathway from the interpositus to the inferior olive. This feedback pathway is theorized to calculate error-correction between US expectancy and US presentation (a la Rescorla-Wagner, 1972) and is the neural mechanism theorized to underlie many learning phenomena including blocking, conditioned inhibition, overshadowing, positive patterning, and negative patterning.

The Gluck et al. (in press) cerebellar model is more physiologically detailed than previous modeling efforts in that it includes separate layers for the cortical inputs of stimuli, a layer representing the Purkinje cells, and an output node representing the interpositus based on a cerebellar circuit simplified from Thompson (1986; Figure 1A). It also maintains the direct inhibitory feedback loop from the interpositus to the inferior olive and has a direct excitatory feedback loop from the interpositus to the pontine nuclei.

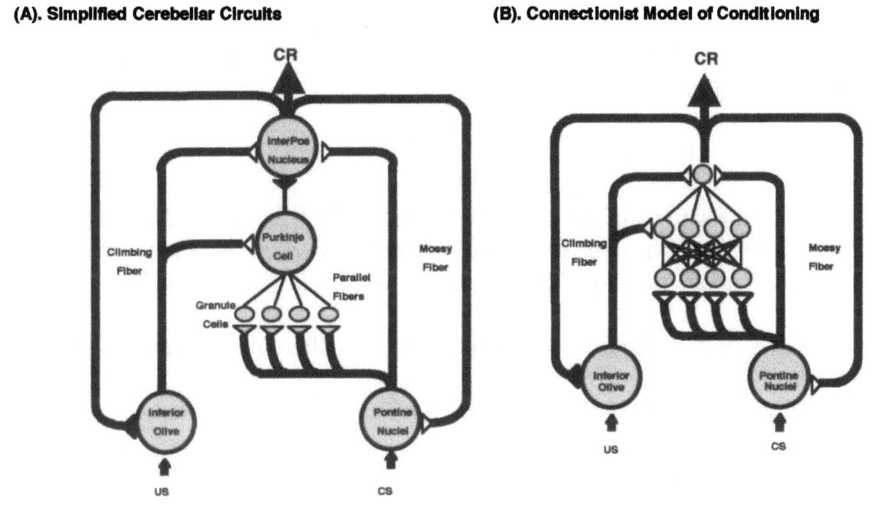

Figure 1. Shows simplifications which have been made to adapt the cerebellar anatomy into the connectionist architecture in the Gluck et al. (in press) computational model of the cerebellum. (A) shows a cerebellar circuit diagram which has been simplified from the cerebellar circuitry from Thompson (1986). The cerebellar cortex has been simplified into a layer which represents the granule cells, a node which represents the Purkinje cells, and node which represents the interpositus nucleus. (B) shows the connectionist model of conditioning which has been designed based on the simplified cerebellar circuit in A. The input layer represents the granule cells. The internal layer represents the Purkinje cells and the output node represents the interpositus nucleus.

The major simplification adopted is to represent the cerebellar cortex and interpositus nucleus as a two-layer module with inputs to these layers that represent the CS, US, and recurrent CR information (Figure 1B; Gluck et al., in press). The input-layer nodes each represent possible CSs, and become active when that CS is present. This information, corresponding to pontine projections, projects to an internal layer representing cerebellar cortex and an output layer representing the interpositus nucleus. The output from this node is the behavioral CR. The internal level input weights to the internal layer are random and fixed while the weights to the output nodes are trained by the LMS rule (Widrow & Hoff, 1960) using error = IO = (US-CR) which is equivalent to the term $\left(\lambda - \sum_j CS_j\, w_j\right)$ in the Rescorla Wagner rule (Equation 1). This computation of error is done in the inferior olive, which outputs proportionally to the difference between excitatory US information and inhibitory CR information. The activity of the output node also has excitatory recurrent connections to the CS inputs along with inhibitory recurrent connections to the US inputs. Within this circuit model, this negative feedback loop is implemented with a non-modifiable synapse of value -1 between the adaptive node and the inferior olive. The functional role of this inhibitory feedback is to compute the error signal measured by the IO's activity. The inferior olive's activity is governed by the following equation:

$$IO = US - CR$$

where, IO is the activity of the inferior olive, US is the US input, and CR is the output of the interpositus. Thus, the inferior olive's output in projected to the internal layer and output node as an "error signal" which is analogous to the term $\left(\lambda - \sum_j CS_j w_j\right)$ in the Rescorla Wagner rule. Implicit in the above discussion is the assumption that activity in the inferior olive can represent both errors of omission and errors of commission. Errors of commission occur, for example, on extinction trails when a response is made but no US occurs. Without a baseline level of activity in the inferior olive, the system has no way to represent a trial on which associative weights should decrease, and errors of commission would have no effect. The need for representing negative errors is accommodated by assuming that the inferior olive has a positive baseline level of firing when no error has occurred. Depressing the inferior olive below this baseline represents negative error. In this way the inferior olive term reflects not the absolute activity level of the inferior olive but rather its activity level relative to baseline. There is clear empirical evidence to support this assumption; the spontaneous discharge rate of inferior olivary neurons is about 2-4 spikes per second in the awake behaving animal (Ito, 1984). As noted earlier, naïve animals show US-evoked activity in the dorsal accessory olive, while as learning occurs the US-evoked activity in the dorsal accessory olive decreases to near zero on paired CS-US trials - just as in the model, IO activity returns to baseline as the CR develops.

The Gluck et al. (in press) model is a discrete time model; this means that at each cycle the model can modify its synapses only once, as opposed to continuous biological systems that continuously modify synapses. In simulations, each "trial" is divided into ten discrete cycles or time intervals. A simulation of delay conditioning involves training the model with repeated "trials" of 10 time cycles; the CS is "on" for cycles 4 through 8 while the US is "on" for cycle 8; thus, CS onset precedes US onset while CS and US co-terminate. The interstimulus-interval (ISI) is 4. At this stage in theory development, no direct mapping is made between the duration of a cycle and an actual time interval. (However, in theory, if one assumed the US length to be about 50 msec and that interval to be the length of each time cycle, one can assume that a 4 cycle ISI would correspond to about a 200 msec ISI).

The model is able to simulate a variety of features of delay conditioning. It shows development of a well-timed response in which the CR peak occurs at about the time of US onset. The timing of the CR peak is correct over a range of ISI lengths from 4 to 18 time cycles (Gluck et al., in press). In animals, (Gormezano, Kehoe & Marshall, 1983), training at different ISI lengths results in different learning rates in that the fastest acquisition occurs for about 250-400 msec ISI and is slower for each successively longer ISI. In the model, this difference in learning rates occurs because the only change in net input from cycle to cycle is the changing CR feedback. The network must learn a set of weights such that the CR remains low for the first part of the ISI and grows rapidly thereafter. With short ISI training, it is appropriate to exhibit CRs much sooner after CS onset; therefore, this task is learned more quickly. The increased complexity of the long ISI task not only increases learning time but also results in a broader CR, consistent with experimental data (Gormezano et al., 1983).

The model can also account for various learning phenomena that are thought to involve stimulus selection and that have been previously explained by the Rescorla-Wagner rule. As described earlier, blocking is the phenomenon where a neutral CS, A, is first repeatedly paired with the US, so that the animal comes to expect the US given A. In the second phase of training, animals receive compound presentations consisting of the previously-trained CS A and a novel CS B paired with the same US. A later test of the individual stimuli alone shows continued high level responding to A but little responding to B. Apparently, the prior conditioning to A blocks the learning to B. In contrast, animals which have received AB+ trials (without the A+ training) showed appreciably more responding when tested with B. Marchant, Mis and Moore (1972) and Solomon (1977) and Kehoe (1981) demonstrated this phenomenon in rabbit eyeblink conditioning while Martin and Levey (1991) demonstrated this phenomenon with human eyeblink conditioning. As expected, the cerebellar model shows robust blocking in these training conditions (Figure 2A; Gluck et al., in press). Conditioned inhibition is a phenomenon where paired presentations of a CS A and the US are intermixed with non-reinforced compound presentations of CS A and a second CS B (AB-). In the second phase, learning is compared between B and a novel cue C. In the first phase, the model quickly learns to generate a strong CR to A+ trials but not on AB- trials. In the second phase, B+ is slower than learning to the novel cue C (Figure 2B; Gluck et al., in press). This result matches with results from rabbit eyeblink conditioning (Marchant et al., 1972; Mahoney, Kwaterski & Moore, 1975; Solomon, 1977).

Positive patterning is a phenomenon in which a cue compound AB is paired with the US but the individual components A and B are not. Therefore, the animal learns to respond to the compound, but not respond to the individual cues (Bellingham, Gillette-Bellingham & Kehoe, 1985; Kehoe & Schreurs, 1986). The model is able to simulate this result (Figure 2C; Gluck et al., in press).

Negative patterning is the opposite phenomenon: CS A and CS B are each individually paired with the US while the compound presentations of AB are not reinforced. The animal must therefore learn to respond when either CS appears alone, but not respond when the compound is presented (Bellingham et al., 1985).

Our cerebellar model is able to properly simulate the negative patterning phenomenon with results similar to those from rabbit eyeblink conditioning. There is strong responding to the individual cues A and B while responding to the compound

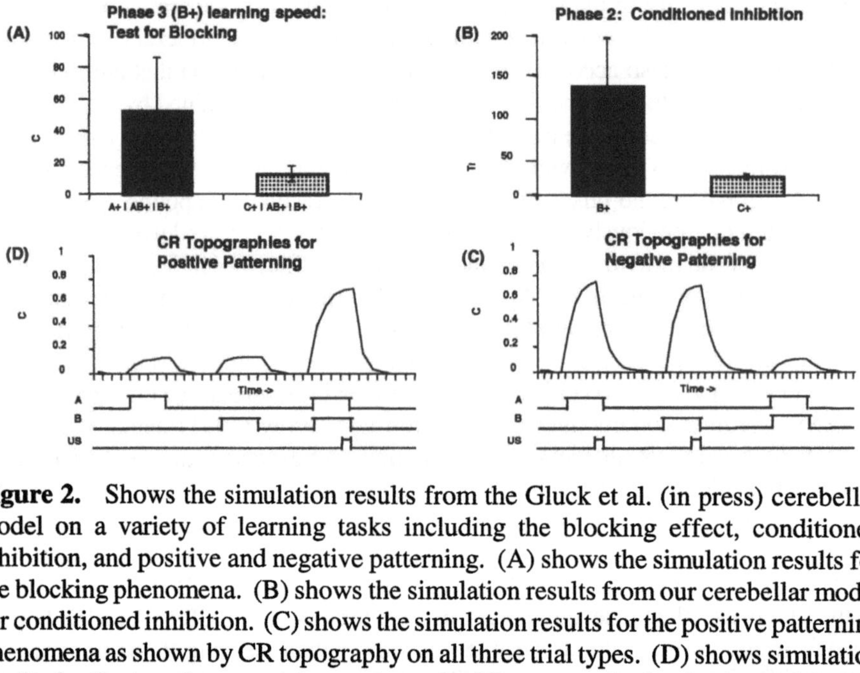

Figure 2. Shows the simulation results from the Gluck et al. (in press) cerebellar model on a variety of learning tasks including the blocking effect, conditioned inhibition, and positive and negative patterning. (A) shows the simulation results for the blocking phenomena. (B) shows the simulation results from our cerebellar model for conditioned inhibition. (C) shows the simulation results for the positive patterning phenomena as shown by CR topography on all three trial types. (D) shows simulation results for the negative patterning as shown by CR topography for the three trial types (A+, B+, AB-).

cue AB in inhibited (Figure 2D; Gluck et al., in press). While the model easily simulates positive patterning, the model has some trouble with negative patterning. Only about fifty to seventy-five percent of the simulations result in correct negative patterning. This bimodal result may be indicative of the complex nature of the task and the problems that have been reported in obtaining the negative patterning result. As we shall see in later sections, negative patterning is a form of a "configural" task which requires sensitivity to CS-CS relationships, a type of task which many have argued depends not just on the cerebellum, but also on the hippocampus (Rudy & Sutherland, 1989). As such, it is not surprising that a model of only the cerebellar contribution to learning would have difficulty reproducing a behavior seen most clearly in animals with intact hippocampal functioning.

Limitations of the Cerebellar Model

While the cerebellar model is somewhat capable of simulating negative patterning, it is not perfect. It also fails to simulate more complex phenomena such as reversal learning following a discrimination task and latent inhibition, in which pre-exposure to a cue retards subsequent learning of the association between that cue and the air puff US. These tasks are also not accounted for by the Rescorla-Wagner rule. All of these tasks require some formation or alternation in the representations of stimuli that involve more than a simple association between a CS and US. These failures of the cerebellar model and Rescorla-Wagner rule led to the exploration of other brain structures and learning rules which could account for these more complex learning phenomena.

HIPPOCAMPAL SUBSTRATES OF EYEBLINK CONDITIONING

The role of the hippocampus in eyeblink conditioning has not been as clearly defined as that of the cerebellum and brainstem circuitry. The circuitry of the hippocampal region is well-established; however, the function of individual structures is not well-defined. Sensory information from all sensory modalities arrives through the superficial entorhinal cortex and travels through the hippocampal formation (dentate gyrus, CA3, CA1, subiculum) before exiting through the deep entorhinal cortex to the sensory and association areas where it originated. There is a second hippocampal input-output pathway through the fornix; among the structures with reciprocal hippocampal connections through the fornix is the basal forebrain, containing several nuclei including the medial septum.

The work on the role of the hippocampus in eyeblink conditioning began with hippocampal lesion studies which resulted in some surprising effects. Schmaltz and Theios (1972) found that aspiration lesions of the hippocampus had no detrimental effect on basic acquisition of the conditioned eyeblink response in a delay paradigm. In delay conditioning, the CS precedes the US, but the two stimuli overlap and co-terminate. There was in fact a facilatory effect in that these hippocampally lesioned rabbits learned faster than non-lesioned controls. This evidence indicated that the hippocampus plays some role in eyeblink conditioning, however it was not necessary for basic acquisition.

As mentioned previously, the cerebellar model of Gluck et al. (in press) is able to simulate stimulus discrimination, but fails to properly simulate reversal of a discrimination task. Berger and Orr (1983) found that hippocampal lesions had no effect on basic discrimination learning between a CS paired with the US and a CS presented alone (i.e., A+, B- training), but did severely disrupt reversal of this initial discrimination. The cerebellar model also fails to demonstrate the latent inhibition effect. Solomon and Moore (1975) found that hippocampal lesions disrupted the latent inhibition effect. These findings, taken together, indicate a role for the hippocampus in tasks which the cerebellum is not capable of solving on its own.

Another form of eyeblink conditioning, trace conditioning, in which the CS offsets prior to the onset of the US, has likewise been found to require the hippocampus.

Trace conditioning has been hypothesized as more difficult than delay conditioning because of the requirement that a representation of the CS must be maintained during the period between the CS offset and US onset during which there are no stimuli present.

One interesting paradox in the work on the role of the hippocampus in eyeblink conditioning is that while removal of the hippocampus has no detrimental effect on simple acquisition of delay conditioning, disruption of hippocampal activity significantly retards learning of delay conditioning. This disruption of hippocampal activity and thereby disruption of learning of the conditioned eyeblink has been demonstrated by a variety of techniques including electrolytic lesions of the medial septum (Berry & Thompson, 1979) sub-seizure electrical stimulation of the hippocampus (Salafia, Romano, Tynan & Host, 1977; Salafia, Chiaia & Ramirez, 1979), and the administration of the cholinergic antagonist scopolamine (Solomon & Gottfried, 1981; Solomon, Van der Schaaf & Perry, 1983).

Overall, it appears that the hippocampus plays some role in eyeblink conditioning, and is required for more complex learning paradigms than simple CS-US acquisition. It also is evident that the septum has some role in hippocampal function, and disruption of this septo-hippocampal system is even more detrimental on eyeblink conditioning than simple removal of the hippocampus. With these empirical results as a foundation, Gluck and Myers (1993) developed a computational model of the role of the hippocampal region in learning and memory in particular in rabbit eyeblink conditioning.

Development of a Hippocampal Model of Conditioning

Our hippocampal computational work has followed a pattern very similar to the cerebellar computational models discussed previously in that it has moved from simplistic representations of a brain structure to more physiologically-accurate neural architectures. In contrast to the cerebellar literature which has very specific empirical results for the function of various brain structures in eyeblink conditioning, the hippocampal literature has little consensus as to the specif roles the hippocampus and its related structures play in learning and memory. Therefore, the hippocampal model has progressed from a "psychological" or "connectionist" model of general hippocampal function to a more physiologically-detailed model of neural substrates.

Gluck and Myers (1993) Hippocampal Model

The approach put forth by Gluck and Myers (1993) was to start with a computational theory of learning in intact animals and then seek to identify a sub-component of this theory that depends on the hippocampal region. This approach led to a computational theory of the functional role of the hippocampal region on mediating stimulus representation. The Gluck-Myers (1993) theory assumes that the hippocampal region develops new stimulus representations that enhance the discriminability of differentially predictive cues (termed predictive differentiation) while compressing the representation of redundant cues (termed redundancy compression). Other brain regions, including cerebral and cerebellar cortices, are presumed to use these hippocampal representations to recode their own stimulus representations. In the absence of an intact hippocampal region, the theory expects that other brain regions can still acquire some associative learning tasks using previously-established fixed representations.

The Gluck-Myers (1993) hippocampal model represented the hippocampal region by way of a connectionist network as shown in Figure 3A.

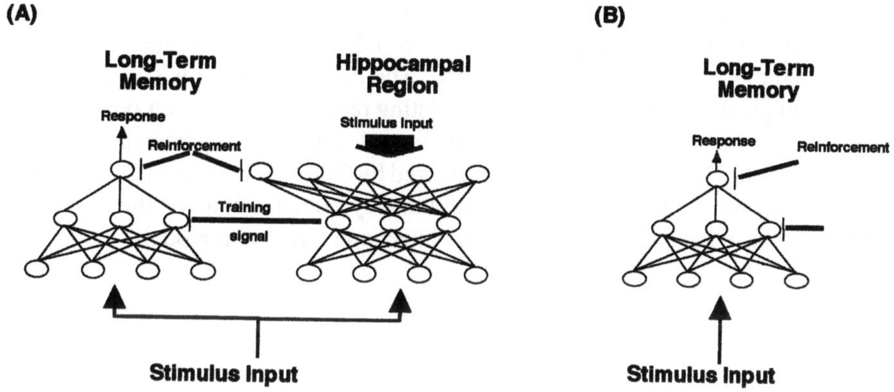

Figure 3. Gluck and Myers (1993) computational model of the hippocampal region. (A) The intact model: Stimulus input is presented to the hippocampal-region network, which can compress and differentiate stimulus representations. The new representations constructed in the hippocampal region network are acquired by the long-term memory network, which simultaneously learns to map from these internal representations to an output interpreted as the system's behavioral response. (B) The HR lesioned model: Broad hippocampal-region damage (the HR lesion) is simulated by disabling the hippocampal-region network. In this case, the remaining long-term memory network cannot form new representations, although it can still learn new mappings to behavioral responses based on its preexisting (and now fixed) internal representations. Reprinted from Gluck and Myers (1993) with permission of the authors.

The basic architecture of the model consists of a three-layered network. Stimulus information enters at the bottom through stimulus (input) nodes. Activation of these input nodes propagates activation through weighted connections to the middle layers of nodes. Activation in this middle layer is a function of the weighted sum of incoming activations from the input layer. The middle layer can be viewed as the network's internal representation of the stimulus pattern. This internal representation can be contrasted with the (external) stimulus represented on the input nodes. The internal pattern of activation is itself propagated on through the next layer of weights to the output (response) layer. Activation in the response layer is a function of the weighted sum of activation in the previous layer.

This network was trained by error back propagation (Parker, 1985; Rumelhart, Hinton & Williams, 1986; Werbos, 1974); it learned to map from inputs representing stimulus activity, through a narrow internal or hidden layer of nodes, to output nodes which learn to reconstruct the stimulus inputs plus a prediction of future events. Because the internal layer is narrow, as compared with the input and output layers, the representations formed in the internal layer must compress redundant information while preserving enough information to all the output to be reconstructed.

The activity from the internal layer is communicated to a long-term memory (cortical) module which represents either cerebral or cerebellar cortex. In the intact hippocampal model, this activity is used by the cortical module in forming its associations. In the hippocampal region-lesion (HR-lesion) model, the hippocampal module is removed as shown in Figure 4B. The cortical module is still capable of forming simple associations based on its existing representations to an output that is interpreted as the behavioral response, but not to develop new representations.

Various learning tasks have been categorized by Gluck and Myers (1993) as either requiring predictive differentiation or redundancy compression for their solution. These tasks have been tested with both the intact and HR-lesion models.

Tests of Redundancy Compression

Gluck and Myers (1993) identified several training procedures in which stimulus representations are altered by redundancy compression in an initial training phase of a two-stage transfer task. Learning and generalization performance on subsequent transfer tasks is either facilitated of retarded, depending on whether or not the initial redundancy in maintained or altered.

The Gluck-Myers (1993) theory expects that non-reinforced exposure to a stimulus will lead to compression of the representation of that stimulus with background contextual cues. For example, in the latent inhibition phenomena, pre-exposure to a stimulus A alone retards subsequent acquisition of conditioned responses to that stimulus (Lubow, 1973). In the intact model, pre-exposure results in compression of the representations of stimulus A and background context. This compression will increase generalization between cue A and context, and therefore retard subsequent learning to respond to the cue A but not the context alone. This compression is assumed to depend on the hippocampal-region. The HR-lesion model, without these compression mechanisms, correctly shows no effect of stimulus exposure (Figure 4A; Gluck & Myers, 1993).

Similarly, if two cues are reliably presented together, their representations will be compressed and generalized with increase between them. This occurs during sensory preconditioning: non-reinforced pre-exposure to a stimulus compound AB, followed by learning a response to A, leads to transfer and responding to B (Figure 4B; Gluck & Myers, 1993). Again, this effect is absent in the HR-lesion model. Similarly, intact rabbits show sensory preconditioning (Thompson, 1972) while animals with hippocampal-region damage (specifically fimbria lesion) do not (Port & Patterson, 1984).

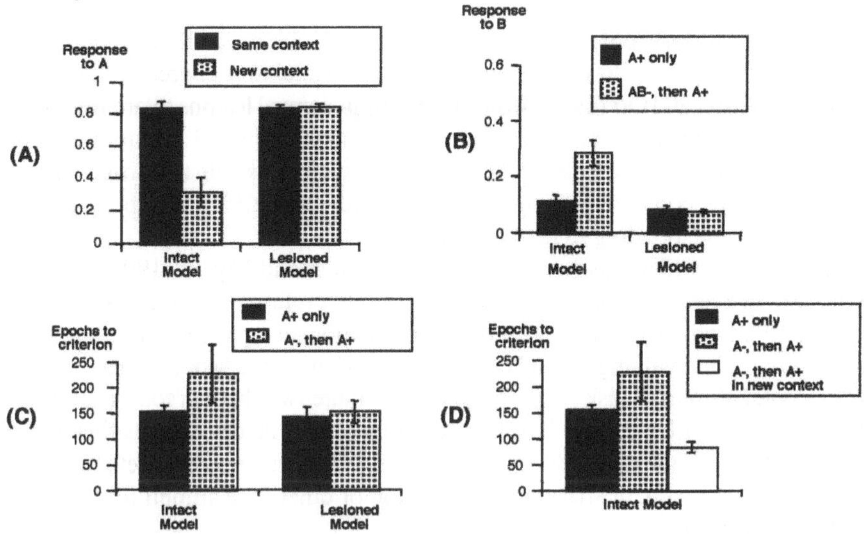

Figure 4. Simulation results with the intact and HR-lesioned models – replotted from results reported in Gluck and Myers (1993); Myers and Gluck (1994). (A). Latent inhibition. Unreinforced pre-exposure to a cue A slows later training to respond to A in the intact but not the HR-lesioned model; consistent with animal results (Kaye & Pearce, 1987; Solomon & Moore, 1975). (B) Sensory preconditioning. Unreinforced pre-exposure to a compound of two stimuli, AB, followed by training to respond to A, results in stronger responding to B alone than in a control condition with no pre-exposure in the intact but not H&EC-lesioned model. Fornix lesion similarly eliminates sensory preconditioning in rabbits (Port & Patterson, 1984). (C) Context shift decrement. After training to respond to a cue A in some context, the intact but not HR-lesioned system shows a decrement in responding to A when presented in a novel context; consistent with animal results (Penick & Solomon, 1991). (D) Context shift after latent inhibition exposure. A context shift between exposure and learning phases interferes with the latent inhibition effect in the intact model; consistent with animal and human results (Lubow, Rifkin & Alek, 1976; Bouton & Brooks, 1993).

Differentiation Tests

We now discuss the ability of the hippocampal model to correctly simulate conditioning results thought to involve differentiation of stimulus representations.

Gluck-Myers' (1993) theory suggest that internal representations of predictive stimuli are pulled apart during discrimination training. If subsequent tasks can make use of this altered representation, learning will be facilitated. The simplest example of this expected facilitation is reversal learning. A reversal task involves an initial phase of learning (A+ B-) followed by a phase of learning (A- B+). With an intact hippocampal region, learning (A+ B-) results in pulling apart stimulus representations for A and B. When the task switches to reversal training (A- B+), the stimulus representations are already very distinct, and it is relatively easy to map them to different responses. In contrast, the Gluck-Myers (1993) theory expects that in the case of hippocampal removal, the reversal should not be facilitated because no stimulus representations have been learned. These simulations agree with empirical findings of Berger and Orr (1983) which found hippocampal lesions retard reversal but not initial discrimination. In particular, hippocampal lesioned rabbits show high responding to both CS A and B. In other words, the rabbit is able to normally acquire a conditioned response to the new CS+, but without the hippocampus it fails to properly inhibit responding to the previous CS+.

Another task which has been theorized by Gluck and Myers (1993) to require predictive differentiation is easy-hard transfer (also referred to as transfer along a continuum), in which learning a "hard" discrimination along a stimulus continuum is facilitated by prior training on an "easy" version of the same task (Lawrence, 1952). For example, an "easy" task might be to differentiate two distinct tone stimuli (e.g., 400 kHz vs. 1200 kHz tones). The Gluck-Myers (1993) theory expects this learning should stretch the internal representation of the tone dimension. This stretching should then facilitate subsequent "hard" discrimination of other tone stimuli (e.g., 800 kHz vs. 900 kHz tones).

For example, an easy task for the model is to learn to respond when stimulus A has a value of 0.9 but not when it has a value of 0.1: (A = 0.9+, A = 0.1-). Following training, the distance between the representations activated by A = 0.9 and A = 0.1 should increase, stretching apart all feature values along this stimulus continuum. Prior training on this easy task facilitates learning a second harder discrimination of intermediate stimulus values (A = 0.6+, A = 0.4-). Learning the harder second task is much quicker for this pre-trained group than for a control group that was not pre-trained on the easy (A = 0.9+, A = 0.1-) discrimination. In fact, training on the easy task facilitates learning the hard task more than an equal amount of training on the hard task itself.

The Gluck-Myers (1993) cortico-hippocampal model makes a novel prediction about easy-hard learning after hippocampal lesion. In the HR-lesion model, the easy task does not cause representational stretching, so there is minimal facilitation of the subsequent hard task. Gluck and Myers predict that there will likewise be no easy-hard facilitation in hippocampal-lesioned animals as compared to control levels of stimulus generalization.

Hippocampal Model of Context

The latent inhibition results shown in Figure 4A suggest that the Gluck-Myers (1993) model can be applied to contextual effects in classical conditioning (Myers & Gluck, 1994). The model predicts that hippocampal representations include contextual information in every learned association. Because all stimuli present are included in the internal representation, the representation of any one stimulus is affected by the other stimuli present. This process ensures that the representation of a stimulus will include information about the context in which that stimulus occurred.

One form of contextual effect on conditioning is a decrement in responding seen following a salient change in context. This contextual shift effect has been seen in many conditioning paradigms including eyeblink conditioning. Penick and Solomon

(1991) found a decrement in responding following a context shift in both intact animals and animals with cortical aspiration lesions. However, animals with hippocampal-region aspiration lesions showed no decrement in responding following contextual shift. This result indicates that the contextual shift effect is a hippocampal-region-dependent task.

After the intact model learns to respond to stimulus A in a given context, the response drops when A is presented in a new context (Figure 4C; Myers & Gluck, 1994). Conversely, the HR-lesion model has no facility for forming new representations, and therefore no mechanism for including information about the context in which a response is learned. Therefore, the HR-lesion model shows no change in the strength of responding to A in a new context (Myers & Gluck, 1994). Similarly, hippocampal lesions eliminate the context-shift effect in animals (e.g., Antelman & Brown, 1972; Penick & Solomon, 1991).

Myers and Gluck (1994) also predicted that the context shift effect was dependent on the amount of training to the original response. Early in training, the hippocampal region is assumed to include contextual information in new stimulus representations through redundancy compression. However, as training continues, and stimulus representations become ever more biased by predictive differentiation, the representations come increasingly to distinguish between A-present and A-absent trials. This tends to undo the effects of the previous redundancy compression and make the representation of A less contextually sensitive. The resulting prediction is that over-training to A should eliminate (or lessen) the response decrement after context shift (Myers & Gluck, 1994).

Time-dependence of the context shift effect has also been seen in other learning paradigms (Antelman & Brown, 1972; Hall & Honey, 1990). Tests of this context shift response decrement in aversive conditioning by Hall and Honey (1990) indicated that a response decrement after context shift was observed early in training but absent after further training. This result indicates that over-training should eliminate the context shift response decrement, but this prediction has yet to be tested in rabbit eyeblink conditioning.

Another contextual shift effect is a release from latent inhibition when CS pre-exposure occurs in one context and then acquisition is completed in another context Lubow et al., 1976; Bouton & Brooks, 1993). The Gluck-Myers (1993) model explains this effect as coming about due to representational compression during pre-exposure. Pre-exposure is assumed to result in compression of cue A with context X, which slows later learning to respond to A but not X alone. However, if training occurs in a new context Y, with which A is not compressed, learning is fast - and latent inhibition is eliminated (Figure 4D, Myers & Gluck, 1994). Again, the model predicts that this effect should be absent after hippocampal-region damage, and this prediction remains to be tested in eyeblink conditioning.

The Gluck-Myers (1993) model is capable of simulating various learning phenomena in both intact animals and animals with lesions to the hippocampal region. Many lesion effects previously described were either aspiration or electrolytic and damaged not only the hippocampus but also the overlying cortex and fibers of passage. Therefore, these effects could be due not to damage to the hippocampus but to other related structures. The development of selective lesioning techniques (e.g., Jarrard,

1989) have made it possible to differentiate the role of the hippocampus proper from the hippocampal region in general. Selective neurotoxins like ibotenic acid only damage cell bodies in the region of the injection and spare surrounding tissue and fibers of passage. These techniques have allowed for selective lesion of the hippocampal cell fields alone.

These selective hippocampal lesions have called into question some of the effects which have previously been thought to be due to a "hippocampal" lesion. For example, Good and Honey (1991) found that while hippocampal region lesions disrupted latent inhibition, selective hippocampal lesions had no effect on latent inhibition. This type of data called into question the role of the hippocampus proper in conditioning.

Myers, Gluck and Granger (1995) Entorhinal Model

Given that the processes of redundancy compression and predictive differentiation can be partially dissociated, it is possible that they represent different subfunctions of the hippocampal-region, which may be situated in different anatomical loci. Myers, Gluck and Granger (1995) attempted to delineate the role of the hippocampus proper from the entorhinal cortex, and argued that the anatomy and physiology of the entorhinal cortex are *sufficient* to underlie the representational function of compression based on stimulus-stimulus redundancy. This work was based on a previous model of the highly-similar piriform (olfactory) cortex (Ambros-Ingerson, Granger & Lynch, 1990) which indicated that this type of cortical anatomy made it a likely candidate for compression of representations.

The major input to the entorhinal cortex is from cortical areas including piriform (olfactory) cortex, perirhinal and parahippocampal cortices, multi-modal association areas, and the subicular complex (Schousboe et al., 1993; van Hoesen & Pandya, 1975). In effect, the entorhinal cortex receives highly-processed inputs from multi-modal association areas. If primary sensory cortices are thought of as the beginning of a cortical processing stream, then the entorhinal cortex is anatomically the culmination of that processing. The entorhinal cortex is therefore ideally placed to integrate information across and between modalities. The entorhinal cortex also receives input from many subcortical areas such as the septum, the thalamus and hypothalamus, and the amygdala. A major output of the entorhinal cortex superficial layer is to the dentate gyrus via the perforant path.

The entorhinal cortex model is a network of units representing superficial entorhinal excitatory layer II cells, sparsely afferented by multi-modal inputs (Figure 5A; Myers, Gluck & Granger, 1995). The units are grouped into patches whose members are assumed to contact and be contacted by inhibitory interneurons. The result of excitatory-inhibitory interaction in each patch is the emergence of lateral competition, which modeling has shown causes only the most activated targets to respond, thereby approximating "winner takes all" activity. The activation of these winning units across the network defines a new representation of the stimulus. The winning nodes undergo LTP-like increment to increase their likelihood of winning the competition when similar inputs are presented in the future. This network performs unsupervised learning, since the clusters formed are independent of any reinforcement or stimulus-outcome pairing relationships. Its operation is similar to many other unsupervised competitive clustering networks proposed previously (e.g., Grossberg, 1976; Kohonen, 1984; von der Malsburg, 1973).

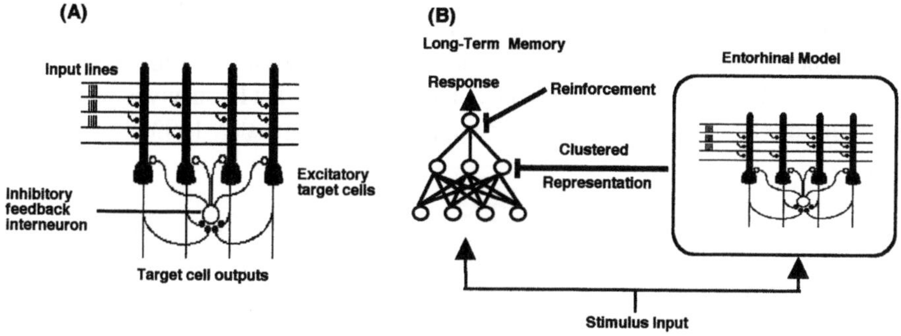

Figure 5. (A) In the Myers, Gluck and Granger (1995) entorhinal model, target cells are excited by sparse afferents, and in turn activate local inhibitory feedback interneurons. Feedback silences all but the most strongly activated target cells; synaptic plasticity makes these "winning" target cells more likely to "win" in response to similar inputs in the future. The resulting network activity is constrained by stimulus-stimulus redundancy compression. (B) The H-lesioned model, in which an entorhinal cortex network provides new, compressed representations to the internal layer of a long-term memory network. Reprinted from Myers, Gluck and Granger (1995) with permission of the authors.

The basic assumption of Myers et al. (1995) is that the anatomy and physiology of the entorhinal cortex make it a candidate for multi-modal redundancy compression leaving other areas (such as the hippocampus proper) to do predictive differentiation. Since compression and differentiation are thought to take place in different sub-components of the hippocampal region, selective lesions of the hippocampus and entorhinal cortex should have different effects based on the representational requirements of the task being tested. In other words, a task which involves redundancy compression for its solution would require an intact entorhinal cortex while a task which involves predictive differentiation for its solution would require an intact hippocampus.

To test the ability of the entorhinal model to accomplish redundancy compression, Myers et al., (1995) developed the selective hippocampal lesion (H-lesion) model (Figure 5B) in which the hippocampal region has been replaced by the entorhinal model; therefore, this H-lesion model should be capable of tasks which require redundancy compression but not predictive differentiation. This H-lesion model was tested on tasks previously found to be disrupted in the HR-lesioned model (Gluck & Myers, 1993; Myers & Gluck, 1994). The H-lesion model was tested on these tasks to determine if redundancy compression alone (within the entorhinal cortex) could account for these phenomena.

For example, latent inhibition (LI) is shown in the intact but not HR-lesioned model (See Figure 4A; Gluck & Myers, 1993). LI reflects several representational processes in the intact model, including redundancy compression, stimulus-stimulus differentiation, and meaning-driven differentiation. In the H-lesion (entorhinal cortex intact) model, by contrast, there is only the mechanism for redundancy compression during the exposure phase. The result is that the representations of cue A and context X are compressed during pre-exposure, retarding subsequent learning to respond to A in X but not to X alone. Thus, *the H-lesion model does show LI* (Figure 6A; Myers et al., 1995). This is consistent with the empirical finding that LI survives selective H-lesion in rats (Honey & Good, 1993; Reilly, Harley & Revusky, 1993).

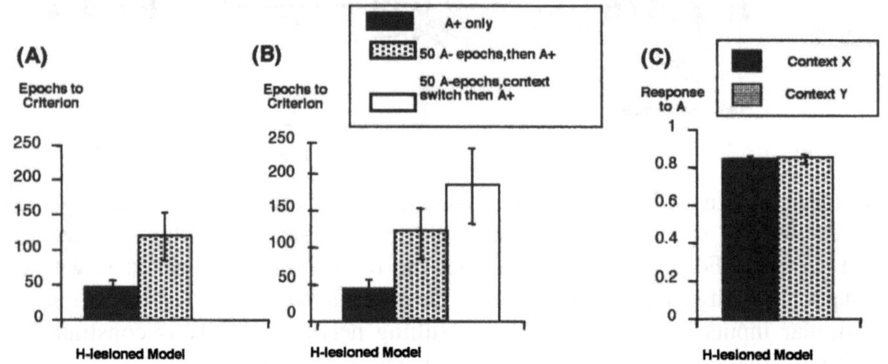

Figure 6. Simulation results from hippocampal lesioned (H-lesioned) model (Myers et al., 1995). (A) Latent inhibition in the H-lesioned model. Learning to respond to cue A, is retarded (reflected in more trials required to reach criterion responding after 50 epochs of un-reinforced pre-exposure to A than in a control condition with no pre-exposure. (B) Latent inhibition is not abolished by a context shift between pre-exposure and acquisition; consistent with results from rats with selective hippocampal ibotenate lesions (Honey & Good, 1993). (C) Absence of response decrement with context shift in the H-lesioned model. After 200 epochs of training to respond to cue A in context X, there is little or no decrement in the response when A is presented in novel context Y; consistent with results from rats with selective hippocampal lesions (Honey & Good, 1993). Reprinted from Myers et al., 1995 with permission of the authors.

However, although both intact and H-lesion models show latent inhibition, there are important and subtle differences. In the H-lesion model, there are no representational differentiation mechanisms to differentiate (un-compress) the representations of A and X during the learning phase. Thus, learning must take place in spite of the fact that the representations of A and X are compressed. The only way for the model to do this is to learn selective responses based on these compressed representations. This can be done by ignoring the parts of the representations that overlap, and focusing on those parts of the representation - however small - which happen to have remained distinct. As long as at least some such distinctions remain, the model can learn to respond when A is present and withhold responding to the context alone. However, learning is slower than in a control condition where there was no prior compression.

Now suppose that there is a context shift between pre-exposure and learning phases. In the intact model, as discussed previously, such a context shift produces a release from LI - pre-exposure in context X does not slow learning in context Y (Myers & Gluck 1994). This is not true in the H-lesion model. Representational compression of A and X, during exposure, means two things: (1) there is increased generalization between A and X, and (2) the overall amount of resources allocated to encode for A (as opposed to A-in-X) is reduced. Shifting to a new context Y may eliminate (1) but not (2). Learning to discriminate the presence of A, and respond selectively to it, still requires identifying aspects of the representation which distinguish A's presence and A's absence. This will still slow learning relative to a control condition with no exposure, and hence no reduction of resources to encode A. Thus, while context shift eliminates LI in the intact model, *context shift does not eliminate LI in the H-lesion model* (Figure 6B; Myers et al., 1995). Consistent with this interpretation, a selective ibotenic acid H-lesion suffices to eliminate the context-sensitivity of LI in rats (Honey & Good, 1993).

A related contextual phenomenon is response decrement with context shift. In the intact model, as previously described, initial compression between cue A and context X leads to decreased responding when A is presented in a new context Y (See Figure 4C; Myers & Gluck, 1994). As training progresses, the representations of A and X are differentiated, so that there may be less effect of a context shift on learned responding to A.

In the selective H-lesioned model, by contrast, only redundancy compression occurs (Myers et al., 1995). By its very nature, this compression impedes the task of learning to respond to A but not to context X alone. In order to master this task, the model must learn to respond to A in spite of the representational compression - focusing on those few aspects of A's representation which happen to differ from that of X. The model must learn to ignore the overlap between the representations of A and X - effectively ignoring the context altogether, and only generating a response when A is present. Thus, when the context is shifted, this makes little difference - since context was already being ignored. Therefore, *the H-lesioned model does not show a response decrement with context shift* (Figure 6C; Myers et al., 1995). This is consistent with the failure of context shift to disrupt learned responding in rats with selective ibotenic acid H-lesion (Honey & Good, 1993).

Real-Time Hippocampal Model and Trace Conditioning

The previously discussed real-time cerebellar model (Gluck et al., in press) can account for temporal behaviors exhibited by hippocampal-damaged animals but not for behaviors requiring an intact hippocampus. Therefore, the cerebellar model can not properly simulate trace conditioning.

The Gluck-Myers (1993) hippocampal model was not a real-time model and therefore can not simulate trace conditioning as defined as a CR which is inhibited during the period between CS offset and US onset until about the time of US onset.

However, a temporally sensitive recurrent network variation of the Gluck-Myers (1993) model has been instantiated by Zackheim, Myers and Gluck (1998). This model was developed to simulate the phenomenon of occasion setting, but has since been applied to trace conditioning (unpublished results). The recurrent hippocampal model is capable of inhibiting responding until about the time of US onset for proper timing of the trace CR.

Computational Model of Septo-Hippocampal Modulation

As previously described, disruption of the septo-hippocampal system has a strong retardation effect on basic acquisition the CS-US association. The mechanism of sept-hippocampal modulation in eyeblink conditioning has been explored by extending the Gluck-Myers (1993) hippocampal model (Myers et al., 1996; Myers, Ermita, Hasselmo & Gluck, 1998).

The model is generalized to incorporate the ideas proposed by Hasselmo and Schnell (1994) that the septo-hippocampal pathways modulate hippocampal processing states between a state of storing new information and recalling previously-stored information. Hasselmo and Schnell (1994) noted that acetylcholine from the medial septum suppresses synaptic transmission at selective synapses in the hippocampus, having more effect at intrinsic, recurrent collaterals than on external afferents. Hasselmo (1995) has interpreted this effect as suggesting a means whereby the dynamics of the hippocampus could vary on a continuum between two modes for the storing of new information or the recall of previously stored information. Septal damage or disruption through pharmacological intervention should disrupt hippocampal functional by reducing the ability to store new information.

In the Gluck-Myers (1993) model, the amount of storage in the hippocampal region network is governed by the learning rate parameter in that network. The rate at which information is transferred from the hippocampus to cortical storage is governed independently by the learning rate on the lower layer of the cortical network. Therefore, altering the hippocampal learning rate is equivalent to selectively reducing hippocampal storage without affecting hippocampal recall and transfer to cortex. Thus, this simple mechanism of adjusting hippocampal learning rate is enough to affect processing in qualitatively the same way as hypothesized by Hasselmo (1995) to occur after septal damage (Myers et al., 1996).

By altering the hippocampal learning rate, the model is able to simulate the disruptive effects of scopolamine on eyeblink conditioning (Myers et al., 1996). The effect of reducing the hippocampal learning rate is to delay the onset of acquisition but not the eventual rate of learning nor the asymptote.

GENERAL DISCUSSION

The cerebellar and hippocampal models discussed here comprise parallel paths in our work utilizing neural networks and computational models to understand the neural substrates of eyeblink classical conditioning. In the intact model (Gluck & Myers,

1993) the hippocampal-region module sends stimulus representations to the cerebellar module, which then maps from them to the appropriate behavioral output. Therefore, the hippocampal-region lesion (HR-lesion) model (Gluck & Myers, 1993) can be viewed as a cerebellum-alone version of the model. This HR-lesion model can simulate the same basic learning phenomena as the Gluck et al., (in press) cerebellar model. These characteristics match with the empirical literature which shows hippocampal-lesioned animals are able to learn basic acquisition (Schmaltz & Theios, 1972) and discrimination (Berger & Orr, 1983). Therefore, both the cerebellar model (Figure 7A; Gluck et al., in press) and the HR-lesioned model (Figure 7B; Gluck & Myers, 1993) can be viewed as developments from the Thompson (1986) cerebellar circuit theorized to underlie eyeblink classical conditioning (Figure 7C).

There are several limitations in our current cerebellar model. The cerebellar cortex is highly simplified to include only granule and Purkinje cells. Future work should include more detailed cerebellar architecture which would include the influences of basket and stellate cells. Also, there is no mechanism to model the actual (physiological) plasticity changes which occur in the Purkinje cells during learning. These intracellular changes need to be included to make the model more physiological accurate. Another limitation of the current model is that there is no UR represented. The model does not include the brainstem motor nuclei which are responsible for the generation of the UR. This brainstem circuitry needs to be added to have a more complete and accurate representation of the mechanics of classical conditioning.

The hippocampal model is limited in that there is no differentiation of the specific contributions of the different sub-components of the hippocampus, specifically the dentate gyrus, and CA1 and CA3. Another limitation is that while there is a long-term memory module which represents the cerebellum, there is no model of cerebral cortex. The addition of cerebral cortex as a long-term memory module would allow for the hippocampal model to be applied to other learning paradigms other than eyeblink conditioning.

Empirical Support for Modeling Predictions

Overall, the modeling work on the role of the cerebellum and hippocampus in classical eyeblink conditioning has not only helped to explain prior empirical results, but has also lead to novel predictions which are currently being tested. The cerebellar prediction about the role of the inferior olive in error correction in tasks such as blocking has been supported by empirical work in which the inhibitory feedback from the interpositus has been blocked by the GABA-ergic antagonist picrotoxin which resulted in a lack of the Kamin (1969) blocking effect (Kim, Krupa & Thompson, 1998). Novel predictions from the Myers et al., (1995) entorhinal model predicting a differentiation between the hippocampus and entorhinal cortex in pre-exposure tasks like latent inhibition and learned irrelevance have also been supported by selective lesion studies (Allen, Chelius & Gluck, 1998). These lesion studies showed that selective entorhinal, but not hippocampal, lesions disrupt a pre-exposure task.

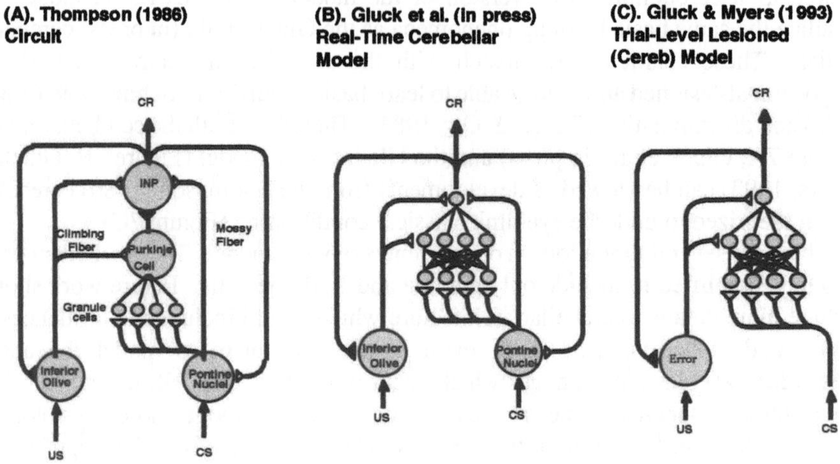

Figure 7. Demonstrates the equivalency between (A) the simplified cerebellar circuit (Thompson, 1986), (B) the Gluck et al., (in press) cerebellar model, and (C) the Gluck-Myers (1993) hippocampal lesioned (cerebellum alone) trial level model.

CONCLUSIONS

We have described our efforts to further the understanding of the neural substrates of rabbit eyeblink conditioning (in particular the cerebellum and hippocampus) through the use of neural networks. Over the years, the initial theoretical assumptions of the computational models have been maintained while more anatomically and physiologically detailed instantiations of these models have been developed. These neural networks have increased our understanding of how classical conditioning occurs in the cerebellum and hippocampus while making novel predictions which are guiding ongoing and future empirical studies. Neural networks result in simulations of various lesion conditions which offer subtle distinctions which may not be evident in a purely qualitative theory.

Neural networks also provide a "tool kit" which can be applied to various data-sets outside of the realm of basic lesion studies which were the basis for the original models. A case in point is the application of the basic Gluck and Myers (1993) hippocampal model to the septo-hippocampal literature in which a manipulation of a basic component (hippocampal learning rate) can account for a variety of cholinergic drug effects (Myers et al., 1996; Myers et al., 1998). In this way, neural networks can be a tool that can be applied to exploring many different aspects of classical eyeblink conditioning in particular and learning and memory in general.

REFERENCES

Allen, M.T., Chelius, L., & Gluck, M.A. (1998). Selective entorhinal ibotenic lesions disrupt the learned irrelevance pre-exposure effect in the classical conditioned rabbit eyeblink response paradigm conditioning. *Society for Neuroscience Abstracts, 24,* 442.

Ambros-Ingerson, J., Granger, R., & Lynch, G. (1990). Simulation of paleocortex performs hierarchical clustering. *Science, 247,* 1344-1348.

Anderson, B.J., & Steinmetz, J.E. (1994). Cerebellar and brainstem circuits involved in classical eyeblink conditioning. *Reviews in neuroscience, 5,* 1-23.

Andersson, G., Garwicz, M., & Hesslow, G. (1988). Evidence for GABA-mediated cerebellar inhibition of the inferior olive in the cat. *Brain Research, 472,* 450-456.

Angaut, P., & Sotelo, C. (1989). Synaptology of the cerebello-olivary pathway: Double labeling with anterograde axonal tracing and GABA iinmunocytochemistry in the rat. *Brain Research, 479,* 361-365

Antelman, S., & Brown, T. (1972). Hippocampal lesions and shuttlebox avoidance behavior: A fear hypothesis. *Physiology and Behavior, 9,* 15-20.

Bartha, G.T., Thompson R.F., & Gluck, M.A. (1991). Sensorimotor learning and the cerebellum. In M. Arbib & J. Ewert (Eds.), *Visual Structures and Integrated Functions,* (pp. 1-16). Berlin: Springer-Verlag.

Bellingham, W.P., Gillette-Bellingham, K., & Kehoe, E.J. (1985). Summation and configuration in patterning schedules with the rat and rabbit. *Animal Learning and Behavior, 13,* 152-164.

Berger, T.W., Alger, B., & Thompson, R.F. (1976). Neuronal substrate of classical conditioning in the hippocampus. *Science, 192,* 483-485.

Berger, T., & Orr, W. (1983). Hippocampectomy selectively disrupts discrimination reversal learning of the rabbit nictitating membrane response. *Behavioral Brain Research, 8,* 49-68.

Berry, S., & Thompson, R. (1979). Medial septal lesions retard classical conditioning of the nictitating membrane response in rabbits. *Science, 205,* 209-211.

Berthier, N.E., & Moore, J.W. (1986). Cerebellar Purkinje cell activity related to the classically conditioned nictitating membrane response. *Experimental Brain Research, 63,* 341-350.

Bouton, M., & Brooks, D. (1993). Time and context effects on performance in a Pavlovian discrimination reversal. *Journal of Experimental Psychology: Animal Behavior Processes, 19,* 1-15.

Donegan, N.H., Gluck, M.A., & Thompson, R.F. (1989). Integrating behavioral and biological models of conditioning. In R.D. Hawkins, & S.G.H. Bower (Eds.), *Psychology of Learning and Motivation,* (pp109-156). New York: Academic Press.

Gibson, A.R., Robinson, F.R., Alam, J., & Houk, J.C. (1987). Somatotopic alignment between climbing fiber input and nuclear output in the cat intermediate cerebellum. *Journal of Comparative Neurology, 260,* 362-377.

Gluck, M.A., Allen, M.T., Myers, C.E., & Thompson, R.F. (in press). Cerebellar substrates for error-correction in motor-reflex conditioning. *Journal of Cognitive Neuroscience.*

Gluck, M.A., & Myers, C.E. (1993). Adaptive stimulus representations: A computational theory of hippocampal-region function. In S. Hanson, J. Cowan & C. Giles (Eds.), *Advances in Neural Information Processing Systems 5,* (pp. 937-944). San Mateo, CA: Morgan Kaufmann

Gluck, M.A., Myers, C.E., & Goebel, J. (1994). A computational perspective on dissociating hippocampal and entorhinal function (Response to Eichenbaum et al.). *Behavioral and Brain Sciences, 17,* 478-479.

Gluck, M.A., Reifsnider, E.S., & Thompson R.F. (1990). Adaptive signal processing and the cerebellum: Models of classical conditioning and VOR adaptation. In M.A. Gluck & D.D. Rumelhart (Eds.), *Neuroscience and Connectionist Theory,* (pp. 131-185). Hillsdale, NJ: Lawrence Erlbaum.

Good, M., & Honey, R.C. (1991). Conditioning and contextual retrieval in hippocampal rats. *Behavioral Neuroscience, 105(4),* 499-509.

Gormezano, I., Kehoe, E.J., & Marshall, B.S. (1983). Twenty years of classical conditioning research with the rabbit. Progress in Psychobiology and Physiological Psychology, 10, 197-275.

Grossberg, S. (1976). Adaptive pattern classification and recoding: Part I. *Biological Cybernetics, 23,* 121-134.

Hall, G., & Honey, R. (1990). Context-specific conditioning in the conditioned-emotional response procedure. *Journal of Experimental Psychology: Animal Behavior Processes, 16(3),* 271-278.

Hasselmo, M. (1995). Neuromodulation and cortical function: Modeling the physiological basis of behavior. *Behavioural Brain Research, 67,* 1-27.

Hasselmo, M., & Schnell, E. (1994). Laminar selectivity of the cholinergic suppression of synaptic transmission in rat hippocampal region CA1: Computational modeling and brain slice physiology.

Journal of Neuroscience, 14(6). 3909-3014.
Honey, R., & Good, M. (1993). Selective hippocampal lesions abolish the contextual specificity of latent inhibition and conditioning. *Behavioral Neuroscience, 107(1),* 23-33.
Houk, J. (1989). Cooperative control of limb movements by the motor cortex, brainstem and cerebellum. In R. Cotterill (Ed.), *Models of Brain Function,* (pp. 309-325). New York: Cambridge University Press.
Ito, M. (1984). *The Cerebellum and Neural Control.* New York: Raven Press.
Jarrard, L.E. (1989). On the use of ibotenic acid to lesion selectively different components of the hippocampal formation. *Journal of Neuroscience Methods, 29,* 251-259.
Kamin, L. (1969). Predictability, surprise, attention and conditioning. In B. Campbell & R. Church (Eds.), *Punishment and Aversive Behavior,* (pp. 279-296). New York: Appleton Century-Crofts.
Kehoe, E.J. (1981). Stimulus selection and combination in classical conditioning with the rabbit. In I. Gormezano, W. Prokasy & R. Thompson (Eds.), *Classical Conditioning.* Hillsdale, NJ: Erlbaum.
Kehoe, E.J. (1988). A layered network model of associative learning. *Psychological Review, 95(4),* 411-433.
Kehoe, E.J., & Schreurs, B.G. (1986). Compound conditioning of the rabbit's nictitating membrane response: Test trial manipulations. *Bulletin of the Psychonomic Society, 24,* 79-81.
Kim, J.J., Krupa, D., & Thompson, R.F. (1998). Inhibitory cerebello-olivary projections and blocking effect in classical conditioning. *Science, 279,* 570-573.
Kim, J.J., & Thompson, R.F. (1997). Cerebellar circuits and synaptic mechanisms involved in classical eyeblink conditioning. *Trends in Neuroscience, 20,* 177-181.
Kohonen, T. (1984). *Self-Organization and Associative Memory.* New York: Springer-Verlag.
Kremer, E.F. (1978). The Rescorla-Wagner model: Losses in associative strength in compound conditioned stimuli. *Journal of Experimental Psychology: Animal Behavior Processes, 4,* 22-36.
Lawrence, D.H. (1952). The transfer of a discrimination along a continuum. *Journal of Comparative and Physiological Psychology, 45,* 511-516.
Lubow, R.E. (1973). Latent inhibition. *Psychological Bulletin, 79,* 398-407.
Lubow, R.E., Rifkin, B., & Alek, M. (1976). The context effect: The relationship between stimulus preexposure and environmental preexposure determines subsequent learning. *Journal of Experimental Psychology: Animal Behavior Processes, 2(1),* 38-47.
Mahoney, W.J., Kwaterski, S.E., & Moore, J.W. (1975). Conditioned inhibition of the rabbit nictitating membrane response as a function of CS-UCS interval. *Bulletin of the Psychonomic Society, 5(2),* 177-179.
Marchant III, H.G., Mis, F.W., & Moore J.W. (1972). Conditioned inhibition of the rabbit's nictitating membrane response. *Journal of Experimental Psychology, 95(2),* 408-411.
Martin, I., & Levey, A.B. (1991). Blocking observed in human eyelid conditioning. *The Quarterly Journal of Experimental Psychology, 43B(3),* 233-256.
Myers, C.D., Ermita, B.E., Harris, K., Hasselmo, M., Solomon, P., & Gluck, M.A. (1996). A computational model of classification conditioning after septo-hippocampal disruption. *Neurobiology of Learning and Memory, 66,* 51-66.
Myers, C.D., Ermita, B.E., Hasselmo, M., & Gluck, M.A. (1998). Further implications of a computational model of septo-hippocampal cholinergic modulation in eyeblink conditioning. *Psychobiology, 26(1),* 1-20.
Myers, C.E., & Gluck, M.A. (1994). Context, conditioning and hippocampal representation. *Behavioral Neuroscience, 108(5),* 835-847.
Myers, C.E., Gluck, M.A., & Granger, R. (1995). Dissociation of hippocampal and entorhinal function in associative learning: A computational approach. *Psychobiology, 23(2),* 116-138.
O'Keefe, J., 7 Nadel, L. (1978). *The Hippocampus as a Cognitive Map.* Oxford: Clarendon University Press.
Parker, D. (1985). *Learning Logic.* Center for Computational Research in Economics and Management Science, MIT Press.
Penick, W., & Solomon, P. (1991). Hippocampus, context, and conditioning. *Behavioral Neuroscience, 105(5),* 611-617.
Port, R., & Patterson, M. (1984). Fimbrial lesions and sensory preconditioning. *Behavioral Neuroscience, 98,* 584-589.
Rescorla, R.A., & Holland P.C. (1977). Associations in Pavlovian conditioned inhibition. *Learning & Motivation, 8,* 429-447.
Rescorla, R.A., & Wagner, A. (1972). A theory of Pavlovian conditioning: Variations in the effectiveness of reinforcement and non-reinforcement. In A. Black & W. Prokasy (Eds.), *Classical Conditioning II:*

Current Research and Theory, (pp. 64-99). New York: Appleton-Century-Crofts.

Reilly, S., Harley, C., & Revusky, S. (1993). Ibotenate lesions of the hippocampus enhance latent inhibition in conditioned taste aversion and increase resistance to extinction in conditioned taste preference. *Behavioral Neuroscience, 107(6),* 996-1004.

Rudy, J., & Sutherland, R. (1989). The hippocampal formation is necessary for rats to learn and remember configural discriminations. *Behavioral Brain Research, 34,* 97-109.

Rumelhart, D., Hinton, G., & Williams, R. (1986). Learning internal representations by error propagation. In D. Rumelhart & J. McClelland (Eds.), *Parallel Distributed Processing: Explorations in the Microstructure Cognition,* (pp. 318-362). Cambridge, MA: MIT Press.

Salafia, W.R., Romano, A.G., Tynan, T., & Host, K.C. (1977). Disruption of rabbit (*oryctolagus cuniculus*) nictitating membrane conditioning by post trial electrical stimulation of hippocampus. *Physiology & Behavior, 18,* 207-212.

Salafia, W.R., Chiaia, N.L., & Ramirez, J.J. (1979). Retardation of rabbit nictitating membrane conditioning by subseizure electrical simulation of hippocampus. *Physiology & Behavior, 22,* 451-455.

Schmaltz, L.W., & Theios, J. (1972). Acquisition and extinction of a classically conditioned response in hippocampectomized rabbits (*oryctolagus cuniculus*). *Journal of Comparative and Physiological Psychology, 79(2),* 328-333.

Schousboe, A., Bachevalier, J., Braak, H., Heinemann, U., Nitsch, R., Schroder, H., & Wetmore, C. (1993). Structural correlates and cellular mechanisms in entorhinal-hippocampal dysfunction. *Hippocampus, 3,* 293-302.

Sears, L.L., & Steinmetz, J.E. (1991). Dorsal accessory inferior olive activity diminishes during acquisition of the rabbit classically conditioned eyelid response. *Brain Research, 545,* 144-122.

Solomon, P. (1977). Role of the hippocampus in blocking and conditioned inhibition of the rabbit's nictitating membrane. *Journal of Comparative and Physiological Psychology, 91(2),* 407-417.

Solomon, P., & Moore, J.W. (1975). Latent inhibition and stimulus generalization of the classically conditioned nictitating membrane response in rabbits *(oryctolagus cuniculus)* following dorsal hippocampal ablation. *Journal of comparative and Physiological Psychology, 89,* 1192-1203.

Solomon, P., & Gottfried, K. (1981). The septohippocampal cholinergic system and classical conditioning of the rabbit's nictitating membrane response. *Journal of Comparative and Physiological Psychology, 95(2), 322-330.*

Solomon, P., Solomon, S., Van der Schaaf, E., & Perry, H. (1983). Altered activity in the hippocampus is more detrimental to classical conditioning than removing the structure. *Science, 220,* 329-331.

Steinmetz, J.E., & Sengelaub, D.R. (1992). Possible conditioned stimulus pathway for classical eyelid conditioning in rabbits: I. Anatomical evidence for direct projections from the pontine nuclei to the cerebellar interpositus nucleus. *Behavioral & Neural Biology, 57,* 103-115.

Thompson, R.F. (1972). Sensory preconditioning. In R. Thompson & J. Voss (Eds.), *Topics in Learning and Performance,* (pp. 105-129). New York: Academic Press.

Thompson, R.F. (1986). The neurobiology of learning and memory. *Science, 233,* 941-947.

van Hoesen, G., & Pandya, D. (1975). Some connections of the entorhinal (area 28) and perirhinal (area 35) cortices of the rhesus monkey. I. Temporal lobe afferents. *Brain Research, 95,* 1-24.

von der Malsburg, C. (1973). Self-organizating of orientation sensitive cells in the striate cortex. *Kybernetik, 14,* 85-100.

Walkenbach, J., Haddad, N.F. (1980). The Rescorla-Wagner theory of conditioning. A review of the literature. *Psychological Record, 30,* 497-509.

Werbos, P. (1974). *Beyond Regression: New Tools for Prediction and Analysis in the Behavioral Science.* Unpublished Ph.D. dissertation: Harvard University.

Widrow, B., & Hoff, M. (1960). Adaptive switching circuits. *Institute of Radio Engineers, Western Electronic Show and Convention Record, 4,* 96-104.

Zackheim, J., Myers, C.E., Gluck, M.A. (1998). A temporally sensitive recurrent network model of occasion setting. In N.A. Schmajuk & P.C. Holland (Eds.), *Occasion Setting: Associative Learning and Cognition in Animals,* (pp. 319-342). Washington, D.C.: American Psychological Association.

11 CLASSICAL CONDITIONING OF AUTONOMIC AND SOMATOMOTOR RESPONSES AND THEIR CENTRAL NERVOUS SYSTEM SUBSTRATES

Donald A. Powell
Dorn VA Medical Center
University of South Carolina
University of South Carolina School of Medicine

Joselyn McLaughlin
Dorn VA Medical Center
University of South Carolina

Mark Chachich
Dorn VA Medical Center

INTRODUCTION

The present chapter addresses issues related to similarities and differences in somatomotor and autonomic classical conditioning, and their underlying neural substrates. Differences in acquisition of these two sets of responses are first discussed. A behavioral stages model of classical conditioning is then described within the context of neural systems that support the early stages of the model, in which autonomic responses are learned and later stages in which somatomotor responses are learned. Although early research first suggested that corticolimbic and extrapyramidal structures provided separate and independent substrates for autonomic, and somatomotor conditioning, respectively, it is now clear that many kinds of conditioning depend on interactions between these two sets of structures. Evidence for the latter conclusion is extensively described, followed by a brief summary indicating directions for future research.

DIFFERENCES IN SOMATOMOTOR AND AUTONOMIC CONDITIONING

We have previously emphasized that the parametric features of Pavlovian conditioned somatomotor responses (e.g., eyeblink or leg flexion conditioned responses), and the concomitantly occurring non-specific visceral responses (e.g., heart rate or skin conductance changes) are very different (e.g., see Powell & Levine-Bryce, 1988). For example, the temporal parameters that are optimal for eyeblink (EB) and heart rate (HR) conditioning may be quite dissimilar (Powell, Lipkin & Milligan, 1974; Schneiderman, 1972). Autonomic conditioned responses (CRs) are typically greatest in magnitude when the interval between the onset of the conditioned and unconditioned stimuli (viz., the interstimulus interval; ISI) is fairly long; e.g., 4-8 sec (Powell & Kazis, 1976). However, little or no EB conditioning occurs at these relatively long ISIs. Rather the ISI that produces the most rapid EB or nictitating membrane (NM) conditioning is 500 msec or less (Schneiderman & Gormezano, 1964; Gormezano, 1972). A second striking difference between learned EB and HR responses is that the latter are acquired within just a few trials (e.g., 10 or less), whereas many trials (up to 100) may be required before the first EB CR occurs (e.g., Powell & Levine-Bryce, 1988); (however, see Lennartz & Weinberger, 1992, 1994; Kehoe & McCrae, 1994 for a discussion of this issue when extremely long inter-session intervals are employed).

Learned autonomic changes have been referred to as nonspecific responses, since they occur regardless of the nature of the conditioning contingencies (e.g., Powell, Buchanan & Gibbs, 1990; Prokasy, 1984; Weinberger & Diamond, 1987). Thus signaled electric shock unconditioned stimuli (USs), delivered to either the orbital region or the foot pad of animals, results in a host of such nonspecific CRs to the signal that are quite similar regardless of the site of application of the US. The learned somatomotor response in each case, however, is specific to the US, consisting of an EB CR in the former case and a leg flexion CR in the latter case. Consequently, such responses are usually referred to as specific conditioned responses.

Figure 1 illustrates the dramatic differences observed in these two response systems in rabbits exposed to classical conditioning contingencies. It depicts the results of an experiment in which a 1216 Hz, 1 sec, 75 db tone was employed as the conditioned stimulus (CS) and a 250 msec, 3 Ma, AC periorbital electric shock train was the US. The top panel of Figure 1 shows percent EB CRs over five acquisition sessions consisting of 60 CS/US presentations each (conditioning group). A nonassociative control group received a random sequence of unpaired CS/US presentations (explicitly unpaired CS/US group). EB CRs increased from a low near-zero rate during session 1 to approximately 80% by session 5 in the conditioning group; the explicitly unpaired group showed virtually no EB responses.

The bottom panel of Figure 1 shows mean change in duration from pre-CS baseline of the third interbeat interval of the electrocardiogram following tone onset, as a function of acquisition sessions in the same two groups of animals. The third interbeat interval was chosen because it was the last one that was available for analysis in all animals before CS offset and the occurrence of the US. This interbeat interval usually represents the largest change from pre-CS baseline (Powell & Levine-Bryce, 1988). The duration of this interbeat interval, referred to as heart period, is the reciprocal of

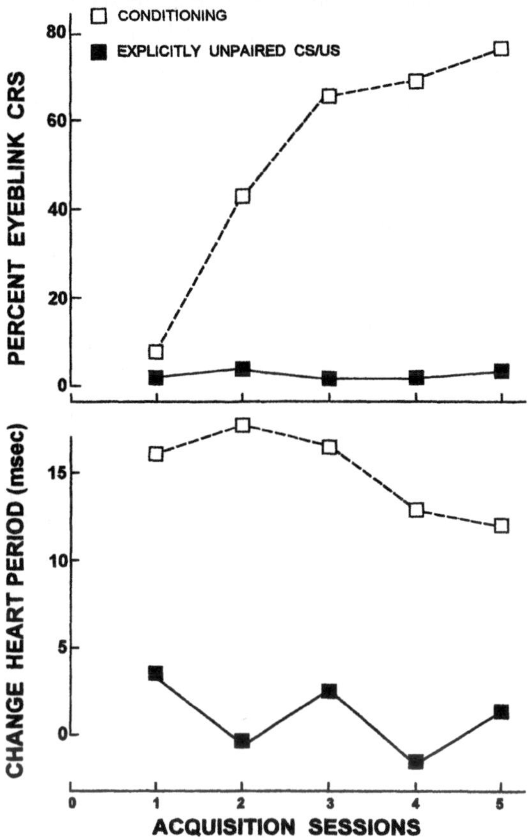

Figure 1 (Top): Conditioned eyeblink responses of rabbits that received CS/US presentations (conditioning group) and rabbits that received explicitly unpaired CS/US presentations (explicitly unpaired group) as a function of five 60-trial conditioning sessions. The CS was a 1 sec, 75 db, 1216 Hz tone that was followed by 250 msec, 3 mA periorbital shock train. **(Bottom)**: Mean change in heart period from pre-CS baseline of the third post-CS interbeat interval of the same rabbits that received conditioning or explicitly unpaired CS/US presentations. The third interbeat interval is shown because it was the last one available for analysis in all animals prior to CS termination and thus is usually associated with the largest heart period change from pre-CS baseline. (From Powell et al., 1990).

HR; as can be seen, it was lengthened by 10-15 msec as a result of training. Thus, HR CRs consisted of decelerations from pre-CS baseline. However, the heart period changes evoked by the tone in the unpaired group were much smaller and more variable, suggesting that the tone-evoked HR decelerations in the paired group were associative. Note, however, that no acquisition function is apparent in the conditioning group, as was the case for the EB data above. The reason for this can be seen in Figure 2. This figure shows mean change in the third interbeat interval over blocks of 2 trials each during the initial session. In Figure 2, the acquisition function for heart period is clearly apparent. Change in heart period decreased in both groups across the first 3 to 5 trials, representing habituation of the decelerative cardiac component of the orienting reflex. The orienting reflex is the initial response to novel stimulation and normally also consists of bradycardia (Powell & Kazis, 1976). After habituation of the orienting reflex, the conditioning group demonstrated a second bradycardiac response of greater than 10-15 msec, whereas the unpaired group continued to show small and variable responses of 1-5 msec. Thus, the decelerative HR CR appeared by trial 5 and had reached its maximum magnitude by trial 10, well before EB CRs began to occur in any animal.

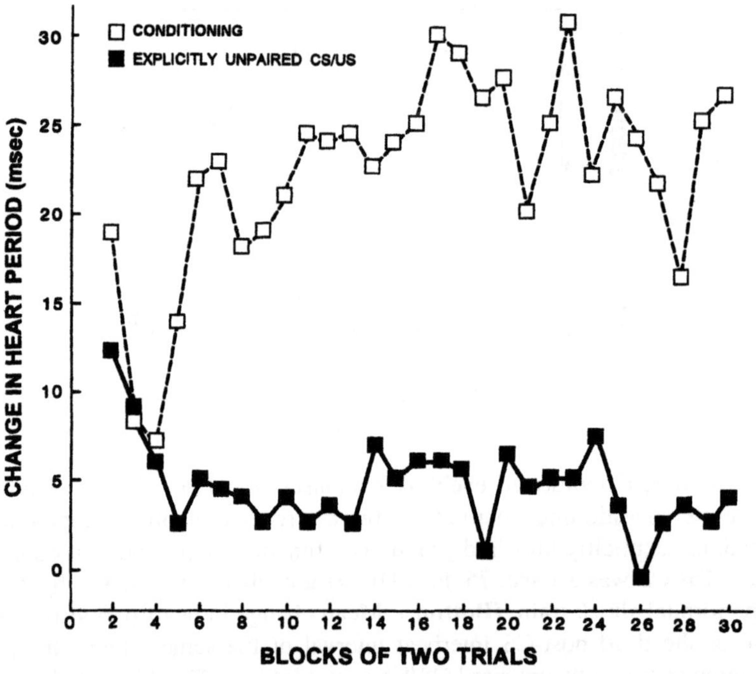

Figure 2: Change from pre-CS baseline in heart period of third interbeat interval of rabbits that received Pavlovian eyeblink conditioning as indicated in Figure 1. The data are again shown for conditioning and explicitly unpaired CS/US groups but are shown as function of blocks of two trials each only during the first session of training.

Plotting the HR change associated with the largest post-CS interbeat interval may, however, mask important temporal changes in the pattern of the HR CR. Thus, when beat x beat changes in CS-evoked HR change are plotted as a function of CS duration, a characteristic pattern of changes are observed. This pattern is shown in Figure 3, which shows the HR change from pre-CS baseline, averaged over trials, as a function of post-CS interbeat intervals of a group of eight rabbits that received differential HR conditioning using a more optimal 4 sec ISI (see Buchanan & Powell, 1989). There is an initial abrupt, but relatively small, HR deceleration during the first, second, and sometimes third interbeat interval. This HR deceleration becomes somewhat larger during subsequent interbeat intervals, however, increasing almost monotonically and reaching a maximum at tone termination when the US would be expected to occur. This regular pattern of the autonomic CR also occurs during human HR and skin conductance conditioning (Ohman, 1988) and has been recognized for some time. The initial small and short-duration component has been referred to as the "registration" or "orienting" component of the CR and the later-occurring and larger magnitude

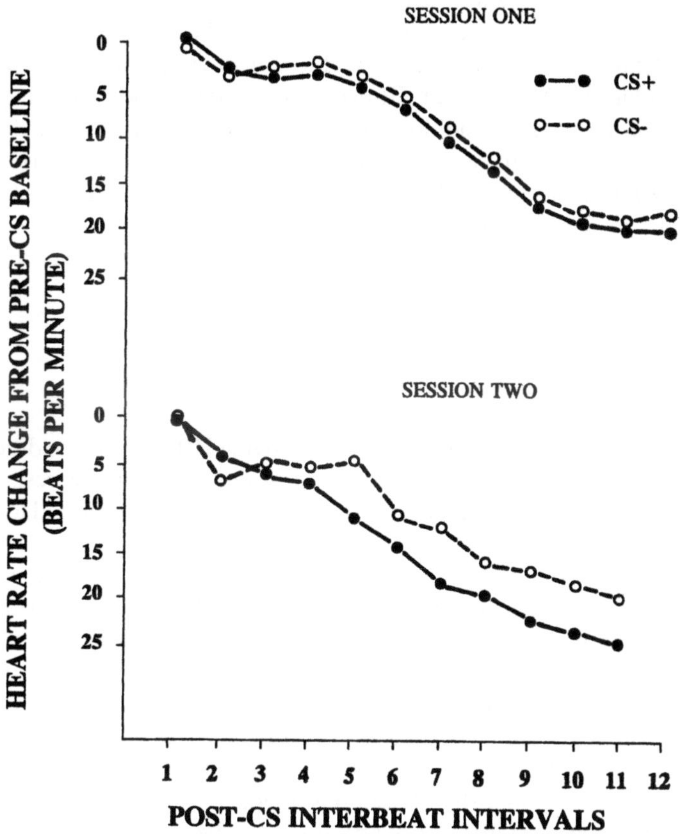

Figure 3: Heart rate change from pre-CS baseline in a group of 8 rabbits that received two sessions of differential conditioning in which either a 1216 Hz or 404 Hz, 75 db, 4.0 sec tone served as either CS+ or CS-. The data are shown in beats per minute, as a function of 12 interbeat intervals after the onset of the CS. (Adapted from Buchanan & Powell, 1989)

response has been referred to as the "contingency" component (Maxwell, Powell & Buchanan, 1994).

This characteristic shape of the HR CR not only has functional implications for the role of conditioned bradycardia with regard to behavior in general but also may be important for understanding the central nervous system (CNS) control of learned autonomic adjustments. For example, separate groups of neurons in the prefrontal cortex show differential CS-evoked changes during the contingency and registration components of the heart rate CR (Maxwell et al, 1994). A similar classification of neurons was also recently discovered in the mediodorsal nucleus of the thalamus, which is the thalamic projection nucleus to the prefrontal cortex (Chachich, Buchanan & Powell, 1997). These conditioned bradycardiac changes have also been shown to occur in a wide variety of Pavlovian conditioning situations, including the use of both visual and tactile CSs and in which either an air puff or sweetened water was used as the US (Powell, Gibbs, Maxwell & Levine-Bryce, 1993). The former of course also elicits EB CRs, but the latter is an appetitive CS and evokes jaw movements as skeletal CRs. Leg flexion conditioning in the rabbit is also accompanied by bradycardia (Powell & Lipkin, 1975). Learned HR decelerations thus appear to be a generalized phenonmena of Pavlovian conditioning, regardless of the type of somatomotor CR elicited. There is also some evidence that interference with the occurrence of this decelerative HR CR may adversely affect acquisition of specific EB CRs (Albiniak & Powell, 1980; Joseph & Powell, 1980; Kazis, Milligan & Powell, 1973; Powell, 1979). Further implications regarding possible relationships between specific and non-specific responses are discussed below.

THEORETICAL IMPLICATIONS

The above-described results suggest that if Pavlovian HR and EB conditioning both represent valid animal models of associative learning they must represent different aspects of learning, since the parametric features of the stimuli required to elicit them and their rate of acquisition are different. Single process models of learning and memory thus may be inadequate to explain even simple associative learning phenomena, such as classical conditioning. This point has also been made by others (e.g., Lennartz & Weinberger, 1992). It is well accepted that different aspects of learning and memory are related to the underlying demands of the task and the type of cognitive resources required (Kilstrom, 1987; Olton, 1979; Schacter, 1992; Squire, 1992; 1994; Tulving, 1985). These theoretical approaches to learning and memory have resulted in a typology of memory in which different kinds of learning and memory are used to accomplish different sets of goals. These models of learning and memory thus assume that different kinds of knowledge exist and therefore separate cognitive systems have evolved to deal with these different kinds of knowledge, and moreover that different CNS substrates underlie the acquisition, storage and retrieval of these different kinds of knowledge (Squire, 1992).

Although memory systems have been characterized in a variety of ways by different theorists, considerable data support a model that includes at least two separate kinds of cognitive functioning. Squire (1992) has characterized these two kinds of processing as declarative versus non-declarative. Declarative processing refers to information that is consciously retrieved and in many cases has been associated with a specific prior event (e.g., episode). This kind of learning thus refers to acquisition of facts regarding objects and relationships in one's environment as well as memory of the specific episodes during which these events occurred. By contrast, non-declarative memory involves acquisition of a) habits and skills, b) priming effects, c) learning of dispositions (including classical and operant conditioning), and d) non-associative effects such as habituation and sensitization (see Squire, 1992). Such learning may not necessarily occur at a conscious level and thus may not be associated with specific episodes in the past. As noted, others have characterized similar but not identical learning and memory systems (see above).

We believe that the separate acquisition functions and different stimulus parameters required for acquisition of the EB CR and other specific responses, such as the leg flexion or jaw movement responses and non-specific visceral responses, such as the HR or skin conductance CRs, also tap different processes and therefore are dependent upon different CNS substrates. A five stage empirical model of somatomotor classical conditioning, depicted in Figure 4, reflects this fact. It indicates a) the hypothetical constructs, b) behavioral correlates, and c) possible neuroanatomical structures associated with each stage. The five behavioral stages represented in this model are meant to describe the sequential events that take place when any mammalian organism is exposed to signals (i.e., CSs) that predict significant events (USs). However, the fact that the behavioral components of this model occur sequentially does not of course mean that the brain mechanisms/changes underlying these various behaviors also occur in a sequential fashion. Indeed, it is highly likely that, depending on the type of paradigm being studied, parallel processing in different brain structures occurs simultaneously. Thus the major point such a model is designed to make is that association-formation, as a result of exposure to classical conditioning contingencies, produces multiple memory traces involving both excitatory and inhibitory processes even at its simpliest level. Such an analysis thus implies that multiple brain structures must be involved. It is now clear that this is the case, as described in more detail below. The brain structures listed in Figure 4, associated with these different stages of learning during classical conditioning, have varying degrees of experimental support, based on current evidence, as is also discussed in more detail below.

A BEHAVIORAL STAGES MODEL OF CLASSICAL CONDITIONING

First, however, a general description of this model is in order. The first stage shown in Figure 4 represents an "attention" and/or "arousal" stage that involves the response to novel stimulation and is associated with the "orienting reflex", alluded to above. Although there may be little skeletal behavior associated with the OR, novel stimuli elicit a well-studied complex of autonomic changes (Sokolov, 1963). If the eliciting stimulus is not paired with a reinforcer (i.e., a US), the orienting reflex habituates. However, pairing of CS and US elicits behaviors associated with the next stage, which is the first step in the development of associative learning. This stage involves the formation of a "significance code" (a term first used by Gabriel, Foster, Orona,

Saltwick & Stanton, 1980), indicating that the CS has become important, because it reliably predicts the US. This significance code is defined as the neuronal representation of stimulus events, their interrelationships and consequences (Gabriel et al, 1980). The development of a central significance code is associated with the appearance of nonspecific autonomic CRs, mediated by corticolimbic structures, as discussed in more detail below.

If appropriate conditioning parameters are employed, a third stage, consisting of the first specific somatomotor CR eventually occurs. This stage represents the initial stage of somatomotor learning (viz. EB, NM, leg flexion, or jaw movement conditioning) and is represented by "heterosynaptic reflex facilitation", which it is suggested involves the basal ganglia for specific skeletal CRs. This occurs in parallel with the development of the significance code. However, as noted, depending on the conditioning parameters, it develops more slowly (or perhaps not at all with relatively long ISIs) and in general ends with the occurrence of the first somatomotor CR. As discussed below, there is considerable evidence suggesting the involvement of the basal ganglia in reflex facilitation.

As conditioning proceeds, a fourth relegation process (again a term first employed by Gabriel et al, 1980), then reassigns the neuronal code representing the somatomotor CR from the basal ganglia to areas which translate and/or store it into a fast motor program in the cerebellum, as evidenced by achievement of asymptotic performance. Also at stage 4, a link or links is/are established to interface the neuronal area mediating the significance code in limbic structures with the fast motor program storage area in the cerebellum, allowing the former to release and execute the motor program. Once the relegation process is complete, integrity of the basal ganglia is no longer necessary for the performance of somatomotor CRs and neither is the limbic system substrate. Again, as discussed below, considerable evidence suggests that the cerebellum is a necessary CNS site for acquisition and performance of somatomotor CRs. This generalization may, however, be limited either to defensive or simple reflexes, such as the EB or NM CR, since preliminary evidence suggests that jaw movement conditioning is unaffected by cerebellar manipulations that affect EB or NM conditioning (Gibbs, 1992).

Stage five, which probably starts from the beginning of conditioning, but is slower to complete than previous stages, involves substantia nigra-modulated caudate inhibition of ascending arousal systems, thereby inhibiting competing responses to similar but nonrelevant cues. The behavioral event corresponding to this stage of learning is the reliable occurrence of conditioned somatomotor responses and a somatomotor discrimination between reinforced (CS+) and non-reinforced (CS-) stimuli in differential conditioning. Thalamo-limbic-striatal interactions appear to be critical to this stage. In summary, when Pavlovian conditioning is conceived as such a multi-stage process it can be viewed as representative of associative learning in general. It thus takes on the character of more complex learning phenomena, which require multiple brain structures and mechanisms. As described below, there is considerable evidence supporting this proposition.

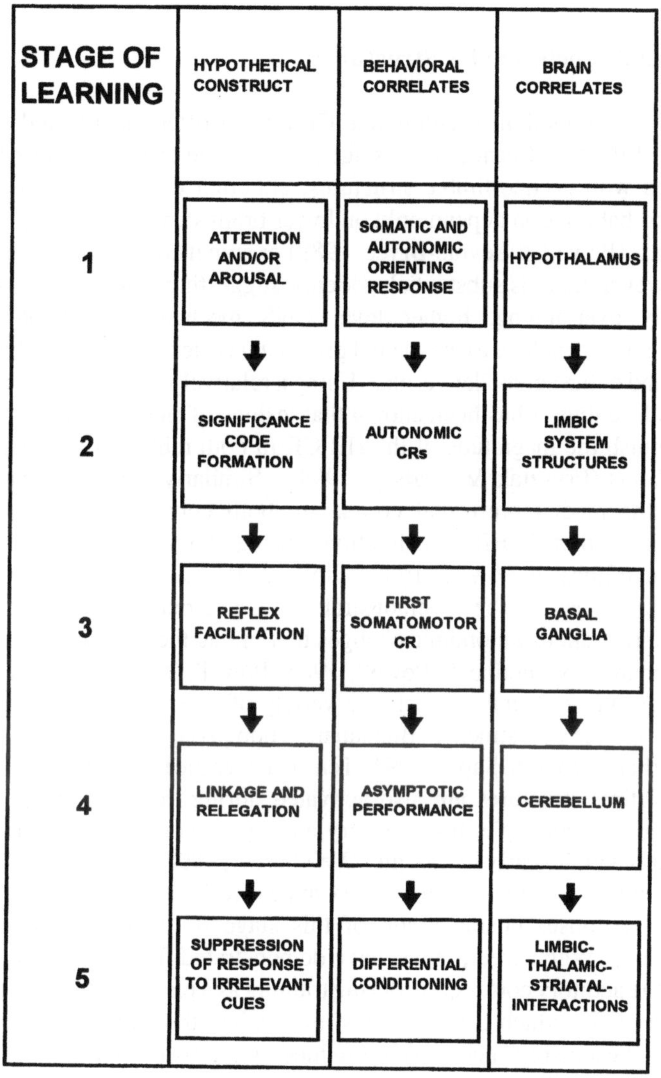

Figure 4: Diagram of a 5-stage model of classical conditioning, showing the hypothetical constructs, behavioral indices, and postulated neuroanatomical structures/mechanisms involved in each stage. The degree of experimental support for the latter varies depending upon the stage involved, but substantial evidence exists implicating the indicated structures in the behaviors listed in each case. Although the model suggests sequential processing in a step wise order, as noted in the text, some types of processing are almost certainly simultaneous and take place in a parallel distributed fashion.

CNS STRUCTURES MEDIATING DIFFERENT STAGES OF CLASSICAL CONDITIONING

Stages 1 and 2: Corticolimbic Structures

It is clear that acquisition of autonomic CRs, most often used to index the initial acquisition of the significance code (stage two) and the orienting reflex (stage one), is associated with cortico-limbic structures, although there is some evidence that orienting and habituation depend only on lower brain stem structures, perhaps in the hypothalamus (Powell & Levine-Bryce, 1989) or spinal cord (Thompson & Spencer, 1966). However, there is substantial evidence suggesting that at least three separate, but partially overlapping, higher level CNS mechanisms mediate autonomic conditioning; these include a) the medial prefrontal cortex, b) several subnuclei of the amygdala, and c) the cerebellar vermis. Using a relatively long, and thus optimum ISI for HR conditioning, it has been shown that lesions of the medial prefrontal cortex greatly diminish the magnitude of the HR CR in both rabbits (Buchanan & Powell, 1982a) and rats (Frysztak & Neafsey, 1994). Similarly, multiple- and single-unit activity in the medial prefrontal cortex are both correlated with acquisition of Pavlovian conditioned HR decelerations using optimum ISIs for autonomic conditioning (Gibbs & Powell, 1988; Gibbs & Powell, 1991; Gibbs, Prescott & Powell, 1992). It has also been demonstrated that electrical stimulation of the medial prefrontal cortex elicits autonomic changes that mimic the CR (Buchanan & Powell, 1982a; Buchanan, Valentine & Powell, 1985; Powell, Watson & Maxwell, 1994); finally, prefrontal efferents project to a variety of subcortical structures known to mediate autonomic adjustments (Buchanan, Thompson, Maxwell & Powell, 1994; Hurley, Herbert, Moga & Saper, 1991; Terreberry & Neafsey, 1983).

Other cortical structures are also activated during the early stages of classical conditioning. For example, both sensory and motor cortex show increases in CS-evoked neural activity early in training (Weinberger, 1998; Woody, 1988). However, neither primary sensory nor motor cortex appear to be necessary for acquisition of nonspecific responses characteristic of this stage of learning. Weinberger and colleagues (e.g., Weinberger, 1998) have demonstrated frequency-specific firing of neurons in the auditory cortex early during training as a result of classical conditioning with auditory CSs, which can be evoked even when the animals are under general anesthesia. Presumably such learning-induced patterns of neuronal firing occur in other cortical areas (Edeline, 1999), depending on the nature of the CS (i.e., visual, tactile, etc.), and are available to guide more complex behavioral changes in response to such stimulation, as Weinberger (1998) suggests. However, as noted, such cortical processing is not necessary for learning the more generalized autonomic response to such stimuli.

There is little doubt, however, that limbic structures are intimately involved in stage 2 processing. For example, it has been widely reported that various nuclei in the amygdala participate in Pavlovian cardiovascular conditioning. Kapp and colleagues (Kapp, Frysinger, Gallagher & Haselton, 1979) have shown that lesions of the amygdala central nucleus greatly attenuate conditioned HR decelerations in the rabbit and that multiple- and single-unit activity in the central nucleus is associated with the acquisition of conditioned HR responses (Applegate, Frysinger, Kapp & Gallagher, 1982; Pascoe & Kapp, 1985). As with the medial prefrontal cortex, electrical stimulation of the central nucleus elicits responses that mimic the CR (Applegate, Kapp, Underwood & McNall, 1983), and efferents from this nucleus also project to autonomic brain stem regulatory nuclei (Schwaber, Kapp, Higgins & Rapp, 1992). LeDoux and colleagues have similarly shown that classically conditioned increases in blood pressure and HR in the rat are associated with medial geniculate input to the lateral nucleus of the amygdala, which provides second-order neurons to the basolateral and central nucleus (LeDoux, 1994). Damage to this circuit abolishes conditioned HR and blood pressure changes (LeDoux Sakaguchi, Iwata & Reis, 1986) and neuronal activity in the lateral nucleus is associated with the occurrence of these HR and blood pressure CRs (Clugnet, LeDoux & Morrison, 1990). McCabe and colleagues have shown that this circuit is also intimately involved in conditioned HR decelerations in the rabbit (McCabe, McEchron, Green & Schneiderman, 1993), and Davis (1992) has demonstrated the participation of the central nucleus and interconnected structures with conditioned enhancement of the startle reflex (viz. "fear-potentiated startle").

The cerebellar vermis has also long been known to participate in cardiovascular, as well as other kinds of autonomic control, as recently reviewed by Ghelarducci and Sebastiani (1996). Moreover, vermal lesions have been shown to impair HR conditioning in both rats (Sebastiani, La Noce, Paton & Ghelarducci, 1992; Supple & Leaton, 1990) and rabbits (Supple & Kapp, 1993). Vermal connections to hypothalamic and brainstem nuclei, e.g., parabrachial nuclei, provide possible anatomical substrates for these effects (Ghelarducci & Sebastiani, 1996), but their functional significance is unknown. Needless to say, the relationship of such cerebellar control of learned autonomic adjustments to similar control by the medial prefrontal cortex and amygdala is also not known at the present time.

Although control experiments in all these studies suggest that none of these areas is involved in unconditioned responding to either the CS or US (e.g., Buchanan & Powell, 1982a; Kapp et al, 1979; Supple & Kapp, 1993), a recent study reported substantial decrements in the cardiac orienting reflex on the first trial of conditioning in rats with amygdala central nucleus lesions (Young & Leaton, 1996). Several earlier studies on primates also found impairments in the orienting reflex as a result of temporal lobe lesions that involved the amygdala (e.g., Bagshaw, Kimble & Pribram, 1965; Pribram, Reitz, McNeil & Spevack, 1979). These findings thus suggest the possibility that the amygdala also participates in the first stage of learning shown in Figure 4, i.e., the occurrence of the orienting reflex. However, the reasons for the differences between these studies and later studies on rabbits and rats (e.g., Kapp et al, 1979; Supple & Leaton, 1990) will have to be worked out before this conclusion can be firmly drawn. These problems are discussed in more detail in a recent paper (Powell et al, 1997).

Considerable evidence also suggests that the hippocampus is intimately involved in the stimulus processing associated with orienting and habituation, as well as classical conditioning of autonomic responses (Buchanan & Powell, 1980; Crowne & Riddell, 1969). Buchanan and Powell (1980) found that hippocampal lesions greatly attenuated the HR decelerations that accompany EB conditioning, but damage to the overlying neocortex, also damaged in the hippocampal lesioned group, attenuated the HR CR in a separate cortical control group as well. These findings were replicated in a second experiment in which a longer more optimal ISI for autonomic conditioning was employed (Buchanan & Powell, 1982b), but not in a third experiment in which the midline neocortex was left intact (Powell & Buchanan, 1980). In the latter experiment, the HR CR was actually enhanced in the hippocampal lesion group compared to cortical control and sham lesioned animals. However, in this experiment damage was primarily focused on the dorsal hippocampus whereas substantial damage occurred in the ventral as well as the dorsal hippocampus in the two earlier experiments. Nevertheless, since midline damage occurred in these two experiments, including substantial portions of the medial prefrontal cortex, this is most probably the explanation of the attenuated HR CR in the cortical control animals in these experiments.

However, more recent experiments provide convincing evidence that the ventral hippocampus and more specifically its subicular efferents participate in autonomic conditioning. It is known that hippocampal CA1 and subicular cells provide efferents to the medial prefrontal cortex (Cavada, Llamas, Reinoso-Suarez, 1983; Ferino, Thierry & Glowinski, 1987; Goldman-Rakic, Selemon & Schwartz, 1984; Swanson, 1981). Moreover, Ruit and Neafsey (1988) found that damage to the medial prefrontal cortex in the rat prevented cardiovascular changes elicited by hippocampal stimulation from occurring. In unlesioned animals hippocampal-evoked autonomic changes were readily elicited; as noted above, such changes can also be elicited in a variety of species by medial prefrontal stimulation (Kaada, 1951; Lofving, 1961; Powell et al, 1994). The data of Ruit and Neafsey (1988) thus suggest that these autonomic effects evoked by stimulation of the medial prefrontal cortex are due to hippocampal input to the prefrontal region. Moreover, it was recently demonstrated that damage limited to the post-subicular region of the hippocampal complex in the rabbit, which contains efferent neurons to the medial prefrontal cortex in this species, dramatically attenuated the HR CR compared to cortical control and sham lesioned animals (Chachich, Penney & Powell, 1996). These more recent experiments, taken as a whole, thus suggest that autonomic plasticity in the medial prefrontal region may be due to its hippocampal input, although clearly more work is needed to definitively draw this conclusion. At the very least, however, these findings suggest that the hippocampus participates in a limbic system circuit that mediates orienting and non-specific classical conditioning, as represented by stages one and two in the model described in Figure 4.

A separate set of studies (e.g., Kim & Fanselow, 1992; Phillips & LeDoux, 1992), suggests that conditioned freezing in rats, induced by contextual cues, is abolished by hippocampal lesions, but freezing induced by the original CS in a novel environment is not. These data are obviously at variance with the data described above with regard to HR conditioning in rabbits. Freezing is another measure of stage 2 conditioning, which is often used in rats, but it may be affected differently by hippocampal manipulations than autonomic measures assessed during this stage of training. Obviously more data are required to verify this hypothesis, but again these studies clearly suggest the participation of the hippocampus in a limbic circuit that underlies stages one and two of the model described in Figure 4.

Stages 3 and 4: Extrapyramidal Structures

Although it is clear that corticolimbic and vermal structures are intimately involved in the early stages of classical conditioning represented in Figure 4 by stages one and two, it has now become equally clear that the later stages of conditioning, during which specific somatomotor responses are acquired, involve extrapyramidal structures. The first experiments compatible with this conclusion showed that damage to the neostriatum in rabbits had a profound effect on acquisition of classically conditioned EB responses, but had no effect on the concomitantly occurring HR CR (Powell, Mankowski & Buchanan, 1978). Later experiments determined that damage to the substantia nigra, which provides the dopamine input to the neostriatum, also impaired acquisition of the EB response, without impairing HR conditioning (Kao & Powell, 1986; Kao & Powell, 1988). These findings are thus compatible with the association of the neostriatum with acquisition of somatomotor CRs, as indicated in stage three of Figure 4. Also compatible with this hypothesis is the finding that neural activity in the neostriatum is correlated with various stages of EB classical conditioning (White et al, 1994).

Somatomotor classical conditioning represents a type of learning variously referred to as stimulus-response learning, habit learning, etc., since it occurs in a slow incremental manner, such as would be expected from a reinforced stimulus-response association (Mishkin, Malamut & Bachevalier, 1984). Such associations involve not only those occurring during classical conditioning but operant conditioning as well. A host of studies suggest that the basal ganglia, including the caudate nucleus, globus pallidus, and nucleus accumbens, may be involved in this type of learning. For example, recent studies in primates have shown important relationships between single unit activity in the caudate nucleus and stimulus-reward learning (e.g., Aosaki, Graybiel & Kimura, 1994; Aosaki, Kimura, & Graybiel, 1995; Schultz, 1994). These studies suggest a tonically active set of neurons, which are presumed to reflect background stimulation, and which are subserved by input from corticolimbic systems. This extrapyramidal system is then modulated by dopaminergic neurons from the substantia nigra, which are presumed to act as reinforcers promoting the consolidation of new behaviors, whether these behaviors are due to classical or operant conditioning contingencies. Interestingly, these studies suggest that such reinforcement is related to ongoing "behavioral plans" rather than specific somatomotor responses. These studies, as well as others indicating the involvement of the neostriatum in associative learning, have been recently reviewed, for example, by White (1997) and Houk and Wise (1995).

Other extrapyramidal structures are also implicated in classical EB conditioning. For example, there is strong evidence that cerebellar structures are intimately involved in both the acquisition and expression of classically conditioned somatomotor behaviors. For example, acquisition of simple EB and leg flexion conditioning is dependent on the deep nuclei of the cerebellum, especially the lateral interpositus nucleus (McCormick & Thompson, 1984), and to some extent the cerebellar cortex (Yeo, Hardiman & Glickstein, 1985). Although the direct participation of the latter in mediation of the classically conditioned EB response has been questioned (Lavond & Steinmetz, 1989; Woodruff-Pak, Lavond, Logan, Steinmetz & Thompson, 1993), there is some indication that the cerebellar cortex may be involved in the specific timing of the response, but is not necessary for acquisition or execution of the learned response per se (Raymond, Lisberger & Mauk, 1996). Like neostriatal lesions, damage to these cerebellar structures does not affect concomitantly conditioned cardiac responses (Lavond, Lincoln, McCormick & Thompson, 1984). It should also be stressed that cerebellar damage completely prevents EB CR acquisition; i.e., after lesions to the lateral interpositus nucleus learning does not occur in the ipsilateral eye regardless of subsequent training (McCormick & Thompson, 1984). Moreover, there is substantial evidence, as recently reviewed (e.g., Lavond, Kim and Thompson, 1993; Thompson, Thompson, Kim, Krupa & Shinkman, 1998; Steinmetz, 1998), indicating that under optimal parametric conditions cerebellar processing is sufficient for acquisition and expression of the EB CR. Although CS processing by other brain structures (e.g., basal ganglia, corticolimbic structures, etc.) obviously also occurs under these conditions, such processing is not necessary for EB CR acquisition. However, such processing does play a role in other aspects of classical conditioning as discussed below. In any case, there are substantial data indicating that cerebellar structures are necessary for the acquisition and expression of classically conditioned somatomotor responses, as indicated in stage four of the model described in Figure 4.

Interactions Between Corticolimbic and Extrapyramidal Structures

At first glance, then, it appears that there may be two separate and non-overlapping CNS substrates, which mediate, respectively, the early-occurring events associated with acquisition of the significance code (i.e., cortico-limbic and cerebellar vermal structures), and the later occurrence of the specific somatomotor response (i.e., extrapyramidal structures, including the basal ganglia and the deep nuclei of the cerebellum, as well as the cerebellar cortex). However, early on there were disconcerting bits of evidence suggesting that corticolimbic system structures might also participate in somatomotor conditioning. For example, hippocampal neuronal activity is highly correlated with the initial development of somatomotor CRs (Berger, Alger & Thompson, 1976), but it was originally reported that hippocampal lesions did not prevent or delay classical EB and NM conditioning (e.g., Powell & Buchanan, 1980; Solomon & Moore, 1975) and in fact may facilitate it (Schmaltz & Theios, 1972). Thus, while electrophysiological data suggested the participation of the hippocampus in EB and NM conditioning, the lesion data did not. More recent research has, however, resolved this enigma. While relatively large (almost complete) hippocampal lesions do not impair acquisition of simple delay classical EB conditioning, they do affect retention of the CR when the response is not over-learned (Akase, Alkon & Disterhoft, 1989).

Moreover, hippocampal lesions also impair acquisition of EB and NM conditioning when the temporal parameters are less than optimal for its occurrence, as in trace conditioning (Moyer, Deyo & Disterhoft, 1990; Port, Romano, Steinmetz & Mikhail, 1986; Solomon, Vander Schaaf, Thompson & Weisz, 1986). In the trace paradigm there is a brief "blank" period between the termination of the CS and the onset of the US. This procedure can be contrasted with the normal "delay" procedure, in which

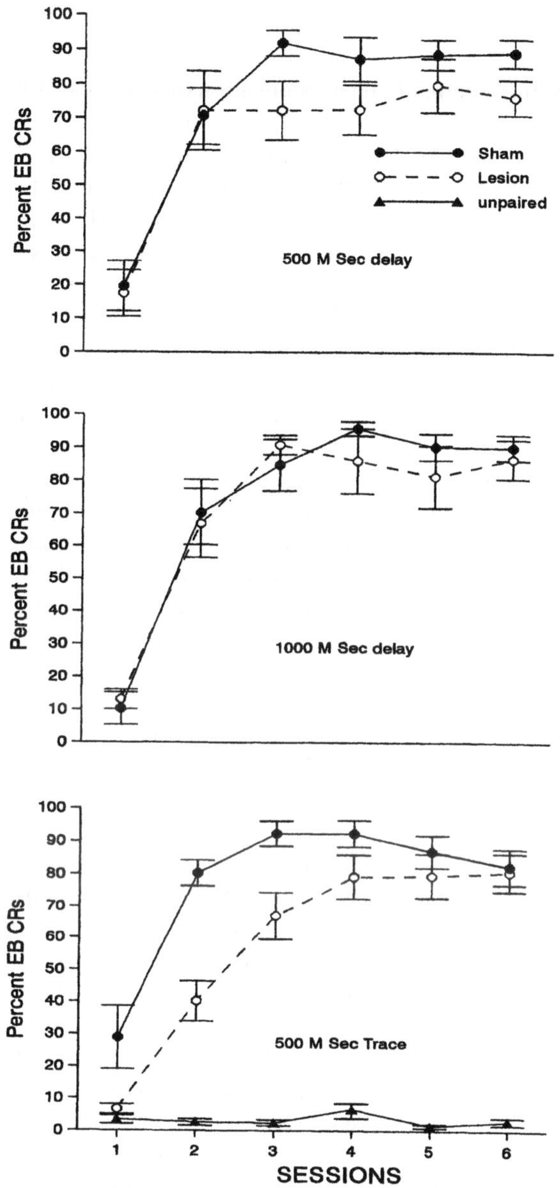

Figure 5: Percent (±SEM) eyeblink conditioned responses (EB CRs) of rabbits with lesions of the medial prefrontal cortex or sham lesions as a function of 6 sessions in which 60 CS/US presentations were presented. The top panel shows animals in which a 500 msec delay procedure was employed; the middle panel animals in which a 1000 msec delay procedure was employed; and the bottom panel animals in which a 500 msec CS was employed, but a 500 msec trace period occurred before the presentation of the periorbital shock US. Also shown in the bottom panel is a group of animals that received explicitly unpaired presentations of the CS and US.

the CS and US either overlap and co-terminate, or US onset occurs simultaneously with CS termination. Acquisition is normally slower using the trace paradigm, and hippocampal lesions differentially impair acquisition (Moyer et al, 1990; Solomon et al, 1990) or timing of the CR (Port et al, 1986), under these circumstances, but, as noted, have no effect on or may actually facilitate acquisition in the delay paradigm. It has also recently been shown that hippocampal lesions impair retention of the trace NM CR if the lesions are made 1 day after training, but not if the damage occurs 4 weeks later (Kim, Clark & Thompson, 1995). However, lesions at neither time affected retention of the delay NM CR.

We have also recently demonstrated that damage to the medial prefrontal cortex impairs trace conditioning in a fashion similar to that described above by hippocampal lesions. Data from an experiment illustrating this finding is shown in Figure 5. This figure shows percent EB CRs of rabbits that received either sham or medial prefrontal lesions during trace conditioning, in which a 1 sec ISI, but a 500 msec duration 75 db, 1000 Hz tone was employed as the CS, thus producing a 500 msec trace period. The top 2 panels of this figure represent similar animals with sham or medial prefrontal lesions that received either 500 msec or 1000 msec delay conditioning. As is illustrated, there is significant impairment of EB conditioning in the lesioned animals in the trace condition that does not occur in either the 500 or 1000 msec delay period conditions. This experiment thus suggests that the medial prefrontal cortex may play a critical role in a circuit involving the integration of information from other limbic structures with autonomic information necessary for producing adaptive behavior under less than optimal circumstances. These kinds of findings also suggest that although separate substrates mediate the autonomic and somatomotor components of associative learning, there are interactions between them, when conditions are not optimal for acquisition.

A recent study of EB conditioning in human subjects, reported by Clark & Squire (1998), dramatically reinforces this conclusion. In this study 4 human subjects with amnesia due to midline diencephalic (viz. hippocampal and/or thalamic) damage, were compared to normal controls on both delay and trace differential conditioning. The amnesic patients showed little evidence of EB conditioning on a trace task with a 250 msec CS and a 1000 msec trace period, but showed normal conditioning on a delay task with a 1250 msec ISI. Even more interesting, a post-experimental true-false test, designed to determine the extent of the subjects' "conscious awareness" of the experimental contingencies, showed that none of the 4 brain damaged subjects were "aware" of these contingencies. Moreover, several normal subjects also failed to show trace conditioning and were also "unaware" of the contingencies, whereas normal subjects that acquired the trace EB CR, were all able to verbalize the contingencies, based on the post-experimental test. Both "aware" and "non-aware" nor nal subjects, however, acquired the delay EB CR. These findings led the authors to conclude that perhaps EB trace conditioning should be classified as a declarative task, since it depends both on "conscious awareness" of the experimental contingencies and intact hippocampal functioning, whereas delay conditioning is non-declarative (viz. procedural), since it was normally acquired by all subjects whether "aware" or "unaware". More importantly it was normally acquired by the brain damaged subjects.

Similar findings in human subjects have been reported by others. For example, Daum and colleagues have shown that patients with temporal lobe lesions are impaired on a conditioned discrimination task in which a visual stimulus served as a signal for the occurrence of an auditory stimulus that signaled a corneal airpuff (Daum, Channon, Polkey & Gray, 1991), but showed normal acquisition, compared to non-brain damaged controls, on an EB simple discrimination task (Daum, Channon & Gray, 1992). Gabrieli et al (1995) also reported intact delay EB conditioning in amnesic patients, whereas this same group reported impaired trace EB conditioning in temporal lobe damaged amnesic patients (McGlinchey-Berrroth, Carrillo, Gabrieli, Brawn & Disterhoft, 1997). An earlier report by Weiskrantz & Warrington (1979) also reported normal delay EB conditioning in amnesic patients. Several reports, however, have indicated that human subjects with cerebellar damage fail to show normal delay EB conditioning (Daum et al, 1993; Lye, O'Boyle, Ramsden & Schady, 1988; Solomon, Stowe & Pendlebury, 1989; Topka, Valls-Sole, Massaquoi & Hallet, 1993; Woodruf-Pak, Papka, & Ivry, 1996.), reinforcing the conclusion based on animal studies, described above, that cerebellar structures are necessary for EB conditioning using the delay paradigm. Thus all human studies reported thus far support conclusions drawn from non-human animals; viz. that cortico-limbic damage has no effects on EB conditioning using optimal delay conditioning parameters, but severely impairs conditioning when these parameters are not optimal, as during a conditioned discrimination paradigm or during trace conditioning. On the other hand, cerebellar damage impairs both delay and trace conditioning, even under optimal circumstances. These findings thus clearly support the conclusion that simple delay conditioning comprises a non-declarative task, whereas other kinds of EB conditioning may be classified as declarative, based upon Squire's definition of these two types of learning and memory (Squire, 1992).

Stage 5: Further Interactions Between Corticolimbic and Extrapyramidal Structures

The fifth stage of learning, illustrated in Figure 4, is also affected by corticolimbic lesions. Discrimination between a reinforced CS+ and a non-reinforced CS- during acquisition of EB differential conditioning is minimally affected by hippocampal damage, as noted above. However, reversal training, in which the two originally reinforced CS+ and CS- are reversed, is severely impaired by hippocampal damage in rabbits (Berger & Orr, 1983; Buchanan & Powell, 1980). Medial prefrontal lesions also severely impair reversal EB conditioning, but have minimal effects on the original discrimination (Chachich & Powell, 1998). The results of an experiment illustrating this finding are shown in Figure 6. The top panel of this figure shows the trials to reach a criterion of three consecutive sessions with a difference between CS+ and CS- of 30% during reversal training in rabbits that met an original similar discrimination criterion of 30% difference between the original CS+ and CS-. One sec tones of 404 and 1216 Hz served as either CS+ or CS- and the CS+ was reinforced with a 3 mA, 250 msec, AC periorbital shock train. One group of rabbits received either sham or amygdala central nucleus lesions, while a second group received sham or medial

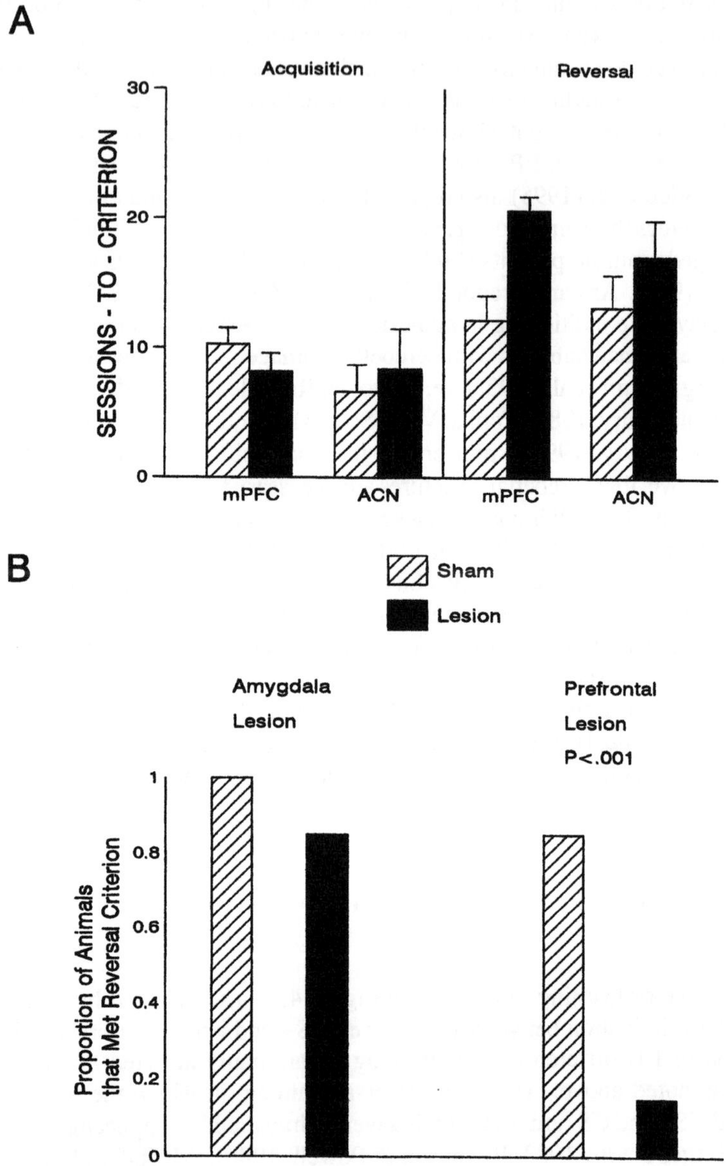

Figure 6: (A) Mean sessions (±SEM) to reach a criterion of a 30% difference over 3 consecutive sessions in percent eyeblink (EB) conditioned responses to a reinforced CS+ and an unreinforced CS- during differential acquisition (15 sessions maximum) and reversal conditioning (20 session maximum) in rabbits with sham, prefrontal (mPFC) or amygdala central nucleus (ACN) lesions. Animals which failed to meet the reversal criterion were arbitrarily assigned a score of 22. (B) Proportion of rabbits to meet the reversal criterion. All animals had previously met an initial discrimination criterion of 30% difference in responding to the original CS+ and CS-, as shown in the top panel. (From Chachich & Powell, 1998).

prefrontal lesions. The top panel indicates that all animals in both groups met the original discrimination criterion; however, animals in the prefrontal lesion group required more sessions than the sham animals to meet the reversal criterion, but animals with central nucleus lesions did not. In fact, as shown in the bottom panel, only one out of seven animals that received prefrontal lesions met this criterion, whereas all but one animal in the amygdala lesion group met it. This research thus also strongly suggests that the medial prefrontal cortex, as well as the hippocampus, may participate in a forebrain circuit that is required for classical somatomotor conditioning under non-optimal circumstances (i.e., reversal conditioning), but is not required under circumstances that are more optimal for learning to occur (original differential conditioning). The fact that prefrontal, but not amygdala lesions, produced an effect on reversal learning may point toward a critical difference between these two structures in mediating the affective or "emotional" components of classical conditioning, assuming that learned autonomic changes index such "emotional" adjustments. Whereas the amygdala may represent an unconscious but extremely relevant component of emotion, which allows for the fast and accurate detection of either dangerous or pleasant circumstances, the higher level processing of the same information by the prefrontal cortex may represent a cortical, perhaps "conscious", integration of emotional/autonomic information with other kinds of information necessary for producing behaviorally relevant somatomotor behaviors that are adaptive.

We have also recently shown that the mediodorsal nucleus of the thalamus, which, as noted above, is the thalamic projection nucleus to the prefrontal cortex plays a role in EB classical conditioning under less-than-optimal circumstances (Buchanan, Penney, Tebbutt & Powell, 1997). In these experiments less than optimal conditioning parameters (i.e., partial reinforcement or lengthened interstimulus intervals) dramatically retarded EB acquisition in rabbits with damage to the thalamic mediodorsal nucleus. The results of these experiments are shown in Figure 7. The right hand panels show EB conditioning in rabbits with sham or mediodorsal nucleus lesions and which received either 50 or 25% reinforcement, while the left hand panels show separate groups of animals with similar lesions that received either a 1 or 1.5 sec ISI. As can be seen in this figure, manipulating both reinforcement frequency, as well as the length of the ISI resulted in impaired EB conditioning. However, performance was considerably more impaired in the lesioned compared to sham animals under the more difficult conditions. It has also been reported that damage to thalamic mediodorsal nucleus severely impairs reversal training of the EB response, similar to that described above by either hippocampal or medial prefrontal lesions (Buchanan, 1991).

These kinds of findings have led Thompson (1991) to suggest that a distributed neural substrate, focused on the hippocampus and its interconnected structures, underlies all classical conditioning, and perhaps associative learning in general, but that neural systems associated with the cerebellum and its interconnected structures provide a localized substrate for the development of specific learned somatomotor responses (i.e., EB and NM CRs). The validity of such a distributive interaction of multiple brain structures during simple classical conditioning has recently received strong support from several studies in which human subjects underwent simple

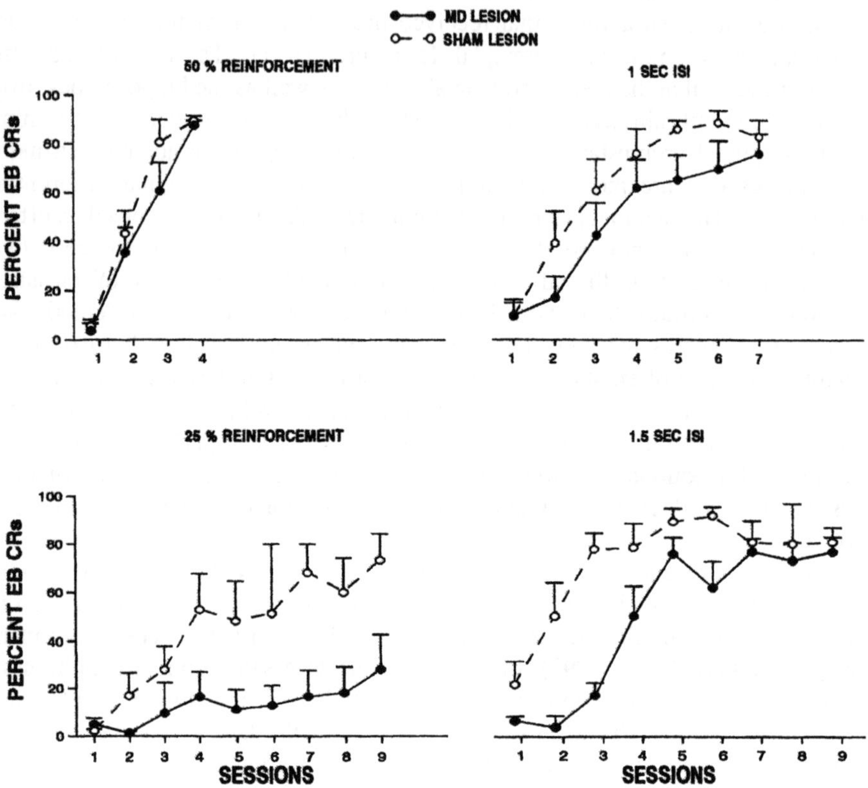

Figure 7: Mean percentage (±SEM) of eyeblink conditioned responses (EB CRs) in animals with lesions of the mediodorsal (MD) nucleus of the thalamus or sham lesions. Left panels show data for animals that received periorbital shock as a US on either 50% or 25% of the trials; right panels show data from animals that received either a 1 sec or 1.5 sec interstimulus interval. Data are shown as a function of varying numbers of acquisition sessions in which 60 trials were presented. A 1216 Hz, 75 db tone was the CS for all conditions. (Adapted from Buchanan et al, 1997).

Pavlovian conditioning, while being subjected to various kinds of brain scans (Blaxton et al, 1996; Fredrikson, Wik, Fischer & Andersson, 1995; Hugdahl et al, 1995; Logan & Grafton, 1995; Molchan, Sunderland, McIntosh, Herscovitch & Schreurs, 1994; Wik, Elbert, Fredrikson, Hoke & Ross, 1996; 1997). These studies have revealed that metabolic activity in several brain areas changed during the learning process, including the temporal lobe and prefrontal structures involved in stages one and two of Figure 4, and extrapyramidal structures postulated to mediate stages three and four. The sensory cortex also showed changes in activity in some cases, which is perhaps not

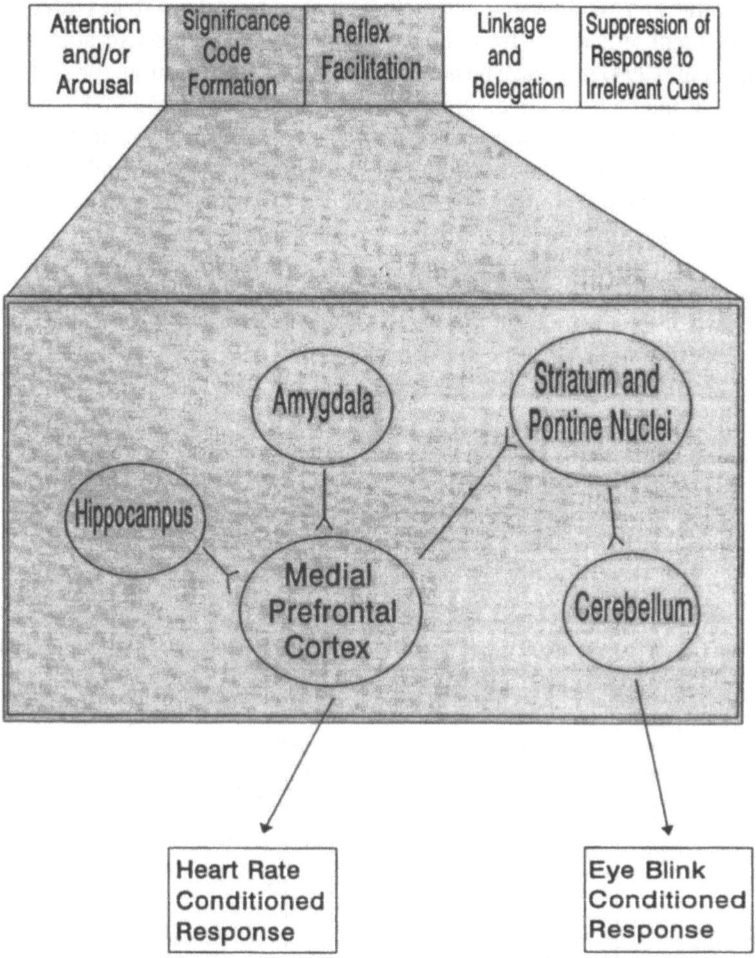

Figure 8: Diagram of known pathways between limbic/cortical structures and extrapyramidal structures that normally participate in classical conditioning. As this figure suggests prefrontal/limbic system interactions are sufficient to produce autonomic CRs such as the heart rate conditioned response. However, extrapyramidal structures, including the neostriatum and cerebellum, mediate acquisition and expression of somatomotor CRs, such as the eyeblink conditioned response. Under some conditions, such as during differential and reversal conditioning or during trace conditioning, a prefrontal/extrapyramidal circuit appears to be involved, as indicated by the connection between medial prefrontal cortex and striatum. These interactions are almost certainly reciprocal, however, and involve the cerebellum, as well. (See Figure 9 below).

surprising, since sensory stimuli must serve as the CS and US (e.g., see Edeline, 1999). These studies thus also strongly suggest the interaction of the cortico-limbic-vermal structures that participate in stages one and two of the classical conditioning process and the thalamic and extrapyramidal structures that participate in stages three through five. The efferent projections from the prefrontal cortex to the neostriatum and pons (Buchanan et al, 1994) provide a possible neuroanatomical substrate for such effects. These kinds of interactions are diagrammatically illustrated in Figure 8. Moreover, the subicular-prefrontal pathway (e.g., Chachich et al, 1996) may be integral to these cortico-limbic/extrapyramidal interactions, suggesting a possible link between the hippocampal and medial prefrontal lesion effects on EB conditioning paradigms that require more processing due to less-than-optimal stimulus parameters.

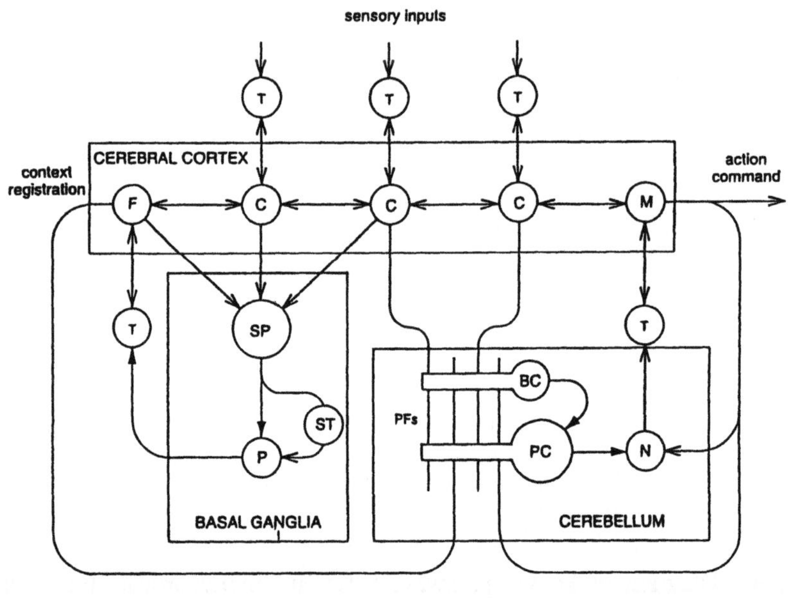

Figure 9: A schema, taken from Houk & Wise (1995), illustrating possible interactions between cortical, thalamic, basal ganglionic and cerebellar modules for registration of a context, mediated by a cortical-basal ganglia (i.e., striatal) module, which results in execution of a specific action command, mediated by cortical-cerebellar interactions. Abbreviations: C = cortical column composed of corticortical, corticothalamic and other projection neurons; E = cortical column in frontal cortex; SP = spiny striatal neuron; ST = subthalamic nucleus neuron; P = palidothalamic neuron; T = thalamocortical neuron; M = motor cortical column; N = deep cerebellar nuclear neuron; BL = Basket cell; PC = Purkinje cell; PFS parallel fibers. Used with permission from Houk & Wise (1995).

The above-described studies thus offer broad support for the interaction of limbic and extrapyramidal mechanisms in the control of even simple kinds of learning, such as EB classical conditioning. Anatcmical studies have shown several interconnections between these structures. For example, the prefrontal, amygdala, midline and intralaminar thalamus and the subiculum and CA1 cells of the hippocampal complex all project to the basal ganglia. Moreover, Finch (1996) has recently demonstrated complex interactions between these inputs to the caudate/putamen and the nucleus accumbens. The medial prefrontal cortex also projects to the lateral pontine nuclei, which provides cerebellar input to the Purkinje cells via mossy fiber input (Buchanan et al, 1994; Wyss & Sripanidkulchai, 1984). Cerebellar input to the prefrontal cortex via the prefrontal projection nuclei of the thalamus has also been recently demonstrated (Middleton & Strick, 1994), suggesting a possible mechanism for cerebellar/prefrontal interactions. Houk and Wise (1995) describe in detail how such interactions might work via prefrontal/striatal and prefrontal/cerebellar modules. Figure 9, taken from Houk and Wise (1995), illustrates how this system might work.

SUMMARY AND CONCLUSIONS

It is clear that a great deal of evidence suggests the interactive participation of several brain areas in somatomotor classical conditioning. Although the activation of these distributive CNS structures is evident during even simple classical conditioning of the EB response under optimal parametric conditions, the brain structure that appears to be necessary and sufficient for acquisition and expression of this response under these conditions includes only cerebellar structures, most probably the deep cerebellar nuclei. Thus, it is only during other manifestations of Pavlovian conditioning (e.g., trace or reversal conditioning) that corticolimbic and other structures become important. These structures include the amygdala, hippocampus, prefrontal cortex and its thalamic connections, and probably connections between the basal ganglia and prefrontal cortex, although evidence for the latter is relatively sparse at the present time.

These considerations have led to the conclusion that some aspects of Pavlovian conditioning require conscious processing and therefore may be classified as declarative processing, whereas simple somatomotor conditioning under optimal parametric conditions would still be classified as a procedural or non-declarative task. This conclusion and the experimental evidence on which it is based has been recently severely criticized (LaBar & Disterhoft, 1998). However, the question of whether conscious awareness is required for classical conditioning to occur has a long history (e.g., see Grant, 1973; Dawson & Furedy, 1976), and suffice it to say we cannot review this literature here. All of this research was conducted on human subjects, but the association of trace EB conditioning with hippocampal and related (i.e., cortical) structures suggests that animal models may also be useful to pursue this question.

A plethora of other questions also remain regarding the interaction of these distributed brain systems and the acquisition, encoding, and retrieval of information required when mammalian organisms are presented with classical conditioning contingencies. Future research, for example, should throw some light on the problem of whether the occurrence of the autonomic measures typically assessed during conditioning of nonspecific processes are necessary for the optimal acquisition and expression of somatomotor classically conditioned responses. Similarly, future research should differentiate the relative roles of different limbic system structures in the acquisition and expression of the nonspecific responses themselves. For example, what specific roles do the cerebellar vermis, amygdala subnuclei, and medial prefrontal cortex play in the elaboration of the complete emotional response to learned contingencies. Using the Pavlovian conditioned EB response as a model system and assessing concomitantly occurring changes in central nervous system processes as well as nonspecific responses at a peripheral level will no doubt answer these as well as other important related questions.

Finally, we should stress that we are aware of the obvious fact that the present five-stage model of somatomotor conditioning is somewhat simplistic. However, it is clear that any explanation of the Pavlovian conditioning process must include at least these five stages, even at its simplest level. A sixth stage, which we have not touched upon involves extinction. The latter may require separate treatment, since there is some evidence that a different set of brain structures mediates extinction than those involved in acquisition and expression of Pavlovian CRs (Morgan & LeDoux, 1995; Hugdahl, 1998). However, again, more research will be required to definitely draw this conclusion.

REFERENCES

Akase, E., Alkon, D.L., & Disterhoft, J.F. (1989). Hippocampal lesions impair memory of short-delay conditioned eye blink in rabbits. *Behavioral Neuroscience, 103*, 935-943.

Albiniak, B.A., & Powell, D.A. (1980). Peripheral autonomic mechanisms and Pavlovian conditioning in the rabbit (Oryctolagus Cuniculus). *Journal of Comparative and Physiological Psychology, 94*, 1101-1113.

Aosaki, T., Graybiel, A.M., & Kimura, M. (1994). Effect of the nigrostriatal dopamine system on acquired neural responses in the striatum of behaving monkeys. *Science, 265*, 412-415.

Aosaki, T., Kimura, M., & Graybiel, A.M. (1995). Temporal and spatial characteristics of tonically active neurons of the primate's striatum. *Journal of Neurophysiology, 73*, 1234-1252.

Applegate, C.D., Frysinger, R.C., Kapp, B.S., & Gallagher, M. (1982). Multiple unit activity recorded from amygdala central nucleus during Pavlovian heart rate conditioning in rabbit. *Brain Research, 238*, 457-462.

Applegate, C.D., Kapp, B.S., Underwood, M. D., & McNall, C.L. (1983). Autonomic and somatomotor effects of amygdala central N. stimulation in awake rabbits. *Physiology and Behavior, 31*, 353-360.

Bagshaw, M.H., Kimble, D.P., & Pribram, K.H. (1965). The GSR of monkeys during orienting and habituation and after ablation of the amygdala, hippocampus, and inferotemporal cortex. *Neuropsychologia, 3*, 111-119.

Berger, T.W., Alger, B., & Thompson, R.F. (1976). Neuronal substrate of classical conditioning in the hippocampus. *Science, 192*, 483-485.

Berger, T.W., & Orr, W.B. (1983). Hippocampectomy selectively disrupts discrimination reversal conditioning of the rabbit nictitating membrane response. *Behavioural Brain Research, 8*, 49-68.

Blaxton, T.A., Zeffiro, T.A., Gabrieli, J.D.E., Bookheimer, S.Y., Carrillo, M.C., Theodore, W.H., & Disterhoft, J.F. (1996). Functional mapping of human learning: A positron emission tomography activation study of eyeblink conditioning. *The Journal of Neuroscience, 16*, 4032-4040.

Buchanan, S.L. (1991). Differential and reversal Pavlovian conditioning in rabbits with mediodorsal thalamic lesions: Assessment of heart rate and eyeblink responses. *Experimental Brain Research, 86*, 174-181.

Buchanan, S.L., Penney, J., Tebbutt, D., & Powell, D.A. (1997). Lesions of the mediodorsal nucleus of the thalamus and classical eyeblink conditioning under less than optimal stimulus conditions: Role of partial reinforcement and interstimulus interval. *Behavioral Neuroscience, 111*, 1075-1085.

Buchanan, S.L., & Powell, D.A. (1980). Divergencies in Pavlovian conditioned heart rate and eyeblink responses produced by hippocampectomy in the rabbit. *Behavioral and Neural Biology, 30*, 20-38.

Buchanan, S.L., & Powell, D.A. (1982a). Cingulate cortex: Its role in Pavlovian conditioning. *Journal of Comparative and Physiological Psychology, 96*, 755-774.

Buchanan, S.L., & Powell, D.A. (1982b). Hippocampal lesions and Pavlovian cardiovascular conditioning. *Pavlovian Journal of Biological Science, 17*, 158-164.

Buchanan, S.L., & Powell, D.A. (1989). Parasagittal thalamic knife cuts and cardiac changes. *Behavioural Brain Research, 32*, 241-253.

Buchanan, S.L., Thompson, R.H., Maxwell, B.L., & Powell, D.A. (1994). Efferent connections of the medial prefrontal cortex in the rabbit. *Experimental Brain Research, 100*, 469-483.

Buchanan, S.L., Valentine, J.D., & Powell, D.A. (1985). Autonomic responses are elicited by electrical stimulation of the medial but not lateral frontal cortex in rabbits. *Behavioural Brain Research, 18*, 51-62.

Cavada, C., Llamas, A., & Reinoso-Suarez, F. (1983). Allocortical afferent connections of the prefrontal cortex in the cat. *Brain Research, 260*, 117-120.

Chachich, M., Buchanan, S., & Powell, D.A. (1997). Characterization of single-unit activity in the mediodorsal nucleus of the thalamus during expression of differential heart rate conditioning in the rabbit. *Neurobiology of Learning and Memory, 67*, 129-141.

Chachich, M., Penney, J., & Powell, D.A. (1996). Subicular lesions disrupt but do not abolish classically conditioned bradycardia in rabbits. *Behavioral Neuroscience, 110*, 707-717.

Chachich, M.E., & Powell, D.A. (1998). Both medial prefrontal and amygdala central nucleus lesions abolish heart rate classical conditioning, but only prefrontal lesions impair reversal of eyeblink differential conditioning. *Neuroscience Letters, 257(3)*: 151-154.

Clark, R.E., & Squire, L.R. (1998). Classical conditioning and brain systems: The role of awareness. *Science, 280*, 77-81.

Clugnet, M., LeDoux, J.E., & Morrison, S.F. (1990). Unit responses evoked in the amygdala and striatum by electrical stimulation of the medial geniculate body. *The Journal of Neuroscience, 10*, 1055-1061.

Crowne, D.P., & Riddell, W.I. (1969). Hippocampal lesions and the cardiac component of the orienting response in the rat. *Journal of Comparative and Physiological Psychology, 69*, 748-755.

Daum, I., Channon, S., & Gray, J.A. (1992). Classical conditioning after temporal lobe lesions in man: Sparing of simple discrimination and extinction. *Behavioural Brain Research, 52*, 159-165.

Daum, I., Channon, S., Polkey, C.E., & Gray, J.A. (1991). Classical conditioning after temporal lobe lesions in man: Impairment in conditional discrimination. *Behavioral Neuroscience, 105*, 396-408.

Daum, I., Schugens, M.M., Ackermann, H., Lutzenberger, W., Dichgans, J., & Birbaumer, N. (1993). Classical conditioning after cerebellar lesions in humans. *Behavioral Neuroscience, 107*, 748-756.

Davis, M. (1992). The role of the amygdala in conditioned fear. In J.P. Aggleton, (Ed.), *The Amygdala: Neurobiological Aspects of Emotion, Memory, and Mental Dysfunction*, (pp. 255-305). Wiley-Liss, Inc., New York, NY.

Dawson, M.E., & Furedy, J.J. (1976). The role of awareness in human differential autonomic classical conditioning: The necessary-gate hypothesis. *Psychophysiology, 13*, 50-53.

Edeline, J.-M. (1999). Learning-induced physiological plasticity in the thalamo-cortical sensory systems: A critical evaluation of receptive field plasticity, map changes and their potential mechanisms. *Progress in Neurobiology, 57*, 165-224.

Ferino, F., Thierry, A.M., & Glowinski, J. (1987). Anatomical and electrophysiological evidence for a direct projection from Ammon's horn to the medial prefrontal cortex in the rat. *Experimental Brain Research, 65*, 421-426.

Finch, D.M. (1996). Neurophysiology of converging synaptic inputs from the rat prefrontal cortex, amygdala, midline thalamus, and hippocampal formation onto single neurons of the caudate/putamen and nucleus accumbens. *Hippocampus, 6*, 495-512.

Fredrikson, M., Wik, G., Fischer, H., & Andersson, J. (1995). Affective and attentive neural networks in humans: A PET study of Pavlovian conditioning. *NeuroReport, 7*, 97-101.

Frysztak, R.J., & Neafsey, E.J. (1994). The effect of medial frontal cortex lesions on cardiovascular conditioned emotional responses in the rat. *Brain Research, 643*, 181-193.

Gabriel, M., Foster, K., Orona, E., Saltwick, S.E., & Stanton, M. (1980). Neuronal activity of cingulate cortex, anteroventral thalamus, and hippocampal formation in discriminative conditioning: encoding and extraction of the significance code of conditional stimuli. In J. Sprague, & A.N. Epstein (Eds.),

Progress in Neurobiology, Physiology and Psychology, Vol. 9, (pp. 126-231). Academic Press, New York, NY.

Gabrieli, J.D.E., McGlinchey-Berroth, R., Carrilo, M.C., Gluck, M.A., Cermak, L.S., & Disterhoft, J.F. (1995). Intact delay-eyeblink classical conditioning in amnesia. *Behavioral Neuroscience, 109,* 819-827.

Ghelarducci, B., & Sebastiani, L. (1996). Contribution of the cerebellar vermis to cardiovascular control. *Journal of the Autonomic Nervous System, 56,* 149-156.

Gibbs, C.M. (1992). Divergent effects of deep cerebellar lesions on two different conditioned somatomotor responses in rabbits. *Brain Research, 585,* 395-399.

Gibbs, C.M., & Powell, D.A. (1988). Neuronal correlates of classically conditioned bradycardia in the rabbit: Studies of the medial prefrontal cortex. *Brain Research, 442,* 86-96.

Gibbs, C.M., & Powell, D. A. (1991). Single-unit activity in the dorsomedial prefrontal cortex during the expression of discriminative bradycardia in rabbits. *Behavioural Brain Research, 43,* 79-92.

Gibbs, C.M., Prescott, L.B., & Powell, D.A. (1992). A comparison of multiple-unit activity in the medial prefrontal and agranular insular cortices during Pavlovian heart rate conditioning in rabbits. *Experimental Brain Research, 89,* 599-610.

Goldman-Rakic, P.S., Selemon, L.D., & Schwartz, M.L. (1984). Dual pathways connecting the dorsolateral prefrontal cortex with the hippocampal formation and parahippocampal cortex in the rhesus monkey. *Neuroscience, 12,* 719-743.

Gormezano, I. (1972). Investigations of defense and reward conditioning in the rabbit. In A. H. Black, & W. F. Prokasy, (Eds.), *Classical Conditioning II: Current research and theory,* (pp. 151-181). Appleton-Century-Crofts, New York, NY.

Grant, D. A. (1973). Cognitive factors in eyelid conditioning. *Psychophysiology, 10,* 75-81.

Houk, J.C., & Wise, S.P. (1995). Distributed modular architectures linking basal ganglia, cerebellum, and cerebral cortex: Their role in planning and controlling action. *Cerebral Cortex, 5,* 95-110.

Hugdahl, K. (1998). Cortical control of human classical conditioning: autonomic and positron emission tomography data. *Psychophysiology, 35,* 170-178.

Hugdahl, K., Berardi, A., Thompson, W.L., Kosslyn, S.M., Macy, R., Baker, D.P., Alpert, N.M., & LeDoux, J.E. (1995). Brain mechanisms in human classical conditioning: A PET blood flow study. *NeuroReport, 6,* 1723-1728.

Hurley, K.M., Herbert, H., Moga, M.M., & Saper, C.B. (1991). Efferent projections of the infralimbic cortex of the rat. *The Journal of Comparative Neurology, 308,* 249-276.

Joseph, J.A., & Powell, D.A. (1980). Peripheral 6-hydroxydopamine administration in the rabbit (oryctolagus cuniculus): Effects on Pavlovian conditioning. *Journal of Comparative and Physiological Psychology, 94,* 1114-1125.

Kaada, B.R. (1951). Somato-motor, autonomic and electrocorticographic responses to electrical stimulation of rhinencephalic and other structures in primates, cat and dog. *Acta Physiologica Scandinavica, 23,* 1-285.

Kao, K., & Powell, D.A. (1986). Lesions of the substantia nigra retard Pavlovian somatomotor learning but do not affect autonomic conditioning. *Neuroscience Letters, 64,* 1-6.

Kao, K., & Powell, D.A. (1988). Lesions of the substantia nigra retard Pavlovian eyeblink but not heart rate conditioning in the rabbit. *Behavioral Neuroscience, 102,* 515-525.

Kapp, B.S., Frysinger, R.C., Gallagher, M., & Haselton, J.R. (1979). Amygdala central nucleus lesions: Effect on heart rate conditioning in the rabbit. *Physiology & Behavior, 23,* 1109-1117.

Kazis, E., Milligan, W.L., & Powell, D.A. (1973). Autonomic-somatic relationships: blockade of heart rate and corneoretinal potential. *Journal of Comparative Physiological Psychology, 84,* 98-110.

Kehoe, E.J., & Macrae, M. (1994). Classical conditioning of the rabbit nictitating membrane response can be fast or slow: Implications for Lennartz and Weinberger's (1992) two-factor theory. *Psychobiology, 22,* 1-4.

Kihlstrom, J.F. (1987). The cognitive unconscious. *Science, 237,* 1445-1452.

Kim, J.J., Clark, R.E., & Thompson, R.F. (1995). Hippocampectomy impairs the memory of recently, but not remotely, acquired trace eyeblink conditioned responses. *Behavioral Neuroscience, 109,* 195-203.

Kim, J.J., & Fanselow, M.S. (1992). Modality-specific retrograde amnesia of fear. *Science, 256,* 675-677.

LaBar, K.S., & Disterhoft, J.F. (1998). Conditioning, awareness, and the hippocampus. *Hippocampus, 8,* 620-626.

Lavond, D.G., Kim, J.J., & Thompson, R.F. (1993). Mammalian brain substrates of aversive classical conditioning. *Annual Review of Psychology, 44,* 317-342.

Lavond, D.G., Lincoln, J.S., McCormick, D.A., & Thompson, R.F. (1984). Effect of bilateral lesions of the dentate and interpositus cerebellar nuclei on conditioning of heart-rate and nictitating membrane/eyelid responses in the rabbit. *Brain Research, 305,* 323-330.

Lavond, D.G., & Steinmetz, J.E. (1989). Acquisition of classical conditioning without cerebellar cortex. *Behavioural Brain Research, 33,* 113-164.

LeDoux, J.E. (1994). Emotion, memory and the brain. *Scientific American, 270,* 50-57.

LeDoux, J.E., Sakaguchi, A., Iwata, J., & Reis, D.J. (1986). Interruption of projections from the medial geniculate body to an arch-neostriatal field disrupts the classical conditioning of emotional responses to acoustic stimuli. *Neuroscience, 17,* 615-627.

Lennartz, R.C., & Weinberger, N.M. (1992). Analysis of response systems in Pavlovian conditioning reveals rapidly versus slowly acquired conditioned responses: Support for two factors, implications for behavior and neurobiology. *Psychobiology, 20,* 93-119.

Lennartz, R.C., & Weinberger, N.M. (1994). A comparison of nonspecific and nictitating membrane conditioned responses: Additional support for two-factor theories. *Psychobiology, 22,* 5-15.

Lofving, B. (1961). Cardiovascular adjustments induced from the rostral cingulate gyrus, with special reference to sympatho-inhibitory mechanisms. *Acta Physiologica Scandinavica, 53* , 1-82.

Logan, C.G., & Grafton, S.T. (1995). Functional anatomy of human eyeblink conditioning determined with regional cerebral glucose metabolism and positron-emission tomography. *Proceedings of the National Academy of Science (USA), 92,* 7500-7504.

Lye, R.H., O'Boyle, D.J., Ramsden, R.T., & Schady, W. (1988). Effects of a unilateral cerebellar lesion on the acquisition of eye-blink conditioning in man. *Journal of Physiology, 403,* 58P.

Maxwell, B., Powell, D.A., & Buchanan, S.L. (1994). Multiple and single unit activity in area 32 (prelimbic region) of the medial prefrontal cortex during Pavlovian heart rate conditioning in the rabbit. *Cerebral Cortex, 4,* 230-246.

McCabe, P.M., McEchron, M.D., Green, E.J., & Schneiderman, N. (1993). Electrolytic and ibotenic acid lesions of the medial subnucleus of the medial geniculate prevent the acquisition of classically conditioned heart rate to a single acoustic stimulus in rabbits. *Brain Research, 619,* 291-298.

McCormick, D.A., & Thompson, R.F. (1984). Cerebellum: Essential involvement in the classically conditioned eyelid response. *Science, 223,* 296-299.

McGlinchey-Berroth, R., Carrillo, M.C., Gabrieli, J.D.E., Brawn, C.M., & Disterhoft, J.F. (1997). Impaired trace eyeblink conditioning in bilateral, medial-temporal lobe amnesia. *Behavioral Neuroscience, 111,* 873-882.

Middleton, F.A., & Strick, P.L. (1994). Anatomical evidence for cerebellar and basal ganglia involvement in higher cognitive function. *Science, 266,* 458-461.

Mishkin, M., Malamut, B., & Bachevalier, J. (1984). Memories and habits: Two neural systems. In G. Lynch, J.M. McGaugh, & N.M. Weinberger, (Eds.), *Neurobiology of Learning and Memory,* (pp. 65-77*).* Guilford Press, New York, NY.

Molchan, S.E., Sunderland, T., McIntosh, A.R., Herscovitch, P., & Schreurs, B.G. (1994). A functional anatomical study of associative learning in humans. *Proceedings of the National Academy of Science (USA), 91,* 8122-8126.

Morgan, M.A., & LeDoux, J.E. (1995). Differential contribution of dorsal and ventral medial prefrontal cortex to the acquisition and extinction of conditioned fear in rats. *Behavioral Neuroscience, 109,* 681-688.

Moyer, J.R., Jr., Deyo, R.A., & Disterhoft, J.F. (1990). Hippocampectomy disrupts trace eye-blink conditioning in rabbits. *Behavioral Neuroscience, 104,* 243-252.

Ohman, A. (1988). Nonconscious control of autonomic responses: A role for Pavlovian conditioning? *Biological Psychology, 27,* 113-135.

Olton, D.S. (1979). Mazes, maps, and memory. *American Psychologist, 34,* 583-596.

Pascoe, J.P., & Kapp, B.S. (1985). Electrophysiological characteristics of amygdaloid central nucleus neurons during Pavlovian fear conditioning in the rabbit. *Behavioural Brain Research, 16,* 117-133.

Phillips, R.G., & LeDoux, J.E. (1992). Differential contribution of amygdala and hippocampus to cued and contextual fear conditioning. *Behavioral Neuroscience, 106,* 274-285.

Port, R.L., Romano, A.G., Steinmetz, J.E., & Mikhail, A.A. (1986). Retention and acquisition of classical trace conditioned responses by rabbits with hippocampal lesions. *Behavioral Neuroscience, 100,* 745-752.

Powell, D.A. (1979). Peripheral and central muscarinic cholinergic blockade: Effects on Pavlovian conditioning. *Bulletin of Psychonomic Society, 14,* 161-164.

Powell, D.A., & Buchanan, S.L. (1980). Autonomic-somatic relationships in the rabbit (Oryctolagus cuniculus): Effects of hippocampal lesions. *Physiological Psychology, 8,* 455-462.

Powell, D.A., Buchanan, S.L., & Gibbs, C.M. (1990). Role of the prefrontal-thalamic axis in classical conditioning. In H.B.M. Uylings, C.G. Van Eden, J.P.C. De Bruin, M.A. Corner, & M.G.P. Feenstra, (Eds.), *Progress In Brain Research, (Vol. 85).* The Prefrontal Cortex: Its Structure, Function and Pathology, (pp. 433-466). Elsevier Science Publishers B.V., Amsterdam, The Netherlands.

Powell, D.A., Chachich, M., Murphy, V., McLaughlin, J., Tebbutt, D., & Buchanan, S.L. (1997). Amygdala-prefrontal interactions and conditioned bradycardia in the rabbit. *Behavioral Neuroscience, 111,* 1056-1074.

Powell, D.A., Gibbs, C.M., Maxwell, B., & Levine-Bryce, D. (1993). On the generality of conditioned bradycardia in rabbits: assessment of CS and US modality. *Animal Learning and Behavior, 21,* 303-313.

Powell, D.A., & Kazis, E. (1976). Blood pressure and heart rate changes accompanying classical eyeblink conditioning in the rabbit (Oryctolagus cuniculus). *Psychophysiology, 13,* 441-447.

Powell, D.A., & Levine-Bryce, D. (1988). A comparison of two model systems of associative learning: Heart rate and eyeblink conditioning in the rabbit. *Psychophysiology, 25,* 672-682.

Powell, D.A., & Levine-Bryce, D. (1989). Conditioned bradycardia in the rabbit: Effects of knife cuts and ibotenic acid lesions in the lateral hypothalamus. *Experimental Brain Research, 76,* 103-121.

Powell, D.A., & Lipkin, M. (1975). Heart rate changes accompanying differential classical conditioning of somatic responses in the rabbit. *Bulletin of the Psychonomic Society, 5,* 28-30.

Powell, D.A., Lipkin, M., & Milligan, M.L. (1974). Concomitant changes in classically conditioned heart rate and corneoretinal potential discrimination in the rabbit (Oryctolagus cuniculus). *Learning and Motivation, 5,* 532-547.

Powell, D.A., Mankowski, D., & Buchanan, S.L. (1978). Concomitant heart rate and corneoretinal potential conditioning in the rabbit (Oryctolagus Cuniculus): Effects of caudate lesions. *Physiology & Behavior, 20,* 143-150.

Powell, D.A., Watson, K., & Maxwell, B. (1994). Involvement of subdivisions of the medial prefrontal cortex in learned cardiac adjustments. *Behavioral Neuroscience, 108,* 294-307.

Pribram, K.H., Reitz, S., McNeil, M., & Spevack, A.A. (1979). The effect of amygdalectomy on orienting and classical conditioning in monkeys. *Pavlovian Journal of Biological Science, 14,* 203-217.

Prokasy, W.F. (1984). Acquisition of skeletal conditioned responses in Pavlovian conditioning. *Psychophysiology, 21,* 1-13.

Raymond, J.L., Lisberger, S.G., & Mauk, M.D. (1996). The cerebellum: A neuronal learning machine? *Science, 272,* 1126-1131.

Ruit, K.G., & Neafsey, E.J. (1988). Cardiovascular and respiratory responses to electrical and chemical stimulation of the hippocampus in anesthetized and awake rats. *Brain Research, 457,* 310-321.

Schacter, D.L. (1992). Understanding implicit memory - A cognitive neuroscience approach. *American Psychologist, 47,* 559-569.

Schmaltz, L.W., & Theios, J. (1972). Acquisition and extinction of a classically conditioned response in hippocampectomized rabbits (Oryctolagus cuniculus). *Journal of Comparative and Physiological Psychology, 79,* 328-333.

Schneiderman, N. (1972). Response system divergencies in aversive classical conditioning. In A.H. Black, & W.F. Prokasy, (Eds.), *Classical Conditioning II: Current theory and research, (pp. 341-376).* Appleton-Century-Crofts, New York, NY.

Schneiderman, N., & Gormezano, I. (1964). Conditioning of the nictitating membrane of the rabbit as a function of CS-US interval. *Journal of Comparative and Physiological Psychology, 57,* 188-195.

Schultz, W. (1994). Behavior-related activity of primate dopamine neurons. *Review of Neurology (Paris), 150,* 634-639.

Schwaber, J.S., Kapp, B.S., Higgins, G.A., & Rapp, P.R. (1982). Amygdaloid and basal forebrain direct connections with the nucleus of the solitary tract and the dorsal motor nucleus. *The Journal of Neuroscience, 2,* 1424-1438.

Sebastiani, L., La Noce, A., Paton, J.F.R., & Ghelarducci, B. (1992). Influence of the cerebellar posterior vermis on the acquisition of the classically conditioned bradycardiac response in the rabbit. *Experimental Brain Research, 88,* 193-198.

Sokolov, E.N. (1963). *Perception and the Conditioned Reflex.* McMillian, New York, NY.

Solomon, P.R., & Moore, J.W. (1975). Latent inhibition and stimulus generalization of the classically conditioned nictitating membrane response in rabbits (Oryctolagus cuniculus) following dorsal hippocampal ablation. *Journal of Comparative and Physiological Psychology, 89,* 1192-1203.

Solomon, P.R., Stowe, G.T., & Pendlebury, W.W. (1989). Disrupted eyelid conditioning in a patient with damage to the cerebellar inputs. *Behavioral Neuroscience, 103,* 898-902.

Solomon, P.R., Vander Schaaf, E., Thompson, R.F., & Weisz, D.J. (1986). Hippocampus and trace conditioning of the rabbit's classically conditioned nictitating membrane response. *Behavioral Neuroscience, 100,* 729-744.

Squire, L.R. (1992). Memory and the hippocampus: a synthesis from findings with rats, monkeys, and humans. *Psychological Review, 99,* 195-231.

Squire, L.R. (1994). Memory and forgetting: Long-term and gradual changes in memory storage. O. Sporns, & G. E. Tononi (Eds.). *Selectionism and the Brain, (pp. 243-269).* Academic Press, New York.

Steinmetz, J.E. (1998). The localization of a simple type of learning and memory: The cerebellum and classical eyeblink conditioning. *Current Directions in Psychological Science, 7,* 72-77.

Supple, W.F., Jr., & Kapp, B.S. (1993). The anterior cerebellar vermis: Essential involvement in classically conditioned bradycardia in the rabbit. *The Journal of Neuroscience, 13,* 3705-3711.

Supple, W. F., Jr., & Leaton, R. N. (1990). Lesions of the cerebellar vermis and cerebellar hemispheres: Effects on heart rate conditioning in rats. *Behavioral Neuroscience, 104,* 934-947.

Swanson, L.W. (1981). A direct projection from Ammon's horn to prefrontal cortex in the rat. *Brain Research, 217,* 150-154.

Terreberry, R.R., & Neafsey, E.J. (1983). Rat medial frontal cortex: A visceral motor region with a direct projection to the solitary nucleus. *Brain Research, 278,* 245-249.

Thompson, R.F. (1991). Are memory traces localized or distributed? *Neuropsychologia, 29,* 571-582.

Thompson, R.F., & Spencer, W.A. (1966). Habituation: A model phenomenon for the study of neuronal substrates of behavior. *Psychological Review, 73,* 16-43.

Thompson, R.F., Thompson, J.K., Kim, J.J., Krupa, D.J., & Shinkman, P.G. (1998). The nature of reinforcement in cerebellar learning. *Neurobiology of Learning and Memory, 70,* 150-176.

Topka, H., Valls-Sole, J., Massaquoi, S.G., & Hallett, M. (1993). Deficit in classical conditioning in patients with cerebellar degeneration. *Brain, 116,* 961-969.

Tulving, A. (1985). How many memory systems are there? *American Psychologist, 40,* 385.

Weinberger, N.M. (1998). Physiological memory in primary auditory cortex: Characteristics and mechanisms. *Neurobiology of Learning and Memory, 70,* 226-251.

Weinberger, N.M., & Diamond, D.M. (1987). Physiological plasticity in auditory cortex: rapid induction by learning. *Progress in Neurobiology, 29,* 1-55.

Weiskrantz, L., & Warrington, E.K. (1979). Conditioning in amnesic patients. *Neuropsychologia, 17,* 187-194.

White, N.M. (1997). Mnemonic functions of the basal ganglia. *Current Opinion in Neurobiology, 7,* 164-169.

White, I.M., Miller, D.P., White, W., Dike, G.L., Rebec, G.V., & Steinmetz, J.E. (1994). Neuronal activity in rabbit neostriatum during classical eyelid conditioning. *Experimental Brain Research, 99,* 179-190.

Wik, G., Elbert, T., Fredrikson, M., Hoke, M., & Ross, B. (1997). Magnetic brain imaging of extinction processes in human classical conditioning. *NeuroReport, 8,* 1789-1792.

Wik, G., Elbert, T., Fredrikson, M., Hoke, M., & Ross, B. (1996). Magnetic imaging in human classical conditioning. *NeuroReport, 7,* 737-740.

Woodruff-Pak, D.S., Lavond, D.G., Logan, C.G., Steinmetz, J.E., & Thompson, R.F. (1993). Cerebellar cortical lesions and reacquisition in classical conditioning of the nictitating membrane response in rabbits. *Brain Research, 608,* 67-77.

Woodruff-Pak, D.S., Papka, M., & Ivry, R. B. (1996). Cerebellar involvement in eyeblink classical conditioning in humans. *Neuropsychology, 10,* 443-458.

Woody, C.D. (1988). Is conditioning supported by modulation of an outward current in pyramidal cells of the motor cortex of cats? In C.D. Woody, D.L. Alkon, & J.L. McGaugh, (Eds.). *Cellular Mechanisms of Conditioning and Behavioral Plasticity, pp. 27-35.* Plenum Press, New York, NY.

Wyss, J.M., & Sripanidkulchai, K. (1984). The topography of the mesencephalic and pontine projections from the cingulate cortex of the rat. *Brain Research, 293,* 1-15.

Yeo, C.H., Hardiman, M.J., & Glickstein, M. (1985). Classical conditioning of the nictitating membrane response of the rabbit. I. Lesions of the cerebellar nuclei. *Experimental Brain Research, 60,* 87-98.

Young, B.J., & Leaton, R.N. (1996). Amygdala central nucleus lesions attenuate acoustic startle stimulus-evoked heart rate changes in rats. *Behavioral Neuroscience, 110,* 228-237.

ACKNOWLEDGMENTS

Preparation of this manuscript was supported by Department of Veterans Affairs Institutional Research Funds awarded to the Wm. Jennings Bryan Dorn VA Medical Center, Columbia, SC. We thank Andrew Pringle for assistance with the illustrations and Elizabeth Hamel for secretarial assistance. We are also greatly indebted to the late Shirley Buchanan, not only for the obvious contributions her research has made to the present paper, but also for her general support and committment toward understanding the CNS substrates underlying classical conditioning.

12 MOTIVATIONAL ISSUES IN AVERSIVE AND APPETITIVE CONDITIONING PARADIGMS

Stephen D. Berry, Matthew A. Seager,
Yukiko Asaka and Ramie L. Borgnis
Miami University

INTRODUCTION

An important theme of this volume is the beneficial impact that studies of classical conditioning have had on our knowledge of simple associative learning. One of the major endeavors of behavioral neuroscience has been the attempt to define, describe, locate and manipulate the neural substrates of this type of learning. Many approaches have been tried, combining the measurement of behavioral plasticity with observation or manipulation of physiological parameters. Such biologically grounded studies have modified or improved theories of learning based solely upon abstractions drawn from behavior. For example, the principle of stimulus equivalence, under which virtually any stimuli chosen by the experimenter may be used as conditioned stimuli in a classically conditioned association (Kimble, 1967) was consistent with philosophical associationist principles current at the turn of the century. More recently, however, it has been limited in scope by biological constraints on what stimuli can be linked with certain types of conditioned behaviors, especially when motivational conditions are changed (for review, see Bolles, 1970). Conditioned taste aversion is a notable demonstration of such seemingly hard-wired biological mechanisms that facilitate some associations (e.g., taste—illness) and may prevent others (e.g., light+sound—illness; Garcia & Koelling, 1966, but see Shettleworth, 1979). Processes that have been invoked to explain differences in the associability of stimuli include species traits such as functional properties of the sensory and motor systems activated, and constructs such as arousal, attention, motivation, etc. that account for variations in the responsiveness of an organism over time and/or under differing experimental conditions (Gazzaniga, Ivry & Mangun, 1998; Hilgard & Bower, 1966; Kimble, 1961; Mook, 1987; Parasuraman, 1998; Petri, 1996).

The concept of motivation and its impact on classical conditioning raises issues that bear on most laboratory studies of learning, since classical conditioning is an important form of associative learning in its own right and is thought to mediate the motivational aspects of instrumental paradigms as well (see, e.g., Bindra, 1974; Rescorla & Solomon, 1967; Scavio, 1987). Significant in our discussion are: (a) the role of global or tonic drive states versus relatively brief or phasic motivational responses (Gazzaniga et al., 1998), (b) the impact of motivational processes on either drive-directed or nonspecific attentional systems (see Posner & Petersen, 1990), and (c) the concept of opponent central processes triggered by stimuli of opposing motivational valences (see Solomon & Corbit, 1974). An essential concept in the literature on learning is incentive motivation, a process that includes both energizing and cue guidance of behavior, triggered by the classically conditioned association of a cue (conditioned stimulus, CS) with reinforcement (unconditioned stimulus, US). Incentives are not the reinforcers or consummatory stimuli themselves, they are cues that activate behavioral systems to bring an organism into contact with appetitive consummatory stimuli (rewards) or away from aversive stimuli (punishments and negative reinforcers; see, e.g., Grastyan, Karmos, Vereczkey & Kellenyi, 1966; Konorski, 1968). Sherrington (1906), in his classic studies of hierarchical spinal and brainstem behavioral mechanisms, speculated that the entire forebrain exists for the purpose of incentive guidance of motivated behavior. That is, learned relationships between (sometimes neutral) environmental events or signals (e.g., CSs) and consummatory stimuli (e.g., USs) serve to motivate and guide the organism into contact with the latter so that instinctive or reflex consummatory responses can respond adaptively. Sherrington's anticipatory—consummatory behavioral dichotomy presaged similar classifications of behavior that emerged in ethology (see Hinde, 1970) and behavioral neuroscience (see Vanderwolf, 1971). For our discussion below, it is interesting that several models suggest that the hippocampus is part of an incentive motivational brain system (Grossberg, 1982; Grossberg & Schmajuk, 1987; Jarrard, 1973).

In this chapter, we will focus on classical conditioning of the rabbit in which recordings, lesions or drugs shed neurobiological light on motivational processes inferred from behavior. All of our studies involve simultaneous recording of neural and behavioral responses during learning, concentrating on the hippocampus and related structures. An impressive literature exists on studies mapping and manipulating neural activity throughout sensory, motor, limbic, cortical and cerebellar structures during rabbit classical conditioning (see, e.g., Gormezano, Prokasy & Thompson, 1987 and other chapters in this volume). Such complementary neural and behavioral data have been extremely productive in specifying critical neural circuitry, resolving ambiguities of interpretation, and providing clear suggestions for the direction of future research on neural substrates of learning.

HIPPOCAMPAL ACTIVITY AND NICTITATING MEMBRANE CONDITIONING

The limbic system has traditionally been linked with such psychological constructs as motivation and emotion (Isaacson, 1982; MacLean, 1955; Papez, 1937). One of the major structures comprising the limbic system, the hippocampus, has also been intimately tied to learning, memory, and incentive processes (see Berger, Berry & Thompson, 1986; Cohen & Eichenbaum, 1993; Grossberg & Schmajuk, 1987; Isaacson & Pribram, 1975a, b; 1986a, b; Scoville & Milner, 1957; Squire, 1992). As a result, much is known about the role that the hippocampus plays in classical eyeblink conditioning, especially in the rabbit. This line of research is reviewed in Chapter 13 by Disterhoft and McEchron (this volume; see also Berger et al., 1986).

Individual Differences in Background State

Neural recording studies have demonstrated massive engagement of hippocampal neurons during learning and performance of the rabbit nictitating membrane (NM) response (Berger, Alger & Thompson, 1976; Berger & Thompson, 1978; see Berger et al., 1986). While unit recordings were revealing learning-related activation of hippocampal neurons, simultaneous recordings of slow-wave (EEG) activity from the pyramidal cell layer of CA1 displayed a striking relationship between a pre-existing brain state of the animal and subsequent acquisition rate.

Berry and Thompson (1978) recorded a free-running two minute sample of EEG just prior to the start of a delay NM conditioning procedure. Sixteen animals were then trained to criterion using standard training procedures. Spectral analysis of the EEG samples revealed that rabbits exhibiting a large proportion of slow wave frequencies in the theta range (2-8 Hz) tended to learn at a faster rate than those that had higher frequencies (8-22 Hz). The correlation between an index of hippocampal frequencies (8-22 Hz/2-8 Hz) and learning rate (trials to criterion) was .72 (see Figure 1). Note that the trials to criterion values ranged from approximately 100 (within the first conditioning session) to almost 500 (4 sessions). The slow wave (EEG) frequency ratios (all computed before the first session) ranged from .2 (a 5:1 dominance of theta) to almost 1.4 (about 60% non theta). Interestingly, post-training samples of EEG taken at the end of the criterion session revealed that the slow and fast learning rabbits' EEG spectra shifted in opposite directions and that this shift was highly related to learning rate (r = -.86; Berry, 1982; Berry, Weisz & Mamounas, 1987). Specifically, fast learners with a large proportion of 2-8 Hz activity before training tended to display more of the higher frequencies (8-22 Hz) after training, while the opposite pattern occurred for slow learners. This is consistent with the idea that identical training experience shifted the animals from their individually different starting points to a more common state, perhaps reflecting motivational and incentive-related processes following NM conditioning.

The pre-training hippocampal EEG not only predicted the rate of behavioral acquisition, but it also predicted the growth and development of conditioned unit responses recorded from the same electrodes. The responses in fast learning animals (i.e., larger standard scores) resulted from a combination of increased mean responsiveness to the CS and US in the fast learners and higher baseline (pre-CS) variability in the slow learners (Berry, 1982). Taken together, these findings indicate that an important determinant of NM acquisition rate is a pre-existing brain state that is reflected by differences in hippocampal slow waves, which predict strong, consistent unit responses in fast-learning rabbits and reduced or variable plasticity of hippocampal neurons in slow learners. As training ends, EEG measures in all animals converge on a pattern that reflects a common, post-learning brain state.

While it is tempting to speculate that this is due to a specific mnemonic function of the hippocampus, supported by the associative conditioned unit responses and the final common EEG state, it is also possible that hippocampal activity participates in a

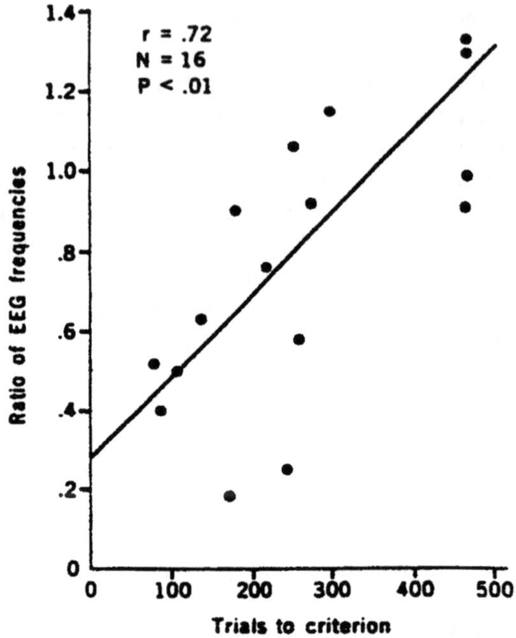

Figure 1. Scatterplot and best-fitting regression line for the relationship between trials to criterion and the EEG frequency ratio (the percentage of 8- to 22-Hz activity divided by the percentage of 2- to 8-Hz activity). [From "Prediction of learning rate from the hippocampal electroencephalogram," by S.D. Berry and R.F. Thompson, 1978, *Science, 200,* p. 1299. Copyright 1978 by the American Association for the Advancement of Science.]

nonassociative process with a major impact on critical circuitry elsewhere (e.g., cerebellum). The latter role is supported by the predictive relationship between pretraining EEG and acquisition rate (which cannot, therefore, be a specific S-R associative process since neither the CS nor US has yet occurred when the slow wave sample is taken) and by the observation that disruptions of hippocampal function (see below) can delay, but in most cases do not prevent, simple classical conditioning. The fact that our recordings of neural activity are related to both the associative and nonassociative features of classical NM conditioning provides a guide to our thinking on the behavioral functions of the hippocampal formation. One candidate would be incentive motivation, a process that combines associative and nonassociative features, i.e., learned cues that can trigger instinctive or hard-wired motivational responses. If this idea holds up under scrutiny, it would support a suggestion by Olds (1975) that the hippocampus may be a neural convergence point for mnemonic and motivational processes.

Disruption of Hippocampal State

Although early lesion studies indicated that removal of the hippocampus did not prevent acquisition of simple delay NM conditioning (Schmaltz & Theios, 1972; Solomon & Moore, 1975), other lesions and drug treatments capable of disrupting the hippocampal theta rhythm were shown to retard acquisition rate. For example, medial septal lesions, which disrupt a major input to the hippocampus and pacemaker for the theta rhythm but leave lateral septal output pathways intact, slow acquisition of the conditioned response without completely preventing it (Berry & Thompson, 1979; Powell, Milligan & Buchanan, 1976). Pharmacological blockade of cholinergic systems, known to disrupt the low frequency theta rhythm, has a similar effect on acquisition rate (Harvey, Gormezano & Cool-Hauser, 1983; 1985; Moore, Goodell & Solomon, 1976; Powell, 1979; Powell, Hernandez & Buchanan, 1985; Salvatierra & Berry, 1989; Solomon & Gottfried, 1981; Solomon, Solomon, Vander Schaaf & Perry, 1983). Although only one of the above studies included chronic electrophysiological recordings that allowed accurate characterization of the actual disruption of hippocampal EEG and unit responses during training (Salvatierra & Berry, 1989), the data reported by Solomon et al. (1983) suggest that the deleterious effects of the drug on conditioning must be due to actions in the hippocampus (because they are absent with hippocampal lesions).

One interpretation of these data is that cholinergic septo-hippocampal mechanisms are part of a specifically mnemonic brain system, disruption of which produces a more or less purely associative deficit. However, pharmacological data indicate that the psychological effects of anticholinergics can range from sedative to hallucinogenic depending upon dosage (Brown, 1990). Thus, the possibility of indirect, modulatory (e.g., attentional or motivational) effects of these drugs on neural substrates of learning in non-cholinergic and/or non-hippocampal systems is still open (see Blokland, 1996; Everitt & Robbins, 1997; Gallagher & Rapp, 1997).

The details of cholinergic disruption of hippocampal activity (Salvatierra & Berry, 1989) may be of some help in interpreting the behavioral findings. First, the disruption of slow waves was not simply a blockade of "atropine sensitive" theta (Vanderwolf, Kramis, Gillespie & Bland, 1975). Slow waves in this frequency range were still clearly present after the drug treatment, but were altered in their proportions and amplitude. The disorganization of frequencies within the theta (2-8 Hz) range suggests that the behavioral deficit was not due to a loss of 2-8 Hz theta *per se*. Neither could it be attributed to the intrusion of incompatible behaviors correlated with higher frequency (8-14 Hz) non-"atropine sensitive" theta, which was not observed in the post drug, pre-training EEG samples. Instead, we must accept the possibility of a more complex relationship between cholinergic inputs and hippocampal function than has been common in the neurobehavioral literature to date. Secondly, there were virtually no conditioned unit responses in the hippocampus or lateral septum after scopolamine, yet behavioral NM conditioning still occurred. This finding was replicated in jaw movement conditioning as well (Seager, Asaka & Berry, 1999). Thus, a process that is parallel or modulatory to the critical learning circuits must be altered by cholinergic antagonists. If one considers the septohippocampal circuit to be part of a larger basal forebrain-to-cortex cholinergic system, then processes like arousal, attention or incentive motivation can be viewed as likely candidates.

A specific attempt to test the relationship between hippocampal slow waves and attentional processes was conducted by Borgnis (1993). She used pretraining stimulus administration to produce latent inhibition (LI), a specific reduction of attention to the conditioning stimuli due to unreinforced preexposure (for review, see Lubow, 1989). As shown in Figure 2, different amounts of preexposure of rabbits to specific stimuli or to the conditioning context produced corresponding degrees of alteration of hippocampal slow waves. As shown on the left, explicitly unpaired exposure produced the greatest increase in slow wave frequency, while no preexposure before paired training produced the least (right). Preexposure to the CS or the context alone produced intermediate increases. Recall that increases in this index predict slower acquisition of the NM response. Consistent with this idea are the data of Best and Best (1976) showing that latent inhibition in rats produced reductions in hippocampal unit responsiveness to a tone CS. These findings suggest that the hippocampus may be involved in LI-induced reductions in attention or stimulus associability. Such an idea is supported by the fact that animals with hippocampal lesions do not show latent inhibition and, therefore, can learn faster than intact rabbits in this paradigm (Schmaltz & Theios, 1972; Solomon & Moore, 1975; see also Honey & Good, 1993; Schmajuk, Lam & Christiansen, 1994).

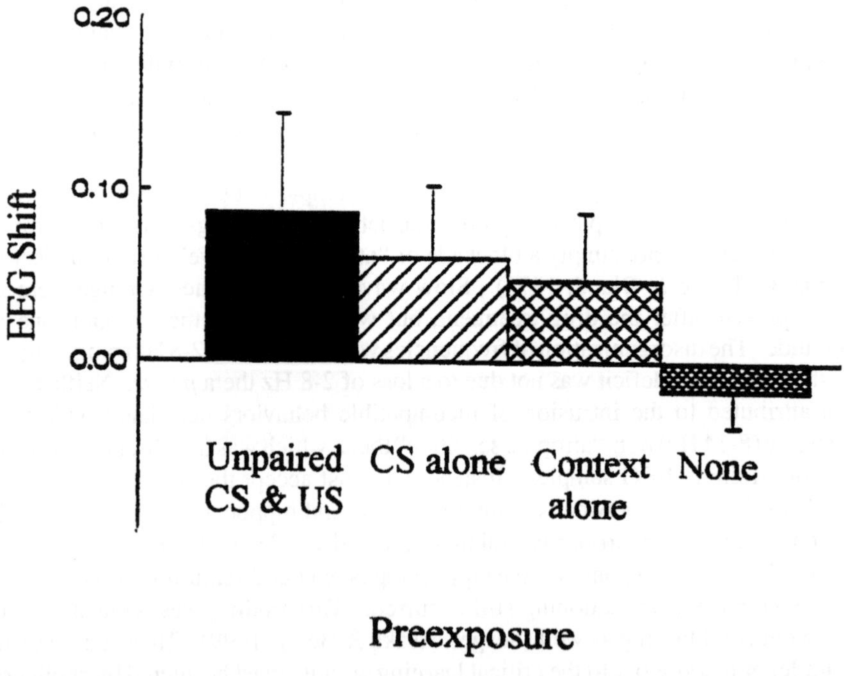

Figure 2. Shift in EEG ratios from Pre-Adaptation to Post-Preexposure as a function of degree and type of preexposure. Error bars = standard error of the mean.

Improvement of State

While it is important to demonstrate the disruption of learning with drugs and lesions of relevant neural systems, seldom have researchers directly improved brain states and facilitated learning, thereby yielding evidence of superior or optimal function (see Berry, Sim & Snyder, 1969; Berry & Snyder, 1978; Destrade, 1982; Deupree, Coppock & Willer, 1982; Galey, Jeantet, Destrade & Jaffard, 1983; Landfield, 1977; Wetzel, Ott & Matthies, 1977; see also Glazer, 1974; Gray, 1972). An attempt to modify or improve hippocampal activity and learning during NM conditioning was conducted in our laboratory using a motivational manipulation (rather than artificial brain stimulation as in the above-cited studies). Berry and Swain (1989) water deprived (22 h restriction) a group of rabbits and trained them in delay NM conditioning. Another group of animals was allowed free access to water before training. Results of the study showed that the motivational manipulation significantly increased the amount of theta in the hippocampus and dramatically enhanced learning rate (mean = 66 and 117 trials, respectively, $p < .001$). The predictive relationship between pre-training EEG and subsequent learning rate obtained by Berry and Thompson (1978) was replicated ($r = .84$; see Figure 3), and the slow wave state was actually a better predictor of individual learning rates than treatment group (deprived vs *ad lib*). Additionally, similar to the findings of Berry and Thompson (1978), an examination of unit responses early in training revealed that deprived animals (which exhibited higher levels of theta activity) had significantly larger conditioned unit responses than the *ad lib* controls, suggesting differences in hippocampal processing that covaried with motivational state.

From these data a question arises as to whether and how hippocampal EEG states can be functionally linked to variations in learning rate. That is, how can this activity modulate other neural systems that form the actual memory trace or engram? There is much evidence indicating a general relationship between patterns of spontaneous or free-running theta activity and the timing and probability of hippocampal cell firing (Berry, Rinaldi, Thompson & Verzeano, 1978; Bland, Andersen, Ganes & Sveen, 1980; Buzsaki, Leung & Vanderwolf, 1983; Fox, Wolfson & Ranck, 1986; Sinclair, Seto & Bland, 1982). Typically, levels of unit activity vary among two or three slow wave states that are defined by size, frequency and waveform characteristics. When synchronous theta is present, units show strong preferred phase relations to the locally recorded slow waves. Additional studies have shown links between patterns of hippocampal slow waves (theta/RSA) and elicited neural activity, including conditioned unit responses (Berry, 1982; Berry & Swain, 1989; Otto, Eichenbaum, Wiener & Wible, 1991), place cell firing (O'Keefe & Recce, 1993; Skaggs, McNaughton, Wilson & Barnes, 1996) and LTP induction (Arai & Lynch, 1992; Holscher, Anwyl & Rowan, 1997; Larson, Wong & Lynch, 1986, Pavlides, Greenstein, Grudman & Winson, 1988; Staubli & Lynch, 1987; Thomas, Watabe, Moody, Makhinson & O'Dell, 1998). Strong functional relationships have also been shown between and among water deprivation, theta, LTP, and behavioral learning during contextual fear conditioning in rats (Maren, DeCola, Swain, Fanselow & Thompson, 1994). Taken together, these findings suggest how state variables reflected in hippocampal slow waves can affect the responsiveness and plasticity of hippocampal output neurons that influence other brain structures.

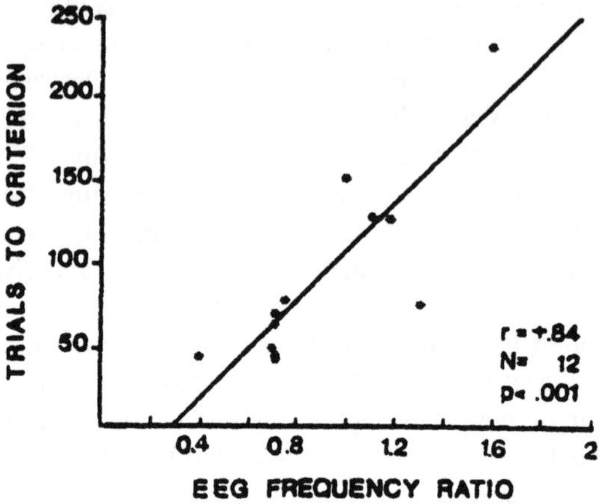

Figure 3. The scatterplot and best-fitting regression line for the relation between trials to criterion and the electroencephalographic (EEG) frequency ratio (amount of 8-22 Hz activity divided by the amount of 2-8 Hz activity). [From "Water deprivation optimizes hippocampal activity and facilitates nictitating membrane conditioning," by S.D. Berry and R.A. Swain, 1989, *Behavioral Neuroscience, 103*(1), p. 74. Copyright 1989 by the American Psychological Association.]

The impact of the "irrelevant" (water deprivation) drive state on NM conditioning in the above study (Berry & Swain, 1989) supports the theoretical assertion of a generalized motivational/attentional process instead of, or in addition to, directed attention biased towards specific motivational or drive-related cues (for background, see Mook, 1987; Petri, 1996). That is, it appears that the motivational state influenced responses to stimuli not associated with the relevant drive (i.e. thirst). More specifically, multi-level models of attentional processes often propose more global levels or states of arousal (correlated with cortical EEG states), within which more specific processes of directed attention operate according to the type of information required from the environment (see Posner & Petersen, 1990; Parasuraman, 1998).

The predictive slow wave relationship in the water deprivation NM study suggests that the hippocampal activity may be reflecting such a generalized process of responsiveness to all environmental cues, rather than to only those associated with reduction of the thirst drive. However, no motivation-relevant cues were given in the above study, so it is impossible to conclude that the hippocampus predicted equal responsivity to all classes of stimuli. In fact, classical conditioning studies in which the stimuli are highly relevant to an induced drive state (appetitive jaw movement conditioning using deprivation and a water US, see below) show even higher levels of theta, rapidly developing and stable hippocampal conditioned unit responses, and extremely fast behavioral learning (Oliver, Swain & Berry, 1993). This finding is consistent with the idea that neural systems are more responsive to cues that are relevant to an ongoing drive or arousal state. In either case, there has been a long-standing link between hippocampal theta rhythm and variables such as attention and/or arousal (Bennett, 1975; Berry & Thompson, 1978; Green & Arduini, 1954; Grossberg & Schmajuk, 1987; Lindsley & Wilson, 1975; Thompson & Berry, 1988).

The latent inhibition study above (Borgnis, 1993) suggests a straightforward role for the hippocampus in general attention, and discrimination studies support this by showing a selective response of hippocampal neurons to CS+ contingencies and not CS- (Berger et al., 1986; Miller & Steinmetz, 1997). On the other hand, lesion studies indicate that the hippocampus is not essential for basic discrimination learning but is necessary for suppression of CS- responding during discrimination reversal (Berger & Orr, 1983; Weikart & Berger, 1986). Solomon's (1980) notion of the hippocampal circuit's involvement in "tuning out irrelevant stimuli" rather than in global attention *per se* (see Posner & Petersen, 1990) appears to fit these data. Relevance in this case is defined in terms of motivational state and prediction of environmental contingencies. Tuning out would be a type of attentional filtering of stimuli that have no unique predictive relation to the US occurrence. In incentive motivational terms, this could be stated as a lack of conditioned positive or negative incentive values for stimuli deemed irrelevant to the motivational state. However, one could argue that the CS- has a strong negative predictive relationship and therefore should not be tuned out perceptually, just not responded to—a behavioral inhibition process (see Gray, 1986; Wasserman & Miller, 1997). Evidence from hippocampal lesions and recording is consistent with both the general state and specific incentive interpretations, so further study will be required, especially using paradigms that place different cognitive and motivational demands on the organism.

Theta-triggered Training

In light of the above-mentioned NM studies correlating hippocampal theta and learning rate, it remains to be determined whether the presence of theta in the pre-training sample primarily reflects a global and/or tonic state of the animal that has a lasting impact throughout a 1-2 h session (e.g., vigilance or arousal in response to the training context), or whether it is important for the animal to be generating theta during the one or two seconds in which the phasic conditioning stimuli are presented in specific CS-US pairings. Such evidence would address questions concerning whether the hippocampus may participate in more specific, directed attentional processes that occur as specific S-S or S-R associations are formed. Therefore, whereas the two previous NM studies (Berry & Thompson, 1978; Berry & Swain, 1989) sampled theta only prior to the first conditioning session, a recent study conducted in our laboratory monitored hippocampal activity "on-line" and initiated individual behavioral training trials contingent upon patterns of this activity (Seager, Asaka, Chabot, Johnson & Berry, 1998). Rather than artificially "driving" or blocking theta with lesions, drugs, or electrical stimulation of septal or other inputs prior to training (Deupree et al., 1982), this study allowed the animal to freely generate theta, permitting us to study the role that naturally occurring theta or its absence plays in learning.

Stainless steel microelectrodes (30-50 um tips) were implanted into stratum oriens of CA1. Slow wave activity from the electrode tip was filtered (1-25 Hz) and digitized at 100 Hz. LabVIEW software (National Instruments) sampled slow wave (EEG) data in 640 ms segments, performed a fast Fourier transform (FFT) and computed a power spectrum. A "theta index" reflecting proportional power in the theta range was calculated from the output of the power spectrum (3.5-8.5 Hz activity in the numerator and 0.5-3.5 Hz and 8.5-22 Hz activity in the denominator). To assess theta continuity, a sliding window continued to sample the incoming slow wave in 160 ms increments and recalculated the ratio (480 ms previous data and 160 ms new data). One group of rabbits (T +) was given trials when this ratio exceeded 1.0 for two consecutive repetitions (total 800 ms) and another group (T -) was given trials only when this ratio fell below 0.3 for two repetitions. Each rabbit was assigned a yoked control that received the same number of trials per day with the same intertrial intervals, regardless of brainwave frequencies.

Results of this experiment revealed that rabbits given trials when exhibiting theta learned significantly faster than rabbits given trials when not exhibiting theta (see Figure 4). The non-theta rabbits took twice as many trials to reach a criterion of eight CRs in any nine consecutive trials (mean = 115 and 58, respectively p = .02;). The yoked control groups learned at an intermediate and more variable rate. Post hoc analyses of pre-trial slow waves are currently under way to sort yoked animals according to the number of trials in theta and relate this to individual differences in learning rate. If this correlation approximates that observed by Berry and Thompson (1978), it will strongly suggest that the original prediction was based on the relationship between pre-session free-running EEG and the probability of theta being present during individual trials within that session.

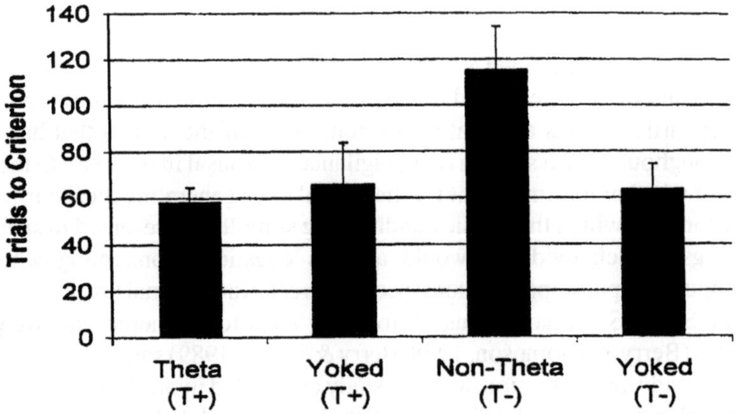

Figure 4. Mean trials to criterion for the theta, nontheta, and yoked control groups. The difference between theta and nontheta groups is statistically significant, p = .02.

The effects of theta-triggered training trials are indicative of a more selective or direct link between patterns of hippocampal slow wave activity, neural conditioning, and the rate of acquisition of a classically conditioned behavioral response. The state of the hippocampal EEG prior to each conditioning trial could have a direct impact on information processing in hippocampal circuits, stronger than that of slow waves at the beginning of a session, which may be predicting only the general probability that individual trials will occur during theta. Thus, through modulation of the firing of output/pyramidal neurons during conditioning trials, slow wave patterns in the hippocampus can facilitate or inhibit other areas responsible for acquisition and elaboration of the behavioral response. If they are disrupted due to lesions, drugs, aging, or latent inhibition, then conditioning is slower. If the slow wave distribution is improved by water deprivation, attentional processes, or trials contingent upon slow wave state, then learning is faster.

APPETITIVE CONDITIONING

In studies of classical conditioning, a number of researchers have investigated the impact of different biologically significant stimuli on learning, invoking explanations such as reinforcement, incentive cueing of behavior, and opponent motivational processes or states (for review, see Rescorla & Solomon, 1972; Grossberg & Schmajuk, 1987; Bindra, 1974). Using rewarding and aversive stimuli either simultaneously (as in US-US conditioning) or sequentially (as in transfer of training and counterconditioning experiments) has revealed that exposure to one motivational class of stimuli alters the responsivity to stimuli of the other class. For example, Tait, Quesnel, and Ten Have (1986) showed that an appetitive US could be used as the CS for an aversive US, but that the reverse was less true (see also Dearing & Dickinson, 1979). Similarly, Scavio (1974) and Scavio and Gormezano (1980) demonstrated that, in transfer experiments, prior training with a CS and aversive US slowed subsequent conditioning of that same CS with an appetitive US. Thus, opponent states appear to be triggered by USs of opposing motivational valences, with reciprocal influences on learning. A major theoretical position maintains that such stimuli trigger opponent processes in central neural systems, thus explaining the negative impact of aversive stimuli on reward training and vice versa (Dickinson & Pearce, 1977; Konorski, 1968; Solomon & Corbit, 1974). Often, the aversive stimuli have a greater negative impact on reward conditioning than exposure to rewarding stimuli have on aversive training (Konorski, 1968; Lovibond & Dickinson, 1982; Scavio, 1987). In fact, Scavio and Gormezano (1980) reported that prior appetitive conditioned jaw movement training can actually facilitate subsequent aversive NM acquisition. Earlier, Konorski (1968) explained such asymmetries by noting the fact that contact with appetitive stimuli reduces the prior drive state (e.g. hunger), whereas contact with aversive stimuli such as shock leaves the prior drive state (e.g., fear) intact. Such motivational influences on learning have important implications for the study of neural substrates. They suggest not only where in the brain to look (e.g., reflex arc, brain stem, limbic system, hypothalamus, sensory systems, cortex), but also what stimulus parameters (e.g., strength; hedonic value) and temporal dimensions of training (e.g., ISI; backward conditioning) may influence neural activity.

To address more directly issues of motivation and the incentive values conditioned by different USs, we began a program of research utilizing a conditioned jaw movement paradigm (CJM) that differed from eyeblink training in important and informative ways. Originally developed by Gormezano (Smith, DiLollo & Gormezano, 1966; Coleman, Patterson & Gormezano, 1966; Sheafor & Gormezano, 1972), this training uses a rewarding intraoral water US rather than an aversive corneal air puff or periorbital shock US. Conditioned jaw movement or similar types of conditioning in the rabbit have been explored by others as well (Di Prisco & Freeman, 1985; McLaughlin & Powell, 1999; Schwartzbaum, 1983). Water restriction prior to conditioning (which is necessary to avoid satiation during such training; see Mitchell & Gormezano, 1970) produces a significantly different motivational context for CJM training sessions than is present for NM/eyeblink conditioning (although see above for the impact of deprivation on NM). Moreover, the occurrence of rewarding USs on each trial may reveal a different distribution of responses throughout the brain, as the CJM paradigm (unlike NM) engages neural systems that respond to positive hedonic stimuli (rewarding, rather than aversive events). This should be the case for the unconditioned responses to the US properties and, importantly, for the learned incentive value of the initially neutral CS. Finally, the behavioral/motor responses and their neural substrates differ, in that while the NM/eyeblink response is a relatively brief (few hundred milliseconds) defensive movement, the jaw movement response is a more complex, rhythmic, and longer lasting appetitive movement mediated by a different motor nucleus (see below).

Neural Substrates of CR and UR

For the NM/eyeblink paradigm, numerous studies have shown that abducens and accessory abducens motor neurons are the final common pathways for conditioned and unconditioned NM responses (see Cegavske, Harrison & Torigoe, 1987). Sensory information from a corneal air puff projects via the trigeminal nerve to the principal and spinal trigeminal nuclei. This sensory information is transferred directly or by way of the reticular formation to motor neurons of the abducens and accessory abducens nuclei (see Cegavske et al., 1987; Anderson & Steinmetz, 1994). These nuclei provide the primary innervation to the retractor bulbi muscle to produce eyeball retraction, allowing for passive extension of the NM. Thus, the final common pathway for the UR and CR has been mapped, and the cerebellum appears to be the critical area of plasticity leading to acquisition and elaboration of the CR (McCormick, Lavond, Clark, Kettner, Rising & Thompson, 1981; Krupa, Thompson & Thompson, 1993; for review see Steinmetz, 1996).

For the CJM paradigm, since neurons located in the motor nucleus of the trigeminal nerve (NVmot) control the muscles of mastication (Donga, Dubuc, Kolta & Lund, 1992), it is assumed that NVmot controls conditioned and unconditioned jaw movement responses (studies are currently underway in our laboratory to confirm this and characterize trigeminal responses in awake, behaving rabbits). Trigeminal motor neurons directly innervate the digastric and masseter muscles that control jaw opening and jaw-closing respectively. Unlike the NM paradigm, cortical areas seem to be important for generation of the response. For example, the area of the cortex known as the cortical masticatory area (CMA) is thought to be involved in rhythmic chewing because electrical stimulation of this area produces rhythmic movement of the jaw (Lund, 1991). The CMA lies below the primary motor cortex in the most inferior part of the precentral gyrus of humans and monkeys (Lund & Lamarre, 1974), and in rabbits and guinea pigs the masticatory area overlies parts of the face area of the primary motor and sensory cortical areas (Goldberg, Chandler & Tal, 1982; Lund, Sasamoto, Murakami & Olsson, 1984). The cortex (CMA) influences the brain stem central pattern generator (CPG) via the corticobulbar tracts (Dellow & Lund, 1971). In the study of movement control systems, rhythmic responses typically rely on a CPG to coordinate neural firing and generate a time base for the rhythm. The CPG often remains a hypothetical construct in the absence of definitive anatomical and neurobiological data. In the case of jaw movement, however, Nozaki, Iriki and Nakamura (1993) demonstrated that neurons in the bulbar parvocellular reticular formation (PCRF) responded with spikes to a short train of depolarizing stimuli in the CMA and showed rhythmic burst activity in association with trigeminal motor neuron activity. They concluded that both excitatory and inhibitory premotor neurons projecting to the masseter and digastric motor neurons were located in the PCRF and that these premotor neurons relay the output of the CPG in the medial bulbar reticular formation to trigeminal motor neurons, inducing rhythmic movement of the jaw. Presumably (but yet to be demonstrated), rhythmic CRs in the CJM paradigm result from the CS activating this pathway. The complexity of the rhythmic response and its neural generators requires further study to map CS and CR pathways and to test modulatory effects by brain structures involved in associative learning. One important difference from the NM paradigm is that cerebellar interpositus nucleus lesions, which disrupt acquisition and retention of NM (for review, see Steinmetz, 1996) fail to disrupt acquisition in the CJM paradigm (Gibbs, 1992; Berry, Steinmetz & Thompson, unpublished observations).

Studies of Hippocampus and CJM

While there are obvious differences in the neural pathways subserving the two types of conditioning, the response of the hippocampus appears to be generally similar for the two tasks. While an opponent process view of appetitive and aversive conditioning would predict opposing neural responses in motivational systems, data obtained in our laboratory are not consistent with such a characterization of the hippocampus. Recordings from the pyramidal cell layer of CA1 during CJM show highly significant increases in firing rate that develop over training (Oliver et al., 1993; Seager, Borgnis & Berry, 1997; 1998; Seager et al., 1999; see Figure 5). Single unit recordings show a number of conditioned response profiles (Borgnis, 1997), which are associative in nature (as in NM) because they are not observed in control rabbits given explicitly unpaired presentations of the conditioning stimuli (see also Oliver et al., 1993). However, consistent differences exist between NM and CJM unit responses, with the often rhythmic, prolonged CJM response easily distinguished from the brief, unimodal NM response. In fact, during a discrimination paradigm where two tone CSs differentiated air puff (NM) and water (CJM) trials, recordings from the

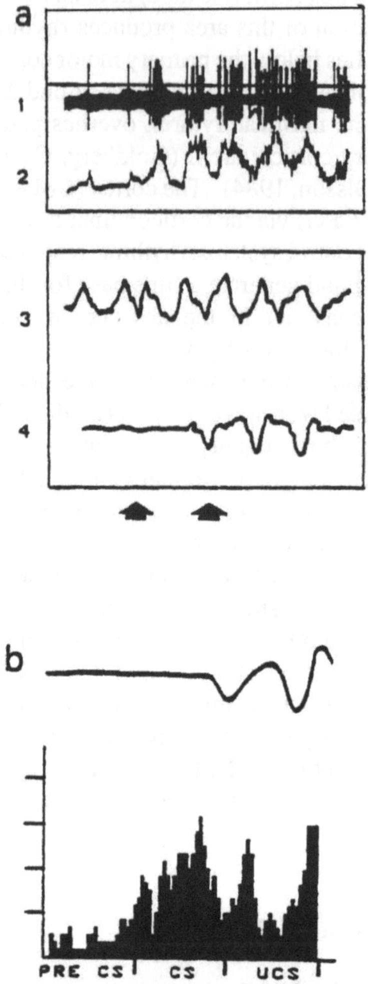

Figure 5. Neural and behavioral responses during CJM training. a: responses on a single training trial. 1. Filtered neural activity, 2. Integrated neural activity; 3. Slow waves from same electrode as 1. 4. Behavioral CJM response. Arrow indicate onset of tone (left) and water (right) at ISI of 250 ms. Horizontal line in 1 shows the window discriminator setting at 25 μV. b: averaged response. Top trace is a behavioral conditioned response from one trial in a trained animal. Bottom trace is an 8-trial averaged histogram of neural activity, showing the relative probability of a spike in each bin on each trial in units of 0.25. Pre CS = 250 ms baseline period; CS = 250 ms after tone onset; UCS = 250 ms after water onset. Each bin reflects 10 ms, and the values are smoothed by a scrolling average of three bins. [From "Hippocampal plasticity during jaw movement conditioning in the rabbit," by C.G. Oliver, R.A. Swain, and S.D. Berry, 1993, *Brain Research, 608,* p. 152. Copyright 1993 by Elsevier Science Inc.]

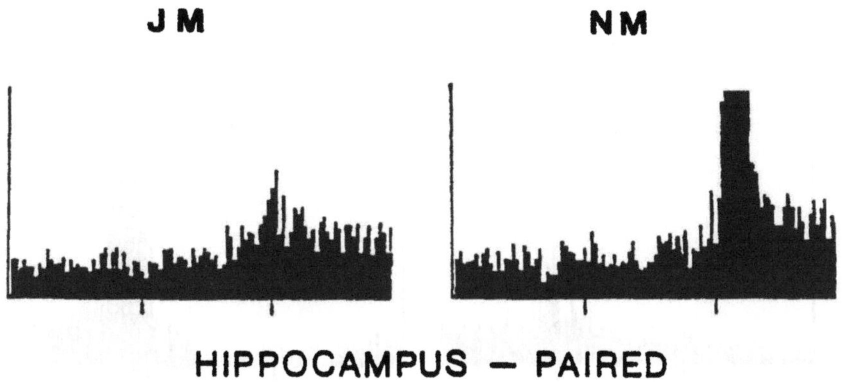

Figure 6. Hippocampal unit histogram responses to CJM trials (left) and NM trials (right) in the paired discrimination training. Markers indicate stimulus onset; ISI = 700 ms.

same electrodes showed different response profiles for the two types of trials (Oliver, 1991; see Figure 6). In both trial types, the responses were excitatory, inconsistent with a simple opponent process view. Differences were shown, however, in the magnitude, latency, duration and rhythmicity of the conditioned unit responses. Since the recordings were taken from small unit clusters, it remains to be determined whether individual cells responded differentially to the two trial types or whether different hippocampal neurons are entrained by the two tasks. A strong indicator that projection cells differentiate the trial types is the fact that lateral septal neurons, which receive projections from hippocampal CA3 pyramidal cells, displayed the same disparity in firing to NM versus CJM trials as seen in hippocampus (Oliver, 1991; see Figure 7).

Hippocampal recordings have been made during other appetitive tasks in rats, but only a few with explicit discrimination between appetitive and aversive learning. For example, Segal, Disterhoft and Olds (1972) reported that, while both appetitive and aversive training produced increases in hippocampal CA1 and CA3 neural firing, the dentate gyrus showed an opponent response—excitation to appetitive and inhibition to aversive. Hirsh's (1974) notion of contextual retrieval,and the data supporting it, are consistent with a role for the hippocampus in differentiating motivational states and influencing retrieval and/or performance strategies depending upon them. The confounding factor in comparing the Segal et al. (1972) study to rabbit classical conditioning is that their paradigm trained locomotion to the reward stimulus and freezing to the aversive. It is possible that the dentate neurons were coding movement processes that are known to accompany patterns of hippocampal slow wave activity generated in the dentate gyrus (see Vanderwolf, 1971; Vanderwolf et al., 1975). It is also important to note that the hippocampal slow wave activity in rabbit conditioning outlined in this chapter is not the same as the movement-related patterns described in rats. It is lower in frequency (2-8 Hz) and is dependent upon cholinergic systems, whereas the locomotion-related slow waves are resistant to cholinergic blockade and are in the 8-14 Hz range (Vanderwolf et al., 1975).

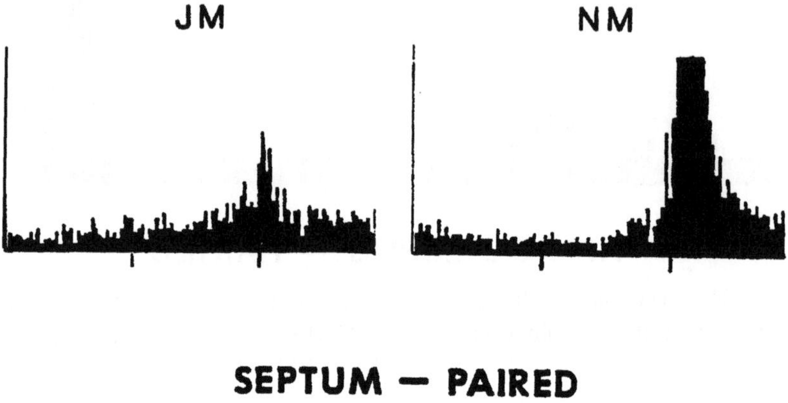

Figure 7. Lateral septal unit histogram responses to CJM trials (left) and NM trials (right) in the paired discrimination training. Markers indicate stimulus onset; ISI = 700 ms.

Aging and CJM

In order to assess whether age-related hippocampal and learning deficits found in eyeblink conditioning would generalize to the appetitive task, Seager et al. (1997) trained two groups of rabbits in a CJM paradigm. Young (3-7 months) and aging (40-49 months) rabbits were trained using a trace CJM paradigm (300 ms tone, 450 ms trace, 200 ms intraoral water) while recording simultaneous hippocampal neural responses from area CA1. Results of the experiment revealed significantly slower acquisition rates in the older animals, consistent with data obtained for eyeblink conditioning (e.g., Coffin & Woodruff-Pak, 1993; Deyo, Straube & Disterhoft, 1989; Graves & Solomon, 1985; Powell, Buchanan & Hernandez, 1981; 1984; Solomon & Groccia-Ellison, 1996; Thompson, Moyer & Disterhoft, 1996; Woodruff-Pak, Lavond, Logan & Thompson, 1987; see Chapter 7; this volume).

Importantly, neural data from the hippocampal electrodes revealed age differences in the magnitude and form of conditioning-related responses which, given the impact of aging on the hippocampus, could be important for interpreting the behavioral differences. Early in training, standard scores corresponding to the latest portion of the trace interval (150 ms before US onset) were significantly larger for young rabbits than for aging rabbits. There was a significant negative correlation (r = -.60) between the magnitude of this response and subsequent learning rate (trials to criterion). The same general relationship held within each of the age groups, indicating that the aging main effect was not responsible for the across-groups correlation. This would suggest that animals that had larger magnitude unit responses just prior to US onset early in training were capable of learning the task at a relatively fast rate.

In addition to significant but expected effects on learning rate and hippocampal responsiveness, an unexpected effect of aging on conditioned movement parameters was observed in this task. Conditioned responses (rhythmic chewing movements beginning after tone onset but before water onset) of aging animals were of a significantly lower frequency (Hz) than CRs of young animals. Upon examination of URs for each age group, an age difference was not found, indicating that the difference in CR frequencies was not secondary to disruptions in motor control systems (see Table 1). This strongly implies that aging affects some neural systems that modulate the central pattern generator during conditioned but not unconditioned responses. No such CR-UR differences have been reported in other aging studies, including NM conditioning, suggesting the CJM paradigm may be especially useful in studies of the neurobiology of aging and its impact on learning and memory systems. Also significant is the fact that the age difference in neural responses occurred during a particularly important part of the trial—the period just prior to arrival of the US. This neural observation suggests that timing or anticipation of the US may differ between groups and help explain the learning deficit.

Table 1
Mean Jaw Movement Frequencies for Aging and Young Rabbits with Accompanying Probabilities of Observed Differences

	CR frequency	UR frequency	Probability of difference
Young	5.20 Hz	5.66 Hz	.13
Aging	4.15 Hz	5.50 Hz	.004
Probability of difference	.02	.73	

[From "Delayed acquisition of behavioral and hippocampal responses during jaw movement conditioning in aging rabbits," by M.A. Seager, R.L. Borgnis, and S.D. Berry, 1997, *Neurobiology of Aging, 18*(6), 631-639. Copyright 1997 by Elsevier Science, Inc.]

Cholinergic Impairment and CJM

A subsequent study to investigate the role of cholinergic systems in the CJM paradigm revealed many parallels between the earlier aging findings and cholinergic impairment. Two groups of young rabbits (3-6 months) were trained to criterion in a trace CJM paradigm (identical to that used in Seager et al., 1997) after daily subcutaneous injections of either scopolamine hydrobromide (HBr) or scopolamine methylbromide (MBr; Seager et al., 1999). Rabbits given HBr took significantly longer to reach a criterion of eight CRs in any nine consecutive trials and gave a significantly lower percentage of CRs early in training. Scopolamine HBr also completely suppressed conditioning-related unit responses in the hippocampus (as in NM, Salvatierra & Berry, 1989). In addition, HBr mimicked the effects of aging on behavioral CR frequency (Hz) measures (see Figure 8). While HBr rabbits exhibited significantly lower CR frequencies than MBr rabbits, UR frequencies were unaffected.

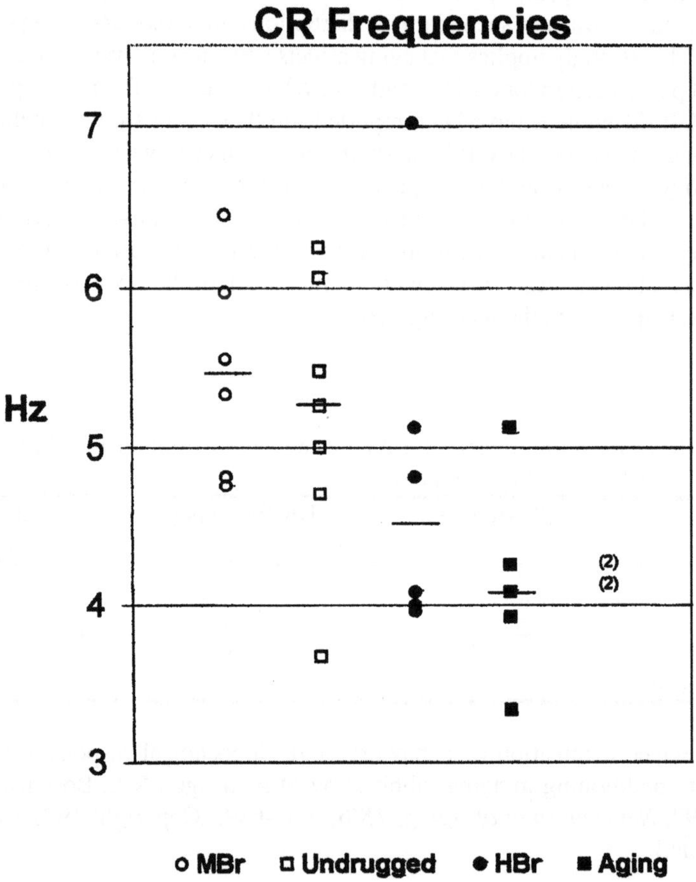

Figure 8. Plot of average CR frequencies for individual rabbits clustered in treatment categories. Figure includes data from young and aging groups in Seager et al. (1997) for comparison between aging and cholinergic impairment. Horizontal lines within each treatment category indicate the median of that group. (2) = two rabbits with identical CR frequencies. [From "Scopolamine disruption of behavioral and hippocampal responses in appetitive trace classical conditioning," by M.A. Seager, Y. Asaka, and S.D. Berry, 1999, *Behavioural Brain Research, 100*(1-2), p. 146. Copyright 1999 by Elsevier Science Inc.]

This study illustrates the utility of the CJM paradigm for studying the involvement of cholinergic systems in memory and the deleterious effects of aging on these systems. Moreover, it hints at how differences in neural control systems might address theoretical questions on the relationship between conditioned and unconditioned responses. If aging and/or drugs can be shown to affect CRs and not URs, then one must explore the possibility of different neural substrates at neurochemical, if not neuroanatomical, levels. Future neurobiological studies can utilize lesions and drugs to exploit the strengths of the CJM paradigm. In many cases they may corroborate findings from NM conditioning but, where differences exist, they may be interpretable in terms of distinct or parallel brain systems mediating appetitive and aversive learning (see, e.g., Gibbs, 1992).

Recordings of slow waves and unit responses in the context of age- or cholinergically-impaired behavior suggest that deficits result from a combination of disrupted brain state (EEG) and impaired unit responses during important parts of training trials. These findings imply that research into treatments should explore the impact of global state or contextual influences as well as highly specific within-trial processes related to stimulus contingencies and timing.

SUMMARY AND CONCLUSIONS

This chapter summarizes studies in classical conditioning of rabbit nictitating membrane and jaw movement responses which reveal similarities and differences in the neural and behavioral effects of aversive and appetitive conditioning. Our observations suggest that, especially in the hippocampal formation, appetitive and aversive conditioning stimuli do not trigger obviously opponent neural responses. The responses differ in important and instructive ways, but in each case, the neural activity in the septohippocampal system appears to increase as a function of the conditioned cue value of the CS in association with the US—a finding in agreement with the concept of incentive motivation.

These investigations began with an unexpected observation of the impact of individual differences in brain state on subsequent NM conditioning rates (Berry & Thompson, 1978). A series of follow-up studies has shown a strong correspondence between the state of the forebrain as reflected by hippocampal activity and the ability of an animal to demonstrate conditioned behavior. Direct manipulations of brain state by lesions (Berry & Thompson, 1979), drugs (Salvatierra & Berry, 1989), or deprivation (Berry & Swain, 1989) have shown the strength of this relationship, and its consistency with the idea of pre-training arousal states and a generalized attention process. A strength of this approach was the simultaneous recording of behavioral and brain activity that allowed each to inform our thinking about the other. That is, some of our drug and lesion studies replicated the behavioral effects reported by others that were often interpreted as possible hippocampal dysfunction. Our observations empirically verified and characterized the changes in hippocampal slow wave and unit activity that were, in fact, occurring before and during the affected behavior. Often, the neural results resolved issues of interpretation that remained ambiguous after analysis of the behavioral data alone.

Our study of theta-triggered training demonstrated the acquisition benefits of having theta present in the hippocampus during the actual arrival of the conditioning stimuli rather than merely as background to the training session. This is consistent with a role for the hippocampus in phasic, selective attentional processes but does not rule out an involvement in more global processes as well (see above). In an exploration of the generality of hippocampal engagement under alternative motivational conditions, we showed that appetitive conditioning of the jaw movement response is accompanied by rhythmic excitation of hippocampal neurons in the trained (but not control) group early in the conditioning process (Oliver et al., 1993). Later, the effects of anticholinergic drugs (Seager et al., 1999) and aging (Seager et al., 1997, 1998) were shown to be generally similar during CJM to what is seen in NM, although the complexity of the behavioral response allowed a more informative analysis of conditioned and unconditioned movement effects in CJM. Simultaneous discrimination between CJM and NM trials showed excitatory responses of different patterns to the different trial types, demonstrating selectivity of hippocampal responses but no strong evidence of opponent processes triggered by USs of opposing valences at this level of the nervous system.

As a result of these studies and a reading of the literature, we are considering some ideas to guide our thinking on hippocampal function(s) during classical conditioning. First, it is clear from the pattern of lesion and recording results that the hippocampus is part of a parallel system that modulates essential conditioning circuits elsewhere (e.g., cerebellum). Second, its function is perhaps related to "declarative" or awareness-based processes (Clark & Squire, 1998) that accompany (but are not essential for the simplest forms of) classical conditioning. Third, conditioned unit responses correspond to the patterns we would expect from cells in an incentive motivational system, with excitatory responses to biologically significant stimuli (USs) and to the cues (CSs) that predict them. Finally, the well known recent declarative memory deficits after hippocampal lesions may be interpretable as a loss of low-level incentive-based reactions (e.g., recognition of familiarity or novelty; nonspecific push/pull "gut" reactions, see Grastyan et al., 1966). Such responses may be necessary for memory retrieval or guidance of recently learned behaviors until traces are established elsewhere in increasingly independent (presumably cortical) systems.

The insights derived from our electrophysiological recordings in intact, lesioned, and drugged animals suggest that EEG or slow wave predictions are related to the state of preparedness of the animal to process exteroceptive events and relationships. The specific conditioned unit responses may provide incentive motivational processes to energize and guide acquired behaviors. These would play a role in the elicitation of the appropriate behavior by cues (CSs) and the adaptation of the conditioned response to the temporal parameters of the training paradigm. To explore these ideas, we plan to continue comparing classical conditioning of positive and negative incentives while mapping limbic and related brain systems.

Descriptions of the impact of motivational variables on classical conditioning are important to a comprehensive characterization of the neural substrates of associative learning. If, in fact, different behavioral or neural processes are involved in the adaptive learning of pleasurable and unpleasant places or events in the environment (see Bolles, 1970; LeDoux, 1995), then close comparisons of the two must be done.

Classical conditioning, with its precise experimental control of cueing, timing, motor systems and motivational responses should play a critical role in this exploration. One goal of this chapter has been to argue the benefit of simultaneous recording of behavioral and neural measurements following manipulation of the brain or behavior. As a complement to lesion studies, such converging operations provide better information on neural substrates and mechanisms than techniques that measure either behavioral or neural domains alone. The addition of physiological dependent measures, and the ability to compare them in detail with the animal's performance on a trial by trial basis, should help to reveal critical brain circuitry for learning, improve our logical inferences about behavioral phenomena, and serve as a productive guide to future research and applications in the psychology of learning and memory.

REFERENCES

Anderson, B.J., & Steinmetz, J.E. (1994). Cerebellar and brainstem circuits involved in classical eyeblink conditioning. *Reviews in the Neurosciences, 5,* 251-273.

Arai, A., & Lynch, G. (1992). Factors regulating the magnitude of long-term potentiation induced by theta pattern stimulation. *Brain Research, 598,* 173-184.

Bennett, T.L. (1975). The electrical activity of the hippocampus and processes of attention. In R.L. Isaacson & K.H. Pribram (Eds.), *The Hippocampus* (Vol. 2, pp. 71-99). New York: Plenum Press.

Berger, T.W., Alger, B., & Thompson, R.F. (1976). Neuronal substrate of classical conditioning in the hippocampus. *Science, 192,* 483-485.

Berger, T.W., Berry, S.D., & Thompson, R.F. (1986). Role of the hippocampus in classical conditioning of aversive and appetitive behaviors. In R.L. Isaacson & K.H. Pribram (Eds.), *The Hippocampus* (Vol. 4, pp. 203-239). New York: Plenum Press.

Berger, T.W., & Orr, W.B. (1983). Hippocampectomy selectively disrupts discrimination reversal conditioning of the rabbit nictitating membrane response. *Behavioural Brain Research, 8,* 49-68.

Berger, T.W., & Thompson, R.F. (1978). Neuronal plasticity in the limbic system during classical conditioning of the rabbit nictitating membrane response. I. The hippocampus. *Brain Research, 145,* 323-346.

Berry, S.D. (1982). Septo-hippocampal activity and learning rate. In C.D. Woody (Ed.), *Conditioning: Representation of Involved Neural Functions* (pp. 417-431). New York: Plenum Press.

Berry, S.D., Rinaldi, P.C., Thompson, R.F., & Verzeano, M. (1978). Analysis of temporal relations among units and slow waves in rabbit hippocampus. *Brain Research Bulletin, 3,* 509-518.

Berry, S.D., Sim, D.G., & Snyder, C.W. (1969). Cortical polarization effects on consolidation of avoidance learning in rats. *Psychonomic Science, 16*(1), 20-21.

Berry, S.D., & Snyder, C.W. (1978). Intensity effects of cortical polarization during consolidation. *Physiological Psychology, 6*(2), 223-225.

Berry, S.D., & Swain, R.A. (1989). Water deprivation optimizes hippocampal activity and facilitates nictitating membrane conditioning. *Behavioral Neuroscience, 103*(1), 71-76.

Berry, S.D., & Thompson, R.F. (1978). Prediction of learning rate from the hippocampal electroencephalogram. *Science, 200,* 1298-1300.

Berry, S.D., & Thompson, R.F. (1979). Medial septal lesions retard classical conditioning of the rabbit nictitating membrane response in rabbits. *Science, 205,* 209-211.

Berry, S.D., Weisz, D.J., & Mamounas, L.A. (1987). Neural correlates of acquisition rate. In I. Gormezano, W.F. Prokasy, & R.F. Thompson (Eds.), *Classical Conditioning* (3rd ed., pp. 255-274). Hillsdale, NJ: Lawrence Erlbaum.

Best, M.R., & Best, P.J. (1976). The effects of state of consciousness and latent inhibition on hippocampal unit activity in the rat during conditioning. *Experimental Neurology, 51,* 564-573.

Bindra, D. (1974). A motivational view of learning, performance, and behavior modification. *Psychological Review, 81*(3), 199-213.

Bland, B.H., Andersen, P., Ganes, T., & Sveen, O. (1980). Automated analysis of rhythmicity of physiologically identified hippocampal formation neurons. *Experimental Brain Research, 38*(2), 205-

19.
Blokland, A. (1996). Acetylcholine: A neurotransmitter for learning and memory? *Brain Research Review, 21,* 285-300.
Bolles, R.C. (1970). Species-specific defense reactions and avoidance learning. *Psychological Review, 77*(1), 32-48.
Borgnis, R.L. (1993). *Latent inhibition of multiple unit activity and EEG in rabbit hippocampus.* Unpublished master's thesis, Miami University, Oxford, OH.
Borgnis, R.L. (1997). Characterization of hippocampal single unit activity and unit/slow wave relations during classical conditioning in the rabbit. *Dissertation Abstracts International, 58*(8-B), 4071.
Brown, J.H. (1990). Atropine, scopolamine, and related belladonna alkaloids. In A.G. Gilman, T.W. Rall, A.S. Nies, & R. Taylor (Eds.), *Goodman and Gilman's thePpharmacological Basis of theRapeutics* (8th ed., pp. 150-165). New York: Pergamon Press.
Buzsaki, G., Leung, L.-W.S., & Vanderwolf, C.H. (1983). Cellular bases of hippocampal EEG in the behaving rat. *Brain Research Reviews, 6,* 139-171.
Cegavske, C.F., Harrison, T.A., & Torigoe, Y. (1987). Identification of the substrates of the unconditioned response in the classically conditioned, rabbit, nictitating-membrane preparation. In I. Gormezano, W.F. Prokasy, & R.F. Thompson (Eds.), *Classical Conditioning* (3rd ed., pp. 65-91). Hillsdale, NJ: Lawrence Erlbaum.
Clark, R.E., & Squire, L.R. (1998). Classical conditioning and brain systems: The role of awareness. *Science, 280,* 77-81.
Cohen, N.J., & Eichenbaum, H. (1993). *Memory, Amnesia, and the Hippocampal System.* Cambridge, MA: MIT Press.
Coffin, J.M., & Woodruff-Pak, D.S. (1993). Delay classical conditioning in young and older rabbits: Initial acquisition and retention at 12 and 18 months. *Behavioral Neuroscience, 107*(1), 63-71.
Coleman, S.R., Patterson, M.M., & Gormezano, I. (1966). Conditioned jaw movement in the rabbit: Deprivation procedure and saccharin concentration. *Psychonomic Science, 6*(1), 39-40.
Dearing, M.F., & Dickinson, A. (1979). Counterconditioning of shock by a water reinforcer in rabbits. *Animal Learning & Behavior, 7*(3), 360-366.
Dellow, P.G., & Lund, J.P. (1971). Evidence for central timing of rhythmical mastication. *Journal of Physiology, 215,* 1-13.
Destrade, C. (1982). Two types of diencephalically-driven RSA (theta) as a means of studying memory formation in mice. *Brain Research, 234,* 486-493.
Deupree, D., Coppock, W., & Willer, H. (1982). Pretraining septal driving of hippocampal rhythmic slow activity facilitates acquisition of visual discrimination. *Journal of Comparative and Physiological Psychology, 96,* 557-562.
Deyo, R.A., Straube, K.T., & Disterhoft, J.F. (1989). Nimodipine facilitates associative learning in aging rabbits. *Science, 243,* 809-811.
Dickinson, A., & Pearce, J.M. (1977). Inhibitory interactions between appetitive and aversive stimuli. *Psychological Bulletin, 84*(4), 690-711.
Di Prisco, G.V., & Freeman, W.J. (1985). Odor-related bulbar EEG spatial pattern analysis during appetitive conditioning in rabbits. *Behavioral Neuroscience. 99*(5), 964-78.
Donga, R., Dubuc, R., Kolta, A., & Lund, J.P. (1992). Evidence that the masticatory muscles receive a direct innervation from cell group k in the rabbit. *Neuroscience, 49*(4), 951-961.
Everitt, B.J., & Robbins, T.W. (1997). Central cholinergic systems and cognition. *Annual Review of Psychology, 48,* 649-684.
Fox, S.E., Wolfson, S., & Ranck, J.B., Jr. (1986). Hippocampal theta rhythm and the firing of neurons in walking and urethane anesthetized rats. *Experimental Brain Research, 62,* 495-508.
Galey, D., Jeantet, Y., Destrade, C., & Jaffard, R. (1983). Facilitation of memory consolidation by post-training electrical stimulation of the medial septal nucleus: Is it mediated by changes in rhythmic slow activity. *Behavioral and Neural Biology, 38,* 240-250.
Gallagher, M., & Rapp, P.R. (1997). The use of animal models to study the effects of aging on cognition. *Annual Review of Psychology, 48,* 339-370.
Garcia, J., & Koelling, R.A. (1966). Relation of cue to consequence in avoidance learning. *Psychonomic Science, 4,* 123-124.
Gazzaniga, M.S., Ivry, R.B., & Mangun, G.R. (1998). *Cognitive Neuroscience: The Biology of the Mind.* New York: W.W. Norton.
Gibbs, C.M. (1992). Divergent effects of deep cerebellar lesions on two different conditioned somatomotor responses in rabbits. *Brain Research, 585,* 395-399.

Glazer, H. (1974). Instrumental response persistence following induction of hippocampal theta frequency during fixed-ratio responding in rats. *Journal of Comparative and Physiological Psychology, 86*(6), 1156-1162.

Goldberg, L.J., Chandler, S.H., & Tal, M. (1982). Relationship between jaw movements and trigeminal motoneuron membrane-potential fluctuations during cortically induced rhythmical jaw movements in the guinea pig. *Journal of Neurophysiology, 48,* 110-138.

Gormezano, I., Prokasy, W.F., & Thompson, R.F. (Eds.). (1987). *Classical Conditioning.* (3rd ed.). Hillsdale, NJ: Lawrence Erlbaum.

Grastyan, E., Karmos, G., Vereczkey, L., & Kellenyi, L. (1966). The hippocampal electrical correlates of the homeostatic regulation of motivation. *Electroencephalography and Clinical Neurophysiology, 21,* 34-53.

Graves, C.A., & Solomon, P.R. (1985). Age-related disruption of trace but not delay classical conditioning of the rabbit's nictitating membrane response. *Behavioral Neuroscience, 99*(1), 88-96.

Gray, J.A. (1972). Effects of septal driving of the hippocampal theta rhythm on resistance to extinction. *Physiology & Behavior, 8,* 481-490.

Gray, J.A. (1986). *The Neuropsychology of Anxiety: An Enquiry into the Functions of the Septo-Hippocampal System.* Oxford: Clarendon Press.

Green, J.D., & Arduini, A.A. (1954). Hippocampal electrical activity in arousal. *Journal of Neurophysiology, 17,* 533-557.

Grossberg, S. (1982). Processing of expected and unexpected events during conditioning and attention: A psychophysiological theory. *Psychological Review, 89*(5), 529-572.

Grossberg, S., & Schmajuk, N.A. (1987). Neural dynamics of attentionally modulated Pavlovian conditioning: Conditioned reinforcement, inhibition, and opponent processing. *Psychobiology, 15*(3), 195-240.

Harvey, J.A., Gormezano, I., & Cool-Hauser, V.A. (1983). Effects of scopolamine and methylscopolamine on classical conditioning of the rabbit nictitating membrane response. *Journal of Pharmacology and Experimental Therapeutics, 255,* 42-49.

Harvey, J.A., Gormezano, I., & Cool-Hauser, V.A. (1985). Relationship between heterosynaptic reflex facilitation and acquisition of the nictitating membrane response in control and scopolamine-injected rabbits. *Journal of Neuroscience, 5,* 596-602.

Hilgard, E.R., & Bower, G.H. (1966). *Theories of Learning* (3rd ed.). New York: Appleton-Century-Crofts.

Hinde, R.A. (1970). Animal Behaviour; a Synthesis of Ethology and Comparative Psychology (2nd ed.). New York: McGraw-Hill.

Hirsh, R. (1974). The hippocampus and contextual retrieval of information from memory: A theory. *Behavioral Biology, 12,* 421-444.

Holscher, C., Anwyl, R., & Rowan, M.J. (1997). Stimulation on the positive phase of hippocampal theta rhythm induces long-term potentiation that can be depotentiated by stimulation on the negative phase in area CA1 in vivo. *Journal of Neuroscience, 17*(16), 6470-6477.

Honey, R.C., & Good, M. (1993). Selective hippocampal lesions abolish the contextual specificity of latent inhibition and conditioning. *Behavioral Neuroscience, 107*(1), 23-33.

Isaacson, R.L. (1982). *The Limbic System* (2nd ed.). New York: Plenum Press.

Isaacson, R.L., & Pribram, K.H. (Eds.). (1975). *The Hippocampus* (Vol. 1). New York: Plenum Press.

Isaacson, R.L., & Pribram, K.H. (Eds.). (1975). *The Hippocampus* (Vol. 2). New York: Plenum Press.

Isaacson, R.L., & Pribram, K.H. (Eds.). (1986). *The Hippocampus* (Vol. 3). New York: Plenum Press.

Isaacson, R.L., & Pribram, K.H. (Eds.). (1986). *The Hippocampus* (Vol. 4). New York: Plenum Press.

Jarrard, L.E. (1973). The hippocampus and motivation. *Psychological Bulletin, 79*(1), 1-12.

Kimble, G.A. (1961). *Hilgard and Marquis' Conditioning and Learning.* New York: Appleton-Century-Crofts.

Kimble, G.A. (1967). Pavlov and the experimental study of conditioned reflexes. In G.A. Kimble (Ed.), *Foundations of Conditioning and Learning* (pp. 22-43). New York: Appleton-Century-Crofts.

Konorski, J. (1968). *Conditioned Reflexes and Neuron Organization.* New York: Hafner Publishing.

Krupa, D.J., Thompson, J.K., & Thompson, R.F. (1993). Localization of a memory trace in the mammalian brain. *Science, 260*(5110), 989-991.

Landfield, P.W. (1977). Different effects of posttrial driving or blocking of the theta rhythm on avoidance learning in rats. *Physiology & Behavior, 18,* 439-445.

Larson, J., Wong, D., & Lynch, G. (1986). Patterned stimulation at the theta frequency is optimal for the induction of hippocampal long-term potentiation. *Brain Research, 368,* 347-350.

Ledoux, J.E. (1995). Emotion: Clues from the brain. *Annual Review of Psychology, 46,* 209-35.

Lindsley, D.B., & Wilson, C.L. (1975). Brain stem-hypothalamic systems influencing hippocampal activity and behavior. In R.L. Isaacson & K.H. Pribram (Eds.), *The Hippocampus* (Vol. 2, pp. 247-278). New York: Plenum Press.

Lovibond, P.F., & Dickinson, A. (1982). Counterconditioning of appetitive and defensive CRs in rabbits. *Quarterly Journal of Experimental Psychology, 34B,* 115-126.

Lubow, R.E. (1989). *Latent Inhibition and Conditioned Attention Theory.* Cambridge, England: Cambridge University Press.

Lund, J.P. (1991). Mastication and its control by the brain stem. *Critical Reviews in Oral Biology and Medicine, 2*(1), 33-64.

Lund, J.P., & Lamarre, Y. (1974). Activity of neurons in the lower precentral cortex during voluntary and rhythmical jaw movements in the monkey. *Experimental Brain Research, 19,* 282-299.

Lund, J.P., Sasamoto, K., Murakami, T., & Olsson, K.A. (1984). Analysis of rhythmical jaw movements produced by electrical stimulation of motor-sensory cortex in rabbits. *Journal of Neurophysiology, 52*(6), 1014-1029.

MacLean, P.D. (1955). The limbic system ("visceral brain") and emotional behavior. *Archives of Neurology and Psychiatry, 73,* 130-134.

Maren, S., DeCola, J.P., Swain, R.A., Fanselow, M.S., & Thompson, R.F. (1994). Parallel augmentation of hippocampal long-term potentiation, theta rhythm, and contextual fear conditioning in water-deprived rats. *Behavioral Neuroscience, 108*(1), 44-56.

McCormick, D.A., Lavond, D.G., Clark, G.A., Kettner, R.E., Rising, C.E., & Thompson, R.F. (1981). The engram found? Role of the cerebellum in classical conditioning of nictitating membrane and eyelid responses. *Bulletin of the Psychonomic Society, 18*(3), 103-105.

McLaughlin, J., & Powell, D.A. (1999). Pavlovian heart rate and jaw movement conditioning in the rabbit: Effects of medial prefrontal lesions. *Neurobiology of Learning and Memory, 71*(2), 150-166.

Miller, D.P., & Steinmetz, J.E. (1997). Hippocampal activity during classical discrimination-reversal eyeblink conditioning in rabbits. *Behavioral Neuroscience, 111*(1), 70-79.

Mitchell, D.S., & Gormezano, I. (1970). Effects of water deprivation on classical appetitive conditioning of the rabbit's jaw movement response. *Learning and Motivation, 1*(2), 199-206.

Mook, D.G. (1987). *Motivation: The Organization of Action.* New York: W.W. Norton.

Moore, J.W., Goodell, N., & Solomon, P.R. (1976). Central cholinergic blockade by scopolamine and habituation, classical conditioning, and latent inhibition of the rabbit's nictitating membrane response. *Physiological Psychology, 4,* 395-399.

Nozaki, S., Iriki, A., & Nakamura, Y. (1993). Trigeminal premotor neurons in the bulbar parvocellular reticular formation participating in induction of rhythmical activity of trigeminal motoneurons by repetitive stimulation of the cerebral cortex in the guinea pig. *Journal of Neurophysiology, 69(2),* 595-608.

O'Keefe, J., & Recce, M.L. (1993). Phase relationship between hippocampal place units and the EEG theta rhythm. *Hippocampus, 3*(3), 317-330.

Olds, J. (1975). Mapping the mind onto the brain. In F.G. Worden, J.P. Swazey, & G. Adelman (Eds.), *The Neurosciences: Paths of Discovery* (pp.375-400). Cambridge, MA: MIT Press.

Oliver, C.G. (1991). Hippocampal and septal unit activity during appetitive-aversive discrimination and reversal. *Dissertation Abstracts International, 51*(12-B, Pt. 1), 6145-6146.

Oliver, C.G., Swain, R.A., & Berry, S.D. (1993). Hippocampal plasticity during jaw movement conditioning in the rabbit. *Brain Research, 608,* 150-154.

Otto, T., Eichenbaum, H., Wiener, S.I., & Wible, C.G. (1991). Learning-related patterns of CA1 spike trains parallel stimulation parameters optimal for inducing hippocampal long-term potentiation. *Hippocampus, 1*(2), 181-192.

Papez, J.W. (1937). A proposed mechanism of emotion. *Archives of Neurology and Psychiatry, 38,* 725-743.

Parasuraman, R. (1998). *The Attentive Brain.* Cambridge, MA: MIT Press.

Pavlides, C., Greenstein, Y.J., Grudman, M., & Winson, J. (1988). Long-term potentiation in the dentate gyrus is induced preferentially on the positive phase of theta-rhythm. *Brain Research, 439*(1-2), 383-387.

Petri, H.L. (1996). *Motivation: Theory, Research, and Applications* (4th ed.). Pacific Grove, CA: Brooks/Cole Publishing.

Posner, M.I., & Petersen, S.E. (1990). The attention system of the human brain. *Annual Review of Neuroscience, 13,* 25-42.

Powell, D.A. (1979). Peripheral and central muscarinic cholinergic blockade: Effects on Pavlovian conditioning. *Bulletin of the Psychonomic Society, 14,* 161-164.
Powell, D.A., Buchanan, S.L., & Hernandez, L.L. (1981). Age-related changes in classical (Pavlovian) conditioning in the New Zealand albino rabbit. *Experimental Aging Research, 7*(4), 453-465.
Powell, D.A., Buchanan, S.L., & Hernandez, L.L. (1984). Age-related changes in Pavlovian conditioning: Central nervous system correlates. *Physiology & Behavior, 32,* 609-616.
Powell, D.A., Hernandez, L., & Buchanan, S.L. (1985). Intraseptal scopolamine has differential effects on Pavlovian eye blink and heart rate conditioning. *Behavioral Neuroscience, 99*(1), 75-87.
Powell, D.A., Milligan, W.L., & Buchanan, S.L. (1976). Orienting and classical conditioning in the rabbit (*Oryctolagus cuniculus*): Effects of septal area lesions. *Physiology & Behavior, 17,* 955-962.
Rescorla, R.A., & Solomon, R.L. (1967). Two-process learning theory: Relationships between Pavlovian conditioning and instrumental learning. *Psychological Review, 74*(3), 151-182.
Rescorla, R.A., & Wagner, A.R. (1972). A theory of Pavlovian conditioning: Variations in the effectiveness of reinforcement and nonreinforcement. In A.H. Black & W.F. Prokasy (Eds.), *Classical Conditioning II: Current Theory and Research* (pp. 64-99). New York: Appleton-Century-Crofts.
Salvatierra, A.T., & Berry, S.D. (1989). Scopolamine disruption of septo-hippocampal activity and classical conditioning. *Behavioral Neuroscience, 103*(4), 715-721.
Scavio, M.J., Jr. (1974). Classical-classical transfer: Effects of prior aversive conditioning in the rabbit. *Journal of Comparative and Physiological Psychology, 86,* 107-115.
Scavio, M.J., Jr. (1987). Appetitive-aversive interactions in rabbit conditioning preparations. In I. Gormezano, W.F. Prokasy, & R.F. Thompson (Eds.), *Classical Conditioning* (3rd ed., pp. 319-338). Hillsdale, NJ: Lawrence Erlbaum.
Scavio, M.J., Jr., & Gormezano, I. (1980). Classical-classical transfer: Effects of prior appetitive conditioning upon aversive conditioning in rabbits. *Animal Learning & Behavior, 8,* 218-224.
Schmajuk, N.A, Lam, Y.-W., & Christiansen, B.A. (1994). Latent inhibition of the rat eyeblink response: Effect of hippocampal aspiration lesions. *Physiology & Behavior, 55*(3), 597-601.
Schmaltz, L.W., & Theios, J. (1972). Acquisition and extinction of a classically conditioned response in hippocampectomized rabbits (*Oryctolagus cuniculus*). *Journal of Comparative and Physiological Psychology, 79*(2), 328-333.
Schwartzbaum, J.S. (1983). Electrophysiology of taste-mediated functions in parabrachial nuclei of behaving rabbit. *Brain Research Bulletin, 11,* 61-89.
Scoville, W.B., & Milner, B. (1957). Loss of recent memory after bilateral hippocampal lesions. *Journal of Neurology, Neurosurgery and Psychiatry, 20,* 11-21.
Seager, M.A., Asaka, Y., & Berry, S.D. (1999). Scopolamine disruption of behavioral and hippocampal responses in appetitive trace classical conditioning. *Behavioural Brain Research, 100*(1-2), 143-151.
Seager, M.A., Asaka, Y., Chabot, E.S., Johnson, L.D., & Berry, S.D. (1998). Hippocampal theta-triggered training trials in rabbit classical conditioning: Effect on learning. *Society for Neuroscience Abstracts, 24*(2), 1914.
Seager, M.A., Borgnis, R.L., & Berry, S.D. (1997). Delayed acquisition of behavioral and hippocampal responses during jaw movement conditioning in aging rabbits. *Neurobiology of Aging, 18*(6), 631-639.
Seager, M.A., Borgnis, R.L., & Berry, S.D. (1998). Hippocampal age differences reoccur after modification of stimulus configurations in rabbit jaw movement conditioning. *Neurobiology of Aging, 19*(3), 277-281.
Segal M., Disterhoft, J.F., & Olds, J. (1972). Hippocampal unit activity during classical aversive and appetitive conditioning. *Science, 175,* 792-794.
Sheafor, P.J., & Gormezano, I. (1972). Conditioning the rabbit's (*Oryctolagus cuniculus*) jaw movement response: US magnitude effects on URs, CRs, and pseudo-CRs. *Journal of Comparative and Physiological Psychology, 81*(3), 449-456.
Sherrington, C.S. (1906). *The Integrative Action of the Nervous System.* New York: C. Scribner's Sons.
Shettleworth, S.J. (1979). Constraints on conditioning in the writings of Konorski. In A. Dickinson & R.A. Boakes (Eds.), *Mechanisms of Learning and Motivation: A Memorial Volume to Jerzy Konorski* (pp. 399-416). Hillsdale, NJ: Lawrence Erlbaum.
Sinclair, B.R., Seto, M.G., & Bland, B.H. (1982). Theta-cells in CA1 and dentate layers of hippocampal formation: Relations to slow-wave activity and motor behavior in the freely moving rabbit. *Journal of Neurophysiology, 48*(5), 1214-1225.
Skaggs, W.E., McNaughton, B.L., Wilson, M.A., & Barnes, C.A. (1996). Theta phase precession in hippocampal neuronal populations and the compression of temporal sequences. *Hippocampus, 6,* 149-

172.
Smith, M.C., DiLollo, V., & Gormezano, I. (1966). Conditioned jaw movement in the rabbit. *Journal of Comparative and Physiological Psychology, 62*(3), 479-483.
Solomon, P.R. (1980). A time and a place for everything? Temporal processing views of hippocampal function with special reference to attention. *Physiological Psychology, 8*(2), 254-261.
Solomon, P.R., & Corbit, J.D. (1974). An opponent process theory of motivation. I. The temporal dynamics of affect. *Psychological Review, 81*, 119-145.
Solomon, P.R., & Gottfried, K.E. (1981). The septohippocampal cholinergic system and classical conditioning of the rabbit's nictitating membrane response. *Journal of Comparative and Physiological Psychology, 95*, 322-330.
Solomon, P.R., & Groccia-Ellison, M. (1996). Classic conditioning in aged rabbits: Delay, trace, and long-delay conditioning. *Behavioral Neuroscience, 110*(3), 427-435.
Solomon, P.R., & Moore, J.W. (1975). Latent inhibition and stimulus generalization of the classically conditioned nictitating membrane response in rabbits (*Oryctolagus cuniculus*) following dorsal hippocampal ablation. *Journal of Comparative and Physiological Psychology, 89*(10), 1192-1203.
Solomon, P.R., Solomon, S.E., Vander Schaaf, E., & Perry, H.E. (1983). Altered activity in the hippocampus is more detrimental to classical conditioning than removing the structure. *Science, 220*, 329-331.
Squire, L.R. (1992). Memory and the hippocampus: A synthesis from findings with rats, monkeys, and humans. *Psychological Review, 99*(2), 195-231.
Staubli, U., & Lynch, G. (1987). Stable hippocampal long-term potentiation elicited by 'theta' pattern stimulation. *Brain Research, 435*, 227-234.
Steinmetz, J.E. (1996). The brain substrates of classical eyeblink conditioning in rabbits. In J.R. Bloedel, T.J. Teyler, & S.P. Wise (Eds.), *The Acquisition of Motor Behavior in Vertebrates* (pp. 89-114). Cambridge, MA: MIT Press.
Tait, R.W., Quesnel, L.J., & Ten Have, W.N. (1986). Classical-classical transfer: Excitatory associations between "competing" motivational stimuli during classical conditioning of the rabbit. *Animal Learning & Behavior, 14*(2), 138-143.
Thomas, M.J., Watabe, A.M., Moody, T.D., Makhinson, M., & O'Dell, T.J. (1998). Postsynaptic complex spike bursting enables the induction of LTP by theta frequency synaptic stimulation. *Journal of Neuroscience, 18*(18), 7118-7126.
Thompson, L.T., Moyer, J.R., Jr., & Disterhoft, J.F. (1996). Trace eyeblink conditioning in rabbits demonstrates heterogeneity of learning ability both between and within age groups. *Neurobiology of Aging, 17*(4), 619-629.
Thompson, R. F., & Berry, S. D. (1988). Learning and motivation, an historical overview. In G.C. Galbraith, M.L. Kietzman, & E. Donchin, (Eds.), *Neurophysiology and Psychophysiology: Experimental and Clinical Applications* (pp. 270-297). Hillsdale, New Jersey: Lawrence Erlbaum.
Vanderwolf, C.H. (1971). Limbic-diencephalic mechanisms of voluntary movement. *Psychological Review, 78*, 83-113.
Vanderwolf, C.H., Kramis, R., Gillespie, L.A., & Bland, B.H. (1975). Hippocampal rhythmic slow activity and neocortical low-voltage fast activity: Relations to learning. In R.L. Isaacson & K.H. Pribram (Eds.), *The Hippocampus* (Vol. 2, pp. 101-128). New York: Plenum Press.
Wasserman, E.A., & Miller, R.R. (1997). What's elementary about associative learning? *Annual Review of Psychology, 48*, 573-607.
Weikart, C.L., & Berger, T.W. (1986). Hippocampal lesions disrupt classical conditioning of cross-modality reversal learning of the rabbit nictitating membrane response. *Behavioural Brain Research, 22*, 85-89.
Wetzel, W., Ott, T., & Matthies, H. (1977). Post-training hippocampal rhythmic slow activity ("theta") elicite by septal stimulation improves memory consolidation in rats. *Behavioral Biology, 21*, 32-40.
Woodruff-Pak, D.S., Lavond, D.G., Logan, C.G., & Thompson, R.F. (1987). Classical conditioning in 3-, 30-, and 45-month-old rabbits: Behavioral learning and hippocampal unit activity. *Neurobiology of Aging, 8*, 101-108.

13 CELLULAR ALTERATIONS IN HIPPOCAMPUS DURING ACQUISITION AND CONSOLIDATION OF HIPPOCAMPUS-DEPENDENT TRACE EYEBLINK CONDITIONING

John F. Disterhoft and Matthew D. McEchron
Northwestern University Medical School

INTRODUCTION

The hippocampus has been of particular interest for studies of memory since Scoville and Milner (1957) reported the profound amnesia of patient H.M. following bilateral resection of the hippocampus. Hippocampal lesions in humans and animals cause severe deficits in the ability to transfer information from short- to long-term stores and thus form new memories (Squire, 1987). There are substantial lesion and recording data showing the importance of the hippocampus for learning (O'Keefe & Nadel, 1978; Cohen & Eichenbaum, 1993).

Classical conditioning of the eyeblink reflex has been adopted by many laboratories as a model paradigm to study the neurobiology of learning and memory (Disterhoft, et al., 1976; Thompson et al., 1976; Steinmetz, 1990; Woody, 1986). Trace eyeblink conditioning is a version of the task in which the tone conditioned stimulus (CS) offset is separated from the air puff unconditioned stimulus (US) onset by a blank "trace" interval in which no stimulus is presented. The trace paradigm is hippocampus-dependent when the trace interval is greater than or equal to a critical duration which varies between species: 250 ms in rats (Weiss et al., 1998); 500 ms in rabbits (Solomon et al., 1986; Moyer et al., 1990); and 1,000 ms in humans (McGlinchey-Berroth et al., 1997; Clark & Squire, 1998). Pavlov (1927) referred to this paradigm as trace conditioning to stress the requirement that a very short term memory trace of the CS be formed in order that the subject predict the US onset and perform conditioned responses (CRs) that are timed properly to avoid the US.

Trace eyeblink conditioning apparently engages the hippocampal system's role in forming temporal and/or configural associations and therefore this structure is necessary for learning the task (Solomon, 1979; Cohen & Eichenbaum, 1993;1998; Wallenstein et al., 1998). The trace paradigm is more difficult for rabbits than the delay paradigm in which the tone CS and air puff US are presented contiguously in time, as evidenced by the fact that learning to a given behavioral criterion takes more training trials (Thompson et al., 1996). The fact that trace conditioning is more difficult than delay conditioning makes it a powerful behavioral model system in which to examine the neural changes underlying the multiple stages of learning and consolidation of the associative task. These two processes are more extended over time during trace conditioning and are thus more accessible for analysis.

Berger et al. (1976, 1978a) used the delay version of eyeblink conditioning in which no trace interval separates the CS and US, and reported that hippocampal neurons exhibited "temporal models" of the eyeblink response, i.e., the firing rate correlated with the time and amplitude of the CR. We are especially interested in the involvement of the hippocampus and forebrain structures in the formation of associative conditioned responses. Therefore, we have used the trace paradigm as a behavioral model system for studying the hippocampal contribution to associative learning.

HIPPOCAMPAL SINGLE NEURONS DURING ASYMPTOTIC EYEBLINK CONDITIONING

Our laboratory has been engaged in a series of *in vivo* electrophysiological studies to try to understand how hippocampal single neurons process learning-related information during the acquisition and consolidation of trace eyeblink CRs. In one of these studies young adult rabbits were trained to asymptotic levels of learning in trace eyeblink conditioning, and the activity of hippocampal pyramidal neurons was then examined during trace eyeblink conditioning sessions (Weiss, Kronforst-Collins & Disterhoft, 1996). Subjects were young adult New Zealand White female rabbits approximately 3 months of age. Each animal was surgically implanted with an array of movable single electrodes. Trace conditioned rabbits (n = 12) received daily sessions consisting of 80 trials presented at an intertrial interval of 30-60 s. Each trial consisted of an auditory tone-CS (100 ms; 90 dB; 6 kHz) followed by a 500 ms stimulus free trace period, then an air puff-US presented to the cornea (150 ms; 3 psi). Pseudoconditioned control rabbits (n = 4) received daily sessions consisting of 80 CS-alone trials and 80 US-alone trials. Eyeblink CRs were defined as significant blinks which occurred after CS onset and prior to US onset.

Neuronal activity was recorded during the later sessions of trace eyeblink conditioning in which CRs were emitted on a minimum of 60% of the trials. Single neuron activity was recorded and analyzed with *DataWave Technologies* software. The action potential waveforms were separated according to the waveform characteristics of individual single neurons, and analyzed with respect to CS and US onset. Pyramidal and theta interneurons were distinguished based upon spontaneous firing rate and spike width (Ranck, 1973). The majority of recorded cells were pyramidal neurons from area CA1. A total of 93 pyramidal neurons were recorded from area CA1 during trace conditioning sessions, and 35 pyramidal neurons were recorded during pseudoconditioning.

Overall, the results indicate that 53 of 93 CA1 neurons (57%) recorded from trace conditioned animals showed significant responses during some portion of the CS-US trial. The percentage of neurons exhibiting significant responses during the trial was significantly greater in trace conditioning compared to pseudoconditioning (57% vs. 37%, $X^2 = 11.2$, $p < 0.01$). A large proportion of the pyramidal cells (44 of 93; 47%) showed significant changes in activity during the 500-ms period following the US. About half of these significant responses following the US were excitatory increases in activity (52%) while the other half were significant decreases (48%). A smaller percentage of neurons responded during the 500 ms trace period (28%), and the majority of these significant responses were inhibitory (62%). The 100 ms CS period was found to have the smallest percentage of significantly related cells (23%), most of which were excitatory (62%). Figure 1 shows examples of excitatory and inhibitory pyramidal neuron firing patterns in a trial-by-trial fashion along with the conditioned eyeblink responses on those trials.

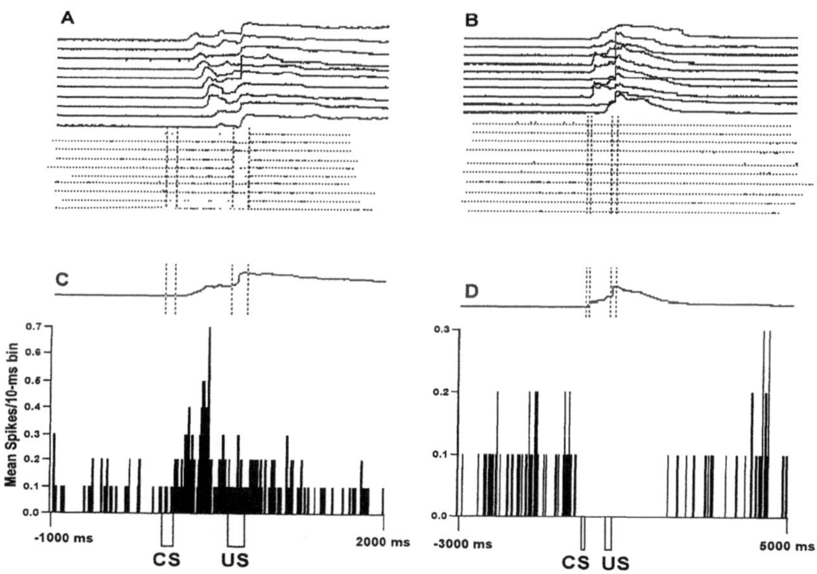

Figure 1. An excitatory pyramidal neuron (left) and an inhibitory pyramidal neuron (right) recorded during trace conditioning. The upper portion of *A* and *B* show 10 individual voltage measures of eyeblink responses (closure upward) sorted according to the latency of response, and raster plots of action potential events (dots) sorted respectively. The time scales are different in the two neurons. The upper portion of *C* and *D* show the average behavioral response for the 10 trials shown in *A* and *B*, while the lower portion shows summed histograms of the action potential events shown in *A* and *B* (0 sec is CS onset). Dashed vertical lines indicate the onset and offset of the CS and US. (Adapted from Weiss et al., 1996.)

This study revealed that there were numerous excitatory and inhibitory patterns of single neuron activity in CA1 during trace eyeblink conditioning. Moreover, these patterns of activity were more complex than those first described by Berger and colleagues (1983), and did not consist solely of a unitary modeling of the behavioral response. Adding to the complexity of these single neuron firing patterns was the large proportion (40%) of "silent cells" encountered in CA1. These silent pyramidal cells fired at rates less than 0.5 Hz during baseline and their firing pattern did not appear to be significantly related to the stimuli involved in trace eyeblink conditioning. The differences between our data and those gathered in previous eyeblink studies may be attributable to the fact that we trained our animals in a hippocampus-dependent task. Furthermore, we were able to employ more sensitive techniques for single neuron recording and separation which had been developed in the 10-20 years separating these studies. The heterogeneous excitatory and inhibitory hippocampal responses that we found were more reminiscent of that reported for primates and rats in hippocampus-dependent tasks (Cohen & Eichenbaum, 1993, for review).

TIME COURSE OF CA1 SINGLE NEURON ACTIVITY

The aim of our next series of experiments was to further understand the excitatory and inhibitory changes in CA1 single neuron activity and to understand the time course of these changes as they relate to the acquisition and consolidation of trace eyeblink CRs (McEchron & Disterhoft, 1997). Changes in single neuron activity in this study were examined with respect to two time periods during the conditioning of each animal: 1) when CRs initially increased early in training; and 2) when CR performance became asymptotic later in training. This information may be particularly important for understanding the role of the hippocampus during acquisition and consolidation.

We used 12 young (3-4 month) New Zealand Albino rabbits surgically implanted with single-ended or tetrode electrodes. Following recovery from surgery and acclimation, single neuron activity was recorded during daily sessions of either trace eyeblink conditioning or pseudoconditioning. Each pseudoconditioned control animal (n = 5) was randomly matched to one of the trace conditioned animals (n = 7) to determine which ordinal day of pseudoconditioning corresponded to the day of initial CR increase. Figure 2A shows that the percentage of CRs for trace conditioned animals showed a sharp increase across the blocks of 20 trials on the day of initial CR increase.

In all cases 2-7 neurons were recorded from each electrode tip and separated with software provided by *DataWave Technologies*. A total of 429 single neurons were recorded from all of the animals used in this study. From these cells, 408 were found to have pyramidal cell characteristics as described by Ranck (1973). Most of these cells were tracked for only a single day of training. Pyramidal cells in CA1 demonstrated several stages of learning-related activity. Figure 2 shows that the pyramidal cells from trace conditioned animals exhibited increases in activity following both the CS and US on the Day of Initial CR Increase. These increases in activity occurred immediately following the CS and 400 ms following the onset of the

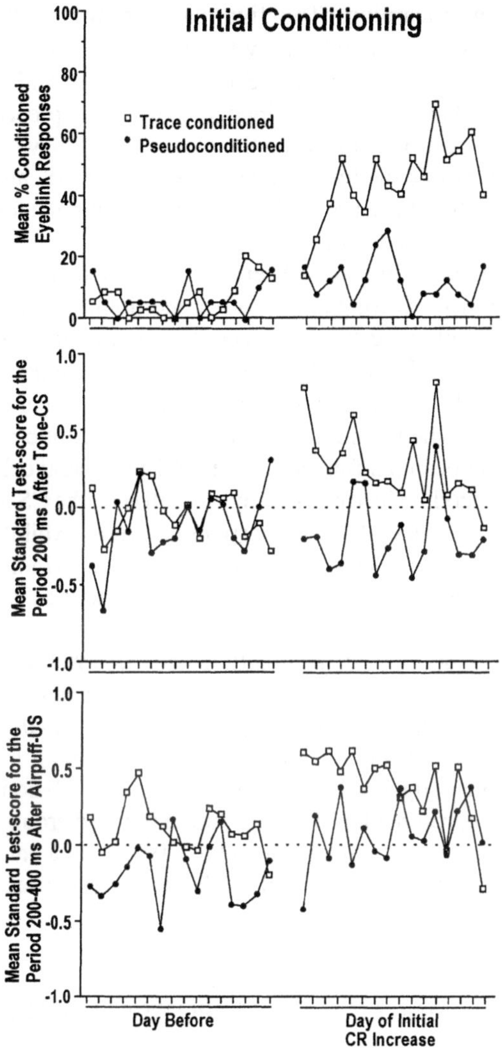

Figure 2. CA1 pyramidal cell activity following the tone conditioned stimulus (CS) and air puff unconditioned stimulus (US) showed learning-related increases before animals initially exhibited increases in conditioned responses (CRs). *A*: Mean percentage of CRs across the 16 5-trial blocks of the training day before and the training day when CRs initially increased. *B*: Mean standard test-score showing the change in pyramidal cell activity from baseline during the 200 ms period following CS onset. *C:* Mean standard test-score showing the change in pyramidal cell activity from baseline during the period 200-400 ms following the US onset. (Adapted from McEchron & Disterhoft, 1997.)

US on the day of initial CR increase. Panels B and C of Figure 2 show that the learning related increases in activity following both the CS and US preceded the behavioral expression of learning. This figure also shows that the learning-related increase in activity was first evident following the onset of the US on the day before the behavioral expression of learning. Similarly, Berger and Thompson (1978) showed that learning-related changes in hippocampal activity preceded delay eyeblink conditioning and first occurred following the US. Thus, it may be necessary for the hippocampus to first encode the importance of the air puff-US, and then to associate the importance of this stimulus with another neutral stimulus, the tone-CS, in order for learning to commence on the day of initial CR increase.

An opposite pattern of activity was observed during asymptotic conditioning when the task was well learned. During asymptotic conditioning pyramidal cells showed decreases in activity following the US. These decreases in activity, or inhibitory responses, are indicated in Figure 3B and 3C by the negative means which occurred during the period 201-400 ms following US onset. Thus, it appears that the emergence of CRs and the period when conditioning becomes asymptotic are two critical and distinct periods of hippocampal function. The CA1 pyramidal cells probably played an important role in encoding learning-related stimuli (i.e., the CS and US) very early in learning, when the first learned responses were exhibited. However, the inhibitory single neuron responses seen late in training seem to indicate that the CS-US information was filtered from CA1 because it was well learned, and no more critical associations were needed for these stimuli. Moreover, this may be a reflection of what the hippocampus was doing after acquisition had occurred, during the period of consolidation. The sharp drop off in activity across days and across the trials within each day may reflect periods when the hippocampus was playing a limited role and other brain regions were playing a larger role in the learning process. This active inhibition in activity may suggest that later during the consolidation of CRs, excitatory information is being represented by a smaller, more focused group of neurons, similar to the notion of sparse coding (McClelland et al., 1995). In a parallel fashion, Rolls et al. (1989) has reported that hippocampal single neuron responses decrease as stimuli become more familiar.

HETEROGENEOUS SINGLE UNIT RESPONSE PROFILES

Up to this point our previous electrophysiological studies had shown that the CA1 single pyramidal neuron response profiles consisted of a number of excitatory and inhibitory response types, few of which show modeling of the behavioral response. Our next set of experiments examined the heterogeneous types of CA1 single neuron responses which occur during trace eyeblink conditioning in young and aged animals (McEchron et al., 1997, 1998). Previous work has shown that aging produces deficits in the ability to acquire trace eyeblink CRs (Coffin & Woodruff-Pak, 1993; Powell et al., 1981; Solomon et al., 1995; Thompson et al., 1996). We also know that aging rabbits require many more trials to acquire the task, *if* they are able to acquire it at all (Thompson et al., 1996). We examined CA1 single neuron activity in young

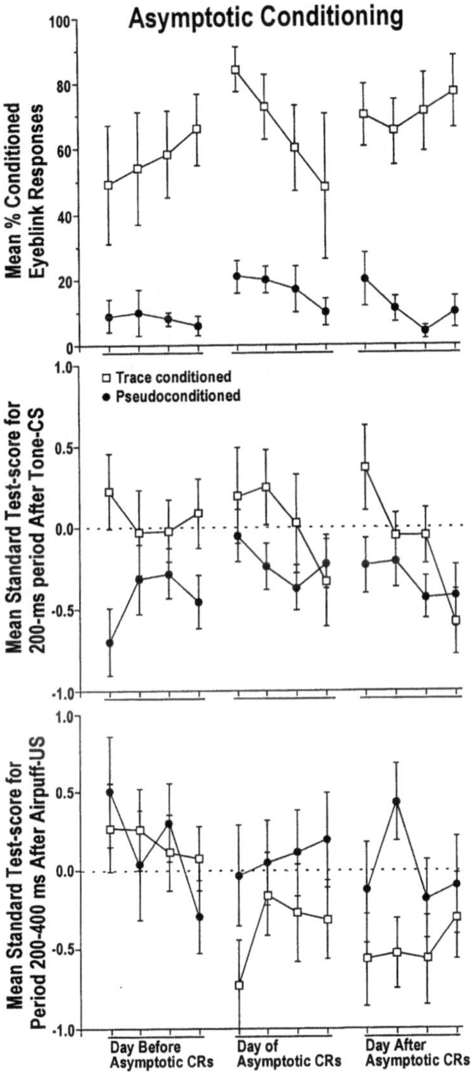

Figure 3. Trace conditioned pyramidal cell activity following the air puff US showed decreases when animals exhibited asymptotic levels of CRs. *A*: Mean percentage of CRs across the four 20-trial blocks of asymptotic conditioning (Day Before Asymptotic CRs, Day of Asymptotic CRs, Day After Asymptotic CRs). *B*: Mean standard test-scores calculated from the activity in the 200 ms period following CS onset. *C*: Mean standard test-scores calculated from the activity in the period 201-400 ms following US. Bars indicate standard error of the mean (SEM). (Adapted from McEchron & Disterhoft, 1997.)

(5-6 month) and aged (30-33 month) New Zealand albino rabbits during trace eyeblink conditioning using a variation of the stereotrode recording technique (Gray et al., 1995; McNaughton et al., 1983). Bundles of 6-8 closely spaced (20-30 μm) wires were surgically implanted in the CA1 area of the hippocampus. Two-wire stereotrode combinations were selected from the implanted probe which provided the largest and most heterogeneous ensembles of single neurons (4-16 neurons). Single neurons were isolated with software from *DataWave Technologies*. This approach allowed us to examine the various types of CA1 single neuron responses which occurred during trace eyeblink conditioning, and to determine if these responses were affected by the aging process.

Following recovery from surgery and acclimation, young (n = 7) and aged rabbits received 10 daily sessions of trace eyeblink conditioning. One half of the aged animals (n = 4) showed few if any CRs. The other half of the aged animals (n = 4) showed normal acquisition very similar to that of the young animals. Figure 4A shows the mean percentage of trace eyeblink CRs across the 10 days of training for these three groups, young, aged learners, and aged non-learners. This figure also shows the percentage of CRs for a group of young control animals (n = 5) which received pseudoconditioning. Clearly, the aged non-learners showed non-associative levels of responding to the CS.

The stereotrode recording techniques allowed us to increase the number of neurons sampled from each stereotrode ensemble (4-16 neurons). This gave us the opportunity to look at the different categories of single neuron responses which occur within local ensembles in CA1 during trace eyeblink conditioning. A total of 1233 pyramidal cells were recorded from the three trace conditioned groups shown in Figure 4. Almost all of these single neurons were tracked for only a single day of training. Daily averages of activity were calculated for each of these neurons, and these averages were then used in an algomerative hierarchical clustering analysis (Everitt & Dunn, 1991). This analysis revealed eight different patterns of single neuron activity. Each of the eight patterns of activity formed a template of the amplitude time course of activity. The averages for each of the 1233 pyramidal cells were then matched statistically to one of the eight templates. Figure 5 shows perievent histograms averaged across all of the cells within each of the eight single neuron response categories. This figure also shows the percentage of the 1233 cells which matched each category. Statistical analyses revealed that for each of the eight single cell response categories there was no significant difference in occurrence across the 10 days of training or across the 3 groups of animals described in this study (young, aged learners, aged non-learners).

The heterogeneous single neuron response profiles shown in Figure 5 provide strong evidence that the activity of hippocampal neurons during trace eyeblink conditioning does not consist solely of a unitary modeling response, but rather is made up of a number of different single neuron response profiles. Previous work from our laboratory and from Richard F. Thompson's group has documented similar examples of heterogeneous single neuron response profiles during delay and trace eyeblink conditioning (Berger et al., 1983; McEchron & Disterhoft, 1997; Weiss et al., 1996). Heterogeneous hippocampal neuron response profiles have also been reported in other spatial and nonspatial learning paradigms (e.g., Shapiro et al., 1997; Hampson et al., 1993).

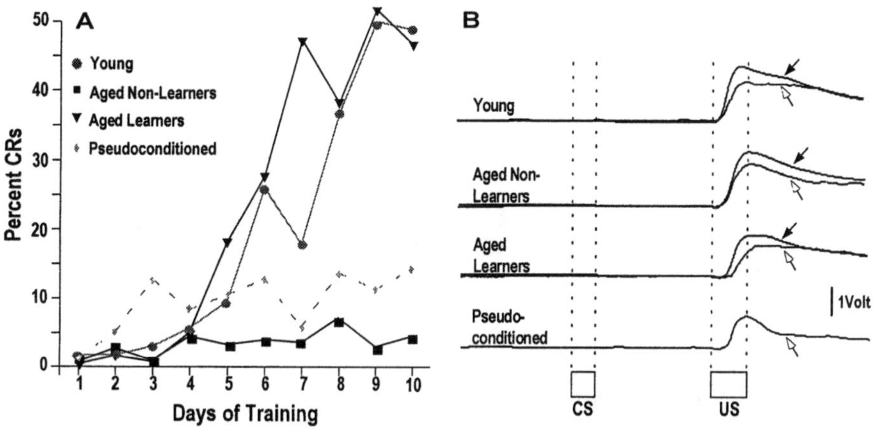

Figure 4. *A.* Daily mean percentage of trace eyeblink CRs for young rabbits (5-6 month; n = 7), aged animals (30-33 month) that acquired trace eyeblink CRs (n = 4); aged animals that did not acquire trace eyeblink CRs (n = 4); and young pseudoconditioned animals (n = 5) which received unpaired CSs and USs. *B.* Voltage measures for eyeblink responses (closure upward) on CS-US trials (closed arrow) and US-alone trials (open arrows) averaged across the first four days of training and across all of the animals from each group. Each eyeblink measure is 1750 ms in duration. (Adapted from McEchron & Disterhoft, 1999.)

There are a number of important observations that can be made from the amplitude time courses of the single neuron response types shown in Figure 5. The majority of the cell types (6/8 response types) showed an excitatory increase in activity to the air puff-US. These air puff excitatory cell types accounted for 58 % of the cells recorded in this study. This suggests that CA1 hippocampal cells encode a significant amount of information about the US, and may actually be primed to respond to US information in the environment. The other important observation is the significant amount of inhibition that was displayed by CA1 single neurons during trace eyeblink conditioning. A total of 3 of the 8 cell types (57.6% of the cells) exhibited some type of inhibitory decrease in activity during the CS-US trial. One of these inhibitory cell types, number four in Figure 5, was also one of the cell types that showed excitation to the US. Inhibitory changes in activity are often overlooked in the hippocampal literature, and the large percentage of inhibitory responses found here underscores the fact that CA1 single neuron responses do not follow the topography of the behavioral response. Analyses revealed that the activity of the majority of the cell types was similar for each of the age groups that received trace conditioning (young, aged learners, aged non-learners). However, three of the cell types that we isolated, types 1, 2, and 7 shown in Figure 5, exhibited significant group differences in activity during

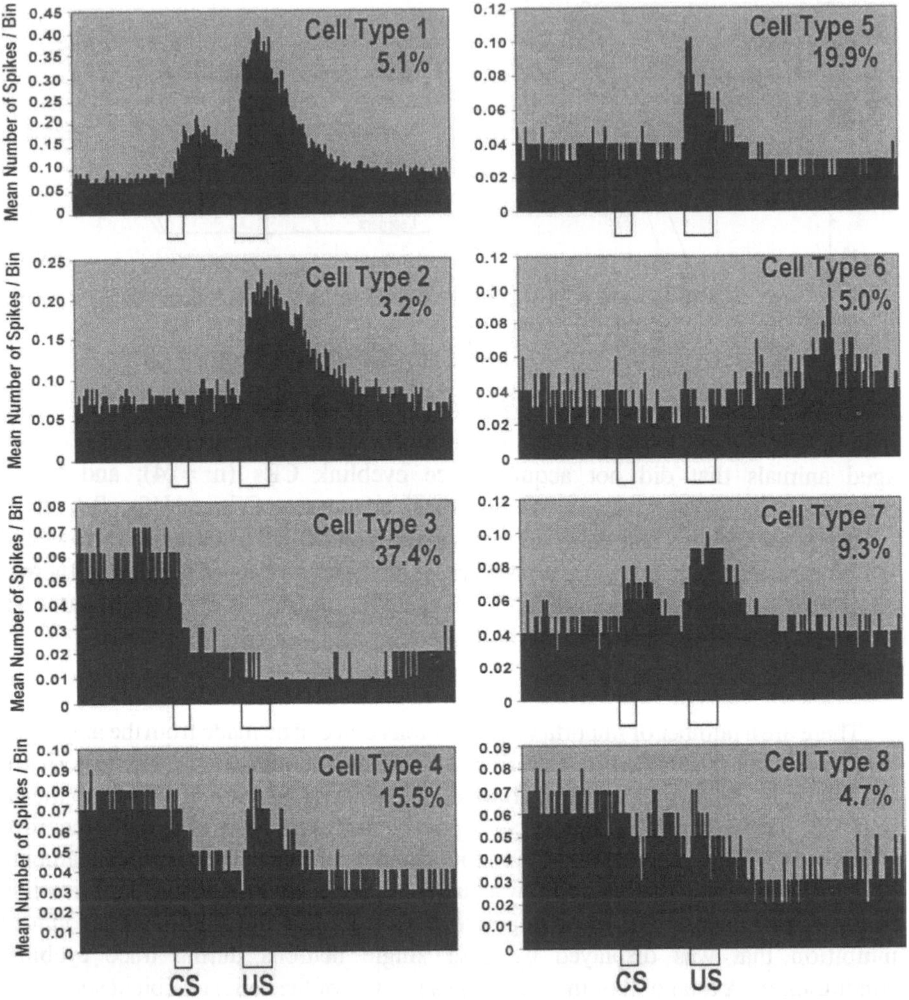

Figure 5. Average perievent histograms (10-ms bins) for eight different pyramidal cell response profiles recorded from young and aged trace conditioned rabbits. For each histogram, action potentials (spikes) from each cell were summed across a single training session, then averaged across cells. The duration of the prestimulus period prior to the onset of the CS was 1000 ms. The percentage of the total cells (1233 cells) belonging to each response category is shown in the corner of each histogram. Pyramidal cell response categories were formed by hierarchical clustering and subsequent template matching. (Adapted from McEchron & Disterhoft, 1999.)

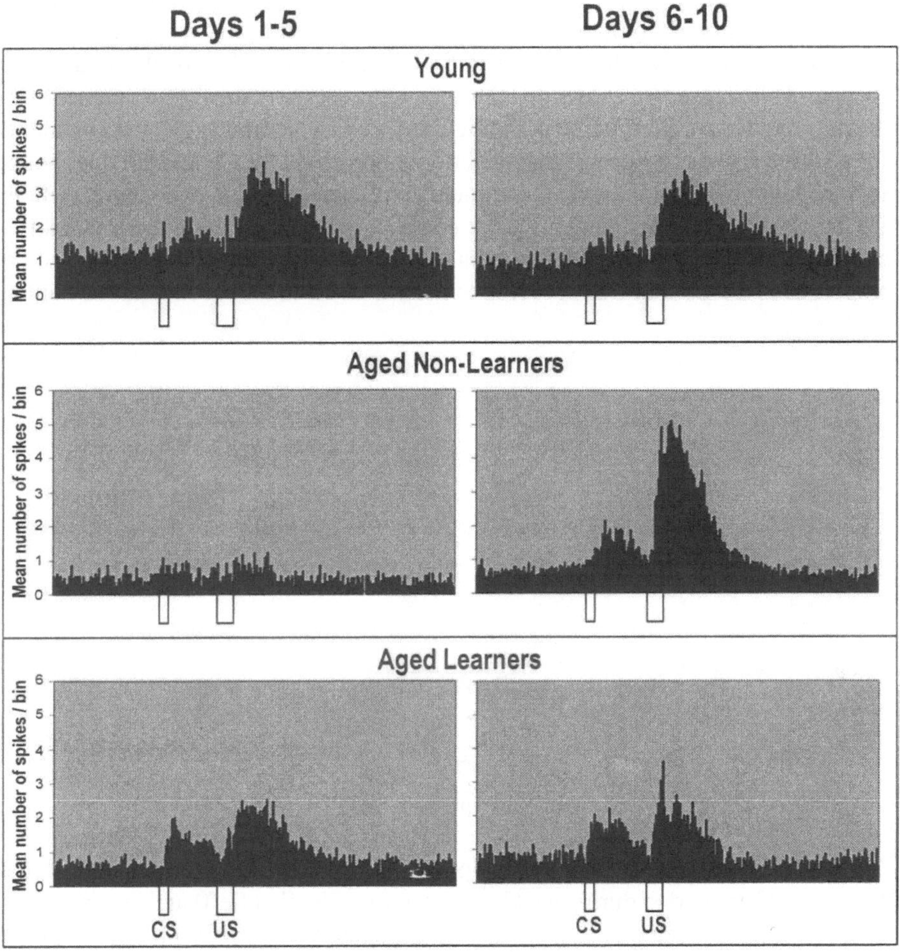

Figure 6. Perievent histograms (10-ms bins) averaged across the pyramidal cells belonging to the response categories 1, 2, and 7 described in Fig. 5. For each histogram, action potentials (spikes) from each cell were summed across a single training session, then averaged across the cells recorded from the first five days of training (left) and the last five days of training (right). The duration of the prestimulus period prior to the onset of the CS is 1000 ms. During the first five days of training pyramidal cells recorded from aged non-learners (middle) showed very little if any increase in activity to the CS and US compared to the cells recorded from young (upper) and aged learners (lower). (Adapted from McEchron & Disterhoft, 1999.)

the first five days of trace conditioning. Figure 6 shows perievent histograms for each group averaged across all of the single neurons classified as types 1, 2, and 7. These histograms show that early in training the single neuron increases in activity to the CS and US were reduced for these cell types in the aged non-learners compared to the young and aged learners. Thus, a specific subset of cells in CA1 encode CS information, and particularly US information during the early stages of training in aged memory impaired animals. This subset makes up less than 18 % of the cells that we recorded. Figure 4B shows that the unconditioned behavioral responses (non-CR responses) to the CS-US trials and the US-alone trials were identical for the three groups. This figure also shows that the unconditioned responses were augmented by the presentation of the CS (reflex facilitation; see Gormezano et al., 1983) similarly for all three groups. It appears that the information about the CS and US does not get into the hippocampus of aged non-learners in a normal fashion, even though CS and US information is clearly entering the central nervous system of these animals as evidenced by the behavioral responses. Figure 6 also shows that single neuron responses to the CS and US recovered to normal levels in the second half of training,

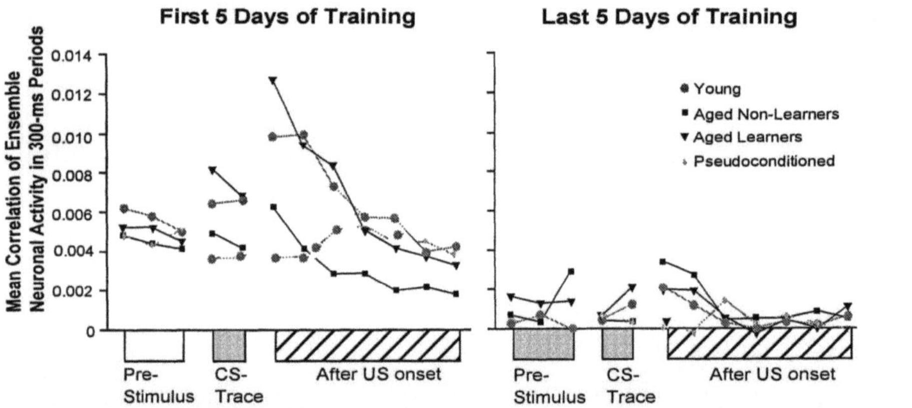

Figure 7. The mean ensemble correlation of CA1 pyramidal neuron activity obtained for each 300-ms period during the CS-US trial from the first (left) and last (right) five days of training. Pearson correlations were computed for each 300-ms period during the trial using 10-ms bins of activity for each neuron pair obtained from each stereotrode ensemble (range 4-16 neurons). A mean correlation was then computed for each stereotrode ensemble. For pseudoconditioned animals 300-ms stereotrode ensemble correlations were obtained for the 3 pre- and 2 post-stimulus onset periods on CS-alone trials, and the 7 post-stimulus periods on US-alone trials. Early in training the ensemble activity following the presentation of the US was more coordinated for young and aged learners compared to the aged non-learners and young pseudoconditioned animals. This suggests that the young and aged learners showed learning-related increases in coordinated activity, and the aged non-learners do not show these increases. (Adapted from McEchron & Disterhoft, 1999.)

even though these animals showed no conditioning in 10 and sometimes as many as 15 days of training. This slow recovery of neural activity suggests that the aged non-learners may have some hippocampal processes which are delayed and would allow them to show some moderate form of conditioning if training were extended for an additional 10 or 20 days. Together these analyses suggest that the activity of a specific subset of cells in the CA1 area of the hippocampus is affected by aging, and that cells exhibiting these response patterns may play an important role in encoding the critical learning-related information about the CS and US early in learning when CRs are initially acquired.

Many studies suggest that the ensemble activity of groups of hippocampal cells encode more information than single or average cell activity (Deadwyler & Hampson, 1995; Deadwyler et al., 1996; Eichenbaum et al., 1989; Sakurai, 1998; Wilson & McNaughton, 1993; 1994). We have also used an ensemble approach to understand the relationship of the heterogeneous single neuron responses in CA1 during trace eyeblink conditioning. We calculated a Pearson correlation coefficient for each possible pair of neurons recorded from each stereotrode-ensemble. (Adapted from McHugh et al., 1996.) The size of the ensembles recorded from each stereotrode ranged from 4 to 16 neurons. The correlation coefficient measured how well the occurrence of two neuron's action potentials was related in time. An average correlation coefficient was then computed for each stereotrode-ensemble during consecutive 300-ms periods of the CS-US trace conditioning trials. Ensemble correlations were also obtained from the stereotrodes implanted in pseudoconditioned animals using both CS- and US-alone trials. Analyses showed that single neuron firing during the first five days of training was significantly more related in time (more coordinated) during the air puff-US in young and aged learners compared to aged non-learners and pseudoconditioned animals (see Figure 7). The low levels of coordinated activity in the pseudoconditioned animals suggest that the increases in coordinated activity following the US onset in the young and aged learners were learning-related. Neuron-ensembles from all groups showed lower levels of coordinated firing during the last five days of training. Thus, the high degree of coordinated activity following the US presentation occurred primarily before CRs were acquired (see Figure 4A). This is another indication that there are several distinct stages of hippocampal function as they relate to the acquisition and consolidation of trace eyeblink CRs. In summary, unitary and ensemble analyses suggest that aged animals which exhibit hippocampal impairments in the capacity for encoding CS and US information early in training are not able to associate these stimuli and acquire trace eyeblink CRs.

TRACE EYEBLINK CONDITIONING INCREASES CA1 AND CA3 PYRAMIDAL NEURON EXCITABILITY WITH A TIME COURSE APPROPRIATE FOR MEMORY CONSOLIDATION

We have also conducted a series of *in vitro* hippocampal slice experiments in order to obtain a more detailed understanding of the cellular mechanisms that are involved in the acquisition and consolidation of trace eyeblink conditioning. In these studies we examined excitability changes recorded in CA1 and CA3 pyramidal neurons after hippocampus-dependent trace eyeblink conditioning (Moyer et al., 1996; Thompson et al., 1996). Some rabbits were trained to a behavioral criterion of 80% CRs per session, while others served as naïve or pseudoconditioned controls. Membrane excitability changes, as evidenced in the size of the post-burst afterhyperpolarization (AHP) and spike frequency accommodation, were studied in neurons from hippocampal slices prepared at time points from 1 hr to 14 days after the rabbits reached behavioral criterion. A reduction in the post-burst AHP, indicating that the pyramidal neurons were more excitable, was observed 1 hr after behavioral acquisition, peaked 24 hr after acquisition, then decayed and returned to a naïve-like state within 7 days (Figures 8 and 9). A similar time course of retention for the excitability changes was seen in both CA1 and CA3 pyramidal neurons. Approximately 50% of the neurons in both regions showed AHP reductions. Spike frequency accommodation is dependent to a large degree upon the size of the AHP (Madison & Nicoll, 1984). It is not surprising, therefore, that this index of excitability also demonstrated a similar time course, i.e., spike frequency accommodation decreased at 1 hr, peaked at 24 hr and was back to naïve baseline within 7 days after behavioral criterion was reached.

Behavioral retention was essentially unchanged and remained asymptotic during the same time interval when the neuronal excitability changes peaked and then returned to baseline. Our interpretation of these data is that postsynaptic excitability changes were maintained in the hippocampus only temporarily, allowing or supporting cellular alterations in other brain regions such as the interconnected neocortex and perhaps the cerebellum for long term or permanent memory storage. A lesion study by Kim et al. (1995) is convergent with our data and our interpretation of them. They showed that rabbits receiving bilateral hippocampal ablations 24 hr after reaching behavioral criterion on the trace eyeblink conditioning task were unable to recall the task and unable to relearn it. Animals showed intact retention when lesioned 30 days after reaching criterion, a period when our observed excitability changes have returned to baseline. In combination, these studies suggest that the functional changes we observed in the hippocampus are required during the initial stages of consolidation, when the excitability changes are maximal. When the excitability changes return to baseline, the representation of the learned association has shifted to other brain regions, and hippocampal lesions have no effect on retention.

One final set of data further substantiates our temporary storage buffer or consolidation hypothesis for the hippocampus. We directly tested the proposition that the storage site had shifted away from the hippocampus at 14 days post-acquisition. Rabbits were trained to behavioral criterion; they remained in their cages without further training for 13 days; on the 14th day, they were trained for a single 80 trial session and exhibited asymptotic retention; 24 h later, slices were prepared and the excitability of CA1 and CA3 pyramidal neurons was evaluated. Our prediction was that, if the hippocampus no longer mediated retention of behavioral performance, the afterhyperpolarization and accommodation changes should also be absent. This is precisely what was observed (see Figures 9A and 9B). Behavioral performance was above criterion but both CA1 and CA3 AHPs and accommodation were comparable to those from naive or pseudoconditioned neurons.

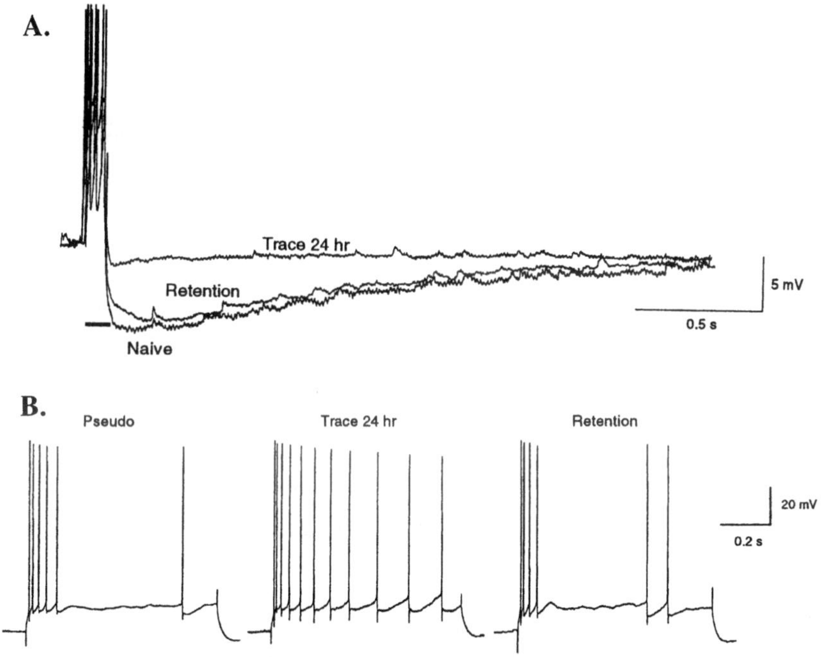

Figure 8. Acquisition of trace eyeblink conditioning increased excitability of hippocampal CA1 pyramidal neurons. *A.* Voltage measures show representative recordings of postburst afterhyperpolarizations (AHPs) in CA1 neurons from a naïve rabbit and from two trace conditioned rabbits. One trace conditioned rabbit was studied 24 hr after reaching 80% CRs, the other 24 hr after receiving an additional session 14 days after reaching 80% CRs (Retention). The AHPs were measured for 5 sec following a 100 ms depolarizing current injection (solid black line). The current was the minimal amount (~0.6 nA) required to reliably evoke a burst of four action potentials. *B.* Examples of typical accommodation responses in CA1 pyramidal cells from rabbits: 24 hr after pseudoconditioning (pseudo), 24 hr after reaching 80 % trace eyeblink CRs, and 24 hr after receiving an additional training session 14 days after reaching 80 % CRs (Retention). (Adapted from Moyer et al., 1996.)

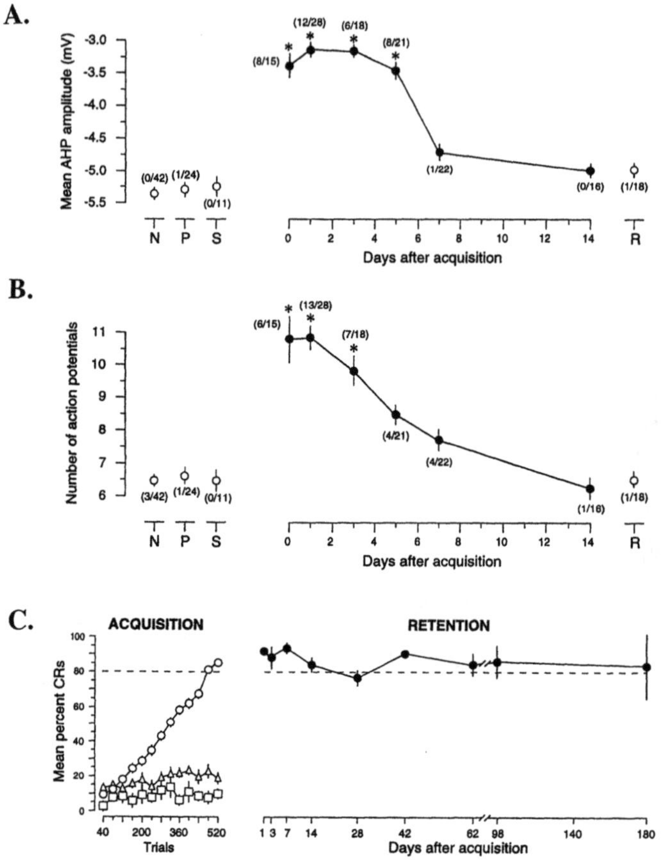

Figure 9. *A.* Learning-related reductions of the AHP amplitude were transient, lasting ~1 week in slices prepared at various times after learning [1 hr (0 d), 1 d, 3 d, 5 d, 7 d, or 14 d]. These changes were not observed in naïve (N), pseudoconditioned (P), or slow-learning (S) control rabbits. Slow learners were did not reach criterion within 15 training sessions. Retention (R) rabbits received an additional 80-trial session 14 days after reaching criterion. *B.* Trace eyeblink conditioning also resulted in a learning-specific transient decrease in spike-frequency adaptation (accommodation) in CA1 neurons. Cells showed accommodation if the number of elicited action potentials was at least 2 SDs more than the mean for all naïve control cells. *C.* The left panel (Acquisition) shows the percent CRs for trace conditioned (O, n = 46) compared with pseudoconditioned (Δ, n = 11) and slow-learning (z, n = 3) rabbits. The right panel (Retention) shows the percent CRs emitted during 20 paired CS-US trials delivered at various time intervals after acquisition. Retention rabbits (●, n = 10) maintained their criterion performance long after acquisition. Parentheses show the ratio of individual cells with increased excitability compared to number of cells studied in that group. Asterisks indicate data significantly different from all three control groups; $p < 0.001$. (From Moyer et al., 1996.)

Our data are consistent with a working hypothesis that the hippocampus holds information during the period necessary for its consolidation in other structures (e.g., Akase et al., 1989; Kim et al., 1995; Squire, 1987). Our data also indicate that the hippocampus has inherent regulatory processes that increase neuronal excitability during learning and return excitability to baseline with a time course of a few days.

The afterhyperpolarization (AHP) which follows a burst of action potentials and spike frequency accommodation are both reduced in CA1 and CA3 pyramidal neurons after hippocampus-dependent trace eyeblink conditioning (Moyer et al., 1994; Thompson et al., 1995). These reductions increase neuronal excitability and are well correlated with behavioral acquisition. Importantly, these excitability increases decay as would be expected if the hippocampus serves as an intermediate storage buffer in acquisition of new associations. These alterations are localized to the hippocampus, as they occur in *in vitro* slices separated from their normal afferent and efferent connections (Disterhoft et al., 1988). They are postsynaptic, as they are evoked by intracellular current injection and persist after block of sodium spike-dependent synaptic transmission (Coulter et al., 1989).

POSTSYNAPTIC POTASSIUM CURRENTS REGULATE NEURONAL EXCITABILITY IN LEARNING

An important conceptual issue regarding our experimental program should be addressed directly. When most neuroscientists think about how information is stored in neural networks during learning, changes located at the synapse are considered first. The description of how "Hebb synapses" might change during a hypothetical learning sequence (Hebb, 1949) has inspired much work on model systems such as long term potentiation (Bliss & Collingridge, 1993). But it should be pointed out that other mechanisms are available for altering synaptic efficacy, e.g., by modulation of excitability at the postsynaptic level (Kazmarek & Levitan, 1987). Adjustment of cellular excitability could amplify or attenuate synaptic changes occurring in distal dendrites, and affect neuronal firing output after learning.

Our data suggest that calcium-mediated outward potassium currents are reduced in a conditioning-specific fashion to increase hippocampal excitability in learning. Similar reductions in these or other outward potassium currents are well documented in invertebrate and mammalian learning models (Alkon, 1984; Byrne, 1987; Woody et al., 1991). The generality of findings across vertebrate and invertebrate species suggests that postsynaptic modulation of outward potassium currents may be an important conserved mechanism often used to mediate neuronal changes after learning.

EXCITABILITY CHANGES IN AGING CA1 NEURONS AFTER TRACE EYEBLINK CONDITIONING

We have recently completed a study examining pyramidal neuron excitability in slices from aging rabbits after acquisition of trace eyeblink conditioning, in addition to studies after learning in young rabbits (Moyer et al., 1998). As was mentioned above in the review of our *in vivo* single neuron recording studies, aging rabbits require many more trials to acquire the task, *if* they are able to acquire it at all (Thompson et al., 1996). We compared the excitability of CA1 neurons from aged rabbits who reached a 60% behavioral criterion, rabbits trained for 30 d that never demonstrated more than 30% CRs per session ("learning-impaired"), and naive aging rabbits. Excitability of CA1 neurons was studied 24 hrs after the last training session. Aged rabbits required significantly more trials to reach a criterion of 60% conditioned responses (CRs) in an 80-trial session than did young rabbits. Aged CA1 neurons from learning intact animals had significantly reduced post-burst afterhyperpolarizations (AHPs) and reduced spike frequency adaptation compared with neurons from control groups of naive and aging rabbits that failed to learn. No differences were seen in resting membrane potential, membrane time constant, neuron input resistance, or action potential characteristics after learning. Neurons from young adult rabbits also showed increased excitability after learning. Although neurons from aging control rabbits had significantly larger AHPs compared with young controls, AHPs from both groups were similar in amplitude, integrated area, and duration after learning.

These data suggest that postsynaptic excitability of CA1 neurons is correlated with learning a hippocampus-dependent trace eyeblink conditioning task in both young adult and aged rabbits. The data also suggest that a similar level of postsynaptic excitability is achieved at the time that learning has occurred regardless of rabbit age and regardless of the actual speed of acquisition of the conditioned response.

IN VIVO AS COMPARED TO *IN VITRO* DATA SETS

The findings from the young and aged *in vitro* analyses converge with the *in vivo* single neuron recording experiments described above. In both the *in vivo* and *in vitro* studies, CA1 pyramidal neurons from aging rabbits that acquired the trace eyeblink conditioned task showed a similar pattern of change as did CA1 pyramidal neurons from young animals that acquired the task. Neurons from aging rabbits that did not learn showed no change from the naïve or pseudoconditioned state. We know from these findings that there is an intimate connection between the *in vivo* and *in vitro* alterations in CA1 pyramidal neurons and hippocampus-dependent learning. Neurons from rabbits that learned showed the cellular alterations in both types of analysis.

There are some fascinating differences between the *in vivo* and *in vitro* data which we would like to point out and discuss. Our *in vivo* recording studies have demonstrated a surprisingly large amount of inhibitory single neuron responding when animals have reached asymptotic levels of CRs (McEchron & Disterhoft, 1997; Weiss et al, 1996). Yet the postsynaptic excitability changes we have recorded *in vitro* should lead to increased, not decreased, neuronal firing. The rabbits in both types of studies have been trained in the same task. And we assume that the alterations we are observing in the same cell populations *in vivo* and *in vitro* must be tightly linked in some integral fashion. Our working assumption is that we have characterized two independent and complementary mechanisms of hippocampal function which are both required for the acquisition and consolidation of trace eyeblink conditioning.

It should be stressed that the postsynaptic excitability changes (AHP and accommodation reductions) are only one factor contributing to the altered pyramidal neuron output during conditioning. We assume that the postsynaptic alterations are rather general, and make the neurons more responsive to inputs on any synapse. They presumably act to amplify patterned inputs at the afferents to the pyramidal neurons, transforming the afferent drive from various inputs to give them a meaning in terms of overall altered hippocampal output. Our *in vivo* recording data show that a relatively small subset of neurons show excitatory changes as learning progresses. Such a subset could use the AHP and accommodation reductions as an important mechanism for enhancing their total output firing level. We suggest that this set of neurons could take advantage of the postsynaptic excitatory changes (which we have shown are occurring) to set up the localized increased firing rates. This approach to integrating our two sets of data is very reminiscent of the "sparse coding" concept that McClelland, McNaughton, and O'Reilly (1995) have discussed. The implication of their hypothesis is that a relatively small subset of pyramidal neurons is responsible for encoding functionally important hippocampal outputs. Our data suggest that the signal to noise level of this active subset is enhanced by the active inhibition which is evident on the surrounding pyramidal neuron population.

Our data are showing us quite clearly that inhibitory input onto the hippocampus becomes dominant as the conditioned reflex arc becomes better learned. There are a large number of inhibitory interneurons, as well as important inhibitory afferent inputs from regions such as the medial septum (Smythe et al., 1992), which could be controlling this dominant response pattern. It is informative to consider our data in relation to observations made in other behavioral tasks. Nonselective medial septal lesions, which eliminate both the GABAergic inhibitory and cholinergic excitatory medial septal neurons, disrupt hippocampus-dependent spatial tasks such as Morris water maze learning (Hagan et al., 1988). These observations are consistent with the concept that there is a major contribution of inhibitory GABAergic drive to the hippocampal functional processing which is involved in tasks that require this structure (Baxter & Gallagher, 1996). The large number of CA1 pyramidal neurons which show active inhibition as measured *in vivo* during trace eyeblink conditioning could be a reflection of the operation of the GABAergic medial septal input during the learning process.

In conclusion, we have two sets of data which are informing us about two different levels of change which occur in hippocampal pyramidal neurons as rabbits acquire the trace eyeblink conditioned reflex. The appropriate explanation of how these two phenomena occur simultaneously in the same neuron population as learning occurs will likely become more obvious as our experiments proceed.

REFERENCES

Akase, E., Alkon, D.L., & Disterhoft, J.F. (1989). Hippocampal lesions impair memory of short-delay conditioned eyeblink in rabbits. *Behavioral Neuroscience, 103*, 935-943.

Baxter, M.G., & Gallagher, M. (1996). Intact spatial learning in both young and aged rats following selective removal of hippocampal cholinergic input. *Behavioral Neuroscience, 110*, 460-467.

Berger, T.W., Alger, B., & Thompson, R.F. (1976). Neuronal substrates of classical conditioning in the hippocampus. *Science, 192*(339), 483-485.

Berger, T.W., Rinaldi, P.C., Weisz, D.J., & Thompson, R.F. (1983). Single-unit analysis of different hippocampal cell types during classical conditioning of rabbit nictitating membrane response. *Journal of Neurophysiology, 50*(346), 1197-1219.

Berger, T.W., & Thompson, R.F. (1978). Identification of pyramidal cells as the critical elements in hippocampal neuronal plasticity during learning. *Proceedings of the National Academy of Sciences, (USA), 75*(354), 1572-1576.

Berger, T.W., & Thompson, R.F. (1978). Neuronal plasticity in the limbic system during classical conditioning of the rabbit nictitating membrane response. I. The hippocampus. *Brain Research, 145*(352), 323-346.

Black, A.H., Nadel, L., & O'Keefe, J. (1977). Hippocampal function in avoidance learning and punishment. *Psychological Bulletin, 84*(419), 1107-1129.

Breese, C.R., Hampson, R.E., & Deadwyler, S.A. (1989). Hippocampal place cells: Stereotypy and plasticity. *Journal of Neuroscience, 9*, 1097-1111.

Coffin, J.M., & Woodruff-Pak, D.S. (1993). Delay classical conditioning in young and older rabbits: Initial acquisition and retention at 12 and 18 months. *Behavioral Neuroscience, 107*(1), 63-71.

Cohen, N.J., & Eichenbaum, H. (1991). The theory that wouldn't die: a critical look at the spatial mapping theory of hippocampal function. *Hippocampus, 1*(3), 265-268.

Deadwyler, S.A., Bunn, T., & Hampson, R.E. (1996). Hippocampal ensemble activity during spatial delayed-nonmatch-to-sample performance in rats. *Journal of Neuroscience, 16*(1), 354-372.

Deadwyler, S.A., & Hampson, R.E. (1995). Ensemble activity and behavior: What's the code? *Science, 270*(5240), 1316-1318.

Disterhoft, J.F., Coulter, D.A., & Alkon, D.L. (1986). Conditioning-specific membrane changes of rabbit hippocampal neurons measured *in vitro*. *Proceedings of the National Academy of Sciences, (USA), 83*, 2733-2737.

Eichenbaum, H., & Cohen, N.J. (1988). Representation in the hippocampus: What do hippocampal neurons encode. *Trends in Neuroscience, 11*(1125), 244-248.

Eichenbaum, H., Kuperstein, M., Fagan, A., & Nagode, J. (1987). Cue-sampling and goal-approach correlates of hippocampal unit activity in rats performing an odor-discrimination task. *Journal of Neuroscience, 7*, 716-732.

Eichenbaum, H., Wiener, S.I., Shapiro, M.L., & Cohen, N.J. (1989). The organization of spatial coding in the hippocampus: A study of neural ensemble activity. *Journal of Neuroscience, 9*(8), 2764-2775.

Everitt, B.S., & Dunn, G. (1991). *Applied multivariate data analysis*. London: Halstead.

Foster, T.C., Christian, E.P., Hampson, R.E., Campbell, K.A., & Deadwyler, S.A. (1987). Sequential dependencies regulate sensory evoked responses of single units in the rat hippocampus. *Brain Research, 408*(1-2), 86-96.

Gluck, M.A., & Myers, C.E. (1993). Hippocampal mediation of stimulus representation: A computational theory. *Hippocampus, 3*(4), 491-516.

Gormezano, I., Kehoe, E.J., & Marshall, B.S. (1983). Twenty years of classical conditioning with the rabbit. *Progress in Psychology and Physiological Psychology, 10*, 198-275.

Gray, C.M., Maldonado, P.E., Wilson, M., & McNaughton, B. (1995). Tetrodes markedly improve the reliability and yield of multiple single- unit isolation from multi-unit recordings in cat striate cortex. *Journal of Neuroscience Methods, 63*(1-2), 43-54.

Hagen, J., Salamone, J.D., Simpson, J., Iversen, S.D., & Morris, R.G.M. (1988). Place navigation in rats is impaired by lesions of medial septum and diagonal band but not nucleus basalis magnocellularis. *Behavioural Brain Research, 27*, 9-20.

Hampson, R.E., Heyser, C.J., & Deadwyler, S.A. (1993). Hippocampal cell firing correlates of delayed-match-to-sample performance in the rat. *Behavioral Neuroscience, 107*(5), 715-739.

Kim, J.J., Clark, R.E., & Thompson, R.F. (1995). Hippocampectomy impairs the memory of recently, but not remotely, acquired trace eyeblink conditioned responses. *Behavioral Neuroscience, 109*(2), 195-203.

Kim, J.J., & Fanselow, M.S. (1992). Modality-specific retrograde amnesia of fear. *Science, 256*, 675-677.

Levy, W.B. (1996). A sequence predicting CA3 is a flexible associator that learns and uses context to solve hippocampal-like tasks. *Hippocampus, 6*(6), 579-590.

McAlonan, G.M., Wilkinson, L.S., Robbins, T.W., & Everitt, B.J. (1995). The effects of AMPA-induced lesions of the septo-hippocampal cholinergic projection on aversive conditioning to explicit and contextual cues and spatial learning in the water maze. *European Journal of Neuroscience, 7*(2), 281-292.

McClelland, J.L., McNaughton, B.L., & O'Reilly, R.C. (1995). Why there are complementary learning systems in the hippocampus and neocortex: Insights from the successes and failures of connectionist models of learning and memory. *Psychological Review, 102*(3), 419-457.

McEchron, M.D., Bouwmeester, H., Tseng, W., Weiss, C., & Disterhoft, J.F. (1999). Hippocampectomy disrupts trace auditory cued fear conditioning and contextual fear conditioning in the rat. *Hippocampus (in press).*

McEchron, M.D., & Disterhoft, J.F. (1997). Sequence of single neuron changes in CA1 hippocampus of rabbits during acquisition of trace eyeblink conditioned responses. *Journal of Neurophysiology, 78*(2), 1030-1044.

McEchron, M.D., & Disterhoft, J.F. (1999). Hippocampal encoding of non-spatial trace conditioning. *Hippocampus, 9*(4), 385-396.

McEchron, M.D., Weible, A.P., & Disterhoft, J.F. (1997). Aging-related changes in single neuron activity in the CA1 area of the rabbit hippocampus during trace eyeblink conditioning in the rabbit. *Society for Neuroscience Abstract, 23*, 1618.

McEchron, M.D., Weible, A.P., & Disterhoft, J.F. (1998). Aging-related alterations in the covariance of CA1 hippocampal single neuron activity in local ensembles during trace eyeblink conditioning in the rabbit. *Society for Neuroscience Abstracts, 24*, 1914.

McHugh, T.J., Blum, K.I., Tsien, J.Z., Tonegawa, S., & Wilson, M.A. (1996). Impaired hippocampal representation of space in CA1-specific NMDAR1 knockout mice. *Cell, 87*(7), 1339-1349.

McNaughton, B.L., O'Keefe, J., & Barnes, C.A. (1983). The stereotrode: A new technique for simultaneous isolation of several single units in the central nervous system from multiple unit records. *Journal of Neuroscience Methods, 8*, 391-397.

Meck, W.H., Church, R.M., & Olton, D.S. (1984). Hippocampus, time, and memory. *Behavioral Neuroscience, 98*, 3-22.

Moore, J.W. (1979). Information processing in space-time by the hippocampus. *Physiological Psychology, 7*, 224-232.

Morris, R.G.M., Garrud, P., Rawlins, N.P., & O'Keefe, J. (1982). Place navigation impaired in rats with hippocampal lesions. *Nature, 297*, 681-683.

Moyer, J.R., Jr., Deyo, R.A., & Disterhoft, J.F. (1990). Hippocampectomy disrupts trace eye-blink conditioning in rabbits. *Behavioral Neuroscience, 104*(2), 243-252.

Moyer, J.R., Jr., Thompson, L.T., & Disterhoft, J.F. (1996). Trace eyeblink conditioning increases CA1 excitability in a transient and learning-specific manner. *Journal of Neuroscience, 16*(17), 5536-5546.

Muller, R.U., & Kubie, J.L. (1987). The effects of changes in the environment on the spatial firing of hippocampal complex-spike cells. *Journal of Neuroscience, 7*, 1951-1968.

Nadel, L. (1991). The hippocampus and space revisited. *Hippocampus, 1*(3), 221-229.

O'Keefe, J., & Nadel, L. (1978). *The Hippocampus as a Cognitive Map.* London: Oxford University Press.

O'Keefe, J., & Speakman, A. (1987). Single unit activity in the rat hippocampus during a spatial memory task. *Experimental Brain Research, 68*, 1-27.

Pavlov, I.P. (1927). *Conditioned Reflexes.* (G.V. Anrep, Translation). London: Oxford University Press.

Powell, D.A., Buchanan, S., & Hernandez, L.L. (1981). Age related changes in classical (Pavlovian) conditioning in the New Zealand albino rabbit. *Experimental Aging Research, 7*, 453-465.

Power, J.M., Thompson, L.T., Moyer, J.R., Jr., & Disterhoft, J.F. (1997). Enhanced synaptic transmission in CA1 hippocampus after eyeblink conditioning. *Journal of Neurophysiology, 78*(2), 1184-1187.

Raffaele, K.C., & Olton, D.S. (1988). Hippocampal and amygdaloid involvement in working memory for nonspatial stimuli. *Behavioral Neuroscience, 102*, 349-355.

Ranck, J. B. (1973). Studies on single neurons in dorsal hippocampal formation and septum in unrestrained rats. I. Behavioral correlates and firing repetoires. *Experimental Neurology, 41*, 461-555.

Rawlins, J.N.P. (1985). Associations across time: The hippocampus as a temporary memory store. *Behavioral and Brain Sciences, 8*, 479-496.

Rawlins, J.N.P., & Tsaltas, E. (1983). The hippocampus, time and working memory. *Behavioural Brain Research, 10*, 233-262.

Rolls, E. (1989). Principles underlying the representation and storage of information in neuronal networks in the primate hippocampus and cerebral cortex. In S. F. Zornetzer, J. L. Davis & C. Lau (Eds.). *An Introduction to Neural and Electronic Networks, (pp. 73-90).* San Diego, CA: Academic Press.

Rolls, E.T., Miyashita, Y., Cahusac, P.M.B., Kesner, R.P., Niki, H., Feigenbaum, J.D., & Bach, L. (1989). Hippocampal neurons in the monkey with activity related to the place in which a stimulus is shown. *Journal of Neuroscience, 9*, 1835-1845.

Ross, R.T., Orr, W.B., Holland, P.C., & Berger, T.W. (1984). Hippocampectomy disrupts acquisition and

retention of learned conditional responding. *Behavioral Neuroscience, 98*, 211-225.
Rudy, J.W., & Sutherland, R.J. (1995). Configural association theory and the hippocampal formation: An appraisal and reconfiguration. *Hippocampus, 5*(5), 375-389.
Sakurai, Y. (1998). Cell-assembly coding in several memory processes. *Neurobiology Learning and Memory, 70*(1-2), 212-225.
Schmajuk, N.A., & Di Carlo, J.J. (1997). Stimulus configuration, classical conditioning, and hippocampal function. *Psychological Review, 99*, 268-305.
Shapiro, M.L., Tanila, H., & Eichenbaum, H. (1997). Cues that hippocampal place cells encode: Dynamic and hierarchical representation of local and distal stimuli. *Hippocampus, 7*(6), 624-642.
Solomon, P.R. (1977). Role of the hippocampus in blocking and conditioned inhibition of the rabbit's nictitating membrane response. *Journal of Comparative and Physiological Psychology, 91*, 407-417.
Solomon, P.R. (1980). A time and a place for everything? Temporal processing views of hippocampal function with special reference to attention. *Physiological Psychology, 8*, 254-261.
Solomon, P.R., Barth, C.L., Wood, M.S., Velazquez, E., Groccia-Ellison, M., & Yang, B.Y. (1995). Age-related deficits in retention of the classically conditioned nictitating membrane response in rabbits. *Behavioral Neuroscience, 109*(1), 18-23.
Solomon, P.R., van der Schaaf, E.V., Thompson, R.F., & Weisz, D.J. (1986). Hippocampus and trace conditioning of the rabbit's classically conditioned nictitating membrane response. *Behavioral Neuroscience, 100*, 729-744.
Squire, L. (1987). *Memory and Brain.* New York: Oxford Press.
Thompson, L.T., Moyer, J.R., Jr., & Disterhoft, J.F. (1996). Trace eyeblink conditioning in rabbits demonstrates heterogeneity of learning ability both between and within age groups. *Neurobiology of Aging, 17*(4), 619-629.
Thompson, L.T., Moyer, J.R., Jr., & Disterhoft, J.F. (1996). Transient changes in excitability of rabbit CA3 neurons with a time course appropriate to support memory consolidation. *Journal of Neurophysiology, 76*(3), 1836-1849.
Tsaltas, E., Preston, G.C., & Gray, J.A. (1983). The effects of dorsal bundle lesions on serial and trace conditioning. *Behavioural Brain Research, 10*(2-3), 361-374.
Wallenstein, G.V., Eichenbaum, H., & Hasselmo, M.E. (1998). The hippocampus as an associator of discontiguous events. *Trends in Neuroscience, 21*(8), 317-323.
Weiss, C., Kronforst-Collins, M.A., & Disterhoft, J.F. (1996). Activity of hippocampal pyramidal neurons during trace eyeblink conditioning. *Hippocampus, 6*(2), 192-209.
Wible, C.G., Findling, R.L., Shapiro, M., Lang, E.J., Crane, S., & Olton, D.S. (1986). Mnemonic correlates of unit activity in the hippocampus. *Brain Research, 399*, 97-110.
Wilson, M.A., & McNaughton, B.L. (1993). Dynamics of the hippocampal ensemble code for space. *Science, 261*, 1055-1058.
Wilson, M.A., & McNaughton, B.L. (1994). Reactivation of hippocampal ensemble memories during sleep. *Science, 265*, 676-679.
Winocur, G. (1990). Anterograde and retrograde amnesia in rats with dorsal hippocampal or dorsomedial thalamic lesions. *Behavioral Brain Research, 38*, 145-154.
Yee, B.K., & Rawlins, J.N. (1994). The effects of hippocampal formation ablation or fimbria-fornix section on performance of a nonspatial radial arm maze task by rats. *Journal of Neuroscience, 14*(6), 3766-3774.
Young, B.J., Fox, G.D., & Eichenbaum, H. (1994). Correlates of hippocampal complex-spike cell activity in rats performing a nonspatial radial maze task. *Journal of Neuroscience, 14*(11 Pt 1), 6553-6563.
Zisper, D. (1985). Computational model of hippocampal place fields. *Behavioral Neuroscience, 99*, 1006-1017.
Zola-Morgan, S.M., & Squire, L.R. (1990). The primate hippocampal formation: Evidence for a time-limited role in memory storage. *Science, 250*, 288-290.

ACKNOWLEDGEMENTS

Supported by NIH grants RO1 MH47340, R37 AG08796 and F32 AG05711. Special thanks to Margaret Bruner for her assistance in preparing this manuscript.

14 COGNITIVE-ENHANCING DRUGS AND EYEBLINK CLASSICAL CONDITIONING

Diana S. Woodruff-Pak and Michael Ewers
Temple University

INTRODUCTION

An aspect of the animal model of classical conditioning of the nictitating membrane (NM)/eyeblink response that extends the validity of the neurobiological results is the convergence of evidence from a variety of neuroscientific techniques. Evidence from lesion, reversible lesion, and electrophysiological recording and stimulation studies presented in Chapters 3 and 4 in this volume and also throughout the book supports a critical role for the cerebellum. The site essential for acquisition and retention of the classically conditioned NM/eyeblink response is the interpositus nucleus ipsilateral to the eye receiving the unconditioned stimulus (US). Cerebellar cortex ipsilateral to the US contributes to the process of acquisition, and an intact cerebellar cortex enables acquisition to occur at a faster rate. As documented in Chapter 2 and elaborated in Chapters 12 and 13, the hippocampus is normally involved during acquisition, and it is essential in some NM/eyeblink classical conditioning procedures.

Pharmacological studies have added some perspective about how the circuitry functions. In the early 1970s, as Richard F. Thompson described in Chapter 2 of this volume, his laboratory utilized the extensive behavioral knowledge base about the rabbit NM/eyeblink conditioning model to investigate the underlying neurobiological mechanisms of associative learning. The first pharmacological studies of NM/eyeblink classical conditioning were also undertaken around that time (Moore, Goodell & Solomon, 1976). Not only have these pharmacological studies extended understanding about the functional relationships between structures engaged during conditioning, they have led to applications in human pharmaco-therapy. Indeed, behavioral and neurobiological parallels between non-human mammals and humans in classical conditioning of the NM/eyeblink response demonstrated that this animal model has utility in behavioral pharmacology for preclinical and clinical trials (Disterhoft, Deyo, Moyer, Straube & Thompson, 1989; Harvey & Gormezano, 1986; Solomon, Groccia-Ellison, Stanton & Pendlebury, 1994; Woodruff-Pak, 1995; Woodruff-Pak, Coffin & Sasse, 1991).

The purpose of this chapter on cognition-enhancement is to trace the background of investigations of pharmacological actions in the NM/eyeblink classical conditioning model. This background actually began with cognition-impairment. Early knowledge about the role of drugs in eyeblink conditioning was established in the 1970s and early-1980s with the muscarinic acetylcholine antagonist, scopolamine. The well-known association between acetylcholine and learning and memory along with the documented action of acetylcholine in eyeblink conditioning have made this neurotransmitter the most studied one in the animal model of eyeblink conditioning. In particular, the majority of strategies of cognition-enhancement involve the cholinergic system, so the major focus of this chapter is on the acetylcholine neurotransmitter system.

Other neurotransmitter systems involved in eyeblink classical conditioning have been investigated primarily to explore their contribution to learning and memory in this paradigm. An interesting strategy has been to use local infusions of antagonists to discrete receptor systems to block the contribution of specific anatomical structures to acquisition and retention. The typical strategy has been to block these neurotransmitters with antagonists. Studies of the role of antagonism in eyeblink classical conditioning in these neurotransmitter systems are beyond the scope of this chapter which addresses cognition enhancement.

Experiments investigating glutamate neurotransmission and the role of long term potentiation (LTP) and long term depression (LTD) in eyeblink conditioning have been reported. Relatively few attempts to explore cognition enhancement via glutamatergic systems have been undertaken, and we will examine them quite briefly in this chapter. We refer the interested reader to Chapter 8 on cellular correlates of conditioning with a central focus on the cerebellum and to Chapter 13 on cellular alterations in hippocampus during conditioning. Both chapters provide insights about molecular and neurochemical mechanisms for plasticity.

Inhibition as well as excitation is essential for learning, especially in a model system with the cerebellum as the major essential structure. Thus, the role of the major inhibitory neurotransmitter, gamma-aminobutyric acid (GABA) is critical in this form of learning. Mamounas, Thompson and Madden (1987) demonstrated in rabbits that microinfusion of GABA antagonists (either bicuculline methiodide or picrotoxin) into specific areas of the medial dentate and lateral interpositus nuclei selectively and reversibly abolished conditioned responses. Microinfusion of GABA antagonists into the cerebellar cortical lobule HVI had a similar effect. These were the first results demonstrating that GABAergic synapses play an essential role in learning in this paradigm. Indeed, some of the clearest evidence of the essential role of the cerebellar interpositus nucleus ipsilateral to the conditioned eye in acquisition of conditioned responses is provided by reversible lesion studies using GABA agonists (Krupa, Thompson & Thompson, 1993; see also Chapter 3). More recently, reversible lesions of cerebellar cortical output with the GABA antagonist picrotoxin was used to demonstrate the role of the cerebellar cortex in the timing of conditioned responses (Garcia & Mauk, 1998).

A cyclic derivative of GABA, N-(2,6-dimethyl-phenyl)-2-(2-oxo-1-pyrrodlidinyl)-acetamide (nefiracetam), attenuates GABA antagonist-induced amnesia by interacting with a portion of $GABA_A$ receptors (Nabeshima, Noda, Tohyama, Itoh & Kameyama, 1990). Nefiracetam also facilitates the release of acetylcholine and has been demonstrated to be a cognition enhancing drug in the eyeblink classical conditioning paradigm (e.g., Woodruff-Pak & Li, 1994). Although we discuss nefiracetam in the context of the cholinergic system, it is possible that it is also acting on the GABAergic system to affect conditioning.

The central focus of this chapter is on preclinical research – that is research with animals. At the present time, we know of no published studies of clinical trials using cognition-enhancing drugs in humans and testing eyeblink classical conditioning. However, the deleterious effect of scopolamine on human eyeblink conditioning has been documented (Bahro, Schreurs, Sunderland & Molchan, 1995; Solomon et al., 1993). The NM response and the eyeblink response in the same eye of the rabbit are highly correlated (r = .99) and show similar patterns of response during classical conditioning (McCormick, Lavond & Thompson, 1982). Because we will discuss implications for humans from the animal studies, the terms eyeblink conditioning and eyeblink classical conditioning will be used for both rabbit and human studies, even though in most cases it is the NM that is measured in rabbits.

CLASSICAL CONDITIONING PROCEDURES FOR TESTING DRUG EFFECTS

The procedure for eyeblink classical conditioning involves the presentation of a neutral stimulus such as a tone or a light conditioned stimulus (CS), followed by a corneal airpuff or mild shock (to the muscles around the eye) unconditioned stimulus (US). The US always causes the organism to blink, thus producing an unconditioned response (UR). Learning occurs with the repeated pairing of the CS and US. The organism learns to blink to the CS before the onset of the US. This learned response is called a conditioned response (CR).

Many studies of drugs and eyeblink conditioning use the delay procedure in which the CS precedes the US by a fixed amount of time and is on while the US is presented. Another frequently used procedure is called trace. The CS and the US do not overlap in the trace procedure because the CS is turned off, a blank period ensues, and then the US occurs. The term, trace, is used because the subject must form a memory trace of the CS to associate it with the later-arriving US. Typically, there are two features of the trace paradigm making it different from the delay paradigm: 1) the presence of the blank trace period; 2) a longer interval between the CS and US.

The interval between the onset of the CS and US plays a significant role in the rate of acquisition. CS-US intervals of less than 100 ms result in little or no conditioning, and CS-US intervals exceeding 500 ms make acquisition more difficult for rabbits. Much of our data on aging rabbits is in the 750 ms delay paradigm, a CS-US interval in which large age-related deficits are apparent (Sasse & Woodruff-Pak, 1990; Sasse, Coffin & Woodruff-Pak, 1991). Using 90 paired CS and US presentations for each daily session, most young rabbits (3-6 months old) attain a learning criterion of eight CRs in nine consecutive trials in four to five sessions (around 400 trials; see Figure 1). Most older rabbits (24 months and older) attain criterion within nine to 10 sessions (around 1,000 trials). Like many forms of learning and memory in aging mammals, conditioning performance in older rabbits is more variable than in young rabbits (see Chapter 7 in this volume).

The long acquisition periods required by the 750 ms delay procedure provide ample time to demonstrate the cognition-enhancing effects of drugs. When experimental designs include the provision that animals are tested for 15 to 20 daily sessions, it is also readily evident when drugs induce cognition-impairment in young rabbits and exacerbate cognition-impairment in older rabbits.

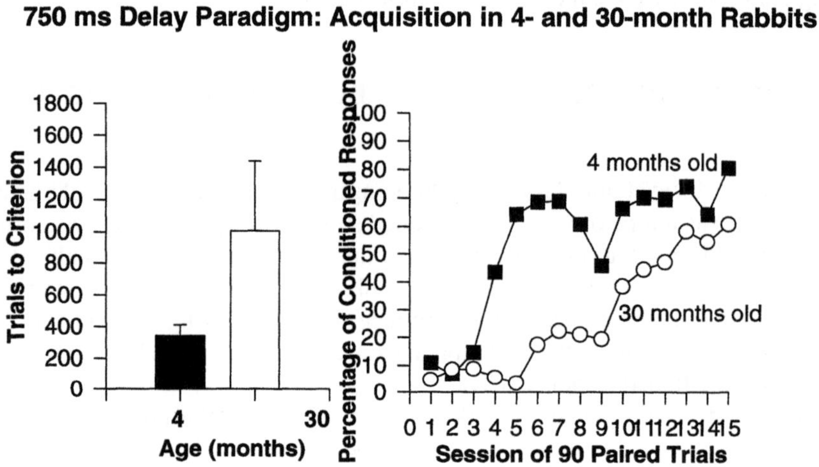

Figure 1. Acquisition in the 750 ms delay paradigm in young and older adult rabbits. Left: Number of trials to attain a learning criterion of eight conditioned responses (CRs) in nine consecutive trials. Error bars are standard deviation. Right: Percentage of CRs per session for fifteen, 90-trial sessions (Woodruff-Pak, unpublished data).

ACETYLCHOLINE, ASSOCIATIVE LEARNING, AND EYEBLINK CONDITIONING

The focus of our discussion about learning and acetylcholine is on hippocampal substrates of eyeblink classical conditioning, however we acknowledge that in the intact organism it is not possible to achieve certainty about the site of action or the mechanism of action of a drug. Whereas it is more likely that cognition-enhancing drugs affecting the cholinergic system are acting in the hippocampus to facilitate learning, we cannot rule out the possibility that the compounds are acting in the cerebellum or in other brain structures.

Cerebellar Purkinje cells are lost in normal aging in rabbits, and we have found a high correlation between number of Purkinje cells and rate of acquisition (Woodruff-Pak, Cronholm, & Sheffield, 1990; Woodruff-Pak & Trojanowski, 1996). Even in a group of young rabbits, the number of Purkinje cells correlated highly with the rate of learning (Woodruff-Pak et al., 1990). Ito (1984) suggested that although the physiological significance of acetylcholine receptors and acetylcholine-related enzymes in Purkinje cells remained obscure, it was possible that acetylcholine modulated synaptic activity of Purkinje cells. The possibility exists that drugs that facilitate acquisition of CRs in rabbits do so by enhancing the responding of Purkinje cells. The fact that many drugs improve acquisition in older rabbits (that presumably have lost Purkinje cells) but do not improve acquisition in young rabbits (with more intact Purkinje cells) could be used to support the contention that the drugs act via the cerebellum. Other possible means for cognition-enhancing drugs to affect eyeblink conditioning via the cerebellum are discussed in Chapter 7 in this volume. Having pointed out a potential role for the cerebellum in cholinergic cognition enhancement, we now turn to the role of the hippocampus.

A classic strategy in behavioral pharmacology to test drugs affecting memory is to determine if these drugs reverse the effects of scopolamine, a muscarinic cholinergic antagonist. The first step in these tests is to identify a behavior that is impaired by scopolamine. Because acetylcholine is one of the neurotransmitters used extensively in the hippocampus, many tests of learning and memory are impaired by the administration of scopolamine.

Cholinergic System Effects on Eyeblink Conditioning and the Hippocampus

The hippocampus and septo-hippocampal cholinergic system have proven to be highly involved in basic associative learning of the sort represented by eyeblink classical conditioning in the rabbit. This was demonstrated initially by Berger, Alger and Thompson (1976) in electrophysiological recording studies of hippocampal neurons and by Moore et al. (1976) in behavioral pharmacology studies. These results provided a point of contact with longstanding interests in the role of the hippocampus and forebrain cholinergic system in human memory.

In the rabbit, neuronal unit activity in the hippocampus increases markedly within trials early in the eyeblink classical conditioning process. Activity recorded in the CA1 region of the hippocampus forms a predictive "model" of the amplitude-time course of the learned behavioral response. The hippocampal modeling of the behavioral CR and UR is generated largely by hippocampal pyramidal neurons in the CA1 and CA3 fields (Berger & Thompson, 1978a; Berger, Rinaldi, Weisz & Thompson, 1983). Firing to the tone-CS and corneal airpuff-US occurs only under conditions where the stimuli are paired and produce behavioral learning (Berger et al., 1976) and only if the cerebellar interpositus nucleus is intact (Clark, McCormick, Lavond & Thompson, 1984; Sears & Steinmetz, 1990). When the CS and US are presented independently in the explicitly unpaired paradigm, there are no hippocampal responses to the tones or air puffs (Berger & Thompson, 1978b). When the interpositus nucleus is lesioned before training begins, there is no hippocampal model of the behavioral CR, although there is a hippocampal response during the behavioral UR (Sears & Steinmetz, 1990).

Muscarinic Cholinergic Effects

The role of the hippocampus during acquisition in delay eyeblink classical conditioning is seemingly paradoxical in that conditioning proceeds normally in animals with bilateral removal of the hippocampus, but manipulation of hippocampal function with drugs can facilitate or impair acquisition. In rabbits, disruption of muscarinic cholinergic receptors with scopolamine injections slows the acquisition of CRs, and this disruption occurs only when the hippocampus is intact (e.g., Solomon, Solomon, Vander Schaaf & Perry, 1983).

Solomon et al. (1983) gave rabbits bilateral hippocampal ablations, ablations of the overlying cortex, or no ablations, and these rabbits were trained after administration of scopolamine or saline. Replicating previous research, bilateral hippocampal ablations had no effect on acquisition of eyeblink conditioning in the delay paradigm, but scopolamine severely retarded acquisition in the cortically lesioned and in the non-lesioned control animals. Significantly, in animals with hippocampal ablations, scopolamine had no effect on conditioning. The scopolamine-treated, hippocampal ablation group conditioned at about the same rate as saline-treated, non-lesioned rabbits. These results suggest that scopolamine acts via the hippocampal cholinergic system to disrupt conditioning.

Scopolamine injections eliminate hippocampal pyramidal cell activity in conjunction with the CR and UR (Salvatierra & Berry, 1989). Microinjections of scopolamine into the medial septum (Solomon & Gottfried, 1981) prolong the rate of acquisition of the classically conditioned eyeblink response in rabbits. As mentioned previously, scopolamine administration also disrupts eyeblink conditioning in humans (Bahro et al., 1995; Solomon et al., 1993).

Reversal of Muscarinic Cholinergic Effects with a Cognition-Enhancing Drug

To use the classic strategy in behavioral pharmacology of testing drugs affecting memory to determine if these drugs reverse the effects of scopolamine, a cognition-enhancing drug must first be identified. Nefiracetam is a drug that ameliorates learning impairment in eyeblink classical conditioning in older rabbits (Woodruff-Pak & Li, 1994). At doses of 10 and 15 mg/kg, but not at a dose of 5 mg/kg, older rabbits attained a learning criterion of eight CRs in nine consecutive trials more rapidly and produced a higher percentage of CRs than did vehicle-treated older rabbits.

Nefiracetam is classified as a nootropic drug. Most compounds developed as nootropic drugs are pyrrolidone derivatives (piracetam, oxiracetam, aniracetam, nefiracetam), and evidence indicates that these drugs activate brain neurotransmitter systems, in particular the cholinergic system (Spignoli & Pepeu, 1987), but also the dopaminergic (Funk & Schmidt, 1984), glutamatergic (Marchi et al., 1990), and GABAergic systems (Nabeshima et al., 1990). Nefiracetam promotes the release of diverse neurotransmitters such as acetylcholine, GABA, and monoamines (Watabe et al., 1993). The mechanism by which nefiracetam facilitates release of a number of neurotransmitters may be activation of the long-lasting N/L-type Ca^{2+} channel currents (Nabeshima, 1994). Yoshii and Watabe (1994) reported that the long-lasting N/L-type Ca^{2+} channel currents were more than doubled by nefiracetam with no effect on the transient T-type current.

Isolating the site of efficacy and the neurotransmitters affected by a drug is challenging – especially when dealing with an intact, behaving organism. In an attempt to understand better how and where nefiracetam was acting to ameliorate eyeblink conditioning impairments in older rabbits, we carried out several experiments with eyeblink classical conditioning in young and older rabbits.

One approach was to determine if the site of action of nefiracetam was in the hippocampus (Woodruff-Pak, Li, Hinchliffe & Port, 1997). The hypothesis was that an effective dose of nefiracetam would work only if the hippocampus was intact. Retired breeder rabbits were tested under drug conditions using a cognition-enhancing dose of nefiracetam (10 mg/kg) or vehicle. There were four lesion conditions: bilateral hippocampectomy, bilateral neocortical removal, sham surgery, and no surgery. This meant that there were eight groups of older rabbits, with 10 mg/kg nefiracetam administered to rabbits with four different types of lesions and vehicle administered to rabbits with four different types of lesions. The three groups of 10 mg/kg nefiracetam-treated rabbits with intact hippocampus acquired CRs more rapidly than the vehicle-treated groups, indicating that this dose of nefiracetam was effective when the hippocampus was intact. Rabbits with bilateral hippocampectomy and treated with nefiracetam learned like vehicle-treated rabbits. The cognition-enhancing drug did not work when the hippocampus was removed. Results suggested that nefiracetam ameliorated learning via the hippocampus. This result made it more likely that it was nefiracetam's effect in promoting acetylcholine that ameliorated eyeblink conditioning because of the known cholinergic input to the hippocampus via the medial septum. Of course this experiment did not rule out the possibility that nefiracetam was effective because it promoted the release of other neurotransmitters. The release of glutamate is clearly another likely mechanism of action that would ameliorate eyeblink conditioning via hippocampal circuitry.

To further explore the efficacy of nefiracetam in the cholinergic system, we carried out the classic pharmacology experiment of testing whether doses of nefiracetam that were effective in ameliorating learning would reverse scopolamine (Woodruff-Pak & Hinchliffe, 1997). Comparisons testing muscarinic cholinergic antagonism and using scopolamine demonstrated that acquisition after injection with a cholinergic antagonist proceeded faster when rabbits also received nefiracetam. In particular, the dose of 10 mg/kg nefiracetam was effective in reversing the effect of scopolamine. Scopolamine impaired acquisition in young rabbits, and when nefiracetam was injected they performed like vehicle-treated rabbits. These results with the muscarinic cholinergic antagonist, scopolamine suggest that nefiracetam does affect the cholinergic system in its amelioration of impairments in eyeblink classical conditioning.

Other evidence of the role of the cholinergic system in eyeblink classical conditioning comes from tests of drugs known to act as cholinesterase inhibitors. Acetylcholinesterase is an enzyme that speeds the degradation of acetylcholine in the synaptic cleft after it is released presynaptically. Drugs that act as cholinesterase inhibitors impair the efficacy of acetylcholinesterase and thus cause more acetylcholine to remain in the synapse to be available for post-synaptic receptors. Physostigmine has long been tested as a cholinesterase inhibitor and cognition-enhancing drug, and more recently donepezil (Aricept) has been tested in animals and eventually approved for use as a cognition-enhancing drug for the treatment of Alzheimer's disease. We have tested these cholinesterase inhibitors in older rabbits using the 750 ms delay eyeblink classical conditioning procedure. At the doses we used, they are moderately effective in ameliorating impairments in acquisition of CRs in older rabbits (Figure 2).

A Role for Nicotinic Cholinergic Receptors in Eyeblink Classical Conditioning

Cholinergic afferents to the hippocampal formation are generated from a single source in the medial septal area (McKinney, Coyle & Hedreen, 1983), and both muscarinic cholinergic receptors (Spencer, Horvath & Raber, 1986) and nicotinic cholinergic receptors (Schwartz, 1986) are present in the same target regions of these afferents. Thus, it is likely that both receptor types are activated in parallel. Cholinergic modulation of hippocampal function probably reflects a complex, dynamic combination of muscarinic receptor and nicotinic receptor activation, rather than an exclusive action of either type of cholinergic receptor. There are a number of nicotinic receptor subtypes that possess varied pharmacological properties including presynaptic facilitation of neurotransmitter release as well as postsynaptic action (Luetje, Wada, Rogers, Abramson, Tsuji, Heinemann & Patrick, 1990).

Mecamylamine: A Nicotinic Antagonist

Previously, we demonstrated that mecamylamine, a drug that blocks nicotinic cholinergic receptors, impairs eyeblink classical conditioning in young rabbits (Woodruff-Pak, Li, Kazmi & Kem, 1994). The dose of mecamylamine was relatively low (0.5 mg/kg) so that nicotinic but not muscarinic receptors would be antagonized. Mecamylamine impaired the performance of young rabbits to the degree that they performed like older rabbits in the 750 ms delay procedure. Research, using a very low dosage level of mecamylamine in young rabbits so that nicotinic cholinergic receptors would be selectively inhibited, demonstrated a role for nicotinic cholinergic receptors in eyeblink conditioning because the acquisition of CRs was severely disrupted.

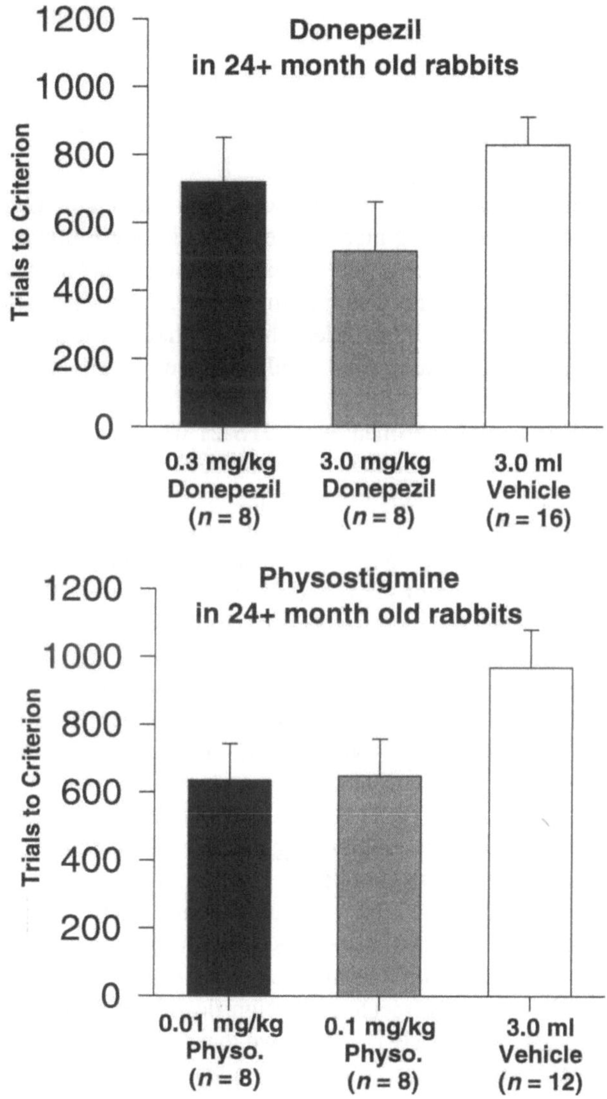

Figure 2. Trials to a learning criterion of eight conditioned responses in nine consecutive trials in the 750 ms delay procedure for older rabbits treated at two doses of donepezil and sterile saline vehicle (Top panel) and two doses of physostigmine (physo.) and sterile saline vehicle (Bottom panel). Error bars are standard error of the mean (Woodruff-Pak, unpublished data).

The acquisition of CRs is now known to be inhibited by both muscarinic and nicotinic cholinergic antagonists. Scopolamine and mecamylamine, respectively, impaired acquisition in several CS-US intervals in the delay procedure. Using the 750 ms trace procedure with a 500 ms trace period, Kaneko and Thompson (1997) demonstrated that acquisition was blocked by a low dose of scopolamine. The effects of muscarinic antagonists were documented in the eyeblink classical conditioning paradigm for two decades, and the effect of nicotinic antagonists were also demonstrated.

A Nicotinic Agonist: GTS-21

Results with cholinergic agonists are more recent than the long-demonstrated effects of scopolamine. A drug affecting nicotinic receptors in development for cognition-enhancement is GTS-21. This drug acts primarily at the alpha 7 nicotinic cholinergic receptor subtype (De Fiebre et al., 1995; Kem, Mahnir, Papke & Lingle, 1997). This drug improves acquisition of CRs in older rabbits so that they learn as well as young rabbits (Woodruff-Pak, Li & Kem, 1994), and it reverses the effect of mecamylamine in the disruption of learning.

To our knowledge, our experiment with GTS-21 was the first to test the efficacy of a nicotinic agonist in older rabbits in the eyeblink classical conditioning paradigm. The nicotinic agonist, GTS-21, ameliorated impaired acquisition in older rabbits in the 750 ms delay eyeblink classical conditioning procedure. The doses that were consistently effective in improving acquisition in older rabbits, as assessed by trials to learning criterion, percentage of CRs, and CR amplitude, were 0.5 and 1.0 mg/kg. These doses did not affect the motor aspects of the response (UR amplitude). A 0.5 mg/kg dose of GTS-21 did not sensitize the older rabbits to the tone CS as the blink rate to the CS was low in the unpaired condition. The conditioning levels achieved in 15 sessions by older rabbits treated with GTS-21 were not significantly different from conditioning levels performed by young rabbits. However, there was a significant difference between the vehicle-treated older and younger rabbits (as seen in the example in Figure 1). Thus, GTS-21 at dose levels of 0.5 and 1.0 mg/kg ameliorated the deficit in eyeblink classical conditioning in older rabbits to the degree that older rabbits perform as well as young rabbits.

Whereas we predicted that the nicotinic agonist, GTS-21, would facilitate acquisition of CRs in older rabbits, it was less clear whether nicotinic receptor binding density in the rabbits' brains would be affected. Single daily injections of GTS-21 15 minutes before training could affect learning significantly without altering the density of nicotinic receptors. Previously it was shown that rodents receiving daily or twice-daily subcutaneous injections of nicotine displayed an up-regulation in the concentration of nicotinic receptors in cortical as well as several other regions of the brain (Collins, Bhat, Pauly & Marks, 1990; Flores, Rogers, Pabreza, Wolfe & Kellar, 1991; Schwartz & Kellar, 1985). Although it is not yet clear if the increase in nicotinic receptors affects cognitive function, evidence for increased nicotine sensitivity has been reported for striatal dopamine release (Rowell & Wonnacott, 1990). Since our experimental protocol for investigating GTS-21 action upon associative learning involved daily injections of this compound over a period of time sufficient for nicotine up-regulation of nicotinic receptors, we measured the concentration of cerebral cortex receptors in the brains of the rabbits used for eyeblink conditioning in order to determine if GTS-21 also influenced receptor concentration (Woodruff-Pak et al., 1994).

The nicotinic receptor estimates for the rabbits administered various doses of GTS-21 were compared with the receptor estimates for the vehicle-treated rabbits, and the data did not reveal evidence for receptor up- or down-regulation by the dose regime of GTS-21 administered. The absence of an observed effect of GTS-21 upon nicotinic receptor concentration may have results from administration of a dose regime which resulted in a much smaller degree of receptor occupation. Alternatively, GTS-21 may differ from nicotine in such a manner that it did not cause receptor up-regulation.

GTS-21, a nicotinic cholinergic agonist, ameliorates the deficit in eyeblink conditioning in older rabbits. Next, we examined whether the effects of mecamylamine on eyeblink conditioning could be reversed with nicotinic agonists (GTS-21 and nicotine; Li, Alvarez & Woodruff-Pak, 1994). Fifteen eyeblink conditioning sessions were run in the 750 ms delay paradigm. Young rabbits were tested in six groups of eight rabbits each with 15 subcutaneous injections that were administered daily, five days per week. Rabbits in the paired CS-US condition were assigned to a control group tested with sterile saline vehicle, and experimental groups tested with 0.5 mg/kg mecamylamine alone, 0.5 mg/kg mecamylamine and 1.0 mg/kg GTS-21, or 0.5 mg/kg mecamylamine and 0.5 mg/kg nicotine. Explicitly unpaired control rabbits were tested in the same 15 session schedule after being injected with sterile saline vehicle or 0.5 mg/kg mecamylamine and1.0 mg/kg GTS-21. Dependent measures (trials to learning criterion, percentage of CRs) indicated that GTS-21 and nicotine reversed the effect of mecamylamine. Rabbits treated with mecamylamine alone took significantly longer to learn, but the effect of mecamylamine on conditioning was reversed by both 1.0 mg/kg GTS-21 and 0.5 mg/kg nicotine.

Retention of CRs as well as acquisition was affected by GTS-21. Retention was exhibited to tone CS-alone trials presented 6 and 13 weeks after the initial training began, with no additional drug administration (Woodruff-Pak, Green, Coleman-Valencia & Pak, in press). Older rabbits treated with 0.5 mg/kg GTS-21 produced more CRs during the first 10 CS-alone trials of retention testing six weeks after the last acquisition session than did vehicle-treated older rabbits. Rabbits treated with 0.5 mg/kg GTS-21 also showed a clear effect of extinction in the second 10 trials of both retention sessions presented in the sixth and thirteenth week of the experiment. Vehicle-treated rabbits produced 13% CRs in the first 10 CS-alone trials in the Retention 1 session in the sixth week of the experiment in striking contrast to the 40% CRs produced in that period by the rabbits treated with 0.5 mg/kg GTS-21. This dramatic difference in retention between older rabbits treated with vehicle or GTS-21 was not present by the thirteenth week of the experiment in the Retention 2 session. Relearning was evident in GTS-21 and vehicle-treated rabbits and was not different between the two groups.

Dual Mechanism of Action: Galantamine

A drug that acts by a dual mechanism of action (i.e. first, an allosteric modulation of nicotinic acetylcholine receptors to increase acetylcholine release and second, reversible, competitive, selective inhibition of acetylcholinesterase) that affects cholinergic neurotransmission is galantamine. Galantamine is a tertiary alkaloid originally derived from the bulbs of the snowdrop and various *Narcissus* species (Parys, 1998). It interacts selectively and competitively with the enzyme acetylcholinesterase (Thomsen & Kewitz, 1990). Research also indicates that galantamine is an allosteric modulator at nicotinic cholinergic receptor sites (Maelicke, Schrattenholz, Periera & Albuquerque, 1998; Schrattenholz et al., 1996). It is proposed that galantamine increases cholinergic function in two ways: (a) increasing the concentration of acetylcholine through a competitive reversible inhibition of acetylcholine hydrolysis by the enzyme acetylcholinesterase; and (b) increasing the release of acetylcholine and other neurotransmitters such as glutamate through an allosteric modulation of acetylcholine effects at nicotinic cholinergic receptor sites. Because galantamine improved cognitive deficits in animal models involving cholinergic deficits, and because the cholinergic system has been demonstrated to be involved in eyeblink classical conditioning, we anticipated that galantamine would be effective in ameliorating conditioning deficits in older rabbits. Our initial aim was to identify a dose or doses of galantamine that showed measurable effects on the acquisition of CRs (Woodruff-Pak & Santos, in press).

Galantamine doses of 0, 1, 2, 3, and 4 mg/kg were tested in daily sessions in 40 older rabbits of a mean age of 29 months in the 750 ms delay conditioning paradigm. A dose of 3 mg/kg galantamine was effective in improving conditioning in older rabbits, enabling them to achieve learning criterion rapidly and to produce a very high percentage of CRs (Figure 3). Control tests of rabbits in explicitly unpaired conditions demonstrated that non-associative factors could not account for the results. The efficacy of galantamine in an associative learning paradigm indicates that the drug works as a cognition-enhancer.

We were impressed by the magnitude and consistency of differences in conditioning produced by the optimal dose of the drug. As indicated in Figure 3, trials to learning criterion, a measure that is larger when learning is poorer, revealed a classical U-shaped response curve. Doses of 1 and 2 mg/kg galantamine produced non-significant effects in comparison to sterile saline vehicle. A dose of 3 mg/kg galantamine reduced the number of trials to learning criterion to a very low mean that was significantly different from the mean for vehicle treatment. A 4 mg/kg dose of galantamine produced a non-significant effect. Mean percentage of CRs per session over the 10 training sessions, a measure that is higher with better performance, produced an inverted-U shaped response curve. Galantamine doses of 1 and 2 mg/kg were under-doses, a dose of 3 mg/kg was optimal, and a dose of 4 mg/kg was an over-dose in the 750 ms delay eyeblink conditioning procedure. Older rabbits treated with 3 mg/kg galantamine produced a high CR percentage early in training and attained a performance level of over 90 percent Crs by Session 10 - a performance level

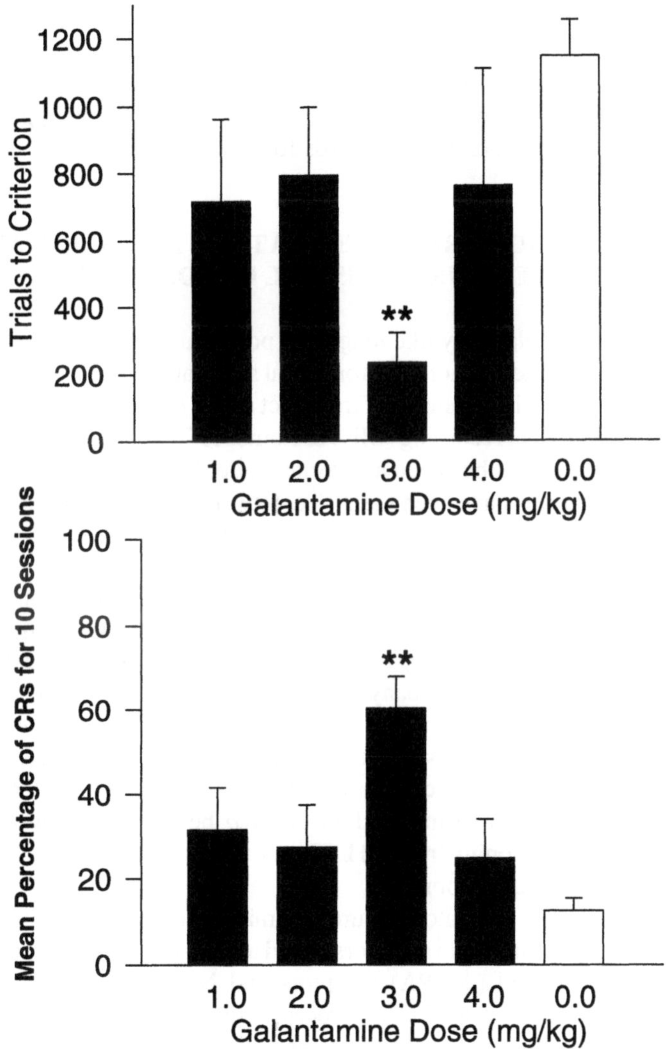

Figure 3. Effect of galantamine at four doses compared to vehicle on trials to a learning criterion of eight conditioned responses (CRs) in nine consecutive trials (Top panel) and mean percentage of CRs per 90-trial session for 10 sessions at four doses of galantamine and vehicle (Bottom panel). ** = $p < .01$. Error bars are standard error of the mean. (Data from Woodruff-Pak & Santos, in press).

typically seen only in young rabbits.

In our laboratory for a period covering almost a decade, hundreds of rabbits of various ages have been treated with drugs or vehicle and tested with the 750-ms delay eyeblink classical conditioning procedure. As mentioned previously and illustrated in Figure 1, young adult rabbits treated with vehicle attain learning criterion in around 400 trials, and retired breeder rabbits treated with vehicle attain learning criterion in around 1,000 trials, with standard deviations of 200 to 300 trials. Older rabbits receiving daily injections of a dose of 3 mg/kg galantamine achieved learning criterion in a mean of 233.0 trials (s.d. = 176.9). The identification of a dose level of galantamine that enables older rabbits to acquire CRs at a rate that is approaching half the number of trials to criterion required by young rabbits is a striking result. The high percentage of CRs maintained by older rabbits treated with 3 mg/kg galantamine is also exceptional by our laboratory standards for older rabbits.

GLUTAMATE, LONG-TERM POTENTIATION, AND NMDA AND AMPA RECEPTORS IN EYEBLINK CLASSICAL CONDITIONING

Processes of synaptic plasticity like long-term potentiation (LTP) are considered by many scientists to be likely candidates for neural substrates underlying some forms of learning. It was in the hippocampus of the intact rabbit that LTP was first discovered with electrophysiological recording (Bliss & Lomo, 1973), although the hippocampal slice preparation in the rat has been a favorite model for studying this phenomenon. A number of similarities have been identified between the learning-induced increase in hippocampal unit activity (particularly in the US period) and the process of LTP in the hippocampus (Thompson, Kim, Krupa & Tocco, 1995).

The learning-induced increase in hippocampus during eyeblink conditioning and hippocampal LTP are expressed by pyramidal neurons in the CA1 and CA3 fields. Both LTP and conditioning develop after very brief stimulation periods, both develop to asymptote over a period of many minutes, both show the same magnitude of increase, and both require very specific parameters of stimulation to develop. A direct demonstration of the parallels between hippocampal LTP and the learning-induced increase in hippocampal unit activity was carried out by Berger (1984) who used perforant path stimulation to induce LTP *in vivo* before rabbits were classically conditioned. Pre-conditioning induced LTP produced significantly faster acquisition in eyeblink conditioning in rabbits.

Glutamate, a major excitatory neurotransmitter has been demonstrated to be involved in LTP, with glutamate receptors called alpha-amino-3-hydroxy-5-methyl-4-isoxazone propionic acid (AMPA) receptors and N-methyl-D-aspartate (NMDA) receptors playing critical roles in this process. Investigations of learning-induced changes in receptor binding in hippocampus as a result of eyeblink classical conditioning using both the delay and trace procedures revealed a substantial and highly significant increase in AMPA receptor binding as a function of conditioning (Tocco et al., 1991; Tocco, Annala, Baudry & Thompson, 1992). In the same rabbits, there were no increases in measures of NMDA receptor binding. The increased AMPA receptor binding occurred in the hippocampal pyramidal dendritic fields in the

CA1 and CA3 regions and in the granule cell dendritic fields. There was a very close correlation in the pattern of increased hippocampal AMPA receptor binding in both eyeblink classical conditioning and *in vivo* LTP.

Shors, Servatius, Thompson, Rogers and Lynch (1995) used a centrally active drug 1-(1,3-benzodioxol-5-ylcarbonyl) perperdine (BNP) that enhanced the amplitude and duration of AMPA receptor gated currents in the hippocampus of freely moving rats to determine if eyeblink conditioning would be affected. Injections of BNP facilitated the rate of acquisition. The mechanism of action may have been to increase the salience of the tone conditioned stimulus, or the learning process itself may have been affected. The investigators concluded that increasing excitatory neurotransmission enhanced the processing of sensory information and may have contributed to subsequent contingency detection.

Pharmacological manipulation of the NMDA receptor markedly facilitated acquisition of CRs in the trace procedure, (Thompson, Dayo & Disterhoft, 1992). D-cycloserine, a drug that acts as a partial agonist to NMDA receptors on the glycine site, was injected intramuscularly and rabbits acquired CRs in about half the number of trials normally required. These results can be interpreted as supporting the hypothesis that learning-induced increases in hippocampal unit activity in eyeblink conditioning parallel LTP. Of course, due to the route of administration, the site(s) of action of the drug are inferred but not demonstrated in this experiment.

Glutamate receptors in the cerebellum could also be affected by agonists. Long term depression (LTD) of AMPA receptors has been proposed as a mechanism underlying adaptive timing of the classically conditioned eyeblink response (Fiala, Grossberg & Bullock, 1996). The investigators hypothesized that Purkinje cell slow responses are produced by activation of metabotropic glutamate receptors and that the latency of the metabotropic glutamate response spans the range of inter-stimulus intervals at which CRs can be acquired. This hypothesis was tested by construction of a mathematical model of the metabotropic glutamate receptor response in Purkinje cells. The model reproduced key features of Purkinje cell responding and behavioral CR acquisition that have been demonstrated empirically in rabbits. Fiala et al. (1996) noted the circuit similarities between the timed cerebellar circuit and a timed dentate-CA3 hippocampal circuit. Such similarities underscore the dilemma for researchers when they test intact organisms and attempt to understand mechanisms and sites of drug action.

COGNITION-ENHANCING DRUGS, ION CHANNELS, AND LEARNING

In Chapter 13 in this volume, the topic of alterations at the cellular level during learning is presented in depth. Here we address changes at the cellular level in calcium channels in relation to the cognition-enhancing drug, nimodipine.

A number of changes occurring in the brain as a function of associative learning are likely mediated by calcium (Alkon, 1984; Coulter et al., 1989). Age-related changes in brain calcium channel activity have been documented (Landfield & Pitler, 1984; Landfield, McGaugh & Lynch, 1978). The amplitude and duration of the post-burst afterhyperpolarization in hippocampal pyramidal cells are mediated by an outward calcium dependent potassium current that serves to reduce neuronal firing rates. Calcium currents are increased in the hippocampus of older animals (Landfield, 1987). Consequently, hippocampal neuronal firing rates may be reduced in older animals, impairing their ability to learn.

There is evidence that hippocampal pyramidal cells are impaired during normal aging. CA1 pyramidal neurons in hippocampal slice preparations taken from aging rabbits are less excitable than neurons in slices from young rabbits (Moyer, Thompson, Black & Disterhoft, 1992). The calcium-dependent afterhyperpolarization is increased in peak amplitude and duration in intracellularly recorded pyramidal cells in aging rats (Landfield & Pitler, 1984) and rabbits (Moyer et al., 1992). It is this larger afterhyperpolarization that prevents the neuron from firing rapidly and thus slows firing rate and decreases excitability.

Disrupted intracellular calcium homeostasis may be a significant factor in age-related learning and memory impairment, and the "calcium hypothesis of aging" has been developed to elucidate calcium's role in this process (Khachaturian, 1984, 1989; Landfield, 1987). Disterhoft, Deyo, Moyer, Straube and Thompson (1989) suggested that blocking calcium channels in older organisms could ameliorate the learning deficit.

The Calcium Channel Antagonist Nimodipine

A drug that is characterized as a calcium channel blocker is nimodipine (a dihydropyridine calcium channel antagonist). This drug is already approved for use in humans for a non-cognitive medical treatment and it is to control for subarachnoid hemorrhage. A number of studies testing the efficacy of nimodipine in the trace eyeblink classical conditioning procedure have been carried out in the laboratory of John Disterhoft. Deyo, Straube and Disterhoft (1989) tested young and older rabbits in a 600 ms trace procedure with the CS duration of 100 ms and a trace of 500 ms. Older rabbits received vehicle only or 1.0 ug/kg/min of nimodipine. The drug was administered via a chronic indwelling intrajugular catheter. Nimodipine has a demonstrated facilitatory effect on the acquisition of CRs in older rabbits, ameliorating the learning deficit. Young rabbits' associative learning was not significantly improved in this paradigm, but nimodipine-treated older rabbits acquired CRs about as well as young rabbits. Vehicle-treated older rabbits performed significantly more poorly than nimodipine-treated older rabbits or young rabbits. Kowalska and Disterhoft (1994) replicated the Deyo et al. (1989) results with eyeblink classical conditioning using a number of doses of nimodipine with the same trace procedure in older rabbits and demonstrated that statistically significant effects on learning occurred with doses starting at 0.5 ug/kg/min. A dose of 1 ug/kg/min was optimally effective in ameliorating deficits in eyeblink conditioning in older rabbits, and doses of 3 and 5 ug/kg/min also improved acquisition.

Administration via a chronic indwelling intrajugular catheter was not the only delivery system with which the Disterhoft laboratory demonstrated efficacy of nimodipine on acquisition using the trace eyeblink conditioning procedure. In another study, older rabbits fed rabbit chow containing 860 ppm nimodipine attained a learning criterion of four CRs in a block of five consecutive trials significantly faster than older control rabbits fed a normal diet (Straube, Deyo, Moyer & Disterhoft, 1990).

Demonstration of the efficacy of nimodipine in eyeblink conditioning in older rabbits has been replicated in other laboratories using different conditioning procedures and routes of drug administration. Using the 750 ms delay eyeblink conditioning paradigm, we gave daily subcutaneous injections of 1.0 and 5.0 mg/kg nimodipine to older rabbits and compared their performance to vehicle-treated and unpaired control older rabbits (Woodruff-Pak, Chi, Li & Fanelli, 1997). Acquisition was significantly faster in the rabbits treated with nimodipine. Post hoc analyses of the trials to learning criterion data indicated that the 5 mg/kg dose was the most effective.

Nimodipine was detected in extracts from the brains of rabbits that were classically conditioned in the experiment with nimodipine in the 750 ms delay procedure described above. Capillary gas chromatography was used to analyze the samples for the presence of nimodipine. Technicians analyzing cortical nimodipine levels were blind to the experimental condition of the rabbits. Comparison of the cortical levels of nimodipine in three groups of rabbits receiving two dose levels of nimodipine or vehicle demonstrated a significant difference in cortical levels of nimodipine. Post hoc

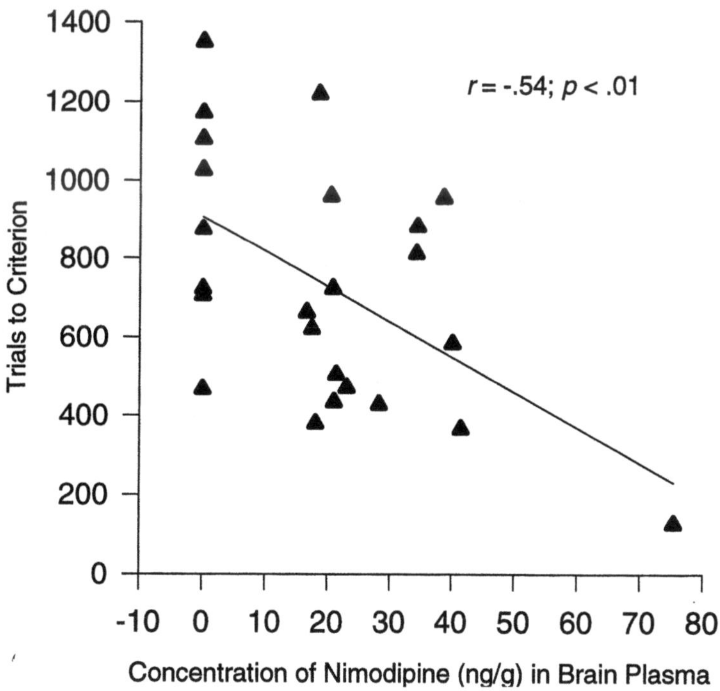

Figure 4. Relationship between trials to learning criterion and brain plasma concentration of cortical nimodipine in 24 older rabbits conditioned in the 750 ms delay conditioning paradigm. (From Woodruff-Pak, Chi, Li, Pak & Fanelli, 1997).

testing using the Dunnett Control Group Comparison test indicated that both groups injected with nimodipine had significantly higher cortical nimodipine levels.

There was a significant relationship between cortical nimodipine level and associative learning. A Pearson product-moment correlation between cortical nimodipine level and trials to learning criterion for the 24 older rabbits in the paired condition was -0.54 ($p < .01$). Rabbits with higher cortical levels of nimodipine attained learning criterion in significantly fewer trials (Figure 4).

Retention of eyeblink conditioning was also enhanced by nimodipine (Solomon et al., 1995). Older rabbits were trained in the delay eyeblink conditioning paradigm in which a 500 ms tone CS was followed 400 ms after its onset with a 100 ms corneal air puff US. One hundred paired CS-US trials were presented each session for 18 sessions. Following acquisition training, rabbits received daily injections of 0, 5, or 15 mg/kg nimodipine for 90 consecutive days. At the end of 30 and 90 days, rabbits' retention was tested by presenting 20 CS-alone presentations. Rabbits given 15 mg/kg nimodipine showed significantly better retention than the vehicle or 5 mg/kg groups. Improved retention was not due to nonassociative factors such as changes in sensitivity to the tone or air puff.

CONCLUSIONS

Eyeblink classical conditioning is of demonstrated utility in preclinical tests of cognition-enhancing drugs. A concern expressed about existing behavioral screening techniques is the poor control of psychological mechanisms that might underlie facilitated performance. Eyeblink classical conditioning is a behavioral paradigm that is well understood, and there are experimental controls and measures to distinguish between effects of perception, motivation, motor functions, and associative learning that have been elaborated extensively. In addition to its parallels with human behavior, a major advantage of using the animal model of eyeblink classical conditioning over the behavioral models commonly used in preclinical trials is that the neural circuitry is almost completely understood. The neurobiological basis of eyeblink classical conditioning in humans is similar to the circuitry demonstrated in non-human mammals (see Volume I on *Eyeblink Classical Conditioning: Applications in Humans*). Thus, using the eyeblink classical conditioning paradigm in preclinical pharmacological studies of cognition-enhancement has clear and direct implications for cognition-enhancement in humans.

REFERENCES

Alkon, D.L. (1984). Calcium-mediated reduction of ionic currents: A biophysical memory trace. *Science, 226*, 1037-1045.

Bahro, M., Schreurs, B.G., Sunderland, T., & Molchan, S.E. (1995). The effects of scopolamine,lorazepam, and glycopyrrolate on classical conditioning of the human eyeblink response. *Psychopharmacology, 122*, 395-400.

Berger, T.W. (1984). Long-term potentiation of hippocampal synaptic transmission affects rate of behavioral learning. *Science, 224*, 627-630.

Berger, T.W., Alger, B.E., & Thompson, R.F. (1976). Neuronal substrate of classical conditioning in the hippocampus. *Science, 192*, 483-485.

Berger, T.W., Rinaldi, P., Weisz, D.J., & Thompson, R. F. (1983). Single unit analysis of different hippocampal cell types during classical conditioning of the rabbit NM response. *Journal of Neurophysiology, 59*, 1197-1219.

Berger, T.W. & Thompson, R.F. (1978a). Identification of pyramidal cells as the critical elements in hippocampal neuronal plasticity during learning. *Proceedings of the National Academy of Science (USA), 75*, 1572-157.

Berger, T.W., & Thompson, R.F. (1978b). Neuronal plasticity in the limbic system during classical conditioning of the rabbit nictitating membrane response. I. The hippocampus. *Brain Research, 145*, 323-346.

Bliss, T.V.P., & Lomo, T. (1973). Long-lasting potentiation of synaptic transmission in the dentate area of the anesthetized rabbit following stimulation of the perforant path. *Journal of Physiology (London), 232*, 331-356.

Clark, G.A., McCormick, D.A., Lavond, D.G., & Thompson, R.F. (1984). Effects of lesions of cerebellar nuclei on conditioned behavioral and hippocampal responses. *Brain Research, 291*, 125-136.

Collins, A.C., Bhat, R.V., Pauly, J.R., & Marks, M.J. (1990). Modulation of nicotine receptors by chronic exposure to nicotinic agonists and antagonists. In: Ciba Foundation Symposium. *The Biology of Nicotine Dependence, (pp. 68-86)*. New York: Wiley.

Coulter, D.A., Lo Turco, J.J., Kubota, M., Disterhoft, J.F., Moore, J. F., & Alkon, D.L. (1989). Classical conditioning reduces amplitude and duration of calcium-dependent afterhyperpolariation in rabbit hippocampal pyramidal cells. *Journal of Neurophysiology, 61*, 971-981.

De Fiebre, C.M., Meyer, E.M., Henry, J.C., Muraskin, S.I., Kem, W.R., & Papke, R.L. (1995). Characterization of a series of anabaseine-derived compounds reveals that the 3-(4)-dimethylaminocinnamylidine derivative is a selective agonist at neuronal nicotinic alpha7/^{125}-alpha-bungarotoxin receptor subtypes. *Molecular Pharmacology, 47*, 164-171.

Deyo, R. A., Straube, K. T., & Disterhoft, J. F. (1989). Nimodipine facilitates associative learning inaging rabbits. Science, 243, 809-811.

Disterhoft, J. F., Deyo, R. A., Moyer, J. R., Straube, K. T., & Thompson, L. T. (1989). Calcium blockers and memory in the aging brain. *CVR&R Supplement*, August, 22-29.

Fiala, J. C., Grossberg, S., & Bullock, D. (1996). Metabotropic glutamate receptor activation in cerebellar Purkinje cells as substrate for adaptive timing of the classically conditioned eye-blink response. *Journal of Neuroscience, 16*, 3760-3774.

Flores, C.M., Rogers, S.W., Pabreza, L.A., Wolfe, B.B. and Kellar, K.J. (1991). A subtype of nicotinic cholinergic receptor in rat brain is composed of alpha 4 and bate 2 subunits and is up-regulated by chronic nicotine treatment. *Molecular Pharmacology, 41*, 31-37.

Funk, K.F. & Schmidt, J. (1984). Changes of dopamine metabolism by hypoxia and effect of nootropic drugs. *Biomedicine and Biochemistry Acta, 11*, 1301-1304.

Garcia, K.S., & Mauk, M.D. (1998). Pharmacological analysis of cerebellar contributions to the timing and expression of conditioned responses. Neuropharmacology, 37, 471-480.

Harvey, J.A., & Gormezano, I. (1986). The assessment of drug effects on learning and stimulus processing by means of classical conditioning. In T. Thompson & N. A. Krasnegor (Eds.), *Developmental Behavioral Pharmacology (, pp. 115-132)*. Hillsdale, NJ: Lawrence Erlbaum Associates.

Ito M (1984). *The Cerebellum and Neural Control*. New York: Raven Press.

Kaneko, T., & Thompson, R.F. (1997). Disruption of trace conditioning of the nictitating membrane response in rabbits by central cholinergic blockade. *Psychopharmacology, 131*, 161-166.

Kem, W.R. Mahnir, V.M., Papke, R.L., & Lingle, C.J. (1997). Anabaseine is a potent agonist on muscle and neuronal alpha-bungarotoxin-sensitive nicotinic receptors. *Pharmacology and Experimental Therapeutics, 283*, 979-992.

Khachaturian, Z.S. (1984). Towards theories of brain aging. In D.W. Kay & G. D. Burrows, (Eds.), *Handbook of Studies in Psychiatry and Old Age, (pp. 7-30)*. New York: Elsevier;

Khachaturian, Z. S. (1989). The role of calcium regulation in brain aging: Reexamination of a hypothesis. *Aging, 1*, 7-34.

Kowalska, M., & Disterhoft, J.F. (1994). Relation of nimodipine dose and serum concentration to learning enhancement in aging rabbits. *Experimental Neurology, 127*, 159-166.

Krupa, D.J., Thompson, J.K., & Thompson, R.F. (1993). Localization of a memory trace in the mammalian brain. *Science, 260*, 989-991.

Landfield, P.W. (1987). "Increased calcium current" hypothesis of brain aging. *Neurobiology of Aging, 8*, 346-354.

Landfield, P.W., McGaugh, J.L., & Lynch, G.S. (1978). Impaired synaptic potentiation processes in the hippocampus of aged, memory-deficient rats. *Brain Research, 150*, 85-101.

Landfield, P.W. & Pitler, T.A. (1984). Prolonged Ca^{2+}-dependent afterhyperpolarization in hippocampal neurons of aged rats. *Science, 226*, 1089-1092.

Li, Y.-T., Alvarez, I., & Woodruff-Pak, D.S. (1994). Mecamylamine-induced deficits in eyeblink conditioning: Reversed by nicotinic agonists. *Society for Neuroscience Abstracts, 20*, 149.

Luetje, C.W., Wada, K., Rogers, S., Abramson, S.N., Tsuji, K., Heinemann, S., & Patrick, J. (1990). Neurotoxins distinguish between different neuronal nicotinic acetylcholine receptor subunit combinations. *Journal of Neurochemistry, 55*, 6732-6740.

Maelicke, A., Schrattenholz, A., Periera, E.F.R., & Albuquerque, E.X. (1998). Nicotinic receptors in the central nervous system: Implications for Alzheimer's disease. Abstract no. 12: 6th International Conference on Alzheimer's Disease and Related Disorders, 18-23 July, Amsterdam.

Mamounas, L.A., Thompson, R.F., & Madden, J., IV. (1987). Cerebellar GABAergic processes: Evidence for critical involvement in a form of simple associative learning in the rabbit. *Proceedings of the National Academy of Science (USA), 84*, 2101-2105.

Marchi ,M., Besana, E., & Raiteri, M. (1990). Oxiracetam increases the release of endogenous Glutamate from depolarized rat hippocampal slices. *European Journal of Pharmacology, 185*, 247-249.

McCormick, D.A., Lavond, D.G., & Thompson, R.F. (1982). Concomitant classical conditioning of the rabbit nictitating membrane and eyelid responses: Correlations and implications. *Physiology and Behavior, 28*, 769-775.

McKinney, M., Coyle, J.T., & Hedreen, J.C., (1983). Topographic analysis of the innervation of the rat neocortex and hippocampus by the basal forebrain cholinergic system. *Journal of Comparative Neurology, 217*, 103-111.

Moore, J.W., Goodell, N.A., & Solomon, P.R. (1976). Central cholinergic blockage by scopolamine and habituation, classical conditioning, and latent inhibition of rabbit's nictitating membrane response. *Physiological Psychology, 4*, 395-399.

Moyer, J.R., Thompson, L.F., Black, J., & Disterhoft, J.F. (1992). Nimodipine increases excitability of rabbit CA1 pyramidal neurons in an age- and concentration-dependent manner. *Journal of Neurophysiology, 68*, 2100-2109.

Nabeshima, T. (1994). Ameliorating effects of nefiracetam (DM-9384) on brain dysfunction. *Drugs of Today, 30*, 357-379.

Nabeshima, T., Noda, Y., Tohyama, K., Itoh, J., & Kameyama, T. (1990) Effects on DM-9384 in a model of amnesia based on animals with GABA-ergic neuronal dysfunctions. *European Journal of Pharmacology, 178*, 143-149.

Olpe, H.-R., & Lynch, G. S. (1982). The action of piracetam on the electrical activity of the hippocampal slice preparation: A field potential analysis. *European Journal of Pharmacology, 80*, 415-419.

Rowell, P.P., & Wonnacott, S. (1990). Evidence for functional activity of up-regulated nicotine binding sites in rat striatal synaptosomes. *Journal of Neurochemistry, 55*, 2105-2110.

Salvatierra, A.T., & Berry, S.D. (1989). Scopolamine disruption of septo-hippocampal activity and classical conditioning. *Behavioral Neuroscience, 103*, 715-721.

Sasse, D.K., Coffin, J.M., & Woodruff-Pak, D.S. (1991). Age differences in rabbits in the delay classical conditioning paradigm using 400 and 750 msec CS-US intervals. *Society for Neuroscience Abstracts, 17*, 1140.

Sasse, D.C., & Woodruff-Pak, D.S. (1990). Classical conditioning in young and older rabbits in delay and trace paradigms with a 750 msec CS-US interval. *Society for Neuroscience Abstracts, 16*, 841.

Schrattenholz, A. Pereira, E.F.R., Roth, U., Weber, K.H., Albuquerque, E.X., Maelicke, A. (1996). Agonist responses of neuronal nicotinic acetylcholine receptors are potentiated by a novel class of allosterically acting ligands. *Molecular Pharmacology, 49*, 1-6.

Schwartz, R. D. & Kellar, K. J. (1985). In vivo regulation of [3H]acetylcholine recognition sites in brain by nicotinic cholinergic drugs. *Journal of Neurochemistry, 52*, 483-491.

Sears, L.L., & Steinmetz, J.E. (1990). Acquisition of classically conditioned-related activity in the hippocampus is affected by lesions of the cerebellar interpositus nucleus. *Behavioral Neuroscience, 104*, 681-692.

Shors, T.J., Servatius, R.J., Thompson, R.F., Rogers, G., & Lynch, G. (1995). Enhanced glutamergic neurotransmission facilitates classical conditioning in the freely moving rat. *Neuroscience Letters, 186*, 153-156.

Solomon, P.R., & Gottfried, K.E. (1981). Disruption of acquisition of the classically conditioned rabbit nictitating membrane response following injection of scopolamine into the medial septal nucleus.

Journal of Comparative and Physiological Psychology, 95, 322-330.

Solomon, P.R., Groccia-Ellison, M., Flynn, D., Mirak, J., Edwards, K.R., Dunehew, A., & Stanton, M. E. (1993). Disruption of human eyeblink conditioning after central cholinergic blockade with scopolamine. *Behavioral Neuroscience, 107*, 271-279.

Solomon, P. R., Groccia-Ellison, M., Stanton, M. E., & Pendlebury, W. W. (1994). Strategies for developing animal models of neurotoxicant-induced neurodegenerative disorders. In M.I. Woodruff & A.J. Nonneman (Eds.). *Toxin-induced models of neurological disorders, (pp. 17-38).* New York: Plenum Press.

Solomon, P. R., Solomon, S. D., Vander Schaaf, E. & Perry, H. E. (1983). Altered activity in the hippocampus is more detrimental to classical conditioning than removing the structure. *Science, 220*, 329-331.

Solomon, P.R., Wood, M.S., Groccia-Ellison, M.E., Yang, B.Y., Fanelli, R.J. , & Mervis, R. F. (1995). Nimodipine facilitates retention of the classically conditioned eyeblink response in rabbits over long retention intervals. *Neurobiology of Aging, 17*, 791-796.

Spencer, D.G.Jr., Horvath, E., & Raber, J. (1986). Direct autoradiographic determination of M1 and M2 muscarinic acetylcholine receptor distribution in the rat brain: Relation to cholinergic nuclei and projections. *Brain Research, 380*, 59-68.

Spignoli, G. & Pepeu, G. (1987). Interactions between oxiracetam, quaniracetam and scopolamine on behavior and brain acetylcholine. *Pharmacology, Biochemistry, and Behavior, 27*, 491-495.

Straube, K.T., Deyo, R.A., Moyer, J.R. Jr., & Disterhoft, J.F. (1990). Dietary nimodipine improves associative learning in aging rabbits. *Neurobiology of Aging, 11*, 659-661.

Thompson, L.T., Deyo, R.A., & Disterhoft, J.F. (1992). Hippocampus-dependent learning facilitated by a monoclonal antibody or D-cycloserine. *Nature, 359*, 838-841.

Thompson, R.F., Kim, J.J., Krupa, D.J., & Tocco, G. (1995). Brain substrates of basic associative learning and memory. In D. Ottoson, T. Bartfai, T. Hokfelt & K. Fuxe (Eds.). *Challenges and Perspectives in Neuroscience, (pp. 239-281)*. New York: Pergamon.

Thomsen, T., & Kewitz, H. (1990). Selective inhibition of human acetylcholinesterase by galantamine *in vitro* and *in vivo*. *Life Sciences, 46*, 1553-1558.

Tocco, G., Devgan, K.K., Hauge, S.A., Weiss, C., Baudry, M., & Thompson, R.F. (1991). Classical conditioning selectively increases AMPA/quisqualate receptor binding in rabbit hippocampus. *Brain Research, 559*, 331-336.

Tocco, G., Annala, A.J., Baudry, M., & Thompson, R.F. (1992). Learning of a hippocampal-dependent conditioning task changes the binding properties of AMPA receptors in rabbit hippocampus. *Behavioral and Neural Biology, 58*, 222-231.

Watabe S., Yamaguchi, H., & Ashida, S. (1993). DM-9384, a new cognition-enhancing agent, increases the turnover of components of the GABAergic system in the rat cerebral cortex. *European Journal of Pharmacology, 238*, 303-309.

Woodruff-Pak, D.S. (in press). Insights about learning in Alzheimer's disease from the animal model. In M.E. Carroll & J. B. Overmier (Eds.). *Linking Animal Research and Human Psychological Health.* Washington, D. C.: American Psychological Association.

Woodruff-Pak, D.S., Chi, J., Li, Y.-T., Pak, M.H., & Fanelli, R. (1997). Nimodipine ameliorates impaired eyeblink classical conditioning in older rabbits. *Neurobiology of Aging 18*, 641-649.

Woodruff-Pak, D.S., Coffin, J.M., & Sasse, D.K. (1991). Learning, memory, and aging: Neuralchanges and drug actions. In K.W. Schaie (Ed.). *Annual Review of Gerontology and Geriatrics, (Vol. 11, pp. 23-54).* New York: Springer.

Woodruff-Pak, D.S., Cronholm, J.F., & Sheffield, J.B. (1990). Purkinje cell number related to rate of eyeblink classical conditioning. *NeuroReport, 1*, 165-168.

Woodruff-Pak, D.S., Green, J.T., Coleman-Valencia, C., & Pak, J.T. (in press). A nicotinic cholinergic drug (GTS-21) and eyeblink classical conditioning: Acquisition, retention, and relearning in older rabbits. *Experimental Aging Research.*

Woodruff-Pak, D.S., & Hinchliffe, R.M. (1997). Scopolamine- or mecamylamine- induced learning impairment: Reversed by nefiracetam. *Psychopharmacology, 131*, 130-139.

Woodruff-Pak, D.S., & Li, Y.-T. (1994). Nefiracetam (DM-9384): Effect on classical conditioning in older rabbits. *Psychopharmacology, 114*, 200-208.

Woodruff-Pak, D.S., Li, Y.-T., Hinchliffe, R.M., & Port, R.L. (1997). Hippocampus in delay eyeblink classical conditioning: Essential for nefiracetam amelioration of learning in older rabbits. *Brain Research, 747*, 207-218.

Woodruff-Pak, D.S., Li, Y.-T., Kazmi, A., & Kem, W.R. (1994). Nicotinic cholinergic system involvement

in eyeblink classical conditioning in rabbits. *Behavioral Neuroscience, 108*, 486-493.
Woodruff-Pak, D.S., Li, Y.-T., & Kem, W.R. (1994). A nicotinic agonist (GTS-21), eyeblink classical conditioning, and nicotinic receptor binding in rabbit brain. *Brain Research, 645*, 309-317.
Woodruff-Pak, D.S., & Santos, J. (in press). Nicotinic modulation in an animal model of a form of associative learning impaired in Alzheimer's disease. *Behavioural Brain Research.*
Woodruff-Pak, D.S., & Trojanowski, J.Q. (1996). The older rabbit as an animal model: Implications for Alzheimer's disease. *Neurobiology of Aging, 17*, 283-290.
Yoshii, M., & Watabe, S. (1994). Enhancement of neuronal calcium channel currents by the nootropic agent, nefiracetam (DM-9384), in NG108-14 cells. *Brain Research, 642*, 123-131.

INDEX

Page numbers in *italics* indicate figures. Page numbers followed by "t" indicate tables.

B

C

F

G

H

I

J

K

MIX
Papier aus verantwortungsvollen Quellen
Paper from responsible sources
FSC® C105338

If you have any concerns about our products,
you can contact us on
ProductSafety@springernature.com

In case Publisher is established outside the EU,
the EU authorized representative is:
Springer Nature Customer Service Center GmbH
Europaplatz 3, 69115 Heidelberg, Germany

Printed by Libri Plureos GmbH
in Hamburg, Germany